Warman's
COINS &
CURRENCY

Volumes in the Encyclopedia of Antiques and Collectibles

Warman's Americana & Collectibles, 7th Edition,
edited by Harry L. Rinker

Warman's American Pottery & Porcelain,
by Susan and Al Bagdade

Warman's Coins & Currency, 2nd Edition
by Allen G. Berman and Alex G. Malloy

Warman's Country Antiques & Collectibles, 3rd Edition,
by Dana Gehman Morykan and Harry L. Rinker

Warman's English & Continental Pottery & Porcelain, 2nd Edition,
by Susan and Al Bagdade

Warman's Glass, 2nd Edition,
by Ellen Tischbein Schroy

Warman's Jewelry,
by Christie Romero

Warman's Paper,
by Norman E. Martinus and Harry L. Rinker

Warman's COINS & CURRNECY

Second Edition

ALLEN G. BERMAN
AND
ALEX G. MALLOY

Wallace-Homestead Book Company
Radnor, Pennsylvania

Dedicated to My Parents,
in Plain English

A.B.

Copyright © 1997 by Alex G. Malloy

All Rights Reserved

Published in Radnor, Pennsylvania 19089, by Wallace-Homestead, a division of Chilton Book Company

No portion of this book may be reproduced by any means – electronic, mechanical, or photographic -- nor stored in an electronic storage and retrieval system, without prior written permission from the publisher. Writers and reviewers may excerpt short portions without written permission. All listings and prices have been checked for accuracy but the publisher cannot be responsible for any errors that may have occurred.

A CIP record for this book is available from the Library of Congress.

Designed by Allen G. Berman and Camden W. Percival

Manufactured in the United States of America

1 2 3 4 5 6 7 8 9 6 5 4 3 2 1 0 9 8 7

CONTENTS

Introduction vii
Acknowledgments viii
Organization of the Book 1
Values 2
Choosing a Dealer 2
Abbreviations 3

UNITED STATES COINS
by Allen G. Berman
History of United States Coinage 4
Mintmarks and Grading 5
Impairments and "Do Nots" 7
Slabs 7
Detecting Counterfeit Coins 8
General U.S. References and Periodicals 9
Pre Federal Coinage 9
Half Cents 10
Cents 11
Two Cent Pieces 14
Three Cent Pieces 14
Nickels 15
Half Dimes 17
Dimes 18
Twenty Cent Pieces 22
Quarters 22
Half Dollars 25
Dollars 30
Trade Dollars 31
United States Gold Coinage 34
Commemorative Coinage 42
Recent Commemorative Coinage 48
Proof Sets 53
Mint Sets 53
Special Mint Sets 54
Bullion Issues 54
Patterns 56
Errors 56
Colonial and State Coinages 57
California and Other Private Gold Coinages 63
Hard Times Tokens 64
Civil War Tokens 65
Encased Postage Stamps 66
Confederate Coinage 67
Merchants' Tokens and "Good Fors" 67
Transportation Tokens 68
Campaign Tokens 69
Art Medals 70
Hawaii 71
U.S. Philippines 71

UNITED STATES PAPER MONEY
by Allen G. Berman
Introduction to U.S. Paper 74
Grading Paper Money 74
Continental and State Currency 74
Obsoletes 75
Fractional and Postal Currency 76
Demand Notes 77
Treasury Notes 78
National Bank Notes 78
National Gold Bank Notes 80
United States Notes (Legal Tender Notes) 80
Gold Certificates 81
Silver Certificates 82
Federal Reserve Bank Notes 83
Federal Reserve Notes 83
Interest Bearing Notes, Compound Interest Treasury Notes,
    & Refunding Certificates 86
Confederate Currency 86
Depression and Other Scrip 88
Military Payment Certificates 88
Bank (Personal) Checks 89

CANADIAN COINS
by Allen G. Berman
History 90
Grading 90
Cents 91
Five Cents 92
Ten Cents 93
Twenty Cents 94
Twenty-Five Cents 94
Fifty Cents 96
Silver Dollars 97
BiMetallic Two Dollars 99
Large Denomination Silver, Gold and Platinum 99
Maple Leaf Bullion Coins 102
Canadian Provincial Coinage 103

ANCIENT AND MEDIEVAL COINS
by Alex G. Malloy
Introduction 107
Greek 107
Biblical 111
Egypt and Africa 112
Greek Imperial 113
Roman 113
Byzantine 119
Dark Ages 120

Medieval Islamic 122
Crusader States 124
Asian Christian Kingdoms 125
Middle Ages: Europe 125
    England 125
    France 127
    Low Countries 129
    Italy 129
    Papal 130
    Spain 130
    Portugal 131
    Germany 131
    Switzerland 132
    Austria 132
    Central Europe 132
    Poland 133
    Baltic States 133
    Russia 134
    Balkans 134
    Scandinavia 135

FOREIGN COINS
by Allen G. Berman

Introduction 136
United Kingdom and Ireland 136
British Commonwealth 139
France 143
French Colonial 145
Portugal 146
Portuguese Colonies 147
Spain 148
Spanish Empire 149
Low Countries (Benelux) and Colonies 150

Scandinavia 152
Germany 154
Switzerland 156
Italy 157
Italian Colonies 157
Vatican City and Papal States 158
Austria 158
Central Europe 159
Poland 160
Baltic States 160
Russia 161
Balkan States 162
Islamic Coins 164
Israel 168
Africa 168
Indian Subcontinent 170
Southeast Asia 171
Pacific 173
China 173
Japan and Korea 177
Caribbean and Bahamas 179
Mexico 180
Central and South America 183

FOREIGN PAPER MONEY
by Allen G. Berman

Introduction 187
Listings (alphabetical by country) 187

INDEX 207

PHOTO ACKNOWLEDGMENTS 211

INTRODUCTION

When I was first asked to write *Warman's Coins and Currency*, I questioned that anyone needed another general book on coins. I soon found out that no book quite like this existed on the market. We wanted to create a general reference work on coins and their values that could be used easily by any curious layman, without specialized numismatic (coin) knowledge. We wanted it to be all-encompassing in the sense that enough diverse material would be covered to give anyone with a "mystery coin" a general idea of its value and background. Needless to say such a book cannot include the minute varieties that may add additional value in the eyes of a specialist, but entire libraries can be filled with the vast array of such works. However if a person wished to have just one coin book on his shelf "just in case" this may prove useful a thousand times over.

A Civil War three cent nickel found in my grandfather's antique desk and a bag of change from a relative's trip around the world caught the imagination of an impressionable ten-year-old. I was hooked for life. Since then the love of old coins has brought me from travels in Europe to a graduate degree in history. I have had the rare privilege of having known no other profession, and even on the longest of days, am still grateful. I know of few hobbies which bring together such a wide array of people from diverse states and countries as intimately and amiably as coin collecting. An interest in coins has even been known to improve a student's grades.

Many of my friends have often been captured by the sense of history they feel when examining my coins. Many forms of literature, from science fiction to folk lore, have mused on the idea of time travel. It seems to have been a dream almost as old as the dream of flight. Coins are the travelers through time that tie one end of civilization to another — ours.

Investors will find the sections on choosing a dealer, "slabs" and grading of particular importance. I have spoken very frankly on these matters, and I hope the information I present will be a guide to avoiding needless heartache and financial loss. I must confess however, that I find investing in coins solely for profit objectionable. Coins should be bought by those who enjoy and appreciate them. In the long run, a true collector is likely to find his dealings in better quality coins just as profitable as those of a cold-hearted investor. And the inexpensive coins he picks up along the way will only add to his fun.

One of the most enjoyable parts of numismatics is the camaraderie. There are hundreds of local coin clubs throughout the United States and Canada. They provide collectors an opportunity to get together with folks of like interests, and yak over a (sometimes) good meal. There are a number of important national and international organizations as well. Most will have their own publications and museums or libraries. The most popular is the American Numismatic Association, 818 North Cascade Ave., Colorado Springs, CO 80903. It has a circulating library for members and a code of ethics and arbitration for the conduct of its members. Another excellent organization is the American Numismatic Society, Broadway at 155th St., New York, NY 10032. This is the most important numismatic library in the Western Hemisphere and major research in the field is rarely done without using this facility.

Museums are also fun, and numismatic curators are far less stuffy than the stereotype. In addition to the museums located at the above two organizations, the Smithsonian Institution has one of the world's most impressive numismatic museums, with extensive exhibits on display to the general public.

Caution should be exercised in using the prices listed. The coin market is continuously in flux and what is popular one year may fall out of favor the next. This is especially true on common coins which can be promoted by mass marketers. The price level may escalate wildly while the marketer is seeking coins for his marketing scheme, but when his order has been filled, they may drop to one third their highest level. Many other coins, while worth more than their metal content, may be affected indirectly by the bullion markets. Hence this book should not be considered an offer to buy or sell. During the course of my business I examine millions of coins every year, buying and selling on my own account and for firms whom I represent. The only way a dealer can make you a firm offer on your coins or offer to sell you a coin is by actually inspecting the coin in question. Especially with older coins, no two coins are identical, and these subtle difference affect both the value of a coin and its desirability.

In addition to the active pursuit of buying and selling old coins, I am continuously conducting research on the material covered in this and any of my other books. If I may be of service or if any reader would like to comment on this work they are encouraged to write to:

Allen G. Berman, M.A.,
Professional Numismatist
P.O. Box 605
Fairfield, CT 06430

The Ancient and Medieval sections of this book are designed to give the curious or beginner a point to start. Each area covered lists various coins encountered in collecting, be they common or rare. Most popular books on numismatics rarely acknowledge ancient and medieval coins at all. This presentation of 2100 years of numismatics is designed to pique interest in one of the oldest areas of collecting. Ancient and medieval numismatics has been my life for over 25 years. I highly recommend this hobby as it brings history and our world alive.

Alex G. Malloy
Alex G. Malloy, Inc.
P.O. Box 38
South Salem, NY 10590

ACKNOWLEDGMENTS

No reference book is the work of one individual, and this is no exception. In a work as diverse as this, covering everything from the invention of coinage in ancient times to current technologically advanced paper money, help has been called from many corners. The market for United States coins is certainly among the most price sensitive of all collectible markets. Values change weekly and ten percent is considered a major difference. We are grateful to both Stephen E. Switter of Fairfield (Connecticut) Coin and Collectibles and to Robert Walter of Sam Sloat Coins, Inc. for their willingness to review the accuracy of these prices at a date close enough to press time to be useful, and for making a number of other important suggestions along the way. Mr. Berman is privileged to have been able to call upon his friend David Klein of RaBenco, often at odd hours. He is truly one of the most notable experts in the field of paper money in North America and without his aid the section on United States paper money would have been profoundly flawed. We would also like to express our gratitude to Stephen Album, Lucien Birkler, Frederick Fleischer, Cindy Grellman, Camden Percival, Gordon A. Singer, Chris Taylor, William B. Warden, and Joseph Zannella, K.N.W., for many conversations, advice, and counsels throughout this project. Each brought to this work their own unique background and specialized expertise. We would like to note our appreciation for the many hours of work contributed by Camden W. Percival in production.

The illustrations for this book constitute a work in itself. After much digging, some photographs and drawings from the late nineteenth and very early twentieth centuries were found to be superior to many available today. A large number of new photographs had to be prepared from both private collections and inventories. Still other illustrations were obtained from generous auction houses and private collectors, among others. We owe a particular debt to Stack's, Bowers and Merena Galleries, and Charlton International, Inc. for their gracious permission to use individual coin illustrations where other sources have fallen short. Illustrations from Mr. Berman's own collection of paper money were also supplemented with those photographed from the personal collections of David Klein and Frederick Fleischer. Additional items were lent for the cover montage by Stephen Switter and David Klein. A special thanks to Ira, Laurence, and Marc Goldberg of Superior Stamp & Coin their willingness to allow us to use many of the fine photos from their past auctions of ancient and medieval coins.

It is Harry Rinker whose vision and foresight have made this volume possible. He developed the pattern and the skeleton to which we added the numismatic sinew, meat, and heart. The whole Warman's series is a fine example of this vision. Last but not least, is the assistance of Christopher J. Kuppig and his staff, particularly Troy Vozzella.

ORGANIZATION OF THE BOOK

Warman's Coins and Currency is organized to provide the reader with easy access to basic information on the history and value of the broad spectrum of United States, Canadian, and foreign coins and paper money. It encompasses ancient and medieval as well as modern currency.

History: A brief survey is presented of the origin and evolution of each series. The coins are placed within an historical, economic and/or artistic context that puts them in place and shows their reason for being made.

References: Most coins have at one time or another been the subject of a number of in depth studies. These studies not only indicate which minor varieties are rare or valuable, as compared to other very similar coins, they also give a fuller sense of history and meaning to the coins. Listed in this section will be found the most standard references for each series of coins, occasionally with a brief commentary. Only the author and title are listed as all books currently in print can be obtained by book store proprietors with this information and a Books In Print catalogue. Many of the standard references that have gone out of print can be obtained by specialist coin dealers, but give them time. It requires hunting!

Periodicals: In some instances the information published in books does not begin to cover the series being discussed. When this is the case, a magazine or journal will be listed. Often these are the publications of specialized numismatic organizations, in which case the name of the organization will be indicated.

Counterfeit Alert: Little could be more important. For some series of coins counterfeits or replicas are more common than the real thing. Listed will be coins known to have been counterfeited in any one of several classes: 1) Replicas not intended to fool anybody. 2) Counterfeits intended to circulate but not to be good enough to fool a collector. 3) Counterfeits (or forgeries) of high quality which pose a serious threat even to experienced numismatists. 4) Altered coins, which are real coins illegally modified to appear to be different than they were when first issued.

Hints: There is always some knowledge that falls through the cracks of education and has to be learned by experience. This book attempts to fill in the void in other books by telling the reader about the characteristics, pitfalls and tricks of certain types of coins before they have to learn the hard way. Also mentioned will be reasons a series might be of particular interest.

Listings: All American and Canadian coins are listed in this book in two states of preservation. For most purposes these listings can be considered comprehensive since the founding of these two countries. The same applies to United States paper money as defined by basic types. Foreign coins are listed in the most frequently encountered state of preservation. For some series representative samples are given, with the idea of including common and rare coins as well as "average" samples. A specific year or mint may be used as an example, and a cross section may by sought by listing several coins. Other times a range of dates may be given. This means that most of the coins of this type are valued at the price listed. Needless to say, coins which do not carry dates are also listed this way. Coins are described only to distinguish one from another. Fuller descriptions can be found in more specialized works.

VALUES

The valuations in this book were compiled based on many sources. These include various, often conflicting, price guides, dealers' fixed price lists of coins offered for sale, auctions, local shop price quotes, coin newspaper advertisements, and transactions observed at coin shows. In the case of foreign and ancient coins, these include overseas sources as well.

Every coin has many different values. The values listed in this book are *retail* values, that is, the average price a coin dealer would charge a retail customer for an example in the grade listed. This is not what a dealer would charge a fellow coin dealer. Common sense would dictate that few dealers would be willing to *buy* a coin at the same price they charge for it. The difference is how they pay their operating expenses (rent, advertising, etc.) and earn their living. Nor are they the "bid" price that so many people talk about. Bid is either the low end of the wholesale price range listed in the *Coins Dealer Newsletter* (the high end is "ask") or the price at which a dealer sets his standing offer to buy a type of coin, even before he finds a seller. How then can the owner of a coin determine what he is likely to get for that coin? The percentage of the listed values a dealer will pay will of course be determined by whether he actually wants the coin. Does he have too many in stock? Does he have any customers who collect that type of coin? As a rule, the higher the value of a coin, the larger percentage he will pay. Also, a coin the value of which is based on its bullion value (precious metal content), rather than collector interest will be traded at a smaller mark-up. Hence, an American one ounce gold piece may be bought at 85-90% of its listed price, whereas a circulated, common date wheat-back cent or a British penny from World War II may receive offers of only 5% or less!

CHOOSING A
COIN DEALER

While there is no automatic way to determine if any coin dealer is "ethical" or "knowledgeable," there are many factors in a dealer's background worth investigating. Obviously it is sometimes wise to avoid dealers lacking experience. In the early 1980's many fly-by-night dealers set-up to buy coins from the general public; many more established telemarketing firms to sell "investment grade" coins. Both of these types of dealers were often nowhere to be found just a few years down the road. A dealer with several years invested in the industry, and presumably a vested interest in maintaining customer loyalty over years, also has an interest in buying and selling at a competitive level. Years of experience are also likely to contribute to a dealer's knowledgeability.

Aside from a dealer's longevity in the field, there are other criteria. Members of the American Numismatic Association (ANA), the world's largest such organization, are required to conduct business according to a specific set of standards, and are subject to arbitration if accused of falling short of these ideals. Similar professional organizations which enforce a code of ethics on their members are the Professional Numismatists Guild and the International Association of Professional Numismatists.

Krause Customer Service Award

ANA member logo

IAPN PNG member logos

One should not exclude a coin dealer simply because he is mail order. Because numismatics is a fairly specialized field, it is not always possible for the expert dealer and the active collector or seller to be at the same place at the same time. As a result a thriving mail order industry has developed, with some of the forefathers of American numismatics establishing themselves as mail order dealers over one hundred years ago. Most legitimate mail order coin dealers will provide a return privilege. During a specified time the purchaser of a coin can usually return it for a refund even if the potential purchaser agrees with the dealer's description. Also when coins are offered for sale to a legitimate mail order dealer, he will generally not presume that he has title to the coins until he has confirmed that his offer has been accepted by the seller. Whether buying or selling through the mail, it is important to remember to wrap the coins securely (so they make no noise) and send them registered or insured. Registered mail has an excellent record, losses being extremely rare. Insured mail is less expensive for lower value items.

Most larger numismatic publications will also offer some recourse against misconduct by their advertisers, withdrawing their advertizing privileges if there are inordinate complaints. One major publisher, Krause Publications, will even award a "Customer Service Award" to dealers who meet additional standards of good conduct.

Whether you deal person to person or mail order, it is important to establish a good working relationship with your dealer. When a dealer remembers who you are it is likely to be to your advantage. He is more likely to go out of his way to mention problems in a coin or to let you know that he has acquired something of interest to you. Never be afraid to ask too many questions. There are no "stupid questions" and a good dealer will be happy to answer them.

ABBREVIATIONS

The following list of abbreviations will not only make using this book easier, it will make reading anything coin-related easier. Many of the symbols and abbreviations used in numismatics have become standardized throughout the English-speaking world. Even in Europe some of these will be recognized.

ANA . . . . American Numismatic Association
ANS . . . . American Numismatic Society
IAPN . . . . International Association of Professional Numismatists
PNG . . . . Professional Numismatists Guild

DESCRIBING A COIN

Obv. . . . . Obverse (heads)
Rev. . . . . Reverse (tails)
l. . . . . left
r. . . . . right
mm. . . . . mintmark or mintmaster's mark
mm. . . . . diameter in millimeters
ND . . . . not dated on coin
/ . . . . separates descriptions of obverse
___. . . . . as previous coin
[ ] . . . . does not actually appear on coin

GRADES

AG . . . . About Good
G . . . . Good
VG . . . . Very Good
F . . . . Fine
VF . . . . Very Fine

EF . . . . Extremely Fine
XF . . . . Extremely Fine
AU . . . . About Uncirculated
Unc . . . . .Uncirculated
BU . . . . Brilliant Uncirculated
CU . . . . Crisp Uncirculated
MS . . . . Mint State (uncirculated)
PF . . . . .Proof
Ch . . . . .Choice

METALS

AL . . . . Aluminum
AB . . . . Aluminum-Bronze
B . . . . Brass
Bil. . . . . Billon
C (or AE) . . . . Copper or Bronze
CN . . . . Copper-Nickel alloy
G (or AV) . . . . Gold
GS . . . . German Silver (Nickel Silver)
Or. . . . . Orichalcum
S (or AR) . . . . Silver
WM . . . . White Metal (a tin alloy)
Z . . . . Zinc

UNITED STATES COINS

HISTORY OF UNITED STATES COINAGE

The first federal coinage of the United States was not based on British coinage but rather on Spanish colonial coinage. The economic principles of mercantilism discouraged the export of precious metal from Britain to the Thirteen Colonies. As a result the precious metal coinage in the colonies consisted of whatever could be obtained at the time. Because of the prolific silver mines of the Spanish colonies, two real (or "two bit") pieces struck in Mexico City were more common in New England than the equivalent shilling struck in old England. The colonists even cut the large Mexican Eight-Real coins, or Spanish Milled Dollars as they called them,

Piece of Eight and Cut One Bit

into pieces as small change. It was therefore natural for the new American dollar to be based on the colonial Mexican dollar. Unlike the Mexican dollar, which was divided into eight reales (hence "piece of eight"), the new American dollar was divided into one hundred cents. This decimal system was at the time virtually unknown and must have been considered very progressive.

While the new United States constitution took coinage out of the realm of state governments, providing the nation with a viable currency was not so simple. Congress voted to establish the U.S. mint in 1792, and the land for it was purchased in Philadelphia in May that year. Initially, things were difficult and haphazard. Mint workers were overburdened, working sixty-six hours per week. According to one tale, the federal government was so short on silver bullion that the first experimental coins

were struck on silver from a donation of George Washington's silverware! For the first several decades of the U.S. mint's existence, its output was so small that copper large cents and half cents served more as a local Philadelphia coinage than a true national coinage. Moreover, undervaluation of the silver coinage in terms of the world silver market caused much of that to be exported to Europe to be melted for bullion. Even much of the machinery had to be purchased second hand! Congress even debated shutting down the mint.

Early American coins were hand struck with a screw press. The blanks on which they were struck were hand adjusted with files in order to correct their weights. Even the dies with which they were struck were hand engraved. Because of this many early pieces can have literally hundreds of varieties for each year.

The same coin struck with two different dies.
(note position of date)

Many of the references listed in the bibliographical sections of this book will help those interested identify the actual die combinations used to strike these coins and determine their rarities.

During the 1830s new steam powered minting machinery was imported from Britain. From this time to the present coins have been uniform in diameter and precisely round. Also the originally lettered edges became "reeded" or plain. Edge reeding is the series of ridges which can now be found on coins of dime value or greater. At just about the time of this reform all silver coins were redesigned with a figure of Liberty seated on a rock, and holding a shield beside her and a liberty cap on a pole. Most consider this design to be inspired by the seated Britannia used in British coinage and ultimately derived from an ancient Roman design. In 1853 and 1873 there were minor adjustments to the weight of the silver coins but the purity of U.S.

silver remained a constant 90% from 1837 through the end of circulating silver coinage in 1964.

By 1857 the United States mint was finally producing enough coin to meet the nation's needs and foreign coins such as the Piece of Eight finally ceased to be legal tender. At the same time the government eliminated the half cent and replaced the large cent with a new small cent, the same size in use today but thicker and with a 12% nickel alloy. After a few years and a switch from the Flying Eagle to the Indian Head design, these were changed to the familiar bronze alloy.

Gold coins were initially struck in only small numbers, but with the discovery of small gold deposits in the South and the establishment of branch mints in Georgia and North Carolina, they became more plentiful. Despite many changes of style, American gold coins invariably depicted a Liberty head until the early twentieth century.

At various times the United States has experimented with unusual denominations. The 1850's through the 1880's saw the use of 2¢, 3¢ and $3 pieces, and a 20¢ piece was tried out in the 1870's. No new denominations have been issued to circulation since then.

During most of the nineteenth century the silver dollar did not play a major role in American coinage. Mintages were low when it was issued at all and during some years the only dollar struck was the trade dollar for overseas circulation. As the economy faltered and pressure from the silver increased Congress enacted legislation in 1878, 1890, 1900 and 1918 mandating or encouraging the issue of millions of silver dollars. These had always been unpopular in the East but found wide acceptance in preference to paper money in the West and Alaska. Both the Morgan and Peace dollars were intended to coincide with new legislation and are extremely common today as a result of their lack of popularity at the time. They were simply stored in vaults rather than spent.

The silver minor coins of 1892 to 1916 were competently but conservatively designed by Chief Engraver of the Mint Charles Barber. Theodore Roosevelt sought the complete revision of the designs of United States coins. The President wanted the coinage to be of high artistic merit and went outside the normal staff of the mint to seek well known artists and sculptors to present innovative Classic Revival designs. Some of the most beautiful and famous coins date from this era including the Saint-Gaudens Double Eagle, the Walking Liberty Half and Mercury Dime by Adolph Weinman and the Buffalo Nickel by the sculptor James Earle Fraser.

Double Eagle designed by sculptor Augustus Saint-Gaudens

The next major development in United States coinage was the increase in the issue of commemorative half dollars, struck specifically for sale to collectors and to raise money for events. During the depression dozens of different halves were issued with virtual abandon. However many of these coins serve to capture the artistic trends of that decade in a manner not possible on necessarily conservative regular circulating coinage.

World War II can be seen on the nation's minor coinage. In mid-1942 the composition of the nickel was changed to a strange alloy including silver and manganese which was indicated by a large mint mark placed over the dome of Monticello. The cent was struck in steel in 1943 to save copper for the war but when too many people confused the emergency cent for a dime the alloy was replaced by cents struck on blanks which included spent shell casings in the alloy.

In 1964 the price of silver was rising to such an extent that speculation in silver small change caused a coinage shortage. The government's answer was to remove silver from the dime and quarter, and phase it out in the half dollar, replacing it with a purely fiduciary coinage composed of two layers of cupro-nickel covering a copper core. The alloy of the cent was changed from bronze to zinc plated with bronze in 1982.

Beginning in 1982 a commemorative coin program was re-introduced. At this

writing the wild abandon of the 1930's program seems to be replaying with a vengeance. One senator even caused a commemorative to be issued because he felt a coin should be struck depicting Jefferson on one side and Monticello on the other. Perhaps he was unaware that the U.S. mint was then striking over one billion coins of that description every year in the Jefferson nickel!

MINT MARKS

Many United States and foreign coins indicate where they were manufactured by placing a small letter or letters discretely on the coin. Traditionally these have been located towards the bottom on the reverse. Recently, since 1968, they have been on the obverse. The first mint of the federal government is the one still located at Philadelphia. Because of its original status it very rarely used its P mint mark until 1980. Many other mints are now closed. The mint marks found on American coins are:

none	Philadelphia (1792-date)
P	same (1942-45, 1980-date)
C	Charlotte, NC (1838-61)
CC	Carson City, NV (1870-93)
D	Dahlonega, GA (1838-61)
D	Denver, CO (1906-date)
O	New Orleans, LA (1838-1909)
S	San Francisco, CA (1854-date)
W	West Point, NY (1984-date)
M	Manila, U.S. Philippines (1925-41)

Also it should be mentioned that the United States did not use mint marks in 1965-67, despite the fact that coins were being struck at Philadelphia, Denver, and San Francisco.

GRADING

Grading is an attempt to communicate, in common, agreed upon terms, the degree of wear and handling marks on a coin. As the mail order coin business grew, grading became more necessary in order to describe coins being offered for sale in various print media without illustrations. In order to promote uniformity the ANA has established official grading standards for every United States coin, describing the degree of wear permissible for each part of the coin for a specified grade. These standards are published in *Official A.N.A. Grading Standards for United States Coins*, more commonly known as the "Gray Book." It is available at virtually every

coin shop in America. All ANA members are obliged to use these standards, and third party grading services usually use them in reaching their opinions. Another popular and very convenient reference is *Photograde*, by James F. Ruddy. It covers grades aG to AU.

In addition to words, one may describe the grade of a coin on a scale of numbers from 1 to 70. One is a coin completely worn out. Seventy is a coin that is not only mint state, but perfectly struck and absolutely free from any surface marks or blemishes, even those caused by the mint. Except for proof coins, coins that grade MS-70 (mint state 70) are virtually unheard of. Many colonial and early American coins do not exist in mint state at all.

While it is not possible to describe the individual grading criteria for all coins in a book such as this, the basic principles of grading are summarized below. While details may vary from coin to coin, the basic definitions are the same not only for most United States coins, but also for many machine struck foreign coins. On U.S. and foreign coins struck before the introduction of modern machinery one must also take into consideration the method of striking. Many will be weakly or only partially struck.

Proof (PF): Proof is not a grade but a method of minting a coin. It is often used instead of a condition because Proof coins almost never circulate and hence it is not necessary to describe the degree of wear. A proof coin in most cases is a coin double struck on polished blanks with polished dies. It may have a mirror like surface, it may have a matte finish (sandblast proof), or it may have matte details and mirror like fields (cameo proof).

Uncirculated (Unc.) or **Mint State (MS):** Most people not involved with coins ask the question "What's the difference between Uncirculated and Mint State?" These are simply two different terms for the same thing. They describe a coin which is exactly as it came from the mint, with no wear whatsoever. Mint State is a term more recently favored, but they are both correct and are both used frequently. Because many different abuses can happen to a coin even *before* the mint releases it into circulation, the American Numismatic Association has adopted standards which define the different qualities of Mint State on a scale of 60 to 70, 70 being the ultimate perfect coin. For example, most coins are handled by the mint in bags with thousands of other coins, all hitting against each other, causing minute dents called "bagmarks." These are especially a problem on large, heavy coins or ones with sharp, reeded edges. Also not every coin is fully struck and those which are weakly struck are worth less than well made ones.

Among those who invest in coins the minute, and often subjective, differences between each individual gradation of Mint State can have serious financial implications. While it is intelligent to seek to invest in the highest grade possible, it is truly doubtful that any individual is capable of discerning between eleven grades of Mint State. As the greatest American numismatist of the twentieth century, Walter Breen, once commented when asked if he could tell the difference between MS-61 and MS-62, "No. Neither, I think, can anyone else. It is simply ammunition for those whose motivation is dishonesty and greed."

MS-70: Except for very recent, made for collector coins, this grade is virtually never encountered, even by dealers of long experience. It describes a Mint State (Uncirculated) coin which is perfectly struck with absolutely no bagmarks or imperfections of any kind. It must have full original luster and no discoloration is permissible.

MS-65: A Mint State 65 coin is the highest quality coin commercially available, and only one in one hundred Uncirculated coins qualifies. It will have very slight bag marks, with no significant marks in the field or on the cheek of the portrait. Such a coin may have natural toning and need not be brilliant.

MS-63: This is a coin with fewer than average bag marks, and only slight ones on open areas such as the fields or face. It still has an overall "clean" appearance.

MS-60: This is the lowest grade for coins which have no wear. The coin will show obvious marks from being handled in bags with other coins, edge nicks, or even discoloration, but no signs of circulation or abrasions. It may be poorly struck.

About Uncirculated (AU): Sometimes called Almost Uncirculated, such a coin will have only the slightest trace of wear, detectible by a magnifying glass, on just the highest points. It should have at least a trace of luster. Such a coin, at a quick glance, may appear to be uncirculated.

Extremely Fine (EF or XF): Slight wear will show on all the highest points. Even minor details will be clear but not necessarily sharp. Some traces of luster will often show.

Very Fine (VF): Signs of circulation will be readily noticeable, but the coin is overall bold and clear. Some of the highest details may be worn away. On most coins displaying a LIBERTY band such as the Indian Head cent, and Barber and Liberty Seated coins, the word must be clear and distinct. On Morgan dollars the leaves around the cotton boll in Liberty's wreath must still be separated from the cotton boll itself.

Fine (F): Many consider this to be the lowest collectible grade. The coin will show appreciable wear, but no major design features will be lost. The word LIBERTY on most head bands or shields will be weak but all letters will be visible. On Morgan dollars only two detail lines will be visible on the cotton bolls.

Very Good (VG): This is a well worn but not ugly coin. On Indian cents and Seated Liberty and Barber coins three of the letters in LIBERTY will be visible. On large cents, half cents, Morgan dollars and gold, LIBERTY will be weak but all letters will be visible. Most eagles will only have 20% or so of their feathers.

Good (G): This is a grade considered only desirable for the collecting of rare coins, those unobtainable or prohibitively expensive in higher grades. It will have a generally flat appearance, but all major design features will be outlined. On Indian cents, Seated Liberty and Barber coins, the word LIBERTY will be gone. Liberty will be incomplete on large cents, half cents and gold, and just visible on Morgan dollars. In most cases the rim will be complete.

About Good (aG or AG): An excessively worn coin lacking all details, and retaining only its major types. Even on Morgan dollars the LIBERTY may be incomplete. The rims on such coins may be incomplete.

Choice (Ch.): This is not a grade but an adjective used to indicate that a coin is particularly attractive compared to most other coins of the same grade.

IMPAIRMENTS AND "DO NOTS"

Besides the actual grade, there are other factors which can reduce the value of a coin. Obvious features include scratches and dents. Any signs of having been mounted as jewelry will detract from a coin's value. Such abuse can often be detected by a small solder weld on the edge. The edges of a coin are often subject to dings and knocks, particularly if a coin is heavy or of a soft metal. These will take from the value of a coin depending on their extent. Porosity makes a coin less valuable and metal detector enthusiasts should remember that many "ground finds" bear such a surface. Fingerprints are also a factor which can

reduce the value of a high grade coin. Except for gold and platinum, all coinage metals form chemical reactions. Human skin contains acid and other chemical compounds which react with the exposed surface of a coin. This is particularly true of coins with original mint luster, as this surface still contains raw metal which has not had the chance to form compounds through the natural toning process. It is important to remember to **NEVER TOUCH THE SURFACE OF A COIN**, hold it by its edges only.

Perhaps the greatest threat an owner can present to a coin is cleaning. Virtually without exception, collectors

Coin damaged by touching its surface

prefer to have a coin with a *natural* surface. Any cleaning, buffing, polishing, dipping, or brightening is likely to cause damage detectable by an expert. It is always to the seller's advantage to leave a coin in its original state and to **NEVER CLEAN A COIN**. Moreover, any artificial attempt to retone a cleaned coin or to hide damage is not only likely to be unsuccessful, but under certain circumstances may constitute fraud.

One last factor that can increase or reduce the value of a coin is the subjective element of "eye appeal." While it is beyond this book to analyze this in detail, it is important to note that one of the reasons that people collect coins is for aesthetic pleasure. If a coin has no wear or bag marks but is generally unpleasant to look at, it will be a difficult coin to sell. If its color and depth of toning contribute to its artistic qualities, it will be considered more desirable. As the Romans said, there is no disputing taste, and this is one factor that will vary with practically every individual to examine a coin.

STORAGE

How a coin is stored can affect its value. Certain holders contain chemicals which can leave a harmful residue on the surface of a coin. Such holders are

intended only as a convenient method of handling and transport, and should not be used for long term storage. When purchasing coin holders for permanent storage ask for plactics whic contain no PVC. Mylar is frequently preferred and is generally considered intert.

Also never store coins in a damp or corrosive environent. If they cannot be stored in a controlled environment, at least avoid the basement. Some collectors even choose to place small packets of silaca jel or other desiccants in their safe deposit boxes to remove the moisture from the atmosphere.

SLABS

Since the early 1980's third party grading has gone from the status of popular fad to a well entrenched part of the coin industry. Based on the premise that both buyer and seller have reason for bias in describing the grade of a coin, or that one or the other may lack expertise to do so, independent firms have been established to fill the role of neutral observer. Coins submitted to such grading services are encapsulated, with a certificate of grade and the grading firm's logo, in a transparent non-destructive holder informally called a "slab." These holders are tamper-resistant. Any attempt to open the holder in order to replace the certified coin with an inferior one is usually obvious.

PCGS "slab"

This practice, however, has not been without its problems. It is in a grading service's best interest not to be too strict in applying standards, lest those who own coins choose other services to which to submit their coins. Different grading services apply varying degrees of strictness. As a result the *Coin Dealer*

Newsletter (the "Gray Sheet") has instituted an index for discounting sight-unseen slabbed coins indicating a specific percentage discount for each grading service against the same coin accurately graded. While this discount varies on a weekly basis, a recent average over several weeks has produced the following:

Correctly graded 100%
PCGS (Professional Coin Grading
    Service) 94%
NGC (Numismatic Guaranty Corp. of
    America) 89%
PCI (Photo Certified Coin Inst.) . 85%
ANACS 72%
INS (International Numismatic Soc.)
. . . . 44%
NCI (Numismatic Certification Inst.)
. . . . 43%

At press time, therefore, PCGS was considered the most accurate grading service, NCI the least.

Another problem with slab grading is that conservatively graded coins tend to be broken out of their holders and resubmitted in hopes of receiving a more liberal grade. Liberally graded coins, while bearing certificates indicating grades superior to their actual state, are rarely broken out for resubmission as it is financially advantageous for the coin's owner to honor the slabbed grade. As a result of this process of attrition an appreciable number of slabbed coins are inaccurately graded.

As a whole, slabbing has had the effect of giving sanction to the buying and selling of rare coins based on the inscription on their holders rather than their actual state of preservation. During the early period of their use they especially permitted investment brokers, posing as coin dealers, to actively offer to their clients something of which they had little true knowledge or understanding. Their clients eagerly purchased these coins, believing the plastic case a valid substitute for having to acquire knowledge themselves or do basic investment research. Thousands of investors willingly paid more for slabbing fees on a regular basis than the cost of a simple grading book. Many of these investment brokers and their clients have since moved on to greener pastures, licking their wounds along the way. A fancy holder can never substitute for knowledge gained through careful examination of coins over an extended period.

A new pitfall for those using third party grading services is "official"

cleaning. While it was little publicized, some slabbing services have long used solvents to remove oils from the surface of a coin, without affecting the actual metal or patina. In the last couple of years this practice has expanded to dipping coins in brightening agents which do actually remove some patina, with commercial "eye appeal" the ultimate objective. Unfortunately any evidence of cleaning is still damage, no matter who is the culprit.

PCI "slab"

One outgrowth of slabbing has been the study of population reports of slabbed coins published by the services that certified them. Use of these reports are theoretically an attempt to analyze the relative rarity of certain high grades. As has been noted above, the frequent practice of resubmission causes many coins to be certified by the same grading service as two or more different coins having differing grades. This renders any population reports inaccurate, and as such worthless for the purpose for which they were intended.

NGC "slab"

DETECTING COUNTERFEIT COINS

People have been making false coins almost as long as there have been coins. Fortunately, the technology available to the counterfeiter is almost always inferior to that of the government striking the real thing. Counterfeits are made in two basic ways: casting and striking. Real modern coins are usually made only by striking. When a counterfeit is made by casting the details will be less distinct than a real example, and somewhat blurred. The edge will often show a seam where the two moulds met, although this can either be hidden or filed off. Beware of coins with filed edges. Another clue to detecting a cast counterfeit is the surface which will sometimes have very tiny pimples due to fine pock-marks in the moulds. The weight will often be light. Cast coins will also not be able to "ring" when hit. This can be tested by balancing the coin on the tip of your finger and striking the edge of it with the soft side of a wooden pencil. A quiet ringing sound will continue for several seconds. Of course be careful not to damage the coin or drop it in the testing, lest you injure a real coin. Struck counterfeits will ring like real coins and will have no seam, but they can be detected by other means. Fine details will differ or be absent. The weight may also be wrong and the style of the reeded edge or edge lettering where present may be incorrect. Many counterfeits of both types will be made of lead-tin alloys, and will appear dark gray, as a poor imitation of silver. Other counterfeits will be made of tungsten and plated with gold. Some counterfeits will have a greasy feel to them. If in doubt examine an authentic coin and the coin in question side by side.

Counterfeit made for circulation

More sophisticated counterfeits made to fool collectors will however be made of good metal up to government specifications. The profit of the counterfeiter is made by his choice of coins that trade for well over their bullion value. While most counterfeits are not difficult to detect it is necessary to carefully examine each coin in order to find them out. Truly rare and valuable coins should always be examined and if a conclusion cannot be reached the opinion of an expert dealer or authentication service such as the American Numismatic Association Authentication Bureau should be sought.

Altered coins fall within the scope of this section as they are intended to deceive the collecting public. These are authentic coins cleverly modified to appear to be scarcer coins. This is often done by reengraving the surface or by adding or scraping off a mountmark. The relevant area of the coin will sometimes show signs of this process under high magnification. Always use a good magnifying glass.

Replica Marked COPY

It is important to mention that many early American coins have been reproduced as crude replicas and souvenirs. These are usually obvious casts with heavy edge seams, and since 1973 will usually bear the tiny word COPY as required by the Hobby Protection Act.

References:
American Numismatic Association, *Counterfeit Detection*, 2 vols.
Harshe, Bert, *How to Detect Altered & Counterfeit Coins and Paper Money*.
John, Lonesome, *Detecting Counterfeit Coins*.
John, Lonesome, *Detecting Counterfeit Gold Coins*.

Periodicals: Virtually every issue of *The Numismatist*, the official journal of the American Numismatic Association has large clear photographs of newly discovered counterfeits. The listings in issues before 1988 are in part summarized in the above A.N.A. references.

GENERAL U.S. REFERENCES

The following books provide a good background to United States coins in general. Other books just dealing with one series are listed below with the coins they describe.

American Numismatic Assoc., *Official A.N.A. Grading Standards for United States Coins* (If you don't have this don't spend serious money on coins.)
Breen, Walter, *Walter Breen's Complete Encyclopedia of U.S. and Colonial Coins* (A masterpiece.)
Breen, Walter, *Walter Breen's Encyclopedia of U.S. and Colonial Proof Coins*
Fivaz, Bill and Stanton, J.T., *The Cherry Pickers' Guide to Rare Die Varieties*
Yeoman, R.S., *A Guide Book of United States Coins* (The bible of U.S. coins.)

PERIODICALS

CoinAge (monthly)
Coins (monthly)
Coin World (weekly)
Numismatic News (weekly)
The Numismatist (monthly)

PRE-FEDERAL COINAGE

History: Many private individuals actively sought to stimulate the Congress during the period of the Articles of Confederation to issue a national coinage. The first important pattern is the famous Continental Dollar. More remains unknown than known concerning this coin. The design is that of a sun dial over the words "Mind Your Business" and below the word *Fugio* and the sun. All around is the legend "Continental Currency 1776." The reverse consists of a ring of thirteen interlocking rings each labeled for a state. At its center is a fourteenth ring inscribed "American Congress" containing "We Are One." It has not yet been positively established who created this piece. The design is based on concepts by Benjamin Franklin, but he is not believed to have been directly involved in the coin's creation. Even though this coin was not adopted by the Congress, it may have been an official project. The design was in part used seven years later on an Indian peace medal.

One set of patterns for the nation's first coinage that we do know the origin of is the Nova Constellatio Silver series. Gouverneur Morris of New York proposed the country adopt a decimal system based on 1,000 in order to facilitate conversion from old state currencies. This set was characterized by an eye within a starburst. While it was not adopted, two results did come of it:

the concept of a decimal coinage was accepted, and a prolific series of coppers followed it. The coppers were in essence a national coinage struck at the private expense and initiative of Gouverneur Morris. These are well made coins of the same basic design as his silver patterns, and were engraved and struck in England. Dates of 1783, 1785 and 1786 are known, though some question the authenticity of the 1786 coins. These Nova Constellatio coppers share some dies with the scarcer Immune Columbia coppers, both being engraved by the competent George Wyon at the request of Morris. On these Columbia (another name for America) is seen sitting, holding a balance and a Liberty cap on a pole.

Finally, in 1787, Congress authorized America's first official coin! It was a cent very closely resembling the Continental Dollar proposed earlier. The design had been somewhat simplified, and the words "United States" replaced "American Congress." Three hundred tons of these were ordered to be struck at New Haven, Connecticut. Collectors have called this coin the Fugio Cent, after the Latin word for "I fly" below the sun. While there are many different varieties of Fugio Cent, they may be grouped into two broad categories: Those with the sun having pointed rays and other with club-like rays.

References: Crosby, S.S., *The Early Coins of America*; Kleeberg, John, *Money of Pre-Federal America*; Newman, Eric P., ed., *Studies on Money in Early America*; Vlack, Robert, *Early American Coins*; Yeoman, R.S., *A Guide Book of United States Coins*.
Counterfeit Alert: A great many counterfeits and replicas, of every quality, of the Continental Dollar have been made - possibly tens of thousands.
Hints: Many minor varieties of Fugio Cent command a premium. "Restrikes" of this coin with new dies were made after 1860.

	VG	VF
1776 Continental Dollar, Pewter	1,600.00	4,200.00

	VG	VF
same, Brass	7,500.00	14,000.00
same, Silver		*Rare*

1783 Nova Constellatio "5", Copper
Unique

1783 Nova Constellatio "100", Silver
Rare

1783 Nova Constellatio "500", Silver
legend   *Rare*

1783 Nova Constellatio "500", Silver
no legend   *Rare*

1783 Nova Constellatio "cent", Copper

	75.00	275.00
1785 same	85.00	350.00
1786 same		*Rare*

1785 Immune Columbia / Nova
Constellatio, Copper   *Rare*

1785 Immune Columbia / Eagle,
Copper   450.00   1,750.00

1785 Immune Columbia / George III,
Copper   2,000.00   *Rare*

1785 Immune Columbia / Vermon
Auctori, Copper 2,000.00   *Rare*

1787 Fugio Cent, Pointed rays

100.00	400.00

1787 Fugio Cent, Club rays

200.00	900.00

1792 UNITED STATES MINT ISSUES

History: The issues of 1792 are the first coins of the modern federal republic as we know it today. These coins were little more than patterns but they differ significantly from the Fugios in that they were made at facilities actually owned by the federal government. The common legend on these coins is "Liberty, Parent of Science and Industry." In terms of their symbolism and their arrangement they set the basic trend for the following hundred years, and the monetary system that they initiated is the one that we use today, although greatly modified.

References: See general references.

Counterfeit Alert: Not extensively counterfeited as any example of a 1792 mint issue would attract intense scrutiny from the entire numismatic community.

Hints: Except for the half disme, these are generally too rare to be collectible.

	G	F
1792 Cent, Copper		*Rare*
1792 same with silver center		*Rare*

1792 Large Cent, Copper		*Rare*
1792 same, White Metal		*Rare*
1792 ½ Disme, Silver	1,800.00	5,000.00
1792 same		*Unique*
1792 Dime, Silver		*only 3 known*
1792 same, Copper		*Rare*

1792 Quarter, Copper	*only 2 known*
1792 Quarter, White Metal	*only 2 known*

HALF CENTS

History: The first American half cents were struck in limited numbers under adverse circumstances. Copper was in short supply and many half cents were struck on cut down private tokens. Some ready-made blanks were able to be shipped from England, however, and later from Massachusetts. Half cents were not initially legal tender and many refused to accept them, causing the coin to go out of production for fourteen years after 1811. Many also resented the profit that the mint made on copper. Eventually their low value and lack of popularity, as well as the increasing price of copper, contributed to their permanent suspension in February 1857.

References: Breen, W., *Walter Breen's Encyclopedia of United States Half Cents 1793-1857*, 1983; Cohen, Roger, *American Half Cents, The "Little Half Sisters,"* 1982 ed.

Counterfeit Alert: A struck counterfeit exists of the 1796 no pole variety.

Hints: The different dies used to strike these coins can be identified. This series is actively collected by die. Rare dies and die combinations can command a substantial premium. Excessively worn or pitted specimens are worth a fraction of listed prices. It should be noted that early types generally are found in Good or lower grades.

Basal Type Value, G: 22.00.

LIBERTY CAP TYPE

	VG	VF
1793	2,300.00	5,000.00
1794	375.00	1,400.00
1795	300.00	1,000.00
1796 with pole	10,000.00	20,000.00
1796 no pole	24,000.00	50,000.00
1797	950.00	4,500.00

DRAPED BUST TYPE

1800	40.00	150.00
1802	800.00	4,000.00

	VG	VF
1803	40.00	250.00
1804	37.00	80.00
1804 spiked chin	45.00	100.00
1805	37.00	75.00
1806	37.00	85.00
1807	37.00	85.00
1808	37.00	95.00

CLASSIC HEAD TYPE

1809	32.00	70.00
1810	40.00	125.00
1811	150.00	950.00
1825	35.00	70.00
1826	32.00	60.00
1828	32.00	50.00
1829	32.00	50.00
1831	2,750.00	4,000.00
1831 restrikes	Unc.	7,500.00
1832	32.00	50.00
1833	32.00	50.00
1834	32.00	50.00
1835	32.00	50.00
1836	Proof only	6,000.00
1836 Restrike	Proof only	6,500.00

BRAIDED HAIR TYPE

1840	Proof only	3,700.00
1840 Restrike	Proof only	3,500.00
1841	Proof only	3,700.00
1841 Restrike	Proof only	3,500.00
1842	Proof only	3,900.00
1842 Restrike	Proof only	3,500.00
1843	Proof only	3,800.00
1843 Restrike	Proof only	3,500.00
1844	Proof only	4,500.00
1844 Restrike	Proof only	3,500.00
1845	Proof only	4,700.00
1845 Restrike	Proof only	4,000.00
1846	Proof only	4,300.00
1846 Restrike	Proof only	3,500.00
1847	Proof only	3,700.00
1847 Restrike	Proof only	3,500.00
1848	Proof only	3,700.00
1848 Restrike	Proof only	3,500.00
1849	Proof only	4,100.00
1849 Restrike	Proof only	3,900.00
1849 Large date	38.00	65.00
1850	38.00	65.00
1851	32.00	65.00
1852 all restrikes?	Proof	4,000.00
1853	32.00	55.00
1854	32.00	55.00
1855	32.00	55.00
1856	35.00	60.00
1857	50.00	85.00

LARGE CENTS

History: The first American large cents were struck in limited number under adverse circumstances. Copper was in such short supply that the nation's cents were struck from melted down kettles and copper nails. Some ready-made blanks were able to be shipped from England, however. The chain reverse used on the first cent, intended to represent the unity of the states, proved unpopular, being interpreted as a symbol of oppression. Many also resented the profit that the mint made on copper cents. Nevertheless, the need for this small value coin won out and, with the purchase of new machinery in 1816 adequate quantities of large cents flowed into circulation.

Eventually they even came to be considered good luck. Often one will discover one of these big old coppers with a square nail-hole. These are called "rafter cents" and as the name implies, they were hammered onto the rafter of early American houses to bring good luck! The rising price of copper in the 1850s caused their demise.

References: Sheldon, William, *Penny Whimsey*, 1958 (and later reprints); Newcomb, H., *United States Copper Cents 1816-1857*, 1956.

Counterfeit Alert: 1799, 1803, 1805 over 5, and 1851 over inverted 18 are known.

Hints: The different dies used to strike these coins can be identified. This series in particular is actively collected by die. Rare dies and die combinations can command a substantial premium. Excessively worn or pitted specimens are worth a fraction of listed prices. It should be noted that early types generally are found in Good or lower grades. The wreath on the 1804 is open at top, the restrike has a closed wreath.

Basal Type Value, G: 7.00.

	VG	VF

FLOWING HAIR TYPE

1793 Chain Rev.	4,000.00	9,000.00
1793 Wreath Rev.	1,200.00	3,600.00

LIBERTY CAP TYPE

1793	2,750.00	7,500.00
1794	200.00	700.00
1795	200.00	650.00
1796	275.00	1,100.00

DRAPED BUST TYPE

1796	200.00	800.00
1797	100.00	350.00
1798	60.00	300.00
1799	1,750.00	10,000.00
1800	50.00	300.00
1801	40.00	275.00
1802	40.00	250.00
1803	50.00	250.00
1804	800.00	2,600.00
1804 restrike	Unc.	450.00
1805	40.00	275.00
1806	70.00	400.00
1807	50.00	275.00

CLASSIC HEAD TYPE

1808	70.00	450.00
1809	150.00	800.00
1810	50.00	425.00
1811	100.00	650.00
1812	50.00	425.00
1813	80.00	500.00
1814	50.00	425.00

CORONET TYPE

	VG	VF
1816	15.00	70.00
1817 13 stars	15.00	60.00
1817 15 stars	24.00	100.00
1818	15.00	60.00
1819	12.00	50.00
1820	12.00	50.00
1821	45.00	265.00
1822	14.00	60.00
1823	80.00	400.00
1823 restrike	*Unc.*	600.00
1824	15.00	75.00
1825	15.00	60.00
1826	14.00	60.00
1827	14.00	60.00
1828	14.00	55.00
1829	14.00	55.00
1830	14.00	55.00
1831	14.00	50.00
1832	14.00	50.00
1833	14.00	50.00
1834	12.00	40.00
1835	11.00	40.00
1836	11.00	40.00

1837	10.00	45.00
1838	10.00	45.00
1839	13.00	45.00
1840	10.00	22.00
1841	10.00	22.00
1842	10.00	22.00
1843	10.00	22.00
1844	10.00	25.00
1845	9.00	18.00
1846	9.00	18.00
1847	9.00	18.00
1848	9.00	18.00
1849	9.00	18.00
1850	9.00	18.00
1851	9.00	18.00
1852	9.00	18.00
1853	9.00	18.00
1854	9.00	18.00
1855	9.00	18.00
1856	9.00	18.00
1857	30.00	50.00

FLYING EAGLE CENTS

History: This is the first cent of modern size. It is light brown in color due to the 12% nickel alloy, and is slightly thicker than the modern cent. In order to promote public acceptance of this new smaller cent the government actually sold them at a discount! The eagle depicted on this cent was a mint mascot named Peter.

References: Snow, *Flying Eagle and Indian Cents*, 1992.

Counterfeit Alert: The majority of 1856 Flying Eagle cents are counterfeit. Altered dates are common.

Hints: The 1856 is technically a pattern not issued for circulation.

Basal Type Value, G: 10.00.

	F	EF
1856	3,000.00	5,000.00
1857	20.00	75.00
1858 Lg. Letters	20.00	75.00
1858 Small Letters	20.00	75.00

INDIAN HEAD CENTS

History: The Indian princess depicted on this cent is actually Sarah Longacre, daughter of the engraver. Legend has it that the idea for the cent stemmed from a visit by a real Indian who placed his headdress on the young girl. The reverse of 1859 lacks the shield at top. During 1864 the alloy was changed from 88% copper, 12% nickel to 95% copper, 5% tin and zinc.

References: Snow, *Flying Eagle and Indian Cents*, 1992.

Counterfeit Alert: 1908S and 1909S cents exist with added mintmark. Counterfeits exist of 1877.

Hints: Coins with natural mint red command a premium.

Basal Type Value, G-VG: 1.00.

	F	XF
COPPER-NICKEL ALLOY		
1859	10.00	70.00
1860	8.00	30.00
1861	20.00	70.00
1862	7.50	24.00
1863	7.50	24.00
1864	20.00	35.00
BRONZE		
1864	7.50	28.00
1864 L on ribbon	65.00	175.00
1865	7.50	28.00
1866	40.00	110.00
1867	40.00	110.00
1868	40.00	100.00
1869	135.00	220.00
1870	135.00	230.00
1871	150.00	260.00
1872	175.00	300.00
1873	20.00	80.00
1874	20.00	75.00
1875	20.00	65.00
1876	32.00	90.00
1877	500.00	1,100.00
1878	32.00	88.00
1879	6.50	30.00
1880	3.50	15.00
1881	3.50	13.00
1882	3.50	13.00
1883	3.50	13.00
1884	5.00	15.00
1885	8.50	25.00
1886	7.00	50.00
1887	2.00	10.00
1888	2.00	10.00
1889	2.00	10.00
1890	2.00	10.00
1891	2.00	10.00
1892	2.00	10.00
1893	2.00	10.00
1894	5.00	15.00
1895	1.75	9.00
1896	1.75	9.00
1897	1.75	9.00
1898	1.75	8.50
1899	1.50	8.00
1900	1.50	7.50
1901	1.50	7.50
1902	1.50	7.50
1903	1.50	7.50
1904	1.50	7.50
1905	1.50	7.50
1906	1.50	7.50
1907	1.50	7.50
1908	1.50	7.50
1908S	35.00	75.00
1909	2.00	8.00
1909S	285.00	365.00

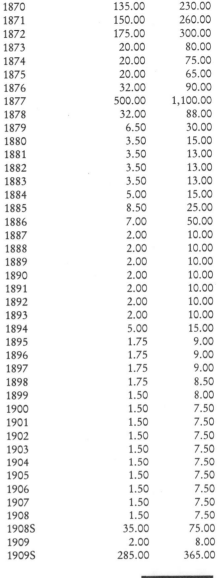

VDB (detail)

LINCOLN CENTS

History: The Lincoln cent was issued as part of an overall trend toward modernizing the coinage and its introduction was intended to coincide with the hundredth anniversary of the birth of Abraham Lincoln. It was the first regular circulating American coin to depict an actual person. The artist Victor David Brenner, a noted sculptor and medalist, executed the design. His initials VDB originally appeared at the bottom of the reverse. They were quickly deleted after complaints that they were "too large," and replaced in 1918 discretely under the shoulder.

References: Taylor, *The Standard Guide to the Lincoln Cent.*

Counterfeit Alert: There exist on the market common Lincolns cleverly altered to appear rare. One should be careful of 1909S VDB, 1909S, 1914D, and 1931S with the mintmark added. Also be aware that many 1922D cents have had their mintmark removed to appear as the 1922 plain. Most apparent 1943 bronze cents are either steel cents plated with bronze or other years with altered dates. Counterfeit 1955 double dies are also known.

Warning: Many apparently brilliant uncirculated steel cents are actually circulated examples privately recoated. 1955 cents with slight "ghosting" at date are not double dies and command little or no premium.

Hints: Early coins with full, natural mint luster command a premium above toned examples. The doubling on the 1995 double die is most evident on the word LIBERTY.

Basal Type Value, G-VG: Wheat reverse 5¢, Memorial 1¢.

WHEAT EARS REVERSE

	VF	Unc
1909 VDB	2.25	10.00
1909S VDB	450.00	600.00
1909	1.00	14.00
1909S	60.00	155.00
1910	.80	14.00
1910S	10.00	75.00
1911	1.25	18.00
1911D	11.00	85.00
1911S	25.00	125.00
1912	3.50	25.00
1912D	14.00	120.00
1912S	18.00	110.00
1913	2.00	20.00
1913D	7.00	80.00
1913S	12.00	100.00
1914	3.00	50.00
1914D	175.00	875.00
1914S	20.00	165.00
1915	9.00	80.00
1915D	3.00	45.00
1915S	12.00	100.00
1916	.75	12.00
1916D	2.00	55.00
1916S	2.50	60.00
1917	.85	12.00
1917D	1.50	55.00
1917S	1.50	60.00
1918	.80	13.00
1918D	1.50	50.00
1918S	1.50	55.00
1919	.50	11.00
1919D	1.25	45.00
1919S	.75	30.00
1920	.40	10.00
1920D	1.00	50.00
1920S	1.00	65.00
1921	1.00	40.00
1921S	3.50	100.00
1922D	10.00	80.00
1922 plain	450.00	4,700.00
1923	.50	12.00
1923S	5.00	175.00
1924	.50	22.00
1924D	20.00	225.00
1924S	2.50	90.00
1925	.50	10.00
1925D	1.00	50.00
1925S	.75	60.00
1926	.50	8.00
1926D	1.25	50.00
1926S	5.00	100.00
1927	.50	8.00
1927D	.85	25.00
1927S	1.65	65.00
1928	.50	8.00
1928D	.75	22.00
1928S	1.25	45.00
1929	.60	7.50
1929D	.65	17.00
1929S	.60	9.00
1930	.40	5.00
1930D	.50	12.00
1930S	.50	8.00
1931	.85	17.00
1931D	4.25	50.00
1931S	40.00	60.00
1932	2.50	17.00
1932D	1.75	15.00
1933	1.50	16.00
1933D	3.00	20.00
1934	.25	4.00
1934D	.45	16.00
1935	.20	2.00
1935D	.25	4.00
1935S	.30	8.00
1936	.25	2.00
1936D	.30	3.00
1936S	.40	4.00
1937	.25	2.00
1937D	.25	2.50
1937S	.30	3.25
1938	.20	2.00
1938D	.45	3.00
1938S	.55	3.50
1939	.15	1.00
1939D	.65	3.50
1939S	.30	2.00
1940	.20	1.50
1940D	.15	1.50
1940S	.15	1.50
1941	.15	1.00
1941D	.15	2.00
1941S	.15	2.25
1942	.15	1.00
1942D	.15	1.00
1942S	.30	6.00
1943 steel	.25	1.75
1943D steel	.25	1.75
1943S steel	.50	4.00
1944	.15	.40
1944D	.15	.50
1944 D over S	135.00	350.00
1944S	.15	.50
1945	.15	.50
1945D	.15	.50
1945S	.15	.50
1946	.15	.50
1946D	.15	.50
1946S	.15	.50
1947	.15	1.00
1947D	.15	.50
1947S	.15	.60
1948	.15	.50
1948D	.15	.50
1948S	.15	.60
1949	.15	.50
1949D	.15	.60
1949S	.15	1.50
1950	.15	.50
1950D	.15	.50
1950S	.15	.50
1951	.15	.50
1951D	.15	.25
1951S	.15	1.00
1952	.15	.25
1952D	.15	.30
1952S	.15	.35
1953	.15	.25
1953D	.15	.25
1953S	.15	.35
1954	.15	.35
1954D	.15	.25
1954S	.15	.25
1955	.15	.25
1955 double die	385.00	650.00
1955D	.15	.25
1955S	.15	.35
1956		.25
1956D		.25
1957		.25
1957D		.25
1958		.25
1958D		.25

LINCOLN MEMORIAL REVERSE

	BU
1959	.15
1959D	.15
1960 large date	.15
1960 small date	3.00

	BU
1960D large date	.15
1960D small date	.25
1961	.15
1961D	.15
1962	.15
1962D	.15
1963	.15
1963D	.15
1964	.15
1964D	.15
1965	.20
1966	.20
1967	.20
1968	.20
1968D	.15
1968S	.15
1969	.35
1969D	.15
1969S	.15
1970	.25
1970D	.15

1970S Large Date

1970S Small Date

1970S small date	35.00
1970S large date	.15
1971	.35
1971D	.35
1971S	.35
1972	.15
1972 double die	250.00
1972D	.15
1972S	.15
1973	.15
1973D	.15
1973S	.15
1974	.15
1974D	.15
1974S	.15
1975	.15
1975D	.15
1975S *proof only*	4.50
1976	.15
1976D	.15
1976S *proof only*	3.00

1977	.15
1977D	.15
1977S *proof only*	2.25
1978	.15
1978D	.15
1978S *proof only*	2.50
1979	.15
1979D	.15
1979S *proof only*	2.50
1980	.15
1980D	.15
1980S *proof only*	1.50
1981	.15
1981D	.15
1981S *proof only*	1.50
1982	.15
1982D	.15
1982S *proof only*	2.00

COPPER PLATED ZINC

1982	.50
1982D	.15
1983	.15
1983 double die rev.	200.00
1983D	.15
1983S *proof only*	2.50
1984	.15
1984 double die	140.00
1984D	.15
1984S *proof only*	4.00
1985	.15
1985D	.15
1985S *proof only*	3.00
1986	.15
1986D	.15
1986S *proof only*	8.00
1987	.15
1987D	.15
1987S *proof only*	3.00
1988	.15
1988D	.15
1988S *proof only*	4.00
1989	.15
1989D	.15
1989S *proof only*	4.00
1990	.15
1990D	.15
1990S *proof only*	6.00
1990S w/o S *proof only*	1,850.00
1991	.15
1991D	.15
1991S *proof only*	6.50
1992	.15
1992D	.15
1992S *proof only*	6.50
1993	.15
1993D	.15
1993S *proof only*	6.00
1994	.15
1994D	.15
1994S *proof only*	4.00
1995	.15
1995 double die	17.00

1995D	.15
1995S *proof only*	4.50
1996	.15
1996D	.15
1996S *proof only*	4.25

TWO CENT PIECES

History: The two-cent piece was first struck during the Civil War when coins, and particularly silver, had been hoarded by an uncertain populace. It was the first coin to bear the motto "In God we trust."

References: Kilman, M., *The Two Cent Piece and Varieties, 1977*; Flynn, Kevin, *Getting Your Two Cents Worth.*

Counterfeit Alert: Not widely counterfeited.

Hints: The easiest way to tell the small from the large motto varieties, is to examine the D in GOD. On the small motto variety its opening is semi-circular; on the large motto it is narrow and vertical.

Basal Type Value, G-VG: 6.50.

	F	Unc
1864 Small motto	85.00	500.00
1864 Large motto	12.00	80.00
1865	12.00	80.00
1866	13.00	80.00
1867	13.00	80.00
1868	13.00	100.00
1869	13.00	150.00
1870	20.00	220.00
1871	20.00	250.00
1872	140.00	700.00
1873 Closed 3	*Proof only*	1,500.00
1873 Open 3	*Restrike*	2,000.00

SILVER THREE CENT PIECES

History: This tiny coin was initially intended to coincide with the value of the then current three cent stamp. Because of its silver composition it is frequently referred to as a "trime."

References: Bowers, Q. David, *U.S. Three-Cent and Five-Cent Pieces.*

Counterfeit Alert: Struck German-silver counterfeits of 1860-61 exist. Also 1864 with flat detail and wiry and undetailed lettering.

Hints: This coin often comes weakly struck in the star. One should be careful not to mistake a weak strike for wear. It also frequently appears bent or dented, and as such has minimal value.

Basal Type Value, G-VG: 9.50.

	F	Unc
No Border Around Star		
1851	17.00	160.00
1851O	30.00	350.00
1852	17.00	160.00
1853	17.00	160.00
Triple Border Around Star		
1854	22.50	275.00
1855	45.00	500.00
1856	20.00	275.00
1857	20.00	275.00
1858	20.00	275.00
Double Border Around Star		
1859	20.00	150.00
1860	20.00	150.00
1861	20.00	150.00
1862	20.00	150.00
1863	70.00	500.00
1864	95.00	525.00
1865	140.00	575.00
1866	95.00	575.00
1867	165.00	575.00
1868	165.00	575.00
1869	165.00	575.00
1870	165.00	575.00
1871	165.00	575.00
1872	250.00	625.00
1873	Proof only	1,200.00

NICKEL THREE CENT PIECES

History: Actually 75% copper, 25% nickel, this coin proved much more convenient then its silver counterpart.

References: Bowers, Q. David, *U.S. Three-Cent and Five-Cent Pieces.*

Counterfeit Alert: Not widely counterfeited.

Hints: These are more frequently encountered in grades of Fine and better, and only rarely in Good.

Basal Type Value, G-VG: 6.00.

	F	Unc
1865	8.00	80.00
1866	8.00	80.00
1867	8.00	80.00
1868	8.00	80.00
1869	8.00	90.00
1870	9.00	90.00

1871	9.00	100.00
1872	9.00	100.00
1873	9.00	100.00
1874	9.00	100.00
1875	12.50	150.00
1876	15.00	150.00
1877 Proof only		1,250.00
1878 Proof only		725.00
1879	55.00	250.00
1880	85.00	270.00
1881	8.00	85.00
1882	80.00	250.00
1883	160.00	350.00
1884	300.00	525.00
1885	415.00	750.00
1886 Proof only		700.00
1887	280.00	475.00
1888	45.00	225.00
1889	75.00	235.00

SHIELD NICKELS

History: Actually 75% copper, this denomination derives its popular name from its white color caused by its 25% nickel content. This design originally featured rays between the stars on the reverse, but these were omitted sometime during 1867.

References: Wescott, Michael, *The United States Nickel Five-Cent Piece.*

Counterfeit Alert: Struck 1870-76 contemporary counterfeits exist.

Hints: The horizontal bands of the shield are sometimes weakly struck.

Basal Type Value, G-VG: 7.00

	F	Unc
1866 Rays	22.00	210.00
1867 Rays	27.00	300.00
1867	10.00	100.00
1868	10.00	100.00
1869	10.00	100.00
1870	10.00	100.00
1871	40.00	275.00
1872	11.00	110.00
1873 Closed 3	25.00	275.00
1873 Open 3	12.00	125.00
1874	17.00	125.00
1875	20.00	150.00
1876	20.00	125.00
1877 Proof only		1,300.00
1878 Proof only		700.00
1879	350.00	600.00
1880	350.00	650.00
1881	200.00	500.00
1882	10.00	100.00
1883	10.00	100.00

1883 3 over 2	125.00	350.00

LIBERTY NICKELS

History: The Liberty, or "V" Nickel both began and ended its existence in scandal. When first released, it lacked the word "cents" below the Roman numeral V for 5. As a result many unscrupulous individuals plated the new coin with gold and passed them as $5 gold pieces. These have come to be known as "Racketeer Nickels."

Although none of these nickels were officially struck in 1913, five were prepared by an unauthorized mint employee. Despite their questionable origin, they have since become one of the most famous and sought after American rarities.

References: Wescott, Michael, *The United States Nickel Five-Cent Piece.*

Counterfeit Alert: The famous 1913 has been extensively counterfeited. 1912D exists altered to 1912S.

Hints: The 1883 no cents is quite common in grades of V.F. to A.U.

Basal Type Value, G-VG: 75¢

	F	Unc
1883 No Cents	4.00	30.00
1883 With Cents	12.00	95.00
1884	15.00	140.00
1885	320.00	850.00
1886	130.00	450.00
1887	14.00	100.00
1888	17.00	120.00
1889	14.00	100.00
1890	14.00	100.00
1891	14.00	100.00
1892	14.00	100.00
1893	14.00	100.00
1894	32.00	150.00
1895	13.00	100.00
1896	14.00	100.00
1897	5.00	95.00
1898	4.00	95.00
1899	3.50	90.00
1900	2.00	70.00
1901	2.00	70.00
1902	2.00	65.00
1903	2.00	65.00
1904	2.00	65.00
1905	2.00	65.00
1905	2.00	65.00
1906	2.00	65.00
1907	2.00	65.00
1908	2.00	70.00

	F	Unc
1909	2.00	80.00
1910	2.00	65.00
1911	2.00	65.00
1912	2.00	65.00
1912D	4.00	180.00
1912S	70.00	625.00
1913		1,485,000.00

BUFFALO NICKELS

History: Three different Indians posed for the noted sculptor James Fraser for the Buffalo or Indian Head Nickel. Originally the Buffalo, actually an American Bison, was depicted standing on a mound upon which were the words "five cents." The realization that the denomination would soon wear off (like the date actually did) caused the mound to be replaced by a plain, with the denomination protected below.

References: Wescott, Michael, *The United States Nickel Five-Cent Piece.*

Counterfeit Alert: Many of the three legged examples encountered are counterfeits reengraved from other dates. Real three legged Buffalos have many subtle differences due to die polishing (see photo). 1921S, 1924S, 1926D and 1926S all exist with added mintmark.

Hints: During the Great Depression some individuals would modify these nickels by hand engraving to bear humorous images. These "Hobo Nickels" often bear a premium, rather than being considered mutilated.

Basal Type Value, G-VG: 50¢

	F	Unc.
1913 Mound	5.00	30.00
1913D Mound	9.00	50.00
1913S Mound	18.00	80.00
1913 Plain	6.00	30.00
1913D Plain	50.00	175.00
1913S Plain	125.00	300.00
1914	7.00	45.00
1914D	50.00	200.00
1914S	11.00	125.00
1915	5.00	40.00
1915D	18.00	125.00
1915S	30.00	300.00
1916	1.50	30.00
1916D	9.00	175.00
1916S	8.00	150.00
1917	1.75	45.00
1917D	12.50	275.00

1917S	15.00	350.00
1918	2.00	50.00
1918 8 over 7	350.00	12,000.00
1918D	16.00	325.00
1918S	12.00	400.00
1919	1.25	40.00
1919D	18.00	450.00
1919S	10.00	475.00
1920	1.25	40.00
1920D	12.00	475.00
1920S	7.50	425.00
1921	2.50	80.00
1921S	48.00	950.00
1923	1.25	40.00
1923S	8.00	400.00
1924	1.50	45.00
1924D	7.50	335.00
1924S	30.00	1,200.00
1925	2.00	40.00
1925D	16.00	300.00
1925S	9.00	450.00
1926	1.00	25.00
1926D	15.00	200.00
1926S	27.00	2,000.00
1927	1.00	25.00
1927D	4.50	125.00
1927S	3.00	550.00
1928	1.00	25.00
1928D	2.50	35.00
1928S	2.00	250.00
1929	1.00	25.00
1929D	1.25	40.00
1929S	1.00	38.00
1930	1.00	20.00
1930S	1.00	35.00
1931S	6.00	50.00
1934	1.00	18.00
1934D	1.00	36.00
1935	.75	15.00
1935D	.75	25.00
1935S	.75	20.00
1936	.75	15.00
1936D	.75	15.00
1936S	.75	15.00
1937	.75	15.00
1937D	.75	15.00

Detail of authentic 1937D 3-legged Buffalo

1937D 3-Legged	260.00	1,300.00
1937S	.75	15.00
1938D	.75	14.00
1938D D over S	7.00	30.00

JEFFERSON NICKELS

History: Our current nickel is one of the first American coins to be designed in an open contest. The winner, Felix Schlag was not permitted to sign his work with his initials until 1966, 28 years later.

During 1942 the alloy was changed to one of 56% copper, 35% silver and 9% manganese. This was indicated by the placement of an enlarged mintmark over the dome of Monticello, and continued until the end of 1945.

References: Wescott, Michael, *The United States Nickel Five-Cent Piece.*

Counterfeit Alert: Crude counterfeits made to pass in circulation were made in the 1940s.

Hints: The steps to Monticello usually occur weakly struck. Those which are *fully* struck command a premium.

Basal Type Value, G-VG: Silver alloy 30¢, regular alloy 5¢.

	VF	BU
1938	.25	2.00
1938D	1.50	3.00
1938S	2.50	5.00
1939	.25	1.00
1939D	4.50	25.00
1939S	1.00	15.00
1940	.25	1.00
1940D	.25	2.50
1940S	.25	2.50
1941	.25	1.00
1941D	.25	2.50
1941S	.25	3.50
1942	.25	1.00
1942D	.25	25.00
Wartime Silver Alloy		
1942P	.50	12.00
1942S	.50	9.00
1943P	.50	5.00
1943P 3 over 2	50.00	375.00
1943D	.50	6.00
1943S	.50	5.00
1944P	.50	5.00
1944D	.50	9.00
1944S	.50	9.00
1945P	.50	6.00
1945D	.50	6.00
1945S	.50	5.00
Regular Alloy		
1946	.25	.75
1946D	.25	.75
1946S	.25	.75
1947	.25	.50
1947D	.25	.75

	VF	BU
1947S	.25	.75
1948	.25	.50
1948D	.25	.85
1948S	.25	.85
1949	.25	1.00
1949D	.25	3.00
1949D D over S	68.00	400.00
1949S	.25	1.50
1950	.25	1.50
1950D	5.50	8.00
1951	.25	1.00
1951D	.25	1.00
1951S	.35	2.50
1952	.25	.75
1952D	.25	1.50
1952S	.25	.50
1953		.25
1953D		.25
1953S		.35
1954		.25
1954D		.25
1954S		.25
1954S S over D	5.00	38.00
1955	.25	.75
1955D		.25
1955D D over S	6.00	65.00
1956		.25
1956D		.25
1957		.25
1957D		.25
1958		.25
1958D		.25
1959		.25
1959D		.25
1960		.25
1960D		.25
1961		.25
1961D		.25
1962		.25
1962D		.25
1963		.25
1963D		.25
1964		.25
1964D		.25
1965		.25
1966		.25
1967		.25
1968D		.25
1968S		.25
1969D		.25
1969S		.25
1970D		.25
1970S		.25
1971		.25
1971D		.25
1971S proof only		1.00
1972		.25
1972D		.25
1972S proof only		1.00
1973		.25
1973D		.25
1973S proof only		1.00
1974		.25

1974D	.25
1974S proof only	1.00
1975	.25
1975D	.25
1975S proof only	1.00
1976	.25
1976D	.25
1976S proof only	1.00
1977	.25
1977D	.25
1977S proof only	.75
1978	.25
1978D	.25
1978S proof only	.75
1979	.25
1979D	.25
1979S proof only	.75
1980	.25
1980D	.25
1980S proof only	.75
1981	.25
1981D	.25
1981S proof only	.75
1982	.25
1982D	.25
1982S proof only	1.00
1983	.25
1983D	.25
1983S proof only	1.75
1984	.25
1984D	.25
1984S proof only	2.50
1985	.25
1985D	.25
1985S proof only	1.50
1986	.25
1986D	.25
1986S proof only	4.50
1987	.25
1987D	.25
1987S proof only	1.50
1988	.25
1988D	.25
1988S proof only	2.50
1989	.25
1989D	.25
1989S proof only	2.00
1990	.25
1990D	.25
1990S proof only	3.00
1991	.25
1991D	.25
1991S proof only	3.25
1992	.25
1992D	.25
1992S proof only	2.50
1993	.25
1993D	.25
1993S proof only	2.00
1994	.25
1994D	.25
1994S proof only	3.00
1995	.25
1995D	.25

1995S proof only	3.00
1996	.25
1996D	.25
1996S proof only	3.00

BUST HALF DIMES

History: The first coinage of half dimes was given high priority due to, as Washington said, "the want of small coins in circulation." Later, because of a vast influx of Mexican small silver, the need was less urgent. The coin was suspended 1806-28.

References: Valentine, D.W., *The United States Half Dimes*, 1931.

Counterfeit Alert: Counterfeits of the 1795 exist.

Hints: The different dies used to strike these coins can be identified. Rare dies and die combinations can command a substantial premium. Excessively worn or bent specimens are worth a fraction of listed prices.

Basal Type Value: AG 7.00.

FLOWING HAIR TYPE

	VG	VF
1794	900.00	1,750.00
1795	650.00	1,300.00

DRAPED BUST / SMALL EAGLE

1796	775.00	1,800.00
1797	800.00	1,900.00

DRAPED BUST / HERALDIC EAGLE

1800	600.00	1,200.00
1801	600.00	1,400.00
1802	12,000.00	30,000.00
1803	600.00	1,200.00
1805	800.00	1,600.00

	VG	VF
CAPPED BUST TYPE		
1829	16.00	50.00
1830	16.00	50.00
1831	16.00	50.00
1832	16.00	50.00
1833	16.00	50.00
1834	16.00	50.00
1835	16.00	50.00
1836	16.00	50.00
1837	16.00	50.00

SEATED LIBERTY HALF DIMES

History: The introduction of this new design coincided with a slight increase in the purity of the silver. The allegory of seated Liberty was probably inspired by the seated Britannia found on English coins for years, but ultimately derives from an ancient Roman type. The addition of arrows next to the date in 1853 indicates a reduction in silver content.

References: Valentine, D.W., *The United States Half Dimes,* 1931; Blythe, Al, *The Complete Guide to Liberty Seated Half Dimes.*

Counterfeit Alert: Not widely counterfeited.

Hints: Excessively worn or bent specimens are worth a fraction of listed prices. 1859-60 issues without United States are rare patterns.

Basal Type Value: G 5.00.

SEATED LIBERTY - OBVERSE FIELD PLAIN

	VG	VF
1837	32.00	90.00
1838O	90.00	350.00

SEATED LIBERTY - STARS ON OBVERSE

	VG	VF
1838	8.00	25.00
1839	8.00	27.00
1839O	11.00	30.00
1840	8.00	27.00
1840O	10.00	40.00
1841	6.00	20.00
1841O	12.00	35.00
1842	6.00	20.00
1842O	28.00	175.00
1843	6.00	20.00
1844	6.00	20.00
1844O	90.00	350.00
1845	6.00	20.00
1846	190.00	550.00
1847	6.00	20.00
1848	6.00	20.00
1848O	16.00	50.00
1849	6.00	20.00
1849 overdates	15.00	45.00
1849O	40.00	225.00
1850	6.00	20.00
1850O	18.00	60.00
1851	6.00	20.00
1851O	15.00	40.00
1852	6.00	20.00
1852O	25.00	125.00
1853 no arrows	30.00	100.00
1853O no arrows	185.00	475.00
1853 arrows	6.00	16.00
1853O arrows	9.00	25.00
1854	6.00	16.00
1854O	7.50	24.00
1855	6.00	16.00
1855O	15.00	45.00
1856	6.00	16.00
1856O	9.00	30.00
1857	6.00	16.00
1857O	9.00	65.00
1858	6.00	16.00
1858O	8.00	25.00
1859	15.00	40.00
1859O	15.00	40.00

SEATED LIBERTY - LEGEND ON OBVERSE

1860	6.00	15.00
1860O	6.00	20.00
1861	6.00	13.00
1862	6.00	15.00
1863	140.00	275.00
1863S	22.00	50.00
1864	275.00	450.00
1864S	32.00	95.00
1865	225.00	350.00
1865S	15.00	50.00
1866	175.00	325.00
1866S	15.00	50.00
1867	325.00	500.00
1867S	15.00	55.00
1868	38.00	100.00
1868S	9.50	25.00
1869	7.00	20.00
1869S	9.50	25.00
1870	6.00	13.00
1870S		*Unique*
1871	6.00	13.00
1871S	12.50	50.00
1872	6.00	13.00
1872S	6.00	13.00
1873	6.00	13.00
1873S	6.00	13.00

BUST DIMES

History: The need for dimes was less pressing than the need for half dimes, postponing its introduction for more than a year. Because of a vast influx of Mexican small silver, the need declined and dime production was suspended for most years 1806-19.

References: Bowers, Q. David, *United States Dimes, Quarters, and Half Dollars.*

Counterfeit Alert: Not widely counterfeited.

Hints: The different dies used to strike these coins can be identified. Rare dies and die combinations can command a substantial premium.

Basal Type Value: G 7.00

DRAPED BUST / SMALL EAGLE

	VG	VF
1796	1,500.00	2,500.00
1797 13 stars	1,000.00	2,300.00
1797 16 stars	1,000.00	2,300.00

DRAPED BUST / HERALDIC EAGLE

1798 over 97, 13 stars		
	1,350.00	4,500.00
1798 over 97, 16 stars		
	575.00	1,350.00
1798	575.00	1,200.00
1800	575.00	1,200.00
1801	575.00	1,200.00
1802	700.00	2,500.00
1803	575.00	1,200.00
1804, 13 stars	1,300.00	3,500.00
1804, 14 stars	1,300.00	3,500.00
1805	500.00	900.00
1807	500.00	900.00

	VG	VF
CAPPED BUST TYPE		
1809	120.00	450.00
1811 over 9	70.00	400.00
1814 Small Date	65.00	175.00
1814 Large Date	25.00	125.00
1820	18.00	100.00
1821 Small Date	20.00	100.00
1821 Large Date	18.00	90.00
1822	400.00	1,100.00
1823, 3 over 2	18.00	90.00
1824, 4 over 2	20.00	200.00
1825	18.00	85.00
1827	18.00	85.00
1828 Large Date	35.00	150.00
1828 Small Date	20.00	100.00
1829 (varieties)	18.00	60.00
1830 30 over 29	35.00	175.00
1830	18.00	50.00
1831	18.00	50.00
1832	18.00	50.00
1833	18.00	50.00
1834	18.00	50.00
1835	18.00	50.00
1836	18.00	50.00
1837	20.00	55.00

SEATED LIBERTY DIMES

History: The introduction of this new design coincided with a slight increase in the purity of the silver. The allegory of seated Liberty was probably inspired by the seated Britannia found on English coins for years, but ultimately derives from an ancient Roman type. The addition of arrows next to the date in 1853 indicates a reduction in silver content. The arrows added in 1873 indicate a slight increase in silver content.
References: Greer, Brian, *The Complete Guide to Liberty Seated Dimes.*
Counterfeit Alert: Some contemporary counterfeits in tin or lead alloy exist.
Hints: Excessively worn or bent specimens are worth a fraction of listed prices. 1859 issues without United States are rare patterns.
Basal Type Value: G 4.00.

	VG	VF

SEATED LIBERTY - OBVERSE FIELD PLAIN

1837	32.00	200.00
1838O	36.00	265.00

SEATED LIBERTY - STARS ON OBVERSE

1838 (varieties)	9.00	20.00
1839	7.00	22.00
1839O	12.00	35.00
1840	7.00	22.00
1840O	12.00	35.00
1840 extra drapery from elbow		
	30.00	125.00
1841	7.00	20.00
1841O	10.00	35.00
1842	7.00	18.00
1842O	8.00	28.00
1843	7.00	18.00
1843O	45.00	185.00
1844	40.00	180.00
1845	7.00	18.00
1845O	20.00	175.00
1846	85.00	275.00
1847	14.00	50.00
1848	12.00	40.00
1849	7.00	18.00
1849O	12.00	85.00
1850	7.00	18.00
1850O	10.00	60.00
1851	7.00	18.00
1851O	12.00	70.00
1852	7.00	18.00
1852O	16.00	95.00
1853 no arrows	40.00	125.00
1853 arrows	6.00	18.00
1853O arrows	8.00	25.00
1854	6.50	18.00
1854O	7.50	22.00
1855	6.50	18.00
1856	6.50	18.00
1856O	6.50	18.00
1856S	75.00	300.00
1857	6.50	16.00
1857O	6.50	20.00
1858	6.50	16.00
1858O	12.00	70.00
1858S	70.00	225.00
1859	6.50	18.00
1859O	7.00	40.00
1859S	75.00	250.00
1860S	20.00	85.00

SEATED LIBERTY - LEGEND ON OBVERSE

1860	6.50	18.00
1860O	350.00	1,000.00
1861	6.00	18.00
1861S	30.00	150.00
1862	6.00	18.00
1862S	30.00	125.00
1863	150.00	400.00
1863S	25.00	75.00
1864	150.00	400.00
1864S	15.00	55.00
1865	150.00	350.00
1865S	15.00	75.00
1866	175.00	500.00
1866S	17.00	60.00
1867	250.00	600.00
1867S	17.00	60.00
1868	7.00	30.00
1868S	10.00	55.00
1869	10.00	40.00
1869S	10.00	35.00
1870	6.00	18.00
1870S	95.00	300.00
1871	6.00	18.00
1871CC	475.00	1,500.00
1871S	10.00	50.00
1872	6.00	18.00
1872CC	250.00	1,000.00
1872S	20.00	95.00
1873 Closed 3	6.00	20.00
1873 Open 3	18.00	75.00
1873CC		Unique
1873 arrows	10.00	40.00
1873CC arrows	500.00	2,400.00
1873S arrows	15.00	55.00
1874	7.00	40.00
1874CC	1,000.00	3,250.00
1874S	20.00	75.00
1875	6.00	12.00
1875CC	6.00	15.00
1875S	6.00	12.00
1876	6.00	12.00
1876CC	6.00	14.50
1876S	6.00	12.00
1877	6.00	12.00
1877CC	6.00	14.00
1877S	6.00	13.00
1878	6.00	12.00
1878CC	35.00	120.00
1879	125.00	300.00
1880	75.00	200.00
1881	75.00	250.00
1882	6.00	12.00
1883	6.00	12.00
1884	6.00	12.00
1884S	15.00	45.00
1885	6.00	12.00
1885S	175.00	600.00
1886	6.00	12.00
1886S	17.00	50.00
1887	6.00	12.00
1887S	6.00	12.00
1888	6.00	12.00

	VG	VF
1888S	6.00	12.00
1889	6.00	12.00
1889S	8.00	35.00
1890	6.00	12.00
1890S	6.50	25.00
1891	6.00	12.00
1891O	6.00	16.00
1891S	6.00	12.00

BARBER DIMES

History: While many considered the depiction of Liberty by Chief Engraver Charles Barber, after whom the coin is named, unartistic, it has over the years come to be regarded as a well balanced portrait. The reverse differs little from that of the Seated Liberty.

References: Lawrence, David, *The Complete Guide to Barber Dimes.*

Counterfeit Alert: Beware of altered 1894S.

Hints: Excessively worn or bent specimens are worth a fraction of listed prices.

Basal Value: G: 75¢.

	F	EF
1892	10.00	25.00
1892O	15.00	35.00
1892S	100.00	150.00
1893, 3 over 2	50.00	150.00
1893	11.00	35.00
1893O	60.00	110.00
1893S	18.00	45.00
1894	50.00	90.00
1894O	125.00	275.00
1894S		extremely rare
1895	200.00	325.00
1895O	500.00	1,300.00
1895S	60.00	110.00
1896	25.00	65.00
1896O	150.00	350.00
1896S	125.00	250.00
1897	2.50	24.00
1897O	150.00	325.00
1897S	45.00	85.00
1898	2.50	22.00
1898O	50.00	120.00
1898S	15.00	40.00
1899	2.50	22.00
1899O	45.00	110.00
1899S	9.00	32.00
1900	2.50	22.00
1900O	50.00	175.00
1900S	6.00	25.00
1901	2.50	22.00
1901O	9.50	40.00
1901S	190.00	400.00
1902	2.50	20.00
1902O	10.00	36.00
1902S	30.00	70.00
1903	2.50	20.00
1903O	6.00	27.00
1903S	235.00	650.00
1904	2.50	20.00
1904S	75.00	225.00
1905	2.50	20.00
1905O	20.00	45.00
1905S	5.50	27.00
1906	2.50	20.00
1906D	5.00	22.00
1906O	30.00	60.00
1906S	8.00	32.00
1907	2.50	20.00
1907D	6.50	30.00
1907O	15.00	40.00
1907S	8.00	35.00
1908	2.50	20.00
1908D	5.50	22.00
1908O	30.00	65.00
1908S	6.00	30.00
1909	2.50	20.00
1909D	45.00	80.00
1909O	7.00	27.00
1909S	50.00	125.00
1910	2.50	20.00
1910D	6.50	32.00
1910S	35.00	75.00
1911	2.50	20.00
1911D	2.50	20.00
1911S	5.50	27.00
1912	2.50	20.00
1912D	2.50	20.00
1912S	4.75	22.00
1913	2.50	20.00
1913S	60.00	160.00
1914	2.50	20.00
1914D	2.50	20.00
1914S	4.75	27.00
1915	2.50	20.00
1915S	18.00	50.00
1916	2.50	20.00
1916S	2.50	20.00

MERCURY DIMES

History: This dime, depicting freedom of thought in the form of Liberty wearing a winged cap, was struck as part of a program to improve the artistic quality of the nation's coinage. It was designed by medalist Adolph Weinman. The fasces on the reverse were an ancient Roman symbol of civic authority.

References: Lange, David W., *The Complete Guide to Mercury Dimes;* Bowers, Q. David, *United States Dimes, Quarters, and Half Dollars.*

Counterfeit Alert: Beware of counterfeit 1916D. Altered coins exist for 1916D, 1921, 1921D, 1931D, 1942/1, 1942/1D. All 1923D are counterfeit.

Hints: Examples with the double-bands which bind the fasces together sharply struck are scarcer. These are referred to as "full split bands."

Basal Value: G: 50¢.

	VF	Unc
1916	5.00	35.00
1916D	1,700.00	3,000.00
1916S	9.50	40.00
1917	5.00	30.00
1917D	15.00	150.00
1917S	5.00	75.00
1918	9.00	85.00
1918D	9.00	120.00
1918S	5.00	95.00
1919	5.00	40.00
1919D	15.00	175.00
1919S	11.00	200.00
1920	5.00	30.00
1920D	6.50	120.00
1920S	6.50	85.00
1921	150.00	1,200.00
1921D	185.00	1,400.00
1923	5.00	30.00
1923S	10.00	150.00
1924	5.00	45.00
1924D	9.00	165.00
1924S	8.00	175.00
1925	4.00	30.00
1925D	25.00	275.00
1925S	8.00	175.00
1926	3.00	30.00
1926D	6.50	85.00
1926S	35.00	900.00
1927	3.50	25.00
1927D	16.00	200.00
1927S	5.50	150.00
1928	3.50	25.00
1928D	12.50	150.00
1928S	4.00	85.00
1929	3.50	22.00
1929D	7.50	30.00
1929S	3.50	36.00
1930	3.50	30.00
1930S	5.50	80.00
1931	4.50	40.00
1931D	15.00	80.00
1931S	6.00	70.00
1934	1.00	15.00
1934D	1.00	25.00
1935	1.00	11.00
1935D	1.00	30.00
1935S	1.00	18.00

	VF	Unc
1936	1.00	15.00
1936D	1.00	22.00
1936S	1.00	14.00
1937	1.00	12.00
1937D	1.00	18.00
1937S	1.00	16.00
1938	1.00	14.00
1938D	1.00	15.00
1938S	1.00	14.00
1939	1.00	10.00
1939D	1.00	12.00
1939S	1.00	18.00
1940	.75	7.00
1940D	.75	10.00
1940S	.75	10.00
1941	.75	7.00
1941D	.75	9.00
1941S	.75	9.00
1942, 2 over 1	240.00	1,600.00
1942D, 2 over 1	240.00	1,300.00
1942	.75	7.00
1942D	.75	9.00
1942S	.75	10.00
1943	.75	7.00
1943D	.75	8.00
1943S	.75	8.00
1944	.75	7.00
1944D	.75	7.00
1944S	.75	8.00
1945	.75	7.00
1945D	.75	7.00
1945S	.75	7.00
1945S micro S	1.75	22.00

ROOSEVELT DIMES

History: John Sinnock designed this as a memorial for the late President Franklin Roosevelt. The choice of the dime denomination was a deliberate attempt to highlight the March of Dimes and its fight against polio. Roosevelt was a victim of polio and was confined to a wheelchair during his presidency.
References: Rapsus, Ginger, *The United States Clad Coinage.*
Counterfeit Alert: Few counterfeits exist for this series.
Hints: Most dates are common in mint state, the 1964 excessively so.
Basal Value: VF: 50¢.

	EF	Unc
1946	.50	1.50
1946D	.50	1.50
1946S	.65	1.50

1947	.50	1.75
1947D	.50	2.50
1947S	.75	2.50
1948	.50	4.00
1948D	.50	3.50
1948S	.75	3.00
1949	.75	10.00
1949D	.50	4.00
1949S	2.25	17.00
1950	.50	2.00
1950D	.50	2.00
1950S	.50	9.00
1950S, S over D	65.00	300.00
1951	.50	1.25
1951D	.50	1.25
1951S	.50	5.00
1952	.50	1.50
1952D	.50	1.50
1952S	.50	3.50
1953	.50	1.50
1953D	.50	1.50
1953S	.50	1.50
1954	.50	1.50
1954D	.50	1.50
1954S	.50	1.50
1955	.50	1.50
1955D	.50	1.50
1955S	.50	1.50
1956		1.00
1956D		1.00
1957		1.00
1957D		1.00
1958		1.00
1958D		1.00
1959		.75
1959D		.75
1960		.75
1960D		.75
1961		.75
1961D		.75
1962		.75
1962D		.75
1963		.75
1963D		.75
1964		.75
1964D		.75

CUPRO-NICKEL CLAD COPPER

1965		.50
1966		.50
1967		.50
1968		.35
1968D		.35
1968S *Proof only*		.75
1969		.50
1969D		.35
1969S *Proof only*		.75
1970		.35
1970D		.35
1970S *Proof only*		.75
1971		.35
1971D		.35
1971S *Proof only*		.75
1972		.35
1972D		.35

1972S *Proof only*	.75
1973	.35
1973D	.35
1973S *Proof only*	.75
1974	.35
1974D	.35
1974S *Proof only*	.75
1975	.35
1975D	.35
1975S *Proof only*	1.00
1976	.35
1976D	.35
1976S *Proof only*	.75
1977	.35
1977D	.35
1977S *Proof only*	.75
1978	.35
1978D	.35
1978S *Proof only*	.75
1979	.35
1979D	.35
1979 thick S *Proof only*	.75
1979 thin S *Proof only*	1.25
1980P	.35
1980D	.35
1980S *Proof only*	.75
1981P	.35
1981D	.35
1981S *Proof only*	.75
1982P	1.50
1982 no mint mark error	150.00
1982D	.35
1982S *Proof only*	.75
1983P	.75
1983D	.75
1983S *Proof only*	.75
1984P	.35
1984D	.35
1984S *Proof only*	1.25
1985P	.35
1985D	.35
1985S *Proof only*	.75
1986P	.35
1986D	.35
1986S *Proof only*	1.50
1987P	.35
1987D	.35
1987S *Proof only*	.75
1988P	.35
1988D	.35
1988S *Proof only*	.75
1989P	.35
1989D	.35
1989S *Proof only*	.75
1990P	.35
1990D	.35
1990S *Proof only*	2.00
1991P	.35
1991D	.35
1991S *Proof only*	2.00
1992P	.35
1992D	.35
1992S *Proof only*	1.25
1992S Silver *Proof only*	2.75

	EF	Unc
1993P		.35
1993D		.35
1993S *Proof only*		2.00
1993S Silver *Proof only*		2.75
1994P		.35
1994D		.35
1994S *Proof only*		2.25
1994S Silver *Proof only*		3.00
1995		.35
1995D		.35
1995S *proof only*		2.25
1995S Silver *proof only*		3.25
1996		.35
1996D		.35
1996W *mint sets only*		
1996S *proof only*		2.00
1996S Silver *proof only*		3.50

TWENTY CENT PIECES

History: Despite the fact that the eagle on this coin faced in the opposite direction, people still confused this odd coin with the quarter. The smooth edge on the twenty cent piece, unlike the reeded edge of the quarter, was also intended to help avoid confusion but to no avail. This experiment was destined to be as unpopular as the Susan B. Anthony dollar, and was eliminated just as quickly.
References: Hammer, Ted, "The Twenty Cent Piece," *The Numismatist*, vol. 60, pp. 167-69.
Counterfeit Alert: Altered 1876CC.
Hints: Mutilated pieces with "reeding" scratched in have been observed.
Basal Type Value: G 35.00.

	F	EF
1875	75.00	200.00
1875CC	75.00	225.00
1875S	68.00	160.00
1876	120.00	325.00
1876CC		*extremely rare*
1877	1,300.00	1,900.00
1878	1,200.00	1,500.00

BUST QUARTERS

History: Few quarters were struck during the early republic. Coinage did not begin until 1796 when a mere 6,146 pieces were struck, and did not resume until 1804. Those up to 1828 have a lettered edge.

From 1831 the edge is reeded as it is today.
References: Browning, A. W., *The Early Quarter Dollars of the United States.*
Counterfeit Alert: Exercise caution in examining 1796-1807 issues. Beware of cleaning.
Hints: The different dies used to strike these coins can be identified. Rare dies and die combinations can command a substantial premium.
Basal Type Value: AG-G: 20.00.

DRAPED BUST / SMALL EAGLE

	VG	VF
1796	5,200.00	11,500.00

DRAPED BUST / HERALDIC EAGLE

1804	1,200.00	3,800.00
1805	250.00	825.00
1806, 6 over 5	250.00	8275.00
1806	250.00	825.00
1807	250.00	825.00

CAPPED BUST TYPE

	VG	VF
1815	70.00	300.00
1818 8 over 5	70.00	325.00
1818	65.00	300.00
1819	65.00	300.00
1820	65.00	250.00
1821	65.00	250.00
1822 25 over 50c	900.00	3,000.00
1822	75.00	350.00
1823, 3 over 2	7,000.00	17,500.00
1824, 4 over 2	85.00	500.00
1825, 5 over 2	85.00	400.00
1825, 5 over 3	60.00	250.00
1825, 5 over 4	60.00	250.00

1827		*extremely rare*
1827 restrike		*extremely rare*
1828	60.00	250.00
1828 25 over 50c	135.00	700.00

NO MOTTO, REDUCED SIZE

1831 Small letters	35.00	95.00
1831 Large letters	35.00	95.00
1832	35.00	95.00
1833	40.00	120.00
1834	35.00	95.00
1835	35.00	95.00
1836	35.00	95.00
1837	35.00	95.00
1838	35.00	95.00

SEATED LIBERTY QUARTERS

History: The introduction of this new design coincided with a slight increase in the purity of the silver. The allegory of seated Liberty was probably inspired by the seated Britannia found on English coins for years, but ultimately derives from an ancient Roman type. The addition of arrows next to the date in 1853 indicates a reduction in weight. The arrows added in 1873 indicate a slight increase in weight.
References: Briggs, Larry, *Liberty Seated Quarters.*
Counterfeit Alert: Counterfeit 1853 no arrows variety exists altered from genuine 1858.
Hints: Excessively worn or bent specimens are worth a fraction of listed prices. 1859 issues without United States are rare patterns.
Basal Type Value: G: 7.00.

NO MOTTO ABOVE EAGLE

	VG	VF
1838	12.00	60.00
1839	12.00	60.00
1840O	13.00	65.00

	VG	VF
1840 extra drapery from elbow		
	20.00	75.00
1840O extra drapery from elbow		
	25.00	80.00
1841	40.00	150.00
1841O	20.00	65.00
1842	75.00	225.00
1842O Small date	385.00	1,250.00
1842O Large date	18.00	65.00
1843	15.00	38.00
1843O	20.00	65.00
1844	15.00	38.00
1844O	18.00	80.00
1845	15.00	35.00
1846	15.00	38.00
1847	15.00	35.00
1847O	27.00	110.00
1848	30.00	110.00
1849	20.00	65.00
1849O	400.00	1,600.00

	VG	VF
1850	30.00	70.00
1850O	30.00	68.00
1851	35.00	120.00
1851O	185.00	585.00
1852	35.00	120.00
1852O	220.00	600.00
1853 no arrows	220.00	500.00

ARROWS AT DATE

1853	8.00	40.00
1853, 3 over 4	70.00	225.00
1853O	11.00	60.00
1854	8.00	30.00
1854O	12.00	45.00
1854O Large O	135.00	275.00
1855	8.00	30.00
1855O	40.00	225.00
1855S	40.00	140.00

ARROWS REMOVED

1856	8.00	25.00
1856O	12.00	38.00
1856S	35.00	175.00
1856S, S over S	50.00	265.00
1857	8.00	25.00
1857O	8.50	30.00
1857S	80.00	300.00
1858	8.00	25.00
1858O	15.00	45.00
1858S	60.00	200.00
1859	9.00	25.00
1859O	20.00	65.00
1859S	95.00	275.00
1860	8.00	25.00

1860O	15.00	40.00
1860S	150.00	600.00
1861	8.00	25.00
1861S	65.00	250.00
1862	9.00	30.00
1862S	45.00	225.00
1863	25.00	65.00
1864	45.00	125.00
1864S	200.00	700.00
1865	50.00	125.00
1865S	75.00	300.00

MOTTO ABOVE EAGLE

1866	225.00	450.00
1866S	175.00	450.00
1867	150.00	300.00
1867S	150.00	300.00
1868	90.00	250.00
1868S	55.00	150.00
1869	200.00	400.00
1869S	80.00	200.00
1870	45.00	135.00
1870CC	1,900.00	6,500.00
1871	30.00	90.00
1871CC	1,000.00	3,800.00
1871S	300.00	550.00
1872	25.00	75.00
1872CC	400.00	1,800.00
1872S	350.00	900.00
1873 Closed 3	80.00	250.00
1873 Open 3	25.00	75.00
1873CC		4 known

ARROWS AT DATE

1873	13.00	60.00
1873CC	1,600.00	5,000.00
1873S	22.00	120.00
1874	15.00	60.00
1874S	20.00	85.00

ARROWS REMOVED

1875	8.00	22.00
1875CC	50.00	185.00
1875S	30.00	90.00
1876	8.00	22.00
1876CC	12.00	32.00
1876S	8.00	22.00
1877	8.00	22.00
1877CC	10.00	32.00
1877S	8.00	26.00
1877S over horizontal S		135.00
1878	8.00	25.00
1878CC	20.00	55.00
1878S	100.00	225.00
1879	130.00	235.00
1880	130.00	235.00
1881	130.00	235.00
1882	130.00	235.00
1883	130.00	235.00
1884	150.00	250.00
1885	130.00	235.00
1886	200.00	325.00
1887	130.00	235.00
1888	130.00	235.00

1888S	10.00	25.00
1889	130.00	235.00
1890	45.00	100.00
1891	8.00	25.00
1891O	140.00	400.00
1891S	10.00	30.00

BARBER QUARTERS

History: While many considered the depiction of Liberty by Chief Engraver Charles Barber, after whom the coin is named, unartistic, it has over the years come to be regarded as a well balanced portrait. It was also used on the dime and half dollar of the same era. The formal heraldic eagle on the reverse was used on the half dollar as well.

References: Lawrence, David, *The Complete Guide to Barber Quarters.*

Counterfeit Alert: Most are poorly made contemporary counterfeits.

Hints: Excessively worn specimens are worth a fraction of listed prices.

Basal Type Value: G: 1.50.

	F	EF
1892	17.00	65.00
1892O	17.00	75.00
1892S	30.00	110.00
1893	15.00	65.00
1893O	20.00	70.00
1893S	24.00	100.00
1894	18.00	65.00
1894O	20.00	70.00
1894S	20.00	70.00
1895	15.00	65.00
1895O	20.00	80.00
1895S	23.00	80.00
1896	15.00	65.00
1896O	40.00	270.00
1896S	600.00	1,350.00
1897	15.00	65.00
1897O	45.00	325.00
1897S	70.00	235.00
1898	15.00	60.00
1898O	30.00	175.00
1898S	20.00	75.00
1899	15.00	60.00
1899O	22.00	80.00
1899S	25.00	85.00
1900	15.00	60.00
1900O	30.00	85.00
1900S	18.00	65.00
1901	15.00	60.00
1901O	60.00	325.00

	F	EF
1901S	3,300.00	6,250.00
1902	15.00	60.00
1902O	20.00	80.00
1902S	23.00	75.00
1903	15.00	60.00
1903O	20.00	85.00
1903S	25.00	95.00
1904	15.00	60.00
1904O	26.00	170.00
1905	15.00	60.00
1905O	22.00	110.00
1905S	17.00	70.00
1906	15.00	60.00
1906D	17.00	62.00
1906O	20.00	70.00
1907	15.00	60.00
1907D	17.00	70.00
1907O	17.00	60.00
1907S	22.00	95.00
1908	15.00	60.00
1908D	15.00	60.00
1908O	15.00	60.00
1908S	42.00	200.00
1909	15.00	60.00
1909D	15.00	60.00
1909O	38.00	180.00
1909S	18.00	72.00
1910	17.00	60.00
1910D	20.00	85.00
1911	15.00	60.00
1911D	65.00	275.00
1911S	18.00	85.00
1912	15.00	60.00
1912S	20.00	80.00
1913	50.00	375.00
1913D	15.00	75.00
1913S	1,600.00	3,100.00
1914	15.00	60.00
1914D	15.00	60.00
1914S	110.00	300.00
1915	15.00	60.00
1915D	15.00	60.00
1915S	17.00	75.00
1916	15.00	60.00
1916D	15.00	60.00

STANDING LIBERTY QUARTER

History: Perhaps one of the most controversial designs ever put in circulation, the Standing Liberty Quarter was initially given a resounding endorsement by the artistic community. Its designer, Hermon MacNeil, was a well known sculptor and its fresh new design was a far cry from Barber's stiff quarter. Later, when the public objected to Miss Liberty's one exposed breast a change was ordered in the design. However so many individuals of importance had endorsed the coin that the legislation ordering the change dwelled on technical matters, how well they stacked and the position of the eagle on the reverse, and tactfully avoided criticism of the offending breast. During 1917 Liberty was clothed in chain mail. As on the Buffalo nickel the date wore off very quickly. To help alleviate this problem it was placed in a recess starting in 1925.

References: Cline, J.H., *Standing Liberty Quarters,* 1986.

Counterfeit Alert: Altered 1916, 1918S 8 over 7, 1923S. On genuine 1923S, 3 must have a flat top.

Hints: Liberty's head is not usually fully struck. Fully struck examples in high grade command a premium. Coins with date worn off are worth only their scrap value.

Basal Type Value: G: 1.25.

	F	EF
1916	1,500.00	2,500.00
1917	15.00	60.00
1917D	25.00	80.00
1917S	20.00	120.00

	F	EF
1917	16.00	40.00
1917D	45.00	80.00
1917S	28.00	65.00
1918	20.00	45.00
1918D	35.00	80.00
1918S	20.00	42.00
1918S, 8 over 7	1,750.00	4,250.00
1919	37.00	60.00
1919D	90.00	250.00
1919S	90.00	335.00
1920	17.00	34.00
1920D	46.00	90.00
1920S	22.00	42.00
1921	110.00	225.00
1923	17.00	35.00
1923S	175.00	400.00
1924	16.00	35.00
1924D	40.00	80.00
1924S	22.00	75.00
1925	5.50	26.00
1926	5.50	26.00
1926D	12.00	50.00
1926S	10.00	82.00

1927	5.50	25.00
1927D	10.00	68.00
1927S	45.00	975.00
1928	5.50	25.00
1928D	8.00	35.00
1928S	5.50	35.00
1929	5.50	25.00
1929D	8.00	32.00
1929S	5.50	28.00
1930	5.50	25.00
1930S	5.50	25.00

WASHINGTON QUARTER

History: The Washington Quarter was originally supposed to be struck for only one year to commemorate the bicentennial of Washington's birth. By the time it was released, however, the celebration was nearly over. Its designer was John Flanagan.

References: Bowers, Q. David, *United States Dimes, Quarters, and Half Dollars;* Rapsus, Ginger, *The United States Clad Coinage.*

Counterfeit Alert: Beware of added mint mark on 1932D and 1932S. 1932 and 1934 counterfeits exist in high grade.

Hints: Dates in the 1930's may have weak rims, but not 1934 and 1935. 1964 may be as common in Unc. as in circulated grades. No quarters were dated 1975.

Basal Type Value: VF 1.00 (silver), Unc 75¢ (clad).

	F	Unc
1932	3.50	20.00
1932D	45.00	400.00
1932S	37.00	200.00
1934	2.00	18.00
1934D	4.00	80.00
1935	2.00	17.00
1935D	4.00	85.00
1935S	3.50	40.00
1936	2.00	16.00
1936D	3.00	285.00
1936S	4.00	40.00
1937	2.50	20.00
1937D	3.50	30.00
1937S	5.00	80.00
1938	3.50	45.00
1938S	4.00	47.00
1939	2.00	12.00

	F	Unc
1939D	3.50	26.00
1939S	3.50	50.00
1940	2.00	11.00
1940D	5.00	42.00
1940S	2.50	14.00
1941	2.00	5.50
1941D	2.00	14.00
1941S	2.00	14.00
1942	2.00	6.00
1942D	2.00	9.00
1942S	2.00	35.00
1943	2.00	5.00
1943D	2.00	12.00
1943S	2.00	18.00
1944	2.00	5.00
1944D	2.00	8.00
1944S	2.00	9.00
1945	2.00	3.50
1945D	2.00	7.00
1945S	2.00	5.00
1946	2.00	3.75
1946D	2.00	5.00

	EF	Unc
1946S	2.50	5.50
1947	2.00	6.00
1947D	2.50	5.00
1947S	2.50	5.00
1948	2.00	3.75
1948D	2.50	5.00
1948S	2.50	7.00
1949	3.00	13.50
1949D	2.50	7.00
1950	2.00	3.00
1950D	2.00	4.00
1950D, D over S	120.00	265.00
1950S	2.00	6.00
1950S, S over D	155.00	300.00
1951	2.00	3.50
1951D	2.00	3.00
1951S	2.00	8.00
1952	1.50	2.75
1952D	2.00	3.00
1952S	2.00	6.50
1953	1.50	3.00
1953D	1.50	2.00
1953S	1.50	3.00
1954	1.50	2.00
1954D	1.50	2.00
1954S	1.50	2.00
1955	1.50	2.00
1955D	1.50	2.00
1956	1.50	2.00
1956D	1.50	2.00
1957	1.50	2.00
1957D	1.50	2.00
1958	1.50	2.00
1958D	1.50	2.00
1959	1.25	1.75
1959D	1.25	1.75
1960		1.75
1960D		1.75
1961		1.75
1961D		1.75

1962	1.75
1962D	1.75
1963	1.50
1963D	1.50
1964	1.25
1964D	1.25

CUPRO-NICKEL CLAD COPPER

1965	.75
1966	.75
1967	.75
1968	.75
1968D	.75
1968S *Proof only*	1.25
1969	.75
1969D	.75
1969S *Proof only*	1.25
1970	.75
1970D	.75
1970S *Proof only*	1.25
1971	.75
1971D	.75
1971S *Proof only*	1.25
1972	.75
1972D	.75
1972S *Proof only*	1.25
1973	.75
1973D	.75
1973S *Proof only*	1.25
1974	.75
1974D	.75
1974S *Proof only*	1.25

1976 Bicentennial	.75
1976D Bicentennial	.75
1976S Bicentennial *Proof only*	1.25
1976S Bicentennial Silver Clad	1.50
1977	.75
1977D	.75
1977S *Proof only*	1.25
1978	.75
1978D	.75
1978S *Proof only*	1.25
1979	.75
1979D	.75
1979 thick S *Proof only*	1.25
1979 thin S *Proof only*	1.50
1980P	.75
1980D	.75
1980S *Proof only*	1.25
1981P	.75
1981D	.75
1981S *Proof only*	1.00
1982P	4.50
1982D	1.50
1982S *Proof only*	1.00
1983P	6.00
1983D	2.50

1983S *Proof only*	1.00
1984P	.75
1984D	1.75
1984S *Proof only*	2.50
1985P	1.25
1985D	3.00
1985S *Proof only*	1.75
1986P	2.00
1986D	2.50
1986S *Proof only*	3.00
1987P	.75
1987D	.75
1987S *Proof only*	1.50
1988P	.75
1988D	.75
1988S *Proof only*	2.00
1989P	.75
1989D	.75
1989S *Proof only*	2.50
1990P	.75
1990D	.75
1990S *Proof only*	2.50
1991P	.75
1991D	.75
1991S *Proof only*	2.50
1992P	.75
1992D	.75
1992S *Proof only*	3.00
1992S Silver *Proof only*	3.50
1993P	.75
1993D	.75
1993S *Proof only*	2.50
1993S Silver *Proof only*	3.50
1994P	.75
1994D	.75
1994S *Proof only*	2.50
1994S Silver *Proof only*	3.50
1995	.75
1995D	.75
1995S *proof only*	2.50
1995S Silver *proof only*	3.75
1996	.75
1996D	.75
1996S *proof only*	2.25
1996S Silver *proof only*	3.75

EARLY HALF DOLLARS

History: While this denomination was issued with some consistency, mintages were generally low. Early half dollars are overwhelmingly scarcer than their contemporary dollars. From 1808 half dollars began to be produced in more reasonable quantities and by the mid-1820's they became one of the more commonly encountered denominations. Later Capped Bust Type halves are often found in high grade due to the fact that some were held in reserve by banks in order to back privately issued paper money. This series also saw the modernization of the half dollar with the introduction of steam powered machinery in the 1830's and the concurrent replacement of the edge inscription with reeding similar to that on half dollars today.

References: Overton, Al C., *Early Half Dollar Die Varieties 1794-1836.*

Counterfeit Alert: A high grade cast of the 1796 exists. Exercise caution in examining these issues. Beware of cleaning, and of plugged holed coins.

Hints: The different dies used to strike these coins can be identified. Rare dies and die combinations can command a substantial premium. Capped bust coins in particular suffer from weak strike. Both the brooch on the obverse and the motto above the eagle on the reverse often occur incompletely struck due to the design on the opposite side using up the metal. Stars are also sometimes weak at center, though difficult to tell from wear to the untrained eye.

Basal Type Value: AG-G: 22.00.

FLOWING HAIR TYPE

	VG	VF
1794	1,500.00	4,200.00
1795 two leaves	500.00	1,500.00
1795 three leaves	1,800.00	5,000.00

DRAPED BUST / SMALL EAGLE

1796, 15 stars	9,900.00	19,000.00
1796, 16 stars	11,500.00	23,000.00
1797	10,700.00	22,000.00

DRAPED BUST / HERALDIC EAGLE

1801	275.00	875.00
1802	225.00	825.00
1803 Small 3	175.00	550.00
1803 Large 3	140.00	335.00
1805, 5 over 4	265.00	825.00
1805	140.00	335.00
1806, 6 over 5	160.00	375.00
1806	150.00	325.00

Note: many varieties of 1806 exist.

1807	150.00	325.00

CAPPED BUST / LETTERED EDGE

	VG	VF
1807 Small stars	90.00	325.00
1807 Large stars	60.00	285.00
1807, 50 over 20	70.00	225.00
1808, 8 over 7	45.00	140.00
1808	40.00	100.00
1809	40.00	100.00
1810	35.00	85.00
1811, 11 over 10	35.00	125.00
1811	35.00	80.00
1812, 2 over 1, small 8,	35.00	135.00
1812, 2 over 1, large 8,	2,000.00	6,000.00
1812	35.00	75.00
1813	35.00	75.00
1813, 50 C over inverted UNI	40.00	125.00
1814, 4 over 3	50.00	140.00
1814	35.00	75.00
1815, 5 over 2	750.00	1,750.00
1817, 7 over 3	90.00	325.00
1817, 7 over 4	20,000.00	70,000.00
1817	35.00	65.00
1818, 8 over 7	35.00	70.00
1818	35.00	55.00
1819, 9 over 8	38.00	90.00
1819	35.00	55.00
1820, 20 over 19	35.00	120.00
1820	35.00	110.00
1821	35.00	65.00
1822, 2 over 1	50.00	125.00
1822	35.00	65.00
1823	35.00	55.00
1824, 4 over 1	32.00	85.00
1824, 4 over 4	32.00	55.00
1824	32.00	55.00
1825	30.00	47.00
1826	30.00	47.00
1827, 7 over 6	30.00	90.00
1827	30.00	47.00

1828	30.00	47.00

Note: date varieties of 1828 exist.

1829, 9 over 7	30.00	65.00
1829	30.00	47.00
1830	30.00	47.00
1831	30.00	47.00
1832	30.00	47.00
1833	30.00	47.00
1834	30.00	47.00
1835	30.00	47.00
1836	30.00	47.00
1836, 50 over 00	45.00	150.00

CAPPED BUST / REEDED EDGE

1836	750.00	1,200.00
1837	30.00	65.00
1838	32.00	67.00
1838O *Proof only*		*Extremely Rare*
1839	32.00	67.00
1839O	150.00	365.00

SEATED LIBERTY HALF DOLLARS

History: The introduction of this new design on the half dollar came somewhat later than its appearance in smaller denominations. The allegory of seated Liberty was probably inspired by the seated Britannia found on English coins for years, but ultimately derives from an ancient Roman type. The addition of arrows next to the date in 1853 indicates a reduction in weight. The arrows added in 1873 indicate a slight increase in weight.

Reference: Bowers, Q. David, *United States Dimes, Quarters and Half Dollars.*

Counterfeit Alert: Beware of 1853O with arrows removed or altered date. Contemporary counterfeits in lead alloy are common.

Hints: Be wary of cleaned and retoned specimens.

Basal Type Value: G: 12.00.

	VG	VF
NO MOTTO ABOVE EAGLE		
1839 No drapery below elbow		
	50.00	240.00
1839 With drapery	27.00	75.00
1840 Sm. rev. letters	35.00	75.00
1840 Med. rev. letters (New Orleans, no		
mintmark	125.00	250.00
1840O	27.00	65.00
1841	38.00	125.00
1841O	25.00	65.00
1842 Small date	35.00	80.00
1842 Med. date	30.00	60.00
1842O Small date	700.00	1,800.00
1842O Medium date	23.00	55.00
1843	21.00	45.00
1843O	25.00	50.00
1844	21.00	45.00
1844O	21.00	46.00
1844O, Double date	200.00	600.00
1845	30.00	75.00
1845O	21.00	55.00
1845O, No Drapery	35.00	100.00
1846	23.00	52.00
1846, 6 over horizontal 6		
	150.00	325.00
1846O, Med. date	18.00	45.00
1846O, Tall date	150.00	450.00
1847, 7 over 6	3,000.00	5,000.00
1847	18.00	42.00
1847O	18.00	45.00
1848	45.00	110.00
1848O	23.00	45.00
1849	30.00	60.00
1849O	23.00	55.00
1850	175.00	325.00
1850O	23.00	55.00
1851	200.00	375.00
1851O	23.00	75.00
1852	250.00	500.00
1852O	60.00	250.00
1853 no arrows		75,000.00

ARROWS AT DATE / RAYS ON REV.

1853	20.00	85.00
1853O	24.00	125.00

ARROWS AT DATE / NO RAYS

1854	20.00	42.00
1854O	20.00	42.00
1855 over 1854	75.00	235.00
1855	24.00	55.00
1855O	20.00	45.00

1855S	400.00	1,500.00
ARROWS REMOVED		
1856	20.00	42.00
1856O	20.00	42.00
1856S	48.00	150.00
1857	20.00	42.00
1857O	20.00	50.00
1857S	60.00	200.00
1858	20.00	42.00
1858O	20.00	42.00
1858S	25.00	90.00
1859	25.00	65.00
1859O	20.00	42.00
1859S	25.00	80.00
1860	22.00	55.00
1860O	20.00	42.00
1860S	22.00	55.00
1861	20.00	42.00
1861O	22.00	55.00

Note: 87% of the 1861O issue was struck by the independent state of Louisiana and then by the Confederate States of America. They include those with a die crack on the obverse, which command a premium.

1861S	20.00	55.00
1862	30.00	80.00
1862S	18.00	45.00
1863	23.00	55.00
1863S	20.00	45.00
1864	30.00	75.00
1864S	20.00	50.00
1865	25.00	55.00
1865S	20.00	50.00
1866		Unique
1866S	90.00	325.00

MOTTO ABOVE EAGLE

1866	25.00	57.00
1866S	20.00	50.00
1867	32.00	75.00
1867S	20.00	45.00
1868	40.00	125.00
1868S	20.00	50.00
1869	25.00	52.00
1869S	20.00	50.00
1870	23.00	55.00
1870CC	725.00	2,300.00
1870S	22.00	55.00
1871	20.00	55.00
1871CC	160.00	450.00
1871S	20.00	45.00
1872	20.00	50.00
1872CC	75.00	260.00
1872S	30.00	80.00
1873 Closed 3	30.00	80.00
1873 Open 3	3,000.00	5,900.00
1873CC	160.00	425.00
1873S	Existence not confirmed	

ARROWS AT DATE

1873	23.00	72.00
1873CC	135.00	425.00
1873S	50.00	175.00
1874	22.00	70.00
1874CC	300.00	750.00
1874S	35.00	150.00

ARROWS REMOVED

1875	20.00	42.00
1875CC	30.00	75.00
1875S	20.00	50.00
1876	20.00	40.00
1876CC	22.00	60.00
1876S	20.00	40.00
1877	20.00	40.00
1877CC	28.00	65.00
1877S	18.00	42.00
1878	25.00	60.00
1878CC	325.00	800.00
1878S	6,000.00	10,000.00
1879	150.00	285.00
1880	135.00	275.00
1881	160.00	275.00
1882	150.00	300.00
1883	160.00	275.00
1884	175.00	300.00
1885	175.00	300.00
1886	250.00	380.00
1887	250.00	450.00
1888	160.00	275.00
1889	160.00	275.00
1890	160.00	275.00
1891	40.00	90.00

BARBER HALF DOLLARS

History: The issue of this new design coincided with the revitalization of the half dollar denomination as well, after more than a decade of little more than ceremonial mintages. While many considered the depiction of Liberty by Chief Engraver Charles Barber, after whom the coin is named, unartistic, it has over the years come to be regarded as a well balanced portrait. It was also used on the dime and half dollar of the same era. The formal heraldic eagle on the reverse was used on the quarter as well.

Reference: Lawrence, David, *The Complete Guide to Barber Halves.*

Counterfeit Alert: Most are contemporary counterfeits in lead or tin alloys. Also beware of 1913, 1914, and 1915 with mintmarks removed.

Hints: This series is particularly difficult to find in strong VF to AU grades with natural surfaces. It is quite common in low grades.

Basal Type Value: G: 3.50.

	VG	VF
1892	23.00	70.00
1892O	125.00	285.00
1892S	125.00	255.00
1893	17.00	65.00
1893O	24.00	100.00
1893S	65.00	250.00
1894	12.50	75.00
1894O	14.00	80.00
1894S	11.00	70.00
1895	11.00	65.00
1895O	15.00	80.00
1895S	20.00	95.00
1896	17.00	80.00
1896O	20.00	125.00
1896S	65.00	165.00
1897	8.00	60.00
1897O	60.00	460.00
	VG	VF
1897S	100.00	350.00
1898	8.00	60.00
1898O	22.00	160.00
1898S	12.50	75.00
1899	8.00	65.00
1899O	10.00	85.00
1899S	10.00	80.00
1900	8.00	65.00
1900O	9.00	80.00
1900S	9.00	65.00
1901	8.00	60.00
1901O	10.00	85.00
1901S	20.00	185.00
1902	8.00	60.00
1902O	9.00	65.00
1902S	23.00	80.00
1903	8.00	65.00
1903O	11.00	70.00
1903S	11.00	65.00
1904	8.00	60.00
1904O	12.50	95.00
1904S	18.00	275.00
1905	10.00	80.00
1905O	15.00	110.00
1905S	8.00	65.00
1906	8.00	60.00
1906D	8.00	60.00
1906O	8.00	65.00
1906S	8.00	65.00
1907	8.00	60.00
1907D	8.00	60.00
1907O	8.00	60.00
1907S	8.00	90.00
1908	8.00	60.00

1908D	8.00	60.00
1908O	8.00	60.00
1908S	10.00	70.00
1909	8.00	55.00
1909O	9.00	75.00
1909S	8.00	60.00
1910	12.50	100.00
1910S	8.00	55.00
1911	8.00	55.00
1911D	9.00	75.00
1911S	8.00	65.00
1912	8.00	55.00
1912D	8.00	55.00
1912S	8.00	60.00
1913	20.00	165.00
1913D	8.00	57.00
1913S	10.00	70.00
1914	30.00	250.00
1914S	8.00	60.00
1915	22.00	175.00
1915D	8.00	55.00
1915S	8.00	55.00

WALKING LIBERTY HALF DOLLAR

History: This coin, depicting Liberty, draped in an American flag, advancing towards a rising sun, was struck as part of a program to improve the artistic quality of the nation's coinage. It was designed by medalist Adolph Weinman. It has always been a very popular design, and was even used on the obverse of the one ounce silver Eagle coins (*see bullion issues*). 1917 issues have mintmark either on the obverse or reverse.

Reference: Fox, Bruce, *The Complete Guide to Walking Liberty Half Dollars.*

Counterfeit Alert: All 1928D halves are counterfeit. Also be careful of altered 1938D.

Hints: Liberty's head is not usually fully struck, nor is the hand held closest to the body. Fully struck examples in high grade command a premium.

Basal Type Value: G: 2.50.

	VG	VF
1916	22.00	100.00
1916D	16.00	70.00
1916S	60.00	265.00
1917	6.00	17.50

1917D Obv.	14.00	80.00
1917D Rev.	10.00	55.00
1917S Obv.	17.00	220.00
1917S Rev.	7.00	23.00
1918	7.00	40.00
1918D	7.00	44.00
1918S	6.00	24.00
1919	13.00	110.00
1919D	12.00	130.00
1919S	11.00	105.00
1920	6.00	22.00
1920D	8.00	110.00
1920S	6.00	40.00
1921	100.00	625.00
1921D	100.00	575.00
1921S	21.00	475.00
1923S	8.00	45.00
1927S	6.00	25.00
1928S	6.00	26.00
1929D	6.00	18.00
1929S	6.00	17.00
1933S	6.00	13.00
	F	**EF**
1934	3.50	11.00
1934D	5.50	24.00
1934S	4.50	23.00
1935	3.50	9.00
1935D	4.50	26.00
1935S	4.00	22.00
1936	3.50	9.00
1936D	4.00	17.00
1936S	4.00	18.00
1937	3.50	9:00
1937D	8.00	28.00
1937S	6.50	17.00
1938	4.00	12.00
1938D	25.00	95.00
1939	3.50	7.50
1939D	4.00	10.00
1939S	6.50	12.50
1940	3.00	8.00
1940S	3.50	9.00
1941	3.00	8.00
1941D	3.00	8.00
1941S	3.00	8.00
1942	3.00	8.00
1942D	3.00	8.00
1942D, D over S	45.00	80.00
1942S	3.00	10.00
1943	3.00	8.00
1943D	3.00	8.00
1943S	3.00	8.00
1944	3.00	8.00
1944D	3.00	8.00
1944S	3.00	8.00
1945	3.00	8.00
1945D	3.00	8.00
1945S	3.00	8.00
1946	3.00	8.00
1946D	5.50	11.00
1946S	3.00	8.00
1947	3.00	8.50
1947D	3.00	9.00

FRANKLIN HALF DOLLAR

History: John Sinnock designed this coin, unusual in that is was the first regular issue half not to bear an eagle as the primary reverse design. In fact the tiny eagle to the right of the Liberty Bell was added *after* the coin was designed in order to comply with an old law requiring its presence on larger denomination silver.

Reference: Bowers, Q. David, *United States Dimes, Quarters and Half Dollars.*

Counterfeit Alert: Few counterfeits exist for this series.

Hints: Many dates are common in mint state. Those uncirculated specimens on which the horizontal lines on the bell are fully struck usually command a premium.

Basal Type Value: F-VF: 2.50.

	EF	Unc
1948	4.00	17.00
1948D	4.00	12.00
1949	4.00	30.00
1949D	4.00	32.00
1949S	5.00	48.00
1950	3.00	25.00
1950D	3.00	20.00
1951	3.00	10.00
1951D	4.00	25.00
1951S	4.00	23.00
1952	3.00	10.00
1952D	3.00	8.00
1952S	4.50	38.00
1953	5.00	18.00
1953D	3.00	8.00
1953S	4.00	12.00
1954	3.00	6.00
1954D	3.00	6.50
1954S	3.00	7.50
1955	5.50	8.00
1955 Bugs Bunny "teeth"		16.00
1956	3.50	6.00
1957	3.00	7.00
1957D	3.00	6.00
1958	3.50	5.00
1958D		5.00
1959		5.00
1959D		5.00
1960		5.00
1960D		5.00
1961		4.50
1961D		4.50

1962	3.50
1962D	4.00
1963	3.00
1963D	3.00

KENNEDY HALF DOLLAR

History: Struck as a memorial to President Kennedy, this coin was placed in circulation within months after the November 22 assassination. The obverse portrait, designed by Gilroy Roberts, is a lower relief modification of his inauguration medal. The reverse, prepared by Frank Gasparro, displays the presidential seal. The only circulation strike in 90% silver was the first year. From 1965 to 1970 these were struck of a clad of 80% pure outer layers bonded to a 21% pure core. Those from 1971 are conventional cupronickel clad. Bicentennial halves dated "1776·1976" depict Independence Hall in Philadelphia on the reverse.

Reference: Rapsus, Ginger, *The United States Clad Coinage.*

Counterfeit Alert: Few counterfeits exist for this series.

Hints: All dates are common in mint state. 1970D, 1987P and 1987D were issued in mint sets only.

Basal Type Value: Silver 2.50, Silver clad 1.00, Cupronickel clad 85¢.

	Unc
1964	2.75
1964D	2.75
SILVER CLAD	
1965	1.25
1966	1.25
1967	1.25
1968D	1.25
1968S *Proof only*	2.50
1969D	1.25
1969S *Proof only*	2.75
1970D	11.00
1970S *Proof only*	6.50
CUPRONICKEL-CLAD COPPER	
1971	1.00
1971D	1.00
1971S *Proof only*	2.25

1972	1.00
1972D	1.00
1972S *Proof only*	2.25
1973	1.25
1973D	1.00
1973S *Proof only*	2.00
1974	1.00
1974D	1.00
1974S *Proof only*	2.00
BICENTENNIAL REVERSE	

1976 Bicentennial	1.00
1976D Bicentennial	1.00
1976S Bicentennial *Proof only*	1.35
	Unc.
1976S Bicentennial Silver Clad	2.75
REGULAR ISSUE CONTINUED	
1977	1.50
1977D	1.50
1977S *Proof only*	1.75
1978	1.50
1978D	1.25
1978S *Proof only*	1.75
1979	1.25
1979D	1.25
1979 Filled S *proof only*	2.00
1979 Clear S *proof only*	12.50
1980P	1.00
1980D	1.00
1980S *Proof only*	2.00
1981P	1.50
1981D	1.50
1981S *Proof only*	2.00
1982P	1.00
1982D	1.00
1982S *Proof only*	2.00
1983P	1.00
1983D	1.00
1983S *Proof only*	2.50
1984P	1.25
1984D	1.00
1984S *Proof only*	4.50
1985P	1.25
1985D	1.25
1985S *Proof only*	3.00
1986P	1.25
1986D	1.25
1986S *Proof only*	12.00
1987P	2.00
1987D	2.00
1987S *Proof only*	2.50
1988P	1.00
1988D	1.00
1988S *Proof only*	5.50

	Unc
1989P	1.00
1989D	1.00
1989S *Proof only*	4.00
1990P	1.00
1990D	1.00
1990S *Proof only*	7.00
1991P	1.00
1991D	1.00
1991S *Proof only*	7.00
1992P	1.00
1992D	1.00
1992S *Proof only*	9.50
1992S Silver *Proof only*	11.00
1993P	1.00
1993D	1.00
1993S *Proof only*	9.50
1993S Silver *Proof only*	13.00
1994P	1.00
1994D	1.00
1994S *Proof only*	7.00
1994S Silver *Proof only*	12.00
1995	1.00
1995D	1.00
1995S *proof only*	7.00
1995S Silver *proof only*	11.00
1996	1.00
1996D	1.00
1996S *proof only*	6.00
1996S Silver *proof only*	10.00

EARLY SILVER DOLLARS

History: Before the introduction of United States coinage the most common silver coins in circulation were the Spanish colonial piece of eight reals or "milled dollar," and its fractions. Even the paper money of the Revolutionary War was often denominated in these coins. So it was only natural that when the U.S. established its own coinage its monetary unit was created to be "of the value of the Spanish milled dollar." The initial portrait and eagle proved unpopular, both being perceived as scrawny. These designs were replaced by fuller designs in 1795 and 1798 respectively. By the latter year mintages of the silver dollar had reached a reasonable number but a shortage of them continued. It seems that most dollar sized coins were popular as payments in international trade, and that the new coin was rapidly being exported. The provision of silver dollars for domestic circulation appearing a futile effort, mintages were reduced to nominal quantities for 1801-04, those struck in the latter year bearing the date 1803.

The famous 1804 dollar, perhaps the king of American coins, was actually struck decades later, initially to be used as diplomatic gifts. Later a small number of additional pieces were struck for collectors.

References: Bolender, M.H., *The United States Early Silver Dollars from 1794 to 1803*, Newman, Eric, and Bressett, Kenneth, *The Fantastic 1804 Dollar*.

Counterfeit Alert: Many counterfeits exist of this series, even of the least rare 1799. Counterfeit 1804 dollars greatly outnumber authentic specimens. Beware of cleaned, plugged and retoned examples.

Hints: Certain kinds of scraping called "adjustment marks," done at the mint will be found on some dollars. These are not considered damage but do somewhat reduce a coin's value. This series is actively collected by die variety, some bringing substantial premiums.

Basal Type Value: abt. G $200.00.

FLOWING HAIR TYPE

	G	F
1794	6,000.00	17,500.00
1795	650.00	1,350.00

DRAPED BUST / SMALL EAGLE

1795	600.00	1,000.00
1796	500.00	1,000.00
1797 9 & 7 stars, Small letters		
	1,100.00	2,300.00
1797 9 & 7 stars, Large letters		
	500.00	950.00
1797 10 stars l. & 6 stars r.		
	500.00	950.00
1798 15 stars	850.00	1,800.00

1798 13 stars	675.00	1,350.00

DRAPED BUST / HERALDIC EAGLE

1798	300.00	480.00
1799, 9 over 8, 15 stars		
	325.00	525.00
1799, 9 over 8, 13 stars		
	325.00	525.00
1799	300.00	480.00
1799 8 stars l. & 5 stars r.		
	325.00	550.00
1800	300.00	480.00
1801	350.00	575.00
1802, 2 over 1	325.00	525.00
1802	325.00	525.00
1802	*Proof Restrike*	70,000.00
1803	325.00	525.00
1803	*Proof Restrike*	70,000.00
1804 (struck 1834-35)	*Proof*	700,000.00
1804 (struck 1859)	*Proof*	200,000.00

GOBRECHT DOLLARS

History: Christian Gobrecht designed these experimental dollars in preparation for the reintroduction of the silver dollar. The reverse design of the flying eagle was rejected however in favor of a less lifelike heraldic version. This rejected reverse was later used on the Flying Eagle Cent. Although Gobrecht also designed the dollar which replaced this issue, his name has come to be attached to this design among collectors. Those examples with the engraver's name in the field *below* the ground and all 1838 issues are patterns.

Reference: Bowers, Q. David, *Silver Dollars and Trade Dollars of the United States: A Complete Encyclopedia*.

Counterfeit Alert: Fewer counterfeits exist of this rare series than would be expected. Beware of cleaned specimens however.

Hints: Restrikes can be distinguished by the die alignments. On them the eagle flies horizontally, not upwards. They are all rare and valuable as well.

STARS ON REVERSE

	VF
1836	3,300.00
1836 (struck 1837) rev. not inverted	3,400.00

STARS ON OBVERSE

1839	3,900.00

SEATED LIBERTY DOLLARS

History: This new obverse design first appeared on the experimental issues of 1836-39. The allegory of seated Liberty was probably inspired by the seated Britannia found on English coins for years, but ultimately derives from an ancient Roman type. As with the smaller silver coins, the motto In God We Trust was added above the eagle on later issues. Mintages for this dollar were always small and only exceeded one million pieces in 1871 and 1872.

Reference: Bowers, Q. David, *Silver Dollars and Trade Dollars of the United States: A Complete Encyclopedia.*

Counterfeit Alert: Counterfeits exist but do not abound.

Hints: Be wary of cleaned and retoned specimens. 1871 is not rare in high grade.

Basal Type Value: G: 85.00.

NO MOTTO ABOVE EAGLE

	F	EF
1840	200.00	400.00
1841	170.00	350.00

1842	150.00	350.00
1843	150.00	350.00
1844	275.00	550.00
1845	250.00	500.00
1846	160.00	350.00
1846O	250.00	550.00
1847	165.00	350.00
1848	425.00	750.00
1849	200.00	350.00
1850	550.00	1,100.00
1850O	325.00	1,300.00
1851 Original	7,000.00	9,000.00
1851 Restrike	*Proof*	20,000.00
1852 Original	7,000.00	9,000.00
1852 Restrike	*Proof*	16,000.00
1853	220.00	550.00
1854	1,150.00	3,000.00
1855	1,000.00	2,600.00
1856	350.00	900.00
1857	350.00	900.00
1858	2,750.00	4,600.00
1859	335.00	525.00
1859O	150.00	275.00
1859S	375.00	1,100.00
1860	275.00	525.00
1860O	150.00	275.00
1861	525.00	1,050.00
1862	500.00	900.00
1863	300.00	625.00
1864	250.00	600.00
1865	250.00	475.00
1866		*2 Known*

MOTTO ABOVE EAGLE

1866	225.00	450.00
1867	250.00	500.00
1868	225.00	450.00
1869	200.00	425.00
1870	160.00	375.00
1870CC	475.00	1,300.00
1870S	50,000.00	100,000.00
1871	160.00	350.00
1871CC	3,100.00	7,300.00
1872	160.00	350.00
1872CC	1,500.00	3,600.00
1872S	350.00	1,000.00
1873	175.00	375.00
1873CC	4,750.00	14,000.00
1873S	*Existence not confirmed*	

TRADE DOLLARS

History: This is the only United States coin to ever have had its legal tender status revoked. It was created to compete with the Mexican dollar in trade with China and the Far East. Liberty is shown seated on the products of the United States, cotton and wheat. While legal tender for up to five dollars initially, their legal tender status was revoked in 1876 with the decline in the price of silver. They were never again considered money but many were redeemed by the government in 1887. Later issues were made specifically for collectors.

References: Bowers, Q. David, *Silver Dollars and Trade Dollars of the United States: A Complete Encyclopedia*; Willem, John M., *The United States Trade Dollar.*

Counterfeit Alert: Counterfeits exist but do not abound.

Hints: Be wary of cleaned specimens. Many of those specimens brought back from the Orient have Chinese characters or "chop marks" punched into them. This was done by merchants to guarantee their purity. Despite marketing promotions to the contrary, they are considered interesting but *damaged* coins and trade at a substantial discount.

Basal Type Value: G: 55.00.

	F	EF
1873	100.00	175.00
1873CC	150.00	475.00
1873S	100.00	200.00
1874	100.00	175.00
1874CC	100.00	180.00
1874S	75.00	150.00
1875	285.00	450.00
1875CC	95.00	200.00
1875S	75.00	130.00
1875S, S over CC	250.00	700.00
1876	75.00	140.00
1876CC	100.00	225.00
1876S	75.00	140.00
1877	75.00	140.00
1877CC	175.00	330.00
1877S	75.00	140.00
1878	*Proof only*	2,000.00

	F	EF
1878CC	550.00	1,450.00
1878S	75.00	140.00
1879	750.00	900.00
1880	750.00	900.00
1881	800.00	1,000.00
1882	750.00	900.00
1883	800.00	1,000.00
1884		*Extremely Rare*
1885		*Extremely Rare*

MORGAN DOLLARS

History: Named after its engraver, George T. Morgan, this dollar is at once one of the most popular coins among both collectors and investors. Its introduction coincides with the revival of the silver dollar after several years' hiatus. It is interesting to note that this is the first American coin to bear Gothic style lettering, perhaps due to Morgan's training at the Royal Mint in England. The master dies were not available in 1921 for the last year of issue, hence they all appear in lower relief and less sculpted in their detail.

The fact that it survives in disproportionate quantities in uncirculated grade has permitted it to be mass marketed on a practical basis. Original bags were continuously available from various sources for most of this century. Additional quantities were sold in distinctive cases directly to the public by the U.S. Government in the 1970's. These are now referred to as "GSA" dollars.

References: Bowers, Q. David, *Silver Dollars and Trade Dollars of the United States: A Complete Encyclopedia*; Van Allen, Leroy, and Mallis, A. George, *Comprehensive Catalogue and Encyclopedia of U.S. Morgan and Peace Silver Dollars.*

Counterfeit Alert: Altered 1879CC, 1889CC, 1892S, 1893S, 1894, 1895, 1895S, 1896S, 1901, 1903S and 1904S exist. Slightly less dangerous cast counterfeits exist of 1878, 1878S, 1879S, 1880O, 1881, 1883, 1883S, 1885, 1888O, 1889, 1889O, 1892O, 1899O, 1901, 1902, 1903, 1904S, 1921D and S.

Hints: Dollars from different mints have different characteristics. Those struck at San Francisco are the best strikes, those of New Orleans the weakest. The eagle's breast is concave on early 1878 strikes, rounded on those struck from later that year until 1904. Be wary of cleaned as well as artificially toned specimens.

Basal Type Value: G: 6.50, except for 1921 all mints, which are 5.00.

	VF	Unc
1878, 8 tail feathers	15.00	50.00
1878, 7 over 8 tail feathers		
	20.00	60.00
1878, 7 feathers	10.00	28.00
1878, same, rev. of 1879		
	12.00	50.00
1878CC	28.00	70.00
1878S	10.00	20.00
1879	9.00	18.00
1879CC	90.00	1,300.00
1879O	10.00	45.00
1879S	10.00	16.00
1880	9.00	16.50
1880CC	62.00	140.00
1880O	9.00	50.00
1880S	10.00	17.00
1881	10.00	19.00
1881CC	105.00	150.00
1881O	9.00	18.00
1881S	9.00	17.00
1882	10.00	18.00
1882CC	35.00	55.00
1882O	10.00	17.00
1882O, O over S	19.00	135.00
1882S	10.00	17.00
1883	9.00	16.50
1883CC	30.00	50.00
1883O	9.00	17.00
1883S	13.00	360.00
1884	9.00	17.00
1884CC	42.00	55.00
1884O	9.00	15.00
1884S	15.00	3,500.00
1885	9.00	16.00
1885CC	160.00	190.00
1885O	9.00	16.00
1885S	15.00	85.00
1886	9.00	16.00
1886O	11.00	280.00
1886S	28.00	125.00
1887, 7 over 6	20.00	140.00
1887	9.00	16.00
1887O, 7 over 6	20.00	265.00
1887O	9.00	29.00
1887S	18.00	64.00
1888	9.00	16.00
1888O	10.00	16.00
1888S	26.00	135.00
1889	10.00	16.00
1889CC	275.00	6,500.00
1889O	10.00	77.00
1889S	22.00	102.00
1890	9.00	16.00
1890CC	30.00	180.00
1890O	10.00	28.00
1890S	10.00	32.00
1891	10.00	38.00
1891CC	34.00	125.00
1891O	11.00	80.00
1891S	10.00	32.00
1892	12.00	120.00
1892CC	62.00	370.00
1892O	12.00	92.00
1892S	40.00	12,500.00
1893	62.00	290.00
1893CC	160.00	1,000.00
1893O	115.00	1,300.00
1893S	1,450.00	25,000.00
1894	280.00	875.00
1894O	30.00	575.00
1894S	38.00	350.00
1895	*Proof only*	14,500.00
1895O	138.00	8,000.00
1895S	175.00	1,000.00
1896	9.00	16.00
1896O	12.00	640.00
1896S	40.00	565.00
1897	11.00	17.00
1897O	11.00	575.00
1897S	10.00	34.00
1898	10.00	16.00
1898O	12.00	16.00
1898S	18.00	120.00
1899	30.00	65.00
1899O	10.00	17.00
1899S	18.00	135.00
1900	9.00	17.00
1900O	10.00	16.00
1900O, O over CC	32.00	165.00
1900S	17.00	95.00
1901	25.00	1,400.00
1901O	9.00	17.00
1901S	21.00	220.00
1902	10.00	33.00
1902O	10.00	16.00
1902S	40.00	175.00
1903	15.00	30.00
1903O	112.00	140.00
1903S	62.00	2,350.00
1904	12.00	60.00
1904O	10.00	16.00
1904S	36.00	860.00
1921	8.00	10.00
1921D	8.00	17.00
1921S	8.00	18.00

PEACE DOLLARS

History: This coin, which depicts a radiant head of Liberty, was struck as part of a program to improve the artistic quality of the nation's coinage. Its reverse bears an eagle perched on a rock inscribed PEACE, to mark the conclusion of World War I. The coin was designed by medalist Anthony De Francisci. Like the Morgan dollar, its introduction coincides with the revival of the silver dollar after several years' hiatus. The 1921 issue has an almost medallic high relief, beautiful in appearance but impractical for mass production. The following year the relief was lowered. Original bags were continuously available from various sources for most of this century.

References: Bowers, Q. David, *Silver Dollars and Trade Dollars of the United States: A Complete Encyclopedia*; Van Allen, Leroy, and Mallis, A. George, *Comprehensive Catalogue and Encyclopedia of U.S. Morgan and Peace Silver Dollars.*
Counterfeit Alert: Beware of counterfeit or altered 1928.
Hints: This coin suffers particularly from bag marks. Uncirculated specimens virtually free of these scuffs command a premium.
Basal Type Value: F: 7.00.

	VF	Unc
1921	31.00	115.00
1922	8.00	10.00
1922D	8.00	20.00
1922S	8.00	20.00
1923	8.00	10.00
1923D	8.00	24.00
1923S	8.00	18.00
1924	8.00	12.00
1924S	13.00	130.00
1925	8.00	11.00
1925S	10.00	45.00
1926	9.00	23.00
1926D	9.00	42.00
1926S	8.00	25.00
1927	15.00	60.00
1927D	14.00	125.00
1927S	12.00	86.00
1928	115.00	155.00
1928S	12.00	68.00
1934	15.00	62.00
1934D	14.00	80.00
1934S	38.00	950.00
1935	11.00	40.00
1935S	12.00	135.00

1964D *None confirmed to have survived*

EISENHOWER DOLLARS
History: This coin was issued shortly after the death of President Dwight D. Eisenhower, but it holds special importance in that it is the first American coin to honor the space program. The reverse is actually a modified version of the emblem and arm patch of Apollo 11, the voyage that first landed man on the moon in 1969. Most issues were struck in the standard cupronickel clad composition of circulating minor coins, but special collector coins were also struck of the silver clad used for the Kennedy halves 1965-70.

Bicentennial dollars dated "1776·1976" depict the Liberty Bell superimposed on the moon on the reverse. Those with block lettering were actually struck in 1975. Those with seriffed lettering were issued both in 1975 and 1976 with no way to distinguish year of striking.
References: Bowers, Q. David, *Silver Dollars and Trade Dollars of the United States: A Complete Encyclopedia*; Rapsus, Ginger, *The United States Clad Coinage.*
Counterfeit Alert: Not generally counterfeited.
Hints: Silver issues were released in blue envelopes (Unc.) and brown boxes (Proof). Those lacking this are traded at a discount.

	BU	PF
1971	2.00	
1971D	2.00	
1971S Silver	3.50	4.50
1972	2.00	
1972D	2.00	
1972S Silver	3.50	4.50
1973	4.00	
1973D	4.00	
1973S *Proof only*		4.00
1973S Silver	4.00	16.00
1974	2.00	
1974D	2.00	1.00
1974S *Proof only*		4.00
1974S Silver	3.50	5.50

BICENTENNIAL REVERSE

1976 Block letters	2.50	
1976 Seriffed	2.00	
1976D Block letters	2.50	
1976D Seriffed	2.00	
1976S Block letters	*Proof only*	4.50
1976S Seriffed	*Proof only*	4.00
1976S Silver, Block letters	6.00	8.00

REGULAR ISSUE CONTINUED

1977	2.00	
1977D	2.00	
1977S *Proof only*		4.00
1978	2.00	
1978D	2.00	
1978S *Proof only*		5.00

SUSAN B. ANTHONY DOLLARS
History: The portrait on this coin depicts Susan B. Anthony, a leader in the movement to gain women the right to vote. The reverse is of the Apollo 11 type used on the Eisenhower dollar. This coin was one of the most unpopular coins ever issued in the United States, and lasted a total of three years, only the first two of which were ever placed in circulation. It was continually being confused with the quarter because of its similar size to that coin. Despite that fact almost a billion were struck, most of which are still in existence.
References: Rapsus, Ginger, *The United States Clad Coinage.*
Counterfeit Alert: Not generally counterfeited.

	BU	PF
1979P Narrow rim, far date	1.50	
1979P Wide rim, near date	5.00	
1979D	1.50	

	BU	PF
1979S	1.50	
1979S Filled S		3.00
1979S Clear S		50.00
1980	1.50	
1980D	1.50	
1980S	1.50	4.50
1981	2.00	
1981D	2.00	
1981S	2.00	
1981S Filled S		5.00
1981S Clear S		70.00

GOLD DOLLARS

History: The tiny gold dollar was not an original American gold coin but was produced in response to pressure from the gold lobby strengthened by the California gold rush. Its small size made it an awkward coin to handle and subject to loss, thus it was made broader and thinner in 1854. Two years later the design was somewhat modified to make the "Indian princess" head larger and bolder. It was discontinued after forty years.

References: Akers, David, *Gold Dollars*; Breen, Walter, *Major Varieties of U.S. Gold Dollars*; Bowers, Q. David, *United States Gold Coins: An Illustrated History*.

Counterfeit Alert: Most dates of gold dollar have been counterfeited, particularly Type II. Of the Type III, 1874, 1883 and 1887 are known.

Hints: Look for traces of mount marks from former use in jewelry, as well as cleaning.

CORONET HEAD - TYPE I

	VF	EF
1849 Open wreath	130.00	165.00
1849 Closed wreath	135.00	165.00
1849C Open wreath		*Rare*
1849C Closed wreath		
	475.00	925.00
1849D	400.00	700.00
1849O	145.00	200.00
1850	135.00	165.00
1850C	625.00	950.00
1850D	600.00	950.00
1850O	265.00	385.00
1851	130.00	165.00
1851C	400.00	650.00
1851D	475.00	800.00
1851O	155.00	200.00
1852	130.00	165.00
1852C	500.00	800.00
1852D	650.00	1,100.00
1852O	150.00	200.00

1853	130.00	165.00
1853C	525.00	1,050.00
1853D	675.00	1,150.00
1853O	150.00	175.00
1854	130.00	165.00
1854D	800.00	1,750.00
1854S	275.00	425.00

SMALL INDIAN PRINCESS HEAD - TYPE II

1854	265.00	400.00
1855	265.00	400.00
1855C	1,000.00	2,100.00
1855D	2,200.00	4,500.00
1855O	400.00	700.00
1856S	600.00	1,100.00

LARGE INDIAN PRINCESS HEAD - TYPE III

1856	130.00	160.00
1856D	3,500.00	6,500.00
1857	130.00	160.00
1857C	500.00	1,050.00
1857D	750.00	1,650.00
1857S	400.00	650.00
1858	130.00	160.00
1858D	750.00	1,250.00
1858S	350.00	550.00
1859	130.00	160.00
1859C	500.00	1,300.00
1859D	700.00	1,400.00
1859S	250.00	525.00
1860	130.00	160.00
1860D	2,500.00	4,600.00
1860S	275.00	450.00
1861	130.00	160.00
1861D	5,900.00	10,050.00

Note: All 1861D gold dollars were struck by the Confederacy.

1862	130.00	160.00
1863	375.00	800.00
1864	350.00	450.00
1865	375.00	550.00
1866	350.00	450.00
1867	375.00	525.00
1868	240.00	350.00
1869	325.00	450.00
1870	275.00	400.00
1870S	450.00	750.00
1871	275.00	375.00
1872	275.00	375.00
1873 Closed 3	350.00	700.00
1873 Open 3	130.00	160.00

1874	130.00	160.00
1875	2,000.00	3,750.00
1876	250.00	325.00
1877	225.00	300.00
1878	225.00	300.00
1879	200.00	275.00
1880	200.00	250.00
1881	180.00	225.00
1882	190.00	235.00
1883	150.00	175.00
1884	180.00	235.00
1885	150.00	175.00
1886	180.00	235.00
1887	160.00	185.00
1888	150.00	175.00
1889	150.00	175.00

GOLD 2½ DOLLARS

History: This denomination, usually referred to as a "quarter eagle" by collectors, was one of those authorized with the original Coinage Act of 1792. The first design bore a bust of Liberty wearing a turban-like hat. In 1808, just before a gap in the coinage followed by a reduction in diameter, the hat was changed to a simple cap. The Classic Head designed by William Kneass and the Coronet Head by Christian Gobrecht are essentially two different artists' interpretations of the same design. The Indian Head type, introduced in 1908, was struck as part of a program instigated by President Theodore Roosevelt to improve the artistic quality of the nation's coinage. The artist was Bela Lyon Pratt. Its radical design is struck completely below the surface of the coin. This prevented wear on the portrait and eagle, but once caused some concern about the "spread of germs."

References: Bowers, Q. David, *United States Gold Coins: An Illustrated History*; Akers, David, *Handbook of 20th-Century United States Gold Coins*.

Counterfeit Alert: Liberty type: 1858 (crude), 1873, 1878, 1883, 1884, 1885, 1899, 1903, 1905, 1905S (all), 1907, Indian type: 1908, 1911, 1914, 1915, 1928. O mint marks have sometimes been seen altered to C mint marks. Beware of added mintmark on 1911D.

Hints: Look for traces of mount marks from former use in jewelry, as well as cleaning.

"TURBAN" BUST RIGHT

	F	VF
1796 No stars on obverse	9,500.00	19,000.00
1796 Stars	8,000.00	12,500.00
1797	7,750.00	9,500.00
1798	3,000.00	4,200.00
1802, 2 over 1	2,600.00	3,600.00
1804, 13 stars	12,000.00	17,000.00
1804, 14 stars	2,650.00	3,500.00
1805	2,500.00	3,700.00
1806, 6 over 4	2,600.00	3,500.00
1806, 6 over 5	4,500.00	6,700.00
1807	2,500.00	3,300.00

CAPPED BUST TYPE

1808	8,000.00	13,000.00
1821	3,000.00	3,600.00
1824, 4 over 1	3,100.00	3,400.00
1825	3,000.00	3,300.00
1826, 6 over 5	3,500.00	4,400.00
1827	3,500.00	4,000.00
1829	2,850.00	3,500.00
1830	2,850.00	3,500.00
1831	2,850.00	3,500.00
1832	2,850.00	3,500.00
1833	2,850.00	3,500.00
1834	6,500.00	9,300.00

CLASSIC HEAD (NO MOTTO)

1834	210.00	260.00
1835	210.00	260.00
1836	210.00	260.00
1837	210.00	260.00
1838	210.00	260.00
1838C	475.00	950.00
1839	210.00	290.00
1839C	400.00	800.00
1839D	450.00	950.00
1839O	360.00	500.00

CORONET TYPE (NO MOTTO)

	VF	EF
1840	250.00	600.00
1840C	570.00	1,300.00
1840D	2,000.00	4,000.00
1840O	275.00	800.00
1841	15,000.00	32,000.00
1841C	550.00	1,200.00
1841D	1,300.00	3,000.00
1842	800.00	2,900.00
1842C	1,100.00	2,800.00
1842D	1,400.00	2,800.00
1842O	450.00	1,300.00
1843	160.00	260.00
1843C, Crosslet 4, small date	2,000.00	4,000.00
1843C, Plain 4, large date	600.00	1,200.00
1843D	575.00	1,200.00
1843O, Crosslet 4, small date	225.00	275.00
1843C, Plain 4, large date	300.00	600.00
1844	450.00	1,100.00
1844C	700.00	1,500.00
1844D	600.00	1,200.00
1845	265.00	350.00
1845D	675.00	1,300.00
1845O	900.00	2,100.00
1846	350.00	725.00
1846C	950.00	1,900.00
1846D	750.00	1,200.00
1846O	250.00	500.00
1847	225.00	400.00
1847C	550.00	950.00
1847D	625.00	1,100.00
1847O	250.00	450.00
1848	500.00	975.00
1848 CAL.	8,000.00	14,000.00

The above 1,389 quarter eagles were struck with California gold supplied by the Dept. of War. The CAL. appears above the eagle.

1848C	650.00	1,400.00
1848D	600.00	1,250.00
1849	250.00	550.00
1849C	700.00	1,700.00
1849D	725.00	1,300.00
1850	165.00	200.00
1850C	700.00	1,500.00
1850D	700.00	1,350.00
1850O	250.00	450.00
1851	145.00	180.00
1851C	625.00	1,400.00
1851D	675.00	1,300.00
1851O	185.00	350.00
1852	160.00	190.00
1852C	600.00	1,500.00
1852D	900.00	2,500.00
1852O	185.600	275.00
1853	145.00	175.00
1853D	1,250.00	2,400.00
1854	145.00	175.00
1854C	700.00	1,500.00
1854D	2,400.00	5,000.00
1854O	185.00	275.00
1854S		Very Rare
1855	155.00	180.00
1855C	1,200.00	2,500.00
1855D	3,500.00	6,500.00

1856	155.00	180.00
1856C	750.00	1,500.00
1856D	6,000.00	11,000.00
1856O	275.00	650.00
1856S	190.00	400.00
1857	145.00	185.00
1857D	975.00	1,900.00
1857O	185.00	340.00
1857S	185.00	350.00
1858	150.00	250.00
1858C	625.00	1,250.00
1859	150.00	275.00
1859D	1,200.00	2,400.00
1859S	400.00	1,200.00
1860	160.00	250.00
1860C	700.00	1,600.00
1860S	250.00	700.00
1861	145.00	185.00
1861S	400.00	1,300.00
1862, 2 over 1	975.00	2,000.00
1862	180.00	275.00
1862S	850.00	2,200.00
1863	Proof only	25,000.00
1863S	450.00	1,400.00
1864	4,500.00	10,000.00
1865	3,750.00	7,000.00
1865S	275.00	800.00
1866	1,100.00	3,000.00
1866S	325.00	800.00
1867	350.00	800.00
1867S	300.00	750.00
1868	275.00	425.00
1868S	250.00	600.00
1869	250.00	375.00
1869S	250.00	600.00
1870	250.00	350.00
1870S	250.00	500.00
1871	250.00	350.00
1871S	200.00	350.00
1872	350.00	950.00
1872S	250.00	500.00
1873 Closed 3	175.00	240.00
1873 Open 3	145.00	165.00
1873S	250.00	500.00
1874	274.00	385.00
1875	3,500.00	5,500.00
1875S	200.00	400.00
1876	300.00	700.00
1876S	225.00	750.00
1877	400.00	725.00
1877S	150.00	185.00
1878	145.00	165.00
1878S	145.00	165.00
1879	145.00	165.00
1879S	150.00	250.00
1880	200.00	375.00
1881	1,300.00	3,250.00
1882	225.00	275.00
1883	225.00	375.00
1884	225.00	375.00
1885	700.00	1,400.00
1886	200.00	275.00
1887	185.00	225.00
1888	175.00	200.00

	VF	EF
1889	175.00	200.00
1890	185.00	200.00
1891	175.00	200.00
1892	200.00	275.00
1893	145.00	165.00
1894	175.00	250.00
1895	145.00	165.00
1896	145.00	165.00
1897	145.00	165.00
1898	145.00	165.00
1899	145.00	165.00
1900	145.00	165.00
1901	145.00	165.00
1902	145.00	165.00
1903	145.00	165.00
1904	145.00	165.00
1905	145.00	165.00
1906	145.00	165.00
1907	145.00	165.00

INDIAN HEAD TYPE

1908	140.00	155.00
1909	140.00	155.00
1910	140.00	155.00
1911	140.00	155.00
1911D	500.00	1,000.00
1912	140.00	155.00
1913	140.00	155.00
1914	140.00	175.00
1914D	140.00	160.00
1915	140.00	155.00
1925D	140.00	155.00
1926	140.00	155.00
1927	140.00	155.00
1928	140.00	155.00
1929	140.00	155.00

THREE DOLLAR GOLD PIECES

History: This strange denomination served little purpose but to buy sheets of 100 three-cent stamps or 100 silver 3-cent pieces! It was not created until 1854, making it the most recently introduced circulating denomination. It was never very popular and was discontinued in 1889 with the gold dollar. Only one type was struck.

References: Bowers, Q. David, *United States Gold Coins: An Illustrated History.*
Counterfeit Alert: Virtually every date of these has been counterfeited. 1857 and 1882/82 among others are known.
Hints: Look for traces of mount marks from former use in jewelry, as well as cleaning.

	VF	EF
1854	485.00	700.00
1854D	6,500.00	10,000.00
1854O	575.00	1,100.00
1855	500.00	725.00
1855S	1,000.00	2,150.00
1856	500.00	750.00
1856S	600.00	1,100.00
1857	500.00	750.00
1857S	800.00	2,400.00
1858	800.00	1,200.00
1859	525.00	800.00
1860	525.00	800.00
1860S	800.00	2,200.00
1861	625.00	875.00
1862	625.00	900.00
1863	625.00	900.00
1864	650.00	925.00
1865	1,000.00	2,250.00
1866	675.00	925.00
1867	675.00	925.00
1868	675.00	900.00
1869	675.00	950.00
1870	675.00	950.00
1870S	*Unique*	900,000.00
1871	675.00	1,000.00
1872	675.00	950.00
1873 Closed 3	3,000.00	4,200.00
1873 Open 3	*Proof only*	25,000.00
1874	485.00	650.00
1875	*Proof only*	55,000.00
1876	*Proof only*	21,000.00
1877	1,000.00	2,400.00
1878	475.00	650.00
1879	525.00	800.00
1880	675.00	1,100.00
1881	850.00	1,600.00
1882	625.00	1,000.00
1883	650.00	1,050.00
1884	900.00	1,350.00
1885	850.00	1,300.00
1886	750.00	1,250.00
1887	525.00	725.00
1888	525.00	725.00
1889	525.00	725.00

FIVE DOLLAR GOLD PIECES

History: This denomination, usually referred to as "half eagle" by collectors, was one of those authorized with the original Coinage Act of 1792. The first design bore a bust of Liberty wearing a turban-like hat. In 1807 the hat was changed to a simple cap. The Classic Head designed by William Kneass and the Coronet Head by Christian Gobrecht are essentially two different artists' interpretations of the same design. The Indian Head type, introduced in 1908, was struck as part of a program instigated by President Theodore Roosevelt to improve the artistic quality of the nation's coinage. The artist was Bela Lyon Pratt. Its radical design is struck completely below the surface of the coin. This prevented wear on the portrait and eagle, but once caused some concern about the "spread of germs."

References: Bowers, Q. David, *United States Gold Coins: An Illustrated History*; Akers, David, *Handbook of 20th-Century United States Gold Coins.*
Counterfeit Alert: Capped Bust - 1811, 1815 (altered from 1813); Coronet type - 1852C (crude), 1858, 1885, 1885S, 1892, 1906S, 1907D, 1908, Indian type - 1908D, 1909D, 1909O, 1914D, 1914S, 1915D (all), and many others. O mint marks have sometimes been seen altered to C mint marks.
Hints: Look for traces of mount marks from former use in jewelry, as well as cleaning.

"TURBAN" BUST / SMALL EAGLE

	F	VF
1795	4,600.00	6,500.00
1796, 6 over 5	5,750.00	7,500.00
1797, 15 stars	7,500.00	10,000.00
1797, 16 stars	7,000.00	9,000.00
1798		23,000.00

"TURBAN" BUST / HERALDIC EAGLE

1795	5,800.00	6,750.00
1797, 7 over 5	4,500.00	7,000.00
1797, 16 star obv.		*Unique*
1798 Small 8	1,500.00	2,000.00
1798 Large 8, 13 star rev.	1,150.00	1,900.00
1798 Large 8, 14 star rev.	1,500.00	2,500.00
1799	1,200.00	1,700.00

	F	VF
1800	1,000.00	1,550.00
1802, 2 over 1	1,000.00	1,550.00
1803, 3 over 2	1,000.00	1,550.00
1804, Small 8	1,050.00	1,550.00
1804, Small 8 over Large 8	1,050.00	1,600.00
1805	1,000.00	1,550.00
1806, Pointed 6	1,200.00	1,700.00
1806, Round 6	1,000.00	1,550.00
1807	1,000.00	1,550.00

CAPPED BUST TYPE

	F	VF
1807	1,100.00	1,650.00
1808, 8 over 7	1,200.00	1,750.00
1808	1,100.00	1,600.00
1809, 9 over 8	1,100.00	1,600.00
1810 Small date, small 5	4,700.00	9,500.00
1810 Small date, tall 5	1,500.00	2,000.00
1810 Large date, small 5	3,000.00	4,700.00
1810 Large date, large 5	1,100.00	1,600.00
1811 Small 5	1,100.00	1,600.00
1811 Tall 5	1,100.00	1,600.00
1812	1,100.00	1,600.00
1813	1,300.00	1,700.00
1814, 4 over 3	1,500.00	2,000.00
1815	EF	35,000.00
1818	1,550.00	2,000.00
1818 STATESOF	1,600.00	2,100.00
1818, 5D over 50	2,100.00	4,000.00
1819		17,000.00
1819, 5D over 50		17,000.00
1820, Curved-base 2	1,500.00	2,000.00
1820, Square-base 2	1,500.00	2,000.00
1821	2,100.00	3,750.00
1822	Only 3 known	
1823	1,650.00	2,050.00
1824	2,000.00	3,700.00
1825, 5 over 1	3,200.00	4,800.00
1825, 5 over 4	Only 2 known	
1826	2,800.00	5,500.00
1827	5,500.00	8,000.00
1828, 8 over 7	5,750.00	8,000.00
1828	6,500.00	9,000.00
1829	Extremely Rare	

CAPPED BUST / REDUCED DIAMETER

	F	VF
1829	20,000.00	35,000.00
1830	3,000.00	4,500.00
1831	3,000.00	4,500.00
1832, 12 stars	Only 6 known	
1832, 13 stars	3,600.00	5,000.00
1833	3,200.00	5,000.00
1834 Plain 4	3,000.00	5,000.00
1834 Crosslet 4	3,800.00	5,300.00

CLASSIC HEAD (NO MOTTO)

	F	VF
1834 Plain 4	235.00	320.00
1834 Crosslet 4	550.00	900.00
1835	235.00	320.00
1836	235.00	320.00
1837	240.00	320.00
1838	235.00	320.00
1838C	900.00	1,650.00
1838D	825.00	1,300.00

CORONET TYPE (NO MOTTO)

	VF	EF
1839	275.00	500.00
1839C	900.00	2,000.00
1839D	850.00	1,900.00
1840	250.00	400.00
1840C	750.00	1,700.00
1840D	700.00	1,300.00
1840O	375.00	800.00
1841	375.00	925.00
1841C	650.00	1,250.00
1841D	625.00	1,200.00
1841O	Existence not verified	
1842 Small letters	300.00	1,100.00
1842 Large letters	600.00	1,800.00
1842C Small date	3,000.00	Rare
1842C Large date	675.00	1,250.00
1842D Small letters	650.00	1,300.00
1842D Large letters	1,800.00	4,250.00
1842O	950.00	4,600.00
1843	175.00	250.00
1843C	650.00	1,200.00
1843D	600.00	1,110.00
1843O Small letters	550.00	1,250.00
1843O Large letters	325.00	985.00
1844	175.00	250.00
1844C	850.00	2,450.00
1844D	600.00	1,100.00
1844O	200.00	500.00
1845	200.00	275.00
1845D	600.00	1,250.00
1845O	350.00	800.00
1846 Small date	200.00	325.00
1846	175.00	300.00
1846C	850.00	2,400.00
1846D	600.00	1,200.00
1846O	425.00	1,150.00
1847	175.00	250.00
1847C	550.00	1,200.00
1847D	550.00	1,200.00
1847O	1,350.00	5,000.00
1848	175.00	250.00
1848C	600.00	1,300.00
1848D	600.00	1,250.00
1849	175.00	275.00
1849C	565.00	1,250.00
1849D	600.00	1,250.00
1850	300.00	975.00
1850C	550.00	1,200.00
1850D	675.00	1,500.00
1851	175.00	210.00
1851C	600.00	1,100.00
1851D	600.00	1,200.00
1851O	535.00	1,300.00
1852	165.00	200.00
1852C	600.00	1,100.00
1852D	575.00	1,100.00
1853	170.00	210.00
1853C	550.00	1,100.00
1853D	575.00	1,100.00
1854	225.00	325.00
1854C	650.00	1,500.00
1854D	575.00	1,050.00
1854O	325.00	500.00
1854S	Extremely Rare	
1855	175.00	265.00
1855C	650.00	1,500.00
1855D	650.00	1,400.00
1855O	700.00	2,200.00
1855S	400.00	1,000.00
1856	170.00	220.00
1856C	600.00	1,200.00
1856D	625.00	1,300.00
1856O	900.00	1,750.00
1856S	300.00	700.00
1857	175.00	225.00
1857C	550.00	1,250.00
1857D	600.00	1,350.00
1857O	700.00	2,000.00
1857S	300.00	700.00
1858	300.00	675.00
1858C	575.00	1,100.00
1858D	625.00	1,150.00
1858S	700.00	2,400.00
1859	300.00	600.00
1859C	600.00	1,350.00
1859D	700.00	1,500.00
1859S	1,250.00	3,500.00
1860	250.00	525.00
1860C	800.00	1,600.00
1860D	800.00	1,600.00
1860S	1,000.00	2,500.00
1861	165.00	210.00
1861C	1,600.00	3,400.00
1861D	4,300.00	7,000.00
1861S	1,000.00	3,400.00
1862	900.00	1,800.00

	VF	EF
1862S	3,000.00	7,000.00
1863	1,100.00	3,000.00
1863S	1,350.00	3,600.00
1864	650.00	1,800.00
1864S	5,000.00	12,000.00
1865	1,250.00	3,400.00
1865S	1,200.00	3,250.00
1866S	1,850.00	4,750.00

CORONET TYPE (WITH MOTTO)

1866	700.00	1,500.00
1866S	900.00	3,800.00
1867	550.00	2,000.00
1867S	1,200.00	3,200.00
1868	575.00	1,4650.00
1868S	500.00	1,500.00
1869	850.00	1,800.00
1869S	600.00	2,400.00
1870	600.00	1,650.00
1870CC	3,500.00	9,000.00
1870S	1,200.00	3,000.00
1871	800.00	1,800.00
1871CC	1,100.00	2,900.00
1871S	550.00	1,700.00
1872	775.00	1,500.00
1872CC	975.00	3,200.00
1872S	450.00	1,650.00
1873 Closed 3	165.00	200.00
1873 Open 3	160.00	190.00
1873CC	2,000.00	5,000.00
1873S	650.00	1,900.00
1874	550.00	1,600.00
1874CC	700.00	2,000.00
1874S	975.00	3,000.00
1875	35,000.00	50,000.00
1875CC	1,300.00	4,500.00
1875S	850.00	2,500.00
1876	850.00	1,800.00
1876CC	1,200.00	3,200.00
1876S	1,800.00	4,800.00
1877	750.00	1,650.00
1877CC	1,000.00	3,000.00
1877S	325.00	850.00
1878	150.00	180.00
1878CC	2,500.00	7,000.00
1878S	160.00	190.00
1879	145.00	165.00
1879CC	600.00	1,500.00
1879S	175.00	200.00
1880	145.00	160.00
1880CC	325.00	750.00
1880S	145.00	160.00
1881, 1 over 0	300.00	600.00
1881	145.00	160.00
1881CC	600.00	1,500.00

1881S	145.00	160.00
1882	145.00	160.00
1882CC	275.00	450.00
1882S	145.00	160.00
1883	145.00	160.00
1883CC	375.00	800.00
1883S	175.00	225.00
1884	150.00	175.00
1884CC	450.00	850.00
1884S	190.00	220.00
1885	145.00	160.00
1885S	145.00	160.00
1886	150.00	165.00
1886S	145.00	160.00
1887	Proof only	25,000.00
1887S	145.00	160.00
1888	160.00	200.00
1888S	165.00	275.00
1889	275.00	500.00
1890	325.00	550.00
1890CC	225.00	300.00
1891	160.00	190.00
1891CC	225.00	275.00
1892	145.00	160.00
1892CC	225.00	325.00
1892O	450.00	1,275.00
1892S	150.00	175.00
1893	145.00	160.00
1893CC	225.00	335.00
1893O	185.00	230.00
1893S	150.00	220.00
1894	145.00	160.00
1894O	160.00	250.00
1894S	200.00	325.00
1895	145.00	160.00
1895S	200.00	325.00
1896	150.00	175.00
1896S	200.00	275.00
1897	145.00	160.00
1897S	160.00	200.00
1898	145.00	160.00
1898S	145.00	165.00
1899	145.00	160.00
1899S	145.00	165.00
1900	145.00	160.00
1900S	145.00	175.00
1901	145.00	160.00
1901S, 1 over 0	165.00	200.00
1901S	145.00	160.00
1902	145.00	160.00
1902S	145.00	160.00
1903	145.00	160.00
1903S	145.00	160.00
1904	145.00	160.00
1904S	150.00	190.00
1905	145.00	160.00
1905S	145.00	160.00
1906	145.00	160.00
1906D	145.00	160.00
1906S	145.00	160.00
1907	145.00	160.00
1907D	145.00	160.00
1908	145.00	160.00

INDIAN HEAD TYPE

	VF	EF
1908	195.00	210.00
1908D	195.00	210.00
1908S	225.00	325.00
1909	195.00	210.00
1909D	195.00	210.00
1909O	600.00	925.00
1909S	200.00	225.00
1910	195.00	210.00
1910D	195.00	210.00
1910S	200.00	250.00
1911	195.00	210.00
1911D	275.00	425.00
1911S	200.00	240.00
1912	195.00	210.00
1912S	200.00	235.00
1913	195.00	210.00
1913S	210.00	275.00
1914	195.00	210.00
1914D	195.00	210.00
1914S	195.00	250.00
1915	195.00	210.00
1915S	225.00	290.00
1916S	195.00	235.00
1929	2,750.00	3,600.00

TEN DOLLAR GOLD PIECES

History: This denomination, traditionally referred to as an "eagle" by collectors, was one of those authorized with the original Coinage Act of 1792. The first design bore a bust of Liberty wearing a turban-like hat. This large denomination was not struck from 1805-1837 inclusive. The Coronet type designed by Christian Gobrecht was introduced when it was revived in 1838. The Indian Head type, introduced in 1908, was struck as part of a program instigated by President Theodore Roosevelt to improve the artistic quality of the nation's coinage. The head of Liberty wearing an Indian war bonnet was created by the famous sculptor Augustus Saint-Gaudens. The first issues of this type lack the motto "In God We Trust" on the reverse, at the personal request of the president, who thought it improper to place the word "God" on a coin. It was replaced on this denomination by law in 1908.

References: Bowers, Q. David, *United States Gold Coins: An Illustrated History*;

Akers, David, *Handbook of 20th-Century United States Gold Coins.*

Counterfeit Alert: Turban type 1799; Coronet type 1858 (removed mintmark), 1901S, 1906D, 1907; Indian type 1908S, 1909S, 1910S, 1911S, 1912S, 1913, 1913S, 1914S, 1915S, 1916S, 1926, 1932, 1933. Most dates after 1870 have been counterfeited.

Hints: Certain kinds of scraping called "adjustment marks," done at the mint, will be found on some very early eagles. These are not considered damage but do somewhat reduce a coin's value. Look for traces of mount marks from former use in jewelry, as well as cleaning.

TURBAN BUST / SMALL EAGLE

	F	VF
1795, 9 leaves below eagle	13,500.00	24,000.00
1795, 13 leaves	5,200.00	8,000.00
1796	5,700.00	8,250.00
1797	6,650.00	11,000.00

TURBAN BUST / HERALDIC EAGLE

	F	VF
1797	2,450.00	3,500.00
1798, 9 stars l., 4 r.	4,500.00	9,000.00
1798, 7 stars l., 6 r.	16,500.00	26,000.00
Note: both above have 8 over 7 in date		
1799	2,200.00	2,600.00
1800	2,400.00	3,000.00
1803	2,200.00	2,800.00
1804	3,300.00	4,100.00

CORONET TYPE (NO MOTTO)

	VF	EF
1838	950.00	2,500.00
1839 Large letters	700.00	1,850.00
1839 Small letters	1,450.00	3,400.00
1840	375.00	750.00
1841	325.00	675.00
1841O	1,900.00	6,500.00
1842 Small date	325.00	600.00
1842 Large date	335.00	700.00
1842O	350.00	850.00
1843	375.00	800.00
1843O	300.00	585.00
1844	1,250.00	3,200.00
1844O	325.00	700.00
1845	675.00	1,650.00
1845O	400.00	825.00
1846	800.00	2,000.00
1846O	500.00	1,200.00
1847	275.00	295.00
1847O	275.00	425.00
1848	285.00	500.00
1848O	500.00	1,200.00
1849	275.00	310.00
1849O	850.00	8,500.00
1850 Large date	275.00	360.00
1850 Small date	575.00	1,500.00
1850O	425.00	900.00
1851	275.00	475.00
1851O	300.00	550.00
1852	275.00	450.00
1852O	650.00	2,400.00
1853, 3 over 2	475.00	950.00
1853	275.00	290.00
1853O	325.00	535.00
1854	325.00	550.00
1854O Small date	325.00	800.00
1854O Large date	450.00	2,000.00
1854S	275.00	500.00
1855	275.00	350.00
1855O	700.00	2,000.00
1855S	1,500.00	3,200.00
1856	275.00	350.00
1856O	800.00	2,250.00
1856S	275.00	625.00
1857	400.00	1,225.00
1857O	1,000.00	2,500.00
1857S	385.00	950.00
1858	5,000.00	10,000.00
1858O	300.00	900.00
1858S	1,700.00	4,500.00
1859	350.00	900.00
1859O	3,000.00	8,000.00
1859S	2,500.00	6,000.00
1860	375.00	950.00
1860O	600.00	1,500.00
1860S	3,000.00	7,000.00
1861	275.00	325.00
1861S	1,600.00	3,000.00
1862	550.00	1,300.00
1862S	1,500.00	3,500.00
1863	3,800.00	9,500.00
1863S	1,500.00	3,500.00
1864	1,600.00	3,600.00

	VF	EF
1864S	4,500.00	10,000.00
1865	1,800.00	4,000.00
1865S	4,500.00	10,000.00
1865S, 865 over inverted 186	3,000.00	6,000.00
1866S	3,200.00	5,400.00

CORONET TYPE (WITH MOTTO)

	VF	EF
1866	800.00	2,500.00
1866S	1,400.00	3,700.00
1867	1,500.00	3,800.00
1867S	2,500.00	6,500.00
1868	800.00	1,400.00
1868S	1,500.00	3,800.00
1869	1,500.00	4,300.00
1869S	1,500.00	4,300.00
1870	750.00	1,400.00
1870CC	7,000.00	14,000.00
1870S	1,700.00	4,000.00
1871	1,500.00	3,100.00
1871CC	1,900.00	4,800.00
1871S	1,800.00	3,500.00
1872	2,400.00	5,000.00
1872CC	2,500.00	5,800.00
1872S	850.00	1,750.00
1873	4,000.00	9,500.00
1873CC	3,000.00	8,000.00
1873S	1,300.00	2,800.00
1874	260.00	290.00
1874CC	1,000.00	3,200.00
1874S	1,500.00	3,800.00
1875	36,000.00	47,000.00
1875CC	2,500.00	7,500.00
1876	2,400.00	7,900.00
1876CC	2,400.00	7,900.00
1876S	1,450.00	2,750.00
1877	2,400.00	5,500.00
1877CC	2,300.00	4,800.00
1877S	800.00	1,400.00
1878	260.00	275.00
1878CC	3,700.00	8,000.00
1878S	700.00	1,850.00
1879	260.00	275.00
1879CC	4,600.00	9,500.00
1879O	2,100.00	5,000.00
1879S	260.00	275.00
1880	260.00	275.00
1880CC	425.00	800.00
1880O	400.00	850.00
1880S	260.00	275.00
1881	260.00	275.00
1881CC	325.00	600.00
1881O	400.00	900.00
1881S	260.00	275.00
1882	260.00	275.00

	VF	EF
1882CC	500.00	1,500.00
1882O	350.00	850.00
1882S	260.00	275.00
1883	260.00	275.00
1883CC	400.00	800.00
1883O	2,600.00	6,500.00
1883S	260.00	275.00
1884	260.00	275.00
1884CC	550.00	1,400.00
1884S	260.00	275.00
1885	260.00	275.00
1885S	260.00	275.00
1886	260.00	275.00
1886S	260.00	275.00
1887	260.00	275.00
1887S	260.00	275.00
1888	260.00	275.00
1888S	260.00	275.00
1889	325.00	500.00
1889S	260.00	275.00
1890	260.00	300.00
1890CC	325.00	375.00
1891	260.00	275.00
1891CC	275.00	350.00
1892	260.00	275.00
1892CC	325.00	450.00
1892O	260.00	275.00
1892S	260.00	275.00
1893	260.00	275.00
1893CC	375.00	800.00
1893O	260.00	275.00
1893S	260.00	275.00
1894	260.00	275.00
1894O	260.00	275.00
1894S	260.00	350.00
1895	260.00	275.00
1895O	260.00	275.00
1895S	275.00	335.00
1896	260.00	275.00
1896S	260.00	325.00
1897	260.00	275.00
1897O	260.00	275.00
1897S	260.00	275.00
1898	260.00	275.00
1898S	260.00	275.00
1899	260.00	275.00
1899O	260.00	275.00
1899S	260.00	275.00
1900	260.00	275.00
1900S	260.00	275.00
1901	260.00	275.00
1901O	260.00	275.00
1901S	260.00	275.00
1902	260.00	275.00
1902S	260.00	275.00
1903	260.00	275.00
1903O	260.00	275.00
1903S	260.00	275.00
1904	260.00	275.00
1904O	260.00	275.00
1905	260.00	275.00
1905S	260.00	275.00
1906	260.00	275.00

1906D	260.00	275.00
1906O	260.00	275.00
1906S	260.00	275.00
1907	260.00	275.00
1907D	260.00	275.00
1907S	260.00	275.00

INDIAN HEAD / NO MOTTO

1907 Wire rim, periods		4,250.00
1907 Rounded rim, periods		12,500.00
1907 No periods	340.00	380.00
1908	375.00	435.00
1908D	375.00	435.00

INDIAN HEAD / WITH MOTTO

1908	360.00	430.00
1908D	380.00	435.00
1908S	420.00	550.00
1909	400.00	420.00
1909D	400.00	420.00
1909S	400.00	420.00
1910	400.00	420.00
1910D	400.00	420.00
1910S	400.00	420.00
1911	400.00	420.00
1911D	415.00	625.00
1911S	400.00	440.00
1912	400.00	420.00
1912S	400.00	420.00
1913	400.00	420.00
1913S	400.00	500.00
1914	400.00	420.00
1914D	400.00	420.00
1914S	400.00	420.00
1915	400.00	420.00
1915S	400.00	475.00
1916S	400.00	420.00
1920S	4,750.00	5,800.00
1926	400.00	420.00
1930S	3,000.00	4,500.00
1932	400.00	420.00
1933	*Unc.*	50,000.00

TWENTY DOLLAR GOLD PIECES

History: This largest regular issue American gold coin was introduced in response to pressure from the gold lobby, strengthened by the California gold rush.

This denomination is traditionally referred to as a "double eagle" by collectors. It was issued concurrently with the one dollar gold piece and shares a similar portrait of Liberty designed by James Longacre of Indian Head cent fame. The 1861 Paquet reverse was used only that year and is most easily recognized by the fact that the ellipse of stars is within and not partially superimposed in the rays above. In 1866 the motto "In God We Trust" was inserted within the ellipse. The type was further modified in 1877 to spell out the word "dollars." The double eagle depicting Liberty carrying a torch toward the viewer was introduced in 1907, as part of a program instigated by President Theodore Roosevelt to improve the artistic quality of the nation's coinage. It was designed by the famous sculptor Augustus Saint-Gaudens and is generally referred to as a "Saint-Gaudens" or simply "Saint" after its creator. Its first issues, while beautiful, bore much too high a relief to strike up readily, and the design had to be modified. Early issues of this type also lack the motto "In God We Trust" on the reverse, at the personal request of the president, who thought it improper to place the word "God" on a coin. It was replaced on this denomination by law in 1908.

References: Bowers, Q. David, *United States Gold Coins: An Illustrated History*; Akers, David, *Handbook of 20th-Century United States Gold Coins*.

Counterfeit Alert: Liberty type: 1879, 1894, 1897S, 1899S, 1900, 1900S, 1901S, 1903S, 1904, 1904S, 1906, 1906S, 1907; Saint-Gaudens type: 1907 high relief, 1908, 1911D, 1919, 1920, 1924 (many), 1925, 1926, 1927 (many), 1928. Added mintmarks exist for 1927D. Needless to say, the United States double eagle is one of the world's most counterfeited gold coins. Most dates after 1870 have been counterfeited. Examine every piece with great care!

Hints: This coin's large diameter and soft metal make it particularly susceptible to bagging. Those high grade pieces relatively free from bag marks command a premium. Also look for traces of mount marks from former use in jewelry, as well as cleaning.

LIBERTY HEAD - TYPE I

	VF	EF
1849		Unique
1850	500.00	650.00
1850O	600.00	1,000.00
1851	500.00	575.00
1851O	535.00	850.00
1852	500.00	575.00
1852O	525.00	700.00
1853, 3 over 2	585.00	1,500.00
1853	500.00	575.00
1853O	550.00	1,100.00
1854	500.00	575.00
1854O	13,500.00	27,500.00
1854S	525.00	625.00
1855	500.00	575.00
1855O	2,750.00	6,000.00
1855S	500.00	600.00
1856	500.00	575.00
1856O	14,500.00	27,000.00
1856S	500.00	575.00
1857	500.00	575.00
1857O	900.00	1,600.00
1857S	500.00	575.00
1858	525.00	650.00
1858O	950.00	1,850.00
1858S	500.00	600.00
1859	850.00	2,200.00
1859O	2,500.00	5,500.00
1859S	500.00	600.00
1860	500.00	575.00
1860O	2,650.00	4,900.00
1860S	500.00	600.00
1861	500.00	575.00
1861O	1,200.00	3,200.00
1861S	500.00	600.00
1861 Paquet rev.	Proof	660,000.00
1861S Paquet rev.	5,000.00	10,000.00
1862	675.00	1,450.00
1862S	500.00	700.00
1863	500.00	725.00
1863S	500.00	650.00
1864	525.00	825.00
1864S	525.00	850.00
1865	500.00	600.00
1865S	500.00	600.00
1866S	1,200.00	4,750.00

LIBERTY HEAD (WITH MOTTO) - TYPE II

1866	480.00	650.00
1866S	525.00	950.00
1867	480.00	525.00
1867S	480.00	750.00
1868	500.00	900.00
1868S	480.00	700.00
1869	480.00	700.00
1869S	480.00	575.00
1870	500.00	875.00
1870CC	27,000.00	50,000.00
1870S	480.00	520.00
1871	550.00	850.00
1871CC	2,000.00	4,500.00
1871S	480.00	520.00
1872	480.00	520.00
1872CC	975.00	1,800.00
1872S	480.00	520.00
1873 Closed 3	600.00	800.00
1873 Open 3	480.00	520.00
1873CC	875.00	1,500.00
1873S	480.00	520.00
1874	480.00	520.00
1874CC	550.00	700.00
1874S	480.00	520.00
1875	480.00	520.00
1875CC	500.00	600.00
1875S	480.00	520.00
1876	480.00	520.00
1876CC	550.00	685.00
1876S	480.00	520.00

LIBERTY HEAD - TYPE III

1877	480.00	500.00
1877CC	650.00	900.00
1877S	480.00	500.00
1878	480.00	500.00
1878CC	850.00	1,800.00
1878S	480.00	500.00
1879	480.00	500.00
1879CC	975.00	2,200.00
1879O	2,750.00	4,250.00
1879S	475.00	500.00
1880	475.00	500.00
1880S	435.00	475.00
1881	3,200.00	6,000.00
1881S	475.00	500.00
1882	6,700.00	15,000.00
1882CC	500.00	650.00
1882S	475.00	500.00
1883	Proof only	40,000.00
1883CC	550.00	700.00
1883S	475.00	500.00
1884	Proof only	40,000.00
1884CC	500.00	600.00
1884S	475.00	500.00
1885	4,500.00	7,000.00
1885CC	950.00	1,800.00
1885S	475.00	500.00
1886	5,500.00	10,500.00
1887	Proof only	30,000.00
1887S	475.00	500.00
1888	475.00	500.00
1888S	475.00	500.00
1889	475.00	500.00
1889CC	625.00	850.00
1889S	475.00	500.00
1890	475.00	500.00
1890CC	565.00	635.00
1890S	475.00	500.00
1891	2,600.00	4,600.00
1891CC	1,400.00	2,500.00
1891S	475.00	500.00
1892	900.00	1,450.00
1892CC	625.00	825.00
1892S	475.00	500.00
1893	475.00	500.00
1893CC	650.00	735.00
1893S	475.00	500.00
1894	475.00	500.00
1894S	475.00	500.00
1895	475.00	500.00
1895S	475.00	500.00
1896	475.00	500.00
1896S	475.00	500.00
1897	475.00	500.00
1897S	475.00	500.00
1898	475.00	500.00
1898S	475.00	500.00
1899	475.00	500.00
1899S	475.00	500.00
1900	475.00	500.00
1900S	475.00	500.00
1901	475.00	500.00
1901S	475.00	500.00
1902	475.00	500.00
1902S	475.00	500.00
1903	475.00	500.00
1903S	475.00	500.00
1904	475.00	500.00
1904S	475.00	500.00
1905	475.00	500.00
1905S	475.00	500.00
1906	475.00	500.00
1906D	475.00	500.00
1906S	475.00	500.00
1907	475.00	500.00
1907D	475.00	500.00
1907S	475.00	500.00

SAINT-GAUDENS / NO MOTTO

1907 High relief, wire rim

	2,700.00	3,700.00

	VF	EF
1907 High relief, flat rim		
	2,700.00	3,700.00
1907 Arabic numerals		
	485.00	510.00
1908	485.00	510.00
1908D	485.00	510.00

SAINT-GAUDENS / WITH MOTTO

1908	485.00	510.00
1908D	485.00	510.00
1908S	500.00	850.00
1909	485.00	510.00
1909D	485.00	575.00
1909S	485.00	510.00
1910	485.00	510.00
1910D	485.00	510.00
1910S	485.00	510.00
1911	485.00	510.00
1911D	485.00	510.00
1911S	485.00	510.00
1912	485.00	510.00
1913	485.00	510.00
1913D	485.00	510.00
1913S	485.00	510.00
1914	485.00	510.00
1914D	485.00	510.00
1914S	485.00	510.00
1915	485.00	510.00
1915S	485.00	510.00
1916S	485.00	510.00
1920	485.00	510.00
1920S	4,500.00	6,400.00
1921	6,000.00	7,600.00
1922	485.00	510.00
1922S	485.00	510.00
1923	485.00	510.00
1923D	485.00	510.00
1924	485.00	510.00
1924D	675.00	850.00
1924S	650.00	900.00
1925	485.00	510.00
1925D	700.00	1,000.00
1925S	700.00	975.00
1926	485.00	510.00
1926D	900.00	1,600.00
1926S	650.00	850.00
1927	485.00	510.00
1927D		Very Rare
1927S		3,500.00
1928	485.00	510.00
1929		5,000.00
1930S		8,200.00
1931		7,500.00

1931D	6,750.00
1932	7,000.00
1933	*Not released into circulation*

COMMEMORATIVE COINAGE

History: The United States' first commemorative coins were issued in order to support what many have considered the largest American cultural event of the 19th century: the World's Columbian Exposition in Chicago, 1892-93. The Isabella Quarter and the Columbian Half Dollar were sold at a premium and the profit went to subsidize the fair. Despite the fact that many unsold halves were put into circulation at face value after the event, the idea was a relative success. During the period 1900 through 1928 a number of memorials and celebrations were funded in this way. But with the period 1934 through 1938 the unrestrained issue of commemoratives reached scandalous proportions. Collectors became financially over-burdened, and much was lost due to speculation. As a result of these abuses commemorative coinage was phased out completely by the mid-1950's. A commemorative coin program was revived in the U.S. in 1982 (*see recent commemoratives below*).

The coins below are listed alphabetically within metal, with silver preceding gold. While a listing in sequence of issue might seem more appropriate, the present sequence has been well established among numismatists for generations and it is thought best to retain it. All are silver half dollars unless noted.

References: Hodder, Michael and Bowers, Q. David, *A Basic Guide to United States Commemorative Coins*; Swiatek, Anthony and Breen, Walter, *Encyclopedia of United States Silver and Gold Commemorative Coins 1892-1989*; Bowers, Q. David, *Commemorative Coins of the United States: A Complete Encyclopedia.*

Counterfeit Alert: The counterfeits of this series are generally of high quality and thus particularly dangerous. Examine scarcer pieces with great care!

Hints: Occasionally these coins are found in their original cases of issue. Premiums for these cases vary from slight (Lexington-Concord) to extreme (Pan-Pacific). Many of these coins, originally bought as souvenirs, have been cleaned; watch for brush marks or artificial color. Commemoratives typically come in very high grade. Those as low as *EF* are often

discounted, those in Fine are often considered undesirable unless rare.

ISABELLA QUARTER

	AU	Unc.
1893	225.00	275.00

Note: Issued for the Columbian Exposition's Board of Lady Managers.

ALABAMA CENTENNIAL

	AU	Unc.
1921, with 2x2	160.00	300.00
1921, no 2x2	100.00	195.00

Note: Gov. Kilby of Alabama is with this piece the first living person to appear on a United States coin.

ALBANY, NEW YORK

1936	190.00	200.00

Note: Struck for the 250th anniversary of the granting of Albany's charter.

ANTIETAM

1937	350.00	380.00

Note: Struck to mark the 75th anniversary of the Civil War battle of Antietam.

Counterfeit Alert: High grade counterfeits are known.

ARKANSAS CENTENNIAL

	AU	Unc.
1935	62.00	75.00
1935D	70.00	80.00
1935S	70.00	80.00
1936	65.00	75.00
1936D	65.00	75.00
1936S	65.00	75.00
1937	65.00	75.00
1937D	65.00	75.00
1937S	65.00	75.00
1938	80.00	110.00
1938D	80.00	110.00
1938S	80.00	110.00
1939	125.00	225.00
1939D	125.00	225.00
1939S	125.00	225.00

Note: Struck for the 100th anniversary of Arkansas' admission to the Union. Also see listing under Robinson-Arkansas.

BAY BRIDGE

1936S	85.00	105.00

Note: Struck to celebrate the opening of the bridge between San Francisco and Oakland, California.

DANIEL BOONE

1934	72.00	80.00
1935	72.00	80.00
1935D	75.00	85.00
1935S	75.00	85.00

	AU	Unc.
1935 w/"1934"	150.00	110.00
1935D w/"1934"	150.00	220.00
1935S w/"1934"	150.00	220.00
1936	72.00	80.00
1936D	75.00	85.00
1936S	75.00	85.00
1937	85.00	110.00
1937D	90.00	220.00
1937S	90.00	220.00
1938	215.00	260.00
1938D	215.00	260.00
1938S	215.00	260.00

Note: Struck to honor the bicentennial of the birth of Daniel Boone in 1834.

BRIDGEPORT, CONNECTICUT

1936	90.00	100.00

Note: Struck to celebrate the centennial of the incorporation of the City of Bridgeport. The portrait is that of the famous circus promoter P.T. Barnum, a former mayor of the city.

CALIFORNIA DIAMOND JUBILEE

1925S	82.00	100.00

Note: Struck to celebrate the 75th anniversary of California's admission to the Union. The obverse depicts a forty-niner.

CARVER - WASHINGTON

1951	10.00	13.00
1951D	12.00	30.00

1951S	12.00	30.00
1952	10.00	12.00
1952D	12.00	30.00
1952S	12.00	30.00
1953	12.00	30.00
1953D	12.00	30.00
1953S	10.00	13.00
1954	12.00	30.00
1954D	12.00	30.00
1954S	10.00	12.00

Note: This coin portrays both George Washington Carver and Booker T. Washington. Profits from its sales went to help stop the spread of Communism among African Americans. See also Booker T. Washington.

CINCINNATI MUSIC CENTER

1936	200.00	230.00
1936D	200.00	230.00
1936S	200.00	230.00

Note: The portrait is that of Stephen Foster, the composer of Oh! Susannah.

Counterfeit Alert: Known counterfeit exists of the Philadelphia issue.

CLEVELAND - GREAT LAKES

1936	57.00	65.00

Note: Struck to celebrate the centennial of Cleveland, where the Great Lakes Exposition was held in 1936.

COLUMBIA, SOUTH CAROLINA

	AU	Unc
1936	160.00	175.00
1936D	160.00	175.00
1936S	160.00	175.00

Note: Struck to subsidize Columbia's sesquicentennial celebrations.

COLUMBIAN EXPOSITION

| 1892 | 13.00 | 38.00 |
| 1893 | 11.00 | 35.00 |

Note: Sold as souvenirs at the World's Columbian Exposition, Chicago, which marked the 400th anniversary of the discovery of America.

Hint: Many of these were placed in circulation after the fair. Well circulated pieces are worth substantially less.

CONNECTICUT TERCENTENARY

| 1935 | 160.00 | 180.00 |

Note: Struck to honor the 300th anniversary of the founding of Connecticut. The tree on the reverse is the Charter Oak where legend has it the colony's charter was hidden from James II who sought to revoke it.

DELAWARE TERCENTENARY

| 1936 | 175.00 | 185.00 |

Note: Struck to honor the 300th anniversary of the Swedish settlement of Delaware.

ELGIN, ILLINOIS

| 1936 | 155.00 | 175.00 |

Note: Struck to honor the centennial of the founding of this city and to help subsidize the construction of the Pioneer Memorial depicted on the reverse.

BATTLE OF GETTYSBURG

| 1936 | 220.00 | 245.00 |

Note: Struck to honor the 75th anniversary of this famous battle.

GRANT MEMORIAL

| 1922 star in r. field | 525.00 | 900.00 |
| 1922 no star | 65.00 | 85.00 |

Note: Issued to mark the centennial of Grant's birth. His birthplace in Point Pleasant, Ohio is on the reverse. The star was removed after only a few thousand coins were struck.

Counterfeit Alert: Altered no star variety exists with star falsely added. Many will have a flat spot on the corresponding area on the reverse.

HAWAII SESQUICENTENNIAL

| 1928 | 900.00 | 1,200.00 |

Note: Issued to commemorate the 150th anniversary of the discovery of Hawaii by Capt. James Cook. It is considered one of the most desirable U.S. commemoratives.

Counterfeit Alert: Dangerous counterfeits exist.

HUDSON, NEW YORK

| 1935 | 385.00 | 415.00 |

Note: While technically struck for the 150th anniversary of the City of Hudson, and not the famous explorer, it is the latter's ship, the Half Moon, which appears on the obverse of this half dollar.

Counterfeit Alert: Various counterfeits exists.

HUGUENOT-WALLOON TERCENTENARY

| 1924 | 75.00 | 85.00 |

Note: This coin marks the founding of New Netherlands (New York) in 1624. The ship on the reverse bears the same name as the colony, Nieuw Nederland.

ILLINOIS STATEHOOD

	AU	Unc.
1918	65.00	80.00

Note: This is the first coin to honor a state's admission to the Union. The obverse depicts a young, beardless Abraham Lincoln.

IOWA STATEHOOD

1918	62.00	70.00

Note: Struck to mark the centennial of Iowa's admission to the Union.
Hints: This coin often comes bag marked. Those perfectly free of such marks command a premium.

LEXINGTON-CONCORD

1925	58.00	72.00

Note: Struck for the 150th anniversary of these two Massachusetts battles that opened the American Revolution.
Hints: The original boxes for this issue are not rare but do command a small premium.

LONG ISLAND TERCENTENARY

1936	58.00	65.00

Note: Struck for the 300th anniversary of the Dutch colonization of Long Island, New York.

LYNCHBURG, VIRGINIA

1936	140.00	155.00

Note: Struck for the sesquicentennial of this city. Virginia Senator Carter Glass, born in Lynchburg, is portrayed on this coin, ten years before he died in office!

MAINE CENTENNIAL

1920	70.00	90.00

Note: Struck for the 100th anniversary of Maine statehood. Unfortunately these coins were not received in Maine until after the celebration.

MARYLAND TERCENTENARY

1934	120.00	130.00

Note: This half was sold to subsidize the celebrations for the 300th anniversary of the founding of Maryland by Cecil Calvert, Lord Baltimore.

MISSOURI CENTENNIAL

1921, 2★4 in l. field	300.00	400.00
1921, no 2★4	200.00	360.00

Note: This half was struck to commemorate the hundredth anniversary of Missouri's admission to the Union.
Counterfeit Alert: Known counterfeit exists of second type.
Hints: The 2★4 on the early issues is incuse, not raised.

MONROE DOCTRINE

1923S	35.00	45.00

Note: This half was struck to commemorate the hundredth anniversary of the Monroe Doctrine, a policy statement against European intervention in the New World.
Hints: This half is relatively common in circulated condition.

NEW ROCHELLE, NEW YORK

1938	250.00	280.00

Note: Struck to commemorate the 250th anniversary of the founding of the city.

NORFOLK, VIRGINIA

	AU	Unc.
1936	315.00	330.00

Note: Struck to commemorate both the 300th anniversary of the founding of Norfolk, and the 200th of its establishment as a royal borough. Its sales were to raise funds for the celebrations for these events.

OREGON TRAIL MEMORIAL

1926	85.00	90.00
1926S	85.00	90.00
1928	120.00	160.00
1933D	185.00	225.00
1934D	115.00	130.00
1936	95.00	110.00
1936S	115.00	150.00
1937D	95.00	110.00
1938	125.00	150.00
1938D	125.00	150.00
1938S	125.00	150.00
1939	350.00	400.00
1939D	350.00	400.00
1939S	350.00	400.00

Note: Struck to memorialize one of the most important pioneer routes to the West.

PANAMA PACIFIC EXPOSITION

1915S	190.00	325.00

Note: The Panama-Pacific Exposition was held in San Francisco in 1915 to celebrate the opening of the Panama Canal. These halves were sold for one dollar each as souvenirs.
Counterfeit Alert: Counterfeit exists, details lack crispness.

PILGRIM TERCENTENARY

1920	65.00	80.00
1921	85.00	110.00

Note: Struck to commemorate the landing of the Pilgrims at Plymouth Rock. The reverse depicts the Mayflower.

RHODE ISLAND TERCENTENARY

1936	65.00	80.00
1936D	65.00	85.00
1936S	65.00	85.00

Note: Struck to commemorate the founding of Providence by Roger Williams, who is depicted on the obverse.

ROANOKE ISLAND, NORTH CAROLINA

1937	150.00	175.00

Note: Struck to commemorate the founding of Roanoke Island by Sir Walter Raleigh and the birth of Virginia Dare, the first child of European descent born in America.

ROBINSON - ARKANSAS

1936	65.00	80.00

Note: Struck for the 100th anniversary of Arkansas' admission to the Union. The reverse bears the portrait of the then still serving Senator Joseph T. Robinson. Also see listing under Arkansas Centennial.

SAN DIEGO - CALIFORNIA PACIFIC

1935S	60.00	65.00
1936D	65.00	70.00

Note: Struck for the California-Pacific Exposition in San Diego in 1935.

SESQUICENTENNIAL OF INDEPENDENCE

1926	60.00	75.00

Note: Struck to commemorate the 150th anniversary of American independence.

OLD SPANISH TRAIL

1935	675.00	725.00

Note: Struck to commemorate the 400th anniversary of the establishment of the Old Spanish Trail.
Counterfeit Alert: Counterfeits exist, at least one lacking normal die polish marks.

STONE MOUNTAIN MEMORIAL

	AU	Unc.
1925	30.00	37.00

Note: Struck to raise funds to carve the giant Confederate war memorial at Stone Mountain, Georgia. Depicted are "Stonewall" Jackson and Robert E. Lee. The sculpture was finally completed forty-five years later in 1970.
Hints: This is particularly common in circulated grades.

TEXAS CENTENNIAL

1934	82.00	90.00
1935	82.00	90.00
1935D	82.00	90.00
1935S	82.00	90.00
1936	82.00	90.00
1936D	82.00	90.00
1936S	82.00	90.00
1937	85.00	95.00
1937D	85.00	95.00
1937S	85.00	95.00
1938	145.00	180.00
1938D	145.00	180.00
1938S	145.00	180.00

Note: Commemorates not the centennial of Texas statehood, but of Texan Independence. Beside the kneeling Victory are portraits of Sam Houston and Stephen Austin.

FORT VANCOUVER

1925	220.00	250.00

Note: Struck to raise funds to pay for the centennial celebration of Fort Vancouver, these coins were sold at one dollar each.

Counterfeit Alert: Counterfeit exists, details lack crispness.

VERMONT SESQUICENTENNIAL

1927	130.00	150.00

Note: Struck to commemorate the Battle of Bennington and the independence of Vermont. Vermont retained its independence until 1791.

BOOKER T. WASHINGTON

1946	10.00	12.00
1946D	10.00	13.00
1946S	10.00	13.00
1947	11.00	15.00
1947D	11.00	15.00
1947S	11.00	15.00
1948	18.00	28.00
1948D	18.00	28.00
1948S	18.00	28.00
1949	40.00	65.00
1949D	40.00	65.00
1949S	40.00	65.00
1950	40.00	60.00
1950D	40.00	60.00
1950S	10.00	12.00
1951	10.00	12.00
1951D	35.00	55.00
1951S	35.00	55.00

Note: Struck to honor the memory and construct memorials to this great educator.
Hints: This coin received wide circulation and is often found in grades of VF-EF but rarely lower.

WISCONSIN CENTENNIAL

1936	155.00	175.00

Note: Struck to commemorate the territorial rather than statehood anniversary of Wisconsin.

YORK COUNTY, MAINE

1936	155.00	165.00

Note: Struck to commemorate tercentenary of the founding of York County, the first established in Maine.

LAFAYETTE DOLLAR

1900	300.00	550.00

Counterfeit Alert: A number of counterfeits have been made of this piece.
Note: This was the first commemorative silver dollar struck and last until the bicentennial in 1976. The obverse depicts both Lafayette and Washington. The reverse depicts a statue of Lafayette given to France by the United States.

GRANT MEMORIAL GOLD DOLLARS

1922 with star	1,100.00	1,400.00
1922 no star	1,000.00	1,200.00

Note: Issued to mark the centennial of Grant's birth. His birthplace in Point Pleasant, Ohio is on the reverse.
Hints: Half the issue has a star above the word GRANT on the obverse.

LEWIS AND CLARK EXPOSITION GOLD DOLLARS

	AU	Unc.
1904	500.00	775.00
1905	500.00	875.00

Note: Issued as a souvenir of the Lewis and Clark Exposition in Portland, Oregon, and to raise money for a memorial to Sacagawea there.

LOUISIANA PURCHASE EXPOSITION GOLD DOLLARS

1903 Jefferson	360.00	450.00
1903 McKinley	335.00	425.00

Note: Despite the 1903 date, which does correspond to the centennial of the Louisiana Purchase, these coins were issued for distribution at the Louisiana Purchase Exposition in St. Louis in 1904. One type bears the portrait of Thomas Jefferson, the other of President McKinley.

WILLIAM McKINLEY MEMORIAL GOLD DOLLARS

1916	310.00	375.00
1917	330.00	460.00

Note: Struck to raise funds for a memorial to the assassinated president in Niles, Ohio, his birthplace.

PANAMA-PACIFIC EXPOSITION GOLD COINS

1915S $1	340.00	420.00

1915S $2½	1,150.00	1,450.00

1915S $50 round	21,500.00	25,000.00
1915S $50 octagonal	19,000.00	21,500.00

Note: The Panama-Pacific Exposition was held in San Francisco in 1915 to celebrate the opening of the Panama Canal. This is the only event ever to be honored with more than one denomination of commemorative gold. It is also the only issue of a $50 gold coin, excluding recent bullion issues.

Note: The case of issue alone for this complete set is of significant value.

INDEPENDENCE SESQUICENTENNIAL $2½ GOLD

	AU	Unc.
1926	300.00	325.00

Note: Struck to commemorate the 150th anniversary of American independence.

RECENT COMMEMORATIVE COINAGE

History: The United States commemorative coin program was revived in 1982 with the Washington Half and quickly fell into old habits. Even the American Numismatic Association has opposed the recent uncontrolled issue of commemoratives. President Ganz of the ANA recently pointed out that the cost of keeping up with new U.S. government issues alone greatly exceeds the annual budget of even most serious collectors. As in the 1930's collectors have became financially over-burdened. As a result so many coins have been "dumped" onto the secondary market that many commemoratives can be purchased at coin shops one or two years after issue at *less* than the original government issue price!

References: Hodder, Michael and Bowers, Q. David, *A Basic Guide to United States Commemorative Coins*; Swiatek, Anthony and Breen, Walter, *Encyclopedia of United States Silver and Gold Commemorative Coins 1892-1989*; Bowers, Q. David, *Commemorative Coins of the United States: A Complete Encyclopedia*.

Counterfeit Alert: Counterfeits of this series are virtually unknown.

Hints: These coins are found almost exclusively in their original cases of issue. Those lacking them are considered less marketable and are traded at a discount.

WASHINGTON HALF DOLLAR

	BU	PF
1982D	4.00	
1982S		4.00

Note: Struck to mark the 250th anniversary of the birth of George Washington.

LOS ANGELES OLYMPICS

1983P	$1 Silver	11.00	
1983D	$1 Silver	14.00	
1983S	$1 Silver	12.00	10.00

		BU	PF
1984P	$1 Silver	15.00	
1984D	$1 Silver	26.00	
1984S	$1 Silver	27.00	12.00

1984P	$10 Gold		255.00
1984D	$10 Gold		240.00
1984S	$10 Gold		235.00
1984W	$10 Gold	230.00	230.00

Note: The first year's dollar depicts a discus thrower, the second the gateway to the Olympic Stadium. The $10 gold, the first since 1933, depicts runners carrying the olympic flame.

STATUE OF LIBERTY

| 1986D | $½ Clad | 4.00 | |
| 1986S | $½ Clad | | 5.00 |

| 1986P | $1 Silver | 11.00 | |
| 1986S | $1 Silver | | 10.00 |

| 1986W | $5 Gold | 140.00 | 140.00 |

Note: While in a narrow sense these coins commemorate the centennial of the Statue of Liberty and Ellis Island Immigration Center, in a broader sense they honor the nation's immigrant heritage as a whole. The $5 gold piece is the first since 1929.

CONSTITUTION BICENTENNIAL

| 1987P | $1 Silver | 10.00 | |
| 1987S | $1 Silver | | 9.50 |

| 1987W | $5 Gold | 130.00 | 125.00 |

Note: The reverse of this dollar, of dubious artistic merits, is intended to represent a cross section of the American people. The gold piece depicts an eagle holding a quill pen.

SEOUL OLYMPICS

| 1988D | $1 Silver | 15.00 | |
| 1988S | $1 Silver | | 10.00 |

| 1988W | $5 Gold | 130.00 | 125.00 |

Note: It was decided to strike coins to honor American participation in the South Korean Olympics of 1988.

CONGRESS BICENTENNIAL

| 1989D | $½ Clad | 12.00 | |
| 1989S | $½ Clad | | 7.50 |

| 1989D | $1 Silver | 21.00 | |
| 1989S | $1 Silver | | 15.00 |

| 1989W | $5 Gold | 135.00 | 125.00 |

Note: Both the half dollar and the dollar depict differing renderings of the statue of Freedom on the Capitol dome. The $5 gold piece depicts the dome itself.

EISENHOWER CENTENNIAL

| 1990W | $1 Silver | 15.00 | |
| 1990P | $1 Silver | | 12.50 |

Note: This very unusual design depicts two opposite facing portraits of Eisenhower, one as general, the other as president. The reverse depicts his home at Gettysburg.

MOUNT RUSHMORE

	BU	PF
1991D $½ Clad	15.00	
1991S $½ Clad		13.00

| 1991P $1 Silver | 32.00 | |
| 1991S $1 Silver | | 28.00 |

| 1989W $5 Gold | 140.00 | 135.00 |

Note: Struck to commemorate the fiftieth anniversary of Mt. Rushmore national monument and to help raise money for its preservation.

KOREAN WAR MEMORIAL

| 1991D $1 Silver | 19.00 | |
| 1991P $1 Silver | | 16.00 |

Note: Struck to commemorate the 38th (sic) anniversary of the end of the Korean War. The reverse of this coin depicts a map of Korea with the 38th parallel indicated.

Any humor in this obvious pun has been lost on this author.

USO ANNIVERSARY

| 1991D $1 Silver | 28.00 | |
| 1991S $1 Silver | | 22.00 |

Note: Struck to honor the 50th anniversary of the United Service Organizations, and to raise money for the USO and the Treasury Department.

BARCELONA OLYMPICS

| 1992P $½ Clad | 7.50 | |
| 1992S $½ Clad | | 10.00 |

| 1992D $1 Silver | 28.00 | |
| 1992S $1 Silver | | 30.00 |

| 1992W $5 Gold | 150.00 | 145.00 |

Note: It was decided to strike coins to honor American participation in the Olympics in Barcelona, Spain, and to raise money for American athletes. The half depicts a

gymnast, the dollar a baseball player, and the $5 piece a sprinter.

WHITE HOUSE BICENTENNIAL

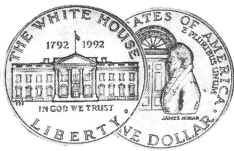

| 1992D $1 Silver | 40.00 | |
| 1992W $1 Silver | | 38.00 |

Note: Struck to mark the 200th anniversary of the White House, the portrait is that of James Hoban, its architect.

COLUMBUS QUINCENTENARY

| 1992D $½ Clad | 13.00 | |
| 1992S $½ Clad | | 12.50 |

| 1992D $1 Silver | 24.00 | |
| 1992P $1 Silver | | 26.00 |

| 1992W $5 Gold | 200.00 | 185.00 |

Note: Struck to commemorate the 500th anniversary of Columbus' discovery of

America. The dollar interestingly combines the twin themes of sea and space exploration. Several other countries also struck coins for this anniversary.

BILL OF RIGHTS

		BU	PF
1993W	$½ Silver	15.00	
1993S	$½ Silver		12.00

| 1993D | $1 Silver | 25.00 | |
| 1993W | $1 Silver | | 28.00 |

| 1993D | $1 Silver | 20.00 | |
| 1993S | $1 Silver | | 20.00 |

1993W $5 Gold   190.00   185.00
Note: Struck as a memorial for those who served in World War Two.

WORLD CUP

| 1994 | $½ Clad | 9.50 |
| 1994 | $½ Silver | 11.00 |

1993W $5 Gold   175.00   175.00
Note: Struck to commemorate the Bill of Rights, the constitutional document guaranteeing the basic freedoms of Americans.

WORLD WAR II

| 1994D | $1 Silver | 25.00 | |
| 1994S | $1 Silver | | 28.00 |

| 1993P | $½ Clad | 11.00 | |
| 1993P | $½ Silver | | 12.50 |

1994W $5 Gold   185.00   195.00
Note: Struck to commemorate the soccer World Cup played in the United States.

JEFFERSON MEMORIAL

| 1993P (1994) | 38.00 | |
| 1993S (1994) | | 38.00 |

Note: Issued to honor Thomas Jefferson on the 250th anniversary of his birth.

VIETNAM WAR MEMORIAL

| 1994P | $1 Silver | 30.00 | |
| 1994S | $1 Silver | | 33.00 |

Note: Struck for the tenth anniversary of the Vietnam Veterans War Memorial in Washington, D.C.

PRISONERS OF WAR

| 1994P | $1 Silver | 31.00 | |
| 1994S | $1 Silver | | 33.00 |

Note: Issued to honor American Prisoners of War.

WOMEN VETERANS

		BU	PF
1994P	$1 Silver	31.00	
1994S	$1 Silver		33.00

Note: Issued to honor the role of women in the U.S. armed forces.

U.S. CAPITOL

1994P	$1 Silver	32.00	
1994S	$1 Silver		35.00

Note: Struck to commemorate the two hundredth anniversary of the U.S. Capitol building.

SPECIAL OLYMPICS

1995W	$1 Silver	36.00	
1995P	$1 Silver		30.00

Note: Issued to commemorate the Special Olympics World Games, held in the United States in 1995, and to honor the Special Olympics movement. The portrait on this coin is somewhat controversial in that it depicts Eunice Kennedy Shriver, founder of the Special Olympics, who was alive at the time.

CIVIL WAR BATTLEFIELDS

1995S	$½ Clad	9.50	
1995S	$½ Clad		11.00

1995P	$1 Silver	32.00	
1995S	$1 Silver		35.00

| 1995W | $5 Gold | 200.00 | 235.00 |

Note: Issued to memorialize the Civil War and to raise money for the preservation of its battlefields.

ATLANTA OLYMPICS

		BU	PF
1995D	$½ Clad Basketball	11.00	
1995S	$½ Clad Basketball		12.00
1995D	$½ Clad Baseball	11.00	
1995S	$½ Clad Baseball		12.00

1995D	$½ Clad Swimming	11.00	
1995S	$½ Clad Swimming		12.00
1995D	$½ Clad Soccer	11.00	
1995S	$½ Clad Soccer		12.00

1995D	$1 Silver Gymanast	33.00	
1995P	$1 Silver same		36.00
1995D	$1 Silver Paralympics	33.00	
1995P	$1 Silver same		36.00
1995D	$1 Silver Track & Field	33.00	
1995P	$1 Silver same		36.00
1995D	$1 Silver Cycling	33.00	
1995P	$1 Silver same		36.00
1996D	$1 Silver Tennis	33.00	
1996P	$1 Silver same		36.00
1996D	$1 Silver Wheelchair Athlete	33.00	
1996P	$1 Silver same		36.00
1996D	$1 Silver Rowing	33.00	
1996P	$1 Silver same		36.00
1996D	$1 Silver High Jump	33.00	
1996P	$1 Silver same		36.00

1995W	$5 Gold Torch Runner	200.00	235.00
1995W	$5 Gold Stadium	200.00	235.00
1995W	$5 Gold Flag Bearer	200.00	235.00
1995W	$5 Gold Cauldron	200.00	235.00

Note: Issued to celebrate the 1996 centennial Olympic Games held in Atlanta.

U.S. PROOF SETS

History: While the first proof sets issued for wide distribution were sold in 1936, American proof coins have a long history. During the nineteenth century proofs were exceedingly rare. They were made as presentation pieces, for a very few wealthy collectors, or occasionally for diplomatic purposes. Proof coins of the late 1800's and early this century are slightly more available. The latter are particularly interesting in that they were matte or sand blast proofs with extreme detail but no brilliance. Most proof coins of the twentieth century have brilliant, mirror-like fields, and either brilliant devices or matte devices. These are called cameo proofs due to their high contrast. Modern proof sets contain one coin of each denomination, but only from the one mint specially designated that year to be the one proof mint. Prestige Sets have been issued since 1983 containing a commemorative dollar. Beginning in 1992 Proof Sets have been issued in both standard coinage metals and with normally clad coins struck in 90% silver. Proof sets were not released for years after 1936 not listed below.

References: Breen, Walter, *Walter Breen's Encyclopedia of United States and Colonial Proof Coins.*

Counterfeit Alert: Proof coins are more difficult to counterfeit due to their fine surfaces. On rare occasions they have, however, been subject to alteration.

Hints: Never breath directly on a proof coin; "carbon spotting" may result. Do not store proof sets in a moist basement. Do not remove proof coins from original government holders without reason; they are worth more in original holders.

Proof Set in Case

1936	3,450.00
1937	2,200.00
1938	1,050.00
1939	950.00
1940	725.00
1941	600.00
1942 one nickel	600.00
1942 both nickels	650.00
1950	375.00
1951	275.00
1952	165.00
1953	130.00
1954	70.00
1955 box	60.00
1955 flat pack	55.00
1956	35.00
1957	15.00
1958	20.00
1959	16.00
1960	12.50

1960 small date cent	24.00
1961	8.00
1962	8.00
1963	8.00
1964	8.00
1968S	5.00
1969S	5.00
1970S	9.00
1970S small date cent	65.00
1970S dime w/o S	450.00
1971S	3.50
1971S nickel w/o S	685.00
1972S	3.50
1973S	5.50
1974S	5.75
1975S	7.00
1975S dime w/o S	*Rare*
1976S	7.75
1976S 3-pc. silver	11.50
1977S	5.00
1978S	6.00
1979S Filled S	7.00
1979S Clear S	68.50
1980S	6.00
1981S	7.00
1982S	4.00
1983S	6.00
1983S dime w/o S	375.00
1983S Prestige	90.00
1984S	11.00
1984S Prestige	30.00
1985S	7.00
1986S	20.00
1986S Prestige	30.00
1987S	6.00
1987S Prestige	20.00

1988S	9.00
1988S Prestige	25.00
1989S	7.50
1989S Prestige	30.00
1990S	13.00
1990S cent w/o S	1,500.00
1990S Prestige	25.00
1990S Prestige, cent w/o S	1,400.00
1991S	18.00
1991S Prestige	60.00
1992S	16.00
1992S Prestige	55.00
1992S Silver	23.00
1992S Silver Premier	26.00
1993S	21.00
1993S Prestige	50.00
1993S Silver	33.00
1993S Silver Premier	35.00
1994S	17.50
1994S Prestige	55.00
1994S Silver	30.00
1994S Silver Premier	32.00
1995S	16.50
1995S Prestige	65.00
1995S Silver	20.00
1995S Silver Premier	36.00
1996S	17.50
1996S Prestige	.00
1996S Silver	.00
1996S Silver Premier	.00

U.S. MINT SETS

History: Mint sets, sometimes labeled Uncirculated Sets, are intended to provide representative samples of regular issue circulating United States coinage. These coins are not intended to be special strikes. Unlike Proof Sets, where one mint is designated to be the proof mint, mint sets contain one sample of every circulating coin, therefore if cents were struck for circulation at three different mints in a given year, a complete mint set will contain three different cents. Mint sets from 1947-1958 are *double* sets containing two examples of each coin. Mint sets were not released for years not listed below, however souvenir sets were sold at the mints for the years 1982 and 1983.

References: See general U.S. references.

Counterfeit Alert: The coins themselves are not subject to counterfeiting but occasionally individuals will insert non-original coins into an early holder. This is a practice generally objected to and can be detected by examining the toning.

Hints: Never breath directly on an uncirculated coin; "carbon spotting" may result. Do not store mint sets in a moist basement. Do not remove coins from original government holders without reason, they are worth more in original holders. Older official holders, particularly those from 1947-1958, will tend to tone the coins. This is not damage and such coins should never be cleaned or dipped as this impairs the natural surface and reduces their value.

1947	625.00
1948	225.00
1949	375.00
1951	350.00
1952	275.00
1953	225.00
1954	105.00
1955	75.00
1956	60.00
1957	100.00
1958	75.00
1959	16.00
1960	14.00
1961	14.00
1962	11.00
1963	9.50
1964	8.00

Following Sets in Red and Blue Plastic Sleeves

1968	3.00
1969	3.50
1970	10.00
1970 small date cent	40.00
1971	2.75
1972	2.75
1973	7.50
1974	6.00
1975	6.00
1976	6.50

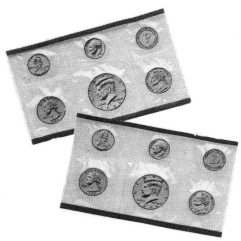

Set in plastic film and envelope

1976S 3-pc. silver	11.00
1977	6.00
1978	6.50
1979	5.50

Note: The 1979S SBA dollar was not included in the above set.

1980	6.50
1981	10.00
1984	4.00
1985	4.50
1986	13.50
1987	6.00
1988	4.00
1989	4.00
1990	5.00
1991	11.00
1992	13.00
1993	8.50
1994	10.00
1995	10.00
1996	

SPECIAL MINT SETS

History: During the period 1965-67 no proof or mint sets were issued and while three different mints were striking coins, they cannot be distinguished because no mint marks were used. Special Mint Sets were sold to collectors as substitutes. While the government initially claimed that these were not of special strike or quality, this is manifestly false. At this point all numismatists acknowledge that these are not circulation strikes. The 1965 set came in a plastic film within an envelope. The 1966 and 1967 sets were packaged in special rigid cases, within a cardboard sleeve.

References: See general U.S. references.

Counterfeit Alert: The coins themselves are not subject to counterfeiting but the rigid holders can be opened and the coins replaced with circulation strikes. This is rare and is usually quite obvious.

Hints: Never breath directly on an uncirculated coin; "carbon spotting" may result. Do not store mint sets in a moist basement. Do not remove coins from original government holders without reason, they are worth less without them.

1965	4.00
1966	4.25
1967	6.50

BULLION ISSUES

History: Beginning in 1980 the U.S. government has struck various gold, and later silver, pieces intended to compete with foreign gold bullion items such as the South African Krugerrand and the Canadian Maple Leaf. The first series, abandoned after only four years, was the American Arts Medallion Series. They bore no face value, and hence have no legal tender status. While intended to be investment items the current series, the American Eagle bullion coins, are not available to the general public in small quantities except as proofs, but can be bought at most local coin shops at a modest premium. The Gold Eagles bear the same obverse as the Augustus Saint-Gaudens $20 gold piece of 1907-33, the silver as the Walking Liberty Half Dollar. Original reverses were introduced, the gold having a family of eagles, the silver an American eagle in a traditional heraldic depiction. While all these coins have denominations most coin dealers avoid referring to them by their denomination and prefer to call them by

Set in Holder with Sleeve 1966-1967

the net amount of precious metal they contain. This is to avoid confusion with the genuine antique gold coins. The $50 contains one ounce of gold, $25 half an ounce, $10 a quarter ounce, $5 one tenth ounce, and $1 contains one ounce of silver, all in addition to small amounts of alloy to provide hardness.

References: See general U.S. references.

Counterfeit Alert: As with all precious metal bullion coins, one should be wary of counterfeits. Also the dollar has been the subject of look-alikes which do not violate counterfeiting laws by slightly changing the inscriptions.

Hints: The one ounce gold piece usually carries the smallest percentage premium of the series, and thus is usually the choice of bullion investors. The small gold and the silver, both in uncirculated and proof grades, have become one of the most popular American gift items, both among collectors and non-collectors. Do not remove proofs from original government holders; they are less desirable without them.

Important: On most of the uncirculated versions the prices will go up and down with the fluctuations of the precious metals prices. The prices below for gold are based on a spot value between $380 and $400. Updated spot prices for gold and silver can be found in most major newspapers.

AMERICAN ARTS MEDALLIONS

1/2 oz. Gold	BU
1980 Marian Anderson	210
1981 Willa Cather	210
1982 Frank Lloyd Wright	210
1983 Alexander Calder	210
1984 John Steinbeck	210

1 oz. Gold	
1980 Grant Wood	425
1981 Mark Twain	425
1982 Louis Armstrong	425
1983 Robert Frost	425
1984 Helen Hayes	430

AMERICAN EAGLE BULLION COINS

1 oz. Silver Eagle	Unc.	PF
1986	12.00	
1986S		18.00
1987	8.00	
1987S		18.00
1988	8.00	
1988S		65.00
1989	8.00	
1989S		16.00
1990	8.00	
1990S		24.00
1991	8.00	
1991S		20.00
1992	8.00	
1992S		20.00
1993	8.00	
1993P		28.00
1994	8.00	
1994S		28.00
1995	8.00	
1995P		45.00
1995W		450.00
1996	8.00	
1996P		29.00

1/10 oz. Gold Eagle		
1986	52.00	
1987	52.00	
1988	60.00	
1988P		60.00
1989	52.00	
1989P		62.00
1990	52.00	
1990P		60.00
1991	52.00	
1991P		60.00
1992	52.00	
1992P		60.00

1993	52.00	
1993P		60.00
1994	52.00	
1994W		75.00
1995	52.00	
1995W		60.00
1996	52.00	
1996W		

1/4 oz. Gold Eagle		
1986	120.00	
1987	120.00	
1988	120.00	
1988P		130.00
1989	130.00	
1989P		130.00
1990	130.00	
1990P		130.00
1991	140.00	
1991P		130.00
1992	120.00	
1992P		130.00
1993	120.00	
1993P		165.00
1994	120.00	
1994W		150.00
1995	120.00	
1995W		60.00
1996	120.00	
1996W		

1/2 oz. Gold Eagle		
1986	230.00	
1987	230.00	
1987P		235.00
1988	230.00	
1988P		230.00
1989	230.00	
1989P		230.00
1990	465.00	
1990P		235.00
1991	400.00	
1991P		250.00
1992	250.00	
1992P		250.00
1993	230.00	
1993P		290.00
1994	230.00	
1994W		275.00
1995	230.00	

	Unc	PF
1995W		260.00
1996	230.00	
1996W		

1 oz. Gold Eagle

	Unc	PF
1986	425.00	
1986W		455.00
1987	425.00	
1987W		455.00
1988	425.00	
1988W		460.00
1989	425.00	
1989W		460.00
1990	425.00	
1990W		460.00
1991	425.00	
1991W		465.00
1992	425.00	
1992W		460.00
1993	425.00	
1993W		475.00
1994	425.00	
1994W		455.00
1995	425.00	
1995W		455.00
1996	425.00	
1996W		

PATTERNS

History: A pattern is a prototype for a coin. It may appear similar to a normal coin but bear a date before that coin's first release, or it may be struck in an alloy never used for that coin (or any other!) In most cases, however, they bear designs that were completely rejected and appear to be the official issues of someone's imagination. They were created as experiments or to present to Congressmen as examples of proposed new coins. While in the nineteenth century "extra" patterns were struck to please wealthy collectors, patterns struck after 1916 are illegal to own and subject to government confiscation. Indeed, even the Smithsonian Institution was forbidden to have a sample of the unissued 1964D Peace Dollar.

Reference: Judd, J. Hewett, *United States Pattern, Experimental and Trial Pieces.*

Counterfeit Alert: Patterns are less prone to being counterfeited than one might expect. Nevertheless, some electrotype copies are known. One should also be careful not to mistake a privately concocted fantasy for an actual government pattern.

Hints: Prices on patterns vary widely. This is a field for the specialist. The above book and some comparison shopping are advised before jumping in with "both feet."

                                    AU-Unc.
1836 $1, Gold, Liberty Cap in rays *Rare*

1855 Large Cent, Copper, Flying Eagle
                                    750.00
1859 1¢ Copper, Seated Liberty   750.00
1860 Half Dime, Seated Liberty but
    UNITED STATES OF AMERICA
    omitted 2,350.00
1866 5¢ Nickel, George Washington,
                                    775.00

1866 5¢ Nickel, Abraham Lincoln,
                                    4,500.00

1872 50¢ Silver, Amazonian Design
                                    8,000.00
1879 Dime, Silver, Obverse as Morgan
    Dollar 950.00
1879 $4 Gold (stella), flowing hair
                                    25,000.00

same, Aluminum   *Rare*
1882 5¢ Aluminum, Liberty head as on
    regular issue of 1883 . . . . 850.00
1896 5¢ Aluminum, Shield 550.00
1909 5¢ Nickel, Shield obverse   *Rare*
1916 Quarter, Silver, Standing Liberty
    type with eagle between branches
                                    Rare
1974 1¢ Aluminum   *Rare*

ERRORS

History: Errors will occur in any manufacturing process, coins included. They occur less frequently because special care is taken not to permit such coins outside the mint, where they are systematically caught and destroyed. As mintages have increased, errors have become more common. Nineteenth century errors are far scarcer than present day errors. Silver dollar, half dollar, gold and commemorative errors are all much more scarce.

References: Spadone, Frank, *Major Variety and Oddity*; Margolis, Arnold, *Error Coin Encyclopedia.*

Counterfeit Alert: Many less than clever laymen have attempted to fool collectors by faking errors. One common attempt involves hammering one coin onto another. Others involving plating with the wrong metal, acid bathing, or cutting two coins in half and gluing the wrong halves together.

Serious counterfeits exist of the 1955, 1972 double dies. Virtually all copper 1943 cents are counterfeit. Check with magnet or for altered date.

End clips are of little value but are easily and often counterfeited.

Hints: Two headed coins are rarely errors, but are usually novelties made outside the mint.

Note: The ranges of values given below are for the Lincoln Memorial cent and the Eisenhower dollar respectively, and are used to show the relative rarity of the different types of errors. Older and larger coins are usually worth more than smaller recent coins. Values will also vary depending on the extent of the error.

                                    AU-BU
Blank (unstruck coin) 50-30.00

Off-Center (blank coin not placed completely on the dies before striking)
. . . . 1.00-200.00

Broadstrike (coin struck without a collar)
. . . . 1.00-150.00
Brockage (coin struck with the previously struck coin still sticking to one of the dies) 12.00-800.00
Cud (Coin struck with a die that has a section of its rim broken off) .75-10.00

	AU	BF

Die Crack (coin struck with a small crack in the die leaving a raised line on the actual coin) 25-4.00

Clashed Die (coin struck with dies that have hit each other with no coin in between, leaving the faint image of one on the other) 50-10.00

Double Die (coin struck with *die* that has the image impressed twice, once shifted) 125.00-*Rare*

Double Struck (coin that has been struck twice, usually having moved slightly between strikes) 15.00-800.00

Struck Through (coin struck with foreign matter between blank and die) 1.00-10.00

Lamination (coin struck on blank with gas trapped in metal) 25-5.00

Die chip (coin struck with tiny bit of metal chipped out of surface of die, producing extra raised spot on coin) 35-5.00

BIE cent (cent with small vertical die chip between B and E in liberty, common for certain years) . . . . .25-*N.A.*

Straight (End) Clip (coin struck from incomplete blank cut out from the flat end of the sheet of metal) 50-7.00

Clip (coin struck on blank which has had part of another blank cut out of it) 75-9.00

Incorrect Blank (coin struck on blank intended for a different type of coin) 40.00-600.00

COLONIAL AND STATE COINAGES

History: During the period before federal coinage was introduced in 1793, hundreds of different types of private, local, state, and colonial coins each competed for popularity. The British government, following the principles of mercantilism, avoided shipping any quantities of gold or silver coin to the American Colonies.

Most precious metal coin circulating in the Colonies at the time was imported from Mexico. The famous piece of eight is here called the Spanish milled dollar after its tamper-proof edge device. Small change was made by cutting these Spanish dollars in parts, as though it were a pie. This is how we get the phrase "two bits" for a quarter. One quarter of a Spanish dollar was 2/8th, each small pie-slice of the coin was called a "bit." Of course silver from other Spanish colonies besides Mexico also flowed in, and there was very little to distinguish the silver struck at Mexico City from that struck at Lima or Potosi. Colonial Americans would accept whatever silver coin they found and then try to guess at its real worth!

Copper coinage was more uniquely American. An appreciable quantity of British regal copper half pence made it to the Colonies, but nowhere near enough to fill the need. Many blacksmiths throughout the Colonies made a part time job of making their own crude counterfeits of British copper. Opportunities afforded by the shortage of small change were not lost on local merchants and very often the same counterfeiters were hired to strike private tokens. Also a number of British firms with interests in the Colonies arranged to ship over their own tokens, often with some royal sanction or authority. Between the Declaration of Independence and the establishment of the United States by the Constitution, a loose association was established under the Articles of Confederation. This left the states with much more sovereignty than they have today and this included the right of coinage. Several of these sovereign states struck their own coinage. Most were cents, the equivalent of the old British halfpenny, and at a glance they even looked like the British halfpenny.

During much of this early period paper money was more common than real money. But that's for later in this book.

References: Crosby, S.S., *The Early Coins of America*; Kleeberg, John, *Money of Pre-Federal America*; Newman, Eric P., ed., *Studies on Money in Early America*; Vlack, Robert, *Early American Coins*; Yeoman, R.S., *A Guide Book of United States Coins*.

Counterfeit Alert: Many quality counterfeits and crude replicas exist. The latter can often be identified by a seam on the edge. See individual sections.

Hints: Many of the coins in these sections are found by metal detectors. "Ground finds" often have pitted or porous surfaces. These coins are not worthless but are worth substantially less than the prices listed.

AMERICAN PLANTATION TOKEN

History: Some of the colonial coins and tokens were not intended to circulate in any restricted area but to be sent wherever they were needed. Most were struck in England and shipped here.

One of these is called the "Plantation token." In 1688 the government gave Richard Holt permission to strike tin tokens with the denomination 1/24th Spanish Real. The reason for this is that the silver circulating in the American Colonies was overwhelmingly Spanish colonial. Tin was used partially because it was the metal the English minor coins were being struck in at the time. The obverse bears King James II on a galloping horse, surrounded by his royal titles. The reverse has his four shields of arms in the form of a cross, surrounded by the value. Restrikes of this piece were made with original dies in 1828.

References: See general works.

Counterfeit Alert: Be aware of restrikes. They can be distinguished from originals by the very large die crack to the right on the obverse, and by the overly fresh surface.

Hints: Pitted or porous coins are the norm on these.

	G	F
James II 1/24 Real	85.00	300.00
same, 4 of 24 sideways		750.00
same, restrike		150.00
copper restrike		600.00

ROSA AMERICANA TOKENS

History: The first serious effort to provide the American Colonies with small change came as a result of a patent given by the crown to William Wood in 1722. He expected to make a handsome profit striking coins for the Colonies at half the weight standard used in Britain. Unfortunately for Wood, the colonists weren't that gullible, and rejected his coinage. These coins bear the portrait of

inscription, *Rosa Americana Utile Dulci* translates "American Rose, Useful [and] Pleasant." These pieces were struck in three sizes, halfpenny, penny, and twopence. Many spelling varieties are known on these coins.

References: See general works.

Counterfeit Alert: Less extensively counterfeited than other series.

Hints: Pitted or porous coins are worth less than the prices listed.

	G	F
No Date 2 pence	65.00	250.00
1722 ½ penny	40.00	200.00

	G	F
1722 Penny	35.00	150.00
1722 2 pence	50.00	225.00
1723 ½ penny	350.00	1,250.00
same with crown	30.00	100.00
1723 Penny	30.00	100.00
1723 2 Pence	50.00	225.00
1724 Penny pattern		Rare
1724 2 pence pattern		Rare
1733 2 pence pattern		Rare

HIBERNIA COINAGE

History: In 1722 William Wood was given a royal patent to strike copper for both the American Colonies (*see previous section*) and Ireland. His Irish coinage started out with a scandal and fared no better. The Lord Lieutenant of Ireland had never been informed, causing much resentment in Ireland. Moreover, he expected to make a handsome profit striking these coins at a below standard weight. The Irish rejected Wood's Hibernia coins as thoroughly as the Americans rejected his Rosa Americana coins. Nevertheless, the rejected Irish coins were gathered and shipped *en masse* to America. They were imported here in such quantity that they are today looked upon as part of the American colonial series. They bear the portrait of George I as on the Rosa Americanas, and a seated allegory of Ireland (Hibernia) playing a harp. They were struck in farthing and halfpenny size. Many varieties are known.

References: See general works.

Counterfeit Alert: Less extensively counterfeited than other series.

Hints: Pitted or porous coins are worth less than the prices listed.

	G	F
1722 Farthing	65.00	325.00
1722 ½ Penny, rocks right (pattern)		425.00
1722 ½ Penny, harp left	20.00	100.00
1722 ½ Penny, harp right	18.00	90.00
1723 Farthing	15.00	45.00

	G	F
same with D:G:	45.00	100.00
1723 ½ penny	15.00	40.00
1724 Farthing	32.00	125.00
1724 ½ penny	25.00	85.00

HIBERNIA / VOCE POPULI COINAGE

History: This private token struck by Mr. Roache of Dublin in 1760 is not properly part of the colonial series. It has become accepted by American collectors however due to its early migration into this country. Voce Populi (the voice of the people) surrounds an anonymous royal head on the obverse. The reverse is similar to the Hibernia coins above. Some pieces bear a P next to the bust. Its meaning is still unknown.

References: See general works.

Counterfeit Alert: Less extensively counterfeited than other series.

Hints: Those pieces dated 1700 were actually struck in 1760. This is a die engraving error. Pitted or porous coins are worth less than the prices listed.

	G	F
1760 Farthing	150.00	350.00
1700 ½ Penny	500.00	1,300.00
1760 ½ Penny	40.00	100.00

	G	F
1760 ½ Penny, P	75.00	175.00
1760 ½ Penny, VOOE	50.00	125.00

PITT TOKENS

History: The Pitt Token was not intended to be a token. It was designed by Paul Revere and struck in Philadelphia as a medal to express gratitude to William Pitt the Elder for his efforts to repeal the Stamp Act.

Once released they seemed to circulate anyway, the large piece as a halfpenny, the small as a farthing. The obverse surrounds Pitt's bust with "The Restorer of Commerce 1766 - No Stamps." The reverse shows a ship approaching the word AMERICA and says "Thanks to the Friends of Liberty and Trade."

References: See general works.

Counterfeit Alert: Less extensively counterfeited than other series.

Hints: All farthings seem to have been struck on cast blanks and should not be mistaken for ground finds.

	VG	F
1766 Farthing	2,300.00	5,500.00

1766 ½ Penny	180.00	425.00

CAROLINA

History: The Carolina Elephant token is one of a group of three related tokens which have been the subject of much questioning. Its reverse says, "God: Preserve: Carolina: And The: Lords: Proprieters. 1694." It shares an obverse design with an earlier English token having a London shield on the back, and with another of 1694 referring to New England. It has been suggested that this token was struck by the Royal African Company from West African copper. The type of elephant is in fact African and not Indian.

Reference: Doty, Richard, "The Carolina and New England Elephant Tokens," in Newman, *Studies on Money in Early America.*

Counterfeit Alert: Struck counterfeits of the second type are known.

Hints: The same reverse die was used for both types. The E can be seen beneath the repunched O.

	VG	VF
1694 ½ Penny PROPRIETERS	3,500.00	7,500.00
1694 ½ Penny PROPRIETORS	2,200.00	5,500.00

CONNECTICUT

History: The very first token to have been struck in Connecticut is one of the few coins to address the user directly. Dr. Samuel Higley of Granby had a small copper mine, and made his own tokens from mine to pocket. The first issue of these halfpenny size tokens bore the legend "The Value Of Three Pence" but when his neighbors refused to accept them at this audacious value he engraved new dies. Not quite willing to accept the reality of their halfpenny value, he had the new tokens tell their users, "Value Me As You Please." The obverse type of these tokens shows a deer or stag, except for one unique example with a wheel. There are two reverses: s: three crowned hammers, and an axe.

The new sovereign State of Connecticut approved a contract for the production of coinage in New Haven in October 1785. The mint ceased operations on June 1, 1787 but the son of one of the partners took some remaining dies, left for Machin Mills, New York, and entered into a new partnership to strike counterfeit, light weight Connecticut cents. Many of these were dated 1788, a year never authorized by the State of Connecticut.

Connecticut cent designs follow a familiar pattern. All bear a royal portrait (pseudo-George II left, or pseudo-George III right) with a seated Liberty on the reverse, very similar in appearance to the Britannia on British halfpennies. The obverse reads *Auctori Connec* for "by the authority of Connecticut." *Inde et Lib* for "Independence and Liberty" surround the figure of Liberty.
References: See general works.
Counterfeit Alert: A number of counterfeits of the first type exist.
Hints: Higley coppers generally come well worn. In this case even ground finds can be of substantial value. Connecticut cents are poorly struck on irregular,

poorly prepared blanks. These coins are crude. Many varieties exist, some worth more than the types below.

	G	F

HIGLEY COPPERS
| 1737 The Value of Three Pence / Connecticut (three crowned hammers) | 4,500.00 | 9,000.00 |
| 1737 The Value of Three Pence / I Am Good Copper (three crowned hammers) | 5,500.00 | 11,000.00 |

1737 Value Me As You Please / I Am Good Copper (three crowned hammers)	4,500.00	9,000.00
[1737] Value Me As You Please / I Cut My Way Through (axe)	5,000.00	9,500.00
[1737] The Wheele Goes Round (wheel) / I Cut My Way Through (axe) *Unique*		
1739 Value Me As You Please / I Cut My Way Through (axe)	6,000.00	12,500.00

STATE COPPERS
1785 Bust left	150.00	500.00
1785 Bust right	40.00	175.00
same, "African Head" variety with fuller features	50.00	275.00
1786 Mailed bust left	35.00	150.00
1786 Draped bust left	55.00	300.00
1786 Hercules bust left	100.00	350.00
1786 Bust right	55.00	250.00
same larger head	65.00	400.00
1787 Bust left	30.00	115.00
same, horn from bust	40.00	175.00
1787 Bust right	90.00	300.00
1788 Mailed bust left	35.00	150.00
1788 Draped bust left	40.00	200.00
1788 Bust right	40.00	175.00

MASSACHUSETTS

History: During the colonial period the British government, following the principles of mercantilism, avoided shipping any quantities of gold or silver coin to the American Colonies. They certainly did not want to authorize the striking of special precious metal coinage for colonial use. But during the 1640's England was embroiled in a civil war between Parliament and the King, whose head would roll by the close of the decade. Before the chaos settled, The Massachusetts General Court ordered that the first silver coins in the English speaking Americas be struck. A local ironworker from Saugus, Massachusetts was asked to engrave the simple dies which were little more than punches. The obverse had the initials NE for New England set in a recessed well. The reverse had Roman numerals within a square indicating the value of each coin in pence. Three denominations were struck: threepence with a III on the reverse, sixpence with VI, and a shilling with XII. This historic coinage was struck only from June 11 to October 19, 1652. By then the government of Massachusetts realized that the simple design not only made counterfeiting easy, but made it difficult to tell if the edges of the coin had been clipped. In reality, the latter was probably the greater worry as few contemporary counterfeits of the NE coinage survive. It was decided that the NE coinage would be replaced with a coinage having a more detailed design. The new coins bore the legends "Masathusets In New England An Dom" with a willow tree on the obverse and 1652 over the value on the reverse. They were not actually struck in 1652, but kept the date so if the English authorities ordered them to cease coining they could point to the date and say that the coins were made before the order arrived. They were really struck from 1653-60. The Willow Tree coins and the NE coins were both struck with a sledge hammer in the primitive medieval method. They are always crude and uneven. In 1660 the tree was changed to an oak and the method of manufacture was changed to the more consistent screw press. This gave a much neater appearance to the coins. The type of the tree was again changed in 1667 to a pine tree. Some time between this year and the end of tree coinage in 1682 the shillings were made smaller and thicker to be more like English coins.

It was not until 1776 that even patterns for new Massachusetts coins were prepared, and little is known of the origin of these mysterious pieces. Finally in 1786 the Massachusetts General Court ordered that a mint be erected and coins be struck. The mint, located in Boston, struck cents and half cents, the first circulating coinage in the Americas to use the "cent." The design of both consisted of an Indian on one side, an eagle on the other, the inscriptions reading "Commonwealth [of] Massachusetts." The mint was deemed unprofitable and plans were made to shut it down in the Fall of 1788.

References: Noe, Sydney, *The New England and Willow Tree Coinage of Massachusetts*; Noe, Sydney, *The Oak Tree Coinage of Massachusetts*; Noe, Sydney, *The Pine Tree Coinage of Massachusetts*; and general works.

Counterfeit Alert: NE sixpence and shilling, Oak Tree twopence and shilling, Pine Tree twopence, sixpence, large size shilling. The Pine Tree series is the most counterfeited of the three trees. Very many crude, base metal cast replicas of both tree and Indian coins have been made for sale in museum gift shops and as souvenirs. They can be identified by a seam on the edge.

Hints: Pitted or porous coins are worth less than the prices listed. Even the finest NE and Willow coins are very crude. Indian types will be neat, but have many varieties.

	G	F
NE 3 pence		*Unique*
NE 6 pence		*Rare*

NE Shilling	5,000.00	16,000.00
1652 Willow 3 pence		*only 3 known*
1652 Willow 6 pence		20,000.00

	G	F
1652 Willow Shilling	5,000.00	17,000.00
1662 Oak 2 pence	350.00	1,200.00
1652 Oak 3 pence	750.00	1,700.00
1652 Oak 6 pence	325.00	1,700.00

1652 Oak Shilling	350.00	1,700.00
1652 Pine 3 pence	300.00	900.00
1652 Pine 6 pence	325.00	1,200.00

1652 Pine Shilling	375.00	1,250.00
1652 Pine Shilling (small diameter)		
	350.00	1,000.00

	VG	VF
1787 ½ cent	100.00	350.00
1787 Cent, arrows to viewer's right		
	3,500.00	*Rare*
1787 Cent, arrows to viewer's left		
	100.00	350.00
1788 ½ cent	125.00	375.00
1788 Cent	100.00	375.00

MARYLAND

History: As practical feudal lord over Maryland, Cecil Calvert, Second Lord Baltimore, ordered coinage for his lands. He was aware that the colonists there were reduced to barter and sought to remedy the situation. Dies were prepared in England in 1659 and, after an initial challenge by the British government was decided in Calvert's favor, the Royal Mint was contracted to strike the coins. Three silver denominations were struck for circulation, fourpence, sixpence and shilling. Their designs were strictly in the pattern of European feudal coinage. The obverse bore Calvert's royal titles in Latin, surrounding his bust. The reverse bore his crowned shield of arms, along with a Latin motto and the denomination. A copper penny was originally considered as well but this

denomination never got past the pattern stage and it is today quite rare.

In 1783, more than a century after the Lord Baltimore coinage, an Annapolis silversmith named John Chalmers struck another series of silver coins. Exasperated by the chiselling whereby people would attempted to cut Spanish pieces of eight into, for example, nine segments and them pass them off as full bits, Chalmers decided to take matters into his own hands. He bought the pieces at silver value, and struck his own coin. His was also light in weight, but his good reputation and promise to honor the pieces encouraged their popularity. Chalmers struck shillings, sixpence and threepence. Seven years later Standish Barry, a Baltimore silversmith, followed suit, striking his own silver threepence. All of Chalmers' silver bears clasped hands as an obverse motif; Barry's threepence carries a portrait of George Washington. The issuers' names are clearly indicated on the tokens, as are their dates of issue.

References: See general listings.

Counterfeit Alert: Struck counterfeits exist of the Lord Baltimore penny. Crude replicas of the Lord Baltimore coins have been made for sale in museum gift shops and as souvenirs. They can be identified by a seam on the edge.

Hints: Pitted or porous coins are worth less than the prices listed.

	G	F
LORD BALTIMORE		
Penny (Denarium)		*only 5 known*
Fourpence (IV)	1,200.00	4,600.00
Sixpence (VI)	1,000.00	4,500.00
Shilling (XII)	1,200.00	4,700.00
	VG	VF
JOHN CHALMERS		
1783 3 pence	950.00	2,500.00
1783 6 pence	1,100.00	3,100.00
1783 Shilling, birds on rev.		
	675.00	2,100.00
1783 Shilling, circle of rings on rev.		
	9,000.00	30,000.00
STANDISH BARRY		
1790 3 pence	2,000.00	8,000.00

NEW ENGLAND

History: The New England Elephant Token is one of a group of three related tokens which have been the subject of

much questioning. Its reverse says, "God: Preserve New England. 1694." It shares an obverse design with an earlier English token having a London shield on the back, and with another of 1694 referring to Carolina. It has been suggested that this token was struck by the Royal African Company from West African copper. The type of elephant is in fact African and not Indian.
Reference: Doty, Richard, "The Carolina and New England Elephant Tokens," in Newman, *Studies on Money in Early America.*
Counterfeit Alert: Struck counterfeits are known.

	VG	VF
1694 ½ Penny	16,000.00	30,000.00

NEW HAMPSHIRE

History: Despite the fact that New Hampshire had no experience with local coinage during the colonial period, it was the first state to investigate the matter when independence was imminent, preceding the declaration by over a month. Several copper patterns bearing a pine tree and harp are known, and its House of Representatives had already provided for a coin to be worth 1/108th of a Spanish milled dollar. It is doubted that any were ever authorized for circulation though.
References: See general references.
Counterfeit Alert: Struck counterfeits are known.
Hints: New Hampshire pieces with a large WM are not counterfeits but rather complete fabrications.

	VG
1776 ½ Penny	13,000.00

NEW JERSEY

History: The first New Jersey coinage was not actually made for New Jersey.

When Mark Newby led a group of immigrants to New Jersey from Ireland he planned ahead. Knowing of the acute coinage shortage in the colonies, he brought with him a large quantity of private tokens believed to have been struck in Dublin in 1670-75. Within six months of his arrival he managed to get the New Jersey Legislature to enact them legal tender for all debts. All these pieces have St. Patrick on them. On the halfpenny he is preaching to the masses (next to the arms of Dublin), on the farthing (quarter penny) he is driving the snakes out of Ireland. The obverse of both coins shows King David playing the harp, with a large crown below. One interesting feature of these coppers is that the large crown on the obverse is struck over a specially applied brass plug, thus giving the crown the appearance of gold. Some scholars have suggested that the denominations are actually penny and halfpenny.

In 1786 the New Jersey Legislature authorized a partnership to strike 3,000,000 coppers on its behalf, in exchange for 10% of the coins struck. These cents have a horse head over a plow on one side, the United States' shield on the other. The legends were *Nova Caesarea* and *E Pluribus Unum* respectively.
Reference: Maris, Edward, *A Historical Sketch of the Coins of New Jersey.*
Counterfeit Alert: Struck counterfeits exist of the silver farthing.
Hints: New Jersey cents are among the most common state coppers and feature a great many varieties, some of which carry a premium. Pitted or porous coins are worth less than the prices listed.

	G	F
St. Patrick Farthing	35.00	150.00
same but silver	400.00	1,700.00
same but gold		unique
St. Patrick Halfpenny	45.00	250.00

	VG	VF
1786 Cent, date at bottom	75.00	350.00
1786 Cent, date lower right	*Rare*	3,200.00
1787 Cent	75.00	175.00
1788 Cent	70.00	165.00
1788 Cent, tiny fox	150.00	300.00
1788 Cent, horse head left	300.00	650.00

NEW YORK

History: The very first token to be issued in New York is one struck by William Lovelace, governor 1663/68-1673. It is a small farthing inscribed "*New Yorke In America" and bears his eagle crest. The reverse has a scene of Venus and Cupid with trees between. Most known specimens are brass, but some have been found in what has been called pewter by some, lead by others.

One private gold token of notorious fame is the Brasher Doubloon of 1787. New York goldsmith Ephraim Brasher struck these rare pieces with the seal of New York on one side, an heraldic American eagle on the other.

Copper during this period was also a matter for the private sector. The state government declined both to strike its own coin and to contract it out. Upon realizing the impasse both partnerships vying for the contract decided to strike their coppers anyway. The Excelsior coppers resembling the Brasher Doubloon were actually struck by him. Other pieces, the more common Eborac Coppers bear a close resemblance to Connecticut coppers but for the substituted legends *Nova Eborac* and *Virt et Lib*, for "New York, Virtue and Liberty."

Towards the end of the century the trading firm of Talbot, Allum & Lee imported large quantities of well made English tokens. These were so abundant that some of them were used as blanks for early United States government copper.
References: Kleeberg, John, "The New Yorke in America Tokens," *Money of Pre-Federal America*; general references.
Counterfeit Alert: Many crude copies of the Brasher Doubloon exist. They can be detected by a seam on the edge. Good counterfeits exist of the Non Vi Virtute, Excelsior, Clinton and Indian types.
Hints: Some damaged "New Yorke in America" pieces have been theorized to have been cancelled upon redemption.

	VG	F
[1663/8-73] Farthing, Brass		
	3,800.00	7,000.00
same, pewter/lead		
	4,000.00	8,000.00
1786 Cent, Non Vi Virtute Vici (George Washington) / Neo-Eboracensis (seated figure)	3,250.00	5,250.00
1787 Brasher Gold Doubloon		*Extremely Rare*

1787 Cent, Excelsior (New York arms) / E Pluribus Unum (eagle with shield)		
	1,250.00	2,500.00
1787 Cent, George Clinton (bust) / Excelsior (New York arms)		
	6,000.00	10,000.00
1787 Cent, (standing Indian) / as previous	4,000.00	6,000.00

1787 Cent, as previous / (eagle on globe)		
	6,500.00	11,000.00
1787 Cent, as previous / Bust of George III		*only 3 known*

1787 Cent, Nova Eborac (bust) / Virt Et Lib (Liberty seated right)		
	150.00	300.00
same, Liberty left	150.00	300.00

	VG	F
Talbot Allum, & Lee		
1794 Cent, Liberty standing / Ship, New York above	60.00	190.00
same, New York omitted		
	400.00	975.00
1795 Cent, same	60.00	190.00

VERMONT

History: Vermont existed unwillingly as an independent republic until 1791, and some of its earlier coppers actually refer to this. The Republic's first contract for coins called for a coin reading *Vermontis Res Publica, Quarta Decima Stella*, or "Republic of Vermont, the Fourteenth Star." The symbolic designs showed a mountain scene with a plow and sun on one side, a star with an eye at its center on the other. After about a year elapsed practicality forced the change of design to make Vermont's cents more compatible with those of Connecticut and New York. The second series looks similar to the Connecticut cents, except for the legend *Vermon Auctori*. The first series was struck at Rupert, Vermont, the second mostly under contract near Newburgh, New York. Certain unauthorized die combinations were struck at the New York mint, most of which are omitted below.

References: See general works.

Counterfeit Alert: Not extensively counterfeited.

Hints: These coins are always poorly struck on crude blanks, especially the second series. Pitted or porous ground finds a worth substantially less than the prices quoted.

	G	F
PLOW SERIES		
1785 Cent VERMONTS		
	150.00	675.00
same VERMONTIS	200.00	650.00
1786 Cent	125.00	525.00

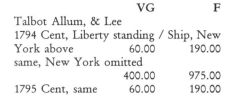

BUST & LIBERTY SERIES

1786 Cent, Bust left	100.00	550.00
1786 Cent, Bust right		
	225.00	750.00
same, BRITANNIA rev.		
	75.00	200.00
1787 Cent, Bust left	950.00	3,500.00
1787 Cent, Bust right	80.00	325.00
1788 Cent	75.00	250.00
1788 Cent, George III obv., normal rev.		
	200.00	850.00

VIRGINIA

History: The very first token to have been struck in Virginia was either a shilling or a pattern for one dated 1714. The inscriptions on the two known specimens combine to read "Gloucester Courthouse Virginia / Righault Dawson Anno Dom 1714." Righault and Dawson were the names of two important families in Gloucester County. The obverse shows said courthouse, the reverse a star. Both specimens are brass.

The only colonial copper that was an official, government issue coin, as opposed to a private or royally authorized token, was the Virginia copper halfpenny. These well made coins were struck in 1773, but by the time they were released in the spring of 1775 it was the eve of the American Revolution and most of them were hoarded. As a result of these hoard coins, some of which were not discovered until the 1800's, these are relatively common in higher grades. The obverse bears a standard portrait of King George III, the reverse his shield of arms with the words "Virginia 1773."

References: See general works.

Counterfeit Alert: Less extensively counterfeited than other series.

Hints: Fairly common in higher grade. Even pieces with mint luster can with effort be obtained.

	F	VF
1714 Shilling		*only 2 known*

	F	VF
1773 ½ Penny	75.00	150.00

WASHINGTON PIECES

History: Private tokens with the portrait of George Washington date to the late 1700s, long before the government started experimenting with patterns for Washington on coins. Most of these tokens circulated as halfpennies, and later as cents. While the majority of these pieces are not from the colonial and pre-federal periods, they are listed here because many bear fictious dates in this period. All have a bust on the obverse. Those with eagle reverse were originally made for circulation in England and were shipped here afterwards.

References: Baker, William, *Medallic Portraits of Washington*.

Counterfeit Alert: There are a great many replicas, some dangerous, and many of nineteenth century origin.

Hints: Early pieces are crude, later ones on a much neater appearance. For pieces of the 1790s numerous varieties and mulings exist. Pieces after the 1820s, generally used as medals, rather than tokens, are not listed here.

	VG	EF
1783 Georgius Triumpho / Voce Popoli, Liberty	75.00	*Rare*
1784 Ugly Head / Chain Cent rev.		*Rare*
1791 Rev. Eagle	100.00	650.00
1792 Same	3,000.00	*Rare*
1792 or ND, Rev. General of the American Armies, etc.	950.00	6,500.00
1793 Rev. Ship	75.00	550.00
1795 Rev. Payable at Clark & Harris..., Grate	40.00	250.00
1795 ½ Penny, Rev. Liberty and Security, Eagle over Shield	50.00	400.00
1795 Penny, same		*Rare*
Same but no date	85.00	600.00

1783 Washington & Independence / United States, Liberty [1820s]
	30.00	300.00
1783 Same / Unity States of America, Wreath [1820s]	70.00	350.00
Washington / One Cent, Bust of Washington [1820s]	35.00	375.00

CALIFORNIA AND OTHER PRIVATE GOLD COINAGES

History: At various times and due to various circumstances the government has been unable to meet the demand for coinage. In areas where the coinage supply was short but the bullion supply was not, private assayers sometimes stepped into the void. They struck coin-like bullion pieces with values (often in dollars) stamped on them. The appearance of private gold tokens such as this usually coincided with a gold rush, or at least the active mining of gold in the immediate vicinity. This is why the most extensive series of such pieces is from California. Some of these pieces are difficult to characterize as either tokens or ingots because they could just as well be rectangular as round. Occasionally they were even polygonal. The designs were very often simple inscriptions without images, but later on they also included Liberty and Indian heads. Some of these pieces may be termed semi-official ingots, such as the issues of Augustus Humbert and F.D. Kohler. They were all made illegal in 1864, but continued to be struck for almost twenty years. A number of unique or of metal test pieces exist, which are outside the scope of this book.

References: Breen, Walter, *Pioneer and Fractional Gold*; Kagin, Donald, *Private Gold Coins and Patterns of the United States*.

Counterfeit Alert: The overwhelming majority of California fractional gold is counterfeit. Fractional gold without the denomination *named* are twentieth century souvenirs, usually of base metal with a gold plate but occasionally of real gold. They will often say "Eureka" or depict a bear on the reverse.

Counterfeits exist of the Baldwin $20. Also many crudely cast base metal replicas exist of larger gold tokens. They bear pronounced edge seams.

Hints: The makers of many California gold $5 and larger coins are indicated on Liberty's coronet. They are frequently abbreviated. Both real and counterfeit fractional gold are generally found only in high grade.

□ = Rectangular shape, ND = No date.

CALIFORNIA — 25¢ through $1

	VF	EF
25¢/$¼ Round	95.00	135.00
25¢/$¼ Octagonal	90.00	120.00
50¢/$½ Round	90.00	140.00
50¢/$½ Octagonal	90.00	140.00
$1 Round	675.00	1,150.00
$1 Octagonal	135.00	225.00

CALIFORNIA — $5 through $50

Augustus Humbert
1852 $10	1,500.00	2,200.00
1852 $20	3,250.00	6,500.00
1851 $50 Lettered edge	9,000.00	12,500.00

same reeded edge	5,000.00	9,500.00

Baldwin & Co.
1850 $5	5,500.00	8,500.00

1850 $10	23,000.00	42,000.00
1851 $10	7,500.00	15,000.00
1851 $20		*Rare*

Cincinnati Mining & Trading Co.
1849 $5		*Unique*
1849 $10		*Rare*

Dubosq & Co.
1850 $5	30,000.00	*Rare*
1850 $10	35,000.00	*Rare*

Dunbar & Co.
1851 $5	45,000.00	70,000.00

Kellogg & Co.
1854 $20	2,000.00	3,000.00
1855 $20	1,800.00	3,000.00
1855 $50		*Rare*

F.D. Kohler, State Assayer

	VF	EF
1850 $50 ☐		200,000.00

Massachusetts & California Co.

1849 $5		Rare

Miners Bank

ND $10	6,000.00	12,000.00

Moffat & Co.

ND $16 ☐		Rare
1849 $5	950.00	2,500.00
1850 $5	950.00	2,500.00

1849 $10	2,200.00	5,000.00
1850 $10	1,500.00	5,500.00
1852 $10	3,000.00	5,000.00
1853 $20	2,500.00	4,000.00

Norris, Gregg & Norris

1849 Half Eagle	4,000.00	6,500.00

J.S. Ormsby

ND $5		Rare
ND $10		Rare

Pacific Company

1849 $5	50,000.00	75,000.00
1849 $10	55,000.00	90,000.00

Schultz ("Schults") & Co.

1851 $5	25,000.00	35,000.00

United States Assay Office of Gold

1852 $10	1,300.00	2,400.00
1853 $10	3,500.00	5,500.00
1853 $20	1,500.00	2,500.00
1852 $50	6,000.00	10,000.00

Wass, Molitor & Co.

1852 $5	3,500.00	6,500.00
1852 $10	2,500.00	4,000.00
1855 $10	14,000.00	21,000.00
1855 $20	10,000.00	18,000.00
1855 $50	12,000.00	20,000.00

COLORADO

Clark, Gruber, & Co

1860 $2½	950.00	1,900.00
1861 $2½	1,200.00	2,400.00
1860 $5	1,350.00	2,250.00
1861 $5	1,350.00	2,800.00
1860 $10	4,000.00	8,000.00
1861 $10	1,500.00	3,000.00

	VF	EF
1860 $20	27,500.00	50,000.00
1861 $20	7,500.00	15,000.00

J.J. Conway & Co.

ND $2½	45,000.00	Rare
ND $5	47,500.00	Rare
ND $10		Rare

John Parsons & Co.

ND $2½	40,000.00	Rare
ND $5	50,000.00	Rare

GEORGIA

Templeton Reid

1830 $2.50	22,000.00	Rare
1830 $5	75,000.00	Rare
1830 $10		Rare
Not dated $10		Rare

NORTH CAROLINA

Christopher Bechtler

$1 Carolina	850.00	1,500.00
$1 N. Carolina	950.00	2,000.00
$2.50 Carolina	1,800.00	4,000.00

$2.50 North Carolina		
	5,000.00	7,000.00
$2.50 Georgia	2,500.00	4,400.00
$5 Carolina	3,000.00	5,000.00
$5 North Carolina	4,000.00	6,500.00

$5 Georgia	3,250.00	5,000.00

August Bechtler

$1 Carolina	700.00	1,000.00
$5 Carolina	2,650.00	4,000.00

OREGON

Oregon Exchange Co.

1849 $5	10,000.00	16,000.00

1849 $10	25,000.00	40,000.00

UTAH

Mormon State of Deseret

1849 $2½	5,000.00	7,500.00

1849 $5	4,000.00	5,500.00
1850 $5	4,500.00	6,500.00
1860 $5	7,750.00	15,000.00
1849 $10		Rare
1849 $20		Rare

HARD TIMES TOKENS

History: During the depressed economic times of the 1830's through 1840's money became scarce. Some merchants thought to remedy the situation by contracting for their own unofficial "large cents" bearing advertisements. Others sought to use this medium to publicize their criticism of the Jackson and Van Buren administrations. When the economy improved both reasons for these tokens faded and they disappeared from circulation.

Reference: Rulau, Russel, *Hard Times Tokens.*

Counterfeit Alert: Not widely counterfeited.

Hints: The Mott token of New York is often mistaken for an earlier period. Low grade, G-VG, tokens are actually scarcer than middle grade, F-VF examples.

VF

NATIONAL ISSUES

Andrew Jackson (head) / The Bank Must
  Perish (wreath) 4,000.00
Andrew Jackson President (bust) /
  Inscription 100.00

Perish Credit Perish Commerce (boar) /
  My Substitute For The U.S. Bank
  (small bust) 12.00
Webster Credit Currency 1841 (ship) /
  Van Buren Metallic Currency 1837
  (ship on rocks) 12.00

VF

William H. Seward Our Next Govnr (bust) / A Faithful Friend to Our Country (eagle) 150.00

Execuitive Experiment (turtle) / Illustrious Predecessor (donkey) 12.00

E Pluribus Unum 1837 (Liberty head) / Millions for Defense Not One Cent for Tribute (wreath) 12.00

Substitute For Shinplasters (phoenix) / as above 12.00

I Take The Responsibility (Jackson in a box) / The Constitution as I Understand It (mule) 12.00

Am I Not a Woman and a Sister 1838 (kneeling female slave) / United States of America 1838 (wreath) 60.00

LOCAL ADVERTISING

Connecticut: JML & WH Scovill Waterbury Con 1837 (phoenix) / Inscription 25.00

Louisiana: (eagle on key) / John A. Merle & Co. ... New Orleans 800.00

Massachusetts: Alfred Willard 149 Washington St. Boston (comb) / Importer of Jewelry, Brushes, Perfumery, ... Fancy Goods, Cutlery, &c. 12.00

New York: 1837 (eagle on snake)/ Feuchtwanger's Composition (wreath) One Cent 65.00

___ : William & John Mott [ca.1839], 1789 over Eagle / Clock 350.00

___ : Merchants Exchange Wall St. (building) / Millions For Defense (wreath) 15.00

South Carolina: Soda Water 1837 (soda urn) / R.L. Baker Charleston S.C. Good For 1 Glass . . . . *Rare*

CIVIL WAR TOKENS

History: During the Civil War citizens of both the Union and the Confederacy lived in fear that any paper currency in circulation would soon become worthless. As a result people hoarded all "hard" money. This included not only gold and silver coins, but also copper. Faced with the shortage of coinage in circulation that resulted, many merchants took it on themselves to produce their own one cent pieces, of similar size and color to our modern cents. Often they bore the name and address of the merchant on one side and a patriotic design on the other. Other examples carried patriotic designs or messages on both sides. The latter were general issues which could be sold by manufacturers to merchants for well below their face value. They are often called "patriotics" while the types with a merchant's name clearly stated are called "store cards." Occasionally Civil War Tokens were struck in other metals such as silver. These were never intended to circulate and are all scarce today. All listings below are copper or bronze cents unless noted.

References: Fuld, George and Melvin, *Patriotic Civil War Tokens*; Fuld, George and Melvin, *U. S. Civil War Store Cards*; Schenkman, David, *Civil War Suttler Tokens and Cardboard Scrip.*

Counterfeit Alert: Counterfeits in a traditional sense are not common, but some dies still survive and recent unknown restrikes may exist. Pieces with inappropriate luster should be examined by an expert, as should all pieces struck in off-metals.

Hints: Many people use Civil War tokens as a way of collecting their own local history. Hundreds of businesses and cities are represented from Maine to Alabama. As a rule, those struck by freelance military provisioners, called "sutlers' tokens," command a premium, as do tokens from states West of Ohio. The tokens listed below are the most common variety of the types described. Rarer die combinations can bring an appreciable premium to a specialized collector.

VF

Alabama: Huntsville, White & Swan 750.00

Connecticut: Bridgeport, A.W. Wallace's Variety Bakery 7.00

Illinois: Belvidere, George B. Ames, Dealer in Drugs, Books, &c. (mortar and pestle) 8.00

___ : Chicago, J.J. Brown's Grocery, 171 West Harrison St. 12.00

___ : El Paso, P.H.Thompkins, Dealer in Dry Goods, Groceries, &C. / Union 1863, Liberty Head 65.00

___ : Lena, W.J. Bollinger, Dealer in Hardware, Iron & Steel (lock) both sides same 12.00

Indiana: Bowling Green, O.H.P. Ash's Cheap Cash Store 10.00

___ : Indianapolis, One Glass Soda Water at J.F. Senour's Drug Store / Drugs and Medicines 1863, Mortar & Pestle 20.00

Iowa: Cedar Rapids, Reynolds & Co. New York Store 135.00

___ : Lansing, Wm. Flemming & Bro., Lumber, Lath & Shingles . . . 135.00

Kansas: Leavenworth, A. Cohen, Clothing and Gents Furnishing Goods, 21 Delaware St. 1250.00

Kentucky: Lexington, John W. Lee, Baker and Confectioner, 10 Main St. / One Half Pint of Milk 50.00

___ : Newport, N'PT & COV Bridge Company 50.00

Maine: Bangor, R.S. Torrey, Inventor of the Maine State Bee Hive, 1864 35.00

Maryland: Baltimore, Shakespeare Club 5 . . . . 225.00

___ : Hagerstown, G.R. Bowman Confectioner 1862 / To Observatory and Telescopes (telescope) . . . 1500.00

Massachusetts: Boston, Merriam & Co., 19 Brattle Sqr. (embossing press in shape of a salamander) 55.00

___ : Nantucket, God Loveth a Cheerful Giver, Great Fair in Aid of the U.S. Sanitary Commission ... August, 1864 . . . . 24.00

VF

Michigan: Detroit, Geo. Beard & Son, Oyster Fruit Fish & Game Depot. 16.00
__:_, Campbell, Linn & Co. Business Card (thistle) / Scotch Store Dry Goods and Millinery 7.00

__: Ionia, James Kennedy 1863 / Exchange Insurance Collection & U.S. War Claim Office 12.00
Minnesota: St. Paul, D.C. Greenleaf, Watch Maker 175.00
__: Winona, C. Benson, Druggist 175.00
Missouri: St. Louis, Henry Jenkins 15.00
New Hampshire: Concord, A.W. Gale, Restorator at Depot / Good for One Cent in Goods 25.00
New Jersey: Atlantic City, Neptune House 1863 / Smick's 12.00

__:_, Newark, Charles Kolb 102 Market St. Restaurant 8.00
New York: J.J.Benson, Good for 25 Cents, Suttler 1st Mtd. Riffles . 75.00
__: Albany, Straight's Elephantine Shoe Store 398 Broadway 1863 (elephant wearing boots) / Redeemed at My Shoe Store 398 Broadway 8.00
__: Brooklyn, Daniel Williams, Grocer Corner Court & Warren Sts / I-O-U 1 Cent 7.00
Note: Brooklyn was not part of New York City at this time.
__: New York, H.J. Bang, Restaurant, 231 Broadway / Importer of Rhine Wines (bunch of grapes) 7.00
__:_, Felix בשר (=Kosher) Dining Saloon 256 Broadway 120.00
__:_ G.A.Defandorf, 233 E.77ᵀᴴ St., Dentist (all incuse) / as obverse .. *Rare*

__:_, Hussey's Special Message Post 50 Wm. St. (small locomotive) ... 10.00
__: Troy, Oliver Boutwell, Miller / Redeemed at My Office 1863 (scroll ornaments) 7.00

Ohio: Camden, C. Chadwick, Dealer in Dry Goods (tiny eagle) 16.00
__: Cincinnati, 500000 Persons Annually Cured by Dr. Bennett's Medicines 7.00
__:_, Carl Haas 493 Vine St. / Carl Haas (rabbit) 493 Vine St. 10.00
__:_, A.B. Wilson Staple & Fancy Grocer 224 W. 6th St. 7.00

Ohio: Marion, A.E. Griffin, Dentist (dentures) 65.00
__: Troy, Rinehart & Gray Cash Druggists * Successors to R. Wright 30.00
Pennsylvania: Lancaster, S.H. Zahm, Dealer in Coins, Tokens, Medals &c 50.00
__: Philadelphia, M.F. Beirn, Magnolia Hotel, 100 So. 8th St. and 416 Library St. 7.00
__: Pittsburgh, Allegheny Valley Railroad Hotel, Opposite Depot 65.00
Rhode Island: Providence, Arcade House 62 Broad St. 8.00
__:_, City Fruit Store, No. 4 Weybosset St. ... Redeemed by Phillips ... 8.00
Tennessee: Memphis, Elliott, Vinson & Co. 150.00

__: Nashville, McKay & Lapsley ** x ** 200.00
Virginia: Norfolk, Pfeiffer & Co., VA in wreath / Good for a Scent 1863, Dog's head 850.00

West Virginia: Wheeling, John Eckhart Manuf'r of Hoisery & C., 187 Main St. 28.00
Wisconsin: Green Bay, F.R. Schettler, Dealer in Hardware 9.00

__: Madison, Madison Brewery Manfr. of Lager Beer * Stock & Cream Ale / J. Rodermund (horse pulling wagon) 50.00

__: Racine, Erhardt & Raps Auctioneers 12.00
Anonymous Patriotics: The Flag of Our Union 1863 (flag) / If Anybody Attempts to Tear It Down, Shoot Him on the Spot (DIX in center) ... 7.00
__: Similar to previous but legend ends in "Spoot." 15.00

__: Our Little Monitor (ironclad ship Monitor) 10.00
__: Knickerbocker Currency (walking figure) 6.00
__: For President * Abraham Lincoln * / For Vice President * Andrew Johnson 45.00
__: The Federal Union, It Must and Shall be Preserved / Army and Navy (within wreath) 6.00

ENCASED POSTAGE STAMPS

History: During the Civil War people lived in fear that any paper currency in circulation would soon become worthless. As a result they hoarded all "hard" money. This included not only gold and silver coins, but also copper. Faced with the shortage of coinage in circulation that resulted, many merchants took it on themselves to produce their own "coinage." In addition to privately manufactured tokens, merchants of the Civil War era fought the coinage shortage with encased postage stamps. This was a natural evolution from the trading of stamps as small change (the government even issued a sort of postage stamp paper money, *see below*). Regular postage stamps were placed in specially prepared round, brass frames which covered their backs and left their printed sides exposed showing their value. The exposed stamp was covered by a window of transparent mica. This unique frame was invented by J. Gault who patented the idea in 1862. The same frame could be used for any denomination and stamps from 1¢ to 90¢ were used. The back side of the brass frame could be used to advertise the merchant's product or service, often with the address of his establishment.
References: Friedberg, Robert, *Paper Money of the United States*; Hodder, Michael J. and Bowers, Q. David,

Standard Catalogue of Encased Postage Stamps.

Counterfeit Alert: Be alert for recently replaced mica.

Hints: Most examples on the market still have the original mica window intact. Those with cracked or missing mica are sold at a discount. Bent and straightened cases are also worth less.

1¢ Aerated Bread Co., New York	725.00
1¢ Take Ayer's Pills	220.00
1¢ Drake's Plantation Bitters	320.00
2¢ J. Gault	*Extremely Rare*
3¢ Ayer's Sarsaparilla	220.00
3¢ J. Gault	385.00
3¢ Lord & Taylor, New York	825.00
5¢ Take Ayer's Pills	220.00
5¢ Pearce, Tolle & Holton, Cincinnati	1,250.00
10¢ J. Gault	360.00
10¢ Schapker & Bussing, Evansville, Ind.	775.00
12¢ F. Buhl & Co., Detroit	825.00
12¢ Ayer's Cathartic Pills	525.00
24¢ J. Gault	1,250.00
30¢ Lord & Taylor, N.Y.	1,850.00
90¢ Burnett's Cocoaine, Kalliston	2,300.00
90¢ Ayer's Sarsaparilla	2,100.00

CONFEDERATE COINAGE

History: It is generally held that the Confederate government contracted with Robert Lovett Jr. of Philadelphia, who avoided completing the contract due to the outbreak of hostilities. Some have, however, suggested that the whole project was devoid of any connection with the Confederate government. In any case, rare nineteenth century restrikes with the original dies exist in proof. For the Civil War Centennial a large number of high quality, non-proof copies were struck with imitation dies. They even reproduce the damage present on the real dies.

That the Confederate half was struck by the Confederacy at the New Orleans mint is certain. Four coins were struck having a distinctive reverse and an obverse die left over from the former Union operations there. Years later restrikes were made with this Confederate die

stamped onto regular 1861O halves that had had their reverses planed off. This same die was also used by J.W. Scott to strike a rare token.

References: General references and Reed, Fred L., III, series of articles, *Coin World*, Oct. 4, Oct. 11, Oct. 18, 1989.

Counterfeit Alert: The late replicas mentioned above abound.

Hints: The restrike half can be distinguished by the flattening of the obverse which resulted from striking a die on an already struck coin.

The Confederacy struck certain coins solely with Union dies. These are genuine Confederate coins a lot less expensive than the Confederate type originals (see listings above).

	Unc.	PF
1861 1¢ Copper-nickel	*only 12 struck*	
1861 1¢ Copper restrike		4,000.00
1861 1¢ Silver restrike		*only 12 struck*
1861 1¢ Gold restrike		*only 7 struck*
1861 1¢ Copper-nickel restrike	10.00	
1861 1¢ Copper-nickel fantasy reverse	4.00	

1861 Half Dollar	*only 4 struck*
same restrike	4,000.00
1861 Scott Token	900.00

1862 The Confederate States of America : 22 February 1862 ★ Deo Vindice ★, Horseman in Wreath / Confederate Arms as original 10.00

Note: Last is a fantasy probably struck for the centennial of the Civil War.

MERCHANTS' TOKENS AND "GOOD FORS"

History: With the end of the Civil War the use and acceptability of private tokens in general commerce decreased markedly. The government contributed to this

process by passing two 1864 laws prohibiting private coinage. Over the past century however, thousands of merchants have struck a variety of tokens which they promised to redeem in goods or services. Other merchant tokens are beautifully engraved advertizing pieces with no commercial function. Still others are receipts of a sort, such as locker checks and welfare tokens. The most common until recently are the small brass or aluminum tokens bearing only simple inscriptions, usually including the words "Good For ... ¢" and the merchant's name. In recent years the most frequently encountered have been arcade tokens, used to operate video games. All these various types are interesting and reflect the details of local history like no national issue can.

References: Alpert, Stephen and Smith, Kenneth E., *Video Arcade, Pinball, Slot Machine, and other Amusement Tokens of North America;* Rulau, Russel, *U.S. Merchant Tokens 1845-60;* Rulau, Russel, *United States Trade Tokens 1866-1889;* Rulau, Russel, *Tokens of the Gay Nineties 1890-1900.*

Periodicals: This is one of the few fields where no general work exists. As a result the best general reference is the ongoing publication of the Token and Medal Society, the *TAMS Journal.*

Counterfeit Alert: Virtually none known and those few that exist are often worth as much as a typical authentic token. The exception to this rule is the large brass bordello tokens, 99% of which are modern replicas.

Hints: Many people use these tokens as a way of collecting their own local history. Hundreds of businesses and cities are represented from Massachusetts to Alaska. Merchant tokens traceable to the Old West, particularly Arizona and New Mexico, command a substantial premium as the earliest numismatic collectables from the Southwestern states. Some tokens may be difficult to sell outside their state of issue, and may trade at a fraction of their values due to lack of interest.

VF

Alabama: Nichols Bros., Nicholsville Alabama / Good for 10 in Trade 4.00

Alaska: ARRC [Alaska Rural Rehabilitation Corp.] 1¢ 12.00
__: same, $10 .... 75.00
__: The Occidental Hotel, Olds & Orton Props, Juneau .../ Good For 12½¢ in Trade, Aluminum [1900-01] ... 8.00

Arizona: Summerfield & Peck, Black Diamond .../ Good For 1 Drink, Brass [1890-1900?] 80.00

VF

Arkansas: See Glade Before You Trade, Glade's Eureka Springs ... / Every Dollar Spent Earns 3% Interest, Worth 3¢ in Trade [c.1920-50] 1.50

California: Berehart Jacoby & Co. St. Francisco (eagle) / General Merchants & Importers (ship), Brass [ca. 1851]
. . . . 150.00

__: Santa Catalina Island, The Casino 1929 (building) / similar inscr. (1 superimposed over ONE), Dollar size, Nickel-silver 2.00

Colorado: Good for 2½¢ in Trade, Meeker Drug Co. / Owl, Square Aluminum [1890-1900] 40.00

Connecticut: The Celluloid Starch Co. New Haven (collar) / A Great Invention Free, Present this Check to Your Grocer & Get One Package Celluloid Starch Free or 3 for 20 Cents, Brass [1890-1900] 3.00

__: This Nickel Worth A Dime, P.T.'s, On Next Purchase (circus tent) / Home of the Steamed Cheese Burger, P.T. Barnum's, 170 Ferry Blvd. Stratford, ..., Wood [1983] 50

__: Arnies Place Arnies Place (AP exaggerated) / rev. same, Brass [Westport, recent] 25

Florida: Onivos N. Xenocles Dealer in Tobaccos / Key West, 1900, Florida, Brass 5.00

Georgia: Richland, Adams Bros., Ga. / Good For One 5¢ Cigar or Soda 4.00

Idaho: Clark & Anderson, Malad, Idaho / Good For 12½¢ at the Bar. Aluminum [1890-00] 10.00

Illinois: Constable & Cleary, 50 Rush St. & 536 Division St. [Chicago] / 2½¢, Copper [1890-1900] 6.00

__: The Elgin National Watch Company of Elgin Ills ★Incorporated 1865★, Winged Father Time / Elgin National etc., This Certifies that Lever Movement N° 747429 Named Elgin Nat^L Watch C° Was manu-factured by Us of the Best Materials and is Warrented a 2000 Time Keeper, White Metal [1880-1900] 10.00

Indiana: Waters Rec. 922 S. Main South Bend, Ind. / Good for 25¢ in Trade [1910-40] 1.00

Indian Territory: see Oklahoma.

Iowa: The Brunswick, Blake, Collender Co. (pool table) / Good For 5¢ J.C. Steepy [Glenwood] in Trade, Brass [1890-1900] 30.00

Louisiana: G.W. Bennett, Good For 25¢ In Goods, Bennettville, LA. 1871 / same, Nickel Silver 65.00

Massachusetts: Crosby's Restaurant, 19 School St. Boston (coat of arms)/ Expansion Souvenir Room "D" Our Latest Addition July 1900, Brass 5.00

Michigan: Good For 5¢ F.B. Crippen in Trade / 5, Brass [Hudson, 1891-92]
. . . . 25.00

VF

Missouri: St. Louis Post Office (eagle over shield) / rev. blank for engraving, Copper [1850's] 150.00

Nevada: Lafayette Hotel Joseph German Prop. Winnemucca ... / We Favor Free Silver Coinage, Aluminum [1896]
. . . . 75.00

New York: Roller Skating Association 1876 (foot in skate) / Brooklyn Rink Skate Check, Brass 15.00

__: Cafe Lindinger, 56 & 58 Liberty St. New York / Fritz Lindinger 2½ 56 & 58 Liberty St., Copper-Nickel [1900]
. . . . 10.00

Oklahoma: Indian Territory Grady Trading Co., Will Pay to the Bearer Five Cents in Merchandise at Any of Its Stores, J.C.Biddle Treas. / Indian Territory Grady Trading Co., 5 Cents, Aluminum [1880-1907] 25.00

Pennsylvania: [Philadelphia] Franklin Institute, Head of Franklin / Building, brass, cent size 25

__: [Philadelphia] J.W., Crowned Arms, 178451, German Silver [1890s] . 12.00
Note: The above is actually an early credit card issued by John Wanamaker Stores.

Texas: Good For A Cow Boy Saloon Drink / Longhorn Steer, Copper-Nickel [Spanish Fort, 1880's] 30.00

Utah: H. & A., Ogden, Utah / Good for 25¢ in Trade [1900-40] 4.00

Virginia: L. Brill 5¢, Brass [Alexandria, 1880-1900] 10.00

Non-Local: Good For 5¢ in Trade / 2 3 7 3 9 (ornament at bottom), ¾ brass with central hole [1920-50] 25

Food Stamp Credit Token Redeemable Only in Eligible Foods 1¢ / at Grand Union Food Stamp Credit Token 1¢, Aluminum [1970's] 25

TRANSPORTATION TOKENS

History: For centuries merchants have been issuing tokens redeemable in goods or services. Transportation tokens are one specialized form of trade token. In this industry such tokens increase the speed with which passengers can be processed by avoiding the need to make change for small and inconvenient amounts or by permitting a passenger to purchase a number of fares simultaneously. In recent years another advantage in their use is that they are less prone to encourage robbery than real coins. In the United States they have been common in commerce since the late nineteenth century, abundant since the 1920's. Most have the name of the issuing authority, private or public, around a simple letter or logo. The majority also have a simple cut out design.

All tokens listed below are approximately dime size and of white metal (nickel alloy) unless noted.

References: Coffee, John, ed., *Atwood's Catalogue of United States and Canadian Transportation Tokens*, 3rd ed. and 1977 Supplement.

Counterfeit Alert: Virtually none known and those few that exist are often worth as much as a typical authentic token.

Hints: Many people use these tokens as a way of collecting their own local history. Hundreds of cities are obtainable from

Massachusetts to Alaska, generally for a minimal price.

VF-EF

Alaska: U.S. Naval Air Base Kodiak AAA / Carpenters Local 2162, quarter size, Brass [WW II] 10.00

California: San Diego Elec. Ry. Co., cut out around S 25

Connecticut: Connecticut Arms / Connecticut Turnpike Good for 1 Fare, Map [1980s] 25
__: Trumbull Coach Lines, cut out around T, quarter sized brass . . 2.00
__: C R & L Lines around C R L CO, cut out around ball 25

Florida: Miami Transit Company around monogram, cut out around ball, quarter sized 35

Georgia: Griffin Motor Coaches, cut outs above and below bus 50

Hawaii: Honolulu Rapid Transit Co. 1924 Ltd., cut out around H 50

Illinois: The Chicago & South Side Rapid Transit R.R. Co. Good for One Continuous Ride around large 31 / Deposit this in Gateman's Box around large 31, 1¼" Aluminum [before 1924] 5.00

Iowa: Des Moines City Railway Co. one fare, shaded diamond, solid Aluminum [1893-1909] 5.00

Kentucky: Bridge Transit Company [Louisville], Zinc 50

Massachusetts: Maverick Coach 1837 / East Boston 1837 (German Silver) 150.00

___: New Bedford & Onset St. Railway Co. One Fare around trolley car, cent size [before 1927] 1.00

Michigan: Detroit & Canada Tunnel Co., solid, Brass 35

Missouri: United Railways Co. of St. Louis 1919, cut out around U 50

New Jersey: Public Service Coordinated Transport [Newark], trolley / bus, cut outs above and below, brass 35

New York: New York City Transit Authority, around NYC, Y cut out, Brass 25

___: Diamond Jubilee Seventy Fifth Anniversary NYC Subway 1904-1979, subway car below cut out diamond 1.00

Ohio: Municipal Traction Co. [Cleveland] / 3 Cent Ticket 1908, nickel size, Aluminum, central hole 2.50

Pennsylvania: Lehigh Valley Transit Co. [Allentown], cut out bell, Zinc . . .50
___: 43rd St. Bridge [Pittsburgh] around 2, nickel size, Brass [1870-1912] . 5.00
___: Pittsburgh Railways Co. 1922, Streetcar / Good For One Fare, Brass, Triangular Cut out 25

Texas: Amarillo Bus Co., cut out around A 25

Utah: U L A T C O Salt Lake City, bee hive, cut outs around 50

Virginia: Virginia Electric & Pwr. Co., N, cut outs around 35

Washington: Seattle Municipal Railway, triangle cut out [ca. 1920], copper .50

CAMPAIGN TOKENS

History: Since the presidential election of 1824, in which Andrew Jackson successfully sought the presidency, medals have been struck with the purpose of advertizing the respective candidates or their policies. Most bear a portrait of the presidential candidate or their running mate on the obverse, an inscription or a patriotic symbol on the reverse. Before 1824 some political medals were struck, but these were not campaign tokens as they were prepared *after* the election as commemoratives of the victory. From the election of 1840 onwards campaign tokens became more common. The typical example was initially quarter size

or slightly larger. By the second quarter of this century they had grown slightly. In recent years they have been overwhelmingly eclipsed by buttons, and as a result have grown in diameter to dollar size, serving the purpose of table medals rather than pocket pieces. Campaign medals have generally been brass throughout their history.

References: Sullivan, Edmund B., *American Political Badges and Medalets 1789-1892.*

Counterfeit Alert: Counterfeits are more prevalent of campaign badges than of medals. The former are outside the scope of this book.

Hints: This series affords an excellent study of the issues that dominated American politics through its history. Many are found holed for wearing.

VF

1824 Andrew Jackson
Bust facing / Wreath 30.00
1828 Andrew Jackson
Bust facing "1829" / Eagle in stars, Large, White metal 400.00
1832 Andrew Jackson
Bust right / The Bank Must Perish, Wreath, Copper 4,000.00
1836 Martin van Buren
Bust right / Temple, Large, White metal 300.00
1840 William Henry Harrison
Bust left / Log Cabin 8.00
1850 Millard Fillmore
Bust right / Eagle 10.00
1856 James Buchanan
Bust right / Eagle 10.00
1864 Abraham Lincoln
Head of Lincoln / Head of Andrew Johnson, Cent size, copper . . . 45.00
1864 George McClellan
Head of McClellan / Army & Navy, Cent size, copper 10.00
1868 U.S. Grant
Bust facing / Inscription 12.00
1868 Horatio Seymour
Jugate busts of Seymour and Blair / General Amnesty, Uniform Currency, Equal Taxes, & Equal Rights, Brass 18.00
1880 James Garfield
Conjoined Busts of Garfield and Arthur / Shield 8.00

VF

1884 Grover Cleveland
Conjoined Busts of Cleveland and
Hendricks / Fasces 8.00
1900 William McKinley
Bust left / Eagle 8.00
1928 or 1932 Herbert Hoover
Elephant / Good for 4 Years of
Prosperity 4.00
1932 Franklin D. Roosevelt
Conjoined busts of Roosevelt and Garner,
Swastika and Anchor / Elect the
Democratic Party, Happy Days are
Here Again 3.00

1960 John F. Kennedy **BU**
Facing Busts of Johnson and Kennedy /
Donkey Head, Large, White metal
.... 4.00
1960 Richard M. Nixon
Facing Busts of Nixon and Lodge /
Elephant head, Large, White Metal
.... 3.00

1972 Richard M. Nixon
Head right / Stylized Elephant, Large,
Bronze 3.00

ART MEDALS

History: Art medals are coin-like items
made without any purpose of trade or
exchange in mind. They are made as
mementos or as an expression of art for
art's sake. As they do not have to be
struck in large numbers or wear well in
circulation, they often will have much
higher relief than coins or tokens. They
will very often be larger than most coins,
often silver dollar size or greater.

Occasionally they will be smaller than a
half dime, struck with the intent to be
novel.

Art medals had their origin in
Renaissance portrait medals. Their use in
the United States became important with
Peace Medals, insignias of good will to
American Indian leaders. The
Continental Congress struck medals,
many of which were restruck by the U.S.
government for the bicentennial. Medals
commemorating presidential inaugura-
tions are on sale at the mint for decades
after the event. This does not even begin
to address the private organizations, from
Ford to the local agriculture club, that
have commissioned medals to honor
anniversaries and individuals.

References: Hibler, Harold and Kappen,
Charles, *So-Called Dollars*; Baker, W.S.,
Medallic Portraits of Washington, among
thousands of others works.

Counterfeit Alert: Few counterfeits.

Hints: On listings below legends are
given first then the designs follow in
parentheses. Note that many dealers have
little interest in the more common art
medals and may offer a small fraction of
the below prices when purchasing such
items for inventory.

Also note that most medals struck by
the Franklin Mint, while of superb
quality, are usually purchased by dealers
solely for their silver value. It is a rare
exception to pay more, regardless of their
retail value due to the minimal demand
for this product on the secondary market.

EF-AU

1863, Lieut. General T.J. Jackson,
Stonewall (head) / Bull Run,
Kernstown, Front Royal ... (wreath), 2",
White Metal 120.00
*Note: The above is the only art medal
authorized by the Confederacy. Struck in
Paris, most examples could not enter the
country due to the Union blockade.*

1876, In Commemoration of the
Hundredth Anniversary of American
Independence (Liberty standing with
Industry and Art kneeling) / These
United Colonies Are, and of Right
Ought to be, Free and Independent
States (kneeling America), 2¼", Bronze
.... 75.00

[1876-80s] Preservando, Beaver Gnawing
Tree / Confederation, Eye above altar,
Bronze 40.00
1883, Two Cities As One New York And
Brooklyn (Brooklyn Bridge) / Souvenir
of the Opening of the East River
Bridge..., Dollar size, WM 16.00
1892-93 World's Columbian Exposition,
Chicago, Dollar size Aluminum, many
varieties depicting various buildings at
fair, each 5.00

1893 World's Columbian Exposition,
Landing of Columbus / A Souvenir of
Pure Aluminum Compliments of
S.H.Quint & Son Manufacturers of
Medals for Advertising and Other
Purposes... .... 7.00
ca. 1893, Head of George Washington /
Lord's Prayer, Smaller than half dime,
Brass 2.50
[1907] Lincoln Plaque, 90x60mm Bronze
by Brenner, struck by Medallic Art Co.
[ca. 1930-60] 250.00
1909 Hendrik Hudson 1609 (bust) /
Nieuw Amsterdam I Daalder MCMIX
(ship), dollar size, Silver 65.00
same but Aluminum 12.00
1926 Sesquicentennial-International-
Exposition Philadelphia (Head of
Washington) / Liberty Riding Pegasus,
dollar size, Brass 15.00

EF-AU

1933 Ford (grill of car) / Thirty Years of Progress (V superimposed on 8), Dollar size, brass 5.00

1938 Tercentenary of Delaware (ship) / (state seal), Dollar size, bronze . 10.00

1939 New York World's Fair (Trylon & perisphere) / Official token, etc., Oval, Silver 35.00

1950 (Minerva head wearing leopard skin) / 1900 1950 Medallic Art Company 50th Anniversary (hand holding obverse of this medal), 2¾", Gilt Bronze 25.00

1959 Olivia (map of Minnesota) / We're Friendly We're Growing, It's Sure Great to Live in Olivia, Dollar size, Gilt bronze 2.00

1968 Martin Luther King Jr (bust facing) / I Have a Dream (eagle behind two workers), 1½", Bronze 10.00

1973 Monroe Connecticut 1823-1973, Two Town Halls / Sesquicentennial, Founding scenes around head of James Monroe, Silver 9.00

1970's In the period ca. 1972-76 many government and municipal bicentennial medals in bronze appeared. The most common types are dollar sized and come sealed in envelopes with transparent windows, or in small black plastic easels. The average retail of these is, in . . . . BU $1-$3.00

1980's Franklin Mint, Twelve Days of Christmas, Copper-Nickel alloy, 12 different, each . . . . Unc. 1.00

EF-AU

1980's American Numismatic Association (lamp and book) / National Coin Week Founded 1924, In Appreciation of Your Participation (wreath), Dollar size, Bronze 2.50

1984 (seven dolphins) / (calendar between dolphins), 3", bronze 15.00

1986 (statue of Liberty amid 12 calendars) / (immigrant family), 3", bronze 15.00

ca. 1986, No inscription (elaborate Winter scene with horse drawn sleigh) / 2 Troy Ounces 999 Silver (bird in wreath), 2", Silver 10.00

1992 [1993] No inscription (battle scene) / Persian Gulf Veterans National Medal, Dedicated ... etc., (eagle below), 38mm, Bronze 12.50

[1993] General Colin Powell Chairman Joint Chiefs... (facing bust) [public distribution bronze strike of Powell's Congressional Medal of Honor] 3" 20.00

same but 1½" 2.00

1994 Florida United Numismatists, Inc. 1955, F U N superimposed over maps / Orange County Convention Center 1994, F.U.N. 39th Annual Convention, Orlando, Fl. Jan. 6,7,8,9, Brass . 2.00

1995 Peace 2000 One World Unit, Dove over world / Peace Through Coinage, Man's Eternal Reach, Hands releasing Dove, Cupronickel 1.50

HAWAII

History: Hawaii first issued coinage as an independent kingdom under Kamehameha III (1825-54). Only copper large cents were issued. In 1833 the Hawaiian government contracted for a silver coinage to be produced at the San Francisco mint. The dies for this coinage were engraved by U.S. mint engraver Charles Barber. Plantation tokens were also commonly used in the late nineteenth century, but often were only accepted at company stores. The majority were of copper or copper alloy. **References:** Krause & Mishler, *Standard Catalog of World Coins*; Gould, Maurice, *Hawaiian Coins, Tokens and Paper Money*. **Counterfeit Alert:** Brass copies of the 1847 cent made for tourists are far more numerous than the real cent. **Hints:** Very many Hawaiian silver coins are found with solder marks from having been used in jewelry. These sell at a heavy discount. Be alert for cleaned and retoned pieces, particularly on the larger silver.

ROYAL COINAGE	F	EF
1847 Cent	225.00	400.00
1883 Dime	32.50	200.00

1883 Quarter	40.00	90.00
1883 Half Dollar	65.00	235.00
1883 Dollar	200.00	625.00

TOKENS

Grove Ranch Plantation (GRP)		
1886 12½¢	275.00	650.00
1887 12½¢	350.00	800.00
Haiku Plantation		
1882 1 Real	150.00	400.00
Thomas Hobron Railroad (RR / THH)		
1879 12½¢	125.00	325.00
1879 25¢		*Rare*
Kahului Railroad		
1891 10¢	250.00	600.00
1891 15¢	250.00	600.00
1891 20¢	250.00	600.00
1891 35¢	250.00	600.00
Wailuku Plantation (HI / WP)		
ND 6¢	175.00	500.00

1880 Half Real	250.00	700.00
1871 12½¢	200.00	650.00
1880 1 Real	175.00	600.00
John Th. Waterhouse [1862]		
(value unstated)	400.00	1,300.00

U.S. PHILIPPINES

History: The Philippine Islands were acquired by the United States as a result of the Spanish-American War in 1898. Coinage was instituted for the colony in 1903, with the standard being adjusted to set the Philippine Peso at two to the U.S.

Dollar in 1907. The obverses of most coins bear allegorical figures. The reverses all bear the legend "United States of America" around a shield of arms surmounted by an eagle. With the change from Colony to Commonwealth in 1935, the shield was changed from that of the United States to that of the Philippines. This change in status was also honored by special commemoratives in 1936, one of which depicts Franklin Roosevelt.

References: Krause & Mishler, *Standard Catalog of World Coins*; Basso, Aldo, *Coins, Medals and Tokens of the Philippines*.

Counterfeit Alert: Cast counterfeits exist of the 1936 commemorative coins.

Hints: Most of the 1936 commemoratives available now were dumped in Manila Bay before the Japanese capture of Corregidor in 1942, and salvaged later. They show obvious pitting and sell actively but at a heavy discount.

HALF CENTAVO / bronze

		VF
1903		.75
1904		1.00
1905	Proof only	100.00
1906	Proof only	80.00
1908	Proof only	80.00

ONE CENTAVO / bronze

1903		.75
1904		.75
1905		.75
1906	Proof only	50.00
1908	Proof only	50.00
1908S		1.50
1909S		5.00
1910S		1.50
1911S		1.50
1912S		1.50
1913S		1.50
1914S		1.50
1915S		12.50
1916S		7.00
1917S, 7 over 6		5.00

1917S		1.50
1918S		1.50
1918S, Large S		8.00
1919S		1.50
1920		1.50
1920S		7.00
1921		1.00
1922		1.00
1925M		.75
1926M		.75
1927M		.75
1928M		.75
1929M		1.25
1930M		1.25
1931M		1.25
1932M		1.50
1933M		.75
1934M		1.50
1936M		.75

1937M		.75
1938M		.75
1939M		.75
1940M		1.00
1941M		1.00
1944S		.25

FIVE CENTAVOS / cupronickel

1903		.75
1904		1.25
1905	Proof only	125.00
1906	Proof only	85.00
1908	Proof only	85.00
1916S		13.50
1917S		1.50
1918S		1.50
1918S mule with 20c rev.		175.00
1919S		2.50
1920		3.00
1921		3.00
1925M		3.00
1926M		4.00
1927M		2.50
1928M		2.50
1930M		1.50
1931M		1.50
1932M		1.50
1934M		2.50
1935M		1.50

1937M		1.25
1938M		1.00
1941M		1.25
1944 Copper-Nickel-Zinc		.25
1944S Copper-Nickel-Zinc		.25
1945S Copper-Nickel-Zinc		.25

TEN CENTAVOS / silver

1903		1.50
1903S		8.00
1904		15.00
1904S		1.50
1905	Proof only	125.00
1906	Proof only	125.00
Reduced Size		
1907		2.50
1907S		2.00
1908	Proof only	125.00
1908S		1.50
1909S		18.00
1910S	Survival not verified	
1911S		3.00
1912S		3.50
1913S		4.00
1914S		4.50
1915S		14.00
1917S		1.50
1918S		1.50
1919S		1.50
1920		5.00
1921		1.50
1929M		1.25
1935M		1.25

1937M		1.00
1938M		1.00
1941M		1.00
1944D		.50
1945D		.50

TWENTY CENTAVOS / silver

| 1903 | | 2.50 |

		VF
1903S		15.00
1904		15.00
1904S		2.50
1905	*Proof only*	175.00
1905S		7.50
1906	*Proof only*	150.00
Reduced Size		
1907		3.50
1907S		2.50
1908	*Proof only*	150.00
1908S		2.50
1909S		7.50
1910S		7.50
1911S		7.50
1912S		4.50
1913S		4.50
1913S, S over S		8.50
1914S		2.50
1915S		2.50
1916S		2.00
1917S		2.00
1918S		1.50
1919S		1.75
1920		2.50
1921		2.00
1928M, 8 over 7		12.00
1929M		2.00

	VF
1937M	1.00
1938M	1.00
1941M	1.00
1944D	.75
1944D, D over S	12.00
1945D	.75

FIFTY CENTAVOS / silver

1903		5.00
1903S		3,000.00
1904		25.00
1904S		6.00
1905	*Proof only*	300.00
1905S		7.50
1906	*Proof only*	250.00
Reduced Size		
1907		4.50
1907S		4.00
1908	*Proof only*	250.00

1908S	4.00
1909S	6.00
1917S	6.00
1918S	3.50
1919S	4.00
1920	5.00
1921	3.75

1936M Commemorative	30.00

1944S	2.00
1945S	2.00

ONE PESO / silver

1903		11.00
1903S		8.00
1904		60.00
1904S		11.00
1905	*Proof only*	550.00
1905S		11.00
1906	*Proof only*	475.00
1906S		600.00
Reduced Size		
1907	*Proof only*	*only 2 known*
1907S		5.50
1908	*Proof only*	350.00
1908S		5.50
1909S		5.50
1910S		5.50
1911S		16.00
1912S		16.00

1936M Roosevelt and Quezon	57.00
1936M Murphy and Quezon	57.00

(See elsewhere for Spanish Colony
and Republic.)

UNITED STATES PAPER MONEY

INTRODUCTION TO U.S. PAPER

History: The first series of U.S. government paper money, Demand Notes, were interest bearing notes issued to help finance the Civil War. The United States has issued several different types of paper money over the years. In many cases the easiest way to identify one from another is by the heading on the note in question. Nineteenth century notes of $1 or more are approximately 7½" by 3 1/8", from the series of 1928 onward they are the current size of 6 1/8" by 2 5/8". Fractional currency, of less than $1 face value, varies in size but is always much smaller than current notes.

References: Friedberg, Robert, *Paper Money of the United States*; Bressett, Kenneth, *Guide Book of United States Currency*.
Periodicals: *Bank Note Reporter*; Society of Paper Money Collectors, *Paper Money*.
Counterfeit Alert: Most American paper money is printed on a special paper composed to a great extent of cloth, with red and blue silk threads appearing to "dive" in and out of the surface. Most counterfeits, particularly those made to pass in circulation, lack these minute threads.
Hints: Series and charter dates appearing on notes are not printing dates, which in some cases are *many years* later.

GRADING PAPER MONEY

Paper money, like coins, is graded on the degree of wear. In short, grades for both U.S. and most foreign paper can be summarized as follows:
Crisp Uncirculated (CU) - This is a perfectly new note — the kind that stick together when you get them at the bank. It will have no folds, bends, holds (see note below), tears, and will have sharp corners.

Extremely Fine (EF) - This is a note which, to an unaccustomed eye, may appear new but will have slight signs of circulation. It will be stiff ("crisp") in its feel. It may have very slight bends but no sharp folds or creases. Minor wrinkles that prevent a note from being better than EF can be seen most easily by holding the note at a sharp angle to a light and then viewing the note from an almost opposite sharp angle, as in the illustration below.

Very Fine (VF) - This note will appear to be circulated but still have some of its stiffness. Its corners may not be pointed. A couple of true folds are permissible, but not to excess. These folds can be distinguished from the minor bends permissible in EF by the fact that the ink over them will be broken. No serious stains or dirt marks are acceptable.
Fine (F) - A Fine note is worn, feeling neither stiff nor limp to the touch. Its edges may be finely rough but no significant tears or rips will be present. No corners or edges will be missing. Again, it must have no serious stains or dirt marks.
Very Good (VG) - This is a worn note with no crispness left in it. Edges many be a bit rough and creases will be evident. A limited amount of staining or ink marks are to be expected.
Good (G) - Notes in this grade are not considered desirable by collectors, who will rarely be willing to buy them except in the case of the rarest notes. They will be limp, worn and stained, with creases causing obvious gaps in the design. Tears are to be expected along the unprinted border of the note.
Hints: Early large size notes will often have minute pin-holes from having been sewn together by bank tellers to prevent theft. If very slight, they will not significantly reduce the value.

When handling a banknote it is important to remember never to touch the corners and especially one must NEVER FOLD PAPER MONEY. If in doubt as to a note's value, it is best to keep it flat in a book until it can be brought to an expert to examine. Also never attempt to clean or iron a note as these are likely to cause damage detectable by an expert.

CONTINENTAL AND STATE CURRENCY

History: The economic policies of England during the colonial era opposed the export of precious metal to the Colonies. One means by which the economic void was filled was by the issue of paper currency by the individual colonial governors. With the outbreak of the American Revolution both the newly independent states and the Continental Congress continued this practice. As neither authority had the full ability to redeem its paper in precious metal, it soon was traded at a massive discount. As a result, the framers of the new American Constitution prohibited government paper money in 1787.

Early colonial notes usually mention King George or show a crown. State notes replace this with the new state arms. Continental notes vary widely in appearance.

Notes of the 1700's bear hand signatures. Some of the signatures on these notes are those of signers of the Declaration of Independence or the Constitution and as such are worth more.
Reference: Newman, Eric, *The Early Paper Money of America*.
Counterfeit Alert: Notes on brittle, crisp yellowed paper are cheap imitations made during the 1950's and 1960's. Real notes are often dull white, and printed on soft or rough-grainy textured paper. More dangerous, accurate counterfeits are less often encountered. Contemporary counterfeits from the 1700's also exist and do have some collector value. New Hampshire counterfeits were made with original plates and are difficult to identify.
Hints: During colonial times damaged

notes were often sewn together with thread. While mutilated, these notes are discounted slightly less than notes ripped in half or having modern tape.

The prices below are for the most common varieties. There are hundreds of design types and any earlier than the 1750's commands a premium.

	VG	VF
Connecticut		
Colony	18.00	50.00
State	18.00	50.00
Delaware		
Colony	20.00	70.00
State	18.00	65.00

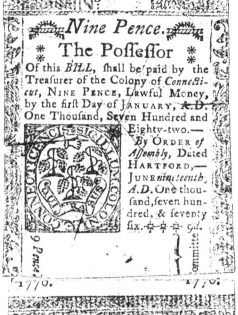

Connecticut Ninepence

Continental Seven Dollars

	VG	VF
Georgia		
Colony		Scarce
State	100.00	235.00
Maryland		
Colony	20.00	70.00
State	18.00	55.00
Massachusetts		
Colony	525.00	Rare
State	18.00	55.00
New Hampshire		
Colony (hole cancelled)	100.00	375.00
State	40.00	160.00
New Jersey		
Colony	18.00	55.00
State	20.00	80.00
New York		
Colony	25.00	85.00
State	30.00	95.00
North Carolina		
Colony / Province	40.00	135.00
State	30.00	85.00
Pennsylvania		
Colony	18.00	55.00
Commonwealth	18.00	45.00
Rhode Island		
Colony	130.00	Scarce
State	18.00	55.00
South Carolina		
Colony		Scarce
State	60.00	225.00
Vermont		
State		Scarce
Virginia		
Colony	45.00	160.00
State	45.00	160.00

Continental Currency		
1775	18.00	70.00
1776	18.00	70.00
1777	30.00	115.00
1778	18.00	65.00
1779	20.00	90.00

OBSOLETES

History: From the late 1700's through the Civil War, most of the paper money circulating in the United States was privately issued by banks. These banknotes were particularly abundant in the 1830's through 1850's. Very often they were backed by Bust Half Dollars or other coin held in reserve. Sometimes however they were backed by nothing. No one was obliged to accept this money, and the decision to do so often depended upon the issuing bank's reputation and proximity. Eventually many of the issuing banks collapsed, giving rise to the term "broken bank notes" and "obsoletes" used by collectors of these notes.

References: Haxby, James, *Obsolete Bank Notes.*

Counterfeit Alert: Notes printed on brittle crisp yellowed paper are cheap modern imitations. Real ones are often dull white and printed on thin, often limp paper. Contemporary nineteenth century counterfeits exhibiting crude engraving but correct paper are not rare and have at least slight collector value.

Hints: Most of these notes are printed on their face only, leaving the back blank.

Obsolete: Connecticut, Fairfield Bank & Trust 1838

	VG	VF
Connecticut: The Connecticut Bank, Bridgeport, 1856 $3		
	22.00	55.00
__: Fairfield Loan & Trust Company, 1839 $1¼	150.00	300.00
__: Southport Bank, 1857 $3		
	75.00	150.00
Delaware: Bank of Wilmington and Brandywine, 1839 $5		
	150.00	300.00
District of Columbia: Columbia Bank, Washington, 1852 $1		
	8.00	20.00
Florida: Bank of St. John's, Jacksonville, 1859 $5	20.00	60.00
Georgia: Mechanics Savings and Loan, Savannah, 1864 $1	5.00	15.00
Illinois: State Bank, Lockport, 1839 $10		
	5.00	15.00
Indiana: Indiana State Bank, Bloomfield, 1856 $2	30.00	90.00
Iowa: Lyons City Treasurer, c.1859 $2		
	20.00	55.00
Mississippi: Jackson, Detroit and St. Joseph Railroad Bank, 1840 $2		
	80.00	200.00
Nebraska: City of Omaha, 1857 $3		
	10.00	30.00

FRACTIONAL AND POSTAL CURRENCY

History: By early 1862 the nation was in the grips of an extreme shortage of coin in circulation. The uncertainties of the Civil War caused hoarding, made worse by the active export of coin to Canada. At first merchants issued their own "neighborhood scrip" but the government made this illegal in July. Postage stamps were authorized for circulation but they often stuck together in a sloppy mess. After the Post Office complained about the run on stamps, the Treasury was authorized to print its own stamps which the Post Office would honor. The idea developed further as these special enlarged stamps took form. The final product, far from the original intent of the law, was a small piece of paper with perforated borders and pictures of stamps, and labeled "Postage Currency." It was redeemable for real stamps, or for the newly issued government banknotes. Serving no purpose, the perforations on the edges were quickly removed. Several different colors of paper were used for this Postage Currency, all of relatively equal value today.

When printing costs from private contractors ran too high and counterfeits began to appear, the Treasury Department decided to issue a completely new set of notes, printed in-house and called "Fractional Currency." This time they did bother to get proper Congressional approval, on March 3, 1863. All second series notes have Washington's portrait in an unusual thick oval overprint of what was intended to be "bronze" ink. The same unusual ink was used to overprint the backs with the denomination. As the quality of the notes improved, so did the quality of the counterfeits. The Treasury attempted to fight this with a third series of more intricately engraved notes beginning in 1864. Certain notes in the series even have real hand signatures as a security measure. The 5¢ note of this series has one of the more unusual stories in United States currency. With no authorization from his superiors at all, Spencer M. Clark, Superintendent of the National Currency Bureau, decided to place his own portrait on the note! He may have been the one who came up with the idea of the government printing its Fractional Currency itself, rather than contracting it out, but most at the time thought this was more than an appropriate level of self-congratulation. Some have suggested that he "misinterpreted" instructions to place the famous explorer William Clark on the notes. A law was promptly passed preventing plates from being engraved depicting any living person. As a matter of economy, however, the plates with Clark's portrait were permitted to continue in use until the 5¢ notes were abolished in 1866. It should not be glossed over, however, that Clark's boss, U.S. Treasurer Spinner also placed his portrait on the 50¢ note of the same series.

On a fourth issue, 1869-75 but dated Act of 1863, a large Treasury seal figures prominently on the face, with the actual design of the note superimposed on it. Two years after the fifth issue was introduced in 1874, Congress authorized the production of extra coins to finally redeem this small and unusual currency.
Reference: Rothert, Matt, *A Guide Book of United States Fractional Currency*.
Counterfeit Alert: Contemporary counterfeits exist, especially of the first and second issues, the latter being of higher quality. Overprints (e.g. bronze ovals) can be chemically removed to appear rare.
Hints: Fractional Currency is far more common than large nineteenth century paper, and is found frequently in all grades from worn out to pristine. Worn out notes have little value.

The bronze ink on the second issue often turns dark or even greenish with age. Such examples are worth less than those with original bright color. Fourth and fifth issue notes with bright pink or blue on front are worth more.

Postal Currency

Fractional Currency - Third Issue

FIRST ISSUE - POSTAGE CURRENCY

	VG	VF
5¢ Washington, perforated edges	15.00	30.00
5¢ Washington, straight edges	5.00	12.00
10¢ Washington, perforated edges	20.00	30.00
10¢ Washington, straight edges	5.00	12.00
25¢ Five Stamps, perforated edges	20.00	40.00
25¢ Five Stamps, straight edges	6.00	15.00
50¢ Five Stamps, perforated edges	20.00	40.00
50¢ Five Stamps, straight edges	12.00	22.00

SECOND ISSUE - 1863-64

5¢ Washington in bronze oval	5.00	11.00
10¢ same	5.00	11.00
25¢ same	8.00	18.00
50¢ same	12.00	30.00

THIRD ISSUE - 1864-69

Note: All say "Act of March 3, 1863"

3¢ Washington	10.00	18.00
5¢ Clark	6.00	13.00
10¢ Washington	6.00	13.00
15¢ *Specimen only*	CU	50.00
25¢ Fessenden	8.00	18.00
50¢ Justice seated	30.00	80.00
50¢ Spinner	24.00	65.00

FOURTH ISSUE - 1869-75

Note: All say "Act of March 3, 1863" and have large Treasury seal.

10¢ Liberty bust	4.00	10.00
15¢ Columbia bust	11.00	25.00
25¢ Washington	6.00	13.00
50¢ Lincoln	16.00	45.00
50¢ Stanton	10.00	20.00
50¢ Samuel Dexter	8.00	18.00

Fractional Currency

FIFTH ISSUE - 1874-76

10¢ Wm. Meredith	3.00	10.00
25¢ Rbt. Walker	3.50	11.00
50¢ Wm. Crawford	8.00	15.00

DEMAND NOTES

History: On July 17, 1861 the United States government, for the first time since the Revolutionary War, authorized the issue of circulating paper money. Earlier experiences with this medium had been a disaster, with notes of both the states and the Continental Congress being discounted to near worthlessness. It was for this reason that the framers of the new Constitution attempted to prohibit government paper money. The pressing needs of the Civil War put an end to these noble intentions. All of these Demand Notes bear the promise "to pay the bearer ... dollars on demand," hence their name. Initially, acceptance of these notes by the public was not obligatory, but became so as a result of separate legislation. While they could be used to pay "all public dues" actual redemption of these notes must have been very difficult for most people. The notes were signed by U.S. Assistant Treasurers at Boston, Cincinnati, New York, Philadelphia and St. Louis "for the Treasurer" and one could redeem a note only at the city of issue!

Unlike the more common, privately issued notes of the time, all these notes bore printed backs. These contained the denomination and the words "United States of America" within an elaborate ornamental frame, all printed in green ink, hence the slang term "greenback" for paper money to this day.

Reference: Donlon, William, et al., *United States Large Size Paper Money 1861 to 1923.*

Counterfeit Alert: Exercise normal caution.

Hints: On very early notes the Assistant Treasurers wrote the words "for the" after their signatures by hand. On most later notes it was already preprinted. Notes with "for the" handwritten command a significant premium above the values indicated.

Demand Notes habitually come in worn state.

Demand Note

All $5 notes show Columbia statue l.,
Alexander Hamilton r.

	G	VG
$5 Boston	350.00	575.00
$5 Cincinnati		Rare
$5 New York	325.00	575.00
$5 Philadelphia	325.00	575.00
$5 St. Louis	2,500.00	5,000.00
$10 Boston	450.00	950.00
$10 Cincinnati		Rare
$10 New York	450.00	1,000.00
$10 Philadelphia	450.00	1,000.00
$10 St. Louis	2,500.00	6,000.00
$20 Boston	4,500.00	8,200.00
$20 Cincinnati		Rare
$20 New York	4,500.00	8,200.00
$20 Philadelphia	4,500.00	8,200.00

amid elaborate ornamentation and a legal statement. Those of the series of 1891 have more open space. The form of the 0's in 100 on the back of the 1890 issue has been likened in appearance to two watermelons, hence its nickname, the Watermelon Note. Of the nine portraits used on these notes, seven are of military leaders.

Reference: Donlon, William, et al., *United States Large Size Paper Money 1861 to 1923.*

Counterfeit Alert: Exercise normal caution.

Hints: All Treasury (Coin) Notes are considered quite scarce and desirable.

	F	VF
$1 1890 Stanton	325.00	525.00
$1 1891 Stanton	65.00	85.00
$2 1890 McPherson	400.00	800.00
$2 1891 McPherson	130.00	250.00
$5 1890 Geo. Thomas	275.00	600.00
$5 1891 Geo. Thomas	160.00	250.00
$10 1890 Sheridan	475.00	950.00
$10 1891 Sheridan	300.00	425.00
$20 1890 Marshall	1,700.00	3,300.00
$20 1891 Marshall	2,300.00	4,000.00
$50 1891 Seward	11,500.00	15,500.00
$100 1890 Farragut	11,500.00	15,500.00
$100 1891 Farragut	17,500.00	21,000.00
$1000 1890 Meade		Rare
$1000 1891 Meade		Rare

NATIONAL BANK NOTES

History: National Bank Notes were first issued by the National Currency Act in 1863. They were joint issues of the federal government and of over 13,000 federally chartered banks. The notes were printed on the order of the individual banks, which were required to keep certain reserves on deposit with the U.S. Treasury to back them. Each chartered bank was named prominently on the face of its notes and, generally, was required to use the word "National" in its title. All these notes bore the words "National Currency." Nationals, as they are called, are classified by collectors as First, Second or Third Charter based on the legislation that permitted their issue. There were two or three series within each charter period and they can be identified by minor

TREASURY NOTES

History: In 1890 the government issued notes which were to be redeemable in gold or silver coins, but the choice of which type of coin was to be left up to the Secretary of the Treasury at the time of redemption. Their promise is simply to "pay to the bearer on demand ... dollars in coin." These are called Treasury Notes or Coin Notes by collectors, and all of them bear the title TREASURY NOTE at the top or bottom of their face. The backs of all of these notes feature the denomination

Treasury Note

design changes. The charter dates and series dates are not actually the dates when the notes were printed, which is often later. In 1929 the size of Nationals was reduced along with the rest of American currency. As of May 20, 1935 no more National Bank Notes were issued.

Reference: Hickman and Oakes, *National Bank Notes.*

Counterfeit Alert: Exercise reasonable caution.

Hints: The values of Nationals vary by bank and by state in which that bank was located. The listings below serve only as a general guide and represent the most common note of each type. Certain states and territories are scarcer and have a premium over the others. These include Alaska, Arizona, Hawaii, Idaho, Indian Territory, Mississippi, Nevada, New Mexico, Puerto Rico, and South Dakota for large size. Premium notes for small size Nationals include Alaska, Arizona, Hawaii, Idaho, Montana, Nevada and Wyoming.

National Bank Note - First Charter

	VG	VF
FIRST CHARTER (1875 and earlier)		
$1 Concord / Pilgrims		
	85.00	225.00
$2 Lazy 2 / Walter Raleigh		
	325.00	850.00
$5 Columbus Sighting Land / Columbus Landing	90.00	225.00
$10 Franklin and Lightning / DeSoto		
	150.00	335.00
$20 Battle of Lexington / Baptism of Pocahontas	450.00	900.00
$50 Washington Crossing Delaware / Pilgrims	1,800.00	3,700.00
$100 Battle of Lake Erie / Signing of Declaration of Independence		
	2,250.00	4,500.00
$500		*Unique*
$1000		*Unique*

SECOND CHARTER / First Series (1882)

All have a large brown charter number on back

$5 James Garfield	60.00	135.00
$10 as 1st charter	70.00	145.00
$20 as 1st charter	100.00	240.00
$50 as 1st charter	550.00	1,100.00
$100 as 1st charter	650.00	1,400.00

SECOND CHARTER / Second Series

All have large "1882*1908" on back

$5 as 1st series	65.00	125.00
$10 as 1st series	70.00	145.00
$20 as 1st series	100.00	210.00
$50 as 1st series	425.00	850.00
$100 as 1st ser.	500.00	1,200.00

SECOND CHARTER / Third Series

All have large, spelled-out value on back

$5 as 2nd series	75.00	225.00
$10 as 2nd series	100.00	240.00
$20 as 2nd series	140.00	365.00
$50 as 2nd series		*Extremely rare*
$100 as 2nd series		*Extremely rare*

THIRD CHARTER / First Series

All have red seal on face

$5 Benjamin Harrison / Pilgrims Landing	65.00	140.00
$10 William McKinley / Female Figure		
	75.00	160.00
$20 Hugh McCulloch / Capitol		
	100.00	200.00
$50 John Sherman / Train		
	475.00	1,300.00
$100 John Knox / Eagle on Shield		
	550.00	1,700.00

THIRD CHARTER / Second Series

All have blue seal on face, dates "1902·1908" on back

$5 as 1st series	22.00	40.00
$10 as 1st series	26.00	45.00
$20 as 1st series	32.00	70.00
$50 as 1st series	170.00	375.00
$100 as 1st series	180.00	400.00

THIRD CHARTER / Third Series

All have blue seal on face, no dates on back

$5 as 1st series	18.00	33.00
$10 as 1st series	22.00	42.00
$20 as 1st series	35.00	70.00
$50 as 1st series	150.00	325.00
$100 as 1st series	170.00	350.00

THIRD CHARTER / Small Size

All series of 1929, with brown seal.

	F	EF
$5	13.00	30.00
$10	15.00	30.00
$20	27.00	40.00
$50	65.00	110.00
$100	115.00	200.00

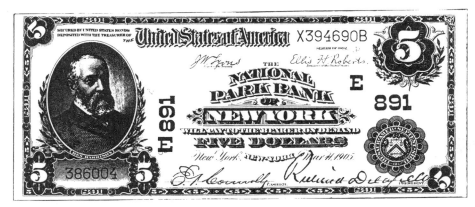

National Bank Note - Third Charter

National Gold Bank Notes

NATIONAL GOLD BANK NOTES

History: These were National banknotes issued under special provisions which made them redeemable in gold coin. They were issued solely in California, in response to that state's aversion to paper money. They bear dates 1870-75.

References: Donlon, William, et. al., *United States Large Size Paper Money 1861 to 1923.*

Counterfeit Alert: Exercise reasonable caution.

Hints: These are usually found in low grade.

All have gold coins as reverse types

	G	F
$5 Columbus Sighting Land	500.00	1,200.00
$10 Franklin and Lightning	700.00	2,700.00
$20 Battle of Lexington	1,800.00	4,800.00
$50 Washington Crossing Delaware	4,500.00	Rare
$100 Battle of Lake Erie	7,500.00	Rare

UNITED STATES NOTES (LEGAL TENDER NOTES)

History: This type of note was first issued in 1862 and continued for more than a century through many different series and design changes. Early notes simply read "The United States will pay to the bearer..." Later on the type of note can be more easily identified by an additional heading on the top of its face, TREASURY NOTE, "This note is legal tender for...," or ultimately the characteristic heading UNITED STATES NOTE. From the series of 1928 onward United States Notes have been the small size used presently. All small size notes have a red seal.

References: Donlon, William, et. al., *United States Large Size Paper Money 1861 to 1923.*

Counterfeit Alert: Contemporary counterfeits exist of the 1863 $50, 1869 $50, and 1863 $100.

Hints: Very late United States notes, while having a small retail premium, may not be found salable to dealers at any premium. The retail premium is simply a small handling charge.

Replacement notes carry a star by the serial number starting with series of 1880 ($20), 1901 ($10), 1907 ($5), and 1917 ($1 and $2). They sometimes carry a premium.

	F	EF
LARGE SIZE (Series of 1862-1923)		
$1 1862 Salmon P. Chase / Circle	150.00	350.00
$1 1869 Columbus scene	185.00	450.00
$1 1874-1917 same / Large X	30.00	55.00
$1 1923 Washington bust right	38.00	80.00
$2 1862 Alexander Hamilton / Circle	275.00	675.00
$2 1869 Jefferson & Capitol / II · 2 · TWO	275.00	675.00
$2 1874-1917 same / "2" only	38.00	65.00
$5 1862-63 Columbia and Hamilton	175.00	450.00
$5 1869 Jackson & Pioneer family / 5 in circle	200.00	350.00
$5 1875-1907 same / Nothing in circle	45.00	85.00
$10 1862-63 Lincoln and Art	425.00	750.00
$10 1869 Webster and Indian Princess scene	300.00	700.00
$10 1875-80 same / No inscription at center	135.00	325.00
$10 1901 Bison / Columbia between pillars	250.00	625.00
$10 1923 Andrew Jackson	400.00	925.00
$20 1862-63 Liberty	650.00	1,250.00
$20 1869 Alexander Hamilton and Victory	675.00	2,000.00
$20 1875-80 same / No inscription at center	175.00	450.00
$50 1862-63 Alexander Hamilton	5,700.00	10,000.00
$50 1869 Henry Clay r.	6,000.00	18,000.00
$50 1874-80 Franklin and Crowned Liberty	1,100.00	2,750.00
$100 1862-63 Eagle	7,000.00	13,000.00
$100 1869 Lincoln and Architecture	7,000.00	14,000.00
$100 1875-80 same / no inscription at center	1,950.00	4,500.00
$500 1862 Albert Gallatin		Rare
$500 1869 John Quincy Adams		Rare
$500 1874-80 Maj. Gen. Joseph Mansfield		Rare
$1000 1862-63 Robert Morris		Rare

	F	EF
$1000 1869-80 Columbus and DeWitt Clinton		24,000.00

SMALL SIZE (Series of 1928-1966)

	F	EF
$1 1928	16.00	30.00
$2 1928	8.00	18.00
$2 1928A	12.00	35.00
$2 1928B	60.00	150.00
$2 1928C	9.00	20.00
$2 1928D	4.00	9.00
$2 1928E	5.00	20.00
$2 1928F	4.00	8.00
$2 1928G	4.00	7.00
$2 1953	3.00	5.00
$2 1953A	3.00	5.00
$2 1953B	3.00	5.00
$2 1953C	3.00	5.00
$2 1963	spend	3.00
$2 1963A	spend	5.00
$5 1928	7.50	12.00
$5 1928A	10.00	16.00
$5 1928B	7.50	12.00
$5 1928C	7.00	12.00
$5 1928D	10.00	45.00
$5 1928E	7.00	12.00
$5 1928F	7.00	11.00
$5 1953	7.00	11.00
$5 1953A	7.00	12.00
$5 1953B	spend	8.50
$5 1953C	spend	11.00
$5 1963	spend	9.00

	F	CU
$100 1966	spend	175.00
$100 1966A	spend	500.00

GOLD CERTIFICATES

History: These notes redeemable in gold coin were intended primarily to facilitate transactions between banks. As a result, the first three issues, all indicating the Act of 1863, are virtually unknown. The last issue, series 1934 are unknown for the same reason. They were first made for circulation in 1882. By the early twentieth century their circulation had increased widely. Gold certificates were reduced in size with the 1928 series. All small size notes have a gold seal. In 1933 the government made a serious attempt to withdraw these notes in connection with the withdrawal of gold coin from circulation. They were actually illegal to own from that year until 1964.

References: See general references.

Counterfeit Alert: Exercise reasonable caution.

Hints: Small size Gold Certificates are somewhat scarce due to their attempted government confiscation in the 1930's.

United States Note (Legal Tender Note)

	F	EF
FOURTH ISSUE - Series of 1882		
$20 Garfield	300.00	800.00
$50 Wright	400.00	900.00
$100 Th. Benton	425.00	950.00
$500 Lincoln		Rare
$1000 Hamilton		Rare
$5000 Madison		Rare
$10,000 Jackson		Rare
FIFTH ISSUE - Series of 1888		
$5000 Madison		Rare
$10,000 Jackson		Rare
SIXTH ISSUE - Series of 1900		
$10,000 Jackson		Rare
SEVENTH ISSUE - Series of 1905-07		
$10 Hillegas	50.00	120.00
$20 Washington 1905 "technicolor"	600.00	2,000.00
$20 Washington 1906	80.00	200.00

	F	EF
EIGHTH ISSUE - Series of 1907		
$1000 Hamilton		Rare
NINTH ISSUE - Series of 1913		
$50 Grant	350.00	675.00
TENTH ISSUE - Series of 1922		
$10 Hillegas	45.00	115.00
$20 Washington	65.00	185.00
$50 Grant	225.00	575.00
$100 Th. Benton	400.00	900.00
$500 Lincoln	Rare	
$1000 Hamilton		Rare
SMALL SIZE - Series of 1928		
$10 Hamilton	22.00	60.00
$20 Jackson	32.00	60.00
$50 Grant	80.00	190.00
$100 Franklin	140.00	225.00
$500 McKinley	750.00	1,500.00
$1000 Cleveland	1,400.00	2,500.00
$5000 Madison		Rare

Gold Certificate

Silver Certificate

SILVER CERTIFICATES

History: First authorized in 1878, this is perhaps the most famous series of American paper money. All these bear the phrase "Silver Dollar(s)" somewhere on the face, and indicate a promise to redeem these notes in actual silver dollars. Until 1968 this could in fact be done. The 1886 and 1891 $2 were memorial commemoratives. The 1896 $1, $2 and $5 are referred to as "Educationals" by collectors and are considered to be among the most artistic notes issued by the United States.

Like other U.S. paper money, the Silver Certificates were reduced in size with the 1928 series. With the series of 1935 the Great Seal of the United States was added to the reverse design. Silver Certificates have not been redeemable in real silver since 1968.

References: See general references.

Counterfeit Alert: Exercise reasonable caution for contemporary counterfeits.

Hints: Very late Silver Certificates, while having a small retail premium, may not be found salable to dealers at any premium. The retail premium is simply a small handling charge.

Replacement notes carrying a star by the serial number were phased in beginning with the series of 1899, and sometimes carry a premium.

	VG	VF
$1 1886 Martha Washington / Inscription	100.00	250.00
$1 1891 same / inscription in rosette	85.00	175.00
$1 1896 History Instructing Youth / George and Martha Washington	90.00	200.00
$1 1899 Eagle	10.00	35.00
$1 1923 Washington	5.00	20.00
$2 1886 Gen. Winfield Scott Hancock	110.00	400.00
$2 1891 Sen. William Windom	100.00	250.00
$2 1896 Science Presenting Steam and Electricity to Commerce and Industry	125.00	500.00
$2 1899 Washington between Mechanics and Agriculture	25.00	100.00
$5 1886 U.S. Grant / Silver Dollars	150.00	500.00
$5 1891 same / Inscription	100.00	350.00
$5 1896 Winged Electricity	185.00	850.00
$5 1899 Sioux Chief "Onepapa"	100.00	350.00
$5 1923 Lincoln / Great Seal "Port-hole Five"	100.00	350.00

$10 1878-80 Robert Morris	235.00	800.00
$10 1886 Thomas Hendricks / Inscription at center	235.00	800.00
$10 1891-1908 same / UNITED STATES in oval	85.00	400.00
$20 1878-80 Stephen Decatur	350.00	1,200.00
$20 1886 Daniel Manning / Double Diamond	600.00	3,500.00
$20 1891 same / Double Circle	200.00	700.00
$50 1878-80 Everett / S I L V E R	2,000.00	7,000.00
$50 1891 same / Inscription	350.00	1,100.00
$100 1878-80 Monroe / S I L V E R	2,500.00	9,500.00
$100 1891 same / Inscription	1,250.00	5,000.00
$500 1878-80 Sumner / S I L V E R	*Rare*	
$1000 1878-91 William Marcy	*Rare*	

SMALL SIZE	VF	EF
$1 1928	8.00	12.00
$1 1928A	5.00	7.00
$1 1928B	6.00	8.00
$1 1928C	75.00	165.00
$1 1928D	65.00	120.00
$1 1928E	275.00	425.00
$1 1934	6.00	9.00
$1 1935	3.00	4.00
$1 1935A	2.00	3.00
$1 1935A HAWAII	9.00	13.00
$1 1935A Yellow seal	8.00	10.00
$1 1935A Red R	20.00	35.00
$1 1935A Red S	16.00	28.00
$1 1935B	2.50	3.50
$1 1935C	2.00	3.00
$1 1935D	2.00	3.00
$1 1935E	1.50	2.00
$1 1935F	1.50	2.00
$1 1935G	1.50	2.00
same with motto	1.50	2.00
$1 1935H	1.50	2.00
$1 1957	spend	1.50
$1 1957A	spend	1.40
$1 1957B	spend	1.40
$5 1934	7.00	10.00
$5 1934A	7.00	10.00
$5 1934A Yellow seal	17.00	30.00
$5 1934B	9.00	12.00
$5 1934C	7.00	10.00
$5 1934D	6.50	9.00
$5 1953	spend	8.00
$5 1953A	spend	7.00
$5 1953B	spend	7.00
$10 1933	1,600.00	3,000.00
$10 1933A		*Rare*

	VF	EF
$10 1934	17.00	20.00
$10 1934A	16.00	20.00
$10 1934 Yellow seal		
	800.00	1,400.00
$10 1934A Yellow seal		
	20.00	30.00
$10 1934B	85.00	150.00
$10 1934C	13.00	16.00
$10 1934D	13.00	16.00
$10 1953	13.00	16.00
$10 1953A	13.00	18.00
$10 1953B	13.00	16.00

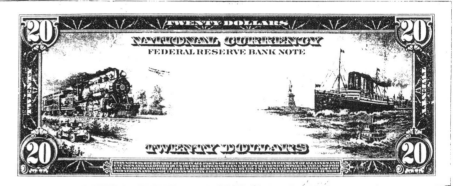

Federal Reserve Bank Note

FEDERAL RESERVE BANK NOTES

History: Like the National Banknotes, these notes bore on their face the words "National Currency." These read "Federal Reserve Bank" as well. Large size notes of the 1915 and 1918 series have a prominent blue seal on the face. Small size notes of the National Currency series of 1929 were actually issued in 1933 as an emergency issue and have a brown seal.

Reference: Schwartz and Oakes, *U.S. Small Size Currency.*

Counterfeit Alert: Reasonable caution should be exercised.

Hints: These should not be confused with Federal Reserve Notes (see below). Replacement star notes are particularly scarce for these notes.

LARGE SIZE	F	EF
$1 1918 George Washington / Eagle with Flag	35.00	60.00
$2 1918 Thomas Jefferson / Battle Ship	150.00	225.00
$5 1915 Abraham Lincoln / Columbus and Pilgrims	75.00	150.00
$5 1918 same	50.00	100.00
$10 1915 Andrew Jackson / Reaper and Factory	225.00	500.00
$10 1918 same	200.00	475.00
$20 1915 Grover Cleveland / Train and Ship	400.00	800.00
$20 1918 same	425.00	800.00
$50 1918 U.S. Grant / Allegory of Panama	2,500.00	4,750.00

SMALL SIZE	F	VF
$5 Boston	10.00	20.00
$5 New York	10.00	15.00
$5 Philadelphia	10.00	20.00
$5 Cleveland	10.00	15.00
$5 Atlanta	10.00	25.00
$5 Chicago	10.00	15.00
$5 St. Louis	90.00	175.00
$5 Minneapolis	15.00	35.00
$5 Kansas City	10.00	15.00
$5 Dallas	10.00	17.00
$5 San Francisco	425.00	800.00
$10 Boston	14.00	25.00
$10 New York	14.00	17.00
$10 Philadelphia	14.00	20.00
$10 Cleveland	14.00	20.00
$10 Richmond	14.00	25.00
$10 Atlanta	14.00	25.00
$10 Chicago	14.00	20.00
$10 St. Louis	14.00	20.00
$10 Minneapolis	14.00	23.00
$10 Kansas City	14.00	22.00
$10 Dallas	300.00	450.00
$10 San Francisco	16.00	38.00
$20 Boston	25.00	45.00
$20 New York	25.00	40.00
$20 Philadelphia	25.00	40.00
$20 Cleveland	25.00	40.00
$20 Richmond	25.00	40.00
$20 Atlanta	25.00	50.00
$20 Chicago	25.00	40.00
$20 St. Louis	25.00	55.00
$20 Minneapolis	25.00	40.00
$20 Kansas City	25.00	40.00
$20 Dallas	30.00	70.00
$20 San Francisco	25.00	45.00
$50 New York	60.00	85.00
$50 Cleveland	60.00	85.00
$50 Chicago	60.00	85.00
$50 Minneapolis	75.00	125.00
$50 Kansas City	60.00	85.00
$50 Dallas	75.00	125.00
$50 San Francisco	65.00	90.00
$100 New York	110.00	130.00
$100 Cleveland	115.00	150.00
$100 Richmond	120.00	175.00
$100 Chicago	110.00	130.00
$100 Minneapolis	115.00	135.00
$100 Kansas City	120.00	150.00
$100 Dallas	120.00	150.00

FEDERAL RESERVE NOTES

History: Authorized with the creation of the Federal Reserve Bank in 1913, these notes bear the words "Federal Reserve Note" on their faces. Beginning with the 1928 series these notes switched to the current small size. All small size have a green seal. This is currently the only form of note issued in the United States.

In 1993 added security devices were incorporated into larger Federal Reserve Notes. These include a filiment strip embedded in the paper and a border of micro printing surrounding the portrait.

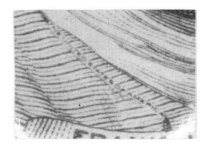

Micro printing (enlargement)

In 1996 the one hundred dollar note underwent its first major redesign since the introduction of small size currency. The new notes have 100 printed in color shifting ink and are printed on watermarked paper.

Reference: Lloyd, H. Robert, *National Bank Notes, Federal Reserve Bank Notes, Federal Reserve Notes 1928-50.*

Counterfeit Alert: Many counterfeits exist, especially of $10 and $20 notes, but most have obvious flaws, easily detectible with reasonable scrutiny.

Hints: These should not be confused with Federal Reserve Bank Notes (see above). Most dealers will not be willing to buy later current size Federal Reserve Notes because of their relatively small retail premium. Most circulated notes are not considered collectable and should simply be spent. The majority of replacement star notes of this series are common and bring no premium.

	F	EF
RED SEAL - SERIES OF 1914		
$5 Abraham Lincoln / Columbus and Pilgrims	35.00	100.00
$10 Andrew Jackson / Reaper and Factory	45.00	100.00
$20 Grover Cleveland / Train and Ship	80.00	300.00
$50 U.S. Grant / Allegory of Panama	300.00	700.00
$100 Franklin / Five Allegorical Figures	400.00	850.00
BLUE SEAL - SERIES OF 1914		
$5 Abraham Lincoln / Columbus and Pilgrims	25.00	38.00
$10 Andrew Jackson / Reaper and Factory	30.00	40.00

$20 Grover Cleveland / Train and Ship 38.00		65.00
$50 U.S. Grant / Allegory of Panama 110.00		225.00
$100 Franklin / Five Allegorical Figures 200.00		335.00
BLUE SEAL - SERIES OF 1918		
$500 John Marshall / DeSoto scene 1,200.00		3,000.00
$1,000 Hamilton / Eagle 2,000.00		3,300.00
$5,000 Madison		*Extremely Rare*
$10,000 Chase		*Extremely Rare*

SMALL SIZE - GREEN SEAL	CU
$1 1963	2.25
$1 1963A	2.25
$1 1963B	3.00
$1 1969	2.25
$1 1969A	2.25
$1 1969B	2.25
$1 1969C	2.25
$1 1969D	2.25
$1 1974	2.00
$1 1977	2.00
$1 1977A	2.00
$1 1981	2.00
$1 1981A	2.00
$1 1985	2.00
$1 1988	2.00
$1 1988A	2.00
$1 1993	2.00

	VF	CU
$1 1995	2.00	
$2 1976 Bicentennial		3.00
same with cancelled stamp		3.25
$5 1928	8.00	35.00
$5 1928A	8.00	35.00
$5 1928B	8.00	35.00
$5 1928C	150.00	450.00
$5 1928D	200.00	850.00
$5 1934	6.50	20.00
$5 1934A	6.50	20.00
$5 1934 HAWAII	27.00	135.00
$5 1934A HAWAII	27.00	110.00
$5 1934B	6.50	25.00
$5 1934C	6.50	25.00
$5 1934D	6.50	25.00
$5 1950		20.00
$5 1950A		12.00
$5 1950A		12.00
$5 1950B		12.00
$5 1950C		12.00
$5 1950D		12.00
$5 1950E		16.00
$5 1963		10.00
$5 1963A		9.50
$5 1969		9.00
$5 1969A		9.00
$5 1969B		8.00
$5 1969C		8.00
$5 1974		8.00
$5 1977		6.50

Federal Reserve Note

	VF	CU
$5 1977A		6.50
$5 1981		6.50
$5 1981A		6.50
$5 1985		6.50
$5 1988		6.50
$5 1988A		6.50
$5 1993		6.50
$5 1995		6.50
$10 1928	20.00	60.00
$10 1928A	15.00	36.00
$10 1928B	14.00	27.00
$10 1928C	30.00	85.00
$10 1934	13.00	25.00
$10 1934A	13.00	22.00
$10 1934A HAWAII	25.00	200.00
$10 1934B	13.00	20.00
$10 1934C	13.00	18.00
$10 1934D	13.00	20.00
$10 1950	13.00	20.00
$10 1950A	13.00	20.00
$10 1950B	13.00	20.00
$10 1950C		18.00
$10 1950D		18.00
$10 1950E		18.00
$10 1963		17.00
$10 1963A		17.00
$10 1969		17.00
$10 1969A		15.00
$10 1969B		18.00
$10 1969C		15.00
$10 1974		14.00
$10 1977		14.00
$10 1977A		14.00
$10 1981		13.00
$10 1981A		13.00
$10 1985		13.00
$10 1988		13.00
$10 1988A		13.00
$10 1993		13.00
$10 1995		13.00
$20 1928	27.00	60.00
$20 1928A	25.00	55.00
$20 1928B	30.00	40.00
$20 1928C	65.00	375.00
$20 1934	25.00	40.00
$20 1934A	25.00	40.00
$20 1934 HAWAII	100.00	750.00
$20 1934A HAWAII	38.00	350.00
$20 1934B	25.00	40.00
$20 1934C	25.00	40.00
$20 1934D		35.00
$20 1950		40.00
$20 1950A		30.00
$20 1950B		30.00
$20 1950C		30.00
$20 1950D		30.00
$20 1950E		40.00
$20 1963		27.00
$20 1963A		27.00

Federal Reserve Note - Hawaii

	CU
$20 1969	27.00
$20 1969A	27.00
$20 1969B	30.00
$20 1969C	27.00
$20 1974	27.00
$20 1977	23.00
$20 1981	23.00
$20 1981A	23.00
$20 1985	23.00
$20 1988A	23.00
$20 1990	23.00
$20 1993	23.00
$20 1995	23.00
$50 1928	145.00
$50 1928A	140.00
$50 1934	100.00
$50 1934A	110.00
$50 1934B	110.00
$50 1934C	90.00
$50 1934D	95.00
$50 1950	90.00
$50 1950A	90.00
$50 1950B	75.00
$50 1950C	75.00
$50 1950D	70.00
$50 1950E	110.00
$50 1963A	60.00
$50 1969	60.00
$50 1969A	60.00
$50 1969B	65.00
$50 1969C	60.00
$50 1974	55.00
$50 1977	55.00
$50 1981	55.00
$50 1981A	55.00
$50 1985	55.00
$50 1988	55.00

	CU
$50 1990	55.00
$50 1993	55.00
$100 1928	230.00
$100 1928A	230.00
$100 1934	150.00
$100 1934A	150.00
$100 1934B	150.00
$100 1934C	135.00
$100 1934D	185.00
$100 1950	140.00
$100 1950A	135.00
$100 1950B	135.00
$100 1950C	135.00
$100 1950D	135.00
$100 1950E	120.00
$100 1963A	120.00
$100 1969	120.00
$100 1969A	110.00
$100 1969C	110.00
$100 1974	110.00
$100 1977	110.00
$100 1981	110.00
$100 1981A	110.00
$100 1988	110.00
$100 1990	110.00
$100 1993	110.00
$100 1996 New Design	110.00

	EF
$500 1928	665.00
$500 1934	650.00
$500 1934A	600.00
$500 1934B	600.00
$500 1934C	600.00
$1000 1928	1,200.00
$1000 1934	1,200.00
$1000 1934A	1,150.00

New Design 1996 Federal Reserve Note

INTEREST BEARING NOTES, COMPOUND INTEREST TREASURY NOTES, & REFUNDING CERTIFICATES

History: The same 1861 Act of Congress that created the nation's first paper money, Demand Notes, also created other notes of higher value which bore interest. These were originally issued in denominations of $50, $100, $500, $1000 and $5000, and paid 7.3% interest. Similar to bonds, each note had coupons attached which could be clipped off at intervals when interest was paid. As paper money became more and more accepted government bonds developed their own separate existence, void of legal tender status. The last note of this kind was issued in 1879 and in 1907 Congress suspended further accrual of interest.

Despite the fact that some later notes were issued with values as low as $10, all were considered quite valuable in their day, and virtually all of them were redeemed for their face value plus interest. Of the several different issues released, every one today is of great rarity. The value of each of these notes is determined on a case by case basis, and is a matter best considered beyond the scope of this book. Below is the most common representative example of this rare series.

References: See general references.

Counterfeit Alert: Should be examined by an expert.

Hints: The bold words "Compound Interest Treasury Note" printed in gold ink on some of these notes has been known to eat through the note itself! Overprints frequently turn green.

	EF		
$1000 1934C	1,150.00	$5000 1934B	13,000.00
$5000 1928	13,000.00	$10,000 1928	25,000.00
$5000 1934	13,000.00	$10,000 1934	25,000.00
$5000 1934A	13,000.00	$10,000 1934A	25,000.00
		$10,000 1934B	25,000.00

	VF
$10 Refunding Certificate 1879 Franklin / T E N	1,100.00

CONFEDERATE CURRENCY

History: One of the most common and most popular types of American paper money is that of the Confederate States of America. The first series of Confederate paper was a small issue of interest bearing notes, backed by cotton crops. Initially they were dated 1861 at Montgomery, Alabama and were actually printed by the

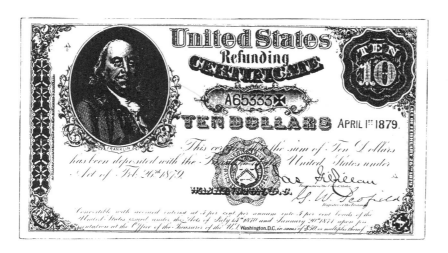

Refunding Certificate

Confederate Currency - $50 Jefferson Davis

National Bank Note Co., New York. When the capitol of the Confederacy was moved to Richmond, Virginia that same year, a new issue mentioning that city was released. These were also printed by a Northern firm, the American Bank Note Co., although through its New Orleans subsidiary, the Southern Bank Note Co. During the Civil War even paper was in short supply in the South. Much of the third issue of Confederate paper was printed on British paper smuggled through the Union naval blockade. Other paper was smuggled in from the North.

Confederate banknotes were redeemable "after the ratification of a treaty of peace between the Confederate States and United States" but whether a note said "six months after..." or "two years after..." varied with the fortunes of the South. The Confederacy at first tried to prevent inflation by limiting the quantity of paper issued, but the war forced it to give in. The first issue of 1861 was limited to $1 million, that of 1863 to approximately $50 million per *month*, and that of 1864 had no limit at all.

Reference: Slabaugh, Arlie, *Confederate States Paper Money.*
Counterfeit Alert: Contemporary counterfeits of Confederate notes are quite common. They usually display notably crude engraving. Except for the 50¢ note, real Confederate notes are hand signed. Those with printed signatures are likely to be counterfeit. Early replicas bear the inscription "Facsimile Confederate Note - Sold wholesale and retail, by S.C. Upham..." and do have some collector value. Notes printed on brittle crisp yellowed paper are cheap modern imitations. Real ones are often printed on thin, often limp paper.
Hints: While up to the 1950's Confederate money was being burned as worthless, it is now popular with both collectors and laymen as historical momentos, even in low grade. Notes bearing the overprint "Accepted as a note Issued under Act of Congress of March 23, 1863." are worth more.

	VG	VF
FIRST ISSUE - MONTGOMERY (1861)		
$50 Hoeing Cotton	700.00	3,000.00
$100 Train	800.00	3,200.00
$500 Cattle	1,300.00	7,500.00
$1000 Calhoun and Jackson	1,500.00	6,800.00
FIRST ISSUE - RICHMOND (1861)		
$50 Industry and Agriculture	110.00	550.00
$100 Train	125.00	600.00
SECOND ISSUE (July 25, 1861)		
$5 Inscription	225.00	1,300.00
$5 Liberty with Eagle, Sailor left	200.00	1,000.00
$10 Liberty with Eagle, Commerce left	35.00	325.00
$20 Ship	18.00	65.00
$20 Diana riding Stag, Industry seated left	18.00	75.00
$50 Washington	22.00	80.00
$100 Ceres and Proserpina	100.00	550.00
THIRD ISSUE (September 2, 1861)		
$2 Confederacy Striking down Union, Judah Benjamin l.	85.00	375.00
$5 Cotton being loaded onto Steam-boat, Indian Princess right	1,250.00	6,500.00
$5 Commerce seated on cotton	15.00	37.00
$5 Commerce, Agriculture, Liberty & Industry seated, Justice standing behind	80.00	375.00
$5 Sailor and cotton bales, C.G. Memminger left	30.00	60.00
$5 Boy's bust left, Blacksmith seated right	125.00	550.00
$5 C.G. Memminger, V at lower right	25.00	70.00
$5 same, but FIVE at lower right	25.00	70.00
$10 Liberty with Eagle left	650.00	3,200.00
$10 Ceres and Commerce left	15.00	60.00
$10 Indian Family	75.00	325.00
$10 Cotton Picker	30.00	150.00
$10 Revolutionary War Generals, Minerva standing r.	15.00	60.00
$10 Wagon with cotton, John Ward left	175.00	850.00
$10 R.M.T. Hunter l., Child r.	25.00	110.00
$10 Hope with Anchor, R.M.T. Hunter left, C.G. Memminger right	20.00	115.00
$10 same, with X X overprint	25.00	90.00
$20 Ceres between Commerce and Navigation	75.00	375.00
$20 Ship	15.00	45.00

	VG	VF
$20 Navigation with globe	335.00	1,300.00
$20 Indian seated behind large 20	10.00	37.00
$20 Alexander Stephens	35.00	150.00
$50 Moneta & chest	18.00	60.00
$50 Train	450.00	2,900.00
$50 Jefferson Davis	25.00	130.00
$100 Loading cotton onto wagon, Sailor left	25.00	70.00

FOURTH ISSUE (1862)

$1 Steamship	20.00	60.00
$1 same with ONE overprint	25.00	90.00
$2 Confederacy striking down Union, Judah Benjamin l.	20.00	60.00
$2 same with "2 TWO" overprint	25.00	90.00
$10 Commerce reclining		*Rare*
$10 Ceres seated		*Rare*
$20 Liberty with shield	600.00	2,900.00
$100 Train	25.00	60.00
$100 Hoeing Cotton	25.00	60.00

FIFTH ISSUE (December 2, 1862)

$1 Clement Clay	25.00	70.00
$2 Judah Benjamin	20.00	60.00
$5 Confederate Capitol, Memminger right	8.00	30.00
$10 South Carolina Capitol, R.M.T. Hunter right	8.00	30.00
$20 Tennessee Capitol, Alexander Stephens right	20.00	75.00
$50 Jefferson Davis	25.00	90.00
$100 Lucy Pickens	30.00	95.00

SIXTH ISSUE (1863)

50¢ Jefferson Davis	8.00	25.00
$1 Clement Clay	20.00	60.00
$2 Judah Benjamin	20.00	80.00
$5 Confederate Capitol, Memminger right	8.00	25.00
$10 South Carolina Capitol, R.M.T. Hunter right	8.00	25.00
$20 Tennessee Capitol, Alexander Stephens right	8.00	30.00
$50 Jefferson Davis	20.00	60.00
$100 Lucy Pickens, Soldiers left, Geo. Randolph right	25.00	70.00

SEVENTH ISSUE (1864)

50¢ Jefferson Davis	7.00	25.00
$1 Clement Clay	30.00	80.00
$2 Judah Benjamin	25.00	70.00
$5 Confederate Capitol, Memminger right	7.00	25.00
$10 Field Artillery, R.M.T. Hunter right	6.00	18.00
$20 Tennessee Capitol, Alexander Stephens right	7.00	20.00

American Numismatic Association Collector Currency

$50 Jefferson Davis	20.00	50.00
$100 Lucy Pickens, Soldiers left, Geo. Randolph right	25.00	55.00
$500 Field and seal left, Stonewall Jackson right	125.00	350.00

DEPRESSION & OTHER SCRIP

History: With the Great Depression of the early 1930's came a general lack of money. Even municipalities and states suffered. In an effort to stimulate the economy these and other entities issued scrip of limited life, sometimes redeemable under restricted circumstances. Many were for amounts under $1.

At many times before and after the Depression various firms and organizations have distributed "money" redeemable in goods or services to stimulate their business. There are thousands of varieties of this sort of scrip, and most consider them to be in the nature of souvenirs.

References: Mitchell, Ralph & Schafer, Neil, *Standard Catalog of Depression Scrip*, Schingoethe, H. and M., *College Currency*.

Counterfeit Alert: Danger of counterfeits varies widely.

Hints: An inexpensive way to collect local history and memories of times gone by.

	EF
Connecticut: [Boy Scouts of America] Fairfield County Council Cub Bucks [1970's] $1	.50
Delaware: Wilmington Delaware Clearing House Association, Bust of Lincoln, 1933 $20	50.00
__: same but SPECIMEN across front	100.00
Florida: St. Petersburg Citizens Emergency Committee, 1933 10¢	35.00
Idaho: Caldwell Dairymen's Co-operative Creamery of Boise Valley, 1935 $14.00	
Illinois: Chicago Clearing House, 1933 $5	5.00
Iowa: Ceder Falls Chamber of Commerce Scrip, 1933 $1	4.00
Utah: Salt Lake City, Latter Day Saints College Currency [1860-1885] $1000	350.00
Non-local: National School Bank, 2 left, girl right [1860-85] $2	30.00
__: American Numismatic Assoc. ANA Collector Currency, 1988 $1	1.00

MILITARY PAYMENT CERTIFICATES

History: Military Payment Certificates are special currency issued by the U.S. government expressly to pay soldiers on American military bases. Its purpose was to prevent speculation in U.S. currency by maintaining a currency that could be withdrawn and replaced at short notice, without adversely affecting the reputation of the U.S. Dollar. The soldiers would be notified and permitted to exchange their "MPC's" but the surrounding population might not be given access to the base during the redemption period.

Reference: Schwan, C.F. and Boling, J.E., *World War II Military Currency.*

Counterfeit Alert: Exercise usual care.

Hints: These often occur in F or CU, not often in VF-EF.

$10 Military Payment Certificate

	VF	CU
Series 481 (1951-54) 10¢ Seated female with globe	2.00	25.00
Series 521 (1954-58) $5 Female with basket	50.00	450.00
Series 641 (1965-68) 5¢ Female head	.75	2.50
Series 661 (1968-69) $5 Female holding flowers	3.00	16.00
Series 692 (1970-73) $10 Indian Chief Hollow Horn Bear	200.00	550.00

BANK (PERSONAL) CHECKS

History: People have been writing checks for hundreds of years, but collecting them for only a tiny fraction of that. From 1862 to 1882, and again in 1898, all personal checks were required to carry a U.S. revenue stamp which was usually printed on the paper, though sometimes affixed like postage stamps. Most checks are of interest only to individuals collecting local history or as an adjunct to a collection of National Bank Notes or United States Revenue Stamps.

Every check bears certain information: the bank on which it is drawn, the maker, recipient, face value, date and sometimes a vignette. The make and recipient are not noted on the examples below.

Certain vignettes command a premium over others. Generic portraits are of little interest; identifiable places and buildings are more desirable.

Reference: Scott Publishing Co., *Specialized Catalogue of United States Stamps.*

Periodicals: Scattered articles throught the volumes of *Bank Note Reporter.*

Bank (Personal) Check - B. Max Mehl, Ft. Worth, Texas

Counterfeit Alert: Not of major concern.

Hints: Checks have appeal to those other than check collectors. It is entirely possible for a check to be virtually worthless of itself but for a rare variety of stamp printed on it to make it valuable. An expert in stamps would be qualified to make this determination. An autograph of a famous individual can also make an otherwise inexpensive check into something valuable and highly sought after. The appraisal of autographs is a separate collecting field and outside the scope of this book.

VF Cancelled

1845 Otsego County Bank of Cooperstown, N.Y., James Fenimore Cooper (maker), $17.50 . . . . . . *Rare*

1874 First National Bank of Rushville, Ill., $112.30, Semi-nude Female Allegory and Eagle Vignettes 2.25

1879 Shawmut National Bank, Boston, Mass., $600.00, Steam Locomotive Vignette 20.00

1881 City National Bank of Bridgeport, Connecticut, $15.45 . . . . 1.50

1895 Centennial National Bank of Philadelphia, $15.00, Bank Building Vignette 30.00

1899 Dime Savings Bank / Western Savings and Deposit Bank, $21.20, three documentary revenue stamps affixed. 5.00

1899 Bank of Clinch Valley, Tazewell, Va., $100.00, one stamp affixed. 75

1906 Central National Bank, Philadelphia, Penn., $27.00 75

1916 The First-Bridgeport National Bank, Connecticut, $7.50 50

1930 Fort Worth National Bank, Ft. Worth, Texas, B. Max Mehl (maker), $30.00, Vignettes of Mehl Building and Fugio Cent 3.00

Note: B. Max Mehl was a noted coin dealer of the early twentieth century.

1969 Bank of America, Seoul Military Post Facilities (maker) $504.75, imprinted "Payable in Military Payment Certificates only. Regulations prohibit sending this check to points outside Japan, Korea and the Philippine Islands." 5.00

Bank (Personal) Check - Rushville, Ill.

CANADIAN COINS

HISTORY OF CANADIAN COINAGE

Canadian coinage, like that of the United States, began as an improvised array of imported foreign coins and private tokens. While a very few coins were struck especially for use in Canada in the eighteenth century, the first quarter of the nineteenth century saw the abundant quantities of distinctly Canadian copper. These were numerous half penny size tokens commissioned by merchants and usually struck in England. Also common were crude local counterfeits of English and Irish regal copper, today referred to as "blacksmith tokens." During the 1830's through 1850's the major banks in Lower and Upper Canada (Quebec and Ontario respectively) took the lead in commissioning new tokens of improved weight with finely engraved designs. At the same time in the Maritime Provinces new official government tokens were struck bearing royal portraits and local motifs. This series even included some denominations in silver.

In 1867 the independent Dominion of Canada was formed, resulting in the end of local Canadian coinage, and the introduction of a new, unified coinage system based on the U.S. gold dollar. While cents through half dollars were struck during the reign of Queen Victoria, the dollar remained only a theoretical denomination. The famous Canadian silver dollar depicting the Voyageur Scene, an early Hudson's Bay Co. agent and a Canadian Indian paddling their canoe past a wooded islet, was not introduced until King George V's jubilee in 1935. With the opening of the new Royal Canadian Mint in 1908, gold sovereigns were first issued of British design and standard but with a discrete "C" mintmark. These were supplemented by distinctly Canadian $5 and $10 gold pieces in 1912.

Among the changes apparent on Canadian coinage over the years is the evolution of the British monarchy as sovereign also of Canada. Queen Victoria is shown to age. Kings Edward VII and George V ascend the throne and their portraits appear on the coinage in 1902 and 1911 respectively. George V's title is changed a year later to include DEI GRA: for "by the Grace of God." George VI's initial 1937 title was changed in 1948 to omit the claim to the emperorship of India. The mint workers were so ill prepared for this change that old 1947 dies had to be used until the new dies were ready. These coins are indicated by a tiny maple leaf after the date. Like Queen Victoria, Elizabeth II is shown to mature from a young girl to dignified sovereign.

George VI's new coinage in 1937 was used as an opportunity to introduce new, less conservative reverse designs on all the minor denominations. These designs, executed by the prolific G.E. Kruger-Gray, as well as Emmanuel Hahn, depict lifelike and distinctly Canadian motifs.

Initially Canadian silver coins were traditional sterling silver (92½% pure) silver. The economic stress of World War I led to a reduction to 80% in 1920. Following a world-wide trend caused by the rising price of silver, Canada phased out circulating silver coins in the 1960's. Ten cent and 25 cent pieces were struck in both 80% and 50% pure silver in 1967. Again, both coins were struck in both 50% silver and pure nickel in 1968, while the dollar and half dollar were struck exclusively on nickel that year. These larger denominations were also made smaller. The dollar was further reduced in 1987 when it was switched to an alloy called "aureate nickel" having the appearance of brass.

Canada has struck commemorative coins at frequent intervals since 1935. Currently the Royal Canadian Mint maintains an active program of collector coins, including commemoratives in silver and gold, and wildlife issues in platinum. Sets of circulating commemorative minor coins were also struck for the centennial and 125th anniversary of the Canadian Confederation.

The Canadian Maple Leaf is one of the world's most successful and popular bullion coins. It is struck in silver, gold, and platinum, in a number of sizes.

GRADING

Because of the consistent patterns of obverse design general rules for the grading of Canadian coins can be easily explained. Of course these basic principles have some limits and it is always best to consult a specialized work on Canadian coins for the particulars of grading any given type.

The most important detail for grading Victoria's young portrait is the braid around the ear. A coin in Extremely Fine (EF) will have complete detail in the braid with only a trace of wear. As a coin wears down to Very Fine (VF) it will begin to lack some detail. The segments of the braid will begin to merge on a coin in Fine (F). By the time a coin wears down to Very Good (VG) the braid will be bold only in its outline, and on a coin in Good (G) it will show it to be worn through.

One unscientific but simple way to judge the grade of a coin with the diademed portrait of Victoria is by the clarity of the diadem. On an EF coin all its details will be sharp and clear. The jewels will be clear but not distinct on a VF coin. As a coin descends to F the jewels in the crown will be less clear and the hair over the ear will lack about half its details. These hair details will be gone on a VG coin as will be a minority of the jewels of the crown. Finally a coin in Good will have a clear rim but a rather flat portrait.

The coins of Edward VII and George V grade similarly. If the band of the crown is sharp and clear in all its details it is EF. If it is bold but not sharp it's VF. If it is complete but lacking detail the coin is Fine. A Very Good coin will have the band about half worn through. The band of the crown will be completely worn through by the time the coin is worn down to Good.

The coins of George VI are only collected in high grade, thus little need be explained. An Extremely Fine coin must have fully detailed hair and a sharp ear. Only traces of wear are permissible. BU coins must have full luster. Toned or baggy coins, while technically Uncirculated are often traded at an *almost* or *about* uncirculated price.

Most coins of Elizabeth II are collected only in Brilliant Uncirculated or nearly so.

REFERENCES

Charlton, J.E., *The Standard Catalogue of Canadian Coins*; Charlton, J.E., *The Charlton Standard Catalogue of Canadian Colonial Tokens*; Haxby, James, *The Royal Canadian Mint and Canadian Coinage: Striking Impressions.*

PERIODICAL

Canadian Coin News.

CENTS

History: Canadian cents are actually older than Canada! The first bronze cents were struck in 1858 for the Province of Canada, nine years before Canadian independence. After a hiatus of several years, the cent was updated replacing the young head of Queen Victoria with a mature head. The large cent was replaced with a small cent in 1920, and the current maple leaf design was adopted in 1937 with the new coinage for George VI. In 1982 the cent was change from round to polygonal.

Counterfeit Alert: The 1936 dot should be examined with great skepticism.

Hints: Small cents listed below under *BU* must have full, natural luster. Toned, smudged, or stained specimens are worth substantially less. Even *EF* cents may command a slight premium with substantial original red.

LARGE CENTS / VICTORIA

	VG	VF
1858	25.00	55.00
1859, 9 over 8	15.00	35.00
1859, Narrow 9	1.00	3.00
1859, Double punched 9 (2 vars.)		
	20.00	50.00
1876H	.85	2.50

1881H	1.50	4.00
1882H	1.00	2.25
1884	1.00	3.25
1886	2.25	5.00
1887	1.75	4.00
1888	.85	2.00
1890H	3.00	9.00
1891 Large date	2.00	8.00
1891 Small date, Large Leaves		
	27.50	65.00
1891 Small date, Small Leaves		
	20.00	50.00
1892	2.00	5.00
1893	1.00	3.00
1894	3.50	9.00
1895	2.00	5.00
1896	1.00	2.00
1897	1.00	2.50
1898H	2.00	6.00
1899	1.00	2.00
1900	4.00	9.50
1900H	1.00	2.00
1901	1.00	2.00

EDWARD VII

1902	.85	1.75
1903	.85	2.00
1904	1.25	3.00
1905	2.00	5.00
1906	.85	2.00
1907	1.25	3.00
1907H	5.00	12.00
1908	1.25	3.50
1909	.85	2.00
1910	.85	1.50

GEORGE V

	F	EF
1911	1.00	3.00
1912	.75	2.25
1913	.75	2.25
1914	1.00	3.50
1915	.75	2.50
1916	.65	2.00
1917	.50	1.50
1918	.50	1.50
1919	.50	1.50

1920	.50	1.50

SMALL CENTS / GEORGE V

1920	.25	1.50
1921	.25	3.50
1922	10.00	20.00
1923	15.00	32.00
1924	4.50	10.00
1925	12.00	27.00
1926	2.00	6.50
1927	.75	3.50
1928	.25	1.50
1929	.25	1.50
1930	1.50	4.50
1931	.75	3.00
1932	.25	1.50
1933	.25	1.50
1934	.25	1.50
1935	.25	1.50
1936	.25	1.50
1936 Dot below date		*Extremely Rare*

GEORGE VI

	EF	BU
1937	1.00	2.50
1938	.35	3.00
1939	.35	2.50
1940	.35	2.00
1941	.50	20.00
1942	.50	15.00
1943	.35	5.00
1944	.50	15.00
1945	.35	2.00
1946	.50	2.00
1947	.35	3.00
1947 Maple Leaf	.35	2.50
1948	.50	4.00
1949	.25	2.00
1950	.25	2.00
1951	.25	2.00
1952	.25	2.00

ELIZABETH II

1953 without fold		1.50

	EF	BU
1953 with fold		12.50
1954 without fold	*Prooflike only*	95.00
1954 with fold		2.00
1955 without fold		*Rare*
1955 with fold		.50
1956		.50
1957		.35
1958		.35
1959		.30
1960		.25
1961		.25
1962		.25
1963		.25
1964		.25

1965 (4 vars.)	.25
1966	.20
1967 Centennial	.20
1968	.20
1969	.20
1970	.20
1971	.15
1972	.15
1973	.15
1974	.15
1975	.15
1976	.15
1977	.15
1978	.15
1979	.15
1980	.15
1981	.15
1982	.15
1983	.15
1984	.15
1985	.15
1986	.15
1987	.15
1988	.15
1989	.15
1990	.15
1991	.15
1992 125th Anniv	.20
1993	.15
1994	.15
1995	.15
1996	.15

FIVE CENTS

History: Canadian five cent pieces were initially tiny silver coins. Like the cent they were also introduced before the Confederation, but the portrait was left relatively unchanged, despite the Queen's age. Soon after Canadian silver was reduced from sterling to 80% these small coins were completely replaced by larger, pure nickel coins. In 1937 the present beaver design was introduced.

The five cent piece has probably been through more changes of alloy than any other Canadian coin. World War II nickel shortages caused its switch to tombac, a brass alloy. After the war, it was struck in chromium-plated steel, and it was even debated at whether or not the commemorative five cent piece for the isolation of nickel would be struck in real nickel. (It was.) The last steel five cent piece was struck in 1954. The famous "Jack Rabbit Nickel" was struck in 1967 for the centennial. From 1982 to the present all have been struck in a copper-nickel alloy.

Counterfeit Alert: Examine all 1921 specimens carefully.

Hints: The thin silver pieces are prone to dents, edge dings, and bends. Coins with this type of damage are sold at a hefty discount. Nickel and steel five cent pieces are often found with "X" shaped counting machine scars and as such are usually avoided by collectors.

SILVER FIVE CENTS / VICTORIA

	VG	VF
1858	5.00	18.00
1858, Large date over small date		
	60.00	220.00
1870 Flat rim	4.00	18.00
1870 Wire rim	4.00	20.00
1871	4.00	18.00
1872H	3.50	15.00
1874H Plain 4	9.00	40.00
1874H Crosslet 4	5.00	30.00
1875H Large date	50.00	250.00
1875H Small date	45.00	200.00
1880H	2.50	11.00
1881H	2.75	12.00
1882H	3.50	15.00
1883H	7.50	38.00
1884	45.00	140.00
1885	3.50	18.00
1886	3.00	13.50
1887	10.00	32.00
1888	2.50	11.00
1889	11.50	40.00
1890H	3.00	15.00
1891	2.00	8.00
1892	3.00	12.00
1893	2.00	8.00
1894	7.00	30.00
1896	2.50	9.00
1897	2.50	9.00
1898	5.00	30.00
1899	1.25	6.00
1900 Oval 0's	2.00	7.00
1900 Round 0's	8.00	35.00
1901	1.25	6.50

EDWARD VII

1902	1.25	3.00
1902H Broad H	1.50	4.00
1902H Narrow H	5.00	19.00
1903	3.00	11.00
1903H	1.25	5.00
1904	1.25	5.50
1905	1.25	5.00
1906	1.25	3.00
1907	1.25	3.00
1908	3.00	10.00
1909	1.25	5.00
1910	1.00	3.00

GEORGE V

	F	EF
1911	2.50	7.50
1912	1.75	5.00
1913	1.75	5.00
1914	1.75	5.50
1915	9.00	38.50
1916	3.25	13.50
1917	1.25	4.00
1918	1.25	4.00
1919	1.25	3.00
1920	1.25	3.00
1921	1,200.00	4,000.00

NICKEL FIVE CENTS / GEORGE V

1922	.50	5.50
1923	1.00	7.50
1924	.50	5.50
1925	32.00	130.00
1926 near 6	4.50	40.00
1926 far 6	85.00	300.00
1927	.50	4.50
1928	.50	4.50
1929	.50	4.50

	F	EF
1930	.50	4.50
1931	.50	4.50
1932	.50	5.50
1933	.75	7.50
1934	.50	4.50
1935	.50	4.50
1936	.50	4.50

GEORGE VI

	EF	BU
1937	2.00	13.00
1938	5.00	70.00
1939	3.00	45.00
1940	1.35	18.00
1941	1.50	20.00
1942 Brass	1.50	5.00
1943 Brass	1.00	5.00
1944 Steel	.50	2.00
1945 Steel	.50	2.00
1946	1.00	11.00
1947	.75	8.00
1947 Dot after date	40.00	250.00
1947 Maple Leaf	.75	8.00
1948	1.50	16.00
1949	.50	4.00
1950	.50	4.00
1951 Steel	.50	2.50

1951 Nickel	.50	2.00
1952 Steel	.50	3.00

ELIZABETH II

1953 Steel, without fold		2.50
1953 Steel, with fold		3.00
1954 Steel		4.00
1955		2.50
1956		2.00
1957		1.35
1958		1.35
1959		.50
1960		.25
1961		.25
1962		.25
1963		.25
1964		.25

1965	.25
1966	.25
1967 Centennial	.25
1968	.25
1969	.25
1970	.65
1971	.25
1972	.25
1973	.25
1974	.25
1975	.25
1976	.25
1977	.25
1978	.25
1979	.25
1980	.25
1981	.25

Cupro-Nickel

1982	.25
1983	.25
1984	.25
1985	.25
1986	.25
1987	.25
1988	.25
1989	.25
1990	.25
1991	.25
1992 125th Anniv	.35
1993	.25
1994	.25
1995	.25
1996	.25

TEN CENTS

History: The early ten cent piece follows the same evolution as the silver five cent piece. It, however, survived beyond World War I in much its original state. The "schooner" placed on its reverse in 1937 is actually the yacht *Bluenose*. The 1967 mackerel reverse commemorates the centennial of confederation. In that year the alloy was reduced, and in the following year all silver was finally removed.

Counterfeit Alert: All 1936 dot coins should be examined with great skepticism.

Hints: The reverses of many early pieces, particularly those of George V will often appear to be a higher grade than the obverse. In most instances the coins are traded at the grade of their obverses. Net silver content, 1920-67 is .060 oz.

VICTORIA

	VG	VF
1858, 8 over 5		Rare
1858	8.00	38.00
1870 Narrow 0	7.50	40.00
1870 Wide 0	10.00	45.00
1871	9.00	45.00
1871H	12.00	60.00
1872H	38.00	170.00
1874H	5.00	25.00
1875H	135.00	465.00
1880H	4.00	20.00
1881H	5.00	28.00
1882H	5.00	25.00
1883H	12.00	70.00
1884	100.00	450.00
1885	10.00	68.00
1886 Small 6	8.00	35.00
1886 Large 6	10.00	45.00
1887	16.00	85.00
1888	4.00	20.00
1889	300.00	1,150.00
1890H	7.50	35.00
1891, 21 leaves	7.50	38.00
1891, 22 leaves	7.50	35.00
1892	6.00	30.00
1893 Flat top 3	9.00	55.00
1893 Round 3	300.00	1,350.00
1894	8.00	40.00
1896	4.00	20.00
1898	4.00	20.00
1899 Small 9's	3.00	20.00
1899 Large 9's	6.00	30.00
1900	1.75	14.00
1901	1.75	14.00

EDWARD VII

1902	2.00	15.00
1902H	1.50	10.00
1903	6.50	40.00
1903H	1.50	12.00
1904	3.00	17.00
1905	2.00	15.00
1906	1.50	10.00
1907	1.50	10.00

	VG	VF
1908	3.50	22.00
1909 Victorian Leaves		
	2.00	14.00
1909 Broad Leaves	3.50	20.00
1910	1.25	7.00

GEORGE V

	F	EF
1911	8.00	40.00
1912	1.75	16.00
1913 Broad Leaves	135.00	600.00
1913 Small Leaves	1.50	14.00
1914	1.50	13.00
1915	8.00	75.00
1916	1.50	8.00
1917	1.00	6.00
1918	1.00	6.00
1919	1.00	6.00
1920	1.00	6.00
1921	1.50	9.50
1928	1.50	8.00
1929	1.50	7.00
1930	2.00	11.00
1931	1.50	8.00
1932	2.00	13.50
1933	3.00	21.00
1934	5.00	45.00
1935	5.00	50.00
1936	1.00	6.00
1936 Dot		*only 4 known*

GEORGE VI

	EF	BU
1937	3.00	15.00
1938	4.00	45.00
1939	5.00	45.00
1940	3.00	17.00
1941	5.00	45.00
1942	2.25	32.00
1943	3.00	15.00
1944	4.00	27.00
1945	3.00	16.00
1946	3.50	28.00
1947	5.00	36.00
1947 Maple Leaf	3.00	13.00
1948	17.00	50.00
1949	1.50	9.00
1950	1.50	8.00
1951	1.50	7.00
1952	1.50	7.00

ELIZABETH II

1953 without fold	1.00	3.00
1953 with fold	1.00	4.00
1954	1.00	6.50
1955	.50	3.00
1956	.50	3.00
1956 Dot below date	4.50	15.00
1957		1.50
1958		1.50
1959		1.00
1960		.75
1961		.75
1962		.65
1963		.65
1964		.65

1965	.50
1966	.50
1967 Centennial	.65
1968	.50
Nickel	
1968	.25
1969	.25
1970	.65
1971	.25
1972	.25
1973	.25
1974	.25
1975	.25
1976	.25
1977	.25
1978	.25
1979	.25
1980	.25
1981	.25
1982	.25
1983	.25
1984	.25
1985	.25
1986	.25
1987	.25
1988	.25
1989	.25
1990	.25
1991	.25
1992 125th Anniv.	.35
1993	.25
1994	.25
1995	.25
1996	.25

TWENTY CENTS

History: In 1858, under British sovereignty, Canada struck a twenty cent coin. As United States quarters frequently circulated in Canada, this coin caused some confusion, and was withdrawn by proclamation in 1870, the same year a Canadian twenty-five cent piece was introduced.

Counterfeit Alert: Not widely counterfeited.

Hints: This is one of the most readily salable Canadian type coins. If you find one that pleases you at a fair price buy it. It won't be in your dealer's case next month.

	VG	VF
1858	45.00	100.00

TWENTY-FIVE CENTS

History: This coin was issued to replace the somewhat confusing twenty cent piece in 1870. It carried the mature portrait of Victoria, unlike the young head on the former coin. All changes in the twenty-five cent piece parallel those of the ten cent piece up to 1992. In that year an immensely popular series of twelve different reverses was struck to commemorate the sesquicentennial of Canadian independence. Each piece depicted a beautifully executed scene illustrative of a different province or territory.

Counterfeit Alert: 1936 dot specimens should be examined with great scrutiny.

Hints: Victorian and Edwardian pieces are disproportionately scarce in middle grades. Net silver content, 1920-67 is .150 oz.

VICTORIA

	VG	VF
1870	7.00	38.00
1871	10.00	50.00

	VG	VF
1871H	12.00	65.00
1872H	4.00	22.00
1874H	4.00	22.00
1875H	165.00	950.00
1880H Narrow 0	22.00	145.00
1880H Wide 0	55.00	275.00
1880H Wide over narrow 0	60.00	300.00
1881H	7.00	50.00
1882H	8.50	60.00
1883H	7.00	38.00
1885	60.00	300.00
1886, 6 over 3	9.00	60.00
1886	6.50	55.00
1887	55.00	300.00
1888	6.50	40.00
1889	70.00	325.00
1890H	10.00	60.00
1891	35.00	170.00
1892	6.00	35.00
1893	45.00	225.00
1894	9.00	60.00
1899	4.00	20.00
1900	2.50	20.00
1901	2.50	20.00

EDWARD VII

1902	4.00	28.00
1902H	3.00	20.00
1903	3.50	27.00
1904	6.00	60.00
1905	3.00	35.00
1906 Small crown		Rare
1906 Large crown	3.00	20.00
1907	2.50	20.00
1908	4.00	30.00
1909	3.00	24.00
1910	2.00	17.00

GEORGE V

	F	EF
1911	13.00	70.00
1912	3.00	25.00
1913	3.00	25.00
1914	4.00	30.00
1915	22.50	275.00
1916	3.00	20.00
1917	2.50	16.00
1918	2.50	16.00
1919	2.50	16.00
1920	2.50	20.00
1921	16.00	140.00
1927	30.00	175.00
1928	2.50	20.00
1929	2.50	20.00
1930	3.00	25.00
1931	3.00	25.00
1932	3.00	28.00
1933	3.50	35.00
1934	5.00	50.00
1935	5.00	36.00
1936	2.00	18.00
1936 Dot	65.00	300.00

GEORGE VI

	EF	BU
1937	4.00	20.00
1938	5.00	80.00
1939	5.00	65.00
1940	2.75	15.00
1941	2.75	20.00
1942	2.75	20.00
1943	2.75	20.00
1944	3.00	35.00
1945	2.75	15.00
1946	5.00	50.00
1947	6.00	60.00
1947 Dot after date	100.00	350.00
1947 Maple Leaf	3.50	22.50
1948	4.50	65.00
1949	1.50	12.00
1950	1.50	10.00
1951	1.50	8.00
1952	1.50	8.00

ELIZABETH II

	EF	BU
1953 without fold	1.25	5.00
1953 with fold	1.25	8.00
1954	4.00	25.00
1955		4.00
1956		3.00
1957		2.00
1958		2.00
1959		1.75
1960		1.50
1961		1.50
1962		1.25
1963		1.25
1964		1.25

1965	1.00
1966	1.00
1967 Centennial	1.00
1968	1.00

Nickel

1968	.50
1969	.50
1970	1.00
1971	.50
1972	.50
1973 Mountie	.50
1974	.50
1975	.50
1976	.50
1977	.50
1978	.50
1979	.50
1980	.50
1981	.50
1982	.50
1983	.50
1984	.50
1985	.50
1986	.50
1987	.50
1988	.50
1989	.50
1990	.50
1991	1.75
1992 125th Anniv.	1.00
1992 Alberta	.75
1992 Alberta Silver Proof	9.00
1992 Br. Columbia	.75
1992 Br. Columbia Silver Proof	9.00
1992 Manitoba	.75
1992 Manitoba Silver Proof	9.00
1992 New Brunswick	.75
1992 New Brunswick Silver Proof	9.00
1992 Newfoundland	.75
1992 Newfoundland Silver Proof	9.00
1992 North West Terr.	.75
1992 North West Terr. Silver Proof	9.00
1992 Nova Scotia	.75
1992 Nova Scotia Silver Proof	9.00
1992 Ontario	.75

	EF	BU
1992 Ontario *Silver Proof*		9.00
1992 Prince Edward Is.		.75
1992 Prince Edw. Is. *Silver Proof*		9.00
1992 Quebec		.75
1992 Quebec *Silver Proof*		9.00
1992 Saskatchewan		.75
1992 Saskatchewan *Silver Proof*		9.00
1992 Yukon		.75
1992 Yukon *Silver Proof*		9.00
1993		.50
1994		.50
1995		.50
1996		.50

FIFTY CENTS

History: Canadian fifty cent pieces begin in 1870, with the introduction of the twenty-five cent piece, and their evolutions share a similar path. Mintages were generally lower for the larger coin, however. Most 1921 pieces were remelted by the mint before they could be released. As a result it is now a great rarity, and is considered by some to be the "king of Canadian coins."

Counterfeit Alert: All 1921 pieces should be examined with great scrutiny.

Hints: Victorian and Edwardian pieces are disproportionately scarce in middle grades. Net silver content 1920-67 is .300 oz.

	VG	VF
VICTORIA		
1870	400.00	1,800.00
1870 LCW	30.00	110.00
1871	35.00	200.00
1871H	55.00	265.00
1872H	30.00	135.00
1872H inverted A over V		
	65.00	325.00
1881H	30.00	100.00
1888	70.00	250.00
1890H	550.00	2,000.00
1892	30.00	125.00
1894	165.00	900.00
1898	30.00	125.00
1899	65.00	335.00
1900	18.00	125.00
1901	24.00	125.00

EDWARD VII		
1902	6.50	70.00
1903H	14.00	100.00
1904	60.00	250.00
1905	75.00	375.00
1906	6.50	60.00
1907	6.50	60.00
1908	18.00	120.00
1909	9.50	85.00
1910 Victorian Leaves	6.00	50.00
1910 Edwardian Leaves		
	6.00	50.00

	F	EF
GEORGE V		
1911	50.00	450.00
1912	15.00	150.00
1913	15.00	150.00
1914	35.00	375.00
1916	13.00	110.00
1917	13.00	85.00
1918	7.00	70.00
1919	6.50	65.00
1920	10.00	120.00
1921	12,500.00	22,000.00
1929	10.00	100.00
1931	20.00	160.00
1932	75.00	425.00
1934	22.50	160.00
1936	20.00	160.00

	EF	BU
GEORGE VI		
1937	8.00	35.00

1938	30.00	150.00
1939	16.00	125.00
1940	4.50	30.00
1941	4.50	30.00
1942	4.50	30.00
1943	4.50	30.00
1944	4.50	30.00
1945	4.50	30.00
1946	6.00	75.00
1946 Hoof in 6	85.00	850.00
1947 Straight 7	11.50	100.00
1947 Curved 7	11.50	100.00
1947 Straight 7, Maple Leaf		
	45.00	165.00
1947 Curved 7, Maple Leaf		
	1,800.00	3,500.00
1948	80.00	200.00
1949	7.50	45.00
1949 Hoof over 9	50.00	400.00
1950	17.50	200.00
1950 Lines in 0	3.00	15.00
1951	3.00	12.50
1952	3.00	12.50

ELIZABETH II		
1953 Small date, without fold		
	2.50	9.00
1953 Large date, without fold		
	8.00	75.00
1953 Large date, with fold		
	2.50	25.00
1954	5.00	25.00
1955	3.00	15.00
1956	2.50	6.00
1957		3.50
1958		3.00
1959		3.00
1960		2.50
1961		2.50
1962		2.50
1963		2.50
1964		2.50

1965		2.25
1966		2.25

	EF	BU
1967 Centennial		2.75
Nickel		
1968		.75
1969		.75
1970		.75
1971		.75
1972		.75
1973		.75
1974		.75
1975		.75
1976		.75
1977		1.35
1978		.75
1979		.75
1980		.75
1981		.75
1982		.75
1983		.75
1984		.75
1985		.75
1986		.75
1987		.75
1988		.75
1989		.75
1990		.75
1991		.75
1992 125th Anniv.		1.00
1993		.75
1994		.75
1995		.75
1996		.75

SILVER DOLLARS

History: As mentioned above, the famous Voyageur Scene, an early Hudson's Bay Co. agent and a Canadian Indian paddling their canoe past a wooded islet, was introduced with the creation of the Canadian silver dollar for King George V's jubilee in 1935. It was the only reverse design considered suitable to retain when the coinage was redesigned for the accession of George VI.

From its inception, the silver dollar was the natural choice for circulating commemorative coins, special reverses being used at frequent intervals. When the circulating dollar became a smaller, pure nickel coin it was not long before a parallel series of large, old style, silver dollars appeared for collectors. The circulating dollar was further reduced in 1987 when it was switched to an alloy called "aureate nickel" having the appearance of brass.

Due to the embarrasing loss of the master dies for the new small, brass-colored dollar, it was introduced with a loon replacing the popular voyageur reverse. The dies were later recovered but the loon was retained. Today there are two dollar coins released every year, a silver one for collectors, and a base one for circulation.

Counterfeit Alert: All 1948 dollars should be carefully examined.

Hints: The net silver content of standard dollars, 1935-1967 is .600 oz. The special series of collector silver dollars is generally bought and sold in the original case of issue. Many consider loose examples less desirable and thus discount them. Since 1981 they have been available in both proof and uncirculated strikings. The more valuable proof versions are listed here.

GEORGE V

	VF	EF
1935 Jubilee	22.50	32.50
1936	12.00	18.00

GEORGE VI

	EF	Unc.
1937	13.00	35.00
1938	38.00	80.00

1939 Visit	9.00	20.00
1945	120.00	225.00
1946	28.00	35.00
1947 Pointed 7	110.00	300.00
1947 Blunt 7	60.00	100.00
1947 Maple Leaf	165.00	275.00
1948	665.00	900.00
1949 Newfoundland	20.00	38.00
1950, 4 water lines	7.00	15.00
1950, Arnprior	12.00	40.00
1951, 4 water lines	7.00	12.00
1951, Arnprior	32.00	100.00
1952, 4 water lines	7.00	12.00
1952, Arnprior	60.00	150.00
1952, No water lines	3.00	12.50

ELIZABETH II

1953 Wire rim, without fold		
	5.00	7.00
1953 Flat rim, with fold		
	5.00	7.00
1954	6.00	12.00
1955, 4 water line	5.50	12.00
1955, Arnprior	70.00	100.00
1956	9.00	15.00
1957, 4 water lines		6.00
1957, Arnprior		9.00

1958 British Columbia		7.00
1959		5.50
1960		5.50

	EF	Unc.
1961		5.50
1962		5.50
1963		5.00
1964 Charlottetown		5.50

1965 (many varieties)		4.75
1966		4.75
1967 Centennial		5.00

	Nickel BU	Silver PL or PF
1968	1.50	
1969	1.50	

1970 Manitoba	2.00	
1971 British Columbia		
	2.00	12.00
1972		2.00

1973 Pr. Edward Is.	2.00	
1973 Mountie		11.00

1974 Winnipeg	2.50	10.00
1975	2.00	
1975 Calgary		8.50
1976	2.00	

1976 Library of Parliament		15.00
1977	2.00	
1977 Jubilee		11.00
1978	2.00	

1978 Games		11.00
1979	2.00	
1979 Ship		23.00
1980	2.00	

1980 Polar Bear		40.00
1981	2.00	
1981 Railroad		30.00

1982 Constitution	2.00	
1982 Regina		8.50
1983	2.00	

1983 Edmonton		12.00
1984	2.00	
1984 Cartier	2.00	

1984 Toronto		10.00
1985	2.00	
1985 National Parks		10.00
1986	2.00	

1986 Vancouver		12.00
1987	2.00	
1987 Davis Ship		20.00

	Brass* BU	Silver PF
1987 Loon	2.00	
1988 Loon	2.00	
1988 Ironworks		45.00
1989 Loon	2.00	
*plated on nickel core		

	BU	PF
1989 MacKenzie River		45.00
1990 Loon	2.00	
1990 Kelsey		23.00
1991 Loon	2.00	

1991 S.S. Frontenac		22.00
1992 125th Anniv. Loon		
	2.00	

1992 125th Anniv. Children, *Nickel*

	2.00	
1992 Stagecoach		21.00
1993 Loon	2.00	

1993 Stanley Cup		21.00
1994 Loon	2.00	
1994 War Memorial	2.00	
1994 RCMP Dog Sled		21.00
1995 Loon	2.00	
1995 Peacekeeping Monument		
	2.00	
1995 Hudson's Bay Co.		21.00

BI-METALLIC TWO DOLLARS

History: This coin follows two worldwide trends. The first is the move to replace low-denominations bills with high value coins. The other is the popular introduction of coins composed of an outer ring of one metal around an inner disc of a different colored metal.

Counterfeit Alert: None known.

Hints: Despite initial reports of these coins falling apart, it is unlikely that there is any consistent pattern of this. It is also doubtful that there will be any lasting premium to the two seperated parts.

	BU	PF
1996 base metal	3.00	20.00
1996 gold alloy		250.00

GOLD FIVE DOLLARS

History: Despite the striking of gold sovereigns within months after the opening of the Royal Canadian Mint, it was four years before these coins bearing Canadian denominations were finally issued. The coat of arms on the reverse is not the current one, as depicted on the current fifty cent piece, but rather the original one, indicating the four original provinces of Ontario, Quebec, Nova Scotia, and New Brunswick.

Counterfeit Alert: Reasonable care should be exercised in examining this type coin.

Hints: Be aware of possible rim dings or cleaning; the latter may be particularly hard to detect. Net gold content .2419 oz.

	VF	EF
1912	135.00	165.00
1913	135.00	165.00
1914	275.00	375.00

SILVER OLYMPIC FIVE DOLLARS

History: These coins were originally sold by subscription in order to raise funds for the 1976 Montreal Olympics. They proved so popular with the non-collecting public that when the massive quantity of sets sold reached the secondary (collector) market they practically outnumbered collectors and thousands of sets were privately melted without remorse.

Counterfeit Alert: None known.

Hints: With the drop in the price of silver many have attempted to spend these coins in recent years, only to find out that their legal tender status has been limited or restricted to some extent. Net silver content .7227 oz.

	BU	PF
1973 Sailboats	5.00	7.00
1973 Map	5.00	7.00
1974 Olympic Symbol		
	5.00	7.00
1974 Ancient Athlete	5.00	7.00
1974 Rower	5.00	7.00
1974 Canoer	5.00	7.00
1975 Runner	5.00	7.00
1975 Javelin Thrower	5.00	7.00
1975 Swimmer	5.00	7.00
1975 Diver	5.00	7.00
1976 Fencers	5.00	8.00
1976 Boxers	5.00	8.00
1976 Village	5.00	8.00
1976 Flame	5.00	8.00

GOLD TEN DOLLARS

History: Despite the striking of gold sovereigns within months after the opening of the Royal Canadian Mint, it was four years before these coins bearing Canadian denominations were finally issued. The coat of arms on the reverse is not the current one, as depicted on the current fifty cent piece, but rather the original one, indicating the four original provinces of Ontario, Quebec, Nova Scotia, and New Brunswick.

Counterfeit Alert: Reasonable care should be exercised in examining this type coin.

Hints: Be aware of possible rim dings or cleaning. The latter may be particularly hard to detect. Net gold content: .4838 oz.

	VF	EF
1912	300.00	375.00
1913	300.00	375.00
1914	310.00	425.00

SILVER OLYMPIC TEN DOLLARS

History: These coins were originally sold by subscription in order to raise funds for the 1976 Montreal Olympics. They proved so popular with the non-collecting public that when the massive quantity of sets sold reached the secondary (collector) market they practically outnumbered collectors and thousands of sets were privately melted without remorse.

Counterfeit Alert: None known.

Hints: With the drop in the price of silver many have attempted to spend these coins in recent years, only to find out that their legal tender status has been limited or restricted to some extent. Net silver content: 1.4454 oz.

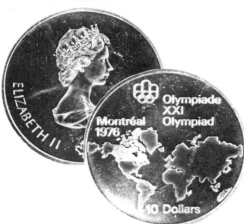

	BU	PF
1973 Montreal	9.50	12.00
1973 Map	9.50	12.00
1974 Map (error)	300.00	
1974 Zeus	9.50	12.00
1974 Ancient Temple	9.50	12.00

1974 Bicycles	9.50	12.00
1974 Lacrosse	9.50	12.00
1975 Indian Head	9.50	12.00
1975 Hand of Shot Putter		
	9.50	12.00
1975 Sailing	9.50	12.00
1975 Paddling river	9.50	12.00
1976 Soccer	9.50	16.00
1976 Field Hockey	9.50	15.00
1976 Round Stadium	9.50	16.00
1976 Velodrome	9.50	16.00

SILVER OLYMPIC FIFTEEN DOLLARS

History: This odd denomination was struck as an Olympic fund raiser.

Counterfeit Alert: None known.

Hints: Legal tender status may be limited. Net silver content: one ounce.

	PF only
1992 Coaching	40.00
1992 3 Athletes	40.00

GOLD TWENTY DOLLARS

History: This coin was struck to commemorate the centennial of Canadian independence. Many of them were sold in sets along with the popular animal coins of smaller denomination.

Counterfeit Alert: High quality counterfeits have been identified.

Hints: Look for possible finger prints or handling marks.

	PF only
1967	225.00

SILVER OLYMPIC TWENTY DOLLARS

History: These were struck to raise funds for the 1988 Calgary Winter Olympics.

Counterfeit Alert: None known.

Hints: Some of these were struck with a plain edge instead of a lettered edge. These are scarce and retail for over $300 each. Legal tender status may be limited.

	PF only
1985 Skier	25.00
1985 Skater	25.00
1986 Biathlon	25.00
1986 Hockey	25.00
1986 Skier	25.00
1986 Ski Jumper	25.00
1987 Figure Skaters	25.00
1987 Curler	25.00
1987 Ski Jumper	25.00
1987 Bobsledders	25.00

SILVER AVIATION TWENTY DOLLARS

History: These coins were struck to honor Canadian pioneers in aviation. Unusual among world coinage, some of these coins have gold surfaced details.

Counterfeit Alert: None known.

Hints: Legal tender status may be limited.

	PF only
1990 Bomber	50.00
1990 Two Airplanes	50.00
1991 Biplane	50.00
1991 Pontoon Plane	50.00
1992 Curtis Jenny	50.00

	PF only
1992 de Haviland Gypsy Moth	50.00
1993 Pontoon Plane	50.00
1993 Lockheed 14 Super Electra	50.00
1994 Curtiss HS-2L & Trees	55.00
1994 Canadian Vickers Vedette	55.00

PLATINUM THIRTY DOLLARS

History: Each year a different animal is featured in four different views, one on each denomination. Issued only in sets of four denominations.

Counterfeit Alert: None known.

Hints: Mintages of these are notably small.

	PF only
1990 Polar Bear Head	75.00
1991 Owl	90.00
1992 Cougar Head	90.00
1993 Fox Head	95.00
1994 Otter Head	95.00
1995 Lynx Head	90.00

PLATINUM 75 DOLLARS

History: See $30 above.

Counterfeit Alert: None known.

Hints: Mintages are notably small.

	PF only
1990 Polar Bear Swimming	220.00
1991 Owls	235.00
1992 Cougar	235.00
1993 Foxes	235.00
1994 Otter	235.00
1995 Lynx kittens	230.00

GOLD 100 DOLLARS

History: These coins carry a different commemorative theme each year. They are struck in proof. Only one coin in the series, the first, was struck with an uncirculated finish also. They contain one quarter ounce of pure gold, except for the proof versions 1976-86.

Counterfeit Alert: Not actively counterfeited.

Hints: These coins are generally collected in their original case or card of issue. Loose examples of the most common types may often be treated as bullion.

	BU	PF
1976 Olympic	110.00	210.00
1977 Jubilee		225.00

1978 Geese (Unity)	210.00
1979 Year of the Child	210.00

1980 Arctic	225.00
1981 National Anthem	225.00

1982 Constitution	225.00
1983 St. John's	225.00

1984 Jacques Cartier	225.00
1985 National Parks	235.00

1986 Peace	225.00
1987 Calgary Olympics	130.00

1988 Whales	200.00
1989 Sainte-Marie	135.00

1990 Literacy	150.00
1991 Ship	200.00

1992 Montreal	200.00
1993 Antique Car	200.00

1994 Home Front	210.00
1995 Louisbourg	210.00

PLATINUM 150 DOLLARS

History: See $30 above.

Counterfeit Alert: None known.

Hints: Mintages are notably small.

	PF only
1990 Polar Bear	375.00
1991 Owl Flying	400.00
1992 Cougars	425.00
1993 Arctic Fox	425.00
1994 Two Otters	435.00
1995 Lynx	435.00

GOLD OLYMPIC 175 DOLLARS

History: See $15 above.
Counterfeit Alert: None known.
Hints: Contains a net gold content of one half ounce.

	PF only
1992	360.00

GOLD 200 DOLLARS

History: These coins carry a different commemorative theme each year. They are struck only in proof. They contain .5042 oz. of pure gold.
Counterfeit Alert: Not actively counterfeited.
Hints: These coins are generally collected in their original case or card of issue. Loose examples of the most common types may often be treated as bullion.

	PF
1990 Flag	275.00
1991 Hockey	300.00

1992 Niagara Falls	325.00

1993 Mounties	325.00

1994 Anne of Green Gables	325.00
1995 Maple Syrup Harvest	325.00

PLATINUM 300 DOLLARS

History: See $30 above.
Counterfeit Alert: None known.
Hints: Mintages are notably small.

	PF only
1990 Polar Bears	750.00
1991 Owl Family	800.00
1992 Cougar in Tree	800.00
1993 Fox Family	800.00
1994 Otter Family	825.00
1995 Lynx Family	850.00

GOLD SOVEREIGNS

History: These sovereigns, bearing the Pistrucci's famous St. George slaying the dragon on their reverse, were of exact British design and standard but with a discrete "C" mintmark. Many of these coins were used to pay British war debts to the United States, thus preventing the risk of shipping gold across the Atlantic during World War I.
Counterfeit Alert: The entire sovereign series has been extensively counterfeited.
Hints: The "C" mintmark which distinguishes this from sovereigns struck elsewhere in the British Empire is found on the ground below the horse's hoof.
Gold Content: .2354 oz.

EDWARD VII	VF	EF
1908C	1,600.00	2,300.00
1909C	235.00	325.00
1910C	165.00	250.00
GEORGE V		
1911C	120.00	130.00
1913C	500.00	750.00
1914C	225.00	325.00
1916C		Rare
1917C	120.00	130.00
1918C	120.00	130.00
1919C	120.00	130.00

SILVER MAPLE LEAF BULLION COINS

History: These coins are not intended to circulate, nor are they intended for the collector market, but rather as a convenient way to hold pure silver. While they bear the face value of $5, most coin dealers avoid refering to them by their denomination and prefer to call them by the net amount of precious metal they contain, one ounce.
Counterfeit Alert: None known.
Hints: To provide detailed listings for these pieces would be beyond the scope of this book. No year to date commands a significant premium.

	BU	PF
1988 to date	7.00	
1989 only		45.00

GOLD MAPLE LEAF BULLION COINS

History: These coins are not intended to circulate, nor are they intended for the collector market, but rather as a convenient way to hold pure, unalloyed gold. While they all bear denominations most coin dealers avoid refering to them by their denomination and prefer to call them by the net amount of precious metal they contain. The $50 contains 1 oz. of gold, $20 half an ounce, $10 a quarter ounce, $5 one tenth ounce.

Counterfeit Alert: Less frequently counterfeited than many other popular bullion coins.

Hints: To provide detailed listings for these pieces would be beyond the scope of this book. No year to date commands a significant premium. Retail values here are given as a percentage above gold spot price a coin dealer would charge when selling a single coin. Prices for quantities are often less.

		BU	PF
1/20 oz. ($1) 1993-	25%		
1/15 oz. ($2) 1994-	22%		
1/10 oz. ($5) 1982—	20%		
1/10 oz. ($5) 1989 only			75.00
1/4 oz. ($10) 1982—	13%		
1/4 oz. ($10) 1989 only			200.00
1/2 oz. ($20) 1986—	9%		
1/2 oz. ($20) 1989 only			350.00
1 oz. ($50) 1979—	7%		
1 oz. ($50) 1989 only			650.00

PLATINUM MAPLE LEAF BULLION COINS

History: These coins are not intended to circulate, nor are they intended for the collector market, but rather as a convenient way to hold pure, unalloyed platinum. While they all bear denominations most coin dealers avoid refering to them by their denomination and prefer to call them by the net amount of precious metal they contain. The $50 contains 1 oz. of gold, $20 half an ounce, $10 a quarter ounce, $5 one tenth ounce.

Counterfeit Alert: Not generally counterfeited.

Hints: To provide detailed listings for these pieces would be beyond the scope of this book. No year to date commands a significant premium. Retail values here are given as a percentage above platinum spot price a coin dealer would charge when selling a single coin. Prices for quantities are often less.

		BU	PF
1/20 oz. ($1) 1993-	25%		
1/15 oz. ($2) 1994-	22%		
1/10 oz. ($5) 1988—	18%		
1/10 oz. ($5) 1989 only			100.00
1/4 oz. ($10) 1988—	13%		
1/4 oz. ($10) 1989 only			275.00
1/2 oz. ($20) 1988—	9%		
1/2 oz. ($20) 1989 only			500.00
1 oz. ($50) 1988—	7%		
1 oz. ($50) 1989 only			875.00

CANADIAN PROVINCIAL COINAGE

History: Before confederation in 1867 Canada was composed of several separate colonies, many of which had their own coinage. These issues varied from private tokens, to semi-official, to official. Early coins were struck on a British sterling standard (i.e. pennies, half pennies), later issues, including all silver, were decimal (i.e. cents). The very last provincial coins were struck for Newfoundland in 1947. That colony joined the Canadian Confederation in 1949.

Reference: Charlton, J.E., *The Charlton Standard Catalogue of Canadian Colonial Tokens.*

Counterfeit Alert: Contemporary counterfeits of George IV Nova Scotia half pennies are common and worth about the same as authentic ones.

Hints: Types and varieties of provincial tokens number in the hundreds. The listings below are only intended to be a representative sample. Even the crudest examples may be rare and valuable. For more information consult the above work by Charlton. Newfoundland fifty cent pieces are more common today than their contemporary Canadian counterparts.

LOWER CANADA

UN SOU / HALF PENNY
BANK TOKEN

	VG	VF
Montreal	1.50	5.00
Bank of Montreal	1.50	5.00
Banque du Peuple	2.50	12.00

	VG	VF
1837 City Bank	1.50	4.00
1837 Bank of Montreal		
	1.50	5.00
1837 Banque du Peuple		
	2.50	6.00
1837 Quebec Bank	1.50	4.00
1838 Bank of Montreal		
	75.00	250.00
1839 Bank of Montreal		
	75.00	250.00
1842 Bank of Montreal		
	1.50	3.00
1844 Bank of Montreal		
	1.50	3.00
1845 Bank of Montreal		*Rare*
1852 Quebec Bank	1.75	4.00

DEUX SOU / ONE PENNY
BANK TOKEN

	VG	VF
1837 City Bank	1.50	6.00
1837 Bank of Montreal		
	1.50	5.00
1837 Banque du Peuple		
	2.00	7.00
1837 Quebec Bank	1.50	6.00
1838 Bank of Montreal		
	150.00	500.00
1839 Bank of Montreal		
	150.00	500.00
1839 Banque du Peuple		*Rare*
1842 Bank of Montreal		
	1.50	5.00
1852 Quebec Bank	2.00	8.00

NEW BRUNSWICK

HALF PENNY

	VG	VF
1843	2.00	10.00
1854	2.00	10.00

PENNY

1843	2.50	12.00
1854	2.25	12.00

HALF CENT

1861	37.50	85.00

CENT

1861	1.25	3.50
1864	1.25	3.50

FIVE CENTS

1862	17.50	85.00
1864	17.50	85.00

TEN CENTS

1862	13.50	85.00
1864	13.50	85.00

TWENTY CENTS

1862	9.50	32.50
1864	9.50	32.50

NEWFOUNDLAND

LARGE CENTS / VICTORIA

	VG	VF
1865	1.25	4.00
1872H	1.25	4.00
1873	1.25	4.00
1876H	1.25	4.00
1880 Round 0	1.25	4.00
1880 Oval 0	35.00	85.00
1885	10.00	25.00
1888	9.00	20.00
1890	1.25	3.50
1894	1.25	3.50
1896	1.25	3.50

LARGE CENTS / EDWARD VII

1904H	3.00	12.00
1907	1.00	3.00
1909	1.00	3.00

LARGE CENTS / GEORGE V

1913	.50	2.00
1917C	.50	2.00
1919C	.50	2.00
1920C	.50	2.00
1929	.50	2.00
1936	.50	1.75

SMALL CENTS / GEORGE VI

	VF	EF
1938	.75	1.75
1940	1.50	4.50
1941C	.50	1.00
1942	.50	1.00
1943C	.50	1.00
1944C	1.25	3.00
1947C	.75	2.00

SILVER FIVE CENTS / VICTORIA

	VG	VF
1865	15.00	55.00
1870	25.00	80.00
1872H	17.00	50.00
1873	25.00	80.00
1873H	675.00	1,750.00
1876H	60.00	165.00
1880	18.00	65.00
1881	12.00	42.00
1882H	8.00	35.00
1885	60.00	185.00
1888	15.00	45.00
1890	5.00	25.00
1894	5.00	25.00
1896	2.50	15.00

SILVER FIVE CENTS / EDWARD VII

1903	1.75	16.00
1904H	1.50	12.00
1908	1.50	11.00

SILVER FIVE CENTS / GEORGE V

1912	.75	4.00
1917C	.75	3.50
1919C	1.50	8.00
1929	.75	3.00

SILVER FIVE CENTS / GEORGE VI

	VF	EF
1938	1.50	3.00
1940C	1.50	3.00
1941C	1.25	2.00
1942C	2.00	3.00
1943C	1.25	2.00
1944C	2.00	3.00
1945C	1.25	2.00
1946C	285.00	385.00
1947C	5.00	13.00

SILVER TEN CENTS / VICTORIA

	VG	VF
1865	9.00	50.00
1870	90.00	300.00
1872H	9.00	45.00
1873	12.00	60.00
1876H	20.00	75.00
1880, 80 over 70	21.00	77.50
1882H	9.00	50.00
1885	40.00	200.00
1888	10.00	50.00
1890	3.50	20.00
1894	3.50	20.00
1896	2.50	18.00

SILVER TEN CENTS / EDWARD VII

| 1903 | 3.00 | 25.00 |
| 1904H | 2.25 | 20.00 |

SILVER TEN CENTS / GEORGE V

1912	1.50	10.00
1917C	1.50	6.00
1919C	2.00	11.00

SILVER TEN CENTS / GEORGE VI

	VF	EF
1938	2.50	6.50
1940	2.00	5.00
1941C	1.75	4.00
1942C	1.75	4.00
1943C	2.00	4.00
1944C	2.00	4.50
1945C	2.00	4.00
1946C	9.00	17.50
1947C	4.50	11.00

SILVER TWENTY CENTS / VICTORIA

	VG	VF
1865	7.00	35.00
1870	10.00	60.00
1872H	7.00	30.00
1873	9.00	40.00
1876H	9.00	40.00
1880, 80 over 70	12.50	60.00
1881	3.50	25.00
1882H	1.50	25.00
1885	5.50	30.00
1888	4.00	27.50
1890	2.50	20.00
1894	2.50	20.00
1896	2.50	17.00
1899	2.00	16.00
1900	2.00	15.00

SILVER TWENTY CENTS / EDWARD VII

| 1904H | 6.50 | 47.50 |

SILVER TWENTY CENTS / GEORGE V

| 1912 | 1.75 | 10.00 |

SILVER TWENTY-FIVE CENTS / GEORGE V

| 1917C | 1.50 | 4.00 |
| 1919C | 1.50 | 4.50 |

SILVER FIFTY CENTS / VICTORIA

	VG	VF
1870	7.00	35.00
1872H	7.00	35.00
1873	15.00	70.00
1874	7.00	50.00
1876H	16.00	75.00
1880	18.00	75.00
1881	7.00	45.00
1882H	5.00	30.00
1885	7.00	45.00
1888	9.00	60.00
1894	4.50	30.00
1896	4.00	24.00
1898	3.75	24.00
1899	3.00	22.00
1900	3.00	22.00

SILVER FIFTY CENTS / EDWARD VII

	VG	VF
1904H	2.50	16.50
1907	3.00	18.00
1908	2.50	13.50
1909	2.50	13.50

SILVER FIFTY CENTS / GEORGE V

1911	2.50	9.00
1917C	2.50	7.00
1918C	2.50	7.00

	VG	VF
1919C	2.50	7.00

GOLD TWO DOLLARS / VICTORIA

	F	EF
1865	160.00	325.00
1870	160.00	325.00
1872	200.00	425.00
1880	900.00	1,750.00
1881	120.00	235.00
1882H	110.00	190.00
1885	120.00	235.00
1888	110.00	190.00

NOVA SCOTIA

HALF PENNY

	VG	VF
1823	2.00	7.50
1824	2.00	12.00
1832	2.00	7.50
1382 (error)	135.00	500.00
1840	1.50	6.50
1843	2.00	8.00
1856	2.00	7.50

PENNY

	VG	VF
1824	2.50	12.00
1832	2.00	9.00
1840	2.00	7.50
1843, 3 over 0	9.00	20.00
1843	2.00	10.00
1856 No LCW	2.00	8.50
1856 with LCW	2.00	7.50

HALF CENT

	VG	VF
1861	1.75	6.00
1864	1.75	6.00

CENT

	VG	VF
1861	1.25	4.00
1862	15.00	35.00
1864	1.25	4.00

PRINCE EDWARD ISLAND

TOKEN

Ships, Colonies & Commerce / Ship

	VG	VF
	2.00	7.00

CENT

	VG	VF
1871	1.00	3.50

UPPER CANADA

HALF PENNY BANK TOKEN

	VG	VF
1850	1.00	2.50
1852	1.00	2.50
1854	1.00	2.50
1854 Crosslet 4	10.00	30.00
1857	1.00	2.25

ONE PENNY BANK TOKEN

	VG	VF
1850	1.50	3.50
1850 Dot between cornucopias		
	2.50	9.50
1852	1.50	3.50
1854	1.50	3.50
1854 Crosslet 4	4.00	12.50
1857	1.50	3.50

ANCIENT COINS

To the general public, ancient coins are often considered something only to be viewed in museums. They are, however, available to everyone and can be found at all price levels. They can be purchased for under $5 or for over $100,000: it's your choice.

Unlike high-grade modern coins, ancients may be held in your hands. Imagine the stories the coin could tell of its circulation and the people who used it. Ted Wear wrote, "That day when I first actually held a coin that was about two thousand years old, was a time I'll never forget. In my hand was a piece of money that might have bought a loaf of bread in ancient Rome, or helped make up the purchase price of a slave, or possibly had been used to bribe some Praetorian Guard."

There are many fine books to guide the new collector into ancients; one should not feel intimidated. Modern coins still use some Latin inscriptions; one does not need to be a scholar to decipher these inscriptions on Roman coins. With minimal effort one can also learn the Greek letter forms, as alpha and beta for a and b.

But it is the images which we can truly enjoy in ancients. You don't need to know ancient history to appreciate them, but you will soon find yourself picking up bits of knowledge of the past.

ANCIENT GREEK

History: The first coinage was produced in Asia Minor by the Lydians in the mid-7th century, B.C. This electrum (natural gold with silver) coinage was so well-accepted that other Greek colonies throughout the Mediterranean world continued this tradition.

As coinage evolved, electrum was refined and separate coinages of gold and silver developed. Greek coinage developed in three metals: gold, silver, and copper or bronze. The silver coinage began in various western Asia Minor cities in the mid 6th century B.C., while copper or bronze coinage was introduced in the early 5th century B.C.

Each Greek city, or region, had its own coinage and these were identified by the badges, or image they wanted to convey to the world. For example, Larissa, in Thessaly, was known for their export trade in fine horses. Their coinage had the image of the city goddess Larissa on the obverse and the reverse featured horses in various poses.

Today, Greek coins are considered to be among the most beautiful coins ever made. Amazingly enough, these fine art collectibles are still priced within the range of anyone's pocketbook.
References: Sear, David; *Greek Coins and their Values.* Vol. I: Europe, Vol. II: Asia and North Africa; *Catalogue of Greek coins in the British Museum*, 29 Volumes; Head, *Historia Numorum*; *Sylloge Numorum Graecorum (SNG) Danish National Museum*; *SNG American Numismatic Society*; *SNG Sammlung von Aulock*; Klawans, *Handbook of Ancient Greek and Roman Coins* (the best book for beginners).

Silver denominations are divided as follows:

Denomination	Diameter in mm.
Decadrachm = 10 drachms	33-35
Tetradrachm = 4 drachms	24-32
Didrachm = 2 drachms	19-24
Drachm = 6 obols	14-19
Tetrobol = 4 obols	13-15
Triobol (Hemidrachm) = 3 obols	11-13
Diobol = 2 obols	10-11
Trihemiobol = 1 1/2 obols	9-11
Obol	8-10
Tritaremorion = 3/4 obol	6-8
Hemiobol = 1/2 obol	5-9
Trihemitartemorion = 3/8 obol	5-8
Tetratemorion = 1/4 obol	5-7
Hemitartemorion = 1/8 obol	4-5

Gold or electrum was under a less universal standard, but the gold stater started by Philip II of Macedon did set the standard after the mid 4th century B.C.

Little is known as to actual names for copper coinage throughout the Greek world. They were circulated close to home, and each city adhered to its own standards. Today, numismatists simply refer to them by diameter, using the abbreviation AE from the Latin word *aes* for copper. Thus a numismatist would refer to an ancient Greek copper or bronze coin 16mm wide as an AE16.

Gods and Goddesses most often encountered on ancient Greek coins are:
Zeus: Always bearded and wearing a crown of laurel or olive leaves, holding a sceptre, eagle or Nike figure.
Apollo: Most common god on Greek coins. Represented in youthful beauty with flowing hair wreathed in laurel, with a laurel branch, a tripod, or holding a lute.
Helios: Sun god with rays from head.
Poseidon: Similar to Zeus, but holding trident.
Dionysus: Can be youthful or bearded, ivy is usually present, often holds wine cup, grapes, or the Bacchic staff.
Herakles: Usually represented bearded or in a lion headdress, with club, or can be found doing one of his famous labors.
Hera: Goddess who wears a low crown or is often veiled.
Athena: Female head in various helmets. Often depicted with an owl, or fighting with shield and spear.
Artemis: Hair in diadem, usually accompanied by dog or stag, equipped with bow, arrows and quiver.
Demeter, Persepone: Hair wreathed in barley corn, Demeter is veiled.
Nike: Winged goddess holds wreath, palm or trophy. Also known as Victory.

Inscriptions will be found in Greek. Often one or two letters will identify the city or the name will be written out; in later Hellenistic times, the king's name will precede the Greek word ΒΑΣΙΛΕΩΣ, meaning "King."
Counterfeit Alert. All Greek gold is subject to modern counterfeiting, along with fine style tetradrachms. Christodoulos made copies which have all been identified. British Museum electrotypes are sometimes passed off as genuine, but shapes and dies can be identified in *A Guide to Principal Coins of the Greeks*.

ARCHAIC GREEK

History: Archaic Greek coins are all coins struck before 480 B.C. These early coins will usually have a reverse of plain incuse, square or whole design in incuse.
Reference: Kraay, *Archaic and Classical Greek Coins.*

VF

Early Lydia
650-561 B.C. Third Stater (Electrum) Lions head/Punch 1,500.00
Croesus, 560-546 B.C. Stater (Electrum) Forepart of bull, lion facing/Punch 4,000.00
Stater (S) similar 1,200.00

Early Western Asia Minor
Ephesus, 650-625 B.C. Hecte (Electrum) Flat striations / Two punch squares 1,500.00
Smyrna, 600-550 B.C. Stater (Electrum) Lions head l./ Square punch 10,000.00

Later Archaic
Metapontum, Lucania, 5th century B.C., Triobol (S) Barley ear / Incuse bucranium 200.00
Poseidonia, Lucania, 525-500 B.C. Drachm (S) Poseidon advancing / Same incuse 450.00

Sybaris, Lucania, 5230-510 B.C. Stater (S) Bull standing / Same incuse. . 1000.00
Croton, Bruttium, 530-510 B.C. Stater (S) Tripod / Tripod incuse 450.00
Selinus, Sicily, 500 B.C. Didrachm (S) Celery leaf / Square incuse with diagonals 850.00

Syracuse, Sicily, 520-500 B.C. Tetradrachm (S) Slow chariot / Head of Arethusa in mill sail incuse square 3,000.00
Thasos, island off Thrace, 510-490 B.C. Stater (S) Icthyphallic satyr with nymph / Incuse square 1,000.00
Mende, Macedonia, 500 B.C. Tetrobol (S) Icthyphallic ass / Square incuse 300.00
Athens, Attica, 500-482 B.C. Tetradrachm, (S) Head of Athena / Owl in incuse square 2,500.00
Aegina, Island, 525- 475 B.C. Stater (S) Sea turtle / Incuse pattern . . 350.00

Cyzicus, Mysia, 550-475 B.C. Stater (Electrum) Forepart of lion, tunny fish below / Incuse square 3,000.00
Mytilene, Lesbos, 485 B.C. Hecte (Electrum) Medusa / Head of Herakles Incuse 800.00
Phocaea, Ionia, 490 B.C.Hecte (Electrum) Head of Athena / Incuse pattern1000.00
Aspendus, Pamphyla, 5th cent B.C. Stater (S) Hoplite / Triskeles in incuse.700.00

Achaemenid Persia
Xerxes and on, 485-337 B.C. Daric (G) King with bow and spear . . 2,000.00
Artaxerxes I, 465-425 B.C. Siglos (S) King with bow and spear 100.00

CELTIC
History: The Celtic tribes occupied various areas in Europe and issued coins from the third to the first century B.C. They are numismatically divided into three groups: Celtic Gaul, Celtic Britain, and Celtic Central Europe and Asia Minor. They were the barbaric tribes that were at odds with Greece and Rome. Their coinage can be described as stylized copies of the Greek and Roman coins with which the Celtic tribes came in contact. The use of billon, which has a small percentage of silver combined with copper and zinc, gives this a silver look.
References: Forrer, *Keltische Numismatik Der Rhein und Donaulande*; De La Tour *Atlas De Monnaies Gauloieses*; Van Arsdell, *Celtic Coinage of Britain*; Nash, *Coinage of the Celtic World*.
Counterfeit Alert: Beware of gold Gallo-Belgic copies
Hints: This series has gained in popularity in recent years.

VF

Celtic Gaul (France)
(All date from late 2nd - mid 1st century B.C.)
The Volcae Tectosages, (S) 15mm, Stylized head l. / Cross, pellets, crescent and axe 125.00
The Allobroges, (S) 15mm, Stylized head of Roma / Hippocamp 125.00

Eastern and Central Tribes
The Aedui, (S) 15mm, Stylized head of Roma / Horse prancing l. . . . 125.00
The Sequani, (Potin) 17mm, helmeted head r. / Lion springing 50.00
Note: Potin is a base metal of copper and tin.

Western Tribes
The Pictones, (S) 19mm, Stylized female head r. / Horseman r. 150.00

The Redones, Stater (G) Stylized head of Apollo / Stylized rider on horseback 1,100.00

Northern Tribes
The Carnutes, (C) 16mm, Stylized head of Herakles / Stylized horseman 75.00

The Veliocasses, Stater (G) Stylized head, large eye and star / Horse, star 800.00
The Remi, (C) 16mm, Three heads Jugate l. / Chariot l. 75.00
The Leuci, (Potin) 19mm, (cast), Very stylized head / Crude boar l. . . 50.00

Celtic Britain   **VF**
Gallo Belgic "Morini" 65-45 B.C. Stater (G) Blank / Disjointed Horse. 500.00

Armorican, Channel Isles, 75-50 B.C. Stater (Billon) Stylized head / Horse with boar. 100.00
Icenci, 30 B.C.-10 A.D. Drachm (S) Two crescents, wreath / Horse . . 150.00
Thames and south, 1st century B.C., Tin coinage, 50 B.C.- 50 A.D., Crude head / Lines as bull 75.00
Durotriges, 60 B.C. - 20 B.C., (S) Stater, very crude head/horse as lines and dots. 100.00

Dynastic Celtic Britain
Tincominnius, 20 B.C.- 5 A.D. Stater (G) TINC / Horseman r. 1,500.00
Catuvellauni, Cunobelin, 10-40 A.D. Stater (G) Ear of corn / Horse 800.00
Coritani, Alesca, 10-60 A.D. (S) 16mm, Boar / Horse 350.00

Celtic Central Europe
(All date from 3rd to 2nd century B.C.)
The Rhine Valley, Stater (Electrum) Triskeles design / 8 circles . 1,200.00
Note: the triskeles is a design of three legs.
Pannonia, imitation of Philip II, Tetradrachm (S) Zeus head / Horseman 350.00
___, Tetradrachm (S) Two-faced head of Zeus / Horseman 800.00
Danubian Celts, imitation of Alexander the Great, Tetradrachm (S) Crude head of Herakles / Zeus 200.00

VF
Danubian Celts, imitation of Thasos, Tetradrachm (S) Dionysus / Herakles, crude 200.00

Celtic Asia Minor
Galatian Celts, imitation of Tarsus, Stater (S) Facing female / Helmeted head. 800.00
___, imitation of Euthydemus, Tetradrachm (S) Head / Herakles, crude. 500.00

ANCIENT SPAIN

History: Ancient Spain saw contact which resulted in Phoenician settlements in the seventh century B.C. The Greeks from Massalia also established colonies. After the Punic wars Rome became a dominant influence. The coinage started around the mid fourth century B.C.
Reference: Heiss, *description Generales Des Monnaies Antiques De L' Espagne*
F

Early Coinage
Emporiae, c. 250 B.C. Drachm (S) Head of Persephone / Pegasus 350.00
Gades, 250-200 B.C., (C) 16mm, Head of Herakles / Two tunny fish . . . 75.00
Balearic Islands — Ebusus, 3rd century B.C., (C) 20mm, facing squatting Cabeiros 100.00

Citerior Province
Emporiae, 218-133 B.C. (C) 30mm, Helmeted Minerva / Pegasus . 100.00

Osca, 204-154 B.C. Drachm (S) Head r. / Horseman with spear 150.00
New Carthage, 1st century B.C. (C) 20mm, Bust of Minerva / Statue 50.00
Celsa, 204-154 B.C. (C) 20mm, Male head, three dolphins / Horseman with palm 150.00
Ilerda, 2nd-1st century B.C. (C) 22mm, Male head / Wolf to r. 70.00
Saguntum, 1st century B.C. (C) 15mm, Scallop shell / Dolphin 65.00
Valentia C. 138 B.C. (C) 29mm, Head of Roma / Cornucopia, thunderbolt. 100.00
Segobriga, 204-154 B.C. (C) 24mm, Young male head, dolphin, palm / Horseman 75.00

Castulo, 204-154 B.C. (C) 28mm, Male head / Sphinx,star 125.00

Ulterior Province
Carmo, 2nd century B.C., (C) 32mm, Helmeted head of Mercury / Two Barley ears 150.00
Carteia, 2nd century B.C. (C) 22mm, Head of Jupiter / Dolphin . . 100.00
Gades, 2nd-1st century B.C., (C) 28mm, Head of Herakles / Two tunny fish. 125.00
Malaca, 2nd-1st century B.C., (C) 22mm, Hd. of Hephaistos/Star,wreath. 110.00
Corduba, 1st century B.C., (C) 22mm, Head of Venus / Cupid 75.00
Obulco, 1st century B.C. (C) 20mm, Head of Apollo / Bull 70.00
Carteia, after 171 B.C., (C) 21mm, Tyche of city / Fisherman on rock . . 70.00
___, (C) 20mm, Dolphin with trident / Rudder 70.00

ANCIENT ITALY AND SICILY

History: Beginning in the eighth century B.C. many Greek colonies were established in Italy and Sicily. The coin production started in archaic times. Many of the great coin artists produced designs for these coins and, as a result, many of the most beautiful Greek coins ever produced came from this area. Some of these fine works of art were signed in the dies.
Hints: For the art connoisseur these coins are highly sought after, especially those in attractive condition. The images are truly beautiful.
Counterfeit Alert: Good Sicilian copies are found of Syracusian tetradrachms, especially the rarer types.

Magna Graecia **VF**
Cales, Campania, 334-268 B.C. Didrachm (S) Helmeted head of Athena / Nike in chariot 350.00
Cumae, Campania, 480-421 B.C. Didrachm (S) Head of Sybil / Mussel shell 350.00
Neapolis, Campania, 325-241 A.D. Didrachm (S) Head of nymph / Man-headed bull 250.00

Arpi, Apulia, 3rd century B.C. (C) 22mm, Head of Zeus / Boar . . 70.00
Tarentum, Calabria, 380-345 B.C. Diobol (S) Club and bow, arrows / Distaff in wreath 110.00
___. 272-235 B.C. Didrachm (S) Nude on horseback / boy on dolphin . 250.00
Heraclea, Lucania, 281-268 B.C. Didrachm (S) Head of Athena / Herakles nude, Nike 300.00

Metapontum, Lucania, 330-300 B.C. Stater (S) Head of Demeter / Ear of barley 315.00
Poseidonia, Lucania, 480-400 B.C. Stater (S) Poseidon striding / Bull . . 250.00
Velia, Lucania, 400-268 B.C. Didrachm (S) Head of Athena / Lion and prey. 250.00
Bruttii, Bruttium, c. 282-203 B.C. Octobol (S) Head of Nike / Dionysus standing 300.00
Croton, Bruttium, c.400 B.C. Stater (S) Eagle / Tripod, Nike 400.00
Rhegium, Bruttium, 270-203 B.C. Tetras (C) Jugate busts of Discouri / Hermes. 125.00

Ancient Sicily **VF**
Agrigentum, 550-472 B.C. Didrachm (S) Eagle / Crab 275.00
Agrigentum, Phintias, 282-279 B.C. (C) 20mm, Hd. of Persephone / Boar 150.00
Catana, 420-413 B.C. Tetradrachm (S) Slow chariot / Apollo 2,000.00

Gela, 490-475 B.C. Didrachm (S) Horseman / Forepart of man-headed bull 600.00
Himera, 450-420 B.C. Hemilitron (C) Gorgon's head / Six pellets . . 150.00
Leontini, 466-422 B.C. Tetradrachm (S) Head of Apollo / Lion's head, barley. 1,000.00
Mamertini, 220-200 B.C. Pentonkion (C) Zeus / Naked warrior 125.00
Panormus, after 409 B.C. Obol (S) Male head / Man-headed bull 200.00
Segesta, 461-415 B.C. Didrachm (S) Head of Segesta 1,000.00

VF

Selinus, 520-490 B.C. Didrachm (S) Leaf / Incuse square. 450.00

Syracuse, Gelon, 485-478 B.C. Didrachm (S) Nude horseman / Head of Artemis. 900.00

___, 474-450 B.C. Tetradrachm (S) Slow chariot / Head of Arethusa,dolphins. 1,200.00

___, 357-353 B.C. 50 Litriai (Electrum) Head of Apollo / Tripod . . . 1000.00

___, Pyrrhos, 278-276 B.C. (C) 23mm. Herakles in lions skin / Athena 125.00

Sicilo-Punic, 410-390 B.C. Tetradrachm (S) Forepart of horse / palm tree. 800.00

MACEDON AND GREECE

History: The Macedonian kingdom emerged on the world scene with Philip II and Alexander the Great; their coins are among the most popular of the Greek series. The heart of the Greek coinage is the Greek mainland cities and the influence of Corinth and Athens is apparent in the coins.

Counterfeit alert: Baltic copies are currently being offered on the international market. In modern Greece tourists can see modern machine-made copies everywhere. Alexander the Great and Athens tetradrachms are the most common.

Macedonia   **VF**

Acanthus, 424-400 B.C. Tetrobol (S) Forepart of bull / Incuse square 150.00

Orthagoreia, c. 350 B.C. Stater (S) Head of Artemis / helmet 1,000.00

Thessalonika, 158-149 B.C., (C) 20mm, Head of Dionysus / Goat 65.00

Kings, Philip II, 359-336 B.C. Tetradrachm (S) Head of Zeus / Youthful horseman 500.00

___, Alexander III, The Great, 336-323 B.C. Stater (G) Head of Athena / Nike 1,700.00

___. Tetradrachm (S) Head of Herakles / Zeus enthroned 300.00

___. (C) 16mm. Herakles in lion skin / Club and bow 50.00

Under Roman rule, 158-146 B.C. Tetradrachm (S) Macedonian shield, Artemis / Club, wreath 600.00

Thrace

Byzantium, 416-357 B.C. Drachm (S) Cow on dolphin / Mill-sail incuse. 125.00

Cherronesos, 400-350 B.C. Hemidrachm (S) Forepart of lion / Incuse, star. 125.00

King Lysimachos, 323-281 B.C. Tetradrachm (S) Head of Alexander the Great / Athena 900.00

Maroneia, 400-350 B.C. (C) 12 mm. Horse prancing / Vine in square. 40.00

Thasos, island, after 146 B.C. Tetradrachm (S) Young Dionysus/ Herakles standing 400.00

Greece

Dyrrhachium, 3rd-2nd cent. B.C. Drachm (S) Cow with calf / Stellate pattern. 75.00

Corcyra, 400-350 B.C. Stater (S) Cow with calf / Stellate pattern. . . 325.00

Larissa, 350-325 B.C. Drachm (S) Nymph facing / Horse 400.00

Thessalian League, 196-146 B.C. Two Victoriatus (S) Zeus / Athena 175.00

Akarnanian Federation, 250-167 B.C. (C) 22 mm, Young Herakles / Bearded head 75.00

Phocis, 480-460 Triobol (S) Facing head of bull / Artemis 150.00

Boeotia, 426-395 B.C. Stater (S) Shield / Amphora 300.00

Histiaea, 196-146 B.C. Tetrobol (S) Head of nymph / Nymph on galley. 100.00

Athens, 460-455 B.C. Tetradrachm (S) Helmeted Athena / Owl . . . 500.00

___, 166-57 B.C. (C) 19mm. Head of Athena / Zeus striding 75.00

Aegina, 456-431 B.C. Stater (S) Tortoise / Incuse 400.00

Corinth, 350-306 B.C. Stater (S) Pegasos / Athena 250.00

___. 306-300 B.C. Drachm (S) Pegasos / Head of Aphrodite 125.00

Sicyon, 4th century B.C. Drachm (S) Chimera / Dove,wreath 125.00

Argos, 3rd century B.C. Hemidrachm (S) Forepart of a wolf / A 125.00

Olympia, after 191 B.C.Drachm (S) Eagle,hare / Thunderbolt . . . 250.00

Achaean League, 196-146 B.C. Hemidrachm (S) Head of Zeus / Ax monogram 75.00

Itanos,, Crete, 320-270 B.C. Didrachm (S) Head of Athena / Eagle. . . . 2,000.00

Melos, Cyclades, 3rd cent. B.C. (C) 21mm. Quince (apple) / Cornucopiae. 100.00

ASIA MINOR

History: The coinage of Asia Minor continued in the Greek tradition, and Alexander the Great also helped to solidify Greek influence. The influence of Rome grew as her legions swept east in the 2nd and 1st century B.C.

VF

Amisus, Pontus, 400-350 B.C. Drachm (S) Head of Tyche / Owl with shield. 200.00

Sinope, Paphlagonia, 2nd-1st cent. B.C. (C) 21mm. Gorgon in Aegis / Nike. 40.00

Cius, Bithynia, 345-330 B.C. Hemidrachm (S) Head of Apollo / Prow. 125.00

Cyzicus, Mysia, 480-450 B.C. Trihemiobol (S) Forepart of boar, tunny fish / Lion 50.00

___, 390-330 B.C. Tetradrachm (S) Head of Persephone / Lion's head,tunny fish 600.00

Parium, Mysia, 350-300 B.C. Hemidrachm (S) Bull / Medusa head. 125.00

Pergamon, Mysia, after 133 B.C. Cistophoric (S) Cista Mystica / Serpents, bow case 150.00

VF
Ephesus, Ionia, 394-387 B.C. Tetradrachm (S) Bee / Palm tree, stag. 500.00
Erythrae, Ionia, 3rd cent. B.C. (C) 15mm. Head of Herakles / EPY inscription. 60.00
Chios, Ionia, 2nd cent. B.C. Drachm (S) Sphinx / Amphora 200.00
Cnidus, Ionia, 390-330 B.C. Tetradrachm (S) Head of Aphrodite / Head of lion. 3,000.00
Caria Satraps, Pixodarus, 340-334 B.C. Drachm (S) Facing Apollo head / Zeus 250.00
Cos, Carian Islands, 167-88 B.C. Tetrobol (S) Asklepius head / Serpent . 175.00
Rhodes, Carian Islands, 230-188 B.C. Tetradrachm (S) Head of Helios facing / Rose 750.00
___, 167-88 B.C. Drachm (S) Helios r. / Rose 150.00
Apameia, Phygria, 133-48 B.C. (C) 23mm. Bust of Athena / Eagle,pattern 65.00
Cragus, Lycia, 168-81 B.C. Drachm (S) Head of Apollo / Lyre 125.00

Aspendus, Pamphylia, 370-330 B.C. Stater (S) Wrestlers / Slinger 300.00
Selge, 3rd cent. B.C. Trihemiobol (S) Medusa head / Athena head . . 55.00
Tarsus, Cilicia, 361-334 B.C. Stater (S) Baal enthroned / Lion on bull 400.00

Cappadocian Kings
Ariobarzanes I, 95-36 B.C. Drachm (S) Head / Athena 75.00

Armenian Kings
Tigranes II (The Great), Tetradrachm (S) Head in tiara / Tyche 1,200.00

Seleucid Kings
Seleucus I, 312-280 B.C. Tetradrachm (S) Head of Zeus / Athena in chariot of elephants 800.00
Antiochus I, 280-261 (C) 18mm. Macedonian shield / Elephant 100.00

Antiochus III (The Great), 223-187 B.C. Tetradrachm (S) Head of king / Apollo seated 650.00
Demetrius I, 162-150 B.C. Drachm (S) Head of king / Zeus Uranius 350.00

Antiochus VIII, 121-96 B.C. Tetradrachm (S) Hd. of king/Zeus standing. 350.00
Demetrius III, 95-88 B.C. (C) 20mm. Head of king / Nike. dated 95/4 B.C. 50.00

BIBLICAL

History: The Biblical coins listed are those from Israel, Phoenicia and Syria: coins minted in the Holy Land, or those referred to in the Bible.
References: Hendin, *Guide to Biblical Coins*; Banks, *Coins of Bible Days*; Hill and Wroth, *Catalogue of Greek Coins in the British Museum, Phoenicia and Syria.*
Counterfeit Alert: Cast leptons are sold in museums as replicas.
Hints: The Jewish leptons and prutot are found and collected in all grades and prices. A good condition coin is actually just as collectible as a very fine, but the prices vary greatly. A good could be valued at $15, a very good at $25, a fine at $45, a very fine at $75, and extremely fine at $135.

JEWISH COINAGE   **F**
Yehund Coins
After 533 B.C., (S) 7.5mm, Head of Ptolemy / Eagle 375.00

Hasmonean
Alexander Jannaeus, 103-76 B.C. Prutah (C) Hebrew in wreath / double cornucopia 35.00

Herodian
Herod I 40-4 B.C. Prutah (C) Anchor / Double cornucopia 40.00
Herod Archelaus 4 B.C.-6 A.D., (C) Prutah, Prow of galley / Inscription in wreath 45.00
Herod Antipas 4 B.C.-40 A.D. (C) 21mm, Reed / Inscription in wreath . 325.00
Agrippa I 37-44 A.D. Prutah (C) Umbrella / Three ears of barley 30.00

Roman Judea: Procurators
Coponius 6-9 A.D. Lepton (C) Ear of barley / Palm tree 30.00

Pontius Pilate 26-36 A.D. Lepton (C) Littus / Date in wreath 55.00
Antonius Felix, 52-59 A.D. Lepton (C) crossed shields/palm tree 35.00

First Revolt of the Jews
66-70 A.D. Lepton (C) Covered amphora / Vine leaf 45.00

Bar Kochba   **VF**
Year Two 133-134 A.D. Tetradrachm (S) Temple of Jerusalem / Lulav. 2,500.00

Holy Land City Coins   **F**
Caesarea, 25mm (C) Head of Trajan (ruled 98-117 A.D.) / Emperor standing 65.00
Neapolis, 22mm (C) Head of Elagabalus (218-222 A.D.) / Mount Gerizim 85.00
Jerusalem (Aelia Capitolina), 22mm (C) Head of antoninus Pius (138-161) / Dioscuri standing 75.00

Phoenicia   **VF**
Aradus, 400-350 B.C. Stater (S) Head of Melqarth / Galley 300.00
Akko-Ptolemais, 1st cent. B.C. (C) 15mm., Zeus / Club 100.00
Berytus, 1st cent. B.C. (C) 22mm., Tyche of city / Poseidon, hippocamps 75.00
Sidon, 3rd cent. B.C. Tetradrachm (S) Veiled Tyche / Eagle 350.00

Syria   **F**
Antioch, 1st cent. B.C. (C) 21mm. Head of Zeus / Zeus enthroned 35.00
Laodicea, 1st cent. B.C. Tetradrachm (S) Bust of Tyche / Zeus enthroned. 200.00
Seleucia, 2nd cent. B.C. (C) 24mm. Head of Zeus / Winged thunderbolt . 30.00
Damascus, 1st cent. B.C. (C) 17mm. Dionysus bust / Cornucopia, basket. 75.00

New Testament-Related Coins   F

Widow's Mite. Alexander Jannaeus, Prutah (C), Anchor / Wheel .. 15.00

Tribute Penny. Tiberius, Denarius (S), Head / Livia seated 275.00

"30 Pieces" of Silver: Tyre Shekel (S), Head of Melqarth / Eagle ... 300.00

Paul's Travels: Antioch, Nero (C) 22mm. SC in wreath 75.00

PARTHIA, BACTRIA AND FARTHER EAST

History: Parthia was the traditional foe of Rome. It roughly covered modern Iran, Iraq, and areas of Afghanistan and Pakistan. Its origin is traced to Arsaces, who founded a kingdom that lasted over 470 years. Sub-Parthian kingdoms were Elymais and Persis. The Bactrian kings ruled Afghanistan and issued bi-lingual Greek-Karosthi coins. Silver tetradrachms and drachms were standard, but nickel coins and square coins are also found. Various other Indo-Greeks also issued coins, including the Indo-Scythians, Indo-Parthians, Sagdiana and Kushan.

References: Shore, *Parthinian Coins and History*; Selwood, *The Coinage of Parthia*; Bopearachchi, *Monnaies Gréco-Bactriennes et Indo-Grecques*; Sear, *Greek Coins and Theri Values,* Vol. II.

Hints: Parthian coins are widely collected. The unusual square Bactrian coins are always sought after. The other Indo-Greeks are found in large quantities and the values stay low. They are a good series to collect for one on a budget.

VF

Parthia *(All obverses have bust of king.)*

Mithradates I, 171-138 B.C. Drachm (S) Bust, long beard / Archer ... 150.00

Artabanus I, 127-124 B.C. Drachm (S) Bust, medium beard / Archer   200.00

Mithradates II, 123-88 B.C. Drachm (S) Bust in long beard / Archer .. 90.00

Orodes I, 90-77 B.C. (C) 16mm. Bust in tiara / Horse 75.00

Phraates IV, 38-2 B.C. Drachm (S) Bust between with star in crescent and eagle / Archer 65.00

Gotarzes II, 40-51 A.D. Tetradrachm (S) Bust with beard / Tyche and king. 175.00

Vologases III, 105-147 A.D. Drachm (S) Bust / Archer 60.00

Osroes II, 190 A.D. Drachm (S) Bust wearing crested tiara / Archer . 65.00

Persis

Darius I, 2nd B.C. Drachm (S) Head / Altar with king 150.00

Kapat, Hemidrachm (S) Head in tiara / Head 75.00

Elymais

Orodes I, 2nd cent. A.D. Drachm (C) Head, anchor / Anchor,dashes   25.00

Bactria   VF

Demetrius, 205-171 B.C. Tetradrachm (S) Head / Athena facing 700.00

Agathokles, 171-160 B.C. Didrachm (Nickel) Head of Dionysus / Panther 100.00

Appollodotos I, 160-150 B.C. Drachm (S) Elephant / Humped Zebu 80.00

Menander, 160-145 B.C. Drachm (S) Diademed bust / Athena 80.00

Epander 135-130 B.C. (C) square 22 by 20mm, Nike advancing / Zebu   60.00

Hermaios, 40-1 B.C. Tetradrachm (S) Bust / Zeus enthroned 150.00

Indo-Greek   VF

Indo-Scythian, Azes I 90-40 B.C. Tetradrachm (S) King on horse / Athena. 100.00

Indo-Scythian, Azes II, 15-5 B.C. Drachm (S) King on horse / Tyche ... 75.00

Indo-Parthian, Gondophares, 20-60 A.D. Tetradrachm (Bil.), similar to above. 60.00

___. Phaares II, 175-200 A.D. (C) 24mm, Bust with tuft / Nike 25.00

Western Satraps, Visvasimha 2nd cent. A.D. Drachm (S) Head / Hill . 15.00

Kushan, Huvishka, 158-195 A.D., (C) 21mm, King standing / Goddess Mao. 15.00

___, Vasu Deva, 193-230 A.D. Stater (G) King standing / Siva 275.00

Pre-Mauryan, 368-321 B.C., Karshapana (S) Punchmarks of sun, mountain, zebu, elephant 20.00

EGYPT AND AFRICA

History: Ptolemaic Egypt was established by Ptolemy I, Alexander the Great's

general, in 305 B.C. The coinage which he began continued until the suicides of Cleopatra VII and Mark Antony. Roman Egyptian coins are those made during the Roman period.

References: *Catalogue of Greek Coins in the British Museum, Ptolemies Kings of Egypt;* Curtis, *The Tetradrachms of Roman Egypt*; *Sylloge Nummorum Graecorum, Copenhagen.*

Counterfeit Alert: Recent crude copies of the tetradrachms are showing up in the market.

Hints: The Ptolemaic series is difficult to categorize as many major references differ in certain attributions. The Danish sylloge is the latest published and their attributions the most reliable.

Ptolemaic Egypt   VF

Ptolemy I, 323-305 B.C. Tetradrachm (S) Head of Alexander / Athena . 400.00

Ptolemy II, 285-246 B.C. (C) 46mm, Head of Zeus / Eagle with spread wings. 250.00

Ptolemy III, 246-221 B.C. Octadrachm (G) Heads of a king and queen / Same. 4,000.00

Ptolemy V, 204-708 B.C. (C) 32mm, Head of Cleopatra / Eagle ... 50.00

Ptolemy VI, 180-145 B.C. (C) 21mm, Zeus / Two eagles 50.00

Ptolemy X, 101-88 B.C. Tetradrachm (S) Ptolemy I head / Eagle 250.00

Cleopatra VII, 51-30 B.C. (C) 80 Drachma, hd of queen/eagle . 900.00

Roman Egypt   VF

All have head of emperor on obverse.

Augustus, 27 B.C.-14 A.D. 80 Drachma (C) Eagle 150.00

Tiberius, Augustus, Tetradrachm (S) Head 250.00

Claudius Diobol (C) Bust of Nilus. 125.00

	VF
Nero, Tetradrachm (Billon) Head of Zeus Olympius	100.00
Vespasian, Tetradrachm (Bil.) Alexandria standing	80.00
Trajan, Tetradrachm (Bil.) Zeus seated.	80.00
Hadrian, Hemidrachm (C) Bull	100.00
Antoninus Pius, Drachma (C) Nilus reclining	200.00
Commodus, Tetradrachm (Bil.) Emperor and Alexandria	90.00
Elagabalus, Tetradrachm (Bil.) Homonia standing	80.00
Maximinus, Tetradrachm (Bil.) Athena standing	75.00
Philip I, Tetradrachm (Bil.) Tyche standing	65.00
Salonina, Tetradrachm (Bil.) Elpis standing	50.00
Probus, Tetradrachm (Potin) Eagle.	35.00
Diocletian, Tetradrachm (Potin) Alexandria standing	35.00
Nomes of Egypt, Menedaite, Drachma (C) Antoninus Pius / Harpokrates	250.00

Africa	VF
Cyrene, 323-305 B.C. Hemidrachm (G) Horseman / Silphium plant	1,500.00

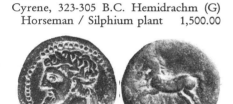

Numidia, Micipsa and brothers, 148-118 B.C. (C) 28mm, Bearded head / Horse galloping 125.00

GREEK IMPERIAL

History: Greek Imperials are those Roman coins minted in the Greek world. The Greek cities were given the right to strike coins, but, as a concession to authority, they had to depict the Roman emperor. This vast series was made from Augustus through Tacitus, and had over 600 mints. The inscriptions are in Greek; Roman colonies are in Latin.
References: Sear, *Greek Imperial Coins and Their Values*; Burnett, Amandry, and Ripolles, *Roman Provincial Coins, Volume I.*
Hints: This series is so vast, and yet fascinating, that one should collect these coins by a theme: one might consider specializing in one area, such as a region, emperor, or city. Many coins in the Greek Imperial category have never been catalogued and are unknown to modern man, yet these same coins can often be had for under $100.00. This is not a series for the condition-conscious. Often Fine is the highest obtainable grade, and most coins have some traces of porosity.

(All have obverse portraits of emperors unless otherwise stated. Listing is by emperor, then city and region.)

	F
Julius Caesar and Augustus, Nemausus, Gaul, (C) 27mm. Two heads / Crocodile,palm tree	175.00
Augustus, Cordoba, Spain, As (C) Inscription in wreath	50.00
___, Parium, Mysia, (C) 19mm. Two priests plowing	50.00
Augustus and Livia, Smyrna, Ionia, (C) 19mm. Two busts / Aphrodite	125.00
Tiberius, Smyrna, Ionia, (C) 18mm. Nike standing	125.00
Caligula, Aezanis, Phrygia (C) 19mm. Zeus standing	200.00
Claudius, Antioch, Syria, (C) 28mm. Large SC in wreath	80.00
Britannicus, son of Claudius, Ephesus, Ionia, (C) 19mm. Cultus statue of Artemis	350.00
Nero, Antioch, Seleucia, Tetradrachm (S) Horseman	100.00
Domitian, Caesarea, Cappadocia, Drachma (S)/Nike running	125.00
Trajan, Bithynia Community (C) 20mm. Large altar	75.00

Hadrian; Caesarea, Cappadocia, Hemidrachm (S) Nike flying. 60.00

Antoninus Pius, Pessinus, Galatia, (C) 25mm. Mên standing 75.00
Marcus Aurelius, Sege, Pisida, (C) 32mm. Aurelius and Verus 100.00
Lucius Verus, Caesarea, Cappadocia, (C) 21mm. Mount Aergaeus 60.00

Commodus, Samos, Ionia, (C) 18mm. Hera Cult Statue	40.00
Septimius Severus, Laodicea, Syria, Tetradrachm (S) Eagle	150.00
Caracalla, Carrhae, Mesopotamia, (C) 20mm. Bust of Tyche	40.00
Elagabalus, Marcianopolis, Moesia (C) 27mm. Askeplios standing	50.00
Severus Alexander, Antioch, Pisidia (C) 33mm. She-wolf, Romulus and Remus.	100.00
__. Aegeae, Cilicia (C) 28mm. Galley.	80.00
Gordian III, Germe, Mysia (C) 20mm. Herakles looking at Kerberos .	40.00
Otacila Severa, Cadi, Phrygia (C) 25mm. Artemis standing	40.00
Herennius Etruscus, Antioch, Seleucia (C) 25mm. Eagle	50.00
Volusian, Antioch, Pisidia (C) 21mm. Eagle between standards	40.00
Gallienus, Ephesus, Ionia (C) 28mm. Diana holding torch	40.00
Aurelian, Cremna, Pisidia (C) 35mm. Fortuna-Nemesis standing	80.00

ROMAN

History: Roman coin collecting is the most popular of the ancient fields. The Romans started issuing coins during the Republican period, in about 290 B.C. It was not long until the Roman monetary system was established with the denarius as the main denomination.

The earliest Roman copper was crudely cast. By the end of the thrid century, however, they were manufactured by striking. This early copper bore simple marks ov value as shown below.

AES Grave (Cast) Copper Standard

Denomination	Value	Mark
AS	12 unciae	I
Semis	6 unciae	S
Triens	4 unciae	....
Quadrans	4 unciae	..
Sextons	2 unciae	..
Uncia		.

Rome's standard denomination continued to be the silver denarius through the mid third century A.D. It was then eclipsed by the double denarius introduced by Caracalla and named *antoninianus* after his proper name. Inflation resulted from the monetary crisis of Valerian; the silver content dropped so much that eventually the antoninianus became a copper coin with a silver wash.

Roman Monetary Standard

(G) aureus = 25 denarii
(G) quinarius = 12.5 denarii
(S) antoninianus = 2 denarii
(S) denarius = 16 (C) asses
(S) quinarius = 8 (C) asses
*(B) double sestertius = 8 (C) asses
(B) sestertius = 4 (C) asses
(B) dupondius = 2 (C) asses
(C) As = 4 (C) quadrantes
(B) Semis = 2 (C) quadrantes
(C) quadrans = ¼ (C) As

*This was agolden-yellow brass alloy, called *orichalcum*, which was introduced by Augustus.

The monetary reforms of Diocletian and Constantius II resulted in new systems:

Diocletian's Reforms

(G) aureus . . . . 24 (S) argentei
(S) argentius . . . . 5 (C) folles
(C) follis . . . . 5 (C) denarii
(C) antoninianus . . . . . 2 (C) denarii
(C) denarius
(C) quinarius . . . . ½ denarius

Constantius II's Reforms

(G) solidus . . . . 1/72 lb. (G)
(G) semis . . . . 1/2 solidus
(S) miliarense . . . . 1/2 solidus
(S) siliqua . . . . 1/24 solidus

The names of many late Roman copper coins are uncertain. Numismatists have grouped them into classes by diameter and refer to them by class number, using the abbreviation AE from the Latin word *aes* (copper). By the following table, one would refer to a late Roman copper 18mm wide as an AE3.

AE 1 . . . . over 25 mm
AE 2 . . . . 24-21 mm
AE 3 . . . . 20-17 mm
AE 4 . . . . under 17 mm

The centenionalis and its half circulated for a short period in the middle 4th century. There are other gold and silver fractionals used in the late Roman period. **References**: Sear, *Roman Coins and their Values*; *Roman Imperial Coinage Vols. 1-10*; Cohen, *Description Historique Des Monneis Frappees Sous L'Empire Romain*; Seaby, *Roman Silver Coins, Vols. I-V*; *Celator* (magazine). **Counterfeit Alert**: Similar problems to those are found on Greek coins. Beware of Becker (a famous counterfeiter of the 19th century) along with copper Paduans made and cast in Italy. The British Museum made copper core electrotypes of

coins in their collection and marked the side with a tiny BM. These are sometimes passed off as genuine. Modern Roman gold aureii are found for almost every emperor. During the Renaissance and later it was not uncommon to find fine sestertius with the fields highly tooled (scraped) to enhance the value. Minor removal of encrustation is acceptable and will not reduce value as long as it does not go below the surface of the metal.

Hints: Roman Imperial coins have been refered to as an ancient rogues' gallery. Each has a Roman emperor's portrait with his name in Latin. It's not hard for the novice to start collecting, as these coins are like holding history in the hand.

ROMAN REPUBLIC

Coins of the Republic reflect Rome under its early form of constitutional covernment. The Punic wars had great influence on the culture and its expansive nature is reflected in the coinage. No Republican bronze was minted after 84 B.C. The denarius became the standard denomination. At the beginning of the second century B.C. the Senate assigned two moneyers to oversee the minting of coins. Each year these moneyers alluded to their names and family images on the coins, resulting in a vast array of coin types.

Counterfeit Alert: Ancient counterfeits are common in Republican silver: the core will usually be copper. These trade on the market at almost the same value, though the value is reduced considerably if the copper core is visible. They are termed fourré.

Aes Grave (cast)   VF
289-245 B.C. As (C) Head of Janus / Prow of ship 1400.00
280-245 B.C. Semis (C) Pegasus flying / Same 600.00
269-240 B.C. Quadrans (C) Two barleycorns / open hand 400.00
225-216 B.C. Triens (C) Helmeted Minerva / prow 350.00

Aes Struck

211-207 B.C. As (C) Head of Janus / Prow 300.00
169-158 B.C. As (C) Head of Janus / Prow, wolf and twins 275.00
189-180 B.C. L. Furius, Quadrans (C) Hercules / Prow, Victory . . . 200.00
169-158 B.C., A. Caecilius, As (C) Head of Janus / A.CAE., prow . . . 250.00

Anonymous Silver
211-207 B.C. Denarius (S) Helmeted head of Roma / Diosouri 125.00

211-207 B.C. Quinarius (S) Roma, V behind / Diosouri 125.00

Republican Moneyer's Issues   VF
(All are denarii unless otherwise stated)
206-200 B.C. A. Terentius Varro (VAR) Roma head / Diosouri galloping.
. . . . 175.00
179-170 B.C. Matienus (MAT), Roma head / Diosouri galloping . . . 100.00
151 B.C. Cornelius Sulla, (P. SVLA) Roma head / Victory in two-horse chariot 100.00
137 B.C. Sex Pompeius, Roma head / Wolf and twins 125.00
131 B.C. M. Opimius, Roma head / Cornucopia in wreath 125.00
127 B.C. Q. Fabius Maximus, Roma head / Cornucopia in wreath 125.00

120 B.C. Caecilia, Roma head / Four-horse chariot 80.00
120 B.C. M. Baebius Pampilus, Roma head / Apollo in chariot 85.00
119 B.C. M. Furius, L.F. Philus, Janus head / Roma, trophy 125.00
116 B.C. M. Sergius Silus, Roma head / Horseman, severed head 100.00
115 B.C., M. Cipius M.F. (M. CIPI. M.F.) Roma head / Victory in chariot 75.00

VF

114-13 B.C., C. Fonteius, Janus head / Galley 135.00
105 B.C., L. Thorius Balbus, Juno head / Bull charging 90.00
100 B.C., P. Servilus Rullus, Minerva bust / Victory in chariot 85.00
96 B.C., A Postumius Albinus, Apollo head / Dioscouri with horses 150.00
90 B.C., L.C. Piso Frugi, Apollo / Horseman, palm 100.00
89 B.C., L. Titurius Sabinus, King Tatius / Rape of Sabine women . . . 125.00
85 B.C., Mn. Fonteius, Apollo head / Cupid on goat 100.00
83-2 B.C., Q. Antonius Balbus, Jupiter head / Victory in chariot . . . 100.00

82-81 B.C., Valeria, Victory bust / Legionary eagle. 100.00
78 B.C., M. Voletus, Jupiter head / Temple 135.00
75 B.C. Rustilius, Roma head / Chariot. 75.00

55 B.C., Q. Cassius Longinus, Liberty head / Eagle 125.00

47-46 B.C., Q.C. Metellus Pius Scipio, Jupiter head / Elephant 150.00
42 B.C., L. Mussidius Longus, Sol bust facing / Shrine of Venus 165.00

ROMAN IMPERATORIAL
First Century B.C.
History: The same numismatic standard is present during the period of the first and second triumvirate and the civil wars.
Hints: This period is strongly collected, as these names are so well known in history.

VF

Pompey the Great, Denarius (S) Head of Numa Pompilius / Prow . . . 400.00
Sextus Pompey, Denarius (S) Head of Pompey the Great / Neptune 650.00

___. Denarius (S) Janiform (two-faced) head of Pompey / Prow 400.00
Julius Caesar, Denarius (S) Head of Caesar / Venus 1,000.00

___. 49-48 B.C., Denarius (S) Elephant / Priestly tools 250.00
Lepidus and M.Antony, Quinarius (S) Staff, raven / Ladle, axe 350.00

Mark Antony (Legion VIII) Denarius (S) Galley / Eagle, two standards 175.00
Mark Antony, 42 B.C. Denarius (S) M.Antony / Temple 400.00
Mark Antony and Octavian, Denarius (S) Head / Head 500.00
Octavian, Denarius (S) Venus bust / Octavian standing 300.00

ROMAN IMPERIAL
TWELVE CAESARS
History: The twelve Caesars include Julius Caesar and the eleven emperors from Augustus to Domitian. These are the most sought after Roman coins. The art is outstanding and the detailed portraits of each emperor make these coins popular.
Counterfeit Alert: Casts from the eastern Balkans are showing up. They can be identified by their smaller size and edge seams, mostly of Nero and Vespasian. Excellent quality counterfeits of silver denarii have been coming from Bulgaria. These will usually appear mint state and fully struck.
(All have portraits of emperor or members of his family).

VF

Augustus, 27 B.C.-14 A.D. Denarius (S) Comet with 8 rays 500.00
___. As (C) Inscription around large S.C. 150.00
Livia, wife of Augustus, Dupondius (C) Inscription around large S.C. . . 300.00

Agrippa, As (C) Neptune standing 200.00
Tiberius, 14-37 A.D., Aureus (G) Livia seated 3,500.00
___. Sestertius (C) Tiberius seated / Inscription S.C. 900.00
Drusus, As (C) Iinscription S.C. 250.00
Germanicus, Dupondius (C) Germanicus, chariot / Germanicus 450.00
Caligula, 37-41 A.D. Denarius (S) S.P.O.R. in wreath 2,600.00

Claudius and Agrippa Jr., Aureus (G) Head / Head 6,000.00
Claudius, 41-54 A.D, As (C) Liberty standing 135.00

Nero, 54-68 A.D. Sesterius (C) Roma seated 600.00
___. Semis (B) Table, wreath . . 125.00
Galba, 68-69 A.D. Denarius (S) Concord seated 500.00
Otho, 69 A.D. Denarius (S) Pax standing 900.00
Vitellius, 69 A.D. As (C) Ceres seated. 500.00

Vespasian, 69-79 A.D. Aureus (G) Annona seated 5,000.00
___. Denarius (S) Pax seated . . 125.00
Titus, 79-81 A.D. Denarius (S) Dolphin, anchor 225.00
Domitian, 81-96 A.D. Denarius (S) Minerva standing 100.00

___ As (C) Fortuna 75.00

ADOPTIVE EMPERORS

History: This period saw Rome at a time of partial peace and its greatest expanse. The coinage was extensive for each emperor.

Counterfeit Alert: Recent copper casts are found for all emperors in asses and dupondii. Cast copper denarii are found that have been toned dark grey to look like silver. Excellent quality counterfeits of silver denarii have been coming from Bulgaria. These will usually appear mint state and fully struck.

(All have portraits of emperor or his family.)

VF

Nerva, 96-98 A.D. Denarius (S) Clasped
  hands 175.00

Trajan, 98-117 A.D. Aureus (G) Basilica
  of Trajan 5,000.00
___. Denarius (S) Fortuna seated   75.00
___. Dupondius (C) Salus feeding
  serpent 75.00
Plotina, wife of Trajan, Denarius (S) Fides
  standing 3,000.00
Marciana, sister of Trajan, Denarius (S)
  Eagle 2,500.00
Hadrian, 117-138 A.D. Denarius (S)
  Moneta standing 85.00
___. Sesterius (C) Diana standing with
  bow 250.00
___, As (C) Ggalley 175.00

Sabina, wife of Hadrian, Denarius (S)
  Concord seated 150.00
Aelius, Caesar, 136-8, As (C) Fortuna-Spes
  standing 150.00
Antonius Pius, 138-161 A.D. Aureus (G)
  Emperor standing 2,500.00
___. Denarius (S) Liberty standing 70.00
___. Sestertius (C) Juno Sospita standing
  with serpent. 350.00
___. As (C) Sow with piglets . .   300.00
Faustina Senior, wife of Pius, Denarius (S)
  Ceres standing 65.00
Marcus Aurelius, 161-180 A.D. Denarius
  (S) Pax standing 75.00
___. Sestertius (C) Liberalitas standing.
  . . . .   150.00
___. Dupondius (C) Minerva standing.
  . . . .   60.00
Faustina Jr., wife of Aurelius, Denarius
  (S), Concord seated 65.00

Lucius Verus, 161-169 A.D. Denarius (S)
  Eagle 125.00
Commodus, 177-192 A.D. Denarius (S)
  Victory seated 85.00

___. Sestertius (C) Cybele riding lion.
  . . . .   500.00

SOLDIER EMPERORS

History: The history of this period is a time of military, political and economic turmoil.   At the end of this period inflation and turmoil gripped the Roman Empire.

Counterfeit Alert: Excellent quality counterfeits of silver denarii have been coming from Bulgaria. These will usually appear mint state and fully struck.

(All have portraits of emperors.)

VF

Pertinax, 193 A.D. Denarius (S) Pertinax
  standing 1,500.00
Clodius Albinus, 195-197 A.D. Denarius
  (S) Providence standing 325.00
Septimius Severus, 193-211 A.D. Aureus
  (G) Jupiter seated 4,000.00
___. Denarius (S) Neptune 55.00
Julia Domna, wife of Severus, As (C)
  Ceres, altar 150.00

Caracalla, 198-217 A.D. Denarius (S) Mars
  standing 60.00
Geta, 209-212 A.D. Denarius (S) Genius
  standing 70.00

Macrinus, 217-218 A.D. Denarius (S)
  Felicity standing. 150.00
Elagabalus, 218-222 A.D. Denarius (S)
  Hilaritas, two children 60.00

Julia Maesa, grandmother of Elagabalus,
  Denarius (S) Felicity 100.00
Severus Alexander 222-223 A.D. Denarius
  (S) Jupiter seated 55.00
Maximinus I, 235-238 A.D. Sestertius (C)
  Pax standing 125.00
Gordian I, 238 A.D., (S) Denarius,
  /Providentia standing 2,000.00

Gordian III, 238-244 A.D. Denarius (S)
  Hercules standing 60.00
Philip I, 244-249 A.D. Antoninianus (S)
  Four standards 40.00

Trajan Decius, 249-251 A.D. Antonini-
  anus (S) Victory walking 40.00
Volusian, 251-253 A.D. Antoninianus (S)
  Concord seated 50.00
Valerian I, 253-260 A.D. Antoninianus (S)
  Fides standing 35.00
Gallienus, 253-260 A.D. Antoninianus (S)
  Antelope walking 35.00
Postumus, 259-268 A.D. Antoninianus
  (Billon) Minerva 35.00
Victorinus, 268-270 A.D. Antoninianus
  (C) Sol advancing 25.00
Claudius II, 268-270 A.D. Antoninianus
  (C) Pax advancing 22.00
Aurelian, 270-275 A.D. Antoninianus (C)
  Concord standing 25.00
Probus, 276-282 A.D. Antoninianus (C)
  Sol in chariot 30.00
Carus, 282-283 A.D. Antoninianus (C)
  Fides, two standards 60.00

Numerian, 283-284 A.D. Antoninianus
  (C) Emperor and Jupiter standing.
  . . . .   65.00

TETRARCHY

History: The coins of Diocletian's reform are plentiful (for the most part) and the large folles are very popular coins. While Constantine I was part of the tetrarchy he is listed under the following category.

Counterfeit Alert: Excellent counterfeits of silver Argentii have been manufactured in Bulgaria. These usually appear mint state and fully struck.

(All have portrait of emperor.)

VF
Diocletian, 284-305 A.D. Argenteus (S) Tetarchs in front of camp . . . 500.00
___. Follis (C) Carthage standing . 75.00
___. Radiate (C) VOT-XX in lines 35.00
Carausius, 287-293 A.D. Antoninianus (C) Pax standing 150.00
Allectus, 293-296 A.D. Antoninianus (C) Pax standing 200.00
Domitus Domitianus, 296-297 A.D. Follis (C) Genius standing 1,000.00

Maximianus 286-310 A.D. Follis (C) Moneta standing 65.00
___ Radiate (C) Maximianus with Victory 30.00
Constantius I, 305-306 A.D. Follis (C) Genius standing 85.00
___. Denarius (C) Genius standing 60.00
___. Radiate (C) VOT-XX in lines 60.00
Severus II 306-307 A.D. Follis (C) Mars advancing 150.00

Galerius, 305-311 A.D. Aureus (G) Felicity seated 3,500.00
___. Follis (C) Moneta standing . 50.00

Galeria Valeria, wife of Galerius, Follis (C) Venus standing 150.00
Maximinus II, 309-313 A.D. Follis (C) Carthage standing 60.00

Maxentius, 306-312 A.D. Follis (C) Roma, emperor in temple 65.00
___. Quarter Follis (C) VOT QQ MVL XX in wreath 60.00
Romulus, son of Maxentius, Quarter Follis (C) Temple 200.00

Licinius I, 308-324 A.D. AE 3 (C) Jupiter standing 25.00
Licinius II 317-324 A.D. AE 3 (C) Jupiter standing 27.00

CONSTANTINIAN PERIOD

History: The period when Constantine the Great drew the empire back to one central ruler saw many numismatic changes. The gold solidus, the silver siliqua and the reduced follis or coller of three unidentified monetary units (C)3 were the new denominations. The (C)3 series struck under Constantine and his descendants is probably the most numerous single ancient group, and is widely collected.

Reference: Carson, Hill and Kent, *Late Roman Bronze Coinage.*

Hints: Many collectors collect this series by mint marks. They are found on the reverse at the bottom. Example: SMANTA– S= sacred, M= money, ANT= Antioch mint, A= First workshop.

Counterfeit Alert: Excellent counterfeits of silver Siliquae have been manufactured in Bulgaria. These usually appear mint state and fully struck.

(All have portrait of emperors unless otherwise noted.)

VF
Constantine I, The Great, 307-337 A.D. Solidus (G) Victory with trophy.
. . . . 2,000.00

___. Siliqua (S) Victory advancing.
. . . . 750.00

___. Follis (C) Genius 75.00
___. Reduced Follis (C) Jupiter standing.
. . . . 40.00
___. AE 3 (C) Camp gate 25.00
Commemorative, 30-346 A.D. AE 3/4 (C) Roma / Wolf and twins 20.00

___, AE 3/4 (C) Constantinopolis / Victory 20.00
Fausta, wife of Constantine AE 3 (C) Fausta with sons 75.00

Helena, mother of Constantine, AE 3 (C) Helena standing 80.00
Crispus, caesar 317-326 A.D. AE 3 (C) VOT X, laurel wreath 35.00
Delmatius, caesar 335-337 A.D. AE 3 (C) Two soldiers, standard 65.00

Hannibalianus, 336-337 A.D. AE 4 (C) River god reclining 500.00
Constantine II, 337-340 A.D. AE 3 (C) Two soldiers with standards . . 25.00
___. AE 3 (C) Campgate 25.00
Constans, 337-350 A.D. AE 4 (C) Two Victories 18.00
Constantius II, 337-361 A.D. Siliqua (S) Legend in wreath 175.00
___. Centenionalis (C) Soldier spearing fallen horseman. 35.00
Magnentius, 350-353 A.D. Centenionalis (C) Emperor spearing foe 100.00
Decentius, caesar, 351-353 A.D. Centenionalis (C) Two Victories with shield 100.00

VF

Vetranio, 350 A.D. Centenionalis (C)
  Vetranio standing 300.00
Constantius Gallus, Caesar 351-354 A.D.
  AE 3 (C) Soldier spearing foe . 35.00
Julian II, 360-363 A.D. AE 1 (C) Bull
  standing 200.00

LATE ROMAN

History: This period of barbarian invasions lasted until the final fall of Rome in 476 A.D, under Romulus Augustus.   The Eastern Empire was thriving and with the reforms of Anastasius I the Eastern Roman (popularly called Byzantine) coinage began.

Reference: Carson, Hills and Kent, *Late Roman Bronze Coinage.*

Counterfeit Alert: Excellent counterfeits of silver Siliquae have been manufactured in Bulgaria. These usually appear mint state and fully struck.

Hints: Late Roman coins are relatively inexpensive and easy to acquire in copper. Gold coins are at a high level of value. *(All coins have portrait of emperor except for usurpers.)*

VF

Valentinian I, 364-375 A.D. Solidus (G)
  Emperor standing 650.00
___. AE 3 (C) Emperor dragging foe
  . . . . 35.00

Valens, 364-378 A.D. AE 3 (C) /Victory
  advancing 35.00
Procopius, 365-366 A.D. AE 3 (C)
  Procopios holding labarum . . 500.00

Gratian, 367-383 A.D. Solidus (G) Two
  emperors enthroned facing . . 800.00
Valentinian II, 375-392 A.D. Siliqua (S)
  Roma seated 150.00
Theodosius I, 379-95 A.D. AE 2 (C)
  Emperor in galley 65.00
___, AE 4 (C) Victory advancing 20.00

Aelia Flaccilla, wife of Theodosius, AE 2
  (C) Victory inscribing shield . 150.00
Magnus Maximus, 383-388 A.D. Siliqua
  (S) Roma seated 175.00
Flavius Victor, 387-388 A.D. AE 4 (C)
  Camp gate 200.00
Eugenius, 392-394 A.D. AE 4 (C) Victory
  advancing 250.00
Arcadius, 383-408 A.D. AE 2 (C)
  Arcadius holding standard 65.00
Eudoxia, wife of Arcadius, AE 3 (C)
  Eudoxia enthroned 135.00

Honorius, 393-423 A.D. Solidus (G)
  Constantinopolis enthroned . 650.00
Johannes, 423-425 A.D. Solidus (G)
  Emperor standing 5,000.00
Theodosius II, 402-450 AD, AE 4 (C)
  Cross in wreath 35.00
Valentinian III, 425-455 A.D. AE 4 (C)
  Victory standing 125.00
Marcian, 450-457 A.D. AE 4 (C)
  Monogram in wreath 50.00

Leo I, 457-474 A.D. AE 4 (C) Lion
  crouching 75.00
Severus III, 461-465 A.D. Tremis (G)
  Cross in wreath 1,200.00
Anthemius, 467-472 A.D. Solidus (G)
  Two emperors 2,000.00

Zeno, 424-491 A.D. Solidus (G) Victory
  with cross 600.00
___. AE 4 (C) Monogram 40.00
Basilucus, 475-476 A.D. Solidus (G)
  Victory with cross 1,000.00

MEDIEVAL COINS

Medieval coins are those coins made after the fall of the Roman Empire in the West. They are all hand struck. Numismatically speaking, this period lasts through the Renaissance up to the 1600s, long after the historical Middle Ages. Medieval coinage ended with the introduction of milling machinery for making coins. This end varied in time with each region, country, and city.

In medieval coins collectors can find their own ethnic and historical roots. Most of the familiar European countries of today had their origin at this time. The fascination today with times past, with knights, castles, monks, the Black Death, the Crusades, and the stories of the *Thousand and one Nights* has increased the collecting of medieval coins.

The gold coins are the most beautiful coins, and usually the best preserved, but in most cases they are beyond most collectors' pocketbooks. The silver, billon (base silver), and copper coins are usually found in lesser quality, and are often crudely designed and struck. Medieval Islamic coinage and other Western Asiatic silver, however, can be collected in Very Fine or Extremely Fine condition. With the advent of the Italian Renaissance there emerged a new higher style of coin engraving in Europe, and many of these pieces are also available in higher grade.

This area of numismatics has traditionally been the least known and understood. Today it is growing in popularity, partially due to the availability and relatively low price of the coins. General introductions in English such as Walker's *Reading Medieval European Coins* and the new translation of Erslev's *Medieval Coins in the Christian J. Thomsen Collection* (the Danish National Museum) are helping to guide beginning collectors in this field.

I would like to thank my co-author, Allen G. Berman, for his important editorial contributions and research in revising and updating this section on medieval coins.

BYZANTINE

History: The Byzantine Empire was in essence the Eastern Roman Empire. Its influence and power lasted for over 962 years. In the Justinian Age, Byzantium held sway in much of the Mediterannean world.

The coinage continued the late Roman system of gold and silver but the reform of the copper coinage by Anastasius was significant.

The copper coinage system is as follows:

40 nummi=	1 follis	M or XXXX
30 nummi=	3/4 follis	or XXX
20 nummi=	1/2 follis	K or XX
16 nummi=	2/5 follis	IS
12 nummi=	3/10 follis	IB
10 nummi=	1/4 follis	I or X
8 nummi=	1/5 follis	H
5 nummi=	1/8 follis	V or E
1 nummus=	1/40 follis	A

The Alexandrian mint struck a 33 nummi (ΛΓ), 6 nummi (S), and 3 nummi (Γ). The late empire saw the introduction of cup-shaped coins known as the gold hyperpyron, electrum aspron trachy, and billon aspron trachy. Numismatists call this cup shap scyphate. A flat copper tetarteron was also introduced.

Reference: Sear, *Byzantine Coins and Their Values.*

Counterfeit Alert: There are false gold coins known from the Beruit school, as noted in Sear. Large follis counterfeits are also encountered.

Hints: Gold starts at under $200.00 for some tremisses (⅓ solidi). The typical grade for copper is Good to Very Good and these can be had for a fraction of the prices given here for Very Fine, sometimes as low as $7 or $8.

(All coins have portrait of emperor.) **VF**
Anastasius I, 491-518 A.D. Large Follis (C) M (Constantinople) 75.00
Justinian I, 527-565, Solidus (G) Victory facing 300.00

___ Large Follis (C) M (Nicomedia). 225.00
___. Half Follis (C) K (Antioch) . 40.00
Justin II, 565-578 Tremissis (G) Winged Victory (Constantinople) . . . 165.00
Justin II (with Sophia) Follis (C) M (Constantinople) 35.00
Tiberius II, 578-582 Tremissis (G) Cross (Constantinople) 300.00
___. ¾ Follis (C) XXX (Cyzicus) 150.00
Maurice Tiberius, 582-602 Solidus (G) Victory facing (Constantinople) 300.00
___. Follis (C) M (Constantinople) 40.00

Phocas, 602-610 Solidus (G) Victory advancing (Constantinople) . . 325.00
___. Follis (C) XXXX (Constantinople). 50.00
Heraclius, 610-641 Hexagram (S) Cross on steps 250.00
___. Three-quarter Follis (C) Λ (Constantinople) 125.00

Constans II, 641-668 Solidus (G) Cross on steps (Constantinople) 275.00
Constantine IV, 668-685 Half Follis (C) K (Constantinople) 125.00
Justinian II, 685-695 Quarter Follis (C) I (Constantinople) 165.00
Leontius, 695-698 Solidus (G) Cross (Constantinople) 1,800.00
Philippicus, 711-713 Half Follis (C) K, (Constantinople) 400.00
Leo III 717-741 Follis (C) Bust facing / M (Constantinople) 150.00
Constantine V, 741-775 Follis with Leo IV (C) Bust of Leo III 50.00
Leo IV, 775-780 Miliaresion (S) Cross / Five-line inscription 225.00
Irene, 797-802 Follis (C) M (Constantinople) 300.00

VF

Leo V, 813-820 Follis (C) Facing bust of
Constantine 65.00
Michael II, 820-829 Solidus (G) Bust
(Syracuse) 650.00
Theophilus, 829-842 Follis (C) 3/4
figure/4 lines 60.00
Basil, 867-886 (C) 18mm. B / Cross
(Cherson) 125.00

Romanus I, 920-944, Miliareson (S) Cross
with medallion / Inscription in five
lines 225.00
Nicephorus II, 963-969, Follis (C) Four
line inscription 90.00
Constantine IX, 1042-1055, Nomisma (G)
Christ enthroned / Bust of the
emperor 300.00
Constantine X, 1059-1067, Follis (C)
Christ facing / Two figures, cross.
. . . . 50.00
Romanus IV, 1068-1071, Nomisma (G)
Christ standing / Three figures 350.00

Michael VII, 1071-1078, Nomisma (G)
Christ / Emperor 250.00
Nicephorus III, 1078-1081, Follis (C)
Enthroned Christ / Cross 50.00
Anonymous, 969-1067, Follis (C) Christ /
Three line inscription, class A . 75.00
___. Follis (C) Christ / Cross, 3 line
inscription, class B 65.00
Alexius I, 1081-1118, Tetarteon (C) Cross
/ Bust 35.00
John II, 1118-1143, Trachy (Electrum)
Christ / Two emperors, cross   300.00

Manuel, 1143-1180, Tetarteon (C) Bust of
Christ / Emperor 35.00
Isaac II, 185-1195, Trachy (Electrum)
Enthroned Christ / Emperor, angel.
. . . . 275.00
Nicaea, John III, Hyperpyron (G) Christ
/ Emperor, Virgin 250.00
Michael VII, 1261-1282, Hyperpyron (G)
Virgin in walls / Christ, Michael and
saint 350.00

Andronicus II, 1328-1341, (G) Trachy,
Virgin/Andronicus and Michael with
Christ 175.00
Andronicus III, 1328-1341, Assarion (C)
St. George / Half figure of emperor.
. . . . 175.00
Manuel II, 1391-1423, 1/16 Hyperpyron
(C) Bust 175.00
John VIII, 1423-1448, Half Hyperpyron
(S) Bust of Christ / Bust of John.
. . . . 175.00

AXUM

History: The ancient kingdom of Axum,
centered in modern Ethiopia, was one of
the first Christian nations. Its coinage is
unique in that many of the coppers
possess a gold inlay in the center.
Reference: Munro-Hay, *The Coinage of
Aksum* .
Counterfeit Alert: Counterfeits exist of
some gold pieces.
Hints: Most coppers occur with pitted
surfaces and as such are discounted.

Axumite Pagan Kings   **F**
Ousanus, 287-317 A.D. (C) 17mm. Bust,
barley / Bust 150.00

VF
Ezanas, 330-370 A.D. Tremissis (G)
Crowned bust / Bald bust . . 1,500.00

Axumite Christian Kings   **F**
Ouazebas, 4th cent. A.D. (C) 18mm. Bust
/ Bust with gold inlay 90.00
Mehadios, 6th cent. A.D. (G) inlay
(C)15mm. Bust / Cross 110.00

Kaleb, 525 A.D. (C) 16mm. Crowned
bust / Cross with gold inlay . . 75.00
Wazen, 7th cent. A.D, (C)17mm. Bust,
palm / Large cross with gold inlay
. . . . 90.00
VF
Armah, 8th cent. A.D. (C) 19mm.
Crowned figure enthroned / Cross with
gold inlay 150.00
Hataz, 9th cent. A.D. (C) 15mm. Facing
bust / Cross and crosslets . . . 200.00

DARK AGES

BARBARIC TRIBES
History: The barbaric tribes north of the
Roman Empire were a constant military
problem to Rome. During periods of
monetary hardship certain barbaric copies
were struck to ease the need for currency.
Reference: Giard, *Catalogue des Monnaies
de L'Empire Romain*, Vol I & II;
American Numismatic Society, *Museum
Notes*, Bastien 143-178.
Hints: This often-overlooked series is
now gaining popularity.

VF
Early Gaul
1st century A.D. As (C) Crude head of
Claudius / Minerva standing . . 50.00
Late Gaul
3rd century A.D. Radiate, copy of
Tetricus I (C) Pax standing . . . 35.00
Alemanni-Franks
Early 4th century A.D. AE 3, copy of
Constantine (C) Helmeted emperor /
Two Victories and altar 65.00

VANDALS
History: The Vandals made their first
appearance at the end of the 4th century.
After stopping briefly in Spain, they
finally established a kingdom in North
Africa including the great city of
Carthage.
Reference: Grierson and Blackburn,
Medieval European Coinage, Volume 1.

Gaiseric, 428-477, Half Siliqua (S) Bust /
Roma, Honorius 250.00

VF

Hilderic, 523-530 A.D. Half Siliqua (S) Bust / Carthage standing . . . 250.00

Gelimer, 530-534, (C) 42mm. Gelimer standing / Horse's head 300.00

OSTROGOTHS

History: The Germanic tribe of the Ostrogoths started their sweep against Rome in the mid-5th century. Theodoric was made king of Italy in 493 A.D.

Reference: Grierson and Blackburn, *Medieval European Coinage, Volume 1.*

Theodoric, 493-526, (S) 1/4 Siliqua, bust/monogram 350.00

Athalaric, 526-534 A.D. 10 Nummi (C) Roma / Athalaric standing . . 325.00

Theodahad, 534-536, Half Siliqua (S) Bust, monogram 600.00

Baduila, 541-552, Tremissis (G) Bust / Victory,name of Anastasius . 1,500.00

___. Minimi (C) Bust/Inscription 100.00

LOMBARDS

History: This Germanic tribe settled in Northern Italy in the late 6th century and made Pavia its capital.

Reference: Grierson and Blackburn, *Medieval European Coinage, Volume 1.*

Anonymous, 6th-7th cent. Quarter Siliqua (S) Bust / Cross in wreath (Justinian). 350.00

Cunincpert, 680-700 A.D. Tremessis (G) Bust / Victory 2,200.00

Lombards in Tuscia, 8th cent. Tremessis (G) Crude bust / Cross . . . 1,500.00

BENEVENTUM

History: Originally part of the Lombard Kingdom in the North of Italy, the South Italian duchy pursued an increasingly independent course after the 570s.

Rombald II 706-731, Solidus (G) Bust facing / Cross (Justinian) . . 3,000.00

Grimoald III, 788-792, Tremissis (G) Bust facing / Cross 2,000.00

VISIGOTHS

History: The Visigoths were a Germanic tribe that settled in Spain at the end of the 5th century, after passing through Gaul. Most of their coins are gold, with some scarcer small bronzes.

Reference: Miles, *The Coinages of the Visigoths of Spain.*

Counterfeit Alert: One of the most commonly counterfeited medieval series, including early counterfeits by Becker.

Anonymous, 565-578, Tremissis (G) Bust of Justin II / Victory 1,500.00

Sisebut, 612-621 Tremissis (G) Facing bust / Facing bust 900.00

Chindasvinta, 642-653, Tremessis (G) Facing bust / Facing bust . . 2,000.00

MEROVINGIANS

History: The Frankish kingdom of Clovis (481-511) established itself in Northern France and Belgium. Known as the Merovingians, the kings ruled until 737.

References: Grierson and Blackburn, *Medieval European Coinage, Volume 1*; Roberts, *Silver Coins of Medieval France.*

Royal Coinage

Chlotar II, 613-629, Tremissis (G) Bust / C-A cross 4,000.00

Sigebert III, 634-656, Tremissis (G) Bust / M-A, cross 4,000.00

Local Coinage by Mint

Baiocas, 7th cent. Tremissis (G) Bust / Latin cross 2,500.00

Massilia, 7th cent. Denier (S) Bust / Cross 500.00

SASANIAN

History: Sometimes referred to as the "fire worshippers," because of the fire-altar on the reverses of most of their coins, the Sasanians were the constant foes of the Roman and Byzantine empires. Their empire covered modern Iraq, Iran, Afghanistan, and Pakistan. The standard coin was the large flat silver drachm. Their beautiful style deteriorated with the passage of time. Also, their thinness caused the design of one side to "ghost" through to the other.

References: Sellwood and Whitting, *Sasanian Coins*; Göbl, *Sasanian Numismatics.*

Counterfeit Alert: Some of the modern counterfeits are identified in Göbl.

Hints: The rulers are identified by their ornate crowns. Some collectors collect by mint and year.

(All coins have portraits of ruler and the reverse has fire altar with or without attendants. All are drachms unless otherwise stated.)

VF

Ardasher I, 224-241 A.D. 200.00

___. Tetradrachm (Billon) 200.00

___. Obol (S) 175.00

Shapur I, 241-272 . . . . 100.00

___, Half Drachm (S) 175.00

___. Obol (S) 150.00

Hormizd I, 272-273 . . . . 2,500.00

Varhran I, 273-276 . . . . 300.00

Varhran II, 276-293, with wife and son. 250.00

Narseh, 293-303 . . . . 150.00

Hormizd II, 303-309 . . . . 175.00

Shapur II, 309-379 . . . . 65.00

___. Chalkous (C) 100.00

Ardasher II, 379-383 . . . . 175.00

Shapur III, 383-388 . . . . 125.00

Varhran IV, 388-399 . . . . 75.00

Yazdgard I, 399-420 . . . . 85.00

Varhran V, 420-438 . . . . 65.00

___. Eastern style, broad 200.00

Yadzgard II, 438-457 . . . . 50.00

Peroz, 457-484 . . . . 30.00

Valkash, 484-488 . . . . 150.00

Kavad, 484-531 . . . . 30.00

Zamasp, 497-499 . . . . 135.00

Hormizd IV, 579-590 . . . . 35.00

Vistahm, 591-597 . . . . 200.00

	VF
Xusro II, 591-628	30.00
Ardasher III, 628-630	125.00
Yazdgard III, 632-651	125.00

SASANIAN KUSHANSHAHS

Ardashir, 270-285, Unit (C)	60.00
Hormizd, 300-325, Unit (C)	35.00
Peroz II, 325-328, Unit (C)	15.00

WHITE HUNS   VF

Napki, 475-576, Dirham (S), Kabul 65.00
Peroz copy, Dirham (S) with Tamgha
before 60.00
Narana-Narendra 5th cent. Drachm (C)
Tall bust / Incuse 45.00

MEDIEVAL ISLAMIC

History: For the most part medieval Islamic coinage may be divided into three categories; first, the early imitative coinage; second, the standard Kufic hammered coinage; third, the iconographic coinage.

The earliest period produced coins that were adapted from the pre-existing coins of Byzantium in the West and the Sasanian Empire in the East; minor modifications were first used and then bolder changes were made.

The standard Islamic hammered coinage started with the Umayyad caliph 'Abd al-Malik. The basic denominations were the gold Dinar, silver Dirham, and copper Fals.

In later dynasties doubles, and multiples appeared and various later series used different names mostly in silver such as the Ottoman Akche, Indian Rupee, Persian Tanka, Abbasi, etc.

On most coins made before the Mongol invasion in the mid 13th century a date mint-mint formula was used in Arabic. It would translate "in the name of Allah, this (denomination) was struck at (mint) in the year (units, tens, hundreds)." The basic inscription would be a declaration of faith or shahada. This declaration from the Koran, "there is only one god, Allah, Muhammad is the apostle of God," was

added to in later times by adding other religious inscriptions from the Koran or justifying the ruler.

The Date: Derived from the flight of Muhammad from Mecca to Medina in 622 A.D. This is the Hegira year. It is converted from AH to AD by taking AH year, subtracting 3% and adding 621.

The Mints: Most Islamic coins have the name of the minting town. There are almost 1000 different mints. Many rare mints will command a high premium to collectors.

The iconographic coins were first struck on early fals. A popular series was begun in the 13th century by newly converted Turkoman tribes and the Rasulids of Yemen; the Mongols also continued this tradition. These coins with images are highly sought after.

References: Album, *Marsden's Numismata Orientalia Illustrata;* Album, *A Check List of Popular Islamic Coins;* Mitchner, *World of Islam;* Spengler Sayles, *Turkoman Figural Bronze Coins and their Iconography,* Vol. I & II.

Hints: Plant's *Reading Islamic Coins* is a helpful aid to this vast series.

ARAB SASANIAN   VF

Name of Yazdigerd III Dirham (S) Bust /Fire altar (Sistan) 95.00
Name of Caliph Mu'aAwiya 662-80 A.D. Dirham (S) Bust/Fire Altar (Darabjird). 160.00
Name of Anti-caliph, Abdallah bin al-Zubayr 680-92 A.D. Dirham (S) Bust/Fire Altar 100.00
Tabaristan: Farkhan, 711-728 Half Dirham (S) Bust / Fire Altar . . 35.00

'Umar bin al-Ala, 770-779 Half Dirham (S) Bust / Fire altar 20.00
Hani, 787-788 - Half Dirham (S) Bust / Fire altar 18.00

ARAB BYZANTINE   F

Anonymous 680-690's (Damascus) Fals (C) Standing emperor /M 30.00
___, (Baalbek) Fals (C) Emperor and son / M 30.00
___, (Tiberias) Fals (C) Three standing figures / M 60.00

___, 694-698 (Damascus) Fals (C) Standing caliph / ○ on staff . . 30.00

UMAYYAD   VF

(All are silver Dirhams unless stated, M=Mint)
'Abd al-Malik, 685-705 Dinar (G) 300.00

Al-Walid I, 705-715, 96 AH, Marw mint.
. . . . 25.00
Sulayman, 715-717. 97 AH, Wasit mint.
. . . . 27.00
'Umar, 717-720. 100 AH, Al-Basra mint.
. . . . 25.00
Yazid 11, 720-724. 105 AH, Wasit mint.
. . . . 25.00
Hisham, 724-743. 123 AH, Wasit mint.
. . . . 20.00
    F
Anonymous, Spain (Al-Andalus) Fals (C).
. . . . 30.00
___. Syria, Fals (C) no mint, pomegranate 20.00
___. Hawk. 25.00
___. Ba'albak mint. 12.00
___. Jerusalem mint. 125.00

ABBASID   VF

(all are silver Dirhams unless stated)
Al-Saffah, 749-754, 133 AH, al-Kufa mint.
. . . . 25.00
Al-Mansur, 754-775, Dinar (G) . 225.00
Al-Mahdi, 775-785, 161 AH, Madinat al-Salam mint 20.00
Al-Rashid, 786-809, 185 AH, Marv mint.
. . . . 50.00
Al-Amin, 809-813, 193 AH, Madinat al-Salam mint 25.00
Al-Ma'mun, 813-83, 199 AH, Dinar (G) Misr mint 225.00
Al-Mu'tazz, 866-869, 251 AH, Surra Man Ra'a 40.00
Al-Muqtadir, 908-932, 300 AH, Jannaba mint (rare mint) 150.00
Al-Qahir, 932-934, 322 AH, Madinat al-Salam mint 35.00
Al-Radi, 934-940, Dinar (G) 324 AH, Tustar min al-Ahwaz mint . . 250.00
Anonymous, Fals (C) Ba'albak mint.
. . . . 25.00
___. Fals (C) Syria. Hims mint . . 25.00

UMAYYAD OF SPAIN   VF
'Abd al-Rahman I, 756-788, Dirham (S).
. . . . 60.00
'Abd al-Rahman II, 912-961, Dirham (S)
343 AH, Madinat al-Zahra mint   45.00
Al-Hakam II, 961-976 A.D. Dirham (S)
359 AH, Madinat al-Zahra mint   35.00
Anonymous, Fals (C) 250-300 AH   35.00

TULUNID
Ahmad, 868-884, Dirham (S), 267 AH, al-
Rafiqa mint (rare mint) 200.00
Harun, 896-905, Dinar (G) Misr mint.
. . . . 200.00

FATIMID
Al-Mu'izz, 953-975, Half Dirham (S) 360
AH, Mahdiya mint 40.00
Al-Hakim, 997-1021 Half Dirham (S).
. . . . 20.00

Al-Zahir, 1021-1036 Dinar (G) . 225.00

MAMLUK - SLAVE KINGS
Baybars I, 1260-1277, Fals (C), Lion,
Dimashq mint 20.00
Kitbugha, 1295-1297 Half Dirham (S).
. . . . 25.00
Al-Zahir Barquq, 1382-1389 Dinar (G)
Qahira mint (heavy, c.18gm.)   400.00
___. Same (light, c.4gm.) 200.00

MUWAHHIDUN   VF
Anonymous, 1160-1269, Square Dirham
(S) 20.00

SAMANID
Ahmad II, 907-914 Dirham (S), 298 AH,
Al-Shash mint 30.00

BUWAYHID
'Adud al-Dawla, 949-983, Dirham (S), 368
AH, Arrajan mint 40.00

KAKWAYHID
Faramurz, 1041-1051, Dinar (G) 435 AH,
Isbahan mint, weak strike . . . 175.00

GHAZNAVID
Mahmud, 998-1030, Bilingual Dirham (S),
418 AH, Mahmudpur mint. Rare type.
. . . . 150.00
___. Multiple Dirham (S) 389 AH,
Andaraba mint 45.00
Ibrahim, 1059-1099 Dirham (Billon)
Lahore mint, Bull 10.00

GREAT SELJUQS
Tughril, 1038-1063 Dinar (G), 436 AH,
Nishapur mint 175.00

HAMMUDID OF QUED-LAOU
Hasan Half Dirham (S), 441 AH, Wadi
Lau mint 100.00

KHWARIZMSHAHS
Muhammad, 1200-1220 Dirham (S).
. . . . 20.00

SELJUQS OF RUM
Kaykhusraw I, 1192-1196, Fals (C)
Horseman / Inscription 35.00

Kaykhusraw II, 1236-1245, Dirham (S),
639 AH, Lion and sun type, Konya
mint 40.00
Kaykhusraw III, 1265-1282, Dirham (S),
672 AH, Lulua mint 30.00
Mes'ud II, 1280-1298, Dirham (S), 681
AH, Sivas mint 20.00

AYYUBIDS OF YEMEN
al-Nasir, 1201-1214, Dirham (S) 605 AH,
Zabid 75.00
Yusuf, 1214-1228, Dirham (S), 620 AH,
Sanaa mint 85.00

GREAT MONGOLS
Genghis Khan, 1206-1227, Dirham
(Billon) 65.00

GOLDEN HORDE
Tole Buqa, 1287-1290, Dirham (S), 687
AH, Khuwarizm mint 60.00

GIRAY KHANS (CRIMEA)
Mengli Giray I, 1466-1514, Akche (S), 900
AH, Kaffa mint 35.00

ILKHANS
Hulagu, 1256-1265, Dirham (S), 669 AH,
al-Jazira mint (rare mint) 75.00

Arghun, 1284-1291, Dirham (S), Tabriz
mint 20.00
Ghazan Mahmud, 1295-1304, Fals (C),
Sunface in square 45.00
Uljaytu, 1304-17, Two Dirhams (S), 710
AH, Jajerm mint 30.00

Abu Sa'id, 1316-1335, Two Dirhams (S),
729 AH, Sultaniyah mint 25.00

MUZAFFARID
Shah Shuja, 1358-1384, Two Dinars (S),
no date, Aydhaj mint 30.00

JALAYRID
Hasan Buzurg, 1335-1356, Dinar (S), 756
AH, Hilla mint 40.00

TIMURID
Timur, 1370-1405, Quarter Tanka (S),
783 AH, Samarqand mint 30.00
Muhammad, 1447-1451, Tanka (S), 851
AH, Abarquh mint 35.00

SHAYBANID
Kuchkunji, 1510-1531, Tanka (S), 934
AH, Bukhara mint 45.00

SAFAVID
Isma'il II, 1576-1578, Two Shahi (S),
Fuman mint 125.00
Sultan Husayn, 1694-1722, Abbasi (S),
Tabriz mint, Inscriptions 15.00

ICONOGRAPHIC
    VF
AYYUBID
Al-Nasir Yusuf I (Saladin), 1169-1193,
Dirham (C), Lion and three stars.
. . . . 100.00

ARTUQID

Alpi, 1152-1176, Dirham (C), Two facing
busts / Two figures 100.00
Husam al-Din, 1184-1201, Dirham (C),
Head left and head facing 90.00

VF

Artuq Arslan, 1200-1239, Dirham (C)
   Centaur shooting 80.00

ZENGIDS

Mosul, Mawdud, 1149-1169, Dirham (C)
   Facing head, two angels 75.00
__, Mahmud, 1219-1233, Dirham (C)
   Prince holding crescent 65.00
Jazira, Mahmud, 1209-1221, Dirham (C)
   Bust, crescent 90.00
Syria, Isma'il, 1174-1181, Fals (C) Bust of
   Constantine 50.00

RASULIDS OF YEMEN

Al-Mujahid, 1322-1363, Dirham (S) Lion
   in center, Mahjam mint 75.00

MEDIEVAL INDIA AND EAST

History: With the collapse of the Gupta
empire, different waves of conquerers
established their empires in the vast
subcontinent. This medieval period can
be divided into the Invasion Period (5th-
13th centuries), and the Period of
Mohammedan States (13th-16th centuries).
The Mogul emperors established their
new empire in India in the mid-16th
century. The culture and coinage of the
far south generally reined quite distinct
from these influences.
Reference: Mitchiner, *Oriental Coins and
their Values;* Mitchiner, *Non-Islamic States
and Western Colonies AD 600-1979;* and
Mitchiner, *The World of Islam.*
Hints: This massive series is very good
for those on a budget, as the values of the
coins are very reasonable.

VF

Vishnukundins, c.475-615 A.D. Unit (C),
   about 20mm. Lion / Shell between
   standards 30.00
Yadavas, Mahadeva, 1261-1270, Unit (G)
   Countermarked, lotus, conch   150.00
Silaharas, anonymous, 12th cent. Drachm
   (Billon) Indo-Sassanian bust / Crude
   horseman 20.00

Western Ganges, anonymous, 1080-1138,
   Pagoda (G) Elephant / Floral scroll.
   . . . . 200.00
Cholas, Uttama Chola, 973-985,
   Kahavand (S) Tiger under canopy, two
   fish to right / Name 35.00

Ghorid, Mohammed bin Sam, 1170-1206,
   Jital (Billon) Horseman 6.00
Vijayanagar, Devaraya I, 1406-22, Pagoda
   (G) Siva & Parvati facing . . . 125.00
Nayakas, Srivira 1500s, Kasu (C) Humped
   bull 10.00

CEYLON

Shasa Malla, 1200-1202, Kahavanu (C)
   King seated / King standing . . 12.00

SULTANS OF DELHI

Mas'aud, 1260-1265, Jital (B) Crude bull /
   Crude horseman 8.00
Firoz Shah II, 1290-1296, Tankal (S) 691
   AH, Hazrat Delhi mint 25.00

Mohammed II, 1296-1316, Jital (B)   8.00
Mubarak Shah I, 1316-1320, Square
   Mohur (G) 300.00

SULTANS OF BENGAL

Sirandar Shah, 1358-1389, Tanka (S) 769
   AH, Firozabad mint 25.00
Yusuf Shah, 1474-1481, Tanka (S) 884
   AH, Dar al-Zarb mint 35.00

SULTANS OF KASMIR

Muhammed Shah, 1481-1514, Fals (C)
   Kasmir mint 5.00

KULBARGA

Ahmad Shah II, 1436-1456, Tanka (S)
   Mohammad-adad mint 100.00

ANGKOR (CAMBODIA)

Khmer Kingdom, 802-1450, Unit (Lead)
   Holed center, floral design . . . 15.00

ARAKAN

Candra kingdom 400-630, Half Unit (S)
   Zebu / Trident 40.00

CRUSADER STATES

History: The Crusader States were
established after the First Crusade in 1098
at Edessa. A large part of the Levant
emerged under Christian sway, including
Jerusalem. After their defeat at the Battle

of Hattin, Crusader influence was greatly
reduced. In 1291, the last coastal
influence was driven out. But, Cyprus,
Rhodes and Chios continued the Crusader
coinage.
   The first coins were like the large
copper follis of Byzantium. Western
influence brought about the sstriking of
small billon (very ase silver) and copper
deniers, obols and pougeoises. Later the
large silver gros was introduced.
Crusader gold copied the issues of
Fatimid Egypt, as well as those of the
Ayyubids of Syria and Egypt. Gold with
Western style designs was struck, but
survives today only as cut fragments.
Reference: Malloy, Preston & Seltman,
Coins of the Crusader States.
Hints: A popular series of issues depict
many holy Christian shrines. Certain
types are readily available to the collector
at attractive prices. The usual condition
encountered is fine.

JERUSALEM   F

Baldwin II, 1143-1163, Denier (B) Cross /
   Tower of David 40.00
Amaury, 1163-1174, Denier (B) Cross /
   Holy sepulchre 50.00
Anonymous, 1187-1220, Fragment cut
   from bar (G) Hexagram /   gate 75.00
Anonymous, c.1250s, Dirham (S)
   Imitation of Damascus type . . 30.00

BEIRUT

Raymond, 1184-1186, Pougeoise (C)
   Tower of David / Star 100.00

TRIPOLI

Raymond II, 1137-1152, Pougeoise (C)
   Star and crescent / Cross 45.00

Raymond III, 1152-1187, Pougeoise (C)
   Cross / Castle 35.00
Bohemond V, 1233-1251, Denier (B)
   Cross / Star 55.00
Bohemond VII, 1275-87, Gros (S) Cross
   / Castle gateway . . . . . . VF 110.00

ANTIOCH

Tancred, 1101-12, Follis (C) St. Peter /
   Inscription 60.00

F
Bohemond III, minority 1149-1163, Denier (Billon) Bare head / Cross.
. . . . 75.00

___. majority 1163-1201, Denier (Bil.) Helmeted head to left / Cross . 30.00
Raymond Rupin, 1216-1219, Denier (Bil.) Helmeted head / Cross 125.00
Bohemond V, 1233-1252, Denier (Bil.) Helmeted head / Cross 60.00

EDESSA
Baldwin II, 1108-18, Follis (C) Count standing / Cross 175.00

CYPRUS
Henry I, 1219-1253, Denier (Bil.) Cross / Gateway 40.00
Hugh IV, 1324-59, Gros (S) King seated / Cross 60.00

FRANKISH GREECE: ACHAEA
Isabelle 1297-1301, Denier (Bil.) Cross / Castle 25.00
Philip of Savoy, 1301-1306, Denier (Bil.) Cross / Castle 25.00
Maud, 1316-1318, Denier (Bil.) Cross / Castle 25.00
John, 1318-33, Denier (Bil.) Cross / Castle 35.00

FRANKISH GREECE: ATHENS
Guy II, 1294-1308, Denier (Bil.) Cross / Castle 25.00

RHODES   **VF**
Helion, 1319-1346, Gigliato (S) Kneeling figure, cross / Cross 200.00

ASIAN CHRISTIAN KINGDOMS
History: These kingdoms were established by ethnic groups, offshoots of the Byzantine empire or later results of the last Crusades.
References: Trebizond: Sear, *Byzantine Coins and their Values*; Armenia: Bedukian, *Coins of Cilician Armenia*; Georgia: Lang, *Studies in the Numismatic History of Georgia in Transcaucasia*; Lesbos and Chios: Schlumberger, *Numismatique de L'orient latin*.
Hints: Armenian copper is usually found in low grade, and as such usually sells for much less than prices listed. Armenian silver is rarely fully struck.

ARMENIA: BARONIAL   **VF**
Gosdantin I, 1095-1099 (C) 21 mm. Cross / Cross 1,000.00

ARMENIA: KINGDOM
Levon I, 1198-1218, Two Tram (S) King enthroned / Lion 250.00
___. Tram (S) King enthroned / Two lions 38.00
___. Tank (C) Head / Patriarchal cross.
. . . . 75.00
Hetoum-Zabel, 1221-1271, Tram (S) King and queen / Lion 30.00

Hetoum I and Kaykhusraw, 1226-1271, Tram (S) Hrseman / Arabic legend.
. . . . 125.00
Levon II, 1270-1289, Tram (S) Horseman / Lion 25.00
Hetoum II, 1289-1296, Kardez (C) Head / Cross 35.00
Smpad, 1296-98, Pough (C) Horseman / Lion 65.00
Levon III, 1301-1307, Takvorin (S) Horseman / Lion 60.00
Oshin, 1308-1320, Pough (C) King seated / Cross 70.00
Gosdantin IV, 1365-1373, Takvorin (Billon) Horseman / Lion . . . 75.00
Levon V, 1374-1385, Obol (S) Bust facing / Cross 175.00

TREBIZOND
Manuel I, 1238-1263, Asper (S) St. Eugenius / King 60.00
John II, 1280-1297, Asper (S) St. Eugenius / King 60.00

Alexius II, 1297-1330, Asper (S) Eugenius on horseback / King 60.00
Alexius III, 1349-1390 (C) 15 mm. Cross / Alexius standing 85.00
John IV, 1446-1458, Reduced Asper (S) St. Eugenius on horseback / John on horseback 70.00

MITELENE (LESBOS)
Francesco I, 1355-1376, Fractional (C) Arms / Cross 250.00

Dorino, 1400-1449, Asper (S) Lamb of God / Cross 500.00

CHIOS
Philip-Marie, 1421-1436, Sequin (G) St. Mark, Doge / Christ. 300.00
Giustiani, anonymous 1342-1566, Quarter Gigliat (S) Castle / Cross . . . 200.00

CAFFA (CRIMEA)
Anonymous, 1265-1475, Aspro (S) Genoese gate / Symbol 250.00

GEORGIA   **VF**
Giorgio III, 1156-1184, Fals (C) (Tiflis) Inscription / Inscription 225.00

Queen T'amar, 1184-1231, Follis (C) Military symbol / Four line inscription 300.00
Dimitri, 1273-1289, Dirham (S) Christian legend / Arabic 175.00
Anonymous, 14th cent. Trebizond copy, Asper (S) St. Eugenius / John II 200.00

ENGLAND
ANGLO-SAXON-NORMAN
History: The Anglo-Saxons were Teutonic raiders who settled in England during the 600's; their reign continued until 1066, when William the Conqueror established Norman rule.

The earliest Anglo-Saxon coins were small, thick silver coins called sceattas, and similar gold pieces called thrymsas. While their designs were often too stylized to interpret, most were ultimately derived from late Roman coins. The silver was eventually debased to nearly pure copper. Gold simply ceased to be struck. The middle period of Anglo-Saxon coinage began when the broad silver penny was introduced, about 780, patterned after the denier used in Charlemagne's France. This continued to be the most important coin in England until the 1350s. The late Anglo-Saxon period is one where a united English Kingdom has replaced the several smaller ones. Its coins uniformly carry a bust of the king, which before was only occasionally used.
References: Seaby, *Coins of England and the United Kingdom*; North, J.J. *English Hammered Coinage*.

Counterfeit Alert: Most false coins were made in the 19th century and are identifiable to the trained modern eye.

Hints: The coins of Henry I through the first issues of Henry II are almost always partially struck. Coins with one-third or more of the design unstruck, even if high grade, are discounted.

EARLY ANGLO-SAXON   VF

Anonymous, 690-725, Sceattas (S) Radiate
    head in square 275.00
___. Porcupine type Sceattas (S)
    Porcupine 225.00
Mercian, 705-730, Sceattas (S) Two heads
    / Birds 375.00
Frisian, 700-750, Sceattas (S) Bust / Cross.
    . . . . 175.00
Northumbrian, Eanred, 810-854 Sceat (S)
    Cross / Cross 175.00

___. Sceat (C) Cross / Wreath . . 80.00
York Archbishops, Wigmund, 837-54,
    Sceat (C) Cross / Cross 125.00

MIDDLE ANGLO SAXON   VF
(All are Silver Pennies.)

Canterbury, Ceolnoth, 833-870, Facing
    bust / Chi-rho monogram . 1,000.00
Mercia, Coenwulf, 796-821, m̄ /Tribrach.
    . . . . 950.00
___, Burgred, 852-874, Bust / Three line
    inscription 350.00

KINGS OF EAST ANGLIA

Edmund, 855-870, Ā / Cross with dot in
    each angle 750.00

VIKING COINAGE

St. Edmund, 870-890, Ā / Cross 350.00
Cnut-Siefred, c.897, Patriarchal cross /
    Cross 375.00

Alfred the Great, 871-899, His bust /
    Monogram 2,500.00
Edward the Elder, 899-924, Cross /
    Name. 375.00

LATE ANGLO-SAXON—
KINGS OF ALL ENGLAND   VF

Aethelstan, 924-939, Cross / Moneyer's
    name 550.00
Eadmund, 939-946, Cross / Moneyer's
    name 500.00

Eadred, 946-955, Cross /Moneyer's
    name 425.00
Eadgar, 959-975, Cross / Cross . 300.00

Aethelred II, 978-1016, Bust / Crux in
    angles of cross 250.00
Cnut, 1016-1035, Bust / Cross . 250.00
Harold I, 1035-1040, Long cross with
    fleur de lis in angles 425.00
Edward the Confessor, 1042-1066, Radiate
    bust / Cross 300.00
Harold II, 1066, Crowned bust / PAX.
    . . . . 950.00

NORMAN

William I, 1066-1087, Bonnet bust /
    Cross. 350.00
William II, 1087-1100, Cross in quatrefoil.
    . . . . 1,200.00
Henry I, 1100-1135, Facing bust / Cross
    fleury 350.00
Stephen, 1134-1154, Cross moline,
    Watford mint 300.00

ENGLAND
POST-NORMAN

History: The silver penny continued to be struck for circulation through the 1600s, being the most important coin until the mid-1300s. By that time half-pennies, farthings (quarter-pennies) and groats (four pence) began to be struck in quantity. Gold coins were also successfully introduced at this time. These pieces were splendid works of Gothic art. Realistic portraiture was first introduced to English coinage toward the end of the reign of Henry VII.

Interestingly, all the coins of Richard the Lionheart and John bear the name of their father, Henry II.

References: North, *English Hammered Coins*; Seaby, *Coins of England and the United Kingdom*.

Counterfeit Alert: Hundreds of different imitations of the English Penny were struck in Germany, Belgium, and the Netherlands during the Middle Ages.

When identifiable by issuer, they command a premium.

Hints: Coins from Philip and Mary through Charles I were struck in very low relief, thus their portraits wore flat very quickly.

(All types have bust of monarch and are London mint unless otherwise noted.)

PLANTAGENET   F

Henry II, 1154-1189, Penny (S) Short
    cross with double-line arms. . . 55.00
Richard the Lion Heart, 1189-1199 Penny
    (S) In name of HENRICVS, Short cross
    with double-line arms. 85.00
John, 1199-1216, Penny (S) In name of
    HENRICVS, Short cross with double-
    line arms. 65.00

Henry III, 1216-1272, Penny (S) Long
    cross with outlined arms 40.00
Edward I, 1272-1307, Penny (S) Long
    cross with solid arms. 25.00
___. Halfpenny (S) Similar 60.00
Edward II, 1307-1327, Penny (S) Long
    cross 30.00

Edward III, 1327-1377 Quarter Noble (G)
    Shield / Cross 275.00
___, Groat (S) Long cross through double
    legend 85.00
Richard II, 1377-1399, Penny (S) Long
    cross 90.00

LANCASTER

Henry IV, 1399-1413, Halfpenny (S) Long
    cross 475.00
Henry V, 1413-1422, Penny (S) Long
    cross, York mint 70.00
Henry VI, 1422-1461 Groat (S) Long cross
    through double legend, Calais mint.
    . . . . 100.00
___. Half Groat (S) 65.00

YORK

Edward IV, first reign 1461-70, Halfgroat
    (S) Similar, Canterbury mint . . 55.00
___, second reign 1471-1483, Groat (S)
    Similar 80.00
Richard III, 1483-1485 Groat (S) Similar.
    . . . . 600.00

F

Richard III. Penny (S) Similar, Durham mint. 500.00

TUDOR

Henry VII, 1485-1509, Halfgroat (S) Similar 75.00

Henry VIII, 1509-1547, Groat (S) Young bust / Shield 135.00
___, Posthumous issue, Groat (S) Bearded bust / Shield, Southwark mint   125.00

Edward VI, 1547-1553 Sixpence (S) VI by bust / Shield 100.00
Mary, 1553-54, Groat (S) Shield   135.00
Philip and Mary, 1554-58, Sixpence (S) Two confronted busts / Shield .   200.00
Elizabeth I, 1558-1603, Angel (G) St. Michael / Ship . . . . VF 850.00
___, Shilling (S) Shield 165.00

STUART

James I, 1603-1625 Sixpence (S) 1603, Shield 75.00
Charles I, 1625-49 Shilling (S) Shield. 65.00
___, Farthing (C) Crown / Crowned harp 18.00
Commonwealth, 1649-1660 Halfgroat (S) Shield in wreath / Two shields   50.00
Charles II, 1660-1685, Shilling (S) Hammered issue, Bust left / Shield. 150.00

SCOTLAND

History: The coinage of Scotland began with David I in 1136. In 1603, James VI, succeeded to the throne of England as James I. (James was the son of Mary, Queen of Scots, who had been executed by her cousin Elizabeth.) Separate Scottish coinage continued until the Act of Union in 1707, during the reign of Queen Anne
Reference: Seaby, *Coins of Scotland, Ireland and the Islands.*

(All have bust obverse and cross reverse unless noted.)   F
William the Lion, 1165-1214, Penny (S) 175.00
Alexander III, 12549-1286, Penny (S) Cross, Edinburgh mint 85.00

David II, 1329-1371, Groat (S) Edinburgh mint 150.00
Robert II, 1371-1390 Halfgroat (S) Perth mint 150.00
Robert III, 1390-1406, Halfgroat (S). 200.00
James I, 1406-1437, Penny (Billon) 150.00
James III, 1460-1488, Plack (Bil.) Shield / Cross 70.00
James IV, 1488-1513, Penny (Bil.)   60.00
James V, 1513-1542, Groat (S) Shield. 150.00
Mary 1542-67, Bawbee (B) Thistle / Cross. 50.00
James VI, 1567-1625, Sword and Sceptre Piece (G) Shield / Crossed sword and sceptre 600.00

IRELAND

History: The earliest Irish coins were silver pennies struck by the Vikangs at Dublin in imitation of English pennies of Aethelred II (978-1016). This design continued to degenerate throughout the 11th century. The coins of the English dominion over Ireland held to stricter standards from the reign of King John, as lord of Ireland (after 1172) through the 15th century.
Reference: Seaby, *Coins of Scotland, Ireland and the Islands.*

VF
Hiberno-Norse issues 1035-1060, Penny (S) Bust / Cross 375.00
John, 1185-1199, Halfpenny (S) Bust in triangle / Cross, crescent and stars in triangle. 150.00

Henry III, 1216-1272, Penny (S) Facing head in triangle / Cross 125.00

Edward I, 1272-1307, Penny (S) Head in inverted triangle / Cross, Dublin mint. 85.00
                              F   VF
Henry VII, 1485-1509, Groat (S) Shield / Three crowns   135.00   250.00

Henry VIII, 1509-1547, Groat (S) Shield / Crowned harp, hΛ (for Henry and Anne Boleyn) at sides.
                    150   125.00
                                       F
Elizabeth I, 1558-1603, Shilling (Billon) Shield / Harp 400.00
James I, 1603-1625, Sixpence (S) Bust / Crowned harp 175.00

ANGLO-GALLIC

History: The English kings inherited vast holdings in France, including Normandy, Anjou, and Aquitaine. Sometimes these lands were larger than those held by the King of France himself, causing perpetual conflict between these two powerful rulers. The coinage of these English-held French territories is called "Anglo-Gallic."
Reference: Elias, *The Anglo-Gallic Coins.*

F
Henry II, 1152-1168, Denier (Billon) Cross / Two line inscription (Aquitaine) 75.00
Richard the Lionheart, 1168-1199, Denier (Bil.) Cross / Three-line inscription (Poitou) 95.00
Eleanor I, 1137-1204, Denier (Bil.) Two small crosses / Cross (Aquitaine). 135.00
Edward I, 1252-1272, Denier (S) Leopard / Cross 85.00
Edward the Black Prince, 1362-1372, Hardi (S) Bust / Cross (Agen)   100.00
Henry V 1413, 1422, Niquet (Bil.) Crowned lion / Cross 100.00
Henry VI, 1422-1458, Denier (Bil.). 100.00

FRANCE
CAROLINGIAN

History: The Carolingian dynasty was founded by Charles Martel, who drove the Moors from France in 753. The first king of the dynasty was Pippin the Short, whose son Charlemagne became one of the major figures in Western history, as the first Holy Roman Emperor..

References: Prou, *Les Monnaies Carolingiennes*; Roberts, *Silver Coins of Medieval France.*; Grierson and Blackburn, *Medieval European Coinage.*

Counterfeit Alert: This series is not plagued by counterfeits, but some deceptive 19th century ones do exist.

Hints: The coins of Charles the Bald's most common type continued to be struck for a century after his death. their style differs. Also be careful not to accept these same deniers being passed off as those of Charlemagne.

                                    VF
Charlemagne, 768-814, Denier (S) CARO-
    LVS / Small cross 3,500.00
Louis the Pious, 814-840, Denier (S) Cross
    / Cross in temple 250.00

Lothaire I, 840-855, Denier (S) Cross / temple. 300.00
Charles II, the Bald, 840-877, Denier (S) Cross / Monogram, Melle mint 200.00
Carloman, 879-884, Denier (S) Cross / Monogram, Arles mint 500.00

Odo, 888-898, Denier (S) O+D+O / Cross 300.00

ROYAL FRANCE

History: Medieval France from Hugh Capet on was a steady progression of the acquisition of power and land. The early coinage followed the Carolingian standard and starting with Saint Louis used gold and the gros. By Philip IV the denominations were vast and varied.

References: Duplessy, *Les Monnaies Francaises Royales*; Mayhew, *coinage in France.*

Counterfeit Alert: Contemporary counterfeits actually made during the Middle Ages and Renaissance are not rare.
                                    F
Hugh Capet, 987-996, Denier (S) Cross / Monogram 300.00

Robert, 996-1031, Denier (S) Facing bust / Bust of bishop 400.00
Philip I, 1060-1108, Denier (S) Mono-gram / Cross 225.00
Louis VI, 1108-1137, Denier (S) OE^X / Cross 125.00
Louis VII, 1137-1180, Denier (S) Head facing / Cross 140.00
Philip II August, 1180-1223, Denier (Billon) FRANCO / Cross . . . 40.00
Louis VIII, 1223-1226, Denier (Bil.) Cross / Castle 35.00

Louis IX (Saint Louis) 1226-1270, Gros (S) Cross / Castle 125.00
Philip III, 1270-1285, Denier Tournois (Bil.) Cross / Castle 30.00
Philip IV, 1285-1314, Double Tournois (S) Double cross / Cathedral spire 30.00
Philip V, 1316-1322, Gros (S) Cross / Castle 150.00
Charles IV, 1322-1328, Royal (G) King standing / Cross . . . . . *VF* 1,200.00
Philip VI, 1328-1350, Denier Parisis (Bil.) FRANCO / Cross 35.00
John, 1350-1364, Mouton (G) Lamb / Cross . . . . *VF* 1,300.00
Charles V, 1364-1380, Blanc (S) Crowned K / Cross 50.00

Charles VI, 1380-1422, Ecu (G) Crown, shield / Cross . . . . *VF* 550.00
Charles VII, 1422-1461, Blanc (called Gruénar) (S) Shield / Cross . . . 40.00
Louis XI, 1461-1483, Ecu (G) Shield / Cross 400.00
Charles VIII, 1483-1497, Liard (Bil.) Dolphin / Cross 30.00
Louis XII, 1497-1515, Hardi (S) King facing / Cross 50.00
Francois I, 1515-1547, Douzain (Bil.) Crowned F / Cross 35.00
Henry II, 1547-1559, Douzin (S) Crowned shield / Floral cross 40.00
Charles IX, 1560-1574, Demi Teston (S) Bust / Crown, shield 70.00
Henry III, 1574-1589, Douzain (Bil.) Shield, crown / Cross 40.00

Henry IV, 1589-1610, Ecu (G) Cross / Shield . . . . *VF* 500.00

___. Quarter Ecu (S) 1606, Floral cross / Crowned arms 65.00
Louis XIII, 1610-1643, Five Sols (S) Bust / Crowned arms 25.00

FEUDAL FRANCE

History: During most of the Middle Ages the French King controlled only part of France directly, with the rest in the hands of his feudal vassals. These vassals, counts, dukes, bishops, etc., had the right to strike their own coins. Thus feudal France provided a prime environment for the development of regional and city coinages. The billon denier was the standard coin, with its fractional obol. As the king took more land and privileges from the feudal nobles, their influence and coinage was diminished. By the 1400s only a few nobles still struck feudal coinage, but this period saw a new diversity of metals and denominations.

References: Roberts, *The Silver Coins of Medieval France*; Boudeau, *Monnaies Francaises (Provincales)*; Mayhew, *coinage in France*; Erslev, *Thomsen Collection*; Poey d'Avant, *Monnaies Féodales de France..*

Counterfeit Alert: This series is generally free of counterfeits.

Hints: French feudal coins are almost never fully struck. Most are either weak in the middle or have a void on one side where the design on the other side is raised. This series is attractively priced for the beginner.

Note: Most coins below are described as silver even if billon if their appearance is that of silver.
                                    F
Amiens, 11th cent. Denier (S) PAX in field / Cross 25.00
Albi, Raymond VII, 1248-1300s, Denier (Bil.) PAX in field / Ccross . . . 25.00

F

Angouleme, 13th cent. Denier (S) Cross / Annulets 25.00
Anjou, Foulques IV, 1060-1109, Denier (S) Cross / Monogram 25.00
Auxerre, 12th cent. Denier (S) Cross / Cross 25.00

Bearn, "Centulle III," 1088-1300, Denier (S) Cross / PAX 25.00
Besançon, 12th cent. Denier (S) Hand / Cross 27.00
Bouillon & Sedan, Henry 1591-1623, Two Liards (C) Bust / Arms 15.00
Brittany, John V. 1399-1442, Blanc (Bil.) Ermine tassels / Cross 40.00
Burgundy, Hugh V, 1305-1315, Denier (Bil.) DVX across / Cross 18.00
Deóls, Raoul VI, 1160-1176, Denier (S) Cross / Star of David 27.00
Gien, Geoffery, c.1100 Denier (S) Cross and crescent / Alpha and omega 25.00
Le Puy, 11-13th century Denier (S) Alpha and omega / Monogram 20.00
Meaux, Etienne, 1161-1171, Denier (S) Bishop's head / Cross 35.00

Melgueil, Anonymous, 1130-1316, Denier (S) Mitred cross / Four annulets 25.00
Metz, Bertram 1179-1212, Denier (S) Figure / Hand 25.00

Nevers, Anonymous, c.1100, Denier (S) Sickle and cross (corrupt monogram of King Louis IV) / Cross 35.00
___. William IV, 1161-1168, Denier (S) C-S cross / Cross 20.00
Poitou, 900-1168, Denier (S) Cross / Metalo 30.00
Sancerre, Etienne, 1152-1191, Denier (S) Head of Julius Caesar / Cross . 30.00
Strasburg, city, 1550, Denier (S) Lis / Lis 15.00

Vienne, 11th cent. Denier (S) Bust / Cross 25.00

LOW COUNTRIES

History: The Low Countries include Belgium, the Netherlands, and Luxembourg. From the tenth century on, local nobles and bishops began to replace Imperial authority in some areas. By the fifteenth century much of this region came under the control of the House of Burgundy, and by later in the century the House of Hapsburg. The Netherlands threw off the yoke of Hapsburg Spain in the late 1500s.

The coinage of the Low Countries through the 1400s bears a strong similarity to Feudal coinage in neighboring regions of France.

References: Erslev, *Medieval Coins in the Christian J. Thomsen Collection.*

Hints: Those coins bearing actual dates before 1500 are much in demand.

F

Brabant, John III, 1312-55, Esterling (S) Shield / Cross 35.00
Flanders, Louis I, 1322-46, Mite (Billon) Ornate L / Cross 27.00
___. Louis II, 1346-48 Gros (S) Lion / Cross 40.00
___. Philip de Hardi, 1384-1404, Double Gros (S) Lion / Cross 150.00

___. Philip the Good, 1419-1467, Gros (S) Two shields / Cross and shield 100.00
___. Charles, 1467-1477, Two Sol (S) Shield / Cross 25.00
Hainault, John II, 1280-1304, Esterlin (S) Bust / Cross 100.00
___. Marguerite II, 1345-1356, Double Gros (S) Monogram / Cross . 150.00
Holland, Florent III, 1157-1190, Suiv (S) Head / Double cross 45.00
Lille, City Coinage, 1220-1250, Petit Denier (S) Edifice / Cross 30.00
Luxemburg, Wenleslas I, 1356-1383, Gros (S) Cross / Crown and shield 100.00

Namur, John IV, 1418-1421, Two Mite (C) Ram / Cross 30.00

MEDIEVAL ITALY

History: The history of Italy in medieval and renaissance times is reflected in its coinage. The doges of Venice ruled the waves, Milan influenced northern Italy, under its Sforza, Visconti, and later Spanish rulers. For the most part, the north was a clutter of smaller rival states and foreign powers. Central Italy was dominated by the Pope (see Papal States below), when his cities were not in revolt. Less confusing, the south consisted of Naples and Sicily, sometimes united, sometimes not. The flowering of the Renaissance is reflected in Italian coins first, reflected in the early introduction of beautiful, realistic portraits on fine quality large silver testone.

References: Erslev, *Medieval Coins in the Christian J. Thomsen Collection; Corpus Nummorum Italicorum I-XX.*

Counterfeit Alert: Venetian gold ducats are found false, along with some florins and other gold.

Hints: A collector can amass a set of coins of most of the doges of Venice at a very moderate cost. The coins of Sicily have been quite reasonable in the last few years. Bases silver (billon) denari in lower grade can be had for several dollars each.

VF

Ancona, 13-15th cent. Denaro (Billon) C•V•S• / Cross 30.00
Aquilea, 1199, Pfenning (Denaro) (S) Crude face / Cross 100.00

Arezzo, 13-14th cent. Grosso (S) Bishop facing / Cross 125.00
Asti, Conrad II, 1140-1356, Denaro (S) REX / Cross 50.00
Bergamo, 1236-1350, Half Grosso (S) Bust of Frederick II / Church . . . 350.00
Bologna, Henry VI, 1191-1337, Bolognino (S) I.P.R.T. / A 75.00
Castro, Luigi Farnese, 1545-1547, Quattrino (Bil.) Arms / Saint . 35.00

VF

Florence, c.1350s, Florin (G) Fleur-de-lis
/ St.John 600.00

Genoa,   Conrad   III,   1138-1152,
Quarterola (Bil.) Gateway / Cross.
. . . . 60.00
___, Anonymous, 1139-1339, Denaro (S)
Gateway / Cross 50.00

Lucca, Otto IV, 13th cent. Grosso (S)
Facing bust / H 250.00
Mantua, Republic, 1200-1329, Denaro (S)
Bust of Vergil / Cross 90.00
Messina, John of Sicily, 1458-1479 Denaro
(Bil.) Eagle / Shield 25.00
Milan, Henry III-V, 1039-1125, Denaro (S)
HE-RIC-N / Cross 65.00
___. Galeazzo II, 1354-1378, Pegione (S)
Bust / Arms 125.00
___. 2nd Republic, 1447-1450, Denaro
(Bil.) Cross / St. Ambrose . . . 40.00
Naples, Ferdinand I, 1458-1494, Coronato
(S) Bust / Cross 200.00
Parma, Otto 1547-1587 Sesino (Bil.) Bust
/ St. Hillary 30.00
Piacenza, Alexander, 1585-91, Scudo (S)
Crowned A / Wolf 35.00
Ravenna, 11-14th cent. Denaro (Bil.)
P.V.S. / Cross 35.00
Reggio, Ercole I, 1471-1505, Bagitino (C)
Bust / Cross 38.00
Salerno, Roger II, 1005-1054, Quarter
Follis (C) Panther / R 50.00
Savoy, Amedeo IX, 1465-1472, Parpagliola
(S) Shield / Cross 125.00
Sicily, Roger II, 1130-1154, Tari (G)
Inscription / Cross 165.00
___. Tancred, 1189-1194, Follaro (S)
Khufic inscription / Latin inscription.
. . . . 40.00
___. Frederick II, 1296-1337, Denaro (Bil.)
Bust / Cross 75.00

___. Ferdinand I, 1458-1494, Coronato
(S) Bust / Angel Michael 250.00
Siena, before 1390, Denaro (S) Backward
S / Cross 75.00
Trento, Frederick, 1207-1218, Grosso (S)
Bust / Cross 150.00
Urbino, Guidobaldo II, 1538-1574, Grosso
(S) 20mm. Seal / St.George . . 150.00
Venice, Orio, Malipiero, 1178-1192,
Denaro (S) Cross / Cross 60.00
___. Pietro Ziani, 1205-1229, Grosso (S)
Doge and St. Mark / Christ . . 75.00
___. Francesco Dandolo, 1328-1339,
Soldino (S) Doge / St. Mark . . 40.00
___. Andrea Contarini, 1368-82,
Tornesello (Bil.) Lion / Cross . . 25.00
___. Antonio Venier, 1382-1460, Zecchino
(G), St. Mark and Doge / Christ.
. . . . 250.00
Verona, Frederick II, 1218-1250, Grosso
(S) Cross / Cross 250.00

PAPAL

History: The Pope, acting as a secular
monarch, ruled the central portion of
Italy from the Middle Ages through 1870.
The earliest Papal coins date from the 8th
century. By the end of the century they
began to resemble the silver deniers of
Charlemagne's France.   Most Popes
thereafter struck coins.   Special *Sede
Vacante* (Vacant See) coins were also
struck between Popes.   Denominations
sometimes varied to fit local needs: Italian
types were struck in Italy, French types
at Avignon in southern France. Initially
gold or silver, many coins in the latter
metal were eventually debased to billon
and later pure copper.
Reference: Berman, *Papal Coins.*
Counterfeit Alert: Early papal denaros
were counterfeited in the 19th century.
Hints: It is helpful for the collector to
become familiar with the papal arms.
Beware of traces of coins having been
mounted for jewelry. such examples are
common and are worth less.

VF

EARLY PAPAL ISSUES

John   VIII,   872-882,   Denaro   (S)
Monogram / Bust St. Peter . 1,500.00

RESTORED PAPAL COINAGE
Clement V 1305-1314, Denaro (Bil.)
Mitred bust / Cross 350.00

Gregory XI, 1370-1378, Bolognino (S)
Mitred bust / U.R.B.I 70.00
Martin V, 1417-1431, Grosso (S) Pope
enthroned / Crossed keys . . . 400.00
Paul II, 1464-1471, Picciolo (Bil.) Arms /
St. Peter 65.00
Alexander VI, 1492-1503, Grosso (S)
Arms / Paul & Peter 150.00
Julius II, 1503-1513, Fiorino (G) Arms /
Sts. Peter and Andrew in boat . 800.00
Leo X, 1513-1521, Giulio (S) Arms / Sts.
Peter and Paul 250.00
Hadrian VI, 1522-1523, Half Giulio (S)
Tiara, crossed keys / Wolf . . 200.00
Clement VII, 1523-1534, Quattrino (Bil.)
Arms / St. Peter 85.00

Paul IV, 1555-1559, Giulio (S) Arms /
St.Paul 150.00
Saint Pius V, 1566-1572, Quattrino (Bil.),
Tiara over crossed keys/St.Peter 35.00
Gregory XIII, 1572-1585, Half Grosso (S)
Arms / Holy Door 125.00
Sixtus V, 1585-1590, Baiocco (Bil.) Bust,
Pope / Holy Spirit 100.00
Paul V, 1605-1621, Testone (S) Arms / St.
Paul 150.00
Sede Vacante, 1676, Half Grosso (S) Arms
under canopy / Dove 95.00

SPAIN

History: The Christians started to regain
control of Spain in the 11th century,
launching attacks on the Moslems from
their mountain retreats in the north.
These Christian kingdoms, including
Castile-Leon and Aragon continued their
expansion.   Finally in 1492 the last
moslem kingdom was defeated and Spain
was united under one rule.
References: Heiss, *Monedas Hispano
Cristianas;* Benedito, Burgos, and Perez,
La Moneda Medieval Hispano Cristiana.
Hints: some of the attributions for this
series are still being debated.

ARAGON   VF
Sancho Ramirez, 1063-94, Dinero (S)
Head / Sceptre, wreath 175.00

LEON

VF

Alfonso I, 1109-1136, Dinero (S) Bust /
Cross, stars 50.00

CASTILE

Alfonso VIII, 1158-1214, Dinero (S) Bust
/ Castle 135.00

CASTILE & LEON

Ferdinand III, 1217-1252, Pepion (S)
Castle / Lion 30.00
Alfonso X, 1252-1284, Noven (Billon)
Castle / Lion 35.00
Sancho IV, 1284-1296, Cornado (S) Bust /
Castle 35.00
Alfonso XI, 1312-1350, Coronado (Bil.)
King's bust / Castle 40.00

Peter I, 1350-1369, Real (S) Crown, P /
Arms 200.00
Henry II, 1368-1379, Obolo (S) Castle /
Lion 60.00
John I, 1379-1390, Blanca (Bil.) Crowned
Y / Lamb of God 65.00
Henry III, 1390-1406, Cruzado (S) Bust /
Cross 80.00
Henry IV, 1454-74, Blanca (S) Bust /
Castle 60.00

UNITED SPAIN

Ferdinand and Isabella, 1469-1516,
Excellente (G) Two busts / Crown,
arms 1,500.00

___. Real (S) Arms / Arrows and yoke.
. . . . 125.00
Philip II, 1556-1598, Four Reales (S)
Crowned shield/Arms (Seville) 175.00
Philip III, 1598-1621. Four Maravedis (C)
1603, Castle /Lion (Segovia) . . 25.00

BARCELONA

Alphonso II, 1285-1291, Groat (S) Bust /
Long cross 85.00

VALENCIA

James I, 1238-1276, Dinero (S) Bust /
Floral sceptre 65.00

MAJORCA

Sancho I, 1311-1324, Dobler (S) Facing
bust / Cross 125.00
James III, 1324-1343, Dinero (S) Facing
bust / Cross 75.00

PORTUGAL

History: The formation of Portugal
began in the 1090s. Alfonso I was the
first king to issue coins. The Dinheiro
was the standard until the 14th century,
when larger coins were introduced by
Peter I, (1357-1367).
References: Vaz, *Livro das Moedas De
Portugal*; Gomes, *Moedas Portuguesas*.
Hints: Medieval Portugese coins are
starting to gain popularity. The earlier
billon dinheiros usually are found in
lower condition and are thus relatively
inexpensive.

VF

Alphonso III, 1248-1279, Dinheiro (Bil.)
Cross / Arms 40.00
Dinis I, 1279-1325, Dinheiro (Bil.) Cross
/ Arms 45.00
Ferdinand I, 1367-1383, Barbuda (Bil.)
Long cross, shield / Helmeted bust.
. . . . 175.00
John I, 1385-1433, Real (Bil.) Crown,
IhnS / Shields & castles 75.00
Alfonso V, 1438-1481, Ceitil (C) Castle /
Arms 35.00

John II, 1481-1495, Vintem (S) Crowned
Y / Arms 60.00
Manuel I, 1495-1521, Tostao (S) Arms /
Cross, stars 250.00
John III, 1521-1557, San Vincente (G)
Arms / St. Vincent 1,600.00
Sebastian, 1557-1578, Real (C) Insciption
/ Crowned S 90.00

GERMANY

History: After the dissolution of the
Carolingian Dynasty the early German
empire evolved, under the Saxon dynasty
and its great emperor Otto I (936-973).
At the same time, the feudal system
preserved regional powers, which were
both ecclesiastical and civic. This form of
Germany lasted until Napoleonic times.
    The early coins were denars, but at
about the turn of the millenium a new

coin concept was introduced. The
bracteate was a paper-thin, broad silver
coin. Bracteates were so thin that they
could only be struck on one side. They
lasted for some 300 years. In the 14th
century the larger silver Groschen was
used. By the late 15th century the
famous taler, ancestor of our silver dollar,
was introduced.
References: Dannenberg, *Die Deutschen
Munzen Der Sachsischen Und Frankischen
Kaiserzeit*; Peus, *Auction 293, Sammlung
Dr. Med Friedrich Bonhoff*; Hess-Leu;
Munzen Der Hohenstaufenzeit, Saurma-
Jeltsch, *Die Saurmasche Munzsammlung*;
Davenport, *German Talers.*(several
volumes).
Hints: The German field is so vast that
collectors are forced to specialize. The
early denars are mostly collected in
Germany, as these are crudely made.
Some collectors outside Germany are
attracted to the braceates, as these are the
most beautiful coins of the medieval
period. German minors are moderately
collected. The most popular German
coins are the talers, which reflect
Renaissance portraiture and heraldry.

F

HOLY ROMAN EMPIRE

Otto III, 983-1002, Denar (S) Cross /
Temple 40.00
Frederick II Hohenstauffen, 1220-1250,
Grosso (S) Eagle / Madonna and Child.
Pisa mint 65.00

GERMAN STATES

Aachen, early dated 1421, Groschen (S)
Charlemagne / Cross 450.00
Altenburg, Frederick II, 1212-1250,
Bracteate (S) Emperor standing 135.00
Bamberg, 1208-1248, Pfennig (S) Bishop /
Angel 50.00
Bavaria, Maximilian I, 1597-1651, Two
Kreuzer (S) Arms / Royal Orb 20.00
Bingen, Johann, 1397-1419, Groschen (S)
St. Peter / Arms 100.00
Brandenburg, Albrecht, 1543-1554, Taler
(S) Bust / Arms 200.00
Brunswick, Heinrich and Albrecht II,
1279-1286, Bracteate (S) Crowned lion
leaping 100.00

Cologne, Conrad II, 1024-1039, Denar (S)
Cross / Temple 100.00

___, Friedrich III, 1371-1414, Gulden (G)
St. Peter enthroned / Shield . 600.00

Saxony, August, 1553-1586, Taler (S)
dated 1571, Bust / Arms 175.00
Worms, Konrad I, 1150-1171, Dunn
Pfennig (S) Bishop facing . . .   100.00
Wurzburg, Gottfried IV, 1443-55, Pfennig
(S) Monogram / Blank 380.00

VF

Erfurt, Heinrich I, 1142-153, Bracteate (S)
Bishop over bridge 350.00
Frankfurt, 15th cent. Hohlpfennig (S)
Helmet 25.00
Goslar, 15th cent. Bracteate (S) Bearded
saint 50.00
Halberstadt, 13th cent. Hohlpfennig (S)
St. Stephan 40.00

Hall, 1180-1300s, Heller (S) Hand / Cross
. . . .   25.00
Julich-Berg, Adolf, 1423-37, Raderalbus (S)
Bust / Five arms 75.00
Lübeck, 1552, Two Schillings (S) Arms
over eagle / Arms over cross . .   25.00
Luneburg, 1547, Taler (S) Tower and wall
/ Man in moon 450.00
Mainz, 15th cent. Hohlpfennig (S) arms.
. . . .   25.00
Meissen, Detrich, 1197-1221, Bracteate (S)
Margrave facing 110.00
Nordlingen, 1518, Pfennig (S) Horns
above arms (one-sided) 35.00
Nurnberg, Frederick, 1495-1536, Half
Schilling (S) Eagle / Arms 50.00
Regensburg, Albert I, 1353-1404, Pfennig
(S) Facing bishop / Crossed keys 35.00
Saxony, Bernhard I, 973-1011, Denar (S)
Diademed head / Small cross .   200.00

SWITZERLAND

History: In 926 Hermann, the count of Franconia, received Swabia and struck denars at Zurich. This early period up until the 11th century saw a progression of growing cities and mints. In this period small bracteates were produced; by the late 14th century two sided coins were struck. In 1433 Basel started striking the silver groschen and gold guldens.

Reference: Metcalf, *Coinage of South Germany*.

VF

Basel, John II, 1335-1365, Bracteate (S)
Mitred bishop 65.00
Geneva, Bishops, c.1200s, Denier (S) St.
Peter / Cross 125.00
Lindau, 1295-1335, Bracteate (S) Tree
branch 65.00
Lusanne, Anonymous, c.1375, Denier (S)
Temple / Cross 60.00
St. Gallen, 1200s, Bracteate (S) Bearded
head facing 75.00
Zofingen, 1250-1300, Bracteate (S)
Crowned helmet 60.00
Zug, 1606, Three Krevzer (S) Arms /
Phoenix 45.00

AUSTRIA

History: The Austrian coinage was not produced in large numbers until the dukes of Austria, in the 11th century, began a series of pfennigs of thin form. In 1276 Austria came under Hapsburg control and the coinage continued.

During the Renaissance the artistic quality of the coinage began to improve, reaching its height with the elaborate Baroque portraiture of the 1600s.

References: Szego, *Coinage of Medieval Austria*; Metcalf, *Coinage of South Germany*; Miller zu Aichholz, et al., *Österreichische Münzprägungen 1519-1938*.

Hints: These coins were made under crude striking conditions and one rarely encounters nicer grade coins. The values are relatively inexpensive.

F

Leopold VI and Eberhard II, 1220-1230,
Pfennig (S) Bust of archbishop /
Similar. 40.00
Ottokar, king 1261-1276, Pfennig (S) Dog
running 30.00

Rudolf, 1276-1281, Pfennig (S) Crowned
bust facing / Eagle 30.00
Albrecht I, 1282-1308, Pfennig (S)
Panther 20.00
Albrecht II, 1330-1437, Grosso (S) Spread
eagle / Double cross 15.00
Albrecht III, 1358-1395, Pfennig (S) Cross
of four hearts 25.00
Ferdinand I, 1521-1564, Pfennig (S) Arms.
. . . .   18.00

CENTRAL EUROPE

HUNGARY

History: Medieval Hungary was a dominating power in central Europe from the reign of their first king, Stephan I. This medieval independent kingdom lasted until the union with Austria in 1527.

The first coins of Stephan are of Carolingian style. By Salomon a small denar and obol system was used. In the 14th century the silver groschen and gold guldens were added, but the denar remained the most common coin until the 17th century.

Reference: Huszar, *Munzkatalog Ungarn*.

Hints: The denars can be found in attractive grades and this, along with availability, results in a devoted collector base. There is a series of Jewish moneyer coins that are quite sought after.

VF

Stephan, 997-1038, Denar (S) Cross /
Cross 200.00

VF

Geza 1064-1074, Denar (S) Cross with rays / Same 150.00

Bela II, 1131-1141, Denar (S) Head.. . . . . 150.00

Bela III, 1172-1196, Follis (C) Two kings / Madonna 60.00

Anonymous, 12th century, Denar (S) Three half circles / Cross 30.00

Bela IV, 1235-1270, Denar (S) Crown, crescent, two lis / Hebrew letter (Jewish moneyer Henok) . . . 100.00

Stephan V, 1270-1272, Obol (S) Bust / Lis. 100.00

Louis I, 1342-1382, Denar (S) Youthful head / Double cross 50.00

Sigismund, 1387-1437, Denar (S) Double cross / Coat of arms 20.00

Wladislaw I, 1440-1444, Denar (S) Eagle / Arms 45.00

Matthias Corvinus, 1458-1490, Gulden (G) Shield / St. Ladislaus 350.00

Ferdinand II, 1526-1564, Denar (S) Shield / Madonna and Child 15.00

TRANSYLVANIA

History: Located in the Carpathian mountains Transylvania or "land across the forest" was part of eastern Hungary. With John I independent rule began in 1538.

References: Resch, *Siebenburgischen Münzen.*

VF

John I, 1538-1540, Ducat (G) Ruler standing / Madonna 1,100.00

John II, 1556, Denar (S) Mother and child / Arms 80.00

Stephan Bocskai, 1607, Three Groschen (S) Bust / Three shields 80.00

Gabriel Bathori, 1613, Groschen (S) Crown / Eagle 50.00

BOHEMIA

History: Boleslav I was the first Duke of Bohemia to issue denars in the 900s. By the reign of Bratislav in 1055, a small but neater denar was introduced in the general trend of Germanic coins of

adjacent regions. These coins portrayed St. Wenceslas on the reverse. In the 1300s Bohemia's Pragergroschen, with its characteristic double-tailed lion, had become the most popular coin in central Europe.

References: Fiala, *Sammlung Max Donebauer;* Cach, *Nejstarsi Ceske Mince.*

F

Ulrich, 1012-1034, Denar (S) Castle / Inscription 150.00

Bretislaus I, 1037-1050, Denar (S) St. Wenceslas / Cross 150.00

Boriwoi II, 1100-1120, Denar (S) Bust / Cross 150.00

Premysl I, 1192-1230, Denar (S) King's bust / Bust 70.00

Wenzel II, 1283-1335, Groschen (S) Crown / Lion 60.00

John of Luxemburg, 1310-1346, Groschen (S) Crown / Lion 50.00

Hussite Period, 1420-1436, Heller, uniface (Bil.) Lion 25.00

Sigimund, 1436-1437, Pennig (S) Lion / Blank 20.00

Wladislaus II, 1471-1516, Groschen (S) Crown / Double-tailed lion 20.00

Ferdinand I, 1526-64, Groschen (S) 1541, Crown / Lion 38.00

Same, without date 20.00

EASTERN EUROPE

POLAND

History: Boleslav I was the first king of Poland in 992-1025. Denars were struck. A Wendenpennig, a small silver coin with turned-up edges was produced by the bishops. Larger denominations were introduced by Casimir the Great in the 14th century. By the 1500s under Sigimund I, gold and heavy silver pieces were in vogue.

References: Gumowski, *Handbuch Des Polnischen Numismatik;* Kopicki, *Podstawowych Typów Monet i Banknotów Polski...*

VF

Bishops,11th century, Wenden, Pfennig (S) Cross / Cross 40.00

Wladislaw II, 1079-1102, Denar (S) Prince / Bishop 150.00

Mieszko Platonogi, 1163-1211, Bracteate (S) Facing figure 150.00

Boleslaw V, 1243-1279, Denar (S) B-O-L-E in cross / Duke and mule . . . 150.00

Wladislaw Jagiello, 1386-1434, Half Groschen (S) Crown / Eagle . . 40.00

Jan Albert 1492-1501, Half Groschen (S) Crown / Eagle 25.00

Sigismund I, 1534, Groschen (S) Crowned bust / City arms (Danzig) 40.00

Sigismund III, 1587-1632, Ducat (G) Bust / Arms 750.00

___. Three Groschen (G) Bust / Inscription 30.00

BALTIC STATES

History: The first coins of the Lithuanians was issued by duke Algirdas in the 14th century. The Teutonic knights also held power in the eastern Baltic. Their first coins were small, one-sided denars struck about 1250. Larger schillings were produced under Master Wynrich ca. 1370. The Dorpat bishops and the Livonian order also struck coins. Sweden and Poland held much of the Baltic region in various periods from the 16th century on.

References: Karys, *Senoves Lietuviv Pinigai;* Fedorov, *Monety Pribatlki XIII-XVIII Stoleti* ; Davenport, *East Baltic Regional Coinage.*

VF

Lithuania, Jogaila, 1377-1395, Denar (S) Cross, knife / Stylized castle . 300.00

___. Sigismund II of Poland, 1568, Groshen (S) Bust / Arms 40.00

___. Stephan of Poland, 1585, Three Groschen (S) Bust / Eagle 40.00

Teutonic Order, 1300s, Bracteate Denar (S) Shield containing cross 75.00

VF
Teutonic Order, Paul von Ruttenberg, 1424-1434, Schilling (S) Cross on arms / Similar 50.00
Livonian Order, Cisso, 1429-1434, Schilling (S) Arms / Cross . . . 65.00
___. Bernd 1471-1483, Artiger (S) Cross / Cross on shield 75.00
Dorpat Bishops, 15th cent. Artiger (S) Sword and key / Sword and key 70.00

Riga, City Coinage, 1575, Schilling (S) Church / Keys crossed 35.00
Riga, Christina, 1632-1654, Schilling (S) Crowned C / Arms 20.00

RUSSIA

History: Except for very rare silver (and a few gold coins dating to the period 978-1054, the coins of Russia started with the small duchies and native states of Moscow, Pskov, Novgorod, Ryazan and Tver in the 1300s. This and subsequent coinage consisted of the silver dengi and later the kopecks. Small copper puls with a wide variety of designs were also struck. First issues of Ivan III Duke of Moscow, who broke Mongol dominance in 1477, were dengi and rare gold ducats. This system was used until Peter the Great's coinage reform.
Reference: Spassky, *Russian Monetary System*; Lapa, *Russian Wire Money*.
Hints: The dengi and kopecks are known in the West as wire money. The values are very reasonable for the more common types. Prices keep falling as new material comes out of Russia.

F
Novgorod, before 1456, Denga (S) Prince / Pellet cross 150.00

Pskov, before 1510, Denga (S) Facing bust of prince / Lion 165.00
Moscow, after 11th cent. Pul (C) Winged serpent / Inscription 40.00
Tver, Mikhail, 1461-1486, Pul (C) Bird / Inscription 60.00
Ivan III, 1462-1505, Denga (S) Horseman / Inscription 65.00

Kazan, Volga region, 16th cent. Kopek (S) Three leaves / Inscription . . . 150.00
Ivan IV (the Terrible) as Duke, 1533-1547, Kopek (S) Horseman / Inscription. 20.00

Ivan IV as Tsar, 1547-1584, Denga (S) Horseman with sword / Inscription. 15.00
Feodor Ivanovich, 1584-1598, Kopek (S) Horseman with spear / Inscription. 15.00
Mikhail Feodorovich, 1613-1645, Kopek (S) Horseman / Inscription . . . 12.00
Alexey Mikhailovich, 1645-1676, Kopek (S) Horseman with spear / Inscription. 13.00
Peter the Great, 1689-1725, Kopek (S) Horseman with spear / Inscription. 12.00

BALKANS

SERBIA

History: Stephan Uros I was the first to strike coins in Serbia. The type was copied from the Venetian matapan. The Serbian empire lasted for over 200 years and was ended by the Ottoman Turks in 1459.
References: Jovanovic, *Srpski Srednjevekovni Novac*; Metcalf, *Coinage of South Eastern Europe*; Ljubic, *Opis, Jogoslavewskih Novaca*.
Hints: The coins of the Balkans have increased in popularity. Many coins are coming to the West now, so the prices are dropping somewhat.

F
Stefan Uros II, 1282-1321, Grosch (S) Christ / King and St. Stephan . 75.00
Stephan Uros IV, 1346-1355, Grosch (S) Christ / Inscription 125.00
___, with Helen, Polugrosch (S) King and queen / Christ 125.00
Lazar, 1371-89, Polugrosch (S) Christ / Lazar standing 75.00

Vuk Brankovic, 1389-1398, Polugrosch (S) Christ / Inscription 75.00
George Brankovic, 1427-56, Grosch (S) Lion / Inscription 80.00

BULGARIA

History: The second kingdom of Bulgaria began under Asen II (1218-44). The coinage was influenced by the close proximity to Byzantium. Most kings struck in silver and copper. The last king was John Shishman (1371-95).
Reference: Mouchmov, *Numismatique Et Sigillographie Bulgare.*
Hints: The values are coming down on this series as material is becoming more available from Bulgarian suppliers.

VF
Asenid Tsars, c.1195, Trachy (Bil.) Bust of Christ / Emperor and St. Constantine. 20.00

Ivan Alexander and Michael, 1313-1355, Grosch (S) Two kings / Christ   45.00
Mikhail Shishman & Ivan Stefan, 1323-1330, Follis (C) Two kings / Trident. 75.00
Ivan Shishman, 1371-1395, Polugosi (S) Tsar / Virgin with Child 40.00
Anonymous, 14th cent. Follis (C) Double headed eagle / Figure 100.00

BOSNIA

History: The earliest Bosnian coinage was issued by Stefan Kotromanic (1322-1353) These issues and later types were grosi and denars.
References: Rengjeo, *Corpus Der Mittelalterlichen Munzen Von Kroatien Slavenien, Dalmatien Und Bosnien*; Lujbic, *Opis Jugoslavenskih Noiaca*.
VF
Tvrtko II, 1420-1443, Groschen (S) Helmet over shield / St. Gregory. 150.00
Tomas Ostojic, 1443-1461, Groschen (S) Crowned helmet, shield / St. George. 150.00

SLAVONIA

History: The coinage of Slavonia started under the sovereignty of Bela IV of Hungary. Zagreb, the main mint, coined Banalis (denars) from 1270-1366.
References: Metcalf, *Coinage in South Eastern Europe;* Rengjeo, *Corpus Der Mittelalterlichen Munzen.*

VF

Duke Koloman, 1235-1241, Denar (S)
Marten / Hungary cross 35.00
King Ladislaus IV, 1272-1290, Denar (S)
Marten / Hungary cross 50.00

WALLACHIA AND MOLDAVIA

History: These areas amount to much of the former province of Roman Dacia, now Romania. Wallachian coinage, the small silver ducat, was minted first by Wladislav I in 1360, and continued through successive rulers to Wladislav V in 1492. Moldavian coins lasted from 1348-1513.
Reference: Buzdugan, Luchian, and Oprescu, *Monede și Bancinote Românesti.*

F

Wallachia, Dan I, 1383-1386, Ducat (S)
Shield / Eagle. 60.00
___. Mircea, 1386-1418, Ducat (S) King standing / Shield 80.00
Moldavia, Alexandru, 1400-1432, Gros (C) Bull's head / Shield 75.00

CROATIA (Dubrovnik/Ragusa)   VF

1372-1421, Denar (S) St. Blazius / Christ. 50.00

SCANDINAVIA

DENMARK

History: The first coins of Denmark were issued under King Sven (985-1014). The coins issued under Cnut the Conqueror are more plentiful and are in the Anglo-Saxon style. In the later 11th Century, constant turmoil resulted in billon and even copper denars. Eric of Pomerania established a more stable system. This was added to with new denominations at various later periods.
References: Hauberg, *Myntforhold Og Udmuntninger I Danmark Indtil 1146*; Hauberg, *Atlas Over Danmarks Monter*; Hedes, *Danmarks Og Norges Monter.*

VF

Knud the Great, 1018-1035, Penny (S) King's bust left / Cross 250.00

Sven Estidsen, 1047-1074, Penny (S)
Christ enthroned / Long cross 350.00
Niels, 1103-1134, Penny (S) Helmeted bust / Castle 175.00

Valdemar II, 1202-1244, Penny (S) Facing bust / Two crosses, sword . . 125.00
Christoffer I, 1252-1259, Penny (S) Cross / Star 40.00
Erik Glipping, 1259-1286, Penny (S) Crown / Cross 80.00
Christoffer II, 1319-1332, Penny (S), A / P 65.00
Eric of Pomerania, 1396-1349, Sterling (S) Crown / Cross 85.00
Christian I, 1448-1481, Hvid (S) Crowned K / Long cross 45.00
Hans, 1481-1513, Hvid (S) Crowned h / Cross and shield 50.00
Christian III, 1534-1559, Two Skilling (S) 1536, Three-quarter king / Three shields 65.00
Frederik II, 1559-1588, Mark (S) 1560, Crowned shield / Inscription . 90.00

SWEDEN

History: The first coins were copies of Anglo-Saxon pennies. Following these early types, small bracteate coins were made until the 14th century. These were so thin that they could only be struck on one side. In 1395 Sweden formed part of a united kingdom under Danish kings; independence from Denmark came with the accession of King Gustav Vasa in 1521.
Reference: Lagerquist, *Svenska Myntunder Vikingatiden.*

VF

Olof Skotonung, 994-1022, Penny (S) Bust R. / Cross C.R.V.X . . 1,800.00

Valdemar, 1250-1275, Small Bracteate (S) Griffin's head 75.00
Gustav Vasa, 1521-1560, Mark (S) King's bust right / Crowned arms . . 200.00
Johan III, 1568-1592, Two Ore (S) 1570, Bust / Crowned arms 150.00

Gotland, Visby, 1380-1390, Ortug (S) Large lis / Lamb of God 80.00

NORWAY

History: Norway's first coins were copied from the Anglo-Saxon Aethelred II "crux" type. Semi-bracteates were then issued which gave way to the small, thin bracteates. These last until 1387 when Norway passed under the Danish sovereignty.
Reference: Skarre, *Coins and Coinage in Viking Age Norway.*

VF

Olaf Tryggvason, 995-1000, Penny (S) Crude bust left / Cross 750.00
Sverre Sigurdsson, 1177-1202, Small Bracteate (S) Bull's eye pattern 150.00

FOREIGN COINS

The collecting of world coins forms one of the most adventurous and exciting areas of numismatics. While at first bewildering to some, there are several "tricks" to make the identification of foreign coins easier. The most important thing to remember is that even if not in English, the names of most foreign countries bear similarities to their English names. Coins that are neatly machine made are usually more recent than coins incompletely stamped on uneven blanks. Nickel alloys have only been popular for 150 years or less. The good reference for the identification of world coins is already in most homes: an atlas. A table of major world alphabets is also useful and found in many large dictionaries.

As the cultures of the world vary, so do the coins they have produced. Because neighboring countries often have coins related to each other, the foreign section of this book is grouped geographically, rather than put into an alphabetical listing. It is hoped that this will make identifying a coin from an unknown country a bit easier. It is also for this reason that some countries are listed by date and some by denomination, the ease of the non-experienced user being considered more important than a rigid system.

Note: Illustrations are shown of the type of coin described immediately below. On coins struck for several years the date may be different than that listed.

GENERAL REFERENCES

Craig, W.D., *Coins of the World 1750-1850.*

Davenport, John S. European Cowns and Talers since 1800.

___, *European Crowns 1700-1800.*

___, *European Crowns 1600-1700.*

___, *European Crowns 1484-1600.*

Doty, Richard G., *The Macmillan Encyclopedic Dictionary of Numismatics*

Friedberg, Robert, *Gold Coins of the World.*

Krause, C. & Mishler, C., *Standard Catalogue of World Coins.*

Yeoman, Richard S., *Current Coins of the World.*

Yeoman, Richard S., *Modern World Coins.*

EUROPEAN AND COLONIAL COINS

UNITED KINGDOM AND IRELAND

History: The coins of Britain are by far the most actively collected, besides North American coins. Modern English coins began with the establishment of a permanent milled coinage during the reign of Charles II. Before that English coins were hand-struck. Most British coins bear no denomination and often no indication of country. The use of BRITANNIARUM or its abbreviation in the royal title is often a clue. Most British coins bear a portrait of the monarch on the obverse. The silver often bears a shield or heraldic motif on the reverse. Copper usually bears the seated figure of Britannia. Since 1797 British coinage has been struck with modern machinery. Silver content was reduced from sterling (92½%) to 50% in 1920 due to war debts, and was finally replaced with cupro-nickel in 1947. Traditionally the British Pound (one sovereign) was divided into 240 pence, twelve of which were equal to one shilling. A farthing was a quarter of a penny and a crown was equal to five shillings. Beginning in 1968 this medieval system was gradually replaced with a decimal system where 100 (new) pence equal one pound.

Scotland had a separate coinage up to the Act of Union in 1707 which joined the two kingdoms which had been ruled by the same monarch for over a century. Scottish issues of this period were often similar in inspiration, and often detail, to English coins. Despite the union of Great Britain and Ireland in 1808, Ireland retained its own coinage until 1823. Post independence Irish coinage, beginning in 1928, bears a distinctive harp design with the word EIRE, Gaelic for Ireland on the obverse. Earlier Irish coins bear the word HIBERNIA, Latin for Ireland. The reverses of recent Irish coins usually show animals.

British copper of the 1700's was widely used in the United States and Canada, where there is some interest among collectors in this series as well. This is particularly true of the Irish "Hibernia" coppers of 1722-24.

During the periods 1648-72, 1780's-1790's, and 1811-12 many private firms, cities and counties throughout the British Isles struck their own tokens to combat acute small change shortages. Their designs often feature local heroes and coats of arms. While they were often inscribed as redeemable in lawful money, many were dishonored. They are common today in medium to high grade. Many tokens of the eighteenth century exist as so-called varieties and are collected along with the real varieties.

The coronation of a new King is always cause for celebration. Official medals for this event have been issued for centuries in gold, silver and bronze. Also a multiplicity of private medals for these events has been issued, often of inferior workmanship. The latter were also produced in cheaper metals such as tin alloys. Many similar jubilee medals, both official and private, also exist. Valuations here are for the medals alone. Those still in their original boxes command a slight premium.

References: Seaby, et. al., *Coins of England*; Seaby, P. and Purvey, F., *Coins of Scotland, Ireland & the Islands*; Seaby et al., *British Tokens and their Values.*

Counterfeit Alert: Contemporary counterfeits of George III eighteenth century half pennies and early nineteenth century silver are common. The former are similar to the real coins except for die work and sometimes weight, and are as popular among collectors as their authentic counterparts. The latter are often silver-plated brass and are worth less. In the last fifty years British gold sovereigns have been very widely counterfeited in real gold. Dangerous counterfeits exist of the 1798 guinea, rare Gothic Crown and 1905 half crown. "Gold" guineas with "good old days" or gibberish legends are not counterfeits but brass game counters of the early nineteenth century.

Hints: Early English coins bear no indication of value. A Crown is a bit larger than a silver dollar, a shilling than a quarter, and a sixpence between a cent and a nickel. Half-pennies are always larger than a quarter, farthings smaller. British copper before 1860 often is found with bruises to the rims. This reduces their value depending on extent.

	VG	VF

CHARLES II (1660-85)
1671 Crown (S), Four Shields

| | 50.00 | 300.00 |

1680 3 pence (S), Three interlocking C's

| | 3.50 | 16.00 |

1673 Halfpenny (C), Britannia seated

| | 5.00 | 85.00 |

1672 Farthing (C), same

| | 3.00 | 45.00 |

JAMES II (1685-88)

1688 Guinea (G), Arms

| | 165.00 | 700.00 |

1686 Half Crown (S), Arms

| | 30.00 | 175.00 |

1685 Halfpenny (Tin), Britannia seated

| | 25.00 | 225.00 |

WILLIAM AND MARY (1688-94)
1689 Half Crown (S), Arms

| | 20.00 | 110.00 |

1691 Halfpenny (Tin), Britannia seated

| | 12.00 | 180.00 |

1694 Halfpenny (C), Britannia seated

| | 4.00 | 45.00 |

1694 Farthing (C), same

| | 5.00 | 60.00 |

WILLIAM III (1694-1702)
1698 Guinea (G), Four shields,

| | 150.00 | 450.00 |

1698 Half Crown (S), similar

| | 23.00 | 115.00 |

1696 Shilling (S), same

| | 10.00 | 45.00 |

1697 Farthing (C), Britannia seated

| | 5.00 | 45.00 |

ANNE (1702-14)
1703 VIGO Crown (S), Four Shields

| | 100.00 | 400.00 |

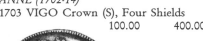

1708 Half Crown (S), same

| | 20.00 | 85.00 |

1711 6 pence (S), same

| | 8.00 | 30.00 |

1714 Farthing (C), Britannia seated

| | 50.00 | 225.00 |

GEORGE I (1714-27)
1716 5 Guinea (G), Four shields

| | 750.00 | 3,000.00 |

1722 Guinea (G), similar

| | 140.00 | 500.00 |

1717 Shilling (S), Four Shields

| | 17.00 | 50.00 |

1719 Farthing (C), Britannia seated

| | 3.00 | 45.00 |

GEORGE II (1727-60)
1745 Half Crown (S), LIMA below bust, Four Shields

| | 24.00 | 85.00 |

1743 Shilling (S), Four shields,

| | 9.00 | 38.00 |

1729 Halfpenny (C), Britannia seated

| | 3.50 | 30.00 |

GEORGE III (1760-1820)
1775 Guinea (G), Rose-shaped Shield

| | 120.00 | 210.00 |

1818 Crown (S), St. George slaying Dragon

| | 10.00 | 36.00 |

1763 Shilling (S), Four shields

| | 65.00 | 275.00 |

1787 Shilling (S), same

| | 7.00 | 15.00 |

1817 Sixpence (S), Arms

| | 2.00 | 10.00 |

1797 Penny (C), Britannia seated

| | 2.00 | 22.00 |

1771 Halfpenny (C), same

| | 3.00 | 25.00 |

1806 Halfpenny (C), same

| | 1.00 | 4.00 |

GEORGE IV (1820-30)

1821 Half Crown (S), Garnished Shield

| | 4.00 | 32.00 |

	VG	VF
1826 Shilling (S), Lion on Crown	2.00	15.00
1826 Halfpenny (C), Britannia seated	1.00	6.00

WILLIAM IV (1830-37)

1835 Half Sovereign (G), Arms (19 mm.)	60.00	200.00

1834 Sixpence (S), Wreath	1.00	15.00
1831 Penny (C), Britannia seated	3.00	35.00

VICTORIA (1837-1901)

1844 ½ Farthing (C)	.75	4.00
1891 Farthing (C), Britannia seated	.25	1.50
1860 Halfpenny (C), same	.25	2.00
1901 Penny (C), same	.25	.75
1901 3 Pence (S)	.25	1.00
1874 Sixpence (S), Wreath	1.00	8.00

1883 Shilling (C), Crown and wreath	1.50	7.00
1887 Shilling (S), Arms	1.25	3.00
1849 Florin (S), Four Shields	6.50	30.00
1880 Florin (S), Four shields	3.00	25.00

1839 Half Crown (S), Young Head / Crowned Arms	80.00	700.00

1900 Half Crown (S), Old Head / Crowned Arms	3.00	12.00

1847 Crown (S), same	225.00	500.00
1887 Crown (S), St. George slaying dragon	7.00	25.00
1900 Sovereign (G), St. George slaying Dragon	105.00	115.00

EDWARD VII (1901-10)

1910 Penny (C), Britannia seated	.25	1.50
1902 Florin (S), Britannia standing	3.00	15.00
1902 Crown (S), St. George slaying Dragon	18.00	50.00

1902 2 Pounds (G), similar	225.00	285.00

GEORGE V (1910-36)

1917 Halfpenny (C), Britannia seated	.25	1.00
1935 3 pence (S), Three acorns	.25	.50
1912 Shilling (S), Lion on crown	1.00	2.25
1931 Florin (S), Four Shields,	1.50	2.50
1915 Half Crown (S), Crowned Shield,	2.50	5.00
1928 Crown (S), Crown in Wreath	35.00	90.00
1935 Crown (S), Modernistic St. George	5.00	8.00

1911 Sovereign (G), St. George slaying dragon		115.00

	VF	EF

GEORGE VI (1936-52)

1943 Halfpenny (C), Ship	.25	.75
1943 3 Pence (B), Plant	.15	.25
1946 Sixpence (S), Crowned monogram		.50
1947 Two Shillings (CN), Crowned rose	.25	1.00
1951 Crown (CN), St. George slaying dragon	*Prooflike*	8.00

ELIZABETH II (1952-date)

	EF	BU
1954 Farthing (C), Wren	.25	1.50
1966 Halfpenny (C), Ship	.15	.25
1953 Penny (C), Britannia seated	1.50	3.00
1967 Penny (C), same	.15	.20

1961 3 Pence (B), Crowned Gate	.10	.50
1963 Two Shillings (CN), Rose and thistles	.25	.75
1965 Crown (CN), Churchill	.75	1.00
1981 Crown (CN), Charles and Diana	1.00	2.00
1971 New Penny (C), Crowned Gate	.10	.15
1989 5 Pounds (G), Queen Enthroned		700.00

BRITISH TOKENS

1793 Coventry, ½ Penny (C), Lady Godiva on Horse / Elephant	3.00	12.00
1794 Wales, Anglesy, ½ Penny (C), Druid / Monogram	2.00	8.00
1814 Birmingham, Penny (C), Work House / Shield	1.50	7.00
[1980s] Trans Atlantic Games / Luckey Prize *monogram* 20p Not Transferable	.10	.20

SCOTLAND F

Charles II 1670 4 Merks (S) Bust r. / Four shields LIII 4 in center 220.00
___, 1679 Bawbee (C) Bust l. / Crowned Thistle 24.00

F

James VII 1687 10 Shillings (S) Bust r. /
X with shields in angles 125.00
William and Mary 1693 20 Shillings (S)
Conjoined Busts 20 below / Crowned
Shield 140.00
___, 1694 5 Shillings (S) Conjoined Busts
V below / Crowned Script Monogram
. . . . 75.00
William II 1701 Pistole (G) Bust l. /
Crowned Arms 2,000.00

___, 1696 Bodle (C) Sword and Scepter /
Crowned Thistle 22.00

Anne 1705 5 Shillings Bust l. 5 below /
Crowned Triple Thistle 35.00
___, 1707E 6 Pence Bust l. E below /
Four Shields 20.00
___, 1709E Half Crown (S) same as above
but 1¼" 175.00

IRELAND   F

Charles II 1683 Halfpenny (C) Bust /
Crowned Harp 20.00
James II 1686 Halfpenny (C) Bust /
Crowned Harp 20.00
___. 1689 Shilling (B) Bust / XII over
Crown 13.00

William and Mary 1693 Halfpenny (C)
Conjoined Busts / Crowned Harp
. . . . 22.00
William III 1696 Halfpenny (C) Bust /
Crowned Harp 35.00
George I 1723 Halfpenny (C) Bust /
Hibernia seated with harp 20.00
George II 1741 Halfpenny (C) Bust /
Crowned Harp 15.00

George III 1805 Halfpenny (C) Bust /
Crowned Harp 5.00
George IV 1823 Penny (C) Bust /
Crowned Harp 8.00

VF

1928 Farthing (C) Woodcock ¼d . 1.00

1928 Sixpence (N) Hound 1.00
1940 Shilling (S) Bull 4.00
1939 Half Crown (S) Horse 7.50
1949 Halfpenny (C) Sow 25
1952 Penny (C) Hen 50

BU

1964 Florin (CN) Trout 1.75
1966 10 Shillings (S) Easter Uprising
. . . . 9.50
1967 3 Pence (CN) Rabbit 50
1983 50 Pence (CN) Woodcock . . 1.00
1988 50 Pence (CN) Dublin Shield 3.00

BRITISH COMMONWEALTH

History: While a few British colonial
coins were struck as early as the reign of
Elizabeth I (1558-1603), this series
becomes really common in the late 1800's
with the formal carving up of the Third
World by the major European powers.
Queen Victoria's portrait appeared on the
coins of more diverse lands than anyone
else in previous history. Many of the
reverses of these early colonials bore
nothing but their value, but some from
the 1920's and later bore symbolic images
of the local flora and fauna, or the coat of
arms of the particular territory. As many
colonies gained their independence after
World War II, and the British Empire
became the British Commonwealth, many
of these new nations kept their close ties
with Britain, and retained the monarch's
portrait on their coinages.

Many of these coins from World War II
were struck in the United States and

carry D and S mintmarks for Denver and
San Francisco.

References: Pridmore, F. *Coins of the
British Commonwealth* (4 vols.).

Counterfeit Alert: In the last fifty years
British Empire gold sovereigns have been
very widely counterfeited in real gold.
Contemporary counterfeits are known of
India half rupees and 8 annas.

Hints: The gold sovereigns of many
colonies cannot be distinguished from
proper British sovereigns except for the
small mintmark on the ground below the
horse's hoof. These mintmarks are: C =
Canada, I = India, M, P and S =
Australia (Melbourne, Perth and Sydney
respectively), and SA = South Africa.

AUSTRALIA   VF

1813 15 pence (S), Value . . F 2,000.00

1892S Sovereign (G), Victoria/St. George
slaying dragon . . . . EF 125.00
1910 3 pence (S), Arms 9.00
1912P Sovereign (G), George V/St.
George slaying dragon . . . EF 105.00
1927 3 pence (S), Arms 3.00
1927 Florin (S), Parliament 6.50
"1934-35" Florin (S), Victoria and
Melbourne 120.00
1936 Penny (C), Value 1.00

1937 Crown (S), Crown . . . EF 20.00
1943S 3 pence (S), Wheat 75
1943S Florin (S), Arms 3.00
1945 Penny (C), Kangaroo 25

EF

1953 Sixpence (S), Arms 17.00
1954 Florin (S), Lion and Kangaroo 4.50
1959 Halfpenny (C), Kangaroo 25
1959 Shilling (S), Ram 1.00
1962 Sixpence (S), Arms 50
1969 Cent (C), Feather-tailed glider . .10
1970 50¢ (CN), Capt. Cook 1.00
1983 20¢ (CN), Platypus 25

1984 $1 (AB), Kangaroos . . . . . *EF* 1.00
                                        BU
1987 $100 (G), Nugget . . . . spot +6%
1988 "Holey Dollar" . . . . *Cased* 22.00
1989 $10 (S), Queensland *Cased* 16.00

BAHAMAS   BU

1806 Penny (C), Ship . . . . . . *F* 30.00
1966 1¢ (B), Starfish 10
1983 5¢ (CN), Pineapple 25
1969 15¢ (CN), Square 25
1966 50¢ (S), Swordfish 2.00

1972 $2 (S), Flamingos 6.50
1973 $5 (S), Arms 8.00
1981 $10 (S), Charles & Diana . . 15.00
1974 $100 (G), Flamingos 80.00
1988 $2,500 (G), Columbus . . 7,000.00

BELIZE   BU
1975 5¢ (B), Queen 35
1975 5¢ (B), Value 1.00
1980 $100 (G), Fish . *PF in case* 70.00

BERMUDA

1793 Penny (C), George III/Ship
 . . . . *VF* 40.00
                                        BU
1964 Crown (S), Arms 4.50
1970 5¢ (CN), Fish 25
1981 $1 (CN), Charles & Diana . . 2.50
1981 $1 (S), same . . . . *PF* 12.00

BRITISH CARIBBEAN TERRITORIES
                                        BU
1955 ½¢ (C), Value 2.00
1965 10¢ (CN), Ship 50
1955 50¢ (CN), Queen standing above
 shields 2.50

BRITISH GUIANA   VF
1836 ½ Guilder (S), Value 36.00
1943 4 pence (S), Value 1.50

BRITISH HONDURAS   F
1904 1¢ (C), Value 7.00
1907 50¢ (S), Value 22.00
1952 25¢ (CN), Value 1.50
1971 1¢ (C), Value . . . . *BU* .35

BRITISH VIRGIN ISLANDS   PF
1973 1¢ (C), Birds 50

1974 $1 (S), Birds 7.50
1985 $20 (S), Artifact 18.00

1988 $25 (S), Artifact 25.00
1975 $100 (G), Bird 140.00

BRITISH WEST AFRICA   VF
1908 1/10 Penny (AL) Star 2.00
1915H Halfpenny (CN) Star . . . 1.75
1920H Penny (CN) Star 1.50
1936 Penny (CN) Edward VIII / Star
 . . . . 1.50
1917H 3 Pence (S) Wreath 2.00
1919H 6 Pence (S) Wreath 4.00
1947 6 Pence (B) Wreath 1.00
1952 6 Pence (B) Wreath 32.50
1936KN Shilling (B) Tree 4.00
1952H Shilling (B) Tree 1.00
1947H 2 Shilling (B) Tree 2.00

BRITISH WEST INDIES   F
1820 1/16 Dollar (S) Anchor . . . 10.00
1822 1/8 Dollar (S) Anchor 7.00

1822 1/4 Dollar (S) Anchor 8.00
1822 1/2 Dollar (S) Anchor 80.00

CAYMAN ISLAND   BU
1972 1¢ (C), Bird 25

1972 $25 (S), Queen & Prince Philip . .
 . . . . *Cased* 20.00
1972 $25 (G), same . . . . . *Cased* 100.00

CEYLON   VF
1815 Stiver (C) Elephant 12.00
1821 Rix Dollar (S) Elephant . . . 35.00
1870 ¼ Cent (C) Tree 2.50
1955 2 Cents (B) Eliz. II . . . . *BU* .35
1870 5 Cents (C) Tree 12.00
1912H 5 Cents (CN) (square) 1.00
1903 50 Cents (S) Tree 7.00
1951 50 Cents (B) Leaves 25

CYPRUS   F
1879 ¼ Piastre (C) Victoria 4.00
1908 ½ Piastre (C) Edward VII . 40.00
1934 1 Piastre (CN) George V . . . 1.00

                                        VF
1928 45 Piastres (S) Lions 24.00
1949 2 Shilling (CN) Lions 2.00
1955 100 Mils (CN) Ship 35

EAST AFRICA   VF
1899 1 Pice (C) Victoria 5.00
1907 Cent (AL) Tusks 6.50
1907 5 Cents (CN) Tusks . . . . . *Rare*
1911 50 Cents (S) Lion 15.00
1920A 50 Cents (S) Lion . . . . . *Rare*
1922H 1 Cent (C) Tusks 35
1936H 5 Cents (C) Edward VIII / Tusks
 . . . . 1.00

	VF
1942 10 Cents (C) Tusks	.50
1949 50 Cents (CN) Lion	.25

	VF
1944SA 1 Shilling (S) Lion	2.00
1964 5 Cents (C) Tusks	.35
1964 10 Cents (C) Tusks	.35

EAST CARIBBEAN STATES   **BU**

1981 2¢ (AL), Square	.10
1981 25¢ (CN), Ship	.25
1981 $1 (AB), Ship	1.00

FIJI   **VF**

1934 Halfpenny (CN) (holed)	2.50
1935 Penny (CN) (holed)	1.00
1936 Penny (CN) Edward VIII (holed)	
	1.00
1950 3 Pence (B) Hut	.75
1934 6 Pence (S) Turtle	2.50
1965 Shilling (CN) Outrigger	.25
1934 Florin (S) Arms	8.50
1942S Florin (S) Arms	4.50

BU

1982 2 Cents (C) Fan	.25
1983 50 Cents (CN) Outrigger	1.50
1974 $25 (S) King's Bust	20.00

GIBRALTAR   **VF**

1802 2 Quarts Token (C)	25.00

1842 2 Quart (C) Castle	35.00
1842 1 Quart (C) Castle	25.00

BU

1967 Crown (CN) Castle	1.50
1990 50 Pence (CN) Dolphins	2.50
1990 Crown (CN) Stamp	7.00

GUERNSEY   **VF**

1830 1 Double (C) Shield	2.50
1885H 2 Doubles (C) Shield	2.25
1902H 4 Doubles (C) Shield	1.50
1949H 8 Doubles (C) Lilies	.25

BU

1956 3 Pence (CN) Cow	1.00

1971 10 Pence (CN) Cow	.50
1983 1 Pound (B) Ship	2.50
1984 1 Pound (B) Value	2.25

HONG KONG   **VF**

1863 1 Mil (C) (hole)	2.00
1902 1 Cent (C) Edward VII	2.00
1888 5 Cent (S) Victoria	1.00
1967 5 Cents (B) Elizabeth II	.10
1936 10 Cents (CN) George V	.35

1889 20 Cents (S) Victoria	11.00
1902 20 Cents (S) Edward VI	22.00
1866 ½ Dollar (S) Ornament	275.00
1891 50 Cents (S) "50"	22.00

BU

1949 5 Cents (B) George VI	2.50
1975 20 Cents (B) Elizabeth II	.25
1960H Dollar (CN) Lion	1.00

INDIA (East India Co.)   **F**

1717 2 Pice (Tin) GR Crown BOMB / Inscription (27 grams)	50.00

1794 1/96 Rupee (C) Arms / Bale Mark (thick border)	5.00
1803 20 (XX) Cash (C) Arms / Inscription	2.00

[1808] ½ Pagoda (S) Building / Deity standing	80.00
1825 ½ Rupee (S) Native inscriptions with small crown on obv.	4.00
1833 ¼ Anna (C) Arms / Scales	1.00

VF

[1831] 1 Pie (C) Inscription	1.00
1857 ½ Anna (C) Arms	1.50
1841 2 Annas (S) Victoria	2.50
1840 ¼ Rupee (S) Victoria	3.50
1835 Rupee (S) William IV	10.00

INDIA (Regal Issues)   **VF**

1862 1/12 Anna (C) Victoria	1.00
1909 1/12 Anna (C) Edward VII	.75
1894 ½ Pice (C) Victoria	1.50

1877 ¼ Anna (C) Victoria	1.00
1907 ¼ Anna (C) Edward VII	1.00
1939 ¼ Anna (C) George VI	.25
1943 Pice (C) (holed)	.25
1862 ½ Anna (C) Victoria	9.00
1942 ½ Anna (B) George VI	.25
1919 1 Anna (C) George V	.25
1878 2 Annas (S) Victoria	2.00

1935 2 Annas (CN) George V	.25
1945 2 Annas (B) George VI	.25
1920 4 Annas (CN) 4 in square	4.00
1919 8 Annas (CN) 8 in square	8.00
1920 8 Annas (CN) 8 in square	20.00
1936 ¼ Rupee (S) George V	2.00
1945 ¼ Rupee (S) George VI	.75
1946 ¼ Rupee (N) Lion	.50
1905 ½ Rupee (S) Edward VII	8.00
1946 ½ Rupee (N) Lion	1.00
1892 Rupee (S) Victoria	6.50

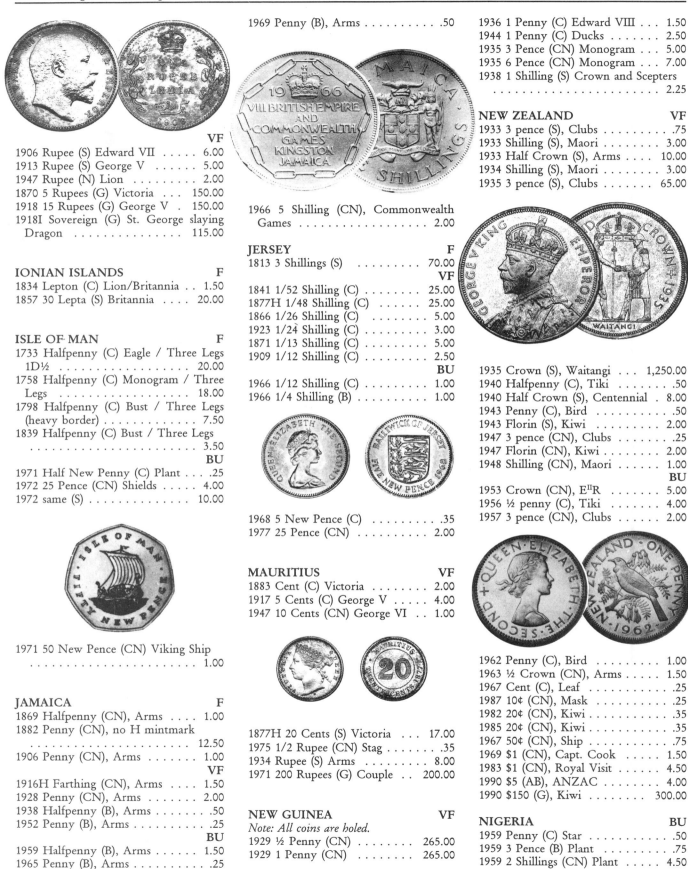

VF

1906 Rupee (S) Edward VII 6.00
1913 Rupee (S) George V 5.00
1947 Rupee (N) Lion 2.00
1870 5 Rupees (G) Victoria . . . 150.00
1918 15 Rupees (G) George V . 150.00
1918I Sovereign (G) St. George slaying
Dragon 115.00

IONIAN ISLANDS   **F**
1834 Lepton (C) Lion/Britannia . . 1.50
1857 30 Lepta (S) Britannia 20.00

ISLE OF MAN   **F**
1733 Halfpenny (C) Eagle / Three Legs
1D½ 20.00
1758 Halfpenny (C) Monogram / Three
Legs 18.00
1798 Halfpenny (C) Bust / Three Legs
(heavy border) 7.50
1839 Halfpenny (C) Bust / Three Legs
. . . . 3.50
                                            BU
1971 Half New Penny (C) Plant 25
1972 25 Pence (CN) Shields 4.00
1972 same (S) 10.00

1971 50 New Pence (CN) Viking Ship
. . . . 1.00

JAMAICA   **F**
1869 Halfpenny (CN), Arms 1.00
1882 Penny (CN), no H mintmark
. . . . 12.50
1906 Penny (CN), Arms 1.00
                                            VF
1916H Farthing (CN), Arms 1.50
1928 Penny (CN), Arms 2.00
1938 Halfpenny (B), Arms 50
1952 Penny (B), Arms 25
                                            BU
1959 Halfpenny (B), Arms 1.50
1965 Penny (B), Arms 25

1969 Penny (B), Arms 50

1966 5 Shilling (CN), Commonwealth
Games 2.00

JERSEY   **F**
1813 3 Shillings (S) 70.00
                                            VF
1841 1/52 Shilling (C) 25.00
1877H 1/48 Shilling (C) 25.00
1866 1/26 Shilling (C) 5.00
1923 1/24 Shilling (C) 3.00
1871 1/13 Shilling (C) 5.00
1909 1/12 Shilling (C) 2.50
                                            BU
1966 1/12 Shilling (C) 1.00
1966 1/4 Shilling (B) 1.00

1968 5 New Pence (C) 35
1977 25 Pence (CN) 2.00

MAURITIUS   **VF**
1883 Cent (C) Victoria 2.00
1917 5 Cents (C) George V 4.00
1947 10 Cents (CN) George VI . . 1.00

1877H 20 Cents (S) Victoria . . . 17.00
1975 1/2 Rupee (CN) Stag 35
1934 Rupee (S) Arms 8.00
1971 200 Rupees (G) Couple . . 200.00

NEW GUINEA   **VF**
Note: All coins are holed.
1929 ½ Penny (CN) 265.00
1929 1 Penny (CN) 265.00

1936 1 Penny (C) Edward VIII . . . 1.50
1944 1 Penny (C) Ducks 2.50
1935 3 Pence (CN) Monogram . . . 5.00
1935 6 Pence (CN) Monogram . . . 7.00
1938 1 Shilling (S) Crown and Scepters
. . . . 2.25

NEW ZEALAND   **VF**
1933 3 pence (S), Clubs 75
1933 Shilling (S), Maori 3.00
1933 Half Crown (S), Arms 10.00
1934 Shilling (S), Maori 3.00
1935 3 pence (S), Clubs 65.00

1935 Crown (S), Waitangi . . . 1,250.00
1940 Halfpenny (C), Tiki 50
1940 Half Crown (S), Centennial . 8.00
1943 Penny (C), Bird 50
1943 Florin (S), Kiwi 2.00
1947 3 pence (CN), Clubs 25
1947 Florin (CN), Kiwi 2.00
1948 Shilling (CN), Maori 1.00
                                            BU
1953 Crown (CN), E^{II}R 5.00
1956 ½ penny (C), Tiki 4.00
1957 3 pence (CN), Clubs 2.00

1962 Penny (C), Bird 1.00
1963 ½ Crown (CN), Arms 1.50
1967 Cent (C), Leaf 25
1987 10¢ (CN), Mask 25
1982 20¢ (CN), Kiwi 35
1985 20¢ (CN), Kiwi 35
1967 50¢ (CN), Ship 75
1969 $1 (CN), Capt. Cook 1.50
1983 $1 (CN), Royal Visit 4.50
1990 $5 (AB), ANZAC 4.00
1990 $150 (G), Kiwi 300.00

NIGERIA   **BU**
1959 Penny (C) Star 50
1959 3 Pence (B) Plant 75
1959 2 Shillings (CN) Plant 4.50

RHODESIA AND NYASALAND

BU
1961 Penny (C), Elephants. *Holed* . 1.00

SEYCHELLES   VF
1948 1 Cent (C) George VI 25

1939 10 Cents (CN) Scalloped . . . 7.00
BU
1972 1 Cent (AL) Cow 15
1972 25 Cents (CN) 25
1974 10 Rupees (CN) Turtle 5.00
same (S) 13.00

SOLOMON ISLANDS   BU
1977 1¢ (C) Cup 25
1977 $1 (C) Spirit Head 2.00
1983FM $5 (S) Crown & Orb *PF* 20.00

SOUTH AFRICA   VF
1924 ¼ Penny (C) Birds 2.00
1936 ½ Penny (C) Ship 4.00

1936 Penny (C), George V/Ship . . 1.00
1939 Penny (C) George VI/Ship . . 1.00
1960 Penny (C) Ship 25
1929 3 Pence (S) Flower 2.00
1941 6 Pence (S) Flower 1.00
1943 Shilling (S) Allegory of Cape
  Provence standing 1.50
1928 Florin (S) Arms 12.00
1952 2 Shillings (S) Arms 2.00
1960 2 Shillings (S) Arms 2.00
1948 2½ Shillings (S) Crowned Arms
  . . . . 50.00
1952 5 Shillings (S) Ship 5.00

1958 5 Shillings (S) Springbok . . . 5.00

SOUTHERN RHODESIA   VF
1934 Halfpenny (CN) Rose 2.00
1937 Penny (CN) Rose 1.00
1942 3 Pence (S) Spears 1.25
1947 Shilling (CN) Stone Bird . . . 1.00
1932 Half Crown (S) Arms 10.00

STRAITS SETTLEMENTS   VF
1888 1 Cent (C) Victoria 4.00
1910 10 Cents (S) Edward VII . . . 2.00
1921 50 Cents (S) George V 2.50

FRANCE

History: Influenced by gradual inflation over the centuries, French coinage up until the Revolution was a natural descendent of its medieval counterpart. The medieval denier continued to be struck into the 1600's, but in copper instead of base silver. The sol or sou of this period is also a holdover from medieval times. The major change in the early modern period was the introduction of the silver écu, similar to a silver dollar. It became a standard of French coinage and many smaller silver coins were named by how many of them it took to make an écu. Gold coins were struck in great quantity by the kings of France at this time as well. Most of the coins of these kings had a portrait, a monogram or a shield on the obverse. The typical reverse was either a shield, a monogram, a cross or sometimes three fleurs-de-lis, the symbol of the Bourbon Kings of France.

With the French Revolution new symbols appeared on the coinage. The ancient Roman fasces (seen in the United States Senate today) with a Liberty Cap atop was put on the reverse. When the king was executed he was replaced by a tablet saying "All men are equal before the law" or an angel representing the spirit of the republic. Napoleon completely abolished the old medieval-based coinage and replaced it with a full decimal system based on a silver franc (the size of a quarter) divided into 100 centimes. However, he also returned to more conservative designs, placing his own portrait on the obverse and a simple wreath on the reverse of most coins.

Throughout the 1800's the French government flip-flopped between kingdom, empire, and republic, finally settling on a republic which it has been since 1871. Through all these changes the

basic concept of Napoleon's reform has remained, suffering only due to inflation. French coins from the early twentieth century are particularly artistic, and those following the monetary reform of 1960 (they lopped off two zeros) are also of high artistic merit.

References: Duplessy, Jean, *Les Monnaies Francaises Royales*, vol. II.

Counterfeit Alert: A great many gold pieces of the 1850's and later have been counterfeited, especially the 20 Franc. Occasional contemporary counterfeits exist from most periods of French coinage. If of low denomination they are worth between 50% and 150% of their authentic counterparts.

Hints: French silver before the revolution often has scrape marks applied to the coin before striking to adjust the weight of the blank. These are not damage but do reduce the value of the coin depending on severity. Two franc pieces are particularly scarce above VG before 1850. Coins which are valued below only for BU have little value in lower grades. Values given are for the most common mint which is usually Paris (mintmark A).

LOUIS XIV (1643-1715)   **F**
1709 Louis d'or (G), Bust / Cross of L's
  and scepters 300.00

1646 Ecu (S), Bust / Crowned Shield
  . . . . 100.00
1692 Quadruple sol (S), Bust / Crowned
  L's 25.00
1693 Quinzain (base S), Eight L's /
  Crowned Arms 20.00
1693 Liard (C), Bust / Three fleurs-de-lis
  . . . . 10.00
1648 Denier tournois (C), Head / Two
  fleurs-de-lis 8.00

LOUIS XV (1715-74)   **F**
1760 2 Louis d'or (G) Head / Two
  Shields Crowned 385.00

F

1741 Ecu (S) Head / Crowned Shield
between branches 40.00
1765 1/10 Ecu (S) same 12.00
1738 2 Sols (base S) Crowned L /
Crowned L monogram 5.00
1771 Sol (C) Head/Crowned shield 6.50

LOUIS XVI (1774-93) **F**
1787 Louis d'or (G) Bust / Crowned
Double Arms 220.00
1783 Ecu (S) Head / Crowned Shield
between branches 40.00

1792 Ecu (S) Head / Angel 75.00
1791 30 Sols (S) Head / Angel . . 30.00
1791 15 Sols (S) same 14.00
1791 2 Sols (C-B) Bust / Fasces in
Wreath 10.00
1786 1 Sol (C) Head / Crowned Arms
. . . . 6.00
1792 3 Deniers (C-B) Bust / Fasces in
Wreath 22.50
1777 1 Liard (C) Head / Crowned Arms
. . . . 4.50

THE FRENCH REVOLUTION **F**
*Note: A special revolutionary calendar was
used, Year (L'an) 1 = 1792-93.*
1793 24 Livres (G) Angel / Wreath
. . . . 900.00
L'An II, 6 Livres (G) same . . . 425.00

1793 2 Sols (B) Tablet / Wreath and
scales 50.00
1793 1 Sol (B) same 35.00
L'An 7, 5 Francs (S) Three Figures /
Wreath 17.00
L'An 5, 5 centimes (C) Head/Wreath
. . . . 5.00
L'An 6, 1 Centime (C) Head 3.50

NAPOLEON I (1799-1815) **F**
1808 10 Centimes (base S) Crowned N /
Value 2.50
1814 1 Decime (C) Crowned N / Wreath
. . . . 15.00
L'An 12, 1 Franc (S) Bust/Wreath 20.00
1811 1 Franc (S) same 12.00

L'An 12, 2 Franc (S) Bust/Wreath 35.00

1813 5 Francs (S) same 30.00

LOUIS XVIII (1814-24)
1815 1 Decime (C) Crowned L / Wreath
. . . . 15.00
1822 1 Franc (S) Bust / Crowned Shield
. . . . 14.00
1817 2 Francs (S) same 35.00
1821 5 Francs (S) same 16.00

CHARLES X (1824-30)
1826 5 Francs (S) Bust / Crowned Shield
. . . . 12.50
1830 20 Francs (G) same 100.00

LOUIS PHILIPPE (1830-48)
1841 ¼ Franc (S) Bust / Wreath . . 3.50
1832 1 Franc (S) same 8.00
1832 2 Francs (S) same 24.00

1832 5 Francs (S) same 8.00

SECOND REPUBLIC (1848-52) **VF**
1848 1 Centime (C) 2.25

1849 1 Franc (S) Ceres Head / Wreath
. . . . 22.50
1849 5 Francs (S) Three Figures /
Wreath 12.00
1852 5 Francs (S) Louis Napoleon
Bonaparte 26.00

NAPOLEON III (1852-70) **VF**
1856 1 Centime (C) Head / Eagle . 4.00
1861 2 Centimes (C) same 2.00
1862 5 Centimes (C) Head/Eagle . 4.00
1862 10 Centimes (C) same 7.00
1867 50 Centimes (S) Head / Crown
. . . . 5.00
1868 1 Franc (S) Head / Arms . . . 7.00
1856 2 Francs (S) Head / Wreath 200.00
1867 2 Francs (S) Head / Arms . 14.00

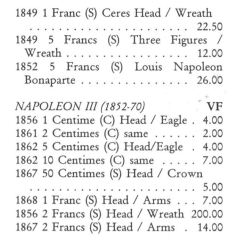

1856 5 Francs (G) Head / Wreath 40.00
1867 5 Francs (S) Head / Arms . 18.00
1861 20 Francs (G) Head / Arms 90.00

3rd-4th REPUBLICS (1871-1958) **VF**
1919 1 Centime (C) Allegory 75
1895 2 Centimes (C) Ceres Head . 2.00
1897 5 Centimes (C) Ceres Head /
Wreath 2.00
1914 10 Centimes (C) Woman and Child
. . . . 1.00
1914 10 Centimes (N) Cap . . . 650.00
1918 10 Centimes (CN) Cap 50
1850 20 Centimes (S) Ceres Head /
Wreath 10.00
1922 50 Centimes (AB) Seated Mercury
. 25
1919 1 Franc (S) Sower 1.00
1887 2 Francs (S) Ceres Head / Wreath
. . . . 12.00
1944 2 Francs (B) FRANCE in Wreath /
Value 2.00
1871 5 Francs (S) Ceres Head / Wreath
. . . . 90.00
1873 5 Francs (S) Three Figures /
Wreath 10.00

	VF
1933 5 Francs (N) Head	1.00
1912 20 Francs (G) Head / Rooster	95.00
1938 20 Francs (S) Head / Wheat Ears	5.00
1953 50 Francs (AB) Head/Rooster	1.00

VICHY FRANCE (ETAT FRANCAIS)
1942 10 Centimes (Z) Wheat Ears/ Oak Leaves ..... .50
1943 50 Centimes (AL) Fasces with Axe ..... .25
1944 2 Francs (AL) same ..... .25

1941 5 Francs (CN) Head of Petain / Fasces with Axe ..... *EF* 175.00

5th REPUBLIC (1959-date) **BU**
1961 1 Centime (Steel) Wheat Ear . .25
1963 5 Centimes (Steel) same ..... .75
1966 10 Centimes (AB) Bust l. ..... .15
1962 50 Centimes (AB) Bust l. ... 3.00
1965 ½ Franc (N) Sower ..... .25
1960 1 Franc (N) Sower ..... .35
1992 1 Franc (N) Head / Wreath . 1.00
1983 10 Francs (CN) Balloon 3.50

1986 100 Francs (S) Statue of Liberty 25.00
same double thick 16.00

FRENCH COLONIAL

History: Among the earliest French colonial coins are the crude hand struck pieces made for the French trading establishments in India. Many of these today cannot be dated simply because the blanks were too small for the design and the date on the dies did not fit onto the coin. These mostly date from the Royal period of French history. During the late 1800's when European colonial expansion was at its height, French colonial coinage was virtually unknown. It was not until the 1920's that it became common and the truly massive quantities seen today only date from 1948 and later. The 1920's issues were mostly struck in aluminum-bronze, the recent ones in aluminum also. During the twentieth century French colonial coin designs have been dominated by Marie-Anne, the allegory of the French Republic, in all her various forms.

References: General works and Bruce, Colin R., *Standard Guide to South Asian Coins and Paper Money.*
Counterfeit Alert: Not extensively counterfeited.
Hints: Many of the pieces of the early period are virtually unknown in superior grade. It is often wise to accept what can be found. The opposite is true of the 1948 and later series.

ALGERIA **VF**
1949 20 Francs (CN) 1.00
1949 50 Francs (CN) 2.00
1950 100 Francs (CN) 2.50

CAMEROON **VF**
1924 50 Centimes (AB) Leaves ... 3.00
1926 1 Franc (AB) same 2.50
1948 1 Franc (AL) Antelope Head . .25
1958 5 Francs (AB) Three Antelope Heads ..... .35
1958 25 Francs (AB) same 1.00

COMOROS ISLANDS **BU**
1964 1 Franc (AL) Palm Trees .... .75

1964 2 Francs (AL) same ..... .85
1964 5 Francs (AL) same 1.00
1964 20 Francs (AB) Shells and Fish 1.65

FRENCH AFARS & ISSAS **BU**
1975 1 Franc (AL) Antelope Head 2.50
1969 10 Francs (AB) Small Boat before Ocean Liner 7.00
1975 50 Francs (CN) Camels 6.50
1975 100 Francs (CN) same 9.50

FRENCH COCHIN CHINA **VF**
1875K Sapeque (France 1 Centime with hole in center) (C) 10.00
1879A 1 Cent (C) Seated Figure . 17.50
1879A 50 Cent. (S) same 150.00

FRENCH COLONIES *(General Issue)* **F**
1825 5 Cent. (C) Charles X 5.00
1841 5 Cent. (C) Louis Philippe I . 5.00
1825 10 Cent. (C) Charles X 8.00
1839 10 Cent. (C) Louis Philippe I 8.00

FRENCH EQUATORIAL AFRICA
VF
1943 10 Centimes (AB) 125.00
1942 50 Centimes (B) Rooster / Cross 2.75
1943 1 Franc (C) same 2.50
BU
1948 1 Franc (AL) Head / Antelope Head 1.50
1948 2 Francs (AL) Head / Antelope Head 3.00

FRENCH GUIANA (CAYENNE) **F**
1789 2 Sous (base S) 5.00
1846 10 Centimes (base S) 16.00

FRENCH INDIA

VG
ND [1700's] 1 Doudou (C) Fleur-de-lis / Inscription (4 gm) 3.50
1836 1 Doudou (C) Rooster / Inscription 6.00
ND [1720-1837] 2 Fanon (S) Crown / Rooster 22.00
1744 1 Fanon (S) Islamic inscription with large **P** 12.00

FRENCH INDO-CHINA **VF**
1887 Sapeque (C) square hole 3.25
1942 ¼ Cent. (Z) 13.00
1939 ½ Cent. (C) Cap ..... .50
1885 1 Cent. (C) Seated figure ... 3.50
1897 1 Cent. (C) Two seated figures (hole) 2.00
1941 1 Cent. (Z) Cap 4.00
1925 5 Cent. (CN) Cornucopiae .. 1.50
1943 5 Cent. (AL) Vichy Issue .... .25
1946 5 Cent. (AL) Bust/Rice Plant . .25
1922 10 Cent. (S) Seated figure ... 2.50
1945 20 Cent. (AL) Bust/Rice Plant .50
1936 50 Cent. (S) Seated figure / Wreath 3.50
1896 1 Piastre (S) same 10.00

1931 1 Piastre (S) Head / Value in ornate frame 9.00
1947 1 Piastre (CN) Bust / Rice Plant,Reeded edge 1.00

VF
same with security edge 15.00

FRENCH OCEANIA   BU
1949 1 Franc (AL) Seated figure . . 3.00
1952 5 Francs (AL) same 5.00

FRENCH POLYNESIA   BU
1965 50 Centimes (AL) Seated figure
. . . . 1.00
1975 1 Franc (AL) same 50
1965 5 Francs (AL) same 1.50

1979 20 Francs (N) Fruit 2.00
1975 50 Francs (N) Mountain . . . 3.50
1976 100 Francs (B) same 3.50

FRENCH SOMALIA   BU
1959 1 Franc (AL) Antelope Head.
. . . . 2.00
1965 5 Francs (AL) same 3.00
1952 20 Francs (AB) Small Boat before
    Ocean Liner 7.50

FRENCH WEST AFRICA   BU
1948 1 Franc (AL) Antelope Head.
. . . . 1.00
1956 5 Francs (AB) same 1.75
1956 25 Francs (AB) same 3.00

GUADELOUPE   F
1921 50 Centimes (CN) Indian Head.
. . . . 4.00
1903 1 Franc (CN) same 4.50

MADAGASCAR   VF
1943 50 Centimes (C) 2.50
1943 1 Franc (C) 5.00
1948 1 Franc (AL) 25
1953 5 Francs (AL) 50

MARTINIQUE   F
1922 50 Centimes (CN) Bust l. . . . 8.00
1922 1 Franc (CN) same 12.00

NEW CALEDONIA   BU
1949 1 Franc (AL) Bird 2.00
1979 2 Franc (AL) Bird 50
1952 5 Francs (AL) Bird 3.00
1972 50 Francs (N) Hut 4.00
1976 100 Francs (B) Hut 5.00

NEW CALEDONIA   BU
1975 1 Franc (B) Bird 50

1979 2 Franc (B) Bird 50
1982 5 Francs (B) Bird 1.00
1972 50 Francs (N) Carving 3.00
1966 100 Francs (S) Carving . . . 13.00

REUNION   BU
1948 1 Franc (AL) 1.50
1948 2 Franc (AL) 2.00
1955 5 Francs (AL) 2.00
1973 50 Francs (AB) 3.00

SAINT PIERRE & MIQUELON   BU
1948 1 Franc (AL) Boat 2.50
1948 2 Francs (AL) Boat 4.00

TOGO   VF
1924 50 Centimes (AB) 5.00
1924 1 Franc (AB) 6.00
1948 1 Franc (AL) 3.00
1956 5 Francs (AB) 2.00

TONKIN PROTECTORATE   AU
1905 1/600 Piastre (Z) 15.00
Note: Hoard quantities exist in AU-Unc.

TUNISIA   VF
1919 5 Centimes (CN) (hole) 50
1945 1 Franc (AB) 25
1939 10 Francs (S) 6.00

PORTUGAL

History: Portugal's coinage tells the story of its people, from its establishment in the middle ages, through the age of exploration, to its modern politics. The coat of arms, which is used by the current republic as well as the former kings, tells the story of how one early ruler of Portugal defeated five Moorish chiefs during the reconquest of the Iberian peninsula. It depicts five shields in the form of a cross, each bearing five pellets. After the overthrow of the monarchy in 1910, the new government added an astrolabe, a medieval navigation device. This recalls Portugal's pioneering role in the voyages of discovery which eventually led to Europe's contact with the New World. Until this century, modern Portuguese coinage consisted mostly of one monetary unit, as opposed to a large one divided into 100 or 1000 smaller ones. Coins were valued in numbers of reis. After 1912 this system was replaced by a large silver Escudo of 100 Centavos.

The Escudo today has become a tiny brass coin due to inflation.

Portuguese coins include many commemoratives, including issues recording the 1974 revolution and the country's 1986 admission to the Common Market.

References: Vaz, F., *Livro das moedas de Portugal.*

Counterfeit Alert: Most known counterfeits of Portuguese coins are of gold. Other metals are counterfeited far less frequently.

Hints: Punchmarks with numbers are found on many Portuguese coins. These are not mutilation but official revaluation marks. They may either increase or decrease value depending on both the mark and the original coin.

JOHN IV 1640-56   **F**
1642 4 Cruzado (G) Crowned Shield /
    Cross with date 400.00
AFONSO VI 1656-83
ND ½ Vintem = 10 reis (S) Four Shields
    / Cross 22.00
PETER II 1683-1706
ND ½ Tostao (S) Crown over XXXX /
    Cross 18.00
JOHN V 1706-50
1713 10 Reis (C) Crowned JV / X in
    wreath 18.00
JOSEPH I 1750-77
1762 200 (=240) Reis (S) Crowned Arms
    / Cross 16.00
MARIA 1777-99
1798 4 Escudos (G) Bust / Crowned
    Arms (1¼") 265.00
1799 5 Reis (C) Arms / V 2.25
JOHN VI (1799-) 1816-26
1814 400 (=480) Reis (S) Arms / Cross
. . . . 22.00
MARIA II 1834-53

1835 400 Reis (S) Arms / Cross . 25.00

LATER ROYAL COINAGE   **VF**
1874 3 Reis (C) Arms / III 4.00
1848 5 Reis (C) Arms / V 7.00
1891 10 Reis (C) Head / Wreath . 1.75
1873 20 Reis (C) Arms / XX 4.00
1900 50 Reis (CN) Arms / Value . 1.00
1909 100 Reis (S) Manuel / Crown 2.00
1854 200 Reis (S) Head / Wreath 18.00

1858 500 Reis (S) Pedro V / Arms 22.00
1908 500 Reis (S) Carlos I / Arms 9.00
1899 1000 Reis (S) same 18.00
1898 1000 Reis (S) Conjoined Busts /
    Cross . . . . *EF* 35.00
1851 2500 Reis (G) Head / Arms 200.00
1879 10,000 Reis (G) Head / Arms
    . . . . 325.00

REPUBLIC   **EF**
1917 1 Centavo (C) Arms 50
1919 4 Centavos (CN) Head 50
1924 1 Escudo (AB) Seated figure /
    Arms 2.00
1961 1 Escudo (CN) Bust 25
1951 2½ Escudos (S) Ship 1.50
                                    BU
1960 5 Escudos (S) Prince Henry the
    Navigator 3.50
1966 20 Escudos (S) Bridge 4.00

1969 50 Escudos (S) Carmona/Arms . .
    . . . . 6.00
1986 50 Escudos (CN) Ship 2.00
1984 250 Escudos (CN) Arms / School of
    Fish 5.00

PORTUGUESE COLONIES

History: Portugal was one of the last European powers to lose its colonial possessions. Most were granted independence around 1975. Most coins

were struck on a standard that closely resembled the home country's, but India, Macao and Timor are notable exceptions. On late issues one side usually bears the arms of Portugal, the other of the colony.
References: Vaz, F., *Livro das moedas de Portugal.*
Counterfeit Alert: Contemporary counterfeits of Brazilian copper are known. All gold should be inspected with scrutiny.
Hints: Punchmarks with numbers are found on many Brazilian coins. These are not mutilation but official revaluation marks. They may either increase or decrease value depending on both the mark and the original coin. Colonial coins of the 1920's and 1930's are usually scarce in high grade except Cape Verde which is available in hoard quantities in BU.

ANGOLA   **F**
1697 20 Reis (C) Arms/XX 18.00
1814 1 Macuta (C) Arms 10.00
1770 8 Macutas (S) Arms 55.00
                                    VF
1927 5 Centavos (CN) Bust 3.00
1922 50 Centavos (N) Bust 8.00
1962 20 Centavos (C) Arms 25
1953 1 Escudos (C) Arms 25
1955 20 Escudos (S) Arms 2.50
1971 20 Escudos (CN) Arms 50

BRAZIL   **F**
1766 5 Reis (C) Crowned V / Globe
    . . . . 4.00
1715 20 Reis (C) Value / Globe . . 4.00
1818 37½ Reis (C) Value / Arms on
    Globe 18.00
1818 75 Reis (C) same 20.00
1754 150 Reis (S) Crowned J / Globe on
    Cross 50.00

1799 640 Reis (S) Crowned Arms / Globe
    on Cross 25.00
1768 800 Reis (G) Head / Arms 100.00
                                    VF
1821 960 Reis (S) Crowned 960 / Arms
    on Cross 30.00
Note: Usually overstruck on Spanish Pieces of Eight.
1740 6400 Reis (G) Bust R or B below /
    Arms (14.34 gm.) 500.00
1725 20,000 Reis (G) Arms / M's in
    angles of Cross 2,000.00

CAPE VERDE   **BU**
1930 5 Centavos (C) Head 4.50
1930 20 Centavos (C) Head 6.00
1968 1 Escudo (C) Arms 2.50
1953 10 Escudos (S) Arms 8.00

PORTUGUESE GUINEA   **VF**
1933 5 Centavos (C) Head 3.75
1933 20 Centavos (C) Head 4.50
1946 1 Escudo (C) Arms 1.50
1952 20 Escudos (S) Arms / Arms 4.00

1973 1 Escudo (C) Arms/Value *EF* 3.00

PORTUGUESE INDIA   **F**
1765 20 Bazarucos (Tin) Arms / Cross
    with date (15 gm.) 36.00
1770 5 Bazarucos (Tin) Arms with B A /
    Cross and date 45.00
1770 5 Bazarucos (Tin) Arms with D A /
    Cross and date 25.00
1769 4 Reis (Tin) Arms with G A / IV
    over 1769 . . . . 30.00
ND ½ Tanga (C) Arms / 30 ½ T in
    Wreath 15.00
ND Tanga (C) Arms / AP over T 16.00
1845 ½ Pardao (S) Head / MEIO P in
    Wreath 38.00
1781 Rupia (S) Bust / Arms 65.00

1793 1 Rupia (S) Maria I / Arms 40.00
1714 10 Xerafins (G) Arms with G A /
    St. Thomas (5.6 gm.) . . . . *Scarce*
                                    VF
1901 1/12 Tanga (C) Head / Arms 3.00
1871 Tanga (C) Arms / Wreath . 27.50
1952 Tanga (C) Arms 50

	VF
1934 4 Tangas (CN) Arms / Arms	5.00
1881 ½ Rupia (S) Head / Arms	7.50
1912 Rupia (S) Bust / Wreath	38.00
1952 Rupia (CN) Arms / Arms	3.00
1961 10 Centavos (C) Arms	.25
1958 3 Escudos (CN) Arms / Arms	1.00

MACAO   EF
1967 5 Avos (B) Arms	.15
1952 10 Avos (C) Arms	.50
1985 20 Avos (B) Arms	.15
1952 1 Pataca (S) Arms / Arms	2.00
1986 100 Patacas (S) Arms/Tiger	35.00

MOZAMBIQUE   F
1820 40 Reis (C) Shield on Globe / Crowned 40	5.00
ND Taler PM countermarked on 1780 restrike Maria Theresa Taler	60.00

Note: The above is often counterfeited.

	VF
1936 10 Centavos (C) Arms	1.00
1974 20 Centavos (C) Arms	10.00
1945 1 Escudo (C) Arms	1.00

1974 1 Escudo (C) Arms	.20
1935 5 Escudos (S) Arms / Arms	4.00
1938 10 Escudos (S) same	11.00
1966 20 Escudos (S) same	3.00

SAINT THOMAS & PRINCE   VF
1813 20 Reis (C) Globe / Crowned 20	22.50
1929 10 Centavos (CN) Bust	2.00
1971 20 Centavos (C) Arms	.25
1929 50 Centavos (CN) Bust	6.00
1939 1 Escudo (CN) Arms	10.00
1962 5 Escudos (S) Arms / Arms	1.00
1939 10 Escudos (S) same	16.00

	BU
1971 20 Escudos (N) same	7.00
1970 50 Escudos (S) Double Arms / Cross	*BU* 9.00

TIMOR   EF
1945 10 Avos (C) Cross	40.00
1951 same	1.50

1945 20 Avos (CN) Bust	30.00
1951 50 Avos (S) Arms	7.00
1970 20 Centavos (C) Arms	.25
1958 60 Centavos (CN)	2.25
1958 1 Escudo (CN)	3.00
1964 10 Escudos (S)	8.00
1970 20 Escudos (CN)	3.00

SPAIN

History: Ferdinand and Isabella were responsible for creating the highly regarded system of Spanish coinage which lasted until the mid-1800's. It was based on a silver coin called the real, eight of which made a "silver dollar," 16 of which were an Escudo. The copper maravedi, 1/34 of a real, was of such little value that only the 4 maravedi and larger were worth striking in quantity. Throughout the 1600's and 1700's heraldry dominated Spanish coinage. Monograms appeared occasionally but the bust of the king would not appear on more than gold and local issues until the late 1700's.

After a few abortive attempts at monetary reform Spain introduced a new coinage in 1869 on the French standard then popular throughout Europe. The portraits and shields on these coins characterized most coins of Spain until recently. The reign of King Juan Carlos has seen intense creativity in coinage design, both in terms of the images depicted as well as the shapes of the coins, some of which are inspired by work of Pablo Picasso and his contemporaries.

References: Castan, C. and Cayon, J., *Las Monedas Espanolas desde los Reyes Catolicos al Estado Espanol.*

Counterfeit Alert: The gold coins of Isabella II were extensively counterfeited at the time.

Hints: The large dates on Spanish coins, 1868-1982 are not the years of striking. The true date is hidden in a six-pointed star, which is a mintmark of Madrid.

The "secret" date (1980) on a Spanish coin

CHARLES II 1665-1700   F
1682 2 Reales (S) Round Arms / Monogram	13.00
1686 2 Reales (S) Arms / Arms	13.00

CHARLES III of AUSTRIA 1701-13
1714 2 Reales (S) Arms / Monogram	25.00

PHILIP V 1700-46
1731 8 Escudos (G) Bust / Arms	1,500.00

1718 2 Reales (S) Crowned Arms / Round Arms	13.00
1720 2 Maravedis (C) Arms / Lion	8.00

LOUIS I 1724
1724 2 Reales (S) Arms / Arms	35.00

FERDINAND VI 1746-59
1757 2 Reales (S) Arms / Arms	18.00

CHARLES III 1759-88
1776 2 Reales (S) Bust / Arms	16.00
	F
1773 2 Escudos (G) same	150.00

CHARLES IV 1788-1808
1801 4 Maravedis (C) Bust / Castles and Lions	7.00
1791 4 Reales (S) Bust / Arms	32.50

JOSEPH NAPOLEON 1808-13
1811 4 Reales (S) Bust / Arms	15.00

FERDINAND VII 1808-33
1829 8 Maravedis (C) Bust / Castles and Lions	7.00
1822 20 Reales (S) Bust / Arms	60.00

ISABEL II 1833-1868
1855 25 Centimos (C) Bust / Arms	3.50

1864 10 Reales (S) Bust / Arms	30.00
1868 10 Escudos (G) same	125.00

AMADEO I 1871-73   VF
1871 5 Pesetas (S) same	18.00

ALFONSO XII 1874-85
1877 10 Centimos (C) same	2.50
1886 1 Peseta (S) same	9.50

ALFONSO XIII 1886-1931
1913 1 Centimo (C) same	1.50
1925 25 Centimos (CN) Ship	.75
1888 5 Pesetas (S) Baby Head/Arms	11.00

REPUBLIC 1931-38   VF
1933 (1934) 1 Peseta (S) España seated /
Arms 3.00
1937 1 Peseta (B) Head / Grapes . . .75

NATIONALIST GOV'T 1937-75   BU
1959 10 Centimos (AL) Franco 10
1973 1 Peseta (AB) Franco / Arms . .25
1954 2½ Pesetas (AB) same 1.50
1957 BA on star 50 Pesetas (CN) Franco
/ Eagle with Arms 100.00
1958 50 Pesetas (CN) same 2.50

JUAN CARLOS I 1975-date
1989 1 Peseta (AL) Face / Arms 10
1989 5 Pesetas (AB) Abstract designs
. 10

1980 25 Pesetas (CN) Soccer Ball in net
. 50
1989 2000 Pesetas (S) King and Queen /
Columbus 28.00

SPANISH EMPIRE

History: Spanish colonial coins can be grouped into two categories. Coins before the independence of Latin America, and coins of the remnant of the Empire many decades later. There were some Philippine coins in between however. The same system created under Ferdinand and Isabella and described above was employed the vast Spanish possessions in the New World, from Argentina to California. Many have heard of the famous treasure fleets sent laden with gold and silver back to Spain. The rich Latin American mines were producing bullion faster than it could be coined. Most of the bullion was either sent back in the form of bars or "cobs." These were odd shaped, hand struck coins made as an expedient. They circulated in the Americas extensively, but their main purpose was to shipped to Spain and melted. About 1732 well made, round coinage replaced these cobs. All silver looked alike: a crowned shield on the obverse, crowned globes between the Pillars of Hercules on the reverse. Many consider this to be their perfect idea of "pirate money." In 1760 new silver was introduced with the portrait of the king and the crowned arms. This combination

had been used on the round gold since its beginning. A number indicating the value was inscribed on the reverse, for example, 8R was 8 reales. All these gold and silver coins were of a relatively uniform design except for their mintmarks and circulated as one coinage. The mintmarks, sometimes shown as monograms, which distinguish these coins are:

Cᴀ	3x	Chihuahua, Mexico
D	2x	Durango, Mexico
G	2x	Guatemala
Gᴀ	2x	Guadalajara, Mexico
Go	3x	Guanajuato, Mexico
LIMAE	1x	Lima, Peru
Mo	1x	Mexico City, Mexico
NG	2x	Nueva Guatemala, Guatemala
NR	3x	Nuevo Reino, Colombia
P	3x	Popayan
P, PTS	1x	Potosi, Bolivia
So	2½x	Santiago, Chile
Zs	1½x	Zacatecas, Mexico

While colonial copper occasionally turns up from Mexico or Santo Domingo, it was far scarcer than the common silver coins.

The restored colonial coinage was small. Most coins had a portrait of the monarch and the coat of arms and were issued for very few years. Generally, no copper was struck.

References: Bruce, Colin R., *Standard Catalog of Mexican Coins*; Sedgwick, Frank, *Practical Book of Cobs*.

Counterfeit Alert: Brass contemporary counterfeits exist of bust type two reales and are considered collectible. Cheap replicas of the Piece of Eight and cob coins have been made by the tens of thousands. Poor quality examples can be found out by the seam around the edge. Serious counterfeits also exist of cob gold pieces.

Hints: Coins recovered from famous shipwrecks have been widely marketed to non-collectors. In most cases there is no need to question if these coins are real. Most are. However sea salvaged coins often have pitting or corrosion due to their prolonged exposure to salt water. Coins from the wreck of the Atocha have been very popular in recent years. Despite the fact that these problems make a coin undesirable to most collectors, the impressive pedigree makes these coins a part of history and often causes these coins to be traded at quite a premium! When buying such sea salvaged coins make sure that the original papers from the salvor accompany the coins. Without these papers they are just corroded old coins. Even with such documentation,

some specialist world coin dealers will consider these coins below their standards and discount them heavily.

The date and mintmark on cob coins are usually not clear. Prices are for those lacking one or the other.

Puerto Rican coins are often found with solder or other mount marks, and as such are discounted.

Values: To determine the value of Spanish colonial coins of 1732-1825 multiply the value given below times the number shown after the table of mintmarks above. Of course, many dates will vary from this table.

PRE-COB COINAGE   VG
Santo Domingo ND 4 maravedi (C), Crowned Y with two tails / Crowned II 16.00
Mexico ND 4 maravedi (C), Crowned K / Crowned I 80.00
Mexico ND 1 Real (S), Crowned shield / Dot between Crowned Columns 27.00

COB COINAGE ca. 1500's-1734
                                              VG
½ Real (S) Monogram / Cross with Castles and Lions 12.50
1 Real (S) Arms / Cross with Castles and Lions 16.00
2 Reales (S) same 18.00
4 Reales (S) same 38.00

8 Reales (S) same 70.00
1 Escudo (G) Arms / Cross . . .   250.00
2 Escudos (G) same 300.00
4 Escudos (G) same 500.00
8 Escudos (G) same 800.00

MILLED SILVER -
SHIELD / CROWNED GLOBES
&PILLARS ca. 1732-60   F
½ Real (S) 7.00
1 Real (S) 10.00

	F
2 Reales (S)	18.00
4 Reales (S)	100.00
8 Reales (S)	100.00

MILLED SILVER, ca. 1760-1825   F
¼ Real (S) Castle / Lion	8.00
¼ Real (C) Monogram / Cross with Castles and Lions	18.00
½ Real (S) Bust / Crowned Arms between Pillars	6.00
1 Real (S) same	8.00
2 Reales (S) same	15.00
4 Reales (S) same	40.00

8 Reales (S) same	38.00

MILLED GOLD - BUST /
CROWNED ARMS 1732-1825   F
½ Escudo (G)	135.00
1 Escudo (G)	150.00
2 Escudos (G)	250.00
4 Escudos (G)	475.00

8 Escudos (G)	575.00

PHILIPPINES   F
1766 Barilla (C) Castle Tower / Lion with Fish Tail	200.00
1826 Quarto (C) Arms / Lion with Sword	20.00

1868 10 Centimos (S) Isabel II / Arms	5.00
1868 20 Centimos (S) same	4.50
1868 50 Centimos (S) same	7.00
1868 Peso (G) same	40.00
1868 2 Pesos (G) same	55.00
1868 4 Pesos (G) same	95.00
	VF
1885 10 Centimos (S) Alfonso XII / Arms	5.50
1885 20 Centimos (S) same	7.50

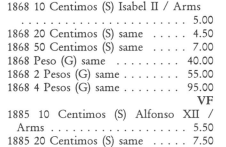

1885 50 Centimos (S) same	8.00
1882 4 Pesos (G) same	700.00
1897 Peso (S) Alfonso XIII / Arms	36.00

PUERTO RICO   VF
1896 5 Centavos (S) Arms / Value	12.00
1896 10 Centavos (S) Alfonso XIII / Arms	15.00
1895 20 Centavos (S) same	35.00
1896 40 Centimos (S) same . . .	215.00

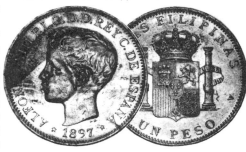

1895 Peso (S) same	240.00

LOW COUNTRIES (BENELUX)

History: Belgium, Netherlands, and Luxembourg form a triangle at the northern border between France and Germany, and share much common history and heritage. They get their name from the low elevation level of their land, particularly of the Netherlands. Until the late 1500's the whole area was owned by the Hapsburg King of Spain. Due largely to religious tensions the Dutch Republic broke away during that century. The area of present day Belgium continued under the Spanish Hapsburgs until it was transferred to the

Austrian branch of the same in 1713. During this period both regions had a number of local coinages, with the Spanish Netherlands (Belgium) striking quite a bit of small and medium silver and the Dutch Republic (Netherlands) striking many small copper duits and large crude dollars (daalders).

The three states took their modern form after Napoleon's defeat. After 15 years Belgium broke away from the Netherlands, and in 1890 the rulers of the Netherlands lost Luxembourg due to inheritance. All local coinage was eliminated. Because Belgium's population is mixed, Flemish and French speaking, most Belgian coins are struck in two varieties, one in each language.

References: Zonnebloem, U., *Catalogus van de Zilvern Munten*, 2 vol.; Mevius, J., *De Nederlandse Munten van 1795 tot Heden*; de Mey, J., *Les Monnaies des Souverains Luxembourgeois*.

Counterfeit Alert: Gold is more often counterfeited than the other metals.

Hints: Dutch Lion Daalders are struck on very crudely formed blanks. Edge cracks are normal. Gold Ducats with BELGII are Dutch not Belgian. Post-1948 coins of Belgium and Luxembourg are often weakly struck in the centers, particularly the cupro-nickel.

BELGIUM   F
1776 Liard (C) Maria Theresa / Inscription	7.50
1793 14 Liards (S) Crossed Sticks X IV / Double headed Eagle with Arms	22.00
1795 Kronenthaler (S) Francis II / X with Crowns	22.00

	VF
1837 5 Centimes (C) Monogram / Lion with Tablets	7.50
1832 10 Centimes (C) similar . . .	70.00
1861 5 Centimes (CN) Value / Lion	1.50
1923 5 Centimes (CN) Crowned A / Branch	.25
1915 10 Centimes (Z) Lion	.25
1911 1 Franc (S) Head / Wreath .	2.00
	VF
1922 1 Franc (N) Woman Kneeling / Caduceus	.25
1843 2 Francs (S) Bust / Wreath	700.00
1870 5 Francs (S) Head / Arms . .	9.50

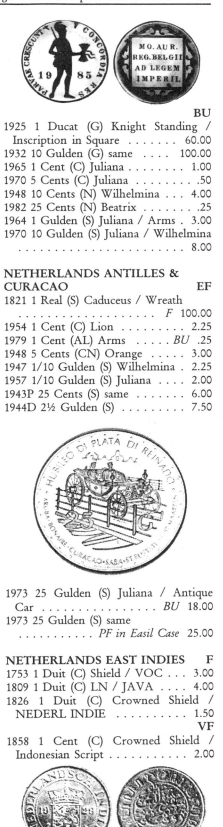

1880 5 Francs (S) Two Kings' Heads / Woman and Lion 175.00
1935 50 Francs (S) St. Michael the Archangel / Train Station ... 100.00
BU
1970 1 Franc (CN) Ceres Head .... .10
1914 20 Francs (G) Bust / Arms 110.00
1948 100 Francs (S) Four Kings / Arms
.... 10.00
1976 250 Francs (S) Head / Crowned B
.... 7.50

BELGIAN CONGO   **VF**
1910 1 Centime (C) Five A's / Star 2.00

1887 2 Centimes (C) Ten L's / Star 2.25
1920 1 Franc (CN) Bust / Tree .. 2.50
1944 1 Franc (B) Elephant 1.00
1944 50 Francs (S) Elephant 50.00
1955 50 centimes (AL) Arms / Tree
.... *BU* 1.00

NETHERLANDS   **F**
1604 Liondaalder (S) Half Knight above
shield / Lion (many provincial
varieties) 60.00
1762 Duit (C) Arms / STAD UTRECHT
.... 3.75

1768 Ducat (S) Knight / Arms . 175.00
1774 similar 55.00

1776 2 Stuiver (S) Arms between 2 S / WEST FRISIAE 4.00
1770 Ducaton (S) Mounted Knight / Arms 38.00
1809 1 Gulden (S) Head of Louis Napoleon / Arms 275.00
VF
1862 ½ Cent (C) Crowned W / Arms
.... 18.00
1938 ½ Cent (C) Lion / Wreath . 2.00
1863 1 Cent (C) Crowned W / Arms
.... 9.00
1922 1 Cent (C) Lion / Wreath .. 1.50
1942 1 Cent (Z) Cross .... .50
1877 2½ Cents (C) Lion / Wreath 6.75
1941 2½ Cents (C) same 2.00
1941 2½ Cents (Z) Prow 4.50
1907 5 Cents (CN) Crown 10.00
1913 5 Cents (CN) Orange 2.00
1819 10 Cents (S) Crowned W / Arms
.... 500.00
1827 10 Cents (S) same 32.00
1885 10 Cents (S) Willem III / Wreath
.... 25.00
1848 25 Cents (S) Willem II / Wreath
.... 38.00

1898 25 Cents (S) Wilhelmina as Girl / Wreath 150.00
1919 25 Cents (S) Wilhelmina as Adult / Wreath 15.00
1928 25 Cents (S) same 2.00

1942 25 Cents (Z) Viking Ship ... 1.00
1898 ½ Gulden (S) Wilhelmina / Arms
.... 50.00
1929 ½ Gulden (S) same 2.50
1847 1 Gulden (S) Willem II/Arms
.... 35.00
1907 1 Gulden (S) Wilhelmina / Arms
.... 35.00
1944P 1 Gulden (S) same (P = made in USA) 20.00
1847 2½ Gulden (S) Willem II / Arms
.... 40.00
1872 2½ Gulden (S) Willem III / Arms
.... 22.00
1898 2½ Gulden (S) Wilhelmina / Arms
.... 250.00
1930 2½ Gulden (S) same 8.00

BU
1925 1 Ducat (G) Knight Standing / Inscription in Square 60.00
1932 10 Gulden (G) same 100.00
1965 1 Cent (C) Juliana 1.00
1970 5 Cents (C) Juliana .... .50
1948 10 Cents (N) Wilhelmina ... 4.00
1982 25 Cents (N) Beatrix .... .25
1964 1 Gulden (S) Juliana / Arms . 3.00
1970 10 Gulden (S) Juliana / Wilhelmina
.... 8.00

NETHERLANDS ANTILLES & CURACAO   **EF**
1821 1 Real (S) Caduceus / Wreath
.... *F* 100.00
1954 1 Cent (C) Lion 2.25
1979 1 Cent (AL) Arms .... *BU* .25
1948 5 Cents (CN) Orange 3.00
1947 1/10 Gulden (S) Wilhelmina . 2.25
1957 1/10 Gulden (S) Juliana 2.00
1943P 25 Cents (S) same 6.00
1944D 2½ Gulden (S) 7.50

1973 25 Gulden (S) Juliana / Antique Car .... *BU* 18.00
1973 25 Gulden (S) same
.... *PF in Easil Case* 25.00

NETHERLANDS EAST INDIES   **F**
1753 1 Duit (C) Shield / VOC ... 3.00
1809 1 Duit (C) LN / JAVA 4.00
1826 1 Duit (C) Crowned Shield / NEDERL INDIE 1.50
VF
1858 1 Cent (C) Crowned Shield / Indonesian Script 2.00

1929 1 Cent (C) similar .... .75

VF

1945P 1 Cent (C) Branch / Flowers
(hole) 25
1858 2½ Cents (C) Crowned Shield /
Indonesian Script 6.00
1945P 2½ Cents (C) same 1.00
1909 1/10 Gulden (S) same 3.00
1945S ¼ Gulden (S) same 75
1834 ½ Gulden (S) Willem I . . . 35.00
1839 1 Gulden (S) Willem I / Crowned
Arms 40.00

LUXEMBOURG   F

1637 1 Sol (base S) Crowned X /
Crowned Arms 50.00
1759 2 Liards (C) Crowned Arms /
Crowned Monogram 30.00

VF

1854 5 Centimes (C) Crowned Shield /
Wreath 3.00
1901 10 Centimes (CN) Head . . . 1.00
1916 25 Centimes (Z) (hole) 2.75
1924 1 Franc (N) Crowned Monogram /
Iron Worker 50

BU

1954 25 Centimes (AL) Crowned Arms /
Branch .15
1929 10 Francs (S) Head / Arms   25.00

1971 10 Francs (CN) Head / Crowned
10F 50

SCANDINAVIA

History: Norway, Sweden, Denmark and
Iceland all share a common language
group and at many times have had
monarchs in common. Finland, while
not sharing the same linguistic root, has
had intimate historical ties with these
countries, in particular Sweden. During
the early modern period Scandinavian
coins often depicted standard European
motifs with a creative flair. Busts were
often half figures, kings, queens, and
Christ were shown standing or three-
quarter length. In Denmark and later in
Norway monograms often used modern
numerals instead of old Roman ones.
Swedish coinage in particular is famous
for its unusual use of copper. Not only
did it frequently use coppers the size of
silver dollars, but for many years it used
small slabs of copper with dies stamped
into them for larger denominations.

These coins called "plate money" could
easily weigh several pounds! During the
late 1800's and somewhat beyond,
Norway, Sweden, Denmark, and Iceland
were part of the Scandinavian Monetary
Union, an agreement to strike a common
standard of coin of equal value. All five
of these countries issue frequent
commemoratives, continuing a long
tradition of such issues dating back
hundreds of years.

Because it was part of Denmark the
coinages of Iceland did not begin until
1922. Finland was under Sweden and
then Russia. Its first coins were dated
1864 and still carried a czarist eagle,
though with a Finnish lion on its chest.
Norwegian coins appear and disappear
throughout history because sometimes
Danish coins were struck in Norway with
only a tiny mint mark to distinguish
them.

References: Hobson, Burton, *Catalogue of
Scandinavian Coins.*

Counterfeit Alert: Contemporary
counterfeits exist of Danish 2 skilling
pieces of the late 1600's. Swedish plate
money has been counterfeited with skill.
Genuine oxidation is one way of
determining authenticity. There are
unauthorized restrikes and possibly
counterfeits of the Finnish 1918 Red
government 5 pennia, counterfeits of the
1951 500 Markkaa.

Hints: Large Swedish coppers of the
1600's often were struck on blanks with
very crude surfaces. Danish and Swedish
commemoratives of the late 1880's and
early 1900's are far more common and
reasonably priced than the quantities
struck would indicate.

Because the coins of these countries are
often similar, it is useful to know the
simple versions of their coats of arms.
Norway's is a lion with a battle axe,
Sweden's is three crowns, and Denmark's
is three lions on a field of hearts. The
native spelling of Iceland is Island, that of
Finland is Suomi.

DENMARK   F

1618 1 Krone (S) King standing / Crown
. . . . 165.00

1659 1 Krone (S) 3F Monogram / Hand
being cut off 325.00
1711 1 Krone (S) King riding horse /
Arms 120.00
1764 4 Skilling (S) Monogram . . . 9.00
1680 2 Skilling (S) Arms 7.00
1771 1 Skilling (C) Monogram . . . 2.00
1762 12 Mark (G) Head / Crown over
XII.M 150.00
1683 4 Ducats (G) C5 Monogram /
Elephant . . . . *Rare*

VF

1867 1 Skilling (C) Monogram . . . 2.50
1871 4 Skilling (S) Head 6.00
1776 1 Daler (S) Monogram / Oval
Arms 80.00
1854 1 Rigsdaler (S) Head 30.00
1863 2 Rigsdaler (S) Head of Christian IX
/ Head of Frederick VII 150.00
1894 1 Ore (C) Monogram / Dolphin and
Wheat 1.00
1907 2 Ore (C) Monogram 1.00
1918 5 Ore (Iron) Monogram 5.00
1907 10 Ore (S) Head 2.25
1926 10 Ore (CN) (hole) 25
1925 ½ Krone (AB) Monogram / Crown
. . . . 4.00
1925 1 Krone (AB) same 1.25
1916 2 Krone (S) Head / Arms . 12.50
1923 2 Kroner (S) Conjoined Heads of
King and Queen / Arms 6.50
1939 2 Kroner (AB) Monogram / Crown
. . . . 2.00

BU

1973 5 Ore (C on Iron) Monogram   .10
1961 25 Ore FR Monogram / Oak
Branches 1.00
1989 50 Ore (B) 50
1945 2 Kroner (S) Wreath 14.00
1953 2 Kroner (S) Map of Greenland
. . . . 28.00
1964 5 Kroner (S) Head of King / Head
of Princess 6.00
1971 5 Kroner (CN) Head / Arms 1.25

1873 20 Kroner (G) Head / Dania seated
. . . . 175.00
1916 20 Kroner (G) Head / Arms 150.00
1990 20 Kroner (AB) Bust of Queen in
Hat 5.00

FINLAND   VF

1875 1 Penni (C) A over II 5.00
1909 1 Penni (C) N over II 50

		VF
1917	1 Penni (C) Czarist Eagle	.50
1889	5 Pennia (C) A over III	5.00
1914	10 Pennia (C) N over II	2.00
1915	1 Markka (S) Czarist Eagle	3.00
1918	5 Pennia (C) Trumpets	27.50
1920	5 Pennia (C) Lion	.25
1953	50 Markkaa (AB) Lion / Tree	.25
1975	10 Markkaa (S) Kekkonen	5.00

1951 500 Markkaa (S) Olympic Rings / Wreath 250.00
1952 500 Markkaa (S) same 25.00

ICELAND   **VF**
1931 1 Eyrir (C) Crowned Monogram
. . . . 1.50
1942 1 Eyrir (C) same 25
1946 5 Aurar (C) Shield 25
1925 1 Krona (AB) Crowned Shield 4.00
1940 2 Kronur (AB) same 1.00
1930 5 Kronur (S) Man in cape . 40.00
1978 50 Kronur (CN) Building 25

1974 1000 Kronur (S) Two men standing by flame 10.00

NORWAY   **F**
1644 2 Skilling (S) Lion and Axe . 9.00
1702 2 Skilling (S) F4 Monogram / Lion Arms 12.00
1785 2 Skilling (S) C7 Monogram / Crowned Oval Shield 5.00
1730 8 Skilling (S) Lion and Axe / VIII etc. 20.00
1796 2/3 Rigsdaler Species (S) Head / Crowned Oval Shield 90.00

1648 Speciedaler (S) Crowned Bust / Lion and Axe 350.00
                                          VF
1867 ½ Skilling (C) Crowned Shield 2.00
1871 2 Skilling (S) same 4.00
1747 24 Skilling (S) Monogram / Lion and axe 40.00
1670 4 Mark (S) Monogram/ Arms
. . . . 175.00
1733 6 Mark (S) Bust / Arms . 1,400.00
1857 1 Specie Daler (S) Bust / Arms
. . . . 200.00
1899 1 Ore (C) O II Arms 3.50
1907 2 Ore (C) H VII Arms 4.00
1951 5 Ore (C) H7 Monogram 25
1876 25 Ore (S) Monogram / Arms
. . . . 12.50
                                          BU
1964 1 Krone (CN) Horse 2.25
1975 5 Kroner (CN) Ship 3.00
1964 10 Kroner (S) Arms / Building
. . . . 6.00
1992 100 Kroner (S) Head / Hockey Players 60.00

SWEDEN   **F**
1597 1 Ore (S) King Standing / Arms
. . . . 50.00
1703 1 Ore (S) Crowned Monogram / Three Crowns 12.50
1722 1 Ore (S) Crowned F / Three Crowns 10.00
1731 1 Ore (C) FF Monogram / Crossed Arrows 5.00
1761 1 Ore (C) AF Monogram / Crossed Arrows 4.00
1758 2 Ore (C) AFSGVR and Arms / Crossed Arrows 5.00
1661 2½ Ore (C) Arms / Three Crowns
. . . . 50.00
1773 16 Ore (S) GIII Monogram Crowned Round Arms 40.00
1701 2 Mark (S) Bust / Three Crowns
. . . . 55.00
1802 1/12 Skilling (C) Monogram / Crossed Arrows 2.00
1819 ½ Skilling (C) same 4.00

1832 1/8 Riksdaler (S) Bust / Arms 8.00
1752 ½ Daler Plate Money (C) Five Punches on copper sheet   *VF* 300.00
1610 1 Riksdaler (S) King standing / Christ Standing 225.00
1646 1 Riksdaler (S) Half figure of Queen / Christ standing 200.00
1715 1 Daler (C) Crown 4.00
1718 1 Daler (C) Warrior & Lion . 5.00
                                          VF

1727 1 Riksdaler (S) Busts of King and Queen / Arms 650.00
1719 1 Ducat (G) Queen / Arms 900.00
1857 ½ Ore (C) Monogram 2.00
1858 1 Ore (C) Head 2.00
1882 1 Ore (C) O II Monogram . . 4.00
1904 1 Ore (C) same 50
1867 2 Ore (C) Head 5.00
1867 5 Ore (C) Head 9.00
1892 5 Ore (C) O II Monogram . . 4.75
1907 5 Ore (C) same 1.50
1934 10 Ore (S) Arms 50
1945 10 Ore (S) Crown 25
1859 25 Ore (S) Head 12.00
1862 50 Ore (S) Head 700.00
1907 50 Ore (S) O II Monogram . . 9.00
1904 1 Krona (S) Head / Arms . . 15.00
1941 1 Krona (S) Head / Arms . . 1.75
                                          Unc
1953 2 Ore (C) Incuse inscriptions 2.50
1967 2 Ore (C) same 25
1976 5 Ore (C) Monogram 25
1956 25 Ore (S) Crown 3.00

1897 2 Kronor (S) Crowned Bust / Arms
. . . . 17.50
1938 2 Kronor (S) Ship 10.00
1954 2 Kronor (S) Arms 4.00

VF
1935 5 Kronor (S) Arms 22.00

1962 5 Kronor (S) Minerva 30.00
1966 5 Kronor (S) Plaque 4.50
1972 10 Kronor (S) Signature 8.00
1991 10 Kronor (AB) Three Crowns upon
    10 . . . . 2.00
1898 20 Kronor (G) Bust / Arms 275.00
1983 200 Kronor (S) Head / Arms 52.00

GERMANY

History: While nominally unified under the Holy Roman (Austrian) Emperor until 1806, German coinage during this period forms a discordant hodge-podge of local authorities and regional standards. The most standard gold coin was the ducat containing .11 ounces of gold. Silver varied more but in general a Taler was a "silver dollar" of varying size, a Gulden was very roughly a "half dollar" and a Kreuzer was a very small coin indeed. Copper coins were called Hellers, Pfennigs, and also Kreuzers. Some of them were struck in a copper-silver alloy called billon.

Each local prince placed his own portrait or shield or monogram on his own coinage. Free cities would often name the Holy Roman Emperor on their coins because they were not subject to local royal authority. Other popular types included the local patron saint, a horse, a Wildman (the German equivalent of the Sasquatch), and an eagle (with one or two heads), as well as a simple denomination.

With the creation of the German Empire in 1871, all German coinage was unified on one standard. All coins of one mark (similar to a U.S. quarter) or smaller were the same throughout the Empire. Two, three, and five marks and gold shared a common reverse, with the local prince or arms on the obverse. After the nobility was forced out in 1918 and the Weimar Republic was created, all German coinage was finally unified.

For a brief time during and shortly after World War I many German municipalities, as well as some firms and banks, issued their own emergency token coinage called *notgeld*. This interesting series was usually struck in inferior metals such as iron and zinc.

From 1948 to 1990 East Germany (DDR) had a separate coinage. In 1991 coins of the Federal Republic of Germany began to be struck in Berlin and circulate in the East as well.

References: Hundreds of books would be necessary to properly cover the coinage of Germany. Aside from the general references suggested above, the sampling here are particularly useful. Schön, G., *Deutscher Münzkatalog 18.Jahrhundert*; Craig, W.D. *Germanic Coinages*; Davenport, *German Church and City Talers, German Secular Talers 1600-1700*, and *German Talers 1700-1800*.

Counterfeit Alert: Contemporary counterfeits of Prussian 1700's base silver coins exist. More dangerous counterfeits exist of a great many 20 Mark gold coins.

Hints: Talers are often found polished or mounted; these coins trade at a discount. Many South German silver coins of the 17th century were struck with roller dies and will have a natural curve. They are not damaged coins. Corroded or spotted zinc or aluminum coins may be considered unsalable. Zinc pieces with full natural mint brightness command a substantial premium and are rare. Base metal coins listed in BU are often virtually worthless in circulated grades.

Imperial 2, 3, and 5 marks, and Weimar and early Federal Republic Commemoratives are popular in Germany and are actively bought in North America for export.

Warning: 1951 and Max Planck 2 marks are no longer legal tender, nor are silver 5 marks.

SEVENTEENTH CENTURY   F
Bavaria 1624 ½ Batzen (S) Shield / Z on
    Orb with Cross 15.00
Brunswick-Lüneburg 1622 3 Flitter (C)
    Lion / III 25.00
Frankfurt 1655 Albus (S) Eagle / Cross
    . . . . 22.00
Lippe-Detmold 1613-27 1 Groschen (S)
    Arms / Orb with cross 20.00
Nurnburg 1632 1 Ducat (G) Arms /
    Lamb . . . . VF 800.00
Pfalz-Zweibruecken 1604 3 Kreuzer (S)
    Arms / Eagle 20.00
Prussia 1682 6 Groschen (S) Bust / Arms
    . . . . 26.00

Saxony 1616 Taler (S) Half Figure with
    Sword / Arms 95.00
Saxony 1630 Groschen (S) Arms / Triple
    Arms 20.00
Saxony 1699 Pfennig (S) Arms / Orb
    with Cross 9.00
Quedlinburg 1617 Taler (S) Arms / Old
    Emperor standing with Sword   975.00
Würzburg 1694 2 Kreuzer (S) Arms /
    Bishop-Saint with Sword and Crozier
    . . . . 20.00
EIGHTEENTH CENTURY   F
Bavaria 1776 10 Kreuzer (S) Bust in
    wreath / Arms 12.50
Bavaria 1772 Taler (S) Bust / Madonna
    and Child 30.00
Brandenburg-Bayreuth 1749 1 Kreuzer (S)
    Bust / Eagle 7.00
Bremen 1752 1 Groten (base S) Key on
    Shield / Eagle 13.00
Brunswick-Luneburg 1715 Ducat (G)
    George I of England / Four Shields
    with Scepters between 300.00
Brunswick-Wolfenbuttel 1753 1/6 Taler
    (S) Horse / Value 10.00
Cologne 1777 1 Stüber (base S) Bust /
    Value 17.00
Frankfurt 1773 1 Kreuzer (S) City View /
    Eagle 6.50
Hamburg 1728 4 Schillings (S) Building
    with three turrets / Eagle 16.50

Hamburg 1730 Taler (S) Arms / Imperial
    Eagle 275.00
Hesse-Darmstadt 1702 1 Albus (S) HD
    over Shield / Wreath 20.00
Hildesheim 1709 1/24 Taler (S) Shield
    with tall crest / 24 on Orb with Cross
    . . . . 25.00

F
Mecklenburg-Strelitz 1763 1/12 Taler (S) Crowned AF Monogram 18.00
Münster 1715 4 Pfennig (C) Crowned Monogram / IIII 10.00
Prussia 1779 1/48 Taler (base S) FR Monogram 6.00
Prussia 1764 1/24 Taler (base S) FR Monogram 10.00
Prussia 1780 Taler (S) Head / Eagle on Cannon 50.00
Wurzburg 1727 1/84 Gulden (S) Triple Arms / 84 inscribed on Orb with Cross 12.00

NINETEENTH CENTURY to 1873   **VF**
Bavaria 1870 1 Kreuzer (base S) Arms 2.50
Bavaria 1868 1 Gulder (S) Ludwig II / Wreath 80.00
Hamburg 1809 Sechsling (S) Building with turrets 2.50
Hannover 1834 1/12 Taler (S) William IV of England 20.00
Lippe-Detmold 1860 1 Groschen (base S) Bearded Bust 13.50
Nassau 1861 1 Kreuzer (C) Arms . 3.00
Prussia 1873 1 Pfennig (C) Arms . 1.00
Prussia 1861 1 Groschen (S) Head . 2.00

Prussia 1861 1 Taler (S) Conjoined busts of King and Queen / Eagle . . . 25.00
Reuss-Greiz 1868 1 Pfennig (C) Arms 3.00
Saxony 1871 1/6 Taler (S) Head / Arms 12.00
Schleswig-Holstein 1850 1 Dreiling (C) Arms in Wreath 6.00
Westphalia 1812 3 Centimes (C) HN Monogram / Value 3.50
Wuerttemburg 1842 Gulden (S) Head / Wreath 45.00

WORLD WAR I RELATED
EMERGENCY TOKENS   **VF**
Aachen 1920 10 Pfennig (Iron) Dog 1.00
Coblenz 1918 10 Pfennig (Iron) Shield 75
Frankenthal 1919 50 Pfennig (Iron) Two Eagles 2.75
Mergentheim 1920 1 Pfennig (Iron) Antler 10.00
Oberammergau 1917 5 Pfennig (Z) Mountain with Cross 2.75

1921 Saxony 20 Pfennig (Porcelain) 3.00

GERMAN STATES 1871 to 1918
Anhalt 1914 3 Mark (S) Conjoined Heads of Duke and Duchess / Eagle . 40.00
Baden 1906 2 Mark (S) Conjoined busts of Grand Duke and Duchess / Eagle 22.00

Baden 1903 5 Mark (S) Head / Eagle 40.00
Bavaria 1876 2 Mark (S) Ludwig II / Eagle 50.00
Bavaria 1908 5 Marks (S) Otto / Eagle 25.00
Hamburg 1909 3 Mark (S) Arms / Eagle 22.50
Hesse 1876 10 Mark (G) Ludwig III / Eagle 165.00
Prussia 1913 3 Mark (S) Horseman surrounded by Crowd / Eagle attacking Snake 10.00
Prussia 1888 5 Mark (S) Friedrich III / Eagle 70.00
Prussia 1908 5 Mark (S) Wilhelm II / Eagle 20.00
Prussia 1906 20 Mark (G) same   110.00

IMPERIAL MINOR COINS 1871-1921
    VF
1892A 1 pfennig (C) Eagle 25
1904A 2 pfennig (C) Eagle 25
1875A 5 pfennig (CN) Eagle 50
1875A 10 pfennig (CN) Eagle 1.50
1875H 10 pfennig (CN) Eagle . . 18.00
1875A 20 pfennig (S) Eagle 6.00
1919D ½ Mark (S) Eagle in Wreath / Wreath 1.00
1875H 1 Mark (S) Eagle / Wreath   5.00

1879A 1 Mark (S) similar 75.00
1906F 1 Mark (S) same 2.00

WEIMAR REPUBLIC AND NAZI STATE: 1921-1945

    VF
1924A 1 Rentenpfennig (C) Sheaf . . .35
1924A 1 Reichspfennig (C) Sheaf . . .25
1938D 2 Reichspfennig (C) Eagle with Swastika 50
1942A 5 Reichspfennig (Z) same 50
1925F 10 Reichspfennig (AB) Six Ears of Grain 25
1924J 50 Rentenpfennig (AB) same   8.00
1924A 50 Reichspfennig (AB) same 800.00
1928A 50 Reichspfennig (N) Eagle   1.75
1939B 50 Reichspfennig (N) Eagle with Swastika 20.00
1940A 50 Reichspfennig (AL) same . .50
1934A 1 Reichsmark (N) Eagle / Wreath 1.50
1937J 2 Reichsmark (S) Hindenburg / Eagle with Swastika 4.50
1923J 3 Mark (AL) Eagle 1.00
1925A 3 Reichsmark (S) Knight standing with large shield / Wreath . . . 35.00
1930 3 Reichsmark (S) Lessing / Eagle 32.50
1930A 3 Reichsmark (S) Zeppelin / Eagle 50.00

1925D 5 Reichsmark (S) Knight standing with large shield / Wreath . . 160.00
1931F 5 Reichsmark (S) Oak Tree / Eagle 75.00
1933A 5 Reichsmark (S) Luther / Eagle 100.00
1935D 5 Reichsmark (S) Church / Eagle 5.50
1936A 5 Reichsmark (S) Hindenburg / Eagle 5.50
1936A 5 Reichsmark (S) same but Eagle has Swastika 6.75
1923A 200 Mark (AL) Eagle 25
1923F 500 Mark (AL) Eagle 1.00

FEDERAL REPUBLIC   **BU**
1949F 1 pfennig (C clad Steel) Oak Sapling 13.00
1950J 1 pfennig (C clad Steel) Oak Sapling 1.00
1966D 2 pfennig (C) same 25
1973D 5 pfennig (B clad Steel) same .25
1971D 50 pfennig (CN) Woman planting Sapling 50
1950D 1 Deutsche Mark (CN) Eagle 30.00

BU
1980D 1 Deutsche Mark (CN) same .75
1975D 2 Deutsche Mark (CN clad N)
Adenauer / Eagle 2.00
1951D 5 Deutsche Mark (S) Eagle 40.00

1955F 5 Deutsche Mark (S) Schiller /
Eagle 1,000.00
1971D 5 Deutsche Mark (S) Large AD /
Eagle 5.00
1972J 5 Deutsche Mark (S) Eagle . 5.00
1974D 5 Deutsche Mark (S) Kant / Eagle
. . . . 5.00
1980F 5 Deutsche Mark (CN clad N)
Cathedral / Eagle 7.50
1972D 10 Deutsche Mark (S) Athletes /
Eagle 7.50
1991A 10 Deutsche Mark (S) Brandenburg
Gate / Eagle 9.50

EAST GERMANY   **BU**
1948A 1 pfennig (AL) Wheat and Gear
. . . . 12.50
1978A 1 pfennig (AL) Arms 25
1952A 5 pfennig (AL) Arms 6.00
1989A 20 pfennig (B) Arms 1.50
1950A 50 pfennig (AB) Factory . 30.00
1956A 1 Mark (AL) Arms 5.00
1977A 1 Mark (AL) Arms 1.00
1969 5 Mark (dark CN) Arms / XX
JAHRE DDR 4.00

1971A 5 Mark (CN) Kepler 30.00
1979A 5 Mark (CN) Einstein . . . 70.00
1983A 20 Mark (CN) Marx 17.50
1990A 20 Mark (CN) Brandenburg Gate
/ Arms 22.50

GERMAN EAST AFRICA   **VF**
1910J 1 Heller (C) Crown / Wreath 2.00
1908J 5 Heller (C) same 25.00
1914J 5 Heller (CH) Crown / Branches
(hole) 7.00
1916T 20 Heller (B) same, no hole (World
War I emergency issue) 5.00

1892 1 Rupie (S) Kaiser in Helmet /
Arms 20.00

GERMAN NEW GUINEA   **EF**
1894 1 Pfennig (C) Inscription . . 90.00

1894 2 Mark (S) Berd of Paradise /
Wreath 460.00

SWITZERLAND

History: Until the time of Napoleon, Swiss coinage closely resembled that of Germany, with each province or "canton" as well as many cities and bishops, striking their own local coinage. Swiss coinage was temporarily unified under the Helvetian Republic, created by Napoleon. In 1850 the modern Swiss Franc was introduced, and, reflecting its famous stability, its design has not changed significantly since 1875. Its composition was changed from silver to pure nickel in 1968, however, along with the ½, 2, and 5 franc pieces. The Swiss gold 20 franc has been one of the world's most recognized bullion coins.

A special commemorative series of large silver coins has been struck since the last century for shooting festivals in various cities.

References: Meier, Albert, *HMZ Katalog*.

Counterfeit Alert: Counterfeits are known of the following gold 20 Francs: 1897B, 1900B, 1902B, 1903B, 1904B, 1911B, 1912B, 1915B, 1919B, 1922B, 1927B, 1930B, 1931B, 1933B, 1935B and possibly others.   1935LB pieces were struck 1945-47.

Hints: Swiss coins give the country name, *Helvetia* or *Confoederatio Helvetica* in Latin only.   One should be careful to watch for signs of cleaning or polishing on shooting commemoratives.
F
Basel ND Rappen (base S) Crozier Head
. . . . 12.00

Schaffhausen 1625 Groschen (S) Ram
leaping from Tower 30.00
Zug 1621 Taler (S) Angel over Arms /
Double headed Eagle 95.00

EIGHTEENTH CENTURY   **F**
Bern 1776 4 Kreuzer Bear / Cross 7.00
Freiburg 1741 2 Kreuzer (S) Shield /
Cross 9.50

St. Gall 1777 Thaler (S) Arms / Bear
. . . . *VF* 250.00
Schwyz 1782 1 Rappen (C) Oval Shield/
Value 5.00

LATER COINAGE   **VF**
Helvetian Republic 1802 ½ Batzen (base
Silver) 15.00
Bern 1818 Batzen (S) Bear CR4 below /
Cross 14.00
Geneva 1839 4 Centimes (Billon) Round
Arms 7.00
Luzern 1815 5 Batzen (S) 40.00
1887B 1 centime (C) 10.00
1967B 1 centime (C) 25
1929B 5 centimes (CN) 25

1851A ½ Franc (S) 125.00
1850A 1 Franc (S) 200.00
1967B 1 Franc (S) 1.25

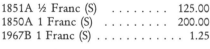

1875B 10 Centimes (Billon) . . . 550.00
1900B 20 Centimes (N) 1.00

	VF
1875 2 Franc (S)	35.00
1845 2 Franc (S)	2.50
1932B 5 Franc (S)	5.00
1922B 20 Franc (G) Bust / Arms	95.00
1865 5 Franc Schaffhausen Shooting Festival	110.00

ITALY

History: Italian coinage can during the early modern period be divided between the North, the Central region, and the South. The Central region was ruled by the Pope and is listed separately under Vatican. Southern Italy and Sicily were long unified as the Kingdom of the Two Sicilies. Its coins are particularly common and are characterized by large copper and silver coins with the royal portrait. The North, however, much like Germany, was divided into numerous petty states, each with its own coinage. Of these states only San Marino survives today. The first coins actually issued in the name of Italy were struck by Napoleon during his occupation of the country, but only for 1807-14. Later in 1860-61, the northern Kingdom of Sardinia under the House of Savoy conquered all the other states and established the country known today as Italy. At first the king, a crown, or his royal arms were featured on the coinage. Later designs became more diverse, and most coins designed under Mussolini allude to the former greatness of the Roman Empire. The change to a republic in 1946 is also seen on the coinage.

References: Hundreds of books would be necessary to properly cover the coinage of Italy. Aside from the general references suggested above, these are particularly popular in the United States and Canada: Davenport, *European Crowns 1484-1600*, *European Crowns 1600-1700*, *European Crowns 1700-1800*; Eklund, O. P., *Copper Coins of Italy*.

Counterfeit Alert: Most post 1860 gold pieces and large silver pieces have been counterfeited. Some examples include 1895 2 Lire, 1898 2 Lire, 1914 5 Lire, all in high grade. Much of the silver is for sale to unsuspecting tourists but occasionally surprisingly good. All rare date or rare type coins struck after Italian Unification should be examined with great care, regardless of size or metal.

Hints: The 20 Lire Mussolini piece is not a coin but a tourist souvenir.

SEVENTEENTH CENTURY **F**

Bologna 1663 Quattrina (C) Lion with Banner / BONONIA DOCET	18.00
Naples 1680 2 Grani (C) Bust, 80 below / Shield	20.00
Venice Soldo (very base S) Winged Lion and Doge / Christ standing	9.50

EIGHTEENTH CENTURY TO ITALIAN UNIFICATION **F**

Gorizia 1741 Soldo (C) Arms	6.00
Sardinia 1826 5 centesimi (C) Shield / Wreath	2.50
Sardinia 1830 1 Lira (S) Head / Crowned Shield	16.00
Lombardy-Venetia 1850 1 centesimo (C) Two Crowns	4.00
Lucca 1752 Scudo (S) Baroque Arms / St. Martin giving clothes to Beggar	55.00
Naples and Sicily 1788 4 Cavalli (C) Head / Grapes	6.50
Naples & Sicily 1847 2 Tornese (C) Head / Crown	2.50
Naples & Sicily 1846 120 Grana (S) Head / Arms	20.00

Tuscany 1712 Tallero (S) Bust / Crown over Castle	225.00
Tuscany 1859 5 Centesimi (C) Crowned Arms	3.50

KINGDOM OF ITALY **VF**

Napoleonic Kingdom 1811 Soldo (C) Napoleon / Crown	F 5.00
Napoleonic Kingdom 1810 20 Lire (G) Napoleon / Arms	135.00
1861M 1 Centesimo (C) Head / Wreath	1.00
1898R 2 Centesimi (C) same	1.00
1921R 5 Centesimi (C) Wheat Ear	.25
1941R 5 Centesimi (AB) Head / Eagle	.50
1926R 10 Centesimi (C) Bee	1.00
1942R 20 Centesimi (Steel) Head / Head with Fasces	.25
1920R 50 Centesimi (N) Head / Chariot of Lions	1.00
1940R 50 Centesimi (Steel) Head / Eagle right	.50
1863M 1 Lire (S) Head / Arms	4.50

1922R 1 Lire (N) Italia seated	1.00
1886R 2 Lire (S) same	10.00
1871M 5 Lire (S) same	18.00
1901R 5 Lire (S) Head / Eagle	Rare
1927R 5 Lire (S) Head / Eagle	2.00

1882R 20 Lire (G) Head / Arms	88.00
1928R 20 Lire (S) Head in Helmet / Fasces with Lion Head	140.00
1923R 100 Lire (G) Head / Fasces	BU 2,200.00

ITALIAN REPUBLIC **BU**

1954 1 Lira (AL) Balance	1.00
1948 2 Lire (AL) Farmer	8.00
1968 5 Lire (AL) Dolphin	.50
1950 10 Lire (AL) Pegasus	8.50
1956 100 Lire (Steel) Minerva with Olive Tree	40.00
1966 100 Lire (Steel) same	2.00
1974 100 Lire (Steel) same	.35
1966 500 Lire (S) Renaissance Portrait / Columbus' Ships	6.00
1992 500 Lire (S) Columbus / Columbus Landing	35.00

SAN MARINO **BU**

1869 5 Centesimi (C) Arms	VF 5.00
1936 5 Centesimi (C) Arms	5.00
1979 100 Lire (Steel) Arms / Helmet	1.00
1988 500 Lire (S) Skier	10.00
1975 2 Scudi (G) Arms	100.00

ITALIAN COLONIES

History: Italian colonial interests mostly focused on the horn of Africa. The 1918 Talero was intended to replace the popular Maria Theresa Taler (*see Austria*). Italian colonial coinage was not extensive and is not common today.

References: Gill, Dennis, *Coinage of Ethiopia, Eritrea and Italian Somalia*.

Counterfeit Alert: Most of the Talleri and 5 Lire of Eritrea encountered are counterfeit.

Hints: Copper of Italian Somalia is sometimes found pitted; prices here are for nice examples without problems or signs of cleaning.

ERITREA **VF**

1891 1 Lira (S) Crowned Bust	40.00
1891 5 Lire (S) Crowned Bust / Eagle	150.00

VF

1918 Tallero (S) Bust of Italia / Eagle
. . . . 60.00

ITALIAN SOMALIA   VF
1909 2 Pesa (C) Bust 22.00
1912 Rupia (S) Head / Crown . . 55.00
1925 5 Lire (S) Crowned Bust / Arms
. . . . 100.00

VATICAN CITY AND PAPAL STATES

History: For many centuries before the Pope ruled the Vatican City, he controlled the entire central third of Italy. This is referred to as the Papal State. In 1870 Italy conquered the small papal army and did not restore to the Pope his current small city-state until 1929.

Initially papal coins were struck at numerous mints throughout central Italy. The Pope gradually phased out these local mints of the Renaissance period by the late 1700's, excluding one last flurry of local copper during the chaos of the Napoleonic era.

The coinage of both the Papal State and the Vatican typically shows the Pope or his coat of arms on one side, and a saint or religious symbol on the other. Coins struck between Popes, called *Sede Vacante* coins, show the arms of the Papal Secretary of State on one side and a dove descending, representing the Holy Ghost on the other. Vatican and Papal coins have been struck in most popular coinage metals, and the coins of most modern Popes are fairly common.

References: Berman, Allen, G., *Papal Coins*; Coffin, Joseph, *Coins of the Popes*; Muntoni, *Le monete dei Papi e degli Stati Pontifici*.

Counterfeit Alert: Many gold pieces and numerous late Papal State large silver pieces have been counterfeited. These include Gregory XVI 50 Lire, Pius IX 20 and 100 Lire, and 1929 100 Lire, among others. Contemporary counterfeits exist of coppers of the 1790's and Pius IX.

Hints: The city in which an early papal coin was struck can often be found by mention or abbreviation on the *reverse*.

Many official and unofficial medals exist and should not be confused with coins. For the last century and a half all coins have carried a denomination. Many of the unofficial medals are low quality strikes for sale to tourists.

PAPAL STATES   F
Urban VIII 1623-44 Piastra (S) St. Michael the Archangel fighting Demons 400.00
Innocent X 1644-55 Half Grosso (S) Arms / Virgin Standing 35.00

Alexander VII 1655-67 Giulio (S) Arms / Table with Money 75.00
Clement IX 1667-69 Grosso (S) Arms / Head of St. Peter 40.00
Clement X 1670-76 ½ Baiocco (C) Arms / MEZO BAIOCCO 30.00
Innocent XI 1676-89 Quattrino (C) Arms / St. Paul stg. 22.00

Sede Vacante 1689 Piastra (S) Arms below canopy / Radiant Dove 350.00
Innocent XII 1691-1700 Testone (S) Arms / Inscription 50.00
Clement XI 1700-21 Quattrino (C) Arms / Bust of St. Peter 25.00
Clement XII 1730-40 Giulio (S) Arms / Inscription 37.50
Sede Vacante 1740 Baiocco (C) Arms / Wreath 35.00
Benedict XIV 1740-58 Half Baiocco (C) Arms / Holy Door 18.00
Pius VI 1775-99, 1796 2½ Baiocchi (C) Bust of St. Peter / Inscription . 15.00
Pius VII 1800-23, Doppia (G) Arms / Allegory of the Church seated in clouds 175.00

Gregory XVI 1831-46, 1834 Scudo (S) Presentation in the Temple . . . 75.00
Pius IX 1846-78, 1847 ½ Baiocco (C) Arms / Wreath 4.00
same, 1865 20 Baiocchi (S) Bust / Wreath
. . . . 6.50
same, 1868 10 Soldi (S) Bust 2.00
same, 1868 20 Lire (G) Bust . . . 125.00

VATICAN CITY   BU
1929 1 Lira (N) Virgin standing . . 6.00

1929 2 Lire (N) Good Sheperd . . 10.00
1951 2 Lire (AL) Fortitude 1.00
1929 5 Lire (S) St. Peter in Boat . 15.00
1939 5 Lire (S) same 9.50
1959 100 Lire (G) Arms 1,050.00
1982 100 Lire (Steel) Parents with Child
. . . . 2.00
1978 1000 Lire (S) John Paul I / Arms
. . . . 25.00

AUSTRIA

History: Austria, under its Hapsburg Emperors, was once one of the most powerful nations on earth. While the diverse provinces under Austrian rule may have had distinctive local shields, the imperial portrait and the standards they were struck on often served to unify this vast coinage. Many Austrian coins from the seventeenth and eighteenth centuries were struck with roller dies, giving them a slight natural curve.

When the Austrian Empire was dismembered after World War I a republic was established. A new unit, the Schilling of 100 groschen, was introduced in 1924. Except for a period of Nazi occupation, Austria has remained a republic and retained the Schilling to this day. Commemorative silver has been issued frequently since 1928.

Many Austrian coins have been restruck with "frozen" earlier dates for bullion purposes. These include the 1780 Maria Theresa Taler, 1915 gold 1 and 4 Ducat, and 20 and 100 Corona, 1912 10 Corona, and 1892 4 and 8 Florin.

References: Schön, G., *Deutscher Münzkatalog 18.Jahrhundert*; Craig, W.D. *Germanic Coinages*; Davenport, *European Crowns 1484-1600, European Crowns 1600-1700, European Crowns 1700-1800*.

Counterfeit Alert: Examine gold pieces with great care.

Hints: The province in which an early imperial coin was issued can often be found by its placement at the *end* of the Latin reverse legend.

Do not confuse Austrian and Russian double headed eagles. The Russian one has St. George slaying a dragon at its center.

SEVENTEENTH CENTURY   **VF**
1697 1 Kreuzer (S) Bust / 1 on Double headed eagle 22.00
1628 3 Kreuzer (S) Bust, 3 below / Double headed eagle 30.00
1670 3 Kreuzer (S) same 27.50

1693 Taler (S) Bust with large jaw / Arms on eagle 140.00

LATER COINAGE   **VF**
1816A 1 Kreuzer (C) Crowned Shield 2.00
1881 1 Kreuzer (C) Double headed eagle / Wreath 25
1860 4 Kreuzer (C) same 8.50
1767 20 Kreuzer (S) Bust in Wreath / Double headed Eagle 15.00
1912 2 Heller (C) Double headed Eagle / Branches 25
1893 1 Corona (S) Head / Crown 2.50
1909 5 Coronae (S) Head / Double headed eagle surrounded by five crowns 13.50
1924 200 Kronen (C) Jerusalem Cross 1.00

1980 2 Groschen (AL) Eagle 10
1948 5 Groschen (Z) Eagle 25
1925 ½ Schilling (S) 1.00
1965 1 Schilling (AB) Flower 25

1928 2 Schilling (S) Schubert 4.00
1964 5 Schilling (S) Stallion 85
1976 100 Schilling (S) Skier 9.00

OFFICIAL RESTRIKES   **BU**
1780SF Maria Theresa Taler 6.50
1914 1 Ducat (G) Head / Double Headed Eagle (original) 135.00
1915 1 Ducat (G) same 50.00

CENTRAL EUROPE

History: These countries all have the common heritage of the Hapsburg empire, and even though their coins have been changing rapidly these days, their origins go back to the Middle Ages. During the early modern period their silver coins were the tiny kreuzer or its multiples up to the dollar-sized taler. They had gold ducats of 1/9 ounce of gold each, and a mixed bag of local copper and base silver. Hungarian coins went in and out of production for years but finally stayed in production from the mid-1800's onward. They are most distinguishable by their frequent use of the radiant Madonna and Child and the Holy Crown of Saint Stephen with the bent cross on top. Bohemian (Czech) coins follow much the same pattern, except that their modern restoration had to wait until after World War I. Its distinguishing characteristic is a Lion with two tails. Slovakia had its own coinage during Nazi occupation, and began striking anew in the early 1990's.

References: Huszar, Lajos, *Münzkatalog Ungarn.*

Counterfeit Alert: Inspect all gold carefully, though more so Hungarian than Czechoslovak.

Hints: Many coins of the 1600's and following were struck with roller dies, giving them a naturally curved appearance. Many Hungarian coins have been officially restruck. This is the case of the gold 10 and 20 Korona 1892, 1895, 100 Korona 1907 and 1908 Proof or

Prooflike. It is also true of proofs of certain commemoratives not originally known in proof.

BOHEMIA   **F**
1686 3 Kreuzer (S) Bust, 3 below / Eagle with double-tailed lion on shield 18.00
1700 1 Kreuzer (S) similar but 1 replaces 3 below bust 17.00
1781 1 Groeschl (C) Crowned shield containing Bohemian lion 6.50
1940 50 Haleru (Z) Lion / Branches .25

HUNGARY   **F**
1751 17 Kreuzer (S) Bust / Madonna and Child over XVII 15.00
1675 15 Kreuzer (S) Bust, XV below / Madonna and Child within radiant ellipse 25.00
1697 1 Duarius (S) Arms / Madonna and Child above DUARIUS 16.00
1704 Poltura (C) Crowned Shield / Madonna and Child 12.00
1763 Poltura (C) Bust / Madonna and Child 12.00
                              VF
1885 1 Kreuzer (C) Arms / Wreath 2.50
1849 Hat (=6) Krajczar (S) Arms . 7.50
1846 20 Kreuzer (S) Head / Madonna and Child 6.00
1895 2 Filler (C) Crown / Wreath . .25
1908 20 Filler (N) same 1.00
1894 1 Korona (S) Head / Crown 2.75
1896 1 Korona (S) Crowned Bust / King on Horse 2.75
                              VF
1904 10 Korona (G) King standing / Arms 47.00
1926 1 Filler (C) Crown 25
                              F
1927 1 Pengo (S) Arms 1.00

                              VF
1938 5 Pengo (S) St. Stephen / Arms 10.00
                              BU
1945 5 Pengo (AL) Parliament Building / Arms 3.50
1954 2 Filler (AL) (hole) 10
1967 50 Filler (AL) Bridge 25
1960 1 Forint (AL) Arms 1.00
                              BU
1956 10 Forint (S) Building 14.00

BU
1961 100 Forint (G) Liszt 175.00
1992 1 Forint (AB) Crowned Arms .50

CZECHOSLOVAKIA **VF**
1923 5 Haleru (C) Lion / Bridge . . .25
1922 1 Koruna (C) Woman harvesting
Wheat 50
BU
1928 10 Korun (S) Masaryk / Arms 8.00
1963 1 Haler (AL) Arms 10
1953 10 Haleru (AL) Lion 25
1991 50 Haleru (CN) CSFR over shield
/ 50h 1.00
1961 1 Korun (AB) Arms / Woman
planting Sapling 50
1964 10 Koruny (S) Arms / Hands 3.50
1949 100 Korun (S) Stalin / Arms 6.00
1990 100 Korun (S) Shield / Two Horses
leaping 12.00

CZECH REPUBLIC **BU**
1993 10 Haler (AL) Lion 20
1993 10 Korun (C clad Steel) Lion /
Church 1.75

SLOVAKIA **VF**
1942 20 Halierov (AL) Shield / Castle
. . . . 1.00
1939 5 Korun (N) Head / Shield . 2.25
1941 20 Korun (S) Shield / Two Saints
. . . . 8.00
BU
1993 50 Haler (AL) Shield / Tower .50
1993 1 Korun (AB) Shield / Madonna and
Child 1.00

POLAND

History: During the Middle Ages and
Renaissance Poland was one of the largest
and most powerful nations in Europe.
One reason for Poland's greatness was its
long union with Lithuania. On many of
its coins the mounted knight of Lithuania
can be seen as well as the Polish eagle.
By the 1700's it was in the process of
being gobbled-up by its neighbors,
Austria, Prussia, and Russia. After the
time of Napoleon Poland was restored as
a separate country, but completely ruled
by Russia. The coins of this period show
an interesting combination of Russian and
Polish characteristics. World War I saw
the birth of a new Polish Republic. The
stern, mustached face of its indomitable
leader, Marshall Pilsudski, appears on
much silver of the 1930's. Even during
the Communist regime Poland made vast
quantities of commemoratives for export
to the West. This has continued to the
present even though for much of the

recent past inflation has forced most of
the real coins out of circulation.
References: Gumowski, Marian,
Handbuch der Polnischen Numismatik.
Counterfeit Alert: Not extensively
counterfeited.
Hints: Unlike most countries, Poland has
sold patterns (Polish, *proba*) freely.
Mintages are high and values are often
not substantially greater than for
approved designs.

KINGDOM **F**
1613 Orte for Gdansk (S) Bust / Arms
. . . . VF 70.00
1664 1 Solidus (C) Head / Eagle . . 7.00

1702 Beichlingen Taler (S) Monograms
around Cross / Arms . . . . . VF 525.00
1753 18 Groszy (S) Heavy Bust r. /
Arms 16.00
1765 1 Grosz (C) Monogram / Round
Arms 6.50
1772 8 Groschen (S) Head / Arms 20.00
1812 3 Groszy (C) Arms 4.00
1813 1/3 Talara (S) Bust / Arms 25.00
1776 Taler (S) Bust / Arms 70.00

UNDER RUSSIAN CZARS **F**
1835 10 Groszy (base S) Eagle . . . 4.00
1818 1 Zloty (S) Head / Arms . . . 9.00
1836 10 Zlotych - 1½ Rubles (S) Eagle
. . . . 32.50

TWENTIETH CENTURY **VF**
1923 1 Grosz (C) Eagle 25
1932 2 Zlote (S) Veiled Bust / Eagle
. . . . 2.00
1933 10 Zlotych (S) Traugutt / Eagle
. . . . 30.00
1936 10 Zlotych (S) Pilsudski / Eagle
. . . . 10.00

BU
1925 20 Zlotych (G) Crowned Bust /
Eagle 150.00
1949 1 Grosz (AL) Eagle 50
1976 10 Groszy (AL) Eagle 10
1967 10 Zlotych (CN) Eagle / Marie
Curie 2.00
1969 10 Zlotych (CN) Eagle / Wheat
(Communist anniversary) 2.00

1971 10 Zlotych (CN) Fish / Arms 2.00
1987 10,000 Zlotych (S) Half figure of
Pope / Eagle 25.00
1988 50,000 Zlotych (S) Pilsudski / Eagle
. . . . 25.00
1992 1 New Grosz (AB) Crowned
Eagle. 25
1992 5 New Zlotych (Bimetallic)
Crowned Eagle 6.00

BALTIC STATES

History: After being dominated by
Russia and Sweden for hundreds of years,
the peoples of Estonia, Latvia, and
Lithuania finally achieved independence
with the collapse of Czarist Russia during
World War I. After little more than two
decades of sovereignty, Stalin's Soviet
Union, with Nazi collusion, annexed and
conquered them. Ultimately, however,
these three countries led the way in the
disintegration of the Soviet Union. The
coins of both generations of Baltic
republics look surprisingly similar,
showing an almost studied attempt to use
their coins to proclaim the continuity of
their states. A perfect example of the
desire for continuity, though not of
traditional design, is a Latvian 1993
commemorative. It honors not the second
anniversary of independence, but the
75th, identifying the new republic with
the old.
References: See general references.
Counterfeit Alert: Not extensively
counterfeited.
Hints: Inspect all silver pieces for signs of
cleaning.

ESTONIA **VF**
1922 1 Mark (CN) Three Lions . . 2.50
1926 5 Marka (CN) same 135.00
1929 1 Sent (C) same 1.25
1933 1 Kroon (S) Arms / Lyre . . 18.00

		VF
1934 1 Kroon (AB) Arms/ Ship		6.50
1930 2 Krooni (S) Castle		8.00
1991 5 Senti (B) Three Lions		.35
1992 1 Kroon (CN) Arms		1.00
1993 5 Krooni (B) Deer		2.75

LATVIA

		VF
1922 1 Santims (C) Arms		1.00
1922 2 Santimi (C) Arms		1.50
1922 5 Santimi (C) Arms		1.25
1922 10 Santimu (N) Arms		1.25
1922 20 Santimu (N) Arms		1.25
1922 50 Santimi (N) Girl at Rudder of		
Ship		3.00
1924 1 Lats (S) Arms / Wreath		2.50
1925 2 Lati (S) same		3.25
1929 5 Lati (S) Head / Arms		12.50
		BU
1992 1 Santims (C) Arms		.35
1992 2 Lati (CN) Arms / Cow		6.50

1973 10 Latu (S) Arms / Ornamental design . . . . *PF* 50.00

LITHUANIA

		VF
1706 3 Groschen (S) Bust / Knight riding		
left		50.00
1925 1 Centas (AB) Knight		4.50
1936 5 Centai (AB) same		5.00
1925 20 Centu (AB) same		4.00
1925 50 Centu (AB) same		10.00
1925 1 Litas (S) Knight / Branch		4.00
1925 2 Litu (S) Knight / Wreath		8.50
1925 5 Litai (S) same		9.00
1936 5 Litai (S) Knight / Bust		8.00
1936 10 Litu (S) Crowned Bust / Knight		
		13.50
		BU
1991 1 Centas (AL) Knight		.35
1991 20 Centu (AB) Knight		.85
1991 5 Litas (CN) Knight / Rays		2.75
<u>1992</u> 10 Litas (CN) Pope / Knight		45.00
<u>1993</u> 10 Litas (CN) Lyres		*PF* 15.00

RUSSIA

History: Modern Russian coinage was created by Peter the Great (1689-1725) in an attempt to Westernize Russia. It has been called the first decimal coinage, based on a silver dollar sized Ruble worth 100 copper Kopeks. Over the years the Ruble tended to shrink somewhat, but was still recognizable as a "silver dollar" well after the Russian Revolution. The copper coinage also became lighter with the years, but was also occasionally made heavier along the way. While czarist Russian coins often depict the czar's portrait or monogram or St. George, the most famous and common design is the Czarist eagle with two heads.

The Communist government used the Soviet coinage as an effective medium to promote the revolution. The famous "Worker Ruble" shows an industrial worker leading a farmer to the dawn of communism. Most coins show the hammer and sickle upon a globe. Around are ribbons, one for each of the constituent Soviet Republics.

Commemoratives were re-introduced in the 1960's and have continued unabated since the fall of Communism.

References: Spassky, I.G. *The Russian Monetary System.*

Counterfeit Alert: Contemporary counterfeits exist of late Czarist 15 and 20 kopeks, and much gold. Most types of Czarist gold have also been counterfeited in the last few decades. The gold 37½ Ruble has recently been restruck in off metal with the mintmark P to distinguish it from the original. Be alert for restrikes with the P removed and plated with gold.

Hints: Do not confuse the Czarist two-headed eagle with the Austrian one. The Czarist one has a horseman at its center.

PETER THE GREAT 1689-1725   **F**
1713 Kopek (C) Peter, with spear, riding horse 30.00
1723 Ruble (S) Bust / Monogram Cross 150.00
ELIZABETH 1741-61
1759 5 Kopek (C) Monogram in wreath / Eagle 35.00

1759 Ruble (S) Bust / Eagle	125.00
1758 Ruble (G) Bust / Monogram	
	110.00

CATHERINE II THE GREAT 1762-96
1770 5 Kopek (C) Monogram in Wreath	
/ Eagle	18.00
1783 15 Kopek (S) Bust / Eagle	25.00
1786 Ruble (S) Bust / Eagle	85.00
PAUL I 1796-1801
1799 1 Kopek (C) Crowned П	7.50
1798 ¼ Ruble (S) Cross of П's / Tablet	
	38.00
ALEXANDER I 1801-25
1818 2 Kopeks (C) Eagle / Wreath	2.25
1801 5 Kopeks (C) Eagle / Circle with	
five dots	25.00
1823 20 Kopeks (S) Eagle	3.00
NICHOLAS I 1825-55
| 1842 1 Kopek (C) Monogram | 2.50 |
| 1836 10 Kopeks (C) Eagle | 15.00 |

1832 Ruble (S) Eagle	20.00
ALEXANDER II 1855-81   **VF**
1859 ½ Kopek (C) Monogram	3.50
1878 Ruble (S) Eagle / Wreath	25.00
1872 5 Rubles (G) Eagle	135.00
ALEXANDER III 1881-94
1888 5 Kopeks (S) Eagle	1.50
1894 50 Kopeks (S) Head / Eagle	30.00
1890 5 Rubles (G) Head / Eagle	125.00
NICHOLAS II 1894-1917
1893 1 Kopek (C) Eagle	.75
1900 10 Kopeks (S) Eagle	1.00
1896 25 Kopeks (S) Head / Eagle	15.00
1897 Ruble (S) same	18.00
1913 Ruble (S) Two Heads / Eagle	25.00
1901 10 Rubles (G) same	115.00

COMMUNIST REGIME   **EF**
1925 ½ Kopek (C) CCCP	7.00
1933 1 Kopek (AB) Arms	.75
1924 2 Kopeks (C) Arms	7.00
1828 2 Kopeks (AB) Arms	.50
1988 3 Kopeks (AB) Arms	.15
1931 10 Kopeks (CN) Arms / Worker	
	1.00
1976 20 Kopeks (CNZ) Arms	.25
1921 50 Kopeks (S) Hammer and Sickle /	
Star	9.00

EF

1924 Ruble (S) Worker and Peasant /
  Arms 25.00
1970 Ruble (CNZ) Lenin 2.00
1979 5 Rubles (S) Olympics 5.00
1989 5 Rubles (CN) Cathedral . . . 4.00
1991 5 Rubles (CN) Tower & Dome .75

RUSSIAN REPUBLIC   **BU**
1992 1 Ruble (B clad S) Two headed
  eagle 50
1992 1 Ruble (CN) Onion Domes /
  Angel (Democracy) 2.00
1992 10 Rubles (CN around AB) Cobra
  . . . . 3.00

SIBERIA   **F**
1771 Kopek (C) Monogram / Two sables
  holding value 33.00
1769 10 Kopeks (C) same 75.00

CAUCASUS

History: Following the collapse of the Soviet Union all three Caucasian republics declared their independence. Georgia immediately became enbroiled in a civil war and Armenia and Azerbaijan have been subject to tensions over a territorial dispute. Few commemoratives have been issued and most minor coins have been eroded by inflation soon after release.
References: General.
Counterfeit Alert: Not commonly counterfeited.
Hints: The coins of Armenia and Azerbaijan can be readily distinguished by their respective emblems.

ARMENIA   **BU**
1994 1 Tram (AL) Arms 75

1994 10 Tram (AL) Arms 2.25

AZERBAIJAN   **BU**
1993 5 Qepik (AL) Ornate frame . . .50
1992 20 Qepik (AL) Star and crescent.50

1993 50 Qepik (Al) Tower 1.00

GEORGIA   **BU**

1993 20 Tetri, Emblem / Deer . . 1.00
1993 50 Tetri (Brass) Emblem / griffin
  . . . . 1.50

BALKAN STATES

History: The modern Balkan states, Greece, Bulgaria, Romania, Albania, and the former Yugoslavia, gained independence throughout the 1800's with the slow collapse of the Ottoman Empire, Greece leading the way in 1821. The first Greek coins emphasized the revival of Greek independence after centuries of occupation by depicting the mythological Phoenix rising from its ashes. Later Greece joined the other new Balkan states with very conservative coins depicting royal portraits, shields of arms and marks of value. Artistic innovation flourished, however, in the 1920's and 1930's with lively designs, often of classical inspiration. Those countries able to continue coinage through and immediately following World War II were forced to use emergency metals such as iron and zinc. These included the Nazi puppet states of Croatia and Serbia. In all but Greece, Communist emblems replaced old heraldic emblems after the war, often accompanied by allegories of Socialist industry and agriculture. With the fall of the dictatorship in Greece and the Communists elsewhere, these countries employed new, often bold references to their respective heritages, often harking back to national heroes of earlier eras. Former Yugoslav republics such as Slovenia, Macedonia, and Croatia have preferred to depict local flora and fauna.
References: See general references.

Counterfeit Alert: Most Albanian gold and large silver has been counterfeited.
Hints: Zinc issues with original mint luster are scarce and command a premium. Early Greek copper is fairly scarce in high grade with no damage. Many early communist issues of Romania are scarce despite their relatively low values. In their native languages Albania is Shqipni, Greece is ΕΛΛΑΣ, Bulgaria is БЪЛГАРИЯ, Croatia is Hrvatska, and Yugoslavia is ЈУГОСЛАВИЈА.

ALBANIA   **VF**
1930 1 Lek (N) Head / Horseman
  . . . . 4.00
1935 1 Frang Ar (S) Head / Arms 9.00

1927V 20 Franga Ari (G) Skanderbeg /
  Winged Lion . . . . *BU* 250.00
1937 20 Franga Ari (G) same *BU* 375.00
1939 0.20 Lek (Steel) Victor Emmanuel in
  helmet / Eagle 2.00
1957 2 Lek (Z) Eagle . . . . *EF* 1.00
          BU
1964 5 Qindarka (AL) Eagle 1.00
1988 5 Leke (CN) Train / Train . 8.00

BOSNIA-HERZEGOVINA   **PF**
1993 500 Dinars (CN) Arms over Mostar
  Bridge / Brontosaurus 7.00

BULGARIA   **VF**
1881 5 Stotinki (C) Arms 4.00
1913 20 Stotinki (CN) Arms 50
1917 20 Stotinki (Z) Arms 1.00
1882 2 Leva (S) Arms 8.50
1894 5 Leva (S) Head 17.00
1930 5 Leva (CN) Horseman 1.00
          BU
1962 1 Stotinka (B) Arms 25
1981 1 Lev (CN) Bulgarian and Soviet
  Flags over clasped hands 3.50

BU
1963 5 Leva (S) Sts. Cyril and Methodus
. . . . *PF only* 16.00
1992 10 Stotinki (AB) Lion 50
1992 10 Leva (CN) Horseman . . . 3.50

CROATIA   BU
1941 2 Kune (Z) U above Arms *EF* 8.00
1993 2 Lipe (AL) Plant 75

1995 2 Kune (CN) Tuna fish 1.50
1993 5 Kuna (CN) Bear 3.50

GREECE   F
1831 10 Lepta (C) Phoenix / Wreath
. . . . 40.00

1850 10 Lepta (C) Arms / Wreath 25.00
1833 1 Drachma (S) Head / Arms 28.00
1882 5 Lepta (C) Head / Wreath . 1.00
1875 5 Drachmai (S) Head / Arms 22.00
                                          VF
1894 10 Lepta (CN) Crown 1.75
1912 20 Lepta (N) Athena standing (hole)
. . . . 1.00
1910 1 Drachma (S) Bust / Figure on
hippocamp 7.00
1926 2 Drachma (CN) Athena . . . 1.00
                                          BU
1954 20 Lepta (AL) Olive branch (hole)
. . . . 1.00
1954 2 Drachmai (CN) Head / Arms
. . . . 2.75
1963 30 Drachmai (S) Five Kings / Map
of Greece 6.00

1976 20 Drachmai (CN) Pericles in
Helmet / Temple 75
1982 2 Drachmes (B) Head 50

MACEDONIA   BU
1993 1 Denar (AB) Dog 1.00

1993 5 Dinari (AB) Lynx 1.75

MOLDOVA   BU
1993 1 Ban (AL) Arms 50
1992 1 Leu (CN) Arms 1.00

MONTENEGRO   VF
1906 1 Para (C) Arms 15.00
1906 10 Para (N) Arms 4.50
1908 20 Para (N) Arms 6.00
1912 1 Perper (S) Head / Arms . 15.00
1909 5 Perpera (S) same 125.00

ROMANIA   VF
1900 1 Ban (C) Head / Arms 2.00
1905 5 Bani (CN) Crown over scroll
(hole) 50
1921 50 Bani (A) Eagle (hole) 1.00
1924 1 Leu (CN) Arms 1.00
1875 2 Lei (S) Arms 15.00
1942 5 Lei (Z) Crown 75
1881 5 Lei (S) Carol I / Arms . . 30.00

1922 20 Lei (G) Ferdinand I / Arms
. . . . *Unc.*275.00
1944 20 Lei (G) Three Kings / Eagle's
Head . . . . *Unc.* 100.00
1944 100 Bani (N clad Steel) Head /
Wreath 1.00
1947 5 Lei (AL) Head / Wheat . . 2.50
1950 1 Leu (CNZ) Oil Drill 2.00

1956 50 Bani (CN) Arms / Worker 2.00
                                          BU
1975 5 Bani (AL) Arms 25
1966 3 Lei (N clad Steel) Factory . 2.50
1992 1 Leu (C clad Steel) Bank
Monogram 1.00
1993 1 Leu (C clad Steel) Arms . . .75
1991 100 Lei (N clad Steel) Renaissance
Bust 7.00

SERBIA   VF
1917 10 Para (CN) Eagle (struck in Rhode
Island) 2.00

1917 20 Para (CN) same 2.25
1879 50 Para (S) Head / Wreath . 12.00
1897 1 Dinar (S) Head / Wreath . 10.00
1882 10 Dinara (G) same 125.00
1942 2 Dinara (Z) Eagle 2.00

SLOVENIA
1993 20 Stotinov (AL) Owl 35
1992 5 Tolarjev (AB) Ibex Head . . 1.00
1993 5 Tolarjev (AB) Bee Hive . . . 2.00

1994 5 Tolarjev (AB) Quill Pen . . 2.00

YUGOSLAVIA   VF
1920 25 Para (CN) Arms 2.00
1925 1 Dinar (CN) Head / Wreath 1.00
1938 1 Dinar (AB) Crown 50
1945 2 Dinara (Z) Arms 1.00
1932 20 Dinara (S) Head / Eagle 25.00
                                          BU
1963 1 Dinar (AL) Arms 25
1955 20 Dinara (AB) Arms / Bust of
Worker with Gear 1.00
1977 200 Dinara (S) Tito / Arms 11.00
1992 2 Dinara (B) Bank Monogram .75

1994 150 New Dinara (G) Dove / Arms
and Building . . . . *Proof* 200.00

ASIAN AND AFRICAN COINS

ISLAMIC COINS

History: Traditionally Islamic coins have been dominated by one overriding consideration: the prohibition of graven images. Islamic coins very rarely have portraits or even animals. The most common designs on Islamic coins are ornate inscriptions, geometrical patterns, and an occasional plant. Also the signature of the Sultan (or now the state itself) formed in a predetermined pattern will also form a central design feature. This is called a tougra and typically looks like this:

In recent decades many Islamic countries have been more lax in observing the restriction on images, to the point where *most* Islamic countries have issued such coins.

Since the Sixteenth century the Ottoman Empire, the ancestor of modern Turkey, ruled most of the Middle East, calling allegiance, if not obedience, from Tunis to Chinese Turkistan (Singkiang). Many of the farther parts of the empire were practically independent by the 1800's. Its final dissolution came after World War I. This is when many modern series of Islamic coins developed. Also some countries, such as Iran and Morocco have a more or less continuous tradition of locally controlled coinage.

References: Mitchiner, M., *World of Islam*; Broome, M., *A Handbook of Islamic Coins*; Plant, Richard, *Arabic Coins and How to Read Them*.

Counterfeit Alert: Many apparently Ottoman coins, having the appearance of gold but barbarous legends, are actually jewelry pieces. Very often they are brass with a gold plating.

Hints: Ottoman coins don't carry regular dates but say when the Sultan ascended the throne and what year of the reign the coin was struck.

Many Ottoman coins are struck on too thin or crudely cast blanks. Throughout the Islamic world coins have served as

traditional jewelry. Many specimens found today will have mount marks from this practice. This is so common that specialized collectors will sometimes accept these pieces, despite their diminished worth.

Numbers and dating: Numbers in Arabic are similar to Western numbers which evolved from them:

١	٢	٣	٤	٥	٦	٧	٨	٩	٠
١	٢	٣	٤	٥	٦	٧	٨	٩	٠

Arabic Numerals

Because the Islamic calendar begins in the year 622 A.D., not the year 1 A.D., the dates on Islamic coins will look deceptively old. The Islamic year in most countries is also 3% shorter. For example, the Islamic year (A.H.) 1300 is the A.D. year 1882, and 1995 A.D. is 1416 A.H. The listings here give the dates actually appearing on the coins.

OTTOMAN EMPIRE   F
Murad II 1421-51 A.D.
834 Akche (S) Inscriptions 7.00

Mohammed II 1451-81 A.D.
855 Akche (S) Inscriptions 5.00
Bayzit II 1481-1512 A.D.
886 Akche (S) Inscriptions 5.00
Suleyman I 1520-66 A.D.
926 Altin (G) Inscriptions 175.00
926 Akche (S) Inscriptions 6.00
Selim II 1566-74 A.D.
974 Para of 4 Akches (S) Inscriptions
. . . . 24.00
Murad III 1574-95 A.D.
982 Akche (S) Inscriptions 6.00
Mohammad III 1595-1603 A.D.
1003 Akche (S) Inscriptions 6.50
Ahmed I 1603-17 A.D.
1012 Akche (S) Inscriptions 5.00
Osman II 1618-22 A.D.
1027 Onluk (S) Inscriptions 30.00
Mustafa I 1617-18, 1622-23 A.D.
1031 Onluk (S) Inscriptions 30.00

Murad IV 1623-40 A.D.
1033 Akche (S) Inscriptions 6.00
Ibrahim 1640-48 A.D.
1049 Akche (S) Inscriptions 6.00
Mohammed IV 1648-87
1058 Altin (G) Inscriptions . . . 175.00
Suleyman II 1687-91 A.D.
1099 Para (C) Toughra / Inscription
. . . . 7.00

Ahmed II 1691-95 A.D.
1102 Yirmilik (S) Inscriptions . . 175.00
Mustafa II 1695-1703 A.D.
1106 Para (S) Inscriptions 10.00
Ahmed III 1703-30
1115 Akche (S) Toughra / Inscriptions
. . . . 10.00
Mahmud I 1730-54
1143 Para (S) same 8.00
Osman III 1754-57
1168 Para (S) same 25.00
Mustafa III 1757-74
[11]80 Para (S) same 5.00
Abdul Hamid I 1774-89
1187 Para (S) same 2.75
Selim III 1789-1807
1203 Para (S) same 2.50
Mustafa IV 1807-08
1222 Para (S) same 25.00
Mahmud II 1808-39
1223 year 23, 100 Para (base S) Toughra in Wreath / Inscription in wreath (15 gm.) 5.00

1223 year 5, 10 Para (S) Toughra in border / Inscription 4.00
Abdul Mejid 1839-61 A.D.   **VF**
1255 year 21, 20 Para (C) Toughra / 20 within inscription 3.00

Abdul Aziz 1861-76 A.D.   **VF**
1277 year 3, Piastre (S) Toughra within
    stars / Inscription within stars . . 6.50
1277 year 8, 20 Piastres (S) same . 18.00
Murad V 1876 A.D.
1293 year 1, Piastre (S) same . . 185.00
Abdul Hamid II 1876-1909 A.D.
1293 year 9, Piastre (S) same 2.00
Mohammed V 1909-1918 A.D.
1327 year 3, 20 Para (N) Toughra in
    beaded border / 20 in border . . 1.00
Mohammed VI 1918-23 A.D.
1336 year 4, 40 Para (CN) same . . 3.00

Turkish Republic   **Unc**
1927 250 Piastres (G) Wreath / Star and
    Crescent 450.00
1948 2½ Kurus (B) (hole) 2.25
1940 10 Kurus (CN) Star and Crescent
    . . . . 10.00
1948 50 Kurus (S) Star and Crescent /
    Wreath 5.00
1985 1 Lira (AL) Head of Mustafa Kemal
   25
1960 2½ Lira (Steel) Mustafa Kemal riding
    horse 3.00
1988 10,000 Lira (S) Bear holding Torch /
    Wreath . . . . *PF only* 30.00

MOROCCO   **F**
1229 Falus (C) Star 5.00

1289 3 Falus (C) Star in border . . 3.00
    VF
1317 1 Dirham (S) Inscriptions . . . 5.00
1340 5 Mazunas (C) Rounded Hexagram
    / star 1.75
    BU
1951 1 Franc (AL) Star 25
1371 10 Francs (AB) Star 1.00
1953 100 Francs (S) Star in Star . . 4.00
1956 500 Francs (S) Bust / Star . 15.00
1974 5 Santimat (B) Arms 25
1978 1 Dirham (CN) Head / Arms . .50

1965 5 Dirhams (S) same 10.00

ALGERIA   **VF**
1124 Sultani (G) Inscriptions . . 250.00
1188 3 Mazunas (S) Inscriptions . 65.00
1240 Budju (S) Inscription / Inscr. in
    ornate circle 30.00

1255 5 Aspers (C) Inscriptions . . 22.50
    BU
1964 1 Centime (AL) Arms 10
1964 10 Centimes (AB) Arms 25
1972 20 Centimes (AB) Cornucopia .50
1987 20 Centimes (AB) Ram's Head .25
1972 1 Dinar (CN) Tractor 1.50
1972 5 Dinars (S) Oil Rig and Wheat
    . . . . 13.00
same but (N) 10.00

TUNISIA   **F**
1112 3 Burben (C) Inscriptions . . 30.00
1186 Piastre (base S) same 55.00
1275 2 Kharub (C) Inscription within
    wreath 10.00
    VF
1289 2 Kharub (C) same 5.00
1914 5 Centimes (C) Arabic / French
    Inscriptions 1.50
1919 5 Centimes (CN) same (hole) . .50
1945 1 Franc (AB) BON POUR 50
1891 1 Franc (S) Arabic between branches
    / French in border 10.00
1916 1 Franc (S) same 2.50
1358 5 Francs (S) same 3.00
1353 10 Francs (S) same 5.00
1904 20 Francs (G) same 92.50
1950 20 Francs (CN) Toughra in Crescent
    / 20 in Crescent 25

    BU
1943 100 Francs (G) Date and Inscriptions
in Borders 700.00
1957 5 Francs (CN) Tougra in Crescent /
5 in crescent 2.00
1960 1 Millim (AL) Tree 25
1983 50 Millim (B) Inscription . . . 1.00
1970 1 Dinar (S) Head / Man climbing
    tree 7.50

LIBYA   **F**
1188 Para (C) Inscription in square /
    Inscription in triangle 18.00
1203 Piastre (S) Toughra / Inscription
    . . . . 150.00
1223 Para (C) Inscriptions 10.00

1223 Para (C) Inscription / Five Stars
    . . . . 20.00
1223 40 Para (base S) Toughra with
    crescent r. / Inscription 90.00
    BU
1952 1 Millieme (C) Bust of King /
    Crown and Wreath 25
1952 2 Piastres (CN) same 1.00
1965 100 Milliemes (CN) Arms . . 3.00
1979 50 Dirhams (CN) Horseman 4.00
1981 70 Dinars (G) Hands 375.00

SUDAN   **F**
1311 10 Piastres (base S) Toughra in
    border / Inscription in border . 90.00

1312 20 Piastres (base S) Toughra above
    branches / Inscription above branches
    . . . . 10.00
    BU
1956 1 Millim (C) Camel Rider 25
1975 5 Millim (B) Bird 25
1987 5 Ghirsh (AB) Building 75
1970 10 Ghirsh (CN) Camel Rider 1.50
1976 5 Pounds (S) Arms /
    Hippopotamus 27.50
1978 5 Pounds (S) Arms / Map of Africa
    . . . . *PF* 18.00

EGYPT   **F**
1003 Falus (C) Inscription / Grill Pattern
    . . . . 5.00
1115 Altin (G) Toughra / Inscription
    . . . . 95.00
1223 5 Para (C) Toughra / Inscription,
    both within wavy border 15.00
1223 Qirsh (S) Toughra / Inscription
    . . . . 28.00

F
1255 year 3, 5 Para (C) Toughra / Inscription 4.00
1255 year 15, 5 Para (C) same but 5 at center of reverse 5.00
VF
1277 year 9, 10 Para (C) Toughra / Inscription 8.00
1277 year 10, 1 Qirsh (S) same . . . 9.00
1293 year 27, 5/10 Qirsh (CN) Toughra in border / 5 within inscription . 1.00
1293 year 29, 5 Qirsh (S) Toughra over quivers 9.00

1293 20 Qirsh (S) Toughra / Inscription 22.00
1327 year 6, 1/10 Qirsh (CN) Toughra in border 1.00
1327 year 6, Qirsh (CN) Toughra in border / Inscr. in stars 3.00
1917 10 Mils (CN) Inscriptions (hole) 1.50
1917 10 Piastres (S) Inscriptions in wreaths 8.00
1920 10 Piastres (S) Inscriptions 36.00
1929 5 Milliemes (CN) Bust in fez   1.50
1933 20 Piastres (S) Military Bust in fez 20.00
1943 10 Milliemes (C) Bust in fez (scalloped edges) 50
1944 2 Piastres (S) same (six sided)   1.50
BU
1955 1 Millieme (AB) Bust of Sphinx 2.00
1956 20 Piastres (S) same 16.00

1955 5 Pounds (G) Ancient Egyptian in Chariot 1,200.00
1967 10 Piastres (CN) Falcon 1.00
1968 Pound (S) Dam 6.50

1984 1 Piastre (AB) Toughra / Pyramids 25
1984 10 Piastres (CN) Mosque 75
1980 Pound (S) Sadat 8.00
1987 5 Pounds (S) Subway 15.00
1983 100 Pounds (G) Nefertiti . 750.00

JORDAN   **BU**
1949 1 Fils (C) Crown 1.75
1955 10 Fils (C) Crown 1.50
1985 10 Fils (C) King Hussein 25
1978 50 Fils (CN) same 1.00
1965 100 Fils (CN) Crown 2.00
1970 ¼ Dinar (CN) King / Tree . 3.00
1969 10 Dinars (G) King / Pope   475.00

LEBANON   **VF**
1925 1 Piastre (CN) Two Lion Heads (hole) 1.50
ND 2½ Piastres (AL) Inscription . 3.00
1924 5 Piastres (AB) Tree 2.50
1940 5 Piastres (AB) Tree / Phoenician Ship 1.50
1929 25 Piastres (S) Tree / Cornucopiae 7.50
BU
1955 1 Piastre (AB) (hole) 25
1972 25 Piastres (AB) Tree 25
1952 50 Piastres (S) Tree 3.00
1978 5 Livres (N) Tree / Fruit . . . 3.75
1980 10 Livres (S) Lake Placid Olympics . . . . *PF only* 27.50

1980 1 Livre (CN) similar   *PF only* 9.00

SYRIA   **VF**
1338 Dinar (G) Arms . . . . *Rare*
ND 2½ Piastres (AL) 12.50
1935 5 Piastres (AB) Crossed grain ears 1.00
1929 25 Piastres (S) Ornamental design 5.50

BU
1971 5 Piastres (AB) Wheat ear 25
1972 25 Piastres (N) Torch 50
1950 1 Lira (S) Falcon 16.00
1950 1 Pound (G) same 135.00

SAUDI ARABIA   **VF**
1348 ¼ Ghirsh (CN) Inscriptions   7.00
1344 ½ Ghirsh (CN) same 10.00
1346 1 Ghirsh (CN) same 8.50
1376 2 Ghirsh (CN) Tree & Swords . . . . *EF* .50

1356 ½ Ghrish (CN) same 5.00
same, reeded edge 75
EF
1378 4 Ghirsh (CN) same 1.00
1374 ¼ Riyal (S) Inscriptions 2.50
1370 Riyal (S) same 5.00
BU
1400 5 Halala (CN) Tree and swords 1.00
1397 50 Halala (CN) same 3.00
1408 100 Halala (CN) same 2.50

AL-FUJAIRAH   **PF**
1969 2 Riyals (S) Richard Nixon . 25.00
1970 2 Riyals (S) same 25.00
1969 25 Riyals (G) same 120.00
1970 25 Riyals (G) same 120.00

SHARJAH   **BU**
1964 5 Rupees (S) John F. Kennedy / Flags 10.00

RAS AL-KHAIMA   **BU**
1970 10 Riyals (S) President Eisenhower 15.00

UNITED ARAB EMIRATES
1975 1 Fils (C) Trees 15
1973 5 Fils (C) Fish 25
1984 10 Fils (C) Dhow 50
1973 50 Fils (CN) Three Oil Derricks 1.00

	BU
1988 100 Fils (CN) Brass Teapot .	1.50
1981 5 Dirhams (CN) Falcon	5.00
1980 750 Dirhams (G) Boy on Horse	
. . . . *PF only*	250.00

YEMEN   VF
1367 1/80 Riyal (AL) Tree 25
1370 1/40 Riyal (C) Inscriptions in crescent 2.00
1383 1/40 Riyal (C) Hand with Torch 1.00
1371 1/8 Riyal (S) Five-sided 4.00
1358 ¼ Riyal (S) Inscriptions . . . 13.50
1373 1 Riyal (S) Inscription with swords below 15.00

	BU
1377 1 Riyal (G) similar	950.00
1963 1 Buqsha (AB) Leaves	.35
1963 20 Buqsha (S) Leaves	5.00
1963 Riyal (S) Leaves	7.00
1974 50 Fils (CN) Arms	1.00

IRAQ   VF
1931 1 Fils (C) Faisal I 2.50
1933 2 Fils (C) Faisal I 4.00
1938 4 Fils (C) Ghazi I 75
1938 10 Fils (CN) Ghazi I 1.50
1931 20 Fils (S) Faisal I 5.00
1953 50 Fils (S) Faisal II 90.00
1953 100 Fils (S) Faisal II 7.00
1932 Riyal (S) Faisal I 16.00
BU
1967 10 Fils (CN) Palm Trees 25
1980 250 Fils (CN) Saddam Hussein 5.00

1971 1 Dinar (S) soldiers 15.00
1971 500 Fils (N) same 8.00

IRAN   F
ND [1700's-1800's] Fals (C) Sun rising over back of Lion, Teheran mint 8.00

similar, Mazandaran mint 10.00
VF
1134 'Abbasi (S) Inscriptions . . . 18.00
1154 10 Shahi (S) Inscription with broad open border 25.00
1273 1 Kran (S) Inscriptions 10.00
1295 50 Dinars (C) Sun Face . . 13.50
1307 100 Dinars (CN) Lion 2.00
1305 2 Krans (S) Lion 6.00
1306 5 Krans (S) Bust facing / Lion 9.00
BU
1322 1 Rial (S) Lion 3.50
1350 1 Rial (CN) Shah / Lion 75
1338 2 Rials (CN) Lion 2.00

1351 20 Rials (CN) Shah / Lion . . 2.00
1357 20 Rials (CN) Shah / Lion over FAO 4.00
1351 Pahlavi (G) Shah / Lion . 110.00
1359 50 Rials (AB) Map of Iran . . 7.00

AFGHANISTAN

	VF
1257 Falus (C) Leaves between Swords	
. . . . *F*	8.00
1214 Rupee (S) Inscription	15.00
1305 Rupee (S) Inscription	13.00
1299 2½ Rupees (S) Toughra / Arms	
. . . .	15.00
1306 2½ Afghani (S) same	22.00
	BU
1316 2 Pul (C)	.75
1961 1 Afghani (N clad Steel)	.50
1357 1 Afghani (CN) Arms	3.00
1352 5 Afghani (CN clad Steel) . .	8.00

PAKISTAN   BU
1974 1 Paisa (AL) Monument with Star and Crescent 10

1948 ¼ Rupee (N) Toughra / Crescent right	.50
1950 ¼ Rupee (N) same, but Crescent left	15.00
1964 50 Paisa (N) Toughra, star and crescent	.50
1976 50 Paisa (CN) Jinnah	.50
1976 150 Rupees (S) Crocodile . .	28.00

CENTRAL ASIA
History: Most of Central Asia has been under Russian influence since the days of the Tsars. Since the fall of the Soviet Union many of these newly indepentdent states have struck either circulating or commemorative coinage. Some have maintained close economic links to Russia as well.
References: General.
Counterfeit Alert: None Known.
Hints: Much of the 1925 and 1937 Mongolian coins encountered have been cleaned, and should be discounted. The silver is more common than the base metal. Tuva coins are found with minor kicks or stains and as such are discounted slightly.

KAZAKHSTAN   BU
1992 1 Tien (Brass) Ornament 50

1993 20 Tenga (CN) Turbaned Bust 3.50

KYRGYZSTAN   PF
1995 10 Som (S) Horseman over mountain 45.00
1995 100 Som (G) Horseman . . 190.00

MONGOLIA   VF
1925 1 Mongo (C) Emblem 10.00
1925 50 Mongo (S) Emblem 10.00
1970 1 Mongo (AL) Horseman 50
1970 50 Mongo (CN) Horseman . 1.00

TUVA *or* TANNU TUVA   VF
1934 1 Kopejek (AB) Inscription 45.00
1934 20 Kopejek (CN) same . . . 55.00

TURKMENISTAN   BU
1993 1 Tennesi (C) President Niyazov 50
1993 20 Tennesi (CN) same 75

UZBEKISTAN　　　　　　　　　BU
1994 1 Tiyin (B clad Steel) Bird 50
1994 50 Tiyin (N clad Steel) Bird . 1.00

ISRAEL

History: After a gap of nearly two thousand years, Israeli coinage began again in 1948. The themes chosen for Israel often depict ancient Jewish coins or engraving. Some coins depict artifacts of the diaspora, or commemorate milestones in Israel's history. Artistic styles vary everywhere from conservative to bizarre.
References: Haffner, Sylvia, *The History of Modern Israel's Money.*
Counterfeit Alert: Not extensively counterfeited.
Hints: Israeli commemoratives are sometimes fully subscribed by those interested in them at the time of issue, leaving reduced demand in the secondary market.

Many Israeli official holders of the 1960's corrode the coins. If possible store the coins separately.

REGULAR ISSUES　　　　　　　BU
1949 25 Mils (AL) Grapes 35.00
1949 1 Prutah (AL) Anchor 1.00
1949 5 Prutot (C) Lyre 1.50
1949 10 Prutot (C) Amphora 2.50
1957 10 Prutot (AL) Amphora . . . 1.50

1949 25 Prutot (CN) Grapes 1.50
1954 50 Prutot (CN) Leaves 1.75
1949 100 Prutot (CN) Palm Tree . 2.00
1949 250 Prutot (CN) Grain 4.00
1949 500 Prutot (S) Three Pomegranates
. . . . 25.00
1965 1 Agora (AL) Grain 25

1963 5 Agorat (AB) Pomegranates . .35
1972 10 Agorat (AB) Palm Tree 25
1979 25 Agorat (AB) Lyre 25
1966 ½ Lira (CN) Menora 25
1980 1 Lira (CN) Pomegranates . . .50
1980 1 New Agorat (AL) Tree 10
1981 ½ Sheqel (CN) Lion 25
1981 1 Sheqel (CN) Chalice 50
1982 5 Sheqalim (AB) Cornucopia 1.00
1984 10 Sheqalim (CN) Ancient Ship .85
1988 1 Agora (AB) Ancient Ship . . .10

1992 10 Agorat (AB) Ancient Coin with
Menora 25
1985 ½ New Sheqel (AB) Lyre 50
1988 1 New Sheqel (CN) Maimonides
. . . . 1.50

COMMEMORATIVES　　　　　　BU
1961 1 Lira (CN) War Elephant . . 7.00
1963 5 Lirot (S) Ocean Liner Smoke-stack
/ Ancient Ship 225.00

1972 5 Lirot (S) Russian Lamp . . . 5.50
1968 10 Lirot (S) Scene of Jerusalem /
Temple 10.00
1976 25 Lirot (S) Five Pomegranate
Branches 7.00
1978 25 Lirot (CN) French Lamp . 4.00
1978 50 Lirot (S) Tree 8.00

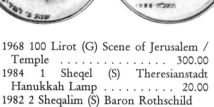

1968 100 Lirot (G) Scene of Jerusalem /
Temple 300.00
1984 1 Sheqel (S) Theresianstadt
Hanukkah Lamp 20.00
1982 2 Sheqalim (S) Baron Rothschild
. . . . 18.00
1989 1 New Sheqel (S) Jaffa 32.00
1995 1 New Sheqel (S) Fox 25.00
1994 10 New Sheqalim (G) Abraham
sacrificing Isaac . . . . *PF only* 400.00

AFRICA

History: The independent coinage of sub-Saharan Africa got a late start. Only three sovereign countries had their own coinage during the colonial period: Ethiopia, Liberia, and the Dutch South African Republic.

Of these by far the most ancient was that of Ethiopia. Ethiopia has a very ancient history and claims (as well does

Armenia) to be the oldest Christian nation on Earth. It certainly is the first country to use the cross as the primary design of a coin. (See Ancient and Medieval section.) The modern coinage of Ethiopia began under Emperor Menelik shortly after he captured the city of Harar from the Moslems. By 1894 majestic portrait of this descendent of King Solomon appeared on the large dollar sized Bir, as did the Lion of Judah, symbol of the Ethiopian Emperors. Even the recent communist government has retained some form of this symbol.

Liberia was founded by freed American slaves. Its first coins were struck by the American Colonization Society which promoted the endeavor. The next decade saw the first appearance of the republic's own coinage. It has traditionally symbolized the principles of freedom that led to Liberia's creation, and many of the coins bear a ship bringing settlers and the motto "The love of liberty brought us here." Ironically, the allegory of Liberia was depicted with European features until 1960, when a new silver coinage was introduced with African features.

The coinage of the Boers of South Africa lasted for barely a decade before it was ended by their defeat and colonization by the British in 1902. Interestingly, British economic influence was already so strong that the Boer coins were all struck to British standards.

Almost all other independent African coinages have their beginnings in the late 1950's, with the independence of some nations being delayed as late as the 1980's. While many of the first coins portrayed leaders and coats of arms, the depiction of wildlife was and has remained popular.
References: Gill, Dennis, *Coinage of Ethiopia, Eritrea and Italian Somalia*; and general references.
Counterfeit Alert: Because the South African Krugerrand has been one of the world's most popular bullion coins, it has been the target of counterfeiters. Some are tungsten with a gold plating. These will "spin" on a desk top but will repeatedly drop to the surface. Other hints on detecting counterfeits can be found in the section on United States coins. Examine every Krugerrand carefully. Weigh it and ring it.
Hints: African coins are particularly popular with collectors. The reasons for this is their beauty, their lack of excessive promotion, and their usually reasonable prices.

ANGOLA　　　　　　　　　　BU
1979 50 Lwei (CN) Arms 65

BU
(1978) 2 Kwanzas (CN) Arms . . . 1.00

BURUNDI   **BU**
1965 1 Franc (B) Arms 2.00

1970 1 Franc (AL) Rising Sun . . . 6.00
1980 1 Franc (AL) Arms 75
1965 50 Francs (G) Bust / Arms   200.00

CAPE VERDE   **BU**
1977 20 Centavos (AL) 75
1994 10 Escudos (N clad Steel) . . . 1.50

CHAD   **EF**
1975 100 Francs (N) Three Gazelles 15.00
1985 500 Francs (CN) Head / Flowers
. . . . 40.00

CENTRAL AFRICAN STATES   **BU**
(currency union of Chad, Central African
Republic, Congo, Gabon and Cameroon)
1978 1 Franc (AL) Three Gazelle Heads
. . . . 1.50
1985 10 Francs (AB) same 1.00
1976 500 Francs (CN) Woman holding
flower 15.00

ETHIOPIA   **VF**
1892 1 Mahaleki (S) Crown . . . 150.00
1897 1/32 Birr (C) Crowned Bust of
Menelik II / Lion of Judah 6.50
1903 1 Gersh (S) same 3.00
1894 1/8 Birr (S) same 25.00

1897 1 Birr (S) same 30.00
1931 25 Matonas (N) Crowned Bust of
Haile Selassie / Lion of Judah . . 2.00
BU
1944 1 Cent (C) Bust of Haile Selassie /
Lion of Judah (struck 1944-75) 25

1966 $50 (G) Haile Selassie / Lion of
Judah . . . . Proof 300.00
1972 $5 (S) Capped Bust of Haile Selassie
/ Lion of Judah . . . . Proof 8.50
1977 1 Cent (AL) Lion Head / Team of
Oxen 50
1982 2 Birr (CN) Lion Head / Soccer
Players and Globes 4.00

GABON   **EF**
1982 100 Francs (N) Three Gazelles 4.00
1985 500 Francs (CN) Head / Flowers
. . . . 6.00

GAMBIA   **BU**
1974 1 Butut (C) Bust / Peanuts 25
1971 1 Dalasi (CN) Bust / Alligator
. . . . 3.00
1987 20 Dalasi (S) Bust / Monkey
. . . . PF only 35.00

GHANA   **BU**
1958 1 Penny (C) Kwame Nkrumah /
Star 25
1958 5 Shillings (S) same . . . PF 10.00
1967 ½ Pesewa (C) Drums / Star . . .25
1984 50 Cedis (CN) Drums / Fishing
from boat 5.00

GUINEA   **VF**
1959 5 Francs (AB) Sekou Toure / Trees
. . . . 3.50
1962 5 Francs (CN) Sekou Toure /
Branches 1.00
BU
1971 50 Cauris (AL) Cowrie shell 10.00
1971 5 Sylis (AL) Bearded Bust . . 10.00
1985 1 Franc (B clad Steel) Arms . . .75

KENYA   **BU**
1975 5 Cents (B) Jomo Kenyatta / Arms
. 25
1970 10 Cents (B) same 25
1969 25 Cents (CN) same 5.00
1966 2 Shillings (CN) same 4.50

1994 5 Shillings (CN) President Moi /
Arms 3.50

1994 10 Shillings (B around CN) Bimetallic 6.00

LIBERIA   **VF**
1833 1 Cent (C) Man with tree . 18.00
1847 1 Cent (C) Head in star cap / Tree
. . . . 12.00
1961 5 Cents (CN) Elephant / Palm tree
and ship . . . . BU .25
1906 10 Cents (S) Head with European
features 9.00

1896 50 Cents (S) same 16.00
BU
1962 1 Dollar (S) Head with African
features 10.00

1966 1 Dollar (CN) same 2.00
1973 5 Dollars (S) Elephant and Map /
Arms . . . . PF 10.00

MALI   **BU**
1961 5 Francs (AL) Hippopotamus 1.00
1975 50 Francs (B) Plant 1.75

MOZAMBIQUE   **BU**
1975 1 Centimo (AL) Head / Plant Rare
1980 2.5 Meticais (AL) Arms / Ship 1.50
1988 1,000 Meticais (CN) Pope / Arms
. . . . 6.50

NAMIBIA   **BU**
1993 $5 (AB) Bird swooping down
toward prey 5.00
1993 5c (CN) Tree 50

NIGERIA   **BU**
1974 1 Kobo (C) Oil Derrick 1.00
1973 25 Kobo (CN) Peanuts 3.50

BU
1991 25 Kobo (C plated Steel) Peanuts
. . . . 1.00

RWANDA

BU
1970 ½ Franc (AL) 1.25
1977 1 Franc (AL) Plant / Arms . . .50
1990 100 Francs (S) Nelson Mandela /
Arms 30.00
1989 1000 Francs (S) Bust / Bank 45.00

SIERRA LEONE   **BU**
1964 ½ Cent (C) Margai / Fish 25
1964 10 Cents (CN) Margai / Cocoa
beans 50

1972 50 Cents (CN) Stevens / Arms 2.00
1983 10 Leones (S) Stevens / Boy Scouts
. . . . 25.00

SOUTH AFRICA   **VF**
1898 1 Penny (C) Paul Kruger / Arms
. . . . 1.75
1897 1 Shilling (S) Paul Kruger / Wreath
. . . . 3.75
BU
1961 ½ Cent (B) Jan Van Riebeeck / Two
Birds 75
1989 1 Cent (C) Arms / Birds 25
1982 2 Cents (C) Vorster / Wildebeest
. 50
1961 20 Cents (S) Jan Van Riebeeck /
Arms 2.50
1977 1 Rand (N) Arms / Springbok 1.50
1994 1 Rand (S) Mandela Presidential
Inauguration . . . . *Proof* 18.00

1975 Krugerrand (G) Paul Kruger /
Springbok (net 1 oz. Gold, gross 33.93
gm.) . . . . spot + 6%

UGANDA   **BU**
1966 5 Cents (C) Tusks 25
1972 5 Shillings (CN) Seven-sided 120.00
1987 5 Shillings (Steel) Seven-sided 1.00

1994 1,000 Shillings (CN) Soccer Player /
Arms . . . . *Proof* 27.00
*Note: The above is marked .999 because the
master die used was also used for a 2,000
Shilling silver version.*

SWAZILAND   **BU**
1974 1 Cent (C) King Sobhuza /
Pineapple 25
1992 1 Lilangeni (B clad Steel) King
Makhosetive / Queen Mother . . . 3.00

TANZANIA   **BU**
1966 5 Senti (C) Julius Nyerere /
Swordfish 25
1992 20 Shilingi (N clad Steel) Nyerere /
Mother and Baby Elephant 3.00

WEST AFRICAN STATES   **BU**
*(currency union of Benin, Burkina Faso,
Ivory Coast, Mali, Niger, Senegal, and
Togo)*
(1976 1 Franc (Steel) Root 25
1990 10 Francs (B) People at Water
Pump 1.00

1985 100 Francs (N) Root 1.00

ZAIRE
1977 5 Makuta (CN) Bust half left 2.50

1975 20 Makuta (CN) Gorillas . . 32.50

ZAMBIA   **BU**
1966 1 Penny (C) (hole) 1.00
1965 5 Shillings (CN) Kenneth Kaunda /
Arms 3.50
1969 1 Ngwee (C) Aardvark 25
1988 20 Ngwee (CN) Reedbuck . . 1.75

ZIMBABWE   **BU**
1988 1 Cent (C) Ancient Stone Bird
Carving / Value 25
1980 20 Cents (CN) Ancient Stone Bird
Carving / Bridge 1.00
1980 50 Cents (CN) same / Sunrise 1.75

INDIAN SUBCONTINENT

History: Modern Indian coins have been influenced by events: the disintegration of the great Moghul Empire, which ruled all but the southern tip of India, and the period of British rule. The basic monetary system based on the silver Rupee was used by the Moghul emperors, but the physical shape of the coins was modified by the British into the ancestor of today's flat rupee.

Indian coins before the colonial coins were hand struck on thick blanks. This has caused them to acquire the nick name "dumps." Special broad versions of the same coins were made, often for presentation purposes; these are called *nazarana*.

After independence most minor Indian coins depict the Asoka Pillar, an ancient sculpture featuring four lions, one facing each direction.

Perhaps among the most exotic in appearance to Western eyes are the coins of Tibet, Nepal and Bhutan, full of religious symbolism and majesty. Conversely, the issues of Bangladesh are quite modern in their appearance. The coins of Tibet are now obsolete due the invasion and conquest of that country by Communist China.

References: Bruce, Colin R., et al., *The Standard Guide to South Asian Coins and Paper Money.*

Counterfeit Alert: Some tiny gold fanams may have been struck at a later date than popularly thought.

Hints: Small test punches are found on many dump style rupees. This reduced the value, but on low to medium grade coins not substantially.

BANGLADESH   BU

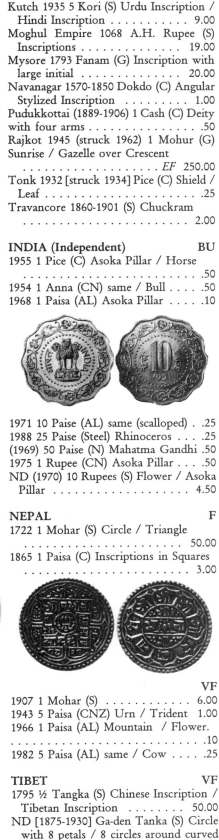

1973 10 Poisha (AL) Flower / Leaf
(scalloped edge) 25
    BU
1979 10 Poisha (AL) Tractor / Flower
(scalloped edge) 25
1975 1 Taka (CN) Family / Flower 1.00

BHUTAN   VF
ND (1790-1820) Deb Rupee (S) Stylized
Inscription 15.00
ND (1835-1927) Deb Rupee (C) same
. . . . 2.75
1928-55 1 Rupee (N) Bust of King /
Symbols in squares 1.50
    BU
ND (1951-55) 1 Pice (C) Symbols in
Square compartments 2.00
1975 5 Chetrums (AL) Bust of King /
Wheel .25

1979 10 Chetrums (C) Shell / Symbols
. 75

INDIA (Pre-Independence)   VF
Assam 1789-99 Rupee (S) Inscriptions
(Octagonal) 18.00

Bikanir 1937 Rupee (S) Facing Bust /
Monogram 15.00
Deccan 854 A.H. Falus (C) Inscriptions
. . . . 7.00
Hydrabad 1340 A.H. Rupee (S) Gateway
with towers 7.50
Hydrabad 1354 A.H. 4 Annas (S) similar
. . . . 2.50
Indore 1886 ¼ Anna Bull 2.00
Jaipur 1913 Nazarana Rupee (S)
Inscription in Border / same with
branch 45.00

Kutch 1935 5 Kori (S) Urdu Inscription /
Hindi Inscription 9.00
Moghul Empire 1068 A.H. Rupee (S)
Inscriptions 19.00
Mysore 1793 Fanam (G) Inscription with
large initial 20.00
Navanagar 1570-1850 Dokdo (C) Angular
Stylized Inscription 1.00
Pudukkottai (1889-1906) 1 Cash (C) Deity
with four arms 50
Rajkot 1945 (struck 1962) 1 Mohur (G)
Sunrise / Gazelle over Crescent
. . . . EF 250.00
Tonk 1932 [struck 1934] Pice (C) Shield /
Leaf 25
Travancore 1860-1901 (S) Chuckram
. . . . 2.00

INDIA (Independent)   BU
1955 1 Pice (C) Asoka Pillar / Horse
. 50
1954 1 Anna (CN) same / Bull 50
1968 1 Paisa (AL) Asoka Pillar 10

1971 10 Paise (AL) same (scalloped) . .25
1988 25 Paise (Steel) Rhinoceros 25
(1969) 50 Paise (N) Mahatma Gandhi .50
1975 1 Rupee (CN) Asoka Pillar 50
ND (1970) 10 Rupees (S) Flower / Asoka
Pillar 4.50

NEPAL   F
1722 1 Mohar (S) Circle / Triangle
. . . . 50.00
1865 1 Paisa (C) Inscriptions in Squares
. . . . 3.00

    VF
1907 1 Mohar (S) 6.00
1943 5 Paisa (CNZ) Urn / Trident 1.00
1966 1 Paisa (AL) Mountain / Flower.
. 10
1982 5 Paisa (AL) same / Cow 25

TIBET   VF
1795 ½ Tangka (S) Chinese Inscription /
Tibetan Inscription 50.00
ND [1875-1930] Ga-den Tanka (S) Circle
with 8 petals / 8 circles around curved
octagon 3.50

1920 5 Skar (C) Lion 3.00
1953 5 Sho (C) Lion before Mountains
. . . . 4.00

1909 1 Srang (S) Lion 325.00
1951 10 Srang (base S) same 5.00
1919 20 Srang (G) Lion 425.00

SOUTHEAST ASIA

History: Southeast Asia has been a crossroads for thousands of years, subject to influences from China, India, Islam, and the West. Its coins are as diverse as these influences, from the modernistic, business-like coins of Singapore to the sometimes mystical coins of Thailand. Most of these countries lost their independence during the nineteenth century, then regained it in the 1950's and 1960's, sometimes producing long gaps filled by European-style colonial coinages.

One very distinct type of coin was struck in Thailand in the 1800's. It is called "bullet money" and was made by punching dies into a short bar of metal bent on itself.

References: Le May, Reginald, *The Coinage of Siam*; Toda, Ed., *Annam and its Minor Currency.*

Counterfeit Alert: Some contemporary counterfeits were made of Siamese coins in the 1800's. A few circulation counterfeits have been made of copper-nickel coins in recent years.

Counterfeits of the cast coins of Annam (early Vietnam) are abundant. Many patinas are false and simply painted. Thousands of souvenir folders with such coins, intermingled with authentic pieces, were produced for sale to G.I.'s during the Vietnam war.

Hints: Cast Annamese coins can *sometimes* be distinguished from Chinese and others by the frequent denomination on the reverse (see illustration). They *never* have Manscript like the Chinese.

ANNAM (early Vietnam)   F
(All have square hole in middle)
1342-69 1 Van (C) Yü-tsung Wang
. . . . 6.00
1655-61 1 Van (C) Vinh-tho 5.00

F

1740-87 1 Van (B) Canh Hung . . . 3.50
1788-92 1 Van (B) Quang Trung
. . . . 2.50
1792-1800 1 Van (B) Canh Thinh
. . . . 2.50
1802-20 1 Van (B) Gia Long 2.00
1820-41 1 Van (B) Minh Mang   1.50
1841-47 1 Van (B) Thieu Tri 1.50
1848-83 6 Van (B) Tu Duc 2.50
1883-84 1 Van (B) Kien Phuc . . . 75.00
1884-85 1 Van (B) Ham Nghi . . 110.00
Note: The vast majority of specimens of the above two are counterfeit.
1885-88 1 Van (B) Dong Khanh   8.00
1888-1907 10 Van (B) Than Thoi
. . . . 1.00

1907-1916 10 Van (B) Duy Tan . . 1.00
1916-25 1 Van (B) Khai Dinh 4.00
1926-45 10 Van (C) Bao Dai 5.00

BURMA   **F**
1865 ½ Anna (C) Peacock 7.00
1852 1 Rupee (S) Peacock 8.00

BU
1949 1 Pe (CN) Lion 3.00
1952 1 Pya (C) Lion 25
1965 25 Pyas (CN) Lion (hexagonal) .75
1976 50 Pyas (B) Rice 1.00

CAMBODIA   **VF**
1800's 1 Pe (base S) Bird (no reverse)
. . . . 7.50

1860 5 Centimes (C) Head / Arms
. . . . 13.00
BU
1860 1 Piastre (S) similar 2,000.00

1959 10 Centimes (AL) Bird 75
1970 1 Riel (CN) Angkor Wat . . 12.50
1979 5 Sen (AL) Arms 4.00

INDONESIA

BU
1970 1 Rupiah (AL) Bird 25
1971 10 Rupiah (CN) 25
(1952) 25 Rupiah (G) Turbaned Bust /
Eagle 200.00
1992 25 Rupiah (AL) Eagle / Nutmeg
. 50
1973 100 Rupia (CN) Building . . . 1.00
1974 2000 Rupiah (S) Tiger 15.00

LAOS   **BU**
1952 20 Cents (AL) Elephants . . . 1.00
1980 50 Att (AL) Arms 1.00
1991 50 Kip (S) Arms / Soccer Ball
. . . . 32.50

MALAYSIA   **VF**
Trengganu 1222 A.H. Pitis (Tin)
Inscriptions (hole) 38.00

Kelantan 1321 A.H. Pitis (Tin)
Inscriptions (hole) 20.00
similar but smaller 5.00
BU
1967 1 Sen (C) Building 10
1989 20 Sen (CN) Boxed Lunch 25
1969 1 Ringgit (CN) Bust 2.50
1990 1 Ringgit (AB) Dagger and
Scabbard 1.50

SINGAPORE   **BU**
1967 1 Cent (C) Building 20
1980 20 Cents (CN) Swordfish 25
1985 1 Dollar (CN) Lion 1.00

1978 10 Dollars (S) Satallite Antenna
. . . . 10.00

THAILAND (Siam)   **VF**
1824-51 ¼ Baht "Bullet Money" (S) 10.00

1851-68 1 Baht "Bullet Money" (S) 30.00
1862 1/8 Fuang (Tin) Three Crowns /
Elephant in ornate border . . . 12.50
1890 2 Att (C) Bust of King / Siam
seated 3.00

1941 1 Satang (C) (hole) 50
1926 5 Satang (N) (hole) 50
1908 1 Baht (S) Bust of King l. /
Elephants 3,750.00
1913 1 Baht (S) Bust of King r. /
Elephants 9.00
BU
1942 (1967-73) 1 Satang (Tin) blank circle
in center 50
1946 10 Satang (Tin) Child Bust / Garuda
Bird 2.00
1987 25 Satang (AB) Bust of King /
Building 15
1979 5 Baht (CN clad C) Bust of King /
Garuda Bird 1.00
1977 10 Baht (N) Bust of Princess /
Crown 2.00

BU
1971 50 Baht (S) Bust of King / Wheel
. . . . 13.50

VIETNAM (North)   **VF**
1946 5 Hao (AL) Stove 10.00
1946 1 Dong (AL) Head / Branch 75.00
1958 5 Xu (AL) (hole) 1.00

VIETNAM (South)   **BU**
1953 20 Su (AL) Three Women . . 1.00
1971 1 Dong (AL) Rice 35

BU
1974 10 Dong (AB clad Steel) Farm Workers 75
1968 20 Dong (N clad Steel) Standing Figure 1.75
1975 50 Dong (N clad Steel) Rice Farmers 500.00

VIETNAM   **BU**
1976 1 Hao (AL) Arms 3.50
1976 1 Dong (AL) Arms 12.00
1986 100 Dong (S) Buffalo 40.00

PACIFIC

History: A great many coins authorized by Pacific islands have been marketed recently to the American public. Very few of these commemoratives have ever been heard of in their home countries. While they are duly authorized money of those nations at the time of striking, their legal tender and redemption status is sometimes extremely limited. The most notorious culprit in recent years is the Marshall Islands.
References: See general references.
Counterfeit Alert: Very few counterfeits known.
Hints: Some of the commemoratives being extensively marketed to the lay public can be purchased later on the after market for less than issue price.

PHILIPPINES   **BU**
1899 2 Centavos (C) Sun over Mountains
. . . . *Rare*

1947S 50 Centavos (S) MacArthur / Arms 4.00
1947S Peso (S) same 12.00

1967 Peso (S) Broken Sword / Arms
. . . . 8.00
1967 1 Sentimo (AL) Lapulapu 10
1979 25 Sentimos (CN) Luna 25
1990 50 Sentimos (CN) M. H. de Pilar / Eagle 30

1970 1 Piso (N) Ferdinand Marcos / Pope Paul VI 2.00
1972 1 Piso (CN) Rizal / Arms 75
                                BU
1977 1 Piso (CN) Rizal 65
1985 1 Piso (CN) Rizal / Bull 50
1975 5 Piso (N) Marcos / Arms . . 1.75
1982 25 Piso (S) Marcos and Reagan / Arms 40.00
1986 25 Piso (S) Pres. Aquino / Pres. Reagan 200.00
1982 1500 Piso (G) Bataan & Corregidor
. . . . 275.00

MARSHALL IS.   **BU**
1988 5 Dollars (CN) Space Shuttle Discovery 5.00
1988 25 Dollars (S) Greg Louganis
. . . . 40.00
1989 50 Dollars (S) First Landing on Moon 35.00

NIUE   **BU**
1987 5 Dollars (CN) Boris Becker . 5.00
1987 5 Dollars (CN) Steffi Graff . 6.00
1988 100 Dollars (S) Franz Beckenbauer
. . . . 115.00

TONGA   **BU**
1967 1 Seniti (C) Head / Turtle 75
1975 2 Seniti (C) Watermelon 15

1968 1 Pa'anga (CN) Head / Arms
. . . . 3.00

1983 1 Pa'anga (CN) Head / Nativity (7-sided) 3.00
1980 2 Pa'anga (CN) Facing Bust / Whale 7.00

WESTERN SAMOA   **BU**
1967 1 Sene (C) Head 25
1974 50 Sene (CN) Banana Tree   1.50
1974 1 Tala (CN) Boxers 4.00
1981 1 Tala (CN) F.D. Roosevelt in Wheelchair 4.00
1981 10 Tala (S) same 19.00

CHINA

History: Unlike Western coinage which has traditionally been manufactured by striking a metal blank with engraved dies, Oriental coinage has, until the past century, been made by casting in molds. The familiar cast "cash" coin of copper or brass featuring a square hole by which it could be strung has its origin over 2,000 years ago. Most of these pieces bear no images whatever, but simply two or four Chinese characters on the obverse, and anywhere from none to several on the reverse.

Chinese coinage, however, even pre-dates these early cast pieces. During the first millennium B.C. an evolution occurred during which the use of the cowrie shell as money gradually passed through stages of development. At first the backs of the shells were removed and filled with clay or earth. Natural cowries were replaced with artificial ones carved out of bone or jade. Then over time these cowrie replacements were themselves replaced with copper versions of the same thing. Other forms of pre-round money existed too. As implements had both a use and a metal content, they became acceptable in trade. Eventually miniature imitations of these tools came to replace the real ones in commerce. These included knives and hoes. The very early examples are often thin and fragile. The very last use of this type of money, 2,000 years ago, was quite sturdy.

Simple round coins were certainly popular before 500 B.C. Frequently they carried marks of value (half ounce, etc.) After several hundred years of coins that carried these "immobilized" inscriptions, inscriptions that did not change from reign to reign, new ones indicating who issued the coins became popular. Most of these are "reign titles," the official name of the emperor, which he could change at will. On occasion mint marks or years would appear on the reverse, but this was the exception until the 1600's when the Manchu dynasty placed Manchu characters indicating the mint on the coins.

With heavy European influence these cast coins were phased out in favor of struck pieces during the late 1800's. Most imperial struck coins have a dragon on one side, and are written in both Chinese and English. The dragon was removed with the overthrow of the Emperor in 1911. Politicians and flags and buildings have dominated the coinage of the Republic under the Nationalists. The Communist Peoples Republic has often preferred to use emblems and allegories rather than specific portraits.

References: Schjoth, F., *Chinese Currency*; Kann, E., *Illustrated Catalog of Chinese Coins*.

Counterfeit Alert: The Chinese have counterfeited their own coins for centuries, partially because formal coin collecting has a longer history in China. Many of the larger diameter cast cash and early implement money are later counterfeits, often detectible by their false, painted on patina. Also the Chinese silver dollars of the late nineteenth and early twentieth centuries have been counterfeited, often being light in weight or too grayish in color.

Hints: Do not be intimidated by Chinese characters. Because most coins have very few, it is easy to match them against illustrations or text. The Chinese series lends itself to collecting as generally or as precisely as the collector prefers.

Iron cast cash will usually be available only in poor grade, until recently certainly so. If you *must* have EF or better, this is not the series to collect.

Avg.

First Millennium B.C. Carved Stone
   Cowrie 100.00
First Millennium B.C. Carved Jade
   Cowrie 150.00

First Millennium B.C. Copper Cowrie
   . . . . 100.00

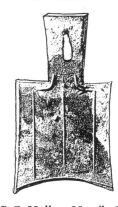

770-375 B.C. Hollow Handle Spade (C)
   . . . . 400.00
after 770 B.C. Ch'i Knife (C) . 250.00

500-250 B.C. Pu Spade Money (C)
   . . . . 30.00

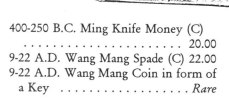

400-250 B.C. Ming Knife Money (C)
   . . . . 20.00
9-22 A.D. Wang Mang Spade (C) 22.00
9-22 A.D. Wang Mang Coin in form of
   a Key . . . . *Rare*

ROUND CAST COINS   F
250-221 B.C. Ming Tao (C) . . . 95.00

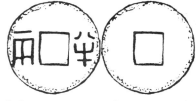

2nd Century B.C. Pan-liang (C) . 4.00

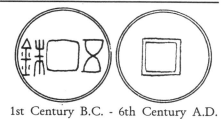

1st Century B.C. - 6th Century A.D.
   Wu-shu (C) 3.50
after 14 A.D. Huo Ch'üan [S-149ff]
   . . . . 4.50
529 A.D. Wu-shu of Eternal Tran-
   quility [239] 18.00
553 A.D. Wu-shu of Constant Equity
   [242] 20.00

600's - 700's A.D. K'ai-yüan 3.00

T'ang Dynasty 618-907
756-62 Ch'ien Yüan chung pao 乹元
重寶 4.00
same but Large Coin 15.00

Five Dynasties Period 907-60
917-42 Ch'ien Heng Chung pao 乹
亨重寶 (Lead) 15.00

960-61 T'ang Kuo t'ung pao
唐國通寶 7.50

Northern Sung Dynasty 960-1127
968-75 Sung Yüan t'ung pao
宋元通寶 2.50
976-84 T'ai P'ing t'ung pao
太平通寶 2.50
990-994 Shun Hua yüan pao
淳化元寶 2.50
995-98 Chih Tao yüan pao
至道元寶 2.50
998-1004 Hsien P'ing yüan pao
咸平元寶 2.50
1004-07 Ching Te yüan pao
景德元寶 2.50
1008-16 Hsiang Fu yüan pao
祥符元寶 2.50
1017-21 T'ien Hsi t'ung pao
天禧通寶 2.50

F

1023-31 T'ien Sheng yüan pao
天 聖 元 寶 2.50
1032-33 Ming Tao yüan pao
明 道 元 寶 5.00
1034-37 Ching Yu yüan pao
景 祐 元 寶 2.50
1038-39 Huang Sung t'ung pao
皇 宋 通 寶 2.50
1040 K'ang Ting yüan pao
康 定 元 寶 4.00
1041-48 Ch'ing Li chung pao
慶 曆 重 寶 20.00
1049-53 Huang yu yüan pao
皇 祐 元 寶 3.00
1054-55 Chih Ho yüan pao
至 和 元 寶 2.50
1056-63 Chia Yu yüan pao
嘉 祐 元 寶 5.00
1064-67 Chih P'ing yüan pao
治 平 元 寶 2.50
1068-77 Hsi Ning yüan pao
熙 寧 元 寶 2.50
1078-85 Yüan Feng t'ung pao
元 豐 通 寶 2.50
1086-93 Yüan Yu t'ung pao
元 祐 通 寶 2.50
1094-97 Shao Sheng yüan pao
紹 聖 元 寶 2.50
1098-1100 Yüan Fu t'ung pao
元 符 通 寶 2.50
1101 Sheng Sung yüan pao
聖 宋 元 寶 2.50
1102-06 Ch'ung Ning t'ung pao
崇 寧 通 寶 8.00

1107-10 Ta Kuan t'ung pao 大 觀
通 寶 Large . . . . VF 30.00
1111-17 Cheng Ho t'ung pao
政 和 通 寶 2.50
1118 Chung Ho t'ung pao
重 和 通 寶 6.00
1119-25 Hsüan Ho t'ung pao
宣 和 通 寶 6.00
1126 Ching K'ang t'ung pao
靖 康 通 寶 6.00

Southern Sung Dynasty 1127-1280
1127-30 Chien Yen t'ung pao
建 炎 通 寶 35.00
1131-62 Shao Hsing yüan pao
紹 興 元 寶 10.00
1163-64 Lung Hsing yüan pao
隆 興 元 寶 50.00
1165-73 Ch'ien Tao yüan pao
乾 道 元 寶 30.00
1174-89 Shun Hsi yüan pao
淳 熙 元 寶 2.75
1190-94 Shao Hsi yüan pao
紹 熙 元 寶 2.75
1195-1200 Ch'ing Yüan t'ung pao 慶 元
通 寶 (Large, Iron) 30.00
same, (C) regular size 2.75
1201-04 Chia T'ai t'ung pao
嘉 泰 通 寶 10.00
1205-07 K'ai Hsi t'ung pao
開 禧 通 寶 10.00
1208-24 Chia Ting t'ung pao
嘉 定 通 寶 4.00
1225-27 Ta Sung yüan pao
大 宋 元 寶 6.00
1228-33 Shao Ting t'ung pao
紹 定 通 寶 3.50
1234-36 Tuan P'ing yüan pao
端 平 元 寶 25.00

1237-40 Chia Hsi t'ung pao
嘉 熙 通 寶 13.00
1241-52 Shun Yu yüan pao
淳 祐 元 寶 2.75
1253-58 Huang Sung yüan pao
皇 宋 元 寶 5.00

F

1259 K'ai Ch'ing t'ung pao
開 慶 通 寶 20.00
1260-64 Ching Ting yüan pao
景 定 元 寶 4.00
1265-74 Hsien Shun yüan pao
咸 淳 元 寶 10.00

Ki-tan Tartar (Liao) Dynasty 907-1125
922-924 T'ien Tsan t'ung pao
天 贊 通 寶 . . . . Scarce
1032-54 Ch'ung Hsi t'ung pao
重 熙 通 寶 . . . . Scarce
1055-65 Ch'ing Ning t'ung pao
清 寧 通 寶 85.00
1066-73 Hsien Yung t'ung pao
咸 雍 通 寶 90.00

1074-82 Ta K'ang yüan [or t'ung] pao
大 康 元 寶 85.00

1083-91 Ta An yüan pao
大 安 元 寶 85.00
1092-1100 Shou Ch'ang yüan pao
壽 昌 元 寶 90.00
1101-09 Ch'ien T'ung yüan pao
乾 統 元 寶 85.00
1110-20 T'ien Ch'ing yüan pao
天 慶 元 寶 85.00

Western Hsia Dynasty 982-1227
1149-68 T'ien Sheng yüan pao
天 盛 元 寶 20.00
1169-93 Ch'ien Yu yüan pao
乾 祐 元 寶 . . . . Scarce
1210-12 Huang Chien yüan pao
皇 建 元 寶 95.00
1212-22 Kuang Ting yüan pao
光 定 元 寶 75.00

Nü-chen Tartars 1115-1260
1156-61 Cheng Lung yüan pao
正 隆 元 寶 5.00
1161-89 Ta Ting t'ung pao
大 定 通 寶 5.00
1201-08 T'ai Ho chung pao
泰 和 重 寶 50.00

Mongol (Yüan) Dynasty 1280-1368
1297-1307 Ta Te t'ung pao
大 德 通 寶 . . . . Scarce
1308-11 Chih Ta t'ung pao
至 大 通 寶 6.00

1308-11 Large Coin with Mongol
Script, Ta Yüan t'ung pao
. . . . 38.00
1312-13 Huang Ch'ing t'ung pao
皇 慶 通 寶   Scarce

F

1341-67 Chih Cheng t'ung pao

至 正 通 寶 . . . . *Scarce*

Ming Dynasty 1368-1644

1368-98 Hung Wu t'ung pao

洪 武 通 寶 3.00

1399-1402 Chien Wen t'ung pao

建 文 通 寶 . . . . *Scarce*

1403-24 Yung Lo t'ung pao

永 樂 通 寶 3.00

1425 Hung Hsi t'ung pao

洪 熙 通 寶 . . . . *Scarce*

1426-35 Hsüan Te t'ung pao

宣 德 通 寶 9.00

1436-49 Cheng T'ung t'ung pao

正 統 通 寶 . . . . *Scarce*

1450-56 Ching T'ai tung pao

景 泰 通 寶 . . . . *Scarce*

1457-64 T'ien Shun t'ung pao

天 順 通 寶 . . . . *Scarce*

1465-87 Ch'eng Hua t'ung pao

成 化 通 寶 . . . . *Scarce*

1488-1505 Hung Chih t'ung pao

弘 治 通 寶 4.00

1506-21 Cheng Te t'ung pao

正 德 通 寶 . . . . *Scarce*

1522-66 Chia Ching t'ung pao

嘉 靖 通 寶 4.50

1567-72 Lung Ch'ing t'ung pao

隆 慶 通 寶 24.00

1573-1619 Wan Li t'ung pao

萬 厯 通 寶 4.00

1620 T'ai Ch'ang t'ung pao

泰 昌 通 寶 18.00

1621-27 T'ien Ch'i t'ung pao

天 啓 通 寶 5.00

1628-44 Ch'ung Chen t'ung pao

崇 禎 通 寶 5.00

Manchu (Ch'ing) Dynasty 1644-1911

1616-27 Imperial Coin of the Heavenly Mandate in Manchu script . . 37.50

1644-61 Shun Chih t'ung pao

順 治 通 寶 3.00

1662-1722 K'ang Hsi t'ung pao

康 熙 通 寶 1.00

1723-35 Yung Cheng t'ung pao

雍 正 通 寶 4.00

1736-95 Ch'ien Lung t'ung pao

乾 隆 通 寶 50

1796-1820 Chia Ch'ing t'ung pao

嘉 慶 通 寶 50

1821-1850 Tao Kuang t'ung pao

道 光 通 寶 50

1851-61 Hsien Feng t'ung pao

咸 豐 通 寶 65

1851-61 50 Cash, Hsien Feng chung pao 咸 豐 重 寶 20.00

1861 Ch'i Hsiang t'ung pao

祺 祥 通 寶 . . . . *Rare*

1862-74 T'ung Chih t'ung pao

同 治 通 寶 75

1875-1908 Kuang Hsu t'ung pao

光 緒 通 寶 2.00

1908-11 Hsüan T'ung t'ung pao

宣 統 通 寶 9.00

Amulets   F

1700's Openwork Amulet 28.00

1900's Openwork Amulet 5.00

1700's Amulet with Figure 22.00

1900's Amulet with Figure 4.00

1700's Amulet without figures . 15.00

1900's Amulet without figures . . 2.00

REPUBLIC (1911-49 on mainland, thereafter on Taiwan)

1912 2 Cash, Flags on rev. 15.00

CHINESE NUMBERS									
1	2	3	4	5	6	7	8	9	10
一	二	三	四	五	六	七	八	九	十
壹	貳	叁	肆	伍	陸	柒	捌	玖	拾

MACHINE STRUCK COINS   VF

Kuang Hsu 1875-1908

1908 1 Cash (B) Dragon 5.00

ND 1 Wen (B) Inscriptions 1.00

1905 2 Cash (B) Dragon 9.00

ND 5 Cash (C) Hu Poo, Dragon 20.00

ND 10 Cash (C) same 2.00

ND 20 Cash (C) same (struck in 1917 from old dies) 1.00

1905 5 Cash (C) Tai-Ching-Ti-Kuo Copper Coin, Dragon 18.00

1907 10 Cash (C) same 1.00

1907 20 Cash (C) same 2.00

1908 10 Cents (S) Tai-Ching-Ti-Kuo Silver Coin, Dragon 38.00

1907 20 Cents (S) same 75.00

1907 50 Cents (S) same 250.00

ND (1908) Dollar (S) same . . 20.00

Hsuan T'ung 1908-11

1909 1 Cash (B) Dragon 70.00

1909 2 Cash (B) Dragon . . . . . . *Rare*

1909 5 Cash (C) Tai-Ching-Ti-Kuo Copper Coin, Dragon . . . . . . *Rare*

1909 10 Cash (C) same 2.00

1911 10 Cash (C) Four characters around Dragon 3.50

1909 20 Cash (C) Tai-Ching-Ti-Kuo Copper Coin, Dragon 4.00

1911 10 Cents (S) Dragon around Value 32.00

1911 20 Cents (S) same 75.00

ND (1910) ¼ Dollar (S) Dragon *Scarce*

ND (1910) ½ Dollar (S) Dragon 75.00

1911 50 Cents (S) Dragon around Value 400.00

1910 Dollar (S) Dragon 265.00

VF

1911 Dollar (S) Dragon around Value
. . . . 20.00

Republic 1911-49   **VF**
(Dated from founding of the republic, year 1 is 1912).
1916 ½ Cent (C) (hole) 8.00
1936 ½ Cent (C) Sun / Spade Coin
. . . . 1.25
ND (1911-27) 10 Cash (C) Crossed Flags
. . . . 1.00
1916 1 Cent (C) (hole) 2.00
1924 1 Cent (C) Inscription / Wreath
. . . . *Scarce*
1928 1 Cent (C) Sun 150.00
1936 1 Cent (C) Sun / Spade Coin
. 50
1939 1 Cent (C) same but small . 38.00
1940 1 Cent (AL) Spade Coin 25
1940 1 Cent (B) Sun / Spade Coin . .50
1948 1 Cent (C) same 9.00
1919 2 Cents (C) Crossed Flags . . 2.00
1933 2 Cents (C) (hole) 50.00
1939 2 Cents (B) Sun / Spade Coin
. . . . 6.50
1940 2 Cents (B) 50
1936 5 Cents (N) Sun Yat Sen / Spade
Coin 50
1940 5 Cents (AL) Spade Coin . . . 1.00
1914 10 Cents (S) General 3.00
1926 10 Cents (S) Bird and Dragon
. . . . 6.50
1927 10 Cents (S) Sun Yat Sen / Flags
. . . . 30.00
1939 10 Cents (N) Sun Yat Sen / Spade
Coin 1.00
1914 20 Cents (S) General 2.00
1926 20 Cents (S) Bird and Dragon
. . . . 7.00
1927 20 Cents (S) Sun Yat Sen / Flags
. . . . 20.00
1942 20 Cents (CN) Sun Yat Sen / Spade
Coin 1.00
1914 ½ Dollar (S) General 13.50
1942 ½ Dollar (CN) Sun Yat Sen / Spade
Coin 75
ND (1912, 1927) Dollar (S) Young Sun
Yat Sen / Momento 7.00
1912 Dollar (S) Capped Bust . . 150.00

1914 Dollar (S) Bust of General in High
Hat / Value 110.00
1916 Dollar (S) Bust of General in High
Hat / Dragon 150.00
1920 Dollar (S) General l. 7.00

1921 Dollar (S) Sun Yat Sen / Junk, birds
above, rising sun right 75.00
1934 Dollar (S) same, no birds or sun
. . . . 7.00
1919 10 Dollars (G) Bust of General /
Value 1,500.00

REPUBLIC (on Taiwan 1949-date) BU
1949 1 Chio (C) Sun Yat Sen / Map
. . . . 3.50
1955 1 Chio (AL) same 1.00
1973 1 Chio (AL) Plant 50
1950 2 Chio (AL) Sun Yat Sen / Map
. . . . 2.50
1949 5 Chio (S) same 5.00
1954 5 Chio (B) same 1.00
1956 5 Chio (B) Flower 50
1988 5 Chio (C) Blossom 25
1960 1 Yuan (CNZ) Blossom / Plant
. 25
1961 1 Yuan (S) Chiang Kai-Shek *Scarce*
1966 1 Yuan (CN) same 1.00
1969 1 Yuan (CNZ) Farmer 1.00
1981 1 Yuan (C) Chiang Kai-Shek . .20
1965 5 Yuan (CN) Sun Yat Sen . . 3.00
1981 5 Yuan (CN) Chiang Kai-Shek .50
1988 5 Yuan (CN) same 35
1965 10 Yuan (CN) Sun Yat Sen . 3.75
1981 10 Yuan (CN) Chiang Kai-Shek .50
1965 50 Yuan (S) Sun Yat Sen / Deer
. . . . 15.00
1965 100 Yuan (S) same 18.00
1965 1000 Yuan (G) Sun Yat Sen 275.00

PEOPLE'S REPUBLIC 1949-date BU
1976 1 Fen (AL) Arms 25
1982 2 Fen (AL) Arms 25
1983 5 Fen (AL) Arms 25
1980 1 Jiao (B) Arms 75
1991 1 Jiao (AL) Arms / Flower . . .65
1981 2 Jiao (B) Arms 75
1980 5 Jiao (B) Arms 75
1990 5 Jiao (B) Arms / Flowers 75
1980 1 Yuan (CN) Great Wall . . . 2.00
1980 1 Yuan (CN) Skier 3.50

1983 5 Yuan (S) Marco Polo . . . 65.00
1988 100 Yuan (1 oz. G) Temple / Panda
. . . . Spot + 10%

JAPAN AND KOREA

History: The numismatic history of Japan and Korea was heavily influenced by China's evolution. In much the same pattern the traditional holed and cast "cash" coins were replaced by Western style machine struck coins. Like in China, the dragon was featured prominently on the coinage. While Korea, split as China is split, has chosen to include portraiture in its repertoire, Japan has followed the more traditional course.

Japanese and older Korean coins are dated by the monarch's reign. For example, the first year of the Showa (Hirohito) reign was 1926. Other Japanese year ones are Meiji 1868, Taiso 1912, and Heisei 1989. The dates below have been translated into A.D. dates for convenience.

References: Mandel, Edgar, *Cast Coinage of Korea*; Japanese Numismatic Dealers Association, *The Catalog of Japanese Coins and Banknotes*.

Counterfeit Alert: Counterfeits are known of the Japanese 1964 Olympic 1000 Yen.

Certain authorities, including Japanese officials, have claimed counterfeits exist of the gold 100,000 Yen, but this judgement has been questioned.

Hints: Cast Korean coins usually have multiple characters on the reverse. Japanese have one or none or a series of curves. Any with script-like Manchu characters on reverse are Chinese. Note that the obverses of all of these, as well as Annamese, use Chinese characters.

JAPAN

Cast Coins   **VF**
708-14 Mon (C)
和 同 開 珎 1,750.00
759-65 Mon (C) 萬 年 通 寳 900.00
765-70 Mon (C)
神 功 開 寳 825.00
1606 Mon (C)
慶 長 通 寳 135.00
1626-1769 Mon (C)
寛 永 通 寳 .... .50
1739-1867 Mon (Iron)
寛 永 通 寳 8.00

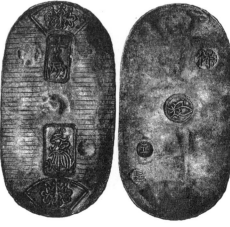

1769-1860 4 Mon (C) rev. Waves . 1.00
1707-09 10 Mon (C) 23.00
Oval Coins
1835-70 100 Mon (B), square hole . 9.00
1736-1818 1 Koban (G) 1,800.00

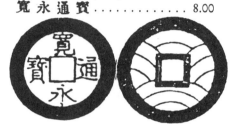

1837-58 1 Koban (G) 1,300.00
Rectangular Coins
1853-69 1 Shu Gin (S) 12.00
1837-69 1 Bu Gin (S) 25.00

                                      VF
1832-69 1 Shu Kin (G) 35.00

1736-1818 1 Bu Kin (G) 135.00
Machine Struck Coins
1883 1 Rin (C) Chrysanthemum . . 2.50
1887 ½ Sen (C) Dragon 1.00
1919 5 Rin (C) Paulowina Plant . . 1.00
1884 1 Sen (C) Dragon 1.00
1913 1 Sen (C) Sun 2.50
1919 1 Sen (C) Paulowina Plant 25
1939 1 Sen (AL) Crow .... .25
1943 1 Sen (AL) Mt. Fuji .... .15
1882 2 Sen (C) Dragon 2.00
1871 5 Sen (S) Dragon / Sun ... 55.00
1877 5 Sen (S) Dragon 18.00
1892 5 Sen (CN) Chrysanthemum . 2.50

1898 5 Sen (CN) Sun 7.00
1937 5 Sen (CN) (hole) .... .50
1946 5 Sen (Tin) Dove .... .25
1916 10 Sen (S) Sun 2.00
1907 20 Sen (S) Sun 3.00

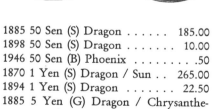

1885 50 Sen (S) Dragon 185.00
1898 50 Sen (S) Dragon 10.00
1946 50 Sen (B) Phoenix .... .50
1870 1 Yen (S) Dragon / Sun .. 265.00
1894 1 Yen (S) Dragon 22.50
1885 5 Yen (G) Dragon / Chrysanthemum and Banners 2,000.00

                                      BU
1925 5 Yen (G) Sunburst / Chrysthemum and Wreath 1,500.00
1974 1 Yen (AL) Sapling .... .10
1955 10 Yen (C) Temple 15.00
1963 10 Yen (C) Temple ...... .50
1958 100 Yen (S) Phoenix 5.00
1964 100 Yen (S) Olympic Flame . 3.00

1976 100 Yen (CN) Bridge 4.00
1992 100 Yen (CN) Three Blossoms 1.25
1964 1000 Yen (S) Mt. Fuji 45.00
1986 100,000 Yen (G) Chrysanthemum / Two Birds 1,100.00

KOREA   **VF**

Cast Coins
1700's-1800's Mun 常 平 通 寳 . 1.00
1679-1752 2 Mun, same 2.00
1883 5 Mun , same 3.50
1866 100 Mun , same 5.00

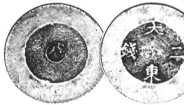

1882-83 2 Chon (Center Enamel) 325.00
Machine Struck Coins
1888 5 Mun (C) Dragon 110.00
1888 10 Mun (C) Dragon 250.00
1888 1 Warn (S) Dragon ...... *Scarce*
1895 1 Fun (C) Dragon 22.50
1898 5 Fun (C) Dragon 3.50
1898 ¼ Yang (CN) Dragon 1.00
1892 1 Yang (S) Dragon 100.00
1892 5 Yang (S) Dragon 1,100.00
1893 1 Whan (S) Dragon 4,800.00
1906 ½ Chon (C) Phoenix 4.00
1902 1 Chon (C) Eagle 1,800.00
1908 1 Chon (C) Phoenix 5.00
1902 5 Chon (CN) Eagle 1,500.00
1905 5 Chon (CN) Phoenix 8.50
1910 10 Chon (S) Dragon 10.00
1908 20 Chon (S) Dragon 24.00
1906 ½ Won (S) Dragon 100.00
1901 ½ Won (S) Eagle 4,800.00
1908 5 Won (G) Dragon .... *Rare*
1906 10 Won (G) Dragon .. 18,000.00

	VF
1906 20 Won (G) Dragon . .	19,000.00

NORTH KOREA — **BU**

	BU
1970 1 Chon (AL) Arms	1.25
1974 5 Chon (AL) Arms	2.00
1959 10 Chon (AL) Arms	2.00
1978 50 Chon (AL) Arms / Monument	3.25
1987 1 Won (CN) Arms / Arch . . . . *Proof only*	4.00
1987 1 Won (AL) Building	3.50
1992 50 Won (S) Kim Il Sung / Arms . . . . *Proof only*	55.00
1989 500 Won (S) Fairy with Flute / Arms . . . . *Proof only*	40.00

SOUTH KOREA — **BU**

	BU
1961 10 Hwan (C) Flower	1.50
1961 50 Hwan (B) Turtle Boat . . .	1.50
1959 100 Hwan (CN) Syngman Rhee	5.00
1967 1 Won (B) Rose	.75

1970 1 Won (AL) Rose	.10
1969 5 Won (C) Turtle Boat	2.25
1983 5 Won (B) Turtle Boat	.10
1970 10 Won (C) Temple	3.50

1979 10 Won (B) Temple	.10
1979 50 Won (CN) Rice	.25
1982 100 Won (CN) Lee Soon-shin .	.30
1992 500 Won (CN) Crane	2.00

1970 1000 Won (G) Gate / Flower	500.00
1984 1000 Won (CN) Church / Cross	4.00
1988 2000 Won (N) Weight Lifter	9.00
1986 10,000 Won (S) Runner . . .	23.00
1988 25,000 Won (G) Kite Flying	285.00

THE AMERICAS

THE CARIBBEAN AND BAHAMAS

History: The coins of the independent Caribbean nations are actively sought by collectors who crave beauty in their collections. Very often these countries have strived to make their coins as appealing to visiting tourists as their beaches. Many coins are struck at different minting facilities, some for collectors and some for circulation. Interestingly, some of the local populations prefer the conservative old colonial designs to the new flora and fauna. This was the case in Belize, where two different design series were struck simultaneously, some with birds and some with the Queen, even after independence.

References: See general references.

Counterfeit Alert: Recent Caribbean coins are not often counterfeited.

Hints: Never remove collector coins from their original holders. Not only does this reduce the salability of the coins, but it increases the risk of damage or fingerprints.

BAHAMAS — **BU**

	BU
1985 1 Cent (C plated Z) Starfish . .	.10
1974 25 Cents (N) Sailing Ship	.25
1974 1 Dollar (S) Conch Shell . . .	2.50

1976 2 Dollars (S) Flamingos .	*PF* 9.00

1974 5 Dollars (CN) Flag	5.00
1992 5 Dollars (S) Columbus . . .	45.00
1975 10 Dollars (S) Flower *Proof*	13.00
1975 50 Dollars (G) Bird	50.00

BARBADOS — **BU**

	BU
1973 1 Cent (C) Trident	.25
1979 5 Cents (B) Lighthouse	.25
1978 25 Cents (CN) Windmill	.50

1973 1 Dollar (CN) Flying Fish . .	1.00

1974 10 Dollars (S) Neptune *Proof*	10.00

BELIZE — **BU**

	BU
1977 1 Cent (AL) Bird	.25
1983 5 Cents (AL) Two Birds	.50
1974 50 Cents (CN) Three Frigate Birds	2.50
1975 5 Dollars (CN) Toucan	6.00
1974 10 Dollars (CN) Bird	8.00
1980 100 Dollars (G) Tropical Fish	*PF* 85.00

CUBA — **VF**

	VF
ca. 1868-77 1 Peso (S) Key Countermark on any one of a variety of Dollar-sized coins. *This is a countermark thought to have been used by revolutionaries.*	125.00
1915 1 Centavo (CN) Arms / Star	1.00
1948 20 Centavos (S) Arms / Star .	1.00
1915 40 Centavos (S) Arms / Star .	5.00
1932 1 Peso (S) Arms / Star	10.00
1934 1 Peso (S) Bust / Arms . . .	25.00

1916 4 Pesos (G) Marti / Arms	130.00
1916 5 Pesos (G) Marti / Arms	118.00
	BU
1984 2 Centavos (AL) Arms / Star .	.25

BU

1962 40 Centavos (CN) Camilo Cienfuegos / Arms 7.00
1987 5 Pesos (S) Che Guevara / Arms
. . . . 15.00

DOMINICAN REPUBLIC   VF
1844 ¼ Real (B) No design 7.50
1877 1 Centavo (B) Inscription . . . 2.00
1888 2½ Centavos (CN) Arms . . . 1.50
1891 10 Centesimos (C) Arms . . . 5.00
1897 20 Centavos (base S) 7.00
1949 1 Centavo (C) Tree 25
1944 5 Centavos (base S) 2.50
1956 25 Centavos (S) Arms / Indian Head 1.75
1891 1 Peso (S) same 85.00
1897 1 Peso (base S) same 55.00
1952 1 Peso (S) same 8.00
BU
1969 1 Centavo (C) same 25
1989 5 Centavos (CN) Drummer . . .25
1984 25 Centavos (CN) Arms / Three Heads 25
1955 1 Peso (S) Trujillo 24.00

1974 1 Peso (S) Arms / Map . . . 12.00
1991 1 Peso (B) Duarte 1.50
1975 100 Pesos (G) Sculpture . . 140.00

HAITI   VF
1807 15 Sols (S) Standing Figure / Arms
. . . . 150.00
1832 1 Centime (C) Fasces 7.00
1895 1 Centime (C) Arms 2.50
1863 5 Centimes (C) Head / Arms 4.00
1949 5 Centimes (CN) same 25
1850 6¼ Centimes (C) Crowned Bust / Arms 9.00
1882 10 Centimes (S) Head / Arms 2.00
1906 10 Centimes (CN) same 1.00
BU
1958 5 Centimes (CNZ) same 25
1953 10 Centimes (CNZ) same . . . 1.00
1975 20 Centimes (CN) same 25
1974 25 Gourdes (S) U.S. Bicentennial
. . . . 5.50

1973 50 Gourdes (S) Cartoons
. . . . *Proof only* 13.00
1981 50 Gourdes (S) Head / Plant 17.00

1981 100 Gourdes (S) Head / Two Naked Youths . . . . *Proof only* 300.00
1974 200 Gourdes (G) Paul VI . . 55.00

JAMAICA   BU
1975 1 Cent (AL) Ackee Plant 15
1969 5 Cents (CN) Crocodile 25

1987 25 Cents (CN) Hummingbird . .75
1976 50 Cents (CN) Garvey 1.00
1982 1 Dollar (CN) Soccer Player . 3.00
1972 10 Dollars (S) Two Heads and Map
. . . . 10.00
1979 10 Dollars (S) Butterfly . . . 18.00
1975 100 Dollars (G) Columbus
. . . . *PF* 135.00

TRINIDAD AND TOBAGO
1966 1 Cent (C) Arms 10
1975 5 Cents (C) Bird of Paradise . . .25
1975 10 Cents (CN) Hibiscus Flower .25
1979 50 Cents (CN) Steel Drums . 1.00

1976 5 Dollars (S) Ibis . . . . . . *PF* 9.50
1976 10 Dollars (S) Map . . . *PF* 10.00

MEXICO
History: Throughout its history Mexico has been world famous for its silver dollars. When Mexico gained its independence it continued to strike these "Pieces of Eight" on the old Spanish colonial standard until 1914! Most Mexican silver coins are measured in eighths of a Peso (a real) or in hundredths (a centavo).

After independence Mexico spent a few years as an empire, but soon abolished this in favor of a new Mexican Republic. Except for a brief period under the ill-fated Hapsburg Emperor Maximillian, the name of the country remained unchanged until 1905. In that year it became the United Mexican States, as can be seen on the coinage.

Commemoratives were unknown in Mexico until this new government, and from the 1950's onwards have been extremely common, especially in silver, of course.

Mexico is also one of the world's major suppliers of gold and silver bullion coins. These were originally restrikes of the 1945 2 and 2½ Peso, 1955 5 Peso, 1959 10 and 20 Peso, and 1947 20 Peso. Today they are struck in even ounces.

References: Bruce, Colin, *Standard Catalog of Mexican Coins.*

Counterfeit Alert: Contemporary counterfeits exist of Cap and Rays type 8 and 2 real pieces. Many modern counterfeits exist of Mexican bullion gold, including the 50 Peso and the Libertad type silver Onza, among others.

Hints: During the 1800's very many date, mintmark, and assayer mark varieties exist. Some are quite scarce and a specialized work should be consulted to identify them. Many scarce pieces are not expensive, but are bought hastily by specialized collectors.

Mexican silver is often weakly struck at the centers, and thus slightly discounted.

Note: The older "Pieces of Eight" are listed under Spanish Colonies.

F

Empire of Augustin Iturbide 1822-23
1823 1/8 Real (C) Arms 35.00
1823 ½ Real (S) Bust / Eagle . . . 12.00

F
1822 8 Real (S) same 50.00
1823 4 Scudos (G) Bust / Arms   900.00

Mexican Republic   VF
1825 ¼ Real (B) Pyramid / Angel   22.00
1831 ¼ Real (C) Eagle / ¼ 12.00
1844 ¼ Real (S) Head / ¼ 7.00
1858 ½ Real (S) Eagle / Cap in Rays
. . . .   5.00
1850 1 Real (S) same 5.00
1827 2 Reales (S) same 10.00
1839 4 Reales (S) same 30.00

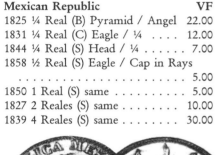

1893 8 Reales (S) same 11.00
1848 ½ Escudo (G) Eagle / Hand, Cap
and Book 62.50
1825 1 Escudo (G) same 100.00
1868 2 Escudos (G) same 200.00
1856 4 Escudos (G) same 500.00
1859 8 Escudos (G) same 435.00
1883 1 Centavo (CN) Quiver 50
1888 1 Centavo (C) Eagle 1.75
1883 2 Centavos (CN) Quiver 50
1882 5 Centavos (CN) Quiver . . .   1.00
1889 5 Centavos (S) Eagle 1.75
1893 10 Centavos (S) Eagle 2.00
1903 20 Centavos (S) Eagle 7.00
1871 25 Centavos (S) Eagle / Balance and
Scroll 12.50
1881 50 Centavos (S) same 24.00
1871 Peso (S) same 20.00
1903 Peso (S) Eagle / Cap with Rays
. . . .   10.00
1902 Peso (G) Eagle 55.00
1872 2½ Pesos (G) Eagle 275.00
1900 5 Pesos (G) Eagle / Balance and
Scroll 300.00
1889 10 Pesos (G) same 475.00
1872 20 Pesos (G) same 600.00

Empire of Maximilian 1864-67   F
1864 1 Centavo (C) Eagle 30.00
1864 5 Centavos (S) Eagle 10.00
1864 10 Centavos (S) Eagle 10.00
1866 50 Centavos (S) Head / Arms
. . . .   30.00

1866 1 Peso (S) Head / Arms with
Griffon Supporters 28.00
1866 20 Pesos (G) same . . .   VF 800.00

United Mexican States (1905-69)   VF
1906 1 Centavo (C) Eagle 75
1915 1 Centavo (C) Zapata 16mm   22.50
1964 1 Centavo (B) Eagle/Wheat BU .25
1915 2 Centavos C) Zapata 20mm   8.00
1939 2 Centavos (C) Eagle 50
1910 5 Centavos (N) Eagle 1.00
1935 5 Centavos (C) Eagle 1.00
1937 5 Centavos (CN) Eagle / Aztec
Calendar Border 25
1944 5 Centavos (C) Eagle / Josefa .   .25
1950 5 Centavos (CN) same 50

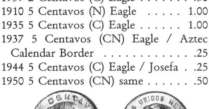

1968 5 Centavos (B) same . . . . BU .25
1914 10 Centavos (S) Eagle 5.00
1919 10 Centavos (S) Eagle 9.00
1935 10 Centavos (C) Eagle 14.00
1933 10 Centavos (S) Eagle 1.50
1946 10 Centavos (CN) Eagle / Aztec
Calendar Border 25
1959 10 Centavos (C) Eagle / Juarez
. . . . BU .50
1907 20 Centavos (S) Eagle 9.00
1919 20 Centavos (S) Eagle 25.00
1935 20 Centavos (C) Eagle 7.00
1943 20 Centavos (S) Eagle 1.00
1946 20 Centavos (C) Eagle / Pyramid
. 85
1968 20 Centavos (C) same . . BU 1.00
1950 25 Centavos (S) Eagle / Balance and
Scroll 50
1964 25 Centavos (CN) Eagle / Madero
. . . . BU .25

1916 50 Centavos (S) Eagle 75.00
1919 50 Centavos (S) without .720   9.00
1935 similar (base S) 2.00
1945 50 Centavos (S) Eagle 3.00
1951 50 Centavos (S) Eagle /
Cuauhtemoc 1.50
1956 50 Centavos (C) same 50
1964 50 Centavos (CN) same . . BU .25

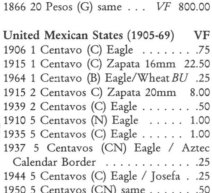

1913 Peso (S) Woman on Horse / Eagle
. . . .   35.00
1919 Peso (S) Eagle 20.00
1932 Peso (S) Eagle 3.00
1947 Peso (S) Eagle / Head of Morelos
. . . .   3.00
1950 Peso (S) Eagle / Bust of Morelos
facing 2.00
1957 Peso (base S) Juarez / Eagle .   4.00

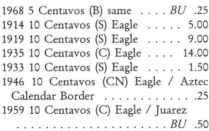

1963 Peso (base S) Bust of Morelos left /
Eagle 50

	VF
1921 2 Pesos (S) Eagle / Liberty	35.00

	BU
1948 5 Pesos (S) Eagle / Cuauhtemoc	8.00
1950 5 Pesos (S) Train / Eagle	55.00
1952 5 Pesos (S) Head of Hidalgo	6.00
1953 5 Pesos (S) Bust of Hidalgo	6.75
1956 5 Pesos (S) Head of Hidalgo	4.50
1957 5 Pesos (S) Juarez / Eagle	13.00
1959 5 Pesos (S) Carranza / Eagle	5.00
1956 10 Pesos (S) Hidalgo / Eagle	8.00
1957 10 Pesos (S) Juarez / Eagle	50.00
1960 10 Pesos (S) Two Busts / Eagle	8.00
1968 25 Pesos (S) Aztec Athlete / Eagle	4.50

United Mexican States (1970-92)   BU

1970 1 Centavo (B) Eagle / Wheat	1.50
1976 5 Centavos (B) Eagle / Josefa	.25
1974 10 Centavos (CN) Corn	.25
1974 20 Centavos (C) Pyramid	1.00
1975 20 Centavos (CN) Eagle / Madero	.25
1984 20 Centavos (C) Eagle / Olmec Head	1.00
1979 50 Centavos (CN) Cuauhtemoc	.25
1983 50 Centavos (Steel) Palenque Head	.50
1970 Peso (CN) Eagle / Morelos	.50
1985 Peso (Steel) same	.50

1977 5 Pesos (CN) Eagle / Guerrero	1.00
1980 5 Pesos (CN) Eagle / Quetzalcoatl	1.00
1988 5 Pesos (B) Eagle	.25
1976 10 Pesos (CN) Eagle / Hidalgo	1.25
1988 10 Pesos (Steel) same	.25
1980 20 Pesos (CN) Eagle / Mayan Sculpture	1.75
1988 20 Pesos (B) Eagle / G. Victoria	.25
1972 25 Pesos (S) Eagle / Juarez	5.50

1985 25 Pesos (S) Eagle / Soccer . . . . *PF cased*	13.50
1984 50 Pesos (CN) Eagle / Coyolxuahqui	2.50
1987 50 Pesos (CN) Eagle / Juarez	.75
1988 50 Pesos (Steel) same	.50
1985 50 Pesos (S) Soccer . . . *PF*	22.00
1988 50 Pesos (S) Oil	15.00
1978 100 Pesos (S) Eagle / Morelos	5.00

1985 100 Pesos (S) Soccer . . *PF*	32.50
1986 100 Pesos (S) Soccer . . *PF*	32.50
1987 100 Pesos (S) Butterflies *PF*	45.00
1988 100 Pesos (S) Oil	30.00
1989 100 Pesos (AB) Eagle / Carranza	.75
1992 100 Pesos (S) Pillars . . . *PF*	40.00
1992 100 Pesos (S) Whale . . *PF*	60.00
1985 200 Pesos (CN) Four Busts	2.50
1986 200 Pesos (CN) Soccer	3.00
1986 200 Pesos (S) Soccer	45.00
1985 250 Pesos (G) Soccer	120.00
1985 500 Pesos (G) Soccer	210.00
1985 500 Pesos (S) Four Busts . . . . *PF*	40.00
1987 500 Pesos (CN) Madero	1.00
1985 1000 Pesos (G) Four Busts . . . . *PF*	250.00
1986 1000 Pesos (G) Soccer . *PF*	600.00
1988 1000 Pesos (G) Oil . . . *PF*	500.00
1989 1000 Pesos (AB) Juana de Asbaje	1.50
1986 2000 Pesos (G) Soccer . .	1,000.00
1988 5000 Pesos (CN) Oil	4.00

New Pesos (1992 to date)   BU

1992 5 Centavos (Steel) Eagle	.25
1992 10 Centavos (Steel) Eagle	.25
1992 20 Centavos (AB) Eagle	.25
1992 50 Centavos (AB) Eagle	.50
1993 1 New Peso (Steel around AB) Eagle	.75
1993 2 New Pesos (Steel around AB)	1.50
1993 5 New Pesos (Steel around AB) Eagle	2.25
1992 10 New Pesos (AB around S) Aztec Calender	4.00

1993 20 New Pesos (AB around S) Hidalgo	7.50

1994 50 New Pesos (AB around S) Six Busts	18.00

Bullion Issues
Note: Values are a handling charge above the metal content, from a 20% premium for pieces worth less than $50 to as low as 4% for a gold 50 Peso. The figures below are the actual contents in gold or silver.

1945 2 Pesos (G)	.048 oz.
1945 2½ Peso (G)	.060 oz.
1955 5 Peso (G)	.120 oz.
1959 10 Peso (G)	.241 oz.
1959 20 Peso (G)	.482 oz.
1947 50 Peso (G)	1.205 oz.
1949 1 Onza (S)	20.00
1980 1 Onza (S)	8.50

1982-date 1 Onza (S) "Libertad"	1.0 oz.
1991 1/10 Onza (G) "Libertad"	.1 oz.
1981 ¼ Onza (G) "Libertad"	.25 oz.
1981 ¼ Onza (G) "Libertad"	.5 oz.
1981 1 Onza (G) "Libertad"	1.0 oz.

Local Coins   VF

Aguascaliens 1915 20 Centavos (C) Eagle	10.00
Chihuahua 1914 5 Centavos (C) Cap with Rays	3.00
Durango 1914 1 Centavos (AL) Eagle	2.00
Oaxaca 1915 10 Centavos (C) Bust of Juarez	4.00
Puebla 1915 5 Centavos (C) Eagle	135.00

CENTRAL AND SOUTH AMERICA

History: Coinage in South America during the nineteenth century was varied, some countries having very conservative coinages with stable standards, and others having rapid inflation or a multiplicity of designs. Bolivia for example introduced new minor silver for propaganda purposes virtually every year. Peru, on the other hand had a changeless and stable dollar or "Sol" for decades. By and large most countries started out with a monetary unit based on the old Spanish Milled Dollar or "Piece of Eight."

With the twentieth century Latin America followed the world trend of abandoning circulating precious metal coins, and reserving it for increased production of commemoratives.

References: Adams, Edgar, *Catalogue of the Collection of Julius Guttag*; and general references.

Counterfeit Alert: Counterfeits exist of many gold pieces, including the more common issues of Peru and Colombia.

Hints: Early issues of Bolivia and Central American Republic are often weakly struck in the centers and when perfectly struck command a premium.

ARGENTINA
Provencias del Rio de la Plata   F
1824 2 Soles (S) Sun/Arms 15.00

1815 4 Reales (S) same 50.00
1836 8 Reales (C) same 75.00

Buenos Aires
1823 Decimo (C) Arms / Wreath . 3.00
1827 5/10 Real (C) Wreath/Value . 4.00
1853 2 Reales (C) Wreath / Wreath 2.00

Republic   VF
1883 1 Centavo (C) Arms/Head . . 1.25
1949 2 Centavos (C) Arms/Value . . .25
1944 5 Centavos (C) Head/Value . . .25
1883 20 Centavos (S) Arms/Head 10.00
1941 50 Centavos (AN) Head/Value .75
1882 Peso (S) Arms / Head 80.00

1959 Peso (N clad Steel) Head / Value
. 25
                                            BU
1960 Peso (N clad Steel) Arms / Building
. . . . 1.00
1961 5 Pesos (N clad Steel) Ship 35
1962 10 Pesos (N clad Steel) Gaucho on
Horse 50
1964 25 Pesos (N clad Steel) Old Coin
. . . . 1.00
1977 50 Pesos (AB) Soccer player/Logo
. . . . 1.00
1985 1 Centavo (AL) Ostrich/Value .25
1989 1 Austral (AL) Building/Value .25
1994 1 Peso (CN around AB) **Arms /
Sun** 2.00

1994 5 Pesos (S) Triple Arms / Book
. . . . *PF* 50.00

BOLIVIA   F
1827 ½ Sol (S) Bolivar / Tree and Two
Llamas 6.00
1849 1 Sol (S) Clasped Hands / AL
GENERAL BELZU, holed . . . 12.00

1853 1 Sol (S) Angel crowning Bust /
City below Mountain, unholed 25.00

Note: The above two coins refering to a living politician are part of a long tradition in Latin America and Spain known as Proclamations. Only in Bolivia did they normally circulate as coins. In other countries they were treated as medals. Most Bolivian proclamations have been holed.

1856 4 Soles (S) Bolivar (S) / Tree and
Two Llamas 17.00
1831 8 Soles (S) Bolivar / Tree and Two
Llamas 22.00
1865 1/8 Melgarejo (S) Bearded Bust /
Dragon 23.00
                                            VF
1883 2 Centavos (C) Arms 8.00
1935 5 Centavos (CN) Mountain Scene /
Caduceus 75

1937 10 Centavos (CN) Mountain Scene
/
Hand with Torch 75
1890 20 Centavos (S) Arms 3.50
1894 ½ Boliviano (S) Arms 4.00
1873 1 Boliviano (S) Arms 20.00
1951 5 Bolivianos (C) Arms 50
1951 10 Bolivianos (C) Bolivar 75
                                            BU
1991 10 Centavos (Steel) Arms 50
1965 20 Centavos (N clad Steel) Mountain
Scene 1.00

1972 1 Peso (N clad Steel) Mountain
Scene 1.50
1976 5 Pesos (N clad Steel) Mountain
Scene 3.50
1979 4000 Pesos (G) Arms / Child
. . . . *PF only* 250.00
Dept. of Cochabamba (1876) 5 Centavo
Quiroga token 8.00

BRAZIL   VF
Empire 1822-1889
(1835) Countermark "20" in circle on old
40 reis (C) 8.50

1869 20 Reis (C) Bust / Arms . . . 2.00
1824 37½ Reis (C) Wreath / Arms
. . . . 45.00
1873 40 Reis (C) Bust / Arms . . . 2.75
1828 80 Reis (C) Wreath / Arms . 8.50
1871 100 Reis (CN) Arms 1.00
1834 400 Reis (S) Wreath / Arms 90.00
1850 500 Reis (S) same 10.00
1888 1000 Reis (S) Bust / Arms . 14.00

Republic
1894 20 Reis (C) Star 1.00
1900 40 Reis (C) Stars 2.00
1919 50 Reis (CN) Head 25
1889 100 Reis (CN) Stars in circle 2.50

VF

1936 200 Reis (CN) Bust / Train . . .50
1932 400 Reis (CN) Map / Cross . 3.00
1936 400 Reis (CN) Cruz / Lamp . . .75
1938 400 Reis (CN) Vargas 25
1913 500 Reis (S) Head / Arms . 2.25
1922 1000 Reis (AB) Two Busts / Crown
    and Cap 50
1922 1000 Reis (AB) same but country
    name misspelled BBASIL 5.00
1927 1000 Reis (AB) Kneeling Figure
    . . . . 1.00

1929 2000 Reis (S) Head / Fasces . 1.50
1932 2000 Reis (S) King / Arms . . 2.25

EF

1932 1000 Reis (AB) da Sousa/Arms 7.00
1935 2000 Reis (S) Caxais / Sword 3.00

1900 4000 Reis (S) Cabral / Two Shields
    . . . . 400.00
1936 5000 Reis (S) Dumont / Wing 3.00
1889 10,000 Reis (G) Bust / Star 235.00

BU

1943 10 Centavos (AB) Vargas 75
1954 1 Cruzeiro (AB) Map 1.00
1961 2 Cruzeiros (AL) Map 50
1976 1 Centavo (Steel) Head 10
1967 20 Centavos (CN) Head / Oil Well
   25
1972 20 Cruzeiros (S) Two Busts
    / Map 5.00

1990 10 Centavos (Steel) Prospector .25

1992 10 Cruzieros (Steel) Farmer . . .25
1993 5 Cruzeiros Reales (Steel) Parrots
   50
1994 1 Real (Steel) Head 2.00

CENTRAL AMERICAN REPUB.   F

1844 ¼ Real (S) Mountains / Tree 6.00
1843 ½ Real (S) same 14.00
1830 1 Real (S) same 13.00
1831 2 Reales (S) same 14.00

1824 8 Reales (S) same 36.00
1847 ½ Escudo (G) same 60.00
1848 1 Escudo (G) same 85.00
1835 2 Escudos (G) same 175.00
1837 4 Escudos (G) same 625.00
1828 8 Escudos (G) same 1,500.00

CHILE   F

1834 1 Real (S) Mountain/Column 20.00
1843 1 Real (S) Condor/Arms . . . 8.00

1842 8 Escudos (G) Arms / Figure leaning
    on Column 375.00

VF

1853 ½ Centavo (C) Star 3.50
1879 2 Centavos (C) Head 5.00
1855 ½ Decimo (S) Condor/Wreath . .
    . . . . 11.00
1908 20 Centavos (S) same 1.00
1875 Peso (S) Condor 10.00
1953 Peso (C) O'Higgins/Wreath . . .25

BU

1975 1 Centavo (Al) Condor/Wreath .
   35
1993 1 Peso (AL) 8-sided 25
1988 5 Pesos (NB) Liberty/Wreath . .35
1989 100 Pesos (AB) Arms/Wreath 1.50

COLOMBIA   VF

1827 ¼ Real (S) Cornucopia . . . 30.00

1820 8 Reales (S) Indian Head /
    Pomegranate 225.00

1858 1 Peso (S) "Nuevo Granada," Arms
    / Wreath 50.00
1881 2½ Centavos (CN) Cap on Pole
   35
1886 5 Centavos (CN) Liberty 50

1902 5 Centavos (CN) same 60.00
1897 10 Centavos (S) Liberty / Arms
    . . . . 1.50
1950 10 Centavos (S) Bolivar 75

1951 20 Centavos (S) Bolivar 1.50
1892 50 Centavos (S) Columbus . . 9.00

BU

1967 1 Centavo (C clad Steel) Cap in
    Wreath 25
1978 10 Centavos (N clad Steel) Bolivar
   25
1978 50 Centavos (N clad Steel) Bolivar
   25
1956 1 Peso (S) Door / Arms . . . 20.00
1989 20 Pesos (AB) Arms 35
1994 500 Pesos (CN around AB) Tree, bi-
    metallic 3.00

COSTA RICA   VF

1874 1 Centavo (CN) Arms 4.00
1918 10 Centavos (B) Arms 2.00
1865 50 Centavos (S) Arms / Ceiba Tree
    . . . . 100.00
1900 2 Colones (G) Columbus / Arms
    . . . . 38.00

BU

1967 5 Centimos (Steel) Arms 25
1970 50 Centimos (Steel) Arms 25

BU
1983 20 Colones (Steel) Arms 1.25
1979 100 Colones (S) Birds in Nest 11.00

ECUADOR   VF
1836 2 Reales (S) Fasces between
Cornucopia/Sun over Mountain 50.00
1902 ½ Decimo (S) Sucre / Arms . 1.00
1894 2 Decimos (S) similar 6.50
1891 5 Decimos (S) similar 18.00

1934 PHILA. 1 Sucre (S) similar . . 2.00
BU
1946 5 Centavos (CN) Arms ..... .25
1974 20 Centavos (CN) Arms .... .25
1943 5 Sucres (S) Sucre / Arms .. 9.00

EL SALVADOR   VF
1915 1 Centavo (CN) Morazán/Value
.... 2.00
1911 10 Centavos (S) Arms/Value   3.50
1892 Peso (S) Arms / Columbus   60.00
1893 Peso (S) same 15.00
Unc
1974 3 Centavos (B) Morazán / Value.
.... .25
1967 5 Centavos (CN) same ...... .25
1953 25 Centavos (S) Priest/Value   3.00
1970 25 Centavos (N) same ...... .50

1985 1 Colon (CN) Columbus . . . 1.50
1988 1 Colon (Steel) Columbus 50

GUATAMALA   VF
1880 ¼ Real (S) Mountains / Value. 1.50

1900 ½ Real (CN) Seated Figure/Arms
.... .50
1862 1 Real (S) Carrera/Arms . . . 6.50
1894 2 Reales (S) Seated Figure / Arms.
.... 4.00
1860 4 reales (G) Carrera / Wreath.
.... 32.00

1894 1 Peso (S) Seated figure / Arms.
.... 13.50
1894 1 Peso (S) made by using ½ Real
dies on foreign Pesos, particularly those
of Peru and Chile. 30.00
1923 1 Peso (B) Bust 1.50
1932 ½ Centavos (B) Arms ...... .50
1944 2 Centavos (B) Quetzal bird / Value.
.... 1.50
1945 10 Centavos (S) Arms / Quetzal
bird 1.00

1943 25 Centavos (S) Bird and map /
Building 4.00
1925 1 Quetzal (S) same 675.00
1926 10 Quetzales (G) same . . . 325.00
BU
1965 1 Centavo (B) Arms / Las Casas.
.... .25
1958 5 Centavos (S) Arms / Tree . 1.00
1993 10 Centavos (CN) Arms / Monolith
.... .25
1965 25 Centavos (CN) Arms / Bust.
.... 1.00
1962 50 Centavos (S) Arms / Flower.
.... 4.00

HONDURAS   F
1833 2 Reales (base S) Mountains / Tree
.... 12.00
1857 8 Reales (C) same 15.00
VF
1869 ¼ Real (CN) Arms 2.50

1870 1 Real (CN) similar 12.00
1920 2 Centavos (C) Arms 2.00
1885 50 Centavos (S) Honduras standing
by Pillar / Arms 20.00
1932 50 Centavos (S) Arms / Indian
Head 2.00
1884 1 Peso (S) Honduras standing by
Pillar / Arms 40.00
1933 1 Lempira (S) Arms / Indian Head
.... 4.00
BU
1957 1 Centavo (C) Arms .... .25
1974 2 Centavos (C clad Steel) Arms .25
1949 5 Centavos (CN) Arms 3.50
1958 20 Centavos (S) Arms / Indian
Head 4.00
1978 50 Centavos (CN) Arms / Indian
Head .... .75

NICARAGUA   VF
1898 5 Centavos (CN) Arms 1.50
1912 10 Centavos (S) Cordoba /
Mountains 3.00

1880 20 Centavos (S) Arms 7.00
1954 50 Centavos (CN) Cordoba /
Mountains .... .35
BU
1962 5 Centavos (CN) same ...... .50
1974 10 Centavos (AL) Map ..... .25
1981 25 Centavos (N Clad Steel) Sandino
.... .50
1994 50 Centavos (Steel) Arms / Dove
.... 1.00

1980 5 Cordobas (CN) Sandino . . 2.50

BU

1967 50 Cordobas (G) Dario / Arms
. . . . 450.00
1988 50 Cordobas (S) Sailboat *PF* 45.00

PANAMA   **VF**
1907 ½ Centesimo (CN) Balboa 75
1935 1 Centesimo (C) Uracca 4.00
1929 5 Centavos (CN) Arms 2.50

1904 5 Centisimos (S) Balboa / Arms
. . . . 4.00
1904 10 Centesimos (S) Balboa / Arms
. . . . 6.00
1930 1/10 Balboa (S) Balboa / Arms
. . . . 2.25
1934 ¼ Balboa (S) Balboa / Arms . 3.50
1930 ½ Balboa (S) same 6.50
1947 1 Balboa (S) Balboa / Panama
standing 6.50

BU

1973 2½ Centavos (CN) Hand / Arms
. 25
1973 1/10 Balboa (CN clad C) Balboa /
Arms 35
1966 ½ Balboa (S clad) Balboa / Arms
. . . . 3.00

1970 5 Balboas (S) Discus Thrower /
Arms 7.00
1972 20 Balboas (S) Bolivar / Arms
. . . . 32.00
1978 75 Balboas (G) Flag . . . *PF* 75.00
1975 100 Balboas (G) Balboa / Arms
. . . . 125.00

PERU   **VF**
1855 ¼ Real (S) Llama / ¼ 6.00
1832 2 Reales (S) Arms / Peru Standing
. . . . 25.00
1838 4 Reales for South Peru (S) Sun /
Fortress and Volcano 50.00
1854 4 Reales (S) Arms / Peru standing
. . . . 18.00

1837 8 Reales for North Peru (S) same
. . . . 35.00

1863 1 Centavo (CN) Sun 2.00
1919 1 Centavo (C) Sun 75
1895 2 Centavos (C) Sun 1.00
1935 5 Centavos (CN) Head / Branch
. . . . 1.00
1951 10 Centavos (B) Head / Branch
. 25
1896 1/5 Sol (S) Arms / Peru seated
. . . . 2.50
1945 ½ Sol (B) Arms 1.00
1864 1 Sol (S) Arms / Peru seated
. . . . 8.00
1935 1 Sol (S) same 5.00

BU

1956 1 Centavo (Z) Sun 1.00
1950 2 Centavos (Z) Sun 2.00
1963 5 Centavos (B) Head / Branch
. 50
1966 1 Sol (B) Arms / Llama 50
1978 10 Soles (B) Tupac Amaru 50
1985 50 Soles (B) Grau 25

1961 100 Soles (G) Arms / Peru seated
. . . . 600.00
1984 100 Soles (B) Arms / Grau 50
1982 10,000 Soles (S) Caceres / Arms
. . . . 5.00

URUGUAY   **VF**
1869 2 Centesimos (C) Sun 2.25
1901 5 Centesimos (CN) Sun 50
1930 10 Centesimos (AB) Head / Cougar
. . . . 2.00

1877 20 Centesimos (S) Arms 4.00
1943 50 Centesimos (S) Artigas / Sunrise
. . . . 1.50
1844 1 Peso (S) Arms 375.00

BU

1959 10 Centesimos (CN) Artigas
. . . . 1.00
1965 50 centesimos (AL) 50
1971 50 Pesos (NB) Rodo / Quill Pen
. . . . 1.50
1989 5 New Pesos (Steel) Sun 25
1984 20 New Pesos (S) Fish . *PF* 16.00

VENEZUELA   **VF**
1819 2 Reales (S) Two Pillars / Spanish
Arms 42.00
1863 10 Reales (S) Esclarecido . . . *Rare*
1858 1 Centavo (C) Liberty Head
. . . . 5.50
1876 2½ Centavos (CN) Arms . . 12.50
1944 5 Centavos (B) Arms 75
1945 5 Centavos (CN) Arms 25
1936 12½ Centavos (CN) Arms 50
1945 ½ Bolivar (S) Bolivar / Arms
. 50
1886 1 Bolivar (S) same 38.00
1900 1 Bolivar (S) same 38.00
1911 1 Bolivar (S) same 4.00
1919 2 Bolivares (S) same 2.50
1879 5 Bolivares (S) same 50.00

1936 5 Bolivares (S) same 8.00

BU

1971 10 Centimos (CN) Arms 25
1977 1 Bolivar (N) Bolivar / Arms . .25
1965 2 Bolivares (N) same 2.50
1973 5 Bolivares (N) same 1.00
1973 10 Bolivares (S) Bolivar in recessed
square 10.00
1912 20 Bolivares (G) Bolivar / Arms
. . . . 125.00
Providencia Leper Colony 1939 0.05
Bolivar (B) Inscription . . . . . *F* 5.00

FOREIGN PAPER MONEY

History: Paper money had its first use during the Yüan dynasty of China. Paper money in the West began a couple of hundred years later. Both of these origins were routed in the various governments' attempts to finance expenditures without actually raising hard cash (coin). This situation reached an extreme during the French Revolution when the first truly common notes, the *assignats*, were issued, theoretically backed by confiscated church property.

Since the mid-to-late nineteenth century, paper money has played an active role in the daily functioning of most currency systems.
References: Pick, Albert, *Standard Catalog of World Paper Money*, Monetary Research Institute, *MRI Bankers' Guide to Foreign Currency*.
Counterfeit Alert: Many foreign notes have been counterfeited. These include British banknotes made by the Nazis. As a general rule look for crispness of printing, and the quality of paper. If in doubt consult an expert.

Hints: Unlike American paper money, banknotes from other countries are frequently rendered void of face value either by government recall or by severe inflation. As a result, notes bearing fantastic denominations such as one billion marks or 100,000 pesos should not automatically be presumed to be valuable.
Note: The size of the illustrations below bears no relationship to the actual size of the notes illustrated. For how to grade paper money, see the introduction to the chapter on United States paper money.

AFGHANISTAN   VF
1298SH 5 Rupees, Building within oval
. . . . 15.00
1340SH 20 Afghanis, King at l. . . 1.00
1358SH 10 Afghanis, Mountains 50

ALGERIA   VF
1942, 5 Francs, Woman at r. 1.00
1964, 50 Dinars, Sheep 22.00

ARGENTINA   F
1884 5 Centavos, Bust at l. 13.50
1891 20 Centavos, Bust at l. / Steer Head 2.50
1895 50 Centavos, Bust at r. / Columbus 10.00
1897 1 Peso, Argentina seated with torch 85.00
                        EF
1935 10 Pesos, similar 4.00
1947 1 Peso, similar 75
ND (1960) 5 Pesos, San Martin / Building 75
Decree-Law 18.188/69 (1974-76) 5 Pesos, Bust of Belgrano 50

ND (1978) 50 Pesos, Old San Martin / Mountains 50
ND (1985) 1 Austral, Stylized portrait of Rivadavia 25

Argentine 1947 1 Peso

Austrian [1919] 1 Krone

AUSTRALIA   EF
[1913] £1, Inscription 3,000.00
[1942] £1, George VI 10.00
[1960] £1, Elizabeth II r. 5.00
1972 1 Dollar, Arms and Elizabeth II
.... 1.25

AUSTRIA   VF
1759 20 Gulden, Inscription .... *scarce*
1848 1 Gulden, Head above, eagle below
.... 20.00
1882, 1 Gulden, Franz Josef both sides
.... 10.00
1902 1000 Kronen, Eagle above, woman
right 3.00
1916 1 Krone, Two heads facing /
Helmeted head left .... .25
[1919] same, overprinted
"DEUTSCHÖSTERREICH" .... .25
1927 10 Schilling, Mercury / Harvest
allegory 10.00
1950 10 Schilling, Rider on Lippizaner /
Castle 1.25
1967 20 Schilling, Ritter von Ghega /
Bridge across mountain ravine .. 2.00

BAHAMAS   EF
1869 1 Pound, Inscription .... *RARE*
ND (1930) 4 Shillings, Ship and George
V 750.00
1936 (1953) 4 Shillings, Ship and Elizabeth
II 18.00

BELGIUM   F
1869 20 Francs, Figures of Agriculture
and Cattle Breeding 225.00
1920 20 Francs, Figure standing with
lion 12.50
1922 1 Franc, Albert I and Elisabeth
.... 1.00
1928 1000 Francs, Albert I, Elisabeth and
allegorical figure 4.00
1944 50 Francs, Woman riding with
Sheaf 1.00
1959 100 Francs, Leopold I 4.00
1958 500 Francs, Leopold II 20.00
1964 20 Francs, Baudouin I ...... .50

BERMUDA   EF
1947 5 Shillings, George V 75.00
1957 10 Shillings, Elizabeth II .. 22.00

BIAFRA   CU
ND (1968-69) 1 Pound, Palm Tree / Coat
of Arms .... .50

Australian [1942] £1

Belgian 1944 50 Francs

BOLIVIA   VF
1902 50 Centavos, Arms 4.00
1911 1 Boliviano, Mercury 5.00
1928 1 Boliviano, Bolivar 1.00
1962 10 Pesos Bolivianos, Busch / Village
before Mountain .... .50
1984 50,000 Pesos Bolivianos, Villaroel /
Refinery .... .25

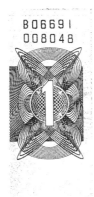

Brazilian [1972] Cruzeiro

BOZNIA AND HERZEGOVINA CU

1992 10 Dinara, Mostar Bridge . . . 1.00
1992 1000 Dinara, same 8.00

BRAZIL F

1833 1000 Reis, Seated Figure . . . 40.00
Estampa 1 (1874) 500 Reis, Pedro II
. . . . 10.00
Estampa 2 (1880) 500 Reis, Pedro II 8.00
Estampa 8 (1880's) 2 Mil Reis, Pedro II
and Building 18.00
Estampa 9 (1888) 5 Mil Reis, Pedro II and
seated figure 40.00
Estampa 7 (1891) 1 Mil Reis, Museum and
Child with Caduceus 8.00
Estampa 9 (1904) 100 Mil Reis, Woman
seated with reading children . 100.00
Estampa 14 (1913) 5 Mil Reis, Bust of Rio
Branco 20.00
Estampa 19 (1925) similar 3.00

(1942) 5 Cruzeiros overprint on above.
. . . . 2.00
Estampa 2 (1953-59) 5 Cruzeiros, Bust of
Rio Branco 25
EF
Estampa 3 (1961-62) 5 Cruzeiros, Sailing
Raft and Indian Head 50
Estampa 2 (1963) 50 Cruzeiros, Princess
Isabel 50
Estampa 1 (1961-64) 100 Cruzeiros, Pedro
II / Woman with Globe 1.00
(1966) 10,000 Cruzeiros, Bust of Dumont
/ Biplane 8.00
ND (1972) 1 Cruzeiro, Woman's head in
medallion 25
ND (1973) 5 Cruzeiros, Pedro I 25
ND (1979) 10 Cruzeiros, Pedro II . . .25
ND (1984) 50,000 Cruzeiros, Microscope
and O. Cruz / Building 4.00

BULGARIA EF

ND [1909] 5 Leva, Arms (note is
vertical) 40.00

1951 50 Leva, Dimitrov / Woman with
baskets 35
1962 1 Lev Arms / Tower 1.00

CAMBODIA CU

(1955) 5 Riels, Stone Head 60.00
(1973) 1000 Riels, Children in class . .50
1991 500 Riels, Angkor Wat 2.00

CAMEROON EF

ND (1962) 100 Francs, Bust / Ship
. . . . 30.00
1985 500 Francs, Statue / Statue Carver
. . . . 3.00
1985 1000 Francs, Bust / Elephant 9.00

Bulgarian 1951 50 Leva

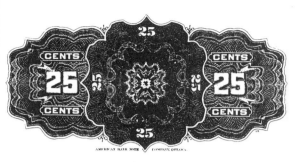

Canadian 1900 25 cents

CANADA

History: The first Canadian notes were issued on the backs of actual playing cards. These are quite rare today. Issues of 1866 were by the Province of Canada, before the independence of the Dominion of Canada the following year. In addition to the issues of the government, many Canadian notes, particularly of larger denominations were issued by private banks. They were finally phased out by the 1940s. Elizabeth II's hair curls, on her first issue, were said by some to resemble a Devil's face, forcing their modification.

References: Charlton, *Standard Catalogue of Canadian Charter Bank Notes* and *Standard Catalogue of Canadian Government Paper Money.*

Counterfeit Alert: Counterfeits are known for some of the early private bank issues. Counterfeits are also known of the $20, $50, $100 and $1000 notes of the 1954 series.

Hints: Well worn notes are common and are worth substatially less. Worn 25 cent notes are worth very little. All 1935 notes were issued in both English and French varieties. Prices here are for the more common of the two.

		F
1714 50 Livres, Inscription on the back of a playing card	. . . .	*RARE*

TWENTY-FIVE CENTS

1870 Bust of Britannia	. . . .	10.00
1900 Britannia seated	. . . .	4.00
1923 Bust of Britannia in oval	. . .	4.00

ONE DOLLAR

1861 Bank of Clifton, Saint George slaying Dragon	. . . .	15.00
1866 Champlain and Cartier	. .	900.00
1870 Jacques Cartier	. . . .	300.00

1878 Countess of Dufferin	. . . . .	65.00
1897 Loggers	. . . .	175.00
1898 similar	. . . .	40.00
1911 Earl and Countess of Grey	.	20.00
1917 Princess of Connaught	. . . .	20.00
1923 George V	. . . .	10.00
1935 George V	. . . .	10.00

TWO DOLLARS

1866 Indian and Sailor	. . . . .	1,100.00
1870 Gen. Wolfe and Montcalm, Indian and train	. . . .	1,800.00
1878 Earl of Dufferin	. . . .	500.00
1887 Marquis and Marchioness of Lansdowne	. . . .	200.00

Canadian 1937 1 Dollar, George VI

Canada (continued)F

1897 Edward VII as Prince of Wales,
  Fisherman on Small Boat 65.00
1914 The Connaughts 40.00
1923 Prince of Wales 25.00
1935 Queen Mary 15.00

FOUR DOLLARS
1882 Marquis of Lorne 150.00
1900 Ship in American Locks .. 150.00
1902 Ship in Canadian Locks .. 250.00

FIVE DOLLARS
1866 Victoria and Ship 2,700.00
1912 Train 75.00
1924 Queen Mary 375.00
1935 Edward VIII as Prince of Wales.
  . . . . 40.00

TEN DOLLARS
1866 Discovery of Land 5,000.00
1935 Princess Mary 25.00

TWENTY DOLLARS
1866 Beavers and Dam 7,000.00
1935 Elizabeth II as little girl .. 100.00

TWENTY-FIVE DOLLARS
1935 Royal Couple 250.00

FIFTY DOLLARS
1866 Mercury 9,000.00
1872 Mercury ..... *PROOFS ONLY*
1935 George VI as Duke of York.
  . . . . 200.00

ONE HUNDRED DOLLARS
1866 Queen Victoria 12,500.00
1935 Duke of Gloucester 175.00

FIVE HUNDRED DOLLARS
1866 Woman with Arms and Lion.
  . . . . *RARE*
1896 Marquis of Lorne 3,500.00
1911 Queen Mary 4,000.00
1925 George V 1,300.00
1935 Sir John Macdonald 1,500.00

ONE THOUSAND DOLLARS
1896 Queen Victoria 5,000.00
1901 Earl Roberts 4,000.00
1911 George V 4,000.00
1924 Earl Roberts 2,500.00
1925 Queen Mary 1,500.00
1935 Sir Wilfred Laurier 450.00
Note: Extremely rare notes of values over
one thousand dollars do exist.

ISSUES OF 1937   VF
1 Dollar, George VI / Allegorical figure
  seated 5.00
2 Dollars, George VI 12.00
5 Dollars, George VI 10.00
10 Dollars, George VI 18.00
20 Dollars, George VI 25.00
50 Dollars, George VI 60.00
100 Dollars, Sir John Macdonald.
  . . . . 120.00
1000 Dollars, Sir Wilfred Laurier.
  . . . . 950.00

RECENT ISSUES   CU
1954 1 Dollar, Elizabeth II / Prairie
  scene 3.00
same but Devil's face in hair ... 20.00

Canadian 1954 1 Dollar, Elizabeth II

1967 1 Dollar, Centennial 2.00
1973 1 Dollar, Elizabeth II / Parliament
  over river with logs 1.50
1954 2 Dollars, Elizabeth II / Rural
  scene 4.00
same but Devil's face in hair ... 35.00
1974 2 Dollars, Elizabeth II / Inuits 3.00
1986 2 Dollars, Elizabeth II / Robins.
  . . . . 2.50
1954 5 Dollars, Elizabeth II / River
  view 12.00
same but Devil's face in hair ... 45.00
1972 5 Dollars, Sir Wilfred Laurier /
  Salmon boat 15.00
1979 5 Dollars, similar 10.00
1986 5 Dollars, similar / Kingfisher 5.00
1954 10 Dollars, Elizabeth II / Rocky
  Mountains 18.00
same but Devil's face in hair ... 52.00
1971 10 Dollars, Sir John Macdonald /
  Oil refinery 15.00
1989 10 Dollars, similar / Osprey 10.00
1954 20 Dollars, Elizabeth II / Hills in
  winter 35.00
same but Devil's face in hair ... 85.00
1969 20 Dollars Elizabeth II / Rocky
  Mountains 35.00
1979 20 Dollars, similar 22.00

1991 20 Dollars, Elizabeth II / Loon.
  . . . . 20.00
1954 50 Dollars, Elizabeth II / Atlantic
  Coast 70.00
same but Devil's face in hair .. 135.00
1975 50 Dollars, MacKenzie King /
  Mounted Police 60.00
1988 50 Dollars, similar / Owl .. 50.00
1954 100 Dollars, Elizabeth II / Mountain
  Lake 110.00
same but Devil's face in hair .. 150.00
1975 100 Dollars, Sir Robert Borden /
  Ships at dock 125.00
1988 100 Dollars, similar / Goose.
  . . . . 100.00
1954 1000 Dollars, Elizabeth II /
  Landscape 950.00
same but Devil's face in hair . 1,200.00
1988 1000 Dollars, Elizabeth II /
  Grosbeaks 900.00

CHILE   F

1881 10 Pesos, Bridge and President.
  . . . . 85.00
1922 5 Peso, Condor and Allegory.
  . . . . 9.00

Chile (1972) 500 Escudos

Chile (continued)   **EF**

ND (1947-59) 5 Pesos / ½ Condor, B.
    O'Higgins 50
ND (1960-61) 5 centesimos overprint on
    back of 50 Pesos, Anibal Pinto . . .25
ND (1962-69) 5 Escudos, M. Bulnes /
    Battle 25
ND (1972) 500 Escudos, Steel worker /
    Open-pit Mining 50
1975 5 Pesos, J.M.Carrera / Courtyard
    with fountain 75

CHINA   **VF**

1368-99, Ming Dynasty, 30 Cash Note
(World's oldest surviving paper money),
depicted are strings of holed coins.
. . . . 1,500.00

Ta Ch'ing Government Bank
1907 $1 Arms 20.00
1909 $5 Bust and Building / Scene
. . . . 40.00

Bank of China
1917 10 cents Temple 20.00
1935 $1 Temple of Heaven 6.00
1935 $1 Farmer plowing / Junk . . 2.00
1936 $1 Sun Yat Sen / Junk 2.50
1940 $5 Sun Yat Sen / Temple of
    Heaven 25

Bank of Communications
1914 $5 Train / Bank 2.00
1941 $5 Oceanliner 75
1942 $100 Train and Ship 8.00

Central Bank of China
ND 10 Coppers Pagoda 8.00
1936 $1 Sun Yat Sen / Confucious and
    Two horse-carts 50
1930 10 Customs Gold Units, Sun Yat
    Sen / Bank building 50
1945 $50 Chaing Kai-Shek 1.00

Federal Reserve Bank of China
(Japanese Puppet)
1938 5 Yuan Dragon and Bust . . . 8.00
1939 5 Fen Bridge 50

Peoples Republic
1948 5 Yuan Junks 6.00
1953 2 Fen Airplane 25
1960 2 Yuan Lathe Worker 50
1962 1 Yuan Farm workers on road .25
(1979) 10 Fen Foreign Exchange
    Certificate 25

Republic (Bank of Taiwan)
1949 5 Cents, Sun Yat Sen / Map   1.00
1949 50 Cents, similar 25
1960 10 Yuan, Sun Yat Sen and Bridge /
    Building 50
1961 1 Yuan, Sun Yat Sen / Building
. 25
1970 100 Yuan Sun Yat Sen 2.50
Hell Bank Note (unofficial issues for
    ceremonial purposes) Traditional
    Portrait / Building 25

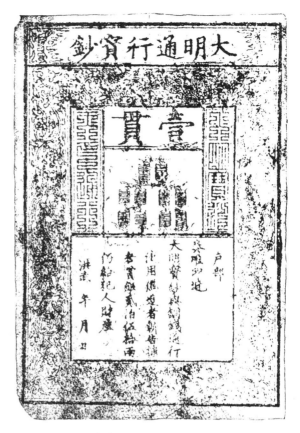

First known note: Chinese 30 Cash

Taiwan 1949 50 Cents

COLOMBIA VF

ND (1819) 6¼ Centavos, Pineapple.
. . . . 125.00
1863 2 Peso, Horseman lassoing Bull.
. . . . 300.00
1895 25 Pesos, Dog's bust 175.00
1900 20 Centavos, Shield 2.50
1915 5 Pesos, Cordoba1 . . . . 5.00
1948 ½ Peso Nariño 2.50
1958 10 Pesos, Nariño and Mercury 1.00
1966 1 Peso Two Busts / Condor . . .25
1973 5 Pesos Policarpa Salavarriata /
Artifact 25
1982 1000 Pesos, Bolivar 1.00

COSTA RICA VG

1865 5 Pesos, Shield and Ship . . 175.00
1902 1 Colon, Columbus and Shield.
. . . . 90.00
1914 10 Colones, Coffee picking 175.00
VF
1953 5 Colones, Carillo 4.00
1973 10 Colones, Brenes / Bank 50
1973 20 Colones, Viquez / Justice 1.50
1992 5000 Colones, Artifact / Stone
Sphere 32.00

CROATIA CU

1941 1000 Kuna, Woman / Mountains.
. . . . 5.00
1991 1 Dinar, Boskovic / Cathedral .50

CUBA VF

1883 1 Peso, Seated figure 75.00
1891 10 Pesos, Mercury 110.00
1896 5 Centavos, Arms / Plant 50
1938 1 Peso, Marti 15.00
1958 20 Pesos, Maceo 2.00
1965 1 Peso, Marti / Castro entering
Havana 1.50
1989 3 Pesos, Che Guevara / Che cutting
sugar cane 3.00

CZECHOSLOVAKIA EF

1934 1000 Korun, Woman and Two
Children 25.00
1949 5 Korun, Lion 1.00
1960 10 Korun, Two Girls 75

DENMARK F

1713 1 Rigsdaler, Inscription . . 800.00
1819 1 Rigsbankdaler, Inscription 75.00
1916 1 Krone, Arms 1.00
EF
1953 10 Kroner, H.Chr.Anderson 15.00
1974 similar 2.00

Ecuador 1920 1 Condor

DOMINICAN
REPUBLIC VF

1849 1 Peso, Arms 325.00
1947 1 Peso, Duarte 6.00
(1952) 20 Pesos, Trujillo 100.00

1978 1 Peso, Duarte 50

ECUADOR VF

1920 1 Sucre, Condor 50

Ethiopian [1966] 1 Dollar

Ecuador (continued) VF

1950 10 Sucres, Conquistador 4.00
1983 5 Sucres, Sucre .... .25

EGYPT F

1898 £1, Two Camels 800.00
1933 £5, Building 12.50
1950 £1, King Farouk 5.00

EF

1961 £1, Tutankhamen Mask 2.00
1976 £20, Mosque / Pharaoh in Chariot
and ancient relief 25.00
1985 25 Piastres, Mosque / Arms .. .50
1987 £5 Mosque / Ramses II 1.00

EL SALVADOR EF

1943 1 Colon, Woman reclining . 25.00
1960 1 Colon, Building 3.00
1972 1 Colon, Cañas / Columbus . 1.00

ETHIOPIA VF

(Illustration on previous page)
1929 5 Thalers, Bank of Abyssinia,
Gazelle head 350.00
1933 5 Thalers, Bank of Ethiopia, Gazelle
head 135.00
(1946) 100 Dollars, Haile Selassie and
Palace 250.00
(1966) 1 Dollar, Harbor and Haile Selassie
/ Lion 4.00
(1966) 100 Dollars, Church and Haile
Selassie / Lion 40.00
1976 1 Birr, Boy / Waterfalls ..... .50
1976 50 Birr, Students / Castle .. 22.00

Fijian 1942 1 Penny

FIJI VF

1871 £1 Two small busts 6,000.00
1872 25 Dollars, Arms 325.00
1934 5 Shillings, George V 200.00
1942 1 Penny, Coin 1.75
1951 5 Shillings, George VI 18.00
1965 5 Shillings, Elizabeth II 5.00
(1968) 50 Cents, Elizabeth II / Thatched
House 2.00

FINLAND VF

1822 1 Ruble, Eagle 550.00
1862 20 Markkaa, Arms 400.00
1922 5 Markkaa, Tree 3.00
1922 500 Markkaa, Nude Crowd, "Litt.
C" above 25.00
1963 5 Markkaa, Fir Branches .. 1.00
1986 10 Markkaa, Nurmi 2.00

FRANCE EF

1719 10 Livres, Inscription . 1,500.00
1793 10 Livres Bust of Louis XVI in
medallion 18.00

1793 50 Sols, Seated allegorical figures
.... 5.00

OLD FRANCS
1863 500 Francs, Seated Figure between
two young standing figures ... *Scarce*
1939 100 Francs, Woman and Child 3.00
1942 10 Francs, Miner / Farm Woman
.... 1.00
1942 100 Francs, Descartes 20.00
1943 5 Francs, Bust of Pyrenean
Shepherd 2.00
1944 5000 Francs, Woman holding
Victory on globe 18.00
1944 2 Francs, Flag (Allied Military
Currency) .... .50
1947 20 Francs, Fisherman 1.50
1951 100 Francs, Farmer / Dock scene.
.... 4.00
1957 1000 Francs, Richelieu 12.00
NEW FRANCS
ND 1959 500 Francs overprinted 5
NOUVEAUX FRANCS 90.00
1959 5 Francs, Building and Victor Hugo
.... 10.00
1967 10 Francs, Voltaire 4.00
1986 500 Francs, Pascal 110.00

GERMAN EAST AFRICA F

1905 50 Rupien, Kaiser Wilhelm II 90.00
1916 1 Rupie, Small Eagle .... .75

German East Africa 1916 Rupie

GERMANY VF

1882 5 Marks, Knight with sword and
shield 250.00
1899 50 Mark, Germania seated 3,000.00
1910 1000 Mark, Shield with women as
supporters 2.00
1914 1 Mark .... .75
1920 50 Mark, Woman with fruit and
flowers .... .75
1923 1,000,000 Mark, no images .. 1.00
1923 21 Gold Mark = 5 Dollars, Small
Eagle 350.00
1942 5 Reichsmark, Youth / Plaza with
Lion statue on pedestal 1.25
1944 1 Mark, Allied Occupation Issue,
Square 1.00
1948 5 Deutsche Mark, Europa riding
Bull 8.00
1960 5 Deutsche Mark, Dürer's Portrait
of Young Venetian Woman ... 4.00

German 1920 Knivsberg

German 1942 5 Reichsmark

Germany (continued)   VF

1970 10 Deutsche Mark, Bust of Young Man with Long Hair / Ship ... 7.50
1980 100 Deutsche Mark, Bust in Floppy Hat / Eagle 70.00
1991 5 Deutsche Mark, Young Woman / Brandenburg Gate 4.00
Knivsberg 50 pfennig, 1920, Allegories of World Powers charging up hill with flags (Called a Plebiscite Note for its political commentary) .... .75
Schneidemuhl, (World War I) 75 pfennig, Arms / Biplane .... .75

GHANA   EF

1962 £1, Bank Building / Coconuts 3.50
1958 £1000, Inscription and Bank Building 125.00
ND (1965) 1 Cedi, Kwame Nkrumah / Bank Building 2.50
1973 10 Cedis, Man smoking Pipe / Dam .... .25
1986 200 Cedis, Old Man / Classroom scene 2.00

GREAT BRITAIN   VF

1797 £1 Cursive Inscription ..... *Rare*
1826 £1 same .... *Rare*
1855 £5 Cursive Inscription ... 800.00
1866 £5 same 300.00
1870 £10 same .... *Rare*
1893 £5 same 300.00
1902 £5 same 175.00
1918 £5 same 100.00
(1922) £1 Britannia and Head of George V
.... 30.00
1925 £100 Cursive inscription . 700.00
1938 £5 same 70.00
1943 £5 same 50.00
[1948] £1 Britannia / Building and 2 St. Georges slaying dragons 5.00
1949 £5 Inscription 35.00
1960 £1 Elizabeth II 4.00

1961 £5 Helmeted Head of Britannia at left 16.00
    CU
(1977) £1 Elizabeth II / Bank Seal   4.50
(1982) £1 Elizabeth II / Sir Isaac Newton 4.00

GREECE   F

1831 5 Phoenix, Inscription ... 800.00
1867 10 Drachmai, G. Stavros and Arms. 1,300.00
1885 1 Drachma, Athena / Arms 35.00
1901 500 Drachmai, Athena standing.
.... 800.00
1923 5 Drachmai, G. Stavros / Head of Heracles 15.00

    VF
1917 1 Drachma, Hermes seated in diamond 2.50
1932 5000 Drachmai, Athena / Bird
.... 5.00
1935 100 Drachmai, Hermes / Woman with basket 4.00
1944 25,000,000 Drachmai, Ancient Coin .... .50
1955 10 Drachmai, King George I / Byzantine Style Church 5.00
1955 100 Drachmai, Pericles / Ships
.... 4.00
    CU
1967 100 Drachmai, Demokritos and Atom / University 3.00
1978 100 Drachmai, Helmeted Head of Athena 2.25
1987 1,000 Drachmai, Apollo and Ancient Coin 15.00

GUATEMALA   VF

1928 2 Quetzales, Bust and Palm Tree at l. 100.00
1934 1 Quetzal, Two Birds on Columns
.... 10.00.00
1945 5 Quetzales, Cargo Ship ... 75.00
1956 1 Quetzal, Building 5.00
1961 10 Quetzales, Stone Carving 15.00
1972 20 Quetzales, Dr. Galvez ... 5.00
1983 ½ Quetzal, Mayan Ruler / Pyramid .... .35
1992 1 Quetzal, Gen. Orellana / Bank Building .... .50

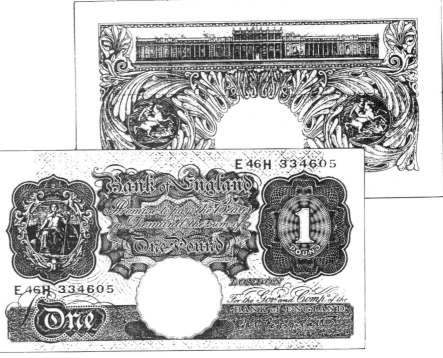

British [1948] £1

Greek 1944 25,000,000 Drachmai

HONG KONG   F
Hong Kong & Shanghai Banking Corp.
1873 1 Dollar, Arms 475.00
1882 5 Dollars, Arms 750.00
1909 100 Dollars, Laborers . . . 800.00
1923 50 Dollars, Greek Bust . . 750.00
1952 100 Dollars, Woman seated with
    book 65.00
                                        EF
1935 1 Dollar, Athena Head . . . 30.00
1975 5 Dollars, Woman reclining.
    . . . . 2.00
1982 100 Dollars, Arms 15.00
Government of Hong Kong
ND (1945) 1 Cent, George VI 50
1949 1 Dollar, George VI 4.00
ND (1952) 1 Cent, Elizabeth II 25
1954 1 Dollar, Elizabeth II 1.50

Hong Kong [1952] 1 Cent

HAITI   F
1875 25 Centimes, Pres. Domingue 10.00
1908 5 Gourdes, Pres. Nord Alexis at
    both l. and r. 400.00
1919 (1925-32) 1 Gourde, Fortifications /
    Arms 8.50
1919 (1967) 1 Gourde, similar 75
*Note: There are many varieties of the above
two note, distinguishable mostly by
signatures and code letters.*
1979 (1985) 5 Gourdes, Jean-Claude
    Duvalier at l. 75
1991 10 Gourdes, Woman seated r. 2.25

HAWAII   VF
ND (1879) 10 Dollars, Cowboy 5,000.00

ND (1879) 20 Dollars, Girl, Woman, and
    Anchor 5,000.00
ND (1879) 50 Dollars, Ram, Woman
    standing, girl 5,000.00
ND (1879), 100 Dollars, Globe 5,000.00
ND (1879), 500 Dollars, Train . *Unique*
1895 5 Dollars, Woman, Building, Steer
    Head . . . . *Rare*
1895 5 Dollars, Tree, Building, Man
    . . . . 5,000.00
1895 10 Dollars, Sugar Cane Harvesting
    . . . . *Rare*
1895 20 Dollars, People before building
    . . . . *Rare*
1895 50 Dollars, Cowboy . . . . . . *Rare*
1895 100 Dollars, Cowboys and Train
    . . . . *Rare*

HUNGARY   VF
1920 100 Korona, St. Stephen . . . 3.00
1923 500 Korona, Prince Arpad . . 1.00
1926 50 Pengo, F. Rakoczi 450.00
1930 100 Pengo, King Matyas 50
1936 10 Pengo, Madonna and Child l.,
    girl r. 50
1945 10,000,000 Pengo, Kossuth 50
1957 20 Forint, Male with Hammer and
    Wheat 2.50
1969 50 Forint, Rakoczi 2.00
                                        CU
1975 500 Forint, E. Ady r. 15.00
1986 50 Forint, F. Rakoczi 1.50
1992 100 Forint, Kossuth r. 1.50

ICELAND   VF
1904 100 Kronur, King / Bird . 275.00
1941 1 Krona, Arms 7.00
1957 10 Kronur, Jon Eiriksson / Dock
    . . . . 2.50
1961 (1981) 50 Kronur, Bishop / Printers
   75

Haiti 1875 25 Centimes

Hungarian 1936 10 Pengo

Indonesia 1964 1 Sen

INDIA   VF
1917 1 Rupee, Coin 2.50
1940 1 Rupee, Coin 50
1951 1 Rupee, Coin 75
1980 1 Rupee, Coin 25
                                                CU
ND (1969-70) 1 Rupee, Coin with Gandhi
. . . . 1.25
ND 2 Rupees, Lion-Column / Satellite.
. . . . 1.00
ND 20 Rupees, Lion-Column / Wheel.
. . . . 2.00

INDONESIA   EF
1947 5 Rupiah, Sukarno 6.00
ND (1957) 100 Rupiah, Squirrel . . 6.50
1964 1 Sen, Man with large hat 25
1964 1 Rupiah, Sukarno 50
1977 100 Rupiah, Rinoceros 50
1984 100 Rupiah, Bird / Dam 50

IRAN   F
1890 1 Toman, Lion & Shah . . 200.00
1938 5 Rials, Shah Roza / Inscription
. . . . 3.00
1944 5 Rials, Portrait of young Shah /
   Tomb of Daniel Nabi 2.00
                                                EF
1332 (1951) 10 Rials, Man and Ram l.,
young Shah r. 4.50
1340 (1961) 10 Rials, Shah r. / Dam 1.50
[1974] 50 Rials, Portrait of Shah / Tomb
   of Cyrus the Great 1.50
[1979] same with overprint obliterating
   portrait of Shah 2.00
[1985] 100 Rials, Ayatolla Moddaress /
   Parliament 1.50

IRAQ   F
1931 1 Dinar, Bearded King r. . . 150.00
1931 (1941) 1 Dinar, Child King r. 40.00
1958 1 Dinar, Star r. 4.00
                                                CU
ND (1973) ½ Dinar, Oil Refinery /
   Ancient Tower 8.00
1986 25 Dinars, Horsemen and Saddam
Hussein / Monument 3.50
1991 25 Dinars, Three Horses / Palace.
. . . . 4.00

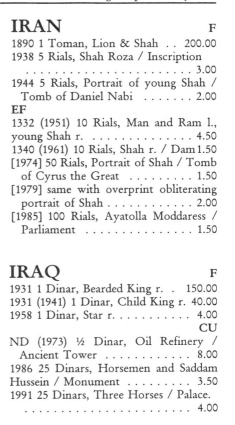

Iranian [1979] 50 Rials

Iraq 25 Dinars 1986

Irish 1984 1 Pound

IRELAND   VF

1928 10 Shillings, Lady Hazel Laverly
. . . . 38.00
1939 1 Pound, Bank of Ireland, Man at
   plough 50.00
1939 1 Pound, Hibernian Bank, same
. . . . 60.00
1939 1 Pound, Munster and Leinster
   Bank, same 60.00
1939 1 Pound, National Bank, same
. . . . 55.00
1939 1 Pound, Ulster Bank, same
. . . . 100.00
1957 1 Pound, Central Bank of Ireland,
   Lady Hazel Laverly 6.00
1984 1 Pound, Central Bank of Ireland,
   Queen Medb / Medieval manuscript
. . . . 1.50
1978 10 Pounds, Jonathan Swift / city
   map 15.00

ISRAEL   EF

(Illustration on following page)
ND (1948) £1, Anglo-Palestine Bank
   Ltd. 50.00
1955 500 Prutot, Ruins of Old Synagogue
   / Modernistic sworl 15.00
1958 1 Lira, Fisherman / Wreath . 2.00
1958 10 Lirot, Scientist / Dead Sea
   Scroll 1.50
1968 5 Lirot, Albert Einstein / Building
. . . . 5.00
1973 10 Lirot, Montefiore / Jaffa Gate
. . . . 1.00
1978 10 Sheqalim, Herzl / Zion Gate
. . . . 1.00
                                            CU
1983 1000 Sheqalim, Maimonides / View
   of Tiberias 4.00
1984 10,000 Sheqalim, Golda Meir /
   Crowd 16.00
1991 200 New Sheqalim, Z. Shazar r. /
   Girl writing 100.00

ITALY   VF

(Illustration on following page)
1888 10 Lire, Umberto I 25.00
1918 25 Lire, Eagle 150.00
1923 5 Lire, Victor Emanuel III on
   Medallion 5.00
1939 10 Lire, Victor Emanuel III . 1.00
1943 1000 Lire, Inscription 7.00
ALLIED MILITARY CURRENCY
1943 1 Lira 25
1943 5 Lire 25
1943 50 Lire 1.50
1943 500 Lire 40.00
REPUBLIC   EF
1951 50 Lire, Helmeted bust of Italia.
. . . . 13.00

Israel 1973 10 Lirot

Italy (continued) — EF

1966 500 Lire, Snake with Eagle l., Arethusa r.	2.00
1976 500 Lire, Winged Head	1.00
1981 1000 Lire, Verdi / La Scala Opera House	1.00
1992 50,000 Lire, Bernini / Equestrian statue	50.00
1977 50 Lire, *Private Scrip*	.50

JAMAICA — VF

1918 5 Shillings, George V / Ship	1,000.00
1950 5 Shillings, George VI	35.00
1960 (1970) 50 Cents, Marcus Garvey	.75
1990 1 Dollar, A. Bustamante	.50

JAPAN — VF

ND (1872) 10 Sen, Two Birds over Two Dragons	65.00
ND (1877) 1 Yen, Sailors	1,150.00
ND (1910) 5 Yen, Bust with Long Beard in circle at center	700.00
ND (1943) 1 Yen, Bust with Long Beard at center	1.00
ND (1944) 5 Sen, Statue of Mounted Warrior	.35
1944 50 Sen, Shrine / Mountain	.35
ND (1946) 1 Yen, Large A	8.00
ND (1945-48) 1 Yen, Large B	1.00
ND (1946) 10 Yen, Building	1.50

Italian 1976 500 Lire

Japan (continued)   VF

ND (1953) 100 Yen, Bust with forked beard 1.50
ND (1969) 500 Yen, Bust in Bowtie / Mt. Fuji l. 6.00
ND (1984) 1000 Yen, Bust / Two Cranes 11.00

Mexico:1943 1 Peso

Japanese 1944 50 Sen

JORDAN   EF

1949 1 Dinar, King in Turban / Ruins.
. . . . 50.00
1959 5 Dinars, King Young Hussein / Petra 35.00
1992 20 Dinars, King Hussein in Arab Headdress / Dome of the Rock . 38.00

KENYA   EF

1966 5 Shillings, Jomo Kenyatta / Coffee Picker 10.00
1978 5 Shillings, same 1.25
1984 5 Shillings, Daniel Moi / Three Rams 1.00

LITHUANIA   CU

1930 20 Litu, Duke and Church / Ship
. . . . 100.00
1991 0.10 Talonas, Shield 35
1991 (1993) 10 Litu, Two Aviators / Old Airplane 5.00

MEXICO   VF

1823 1 Peso, EL IMPERIO MEXICANO
. . . . 50.00
same, cut cancelled 35.00
1914 5 Pesos, Seated figure l., Eagle center
. . . . 2.00

LOCAL ISSUES
REVOLUTIONARY ISSUES
Chihuahua, 1915 1 Peso, Two busts / Building 1.75
Constitutionalist Army, 1914 1 Peso, Eagle 1.50
Sonora, 1914 10 Centavos, Eagle / Coastal scene 1.00

BANCO DE MEXICO   VF
1920 50 Centavos, Helmeted bust.
. . . . 15.00
ND (1935) 1 Peso, Aztec Calender 5.00
1945 1 Peso, similar 2.00
1958 1 Peso, "MEXICO D.F." added.
. 25
1932 5 Pesos, Portrait of Gypsy Girl.
. . . . 15.00
1936 5 Pesos, similar, smaller size.
. . . . 60.00
1949 5 Pesos, similar 1.50

1970 5 Pesos, "MEXICO D.F." added.
. 25
1972 5 Pesos, Josefa 25
1934 10 Pesos, Winged figures holding book of the Law 10.00
1936 10 Pesos, similar, smaller size 25.00
1937 10 Pesos, Girl with large headdress.
. . . . 7.50
1948 10 Pesos, same 1.50
1954 10 Pesos, same 50
1967 10 Pesos, same 50
1954 10 Pesos, same 50
1969 10 Pesos, Bell and Hidalgo 35
1933 20 Pesos, Steam ship at dock and locomotive 60.00
1941 20 Pesos, Josefa / Courtyard.
. . . . 5.00
1959 20 Pesos, same 1.00
1970 20 Pesos, same 1.00
1972 20 Pesos, Morelos / Pyramid . .25
1925 50 Pesos, Allegory of Navigation seated l. 1,500.00
1937 50 Pesos, Zaragoza 150.00
1944 50 Pesos, Allende 5.00
1958 50 Pesos, same 3.00
1965 50 Pesos, same 2.00
1976 50 Pesos, Juarez 75
1981 50 Pesos, same 25

Mexico: Chihuahua 1915 1 Peso

Mexico (continued)   **VF**

1934 100 Pesos, Maritime Commerce
   seated with Youth 150.00
1942 100 Pesos, Madero 30.00
1945 100 Pesos, Hidalgo 20.00
1961 100 Pesos, same 4.00
1970 100 Pesos, same 2.50
1972 100 Pesos, Hidalgo 1.50
1979 100 Pesos, Carranza 50
1982 100 Pesos, Carranza 25
1934 500 Pesos, Electricity 600.00
1943 500 Pesos, Morelos 38.00
1961 500 Pesos, same 12.00
1977 500 Pesos, same 2.00
1979 500 Pesos, Madero / Aztec calendar.
   . . . . 2.50
1983 500 Pesos, same 1.00
1931 1000 Pesos, Wisdom with Globe.
   . . . . 2,000.00
1936 1000 Pesos, Cuauhtemoc / Pyramid.
   . . . . 500.00
1945 1000 Pesos, same 36.00
1965 1000 Pesos, same 8.00
1973 1000 Pesos, same 2.00
1982 1000 Pesos, Nun / Plaza . . . 1.00

1987 2000 Pesos, Sierra and University /
   Courtyard 1.10
1983 5000 Pesos, Cadets 3.00
1950 10,000 Pesos, Romero / Building
   . . . . 400.00
1978 10,000 Pesos, same 12.50
1982 10,000 Pesos, Cardenas / Stone
   carving 2.00
1987 20,000 Pesos, A. Quintana Roo.
   . . . . 3.50
1989 50,000 Pesos, Cuauhtemoc / Aztec
   and Spaniard fighting 8.50
1991 100,000 Pesos, P.E.Calles / Bust of
   Deer 17.50
NEW PESOS   **EF**
1992 10 Pesos, Cardenas / Stone
   Carving 1.75
1992 20 Pesos, A. Quintana Roo . 3.50
1992 50 Pesos, Cuauhtemoc / Aztec and
   Spaniard fighting 8.50
1992 100 Pesos, P.E.Calles / Bust of Deer.
   . . . . 17.50

MOROCCO   VF
1943 5 Francs, Arch 1.50

1944 50 Francs, Coastal Scene / Two
   Stars 13.00
1987 50 Dirhams, King / Horsemen.
   . . . . 10.00

MOZAMBIQUE   VF
1909 1 Libra, Vasco da Gama and sailing
   ships 150.00
1958 50 Escudos, E. Costa at r. . . 2.50
1980 50 Meticais, Soldiers 50

NETHERLANDS   VF
1878 10 Gulden, Ornate border . . *Rare*
1914 1 Gulden 75.00
1926 100 Gulden, Woman seated 1.100.00
1931 50 Gulden, Modernistic Head of
   Minerva 35.00
1943 1 Gulden, Queen Wilhelmina 5.00
1953 100 Gulden, Erasmus writing 55.00
                               CU
1966 5 Gulden, Vondel r. 5.00
1977 100 Gulden, Bird both sides 60.00
1985 250 Gulden, Lighthouse . . 150.00
1992 100 Gulden, Abstract 50.00

NEW ZEALAND   VF
ND (1940-67) 10 Shillings, Capt. Cook /
   Kiwi and Treaty Scene 3.00
                                 CU
ND (1992-) 5 Dollars, Sir Edmund
   Hillary 5.00

NICARAGUA   VF
1894 10 Centavos, Arms 60.00
1938 5 Cordobas, Cattle 40.00
1945 100 Cordobas, Woman offering fruit
   at altar 200.00
1953 1000 Cordobas, Somoza . . 450.00
                               CU
1962 1 Cordoba, Building / Cordoba 3.00
1972 2 Cordobas, Building 1.00
1985 1000 Cordobas, Sandino 2.00
1990 1 Cordoba, Bust of Cordoba 1.25

NIGERIA   EF
1918 1 Shilling, Inscription . *F* 500.00
1958 £1, Coconut harvesting . . . 10.00
ND [1967] £1, Building 1.50
ND [1989] 50 Kobo, Building /
   Logging. 50
ND [1979] 1 Naira, H. Macauley /
   Mask 1.00

NORWAY   VF
1854 1 Speciedaler, Small Shield 1,000.00

Nigeria [1967] 1 Pound

Norway (continued)   **VF**
1950 100 Kroner, Bust / Loggers   50.00
1974 50 Kroner, Bjornson / Church 7.00

PAKISTAN   VF

(1947-48) 1 Rupee note of British India overprinted "Government of Pakistan". 22.00
ND (1975-81) 1 Rupee, Crescent / Tower 25
ND (1975-) 5 Rupiees, Mohammad Ali Jinnah / Tunnel 50

PALESTINE   VF

1927 500 Mills, Rachel's Tomb / Tower of David 350.00
1929 £1, Dome of the Rock / Tower of David 250.00
1939 £5, Crusader Tower / Tower of David 475.00

PANAMA   VF

1941 1 Balboa, Bust of Balboa .   500.00
1941 20 Balboas, Oxcart 2,200.00
Note: Panama issued paper money only in 1941. It traditionally uses United States currency.

PARAGUAY   F

ND (1956) ½ Real, Flowers . . . 75.00
ND (1865) 1 Peso, Bull 10.00
1871 4 Reales, Dog Head . . . . . . *Rare*
1899 50 Centavos, Minerva head / Arms. 4.00
1903 2 Pesos, Building / Arms . . 5.00
    VF
1923 10 Pesos, Church 5.00
1943 5 Guaranies, Bearded Bust . 3.75
1952 5 Guaranies, Woman with jug. .50
1952 10 Guaranies, Bust / Bridge . .50
1952 CIEN = 100 Guaranies, Bearded bust / Ruins 1.00
1952 100 Guaranies, Bearded bust / ship. 2.00
1952 (1982) SA = 100 Guaranies, Bearded bust / Ruins 50

PERU   VF

1879 1 Sol, Woman with fruit .   12.00
1914 ½ Libra, Worker 65.00
1954 5 Soles, Peru seated / Arms   1.00
1968 5 Soles, Pachacutec 50
1968 200 Soles, Bust / Tall Ship . 3.50
1972 10 Soles, Building and Vega / Boats on lake 25

Paraguaian 1952 5 Guaranies

1973 1000 Soles, Two Busts / Machu Picchu 2.50
1985 5000 Soles, Large Head / Miners 25
1987 500 Intis, Tupac Amaru 50

PHILIPPINES   VF

1852 10 Pesos, Isabel II . . . . *Rare*
1883 50 Pesos, Bank Seal . . . . *Rare*
1898 1 Peso, Republic Issue 70.00
1908 5 Pesos, Woman seated . . . 40.00
1912 5 Pesos, Bust of Woman . . 10.00
1915 5 Pesos, Pres. McKinley 5.00
ND (1942) 1 Centavo, Japanese Occupation 25
ND (1943) 5 Pesos, Japanese Occupation. 50
ND (1945) 1000 Pesos, Japanese Occupation 50
ND (1949-66) ½ Peso, Ox cart 50
    BU
[1974-85] 2 Piso, Rizal / 1898 Declaration of Independence 1.00

Peruvian 1972 10 Soles

Philippine [1943] 5 Pesos

Philippines (continued)   BU
1981 2 Piso, same with overprint for Papal visit 1.50
ND (1987) 500 Piso, Benigno Aquino / Various scenes 27.00

POLAND   F
1794 10 Zloty, Inscription . 30.00
1831 1 Zloty, Value 100.00
                       VF
1917 1 Marka, Eagle 2.00
1919 1000 Marek, Bust at right .75
1939 20 Zlotych, Woman wearing cross . . . . Scarce
1944 50 Groszy, Eagle 2.50
1947 500 Zlotych, Woman with Anchor and Oar 18.00
1965 1000 Zlotych, Copernicus in circle / Solar System . . . 20.00
1975 1000 Zlotych, Copernicus.
. 50
1982 20 Zlotych, Traugutt 25
1990 100,000 Zlotych, Building 2.00

PORTUGAL   F
1899 500 Reis, Allegory / Arms.
. . . . 75.00
1910 100,000 Reis, Arrival of Cabral at Lisbon, Republica overprint.
. . . . 800.00
                       VF
1925 20 Centavos, Bust / Building.
. . . . 3.00
1933 50 Escudos, Carneiero 100.00
1949 50 Escudos, Ortigao . 20.00
1954 20 Escudos, de Menezes 2.50
1964 50 Escudos, Queen / City View 1.25
1978 100 Escudos, C. Castello Branco 1.00
1987 5000 Escudos, de Quental / Six Hands 35.00

PUERTO RICO   F
1813 8 Reales, Paschal Lamb . . . Scarce
1819 5 Pesos, Ferdinand VII . . . . Rare
1894 5 Pesos, Queen Mother . 1,700.00
1904 5 Pesos / 5 Dollars, Seated Woman / Paschal Lamb 1,600.00

1909 5 Pesos, Columbus / Woman seated 700.00
same marked CANCELADO.
. . . . 500.00

ROMANIA   VF
1925 500 Lei, Woman with Distaff l., Woman Nursing r. 15.00
1945 100 Lei, King Michael . . .50
1952 25 Lei, Man with Tall Hat.
. . . . 1.00
1966 5 Lei, Arms 25
1991 500 Lei, Brancusi 1.50

RUSSIA   F
1843 5 Rubles, Eagle 400.00
1876 5 Rubles, Eagle / Helmeted Bust
. . . . 350.00
1898 10 Rubles, Allegory of Russia seated 30.00
                       VF
1898 1 Ruble, Eagle / Eagle 75

Russian 1910 100 Rubles

Russia (continued)   VF
1909 5 Rubles, Ornate Frame / Eagle in
  Mantle 1.00
1909 25 Rubles, Alexander III . . . 2.50
1910 100 Rubles, Catherine II the Great
  . . . . 3.00
1912 500 Rubles, Peter I the Great 5.00
1927 3 Chervontsa, Bust of Sower 60.00
1938 1 Ruble, Miner 1.00
1947 1 Ruble, State Seal 75
                                           CU
1961 10 Rubles, Lenin 1.00
1991 100 Rubles, Lenin / Kremlin
Tower 4.00
1993 100 Rubles, Kremlin 1.00

RWANDA   EF
1976 50 Francs Map / Miners . . . 1.25
1978 100 Francs Zebras / Woman and
  Child 2.50
1988 1,000 Francs Watusi Warriors /
  Gorillas 18.00

SAUDI ARABIA   CU
1379 (1961) 5 Riyals, City Wall with
  Tower 100.00
1379 (1977) 1 Riyal, King Faisal / Airport
  . . . . 1.75
1379 (1984) 1 Riyal, Medieval Coin and
  King Fahd / Landscape 1.00

SOUTH AFRICA   VF
1892 1 Pond Paul Kruger (*usually found
  cut in half*) . . . . *Scarce*
1920 £1 Arms 75.00
1947 £1 Ship 10.00
1959 £1 Jan van Riebeeck 5.00
[1975] 1 Rand, same 25

SOUTH KOREA   EF
(1949) 10 Won, Gate at r. 5.00

Saudi Arabia (1977) 1 Riyal

Spanish 1951 1 Peseta

Turkish (1915) 10 Livres

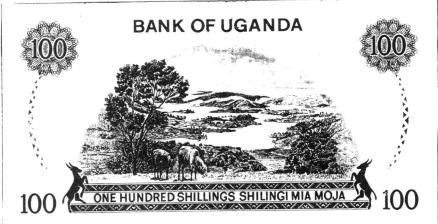

Uganda (1973) 100 Shillings

SWEDEN F

1759 6 Daler, Inscription 85.00
1805 12 Schillingar, Inscription.
. . . . 60.00
1836 2 Riksdaler, Lion and Orb 200.00
1875 1 Krona, Arms 15.00
1914 1 Krona, Arms 6.50
1926 1000 Kronor, Allegory seated /
Gustav Vasa 300.00
EF
1952 5 Kronor, Allegory seated r. /
Gustav Vasa 4.00
1961 5 Kronor, King / Allegory standing
with shield 4.00

SWITZERLAND VF

1907 100 Franken, Helvetia and Cherub
. . . . 600.00
1924 50 Franken, Woman in hat 36.00
1949 500 Franken, Woman left / Three
women embroidering 225.00
1978 20 Franken, DeSaussure / Mountain
climbers 15.00

TURKEY VF

(Illustration on preceding page)
ND (1854) 20 Qirsh, Open radiant oval.
. . . . 250.00
1334 (1915) 10 Livres, Toughra over
inscription 250.00
same but British Military Counterfeit.
. . . . 25.00
CU
ND 5 Lire, Bust of Mustafa Kemal
Ataturk / Waterfall and tree 75

South Korea (continued) EF

4291 = 1958 500 Hwan, Syngman Rhee.
. . . . 50.00
1962 10 Won, Tower / Turtle boat.
. 65

SPAIN F

(Illustration on preceding page)
1876 100 Pesetas, Woman with
Children. 800.00
1886 25 Pesetas, Goya 275.00
VF
1928 50 Pesetas, Velazquez / Velazquez
Painting 1.00
1940 1 Peseta, the Santa Maria . . . 4.00
1951 1 Peseta, Don Quixote 35
1954 5 Pesetas, Alfonso X 35
1957 1000 Pesetas, Ferdinand and
Isabella 10.00

Papal States 1786 35 Scudi

South Vietnam (1956) 1 Dong

Yugoslav 1963 100 Dinar

Turkey (continued)   CU
1970 10,000 Lira, Mosque and Turbaned
    Bust 4.00

UGANDA   CU
(Illustration on preceding page)
ND (1966) 5 Shillings, Arms / Arms
    . . . . 4.00
ND (1973) 100 Shillings, Idi Amin / Lake
    Scene 9.00
ND (1985) 50 Shillings, Milton Obote /
    Dam 2.00

VATICAN
(PAPAL STATES)   G
(Illustration on preceding page)
1786 35 Scudi, Inscription 30.00

VIETNAM   CU
1958 1 Dong, Tower 8.00
1975 50 Xu, Arms 2.50
1980 2 Dong, Arms / River 1.00
1988 1000 Dong, Elephant 1.75
South Vietnam
ND (1956) 1 Dong, Temple r. 1.00

YUGOSLAVIA   EF
1935 500 Dinara, Young King and Eagle
    / Women with Sheaves 9.00
1944 1 Dinar, Soldier.25
1963 100 Dinara, Girl / View of
    Dubrovnik 35
1985 5,000 Dinara, Marshall Tito   20.00

INDEX

A

Abbasid 122
Abbreviations 3
Achaea 125
Afghanistan 112, 121, 167, 187
Africa 112, 113, 120, 140, 143, 145, 146, 156, 157, 164, 165, 168-170
Albania 162
Alexander the Great 108, 110, 112
Al-Fujairah 166
Algeria 145, 165, 187
American Plantation Tokens 57
Angkor 124
Anglo-Gallic 127
Anglo-Saxon 125, 126, 135
Angola 147, 168
Anjou 127
Annam 171, 172
Anthony, Susan B. 33
Anthony Dollars 22, 33
Antioch 111, 112, 113, 119, 124, 125
Aquitaine 127
Arab Byzantine 122
Arab Sasanian 122
Aragon 130
Archaic Greek 107, 108
Argentina 149, 183, 187
Armenia 111, 125, 162, 168
Art Medals 70, 71
Artuqid 123
Asia Minor 107-110
Asian Christian 125
Athens 108, 110, 125
Australia 139, 140, 188
Austria 132, 148, 150, 154, 157-161, 188
Aviation Coins, Canada 100, 101
Axum 120
Ayyubid 123, 124
Azerbaijan 162

B

Bactria 112
Bahamas 140, 179, 188
Balkan States 115, 134, 135, 162, 163
Baltic States 110, 133, 134, 160, 161
Bangladesh 170, 171
Bank (Personal) Checks 89
Barbados 179
Barber, Charles 4, 20, 23, 27, 71
Barber Dimes 6, 7, 20
Barber Half Dollars 6, 7, 27
Barber Quarters 6, 7, 23, 24
Barcelona 131
Beirut 124

Belgian Congo 151
Belgium 121, 126, 129, 150, 151, 188
Belize 140, 179
Beneventum 121
Bengal, sultans 124
Bermuda 140, 188
Bhutan 170, 171
Biafra 188
Biblical Coins 111, 112
Bohemia 133, 159
Bolivia 149, 183, 188
Boone, Daniel 43
Bosnia 134
Bosnia-Herzegovina 162, 189
Brazil 147, 183, 184, 189
British Caribbean Territories 140
British Commonwealth 139-143
British Guiana 140
British Honduras 140
British Tokens 138
British Virgin Islands 140
British West Africa 140
British West Indies 140
Buffalo Nickels 5, 16, 24
Bulgaria 115, 116, 117, 118, 134, 162, 189
Bullion Issues 54, 90, 102, 103, 149, 156, 158, 168, 180, 182
Burma 172
Burundi 169
Bust Dimes 18
Bust Half Dimes 17
Bust Quarters 22
Buwayhid 123
Byzantium 110, 118-121

C

California and Other Private Gold 63, 64
Cambodia 124, 189
Cameroon 145, 169, 189
Campaign Tokens 69, 70
Canada 90-106, 136, 139, 157, 190, 191
Canadian Coins, history 90
Cape Verde 147, 169
Caribbean and Bahamas 179, 180
Carolina 58, 59
Carolingian 127, 128, 131, 132
Carver, George Washington 43
Castile 130, 131
Caucasus 162
Cayenne 145
Cayman Island 140
Celtic 108, 109
Central African Republic 169
Central African States 169
Central American Republic 184

Central and South America 183-186
Central Asia 166, 167
Central Europe 108, 132, 133, 159, 160
Cents, Canada 91, 92
Ceylon 124, 140
Chad 172
Channel Islands 141
Charlemagne 127, 128
Chile 149, 184, 185, 191, 192
China 170, 171, 173-177, 178
Civil War Tokens 65, 66
Colombia 149, 183, 184
Colonial and State Coinages 15, 57
Commemorative Coinage 5, 42-52, 90, 92, 97
Comoros Islands 145
Confederate Coinage 27, 67
Confederate Currency 86-88
Connecticut 59
Continental and State Currency 74, 75
Costa Rica 184, 193
Crimea 125
Croatia 135, 162, 163, 193
Crusader 124, 125
Cuba 179, 180, 193
Curacao 151
Cyprus 124, 125, 140
Czechoslovakia 159, 160, 193
Czech Republic 160

D

Dark Ages 120
Davis, Jefferson 88
De Francisci, Anthony 33
Delhi, Sultans 124
Demand Notes 74, 77, 7842
Denmark 135, 152, 193
Depression and Other Scrip 88
Dollars, Canada 97-99
$2½, U.S. 34
$3 Gold, U.S. 36
$5 Gold, U.S. 36
$10 Gold, U.S. 38
$20 Gold, U.S. 5, 40
Dominican Republic 180, 193
Dorpat Bishops 134
Double Eagle (Gold Twenty Dollars) 5, 40
Dubrovnik 135

E

Eagle (Gold Ten Dollars) 38
Early Half Dollars 25
Early Silver Dollars 30

East Africa 140
East India Co. 141
East Caribbean States 141
East Germany 156
Ecuador 185, 193, 194
Egypt 112, 113, 124, 165, 166, 194
Eisenhower, Dwight D. 33, 49, 166
Eisenhower Dollars 33, 56
El Salvador 185, 194
Elymais 112
Encased Postage Stamps 66
England *(see also Great Britain)* 125-127, 136-138, 154, 155
Eritrea 157, 158
Errors 56, 57
Estonia 160
Ethiopia 120, 168, 169, 194

F
Fatimid 123
Federal Reserve Bank Notes 83
Federal Reserve Notes 83, 84
Fifty Cents, Canada 96
Fiji 141, 194
Finland 152, 153, 194
Five Cents, Canada 92
Flying Eagle Cents 4, 12
Fractional and Postal Currency 74, 76, 77
France 108, 121, 125, 127-129, 143-145, 148, 194
Franklin, Benjamin 9, 29, 68, 79, 80, 84, 86
Franklin Half Dollars 29
Franklin Mint 70, 71
Fraser, James 5, 16
French Afars and Issas 145
French Cochin China 145
French Colonies (general issues) 145
French Equatorial Africa 145
French Guiana 145
French India 145
French Indo China 145
French Oceania 146
French Polynesia 146
French Somalia 146
French West Africa 146

G
Gabon 169
Gambia 169
Georgia 125, 162
Genghis Khan 123
German East Africa 156, 194
German New Guinea 156
Germany 126, 131, 132, 150, 154-156, 194, 195
Ghana 169, 195
Ghaznavid 123
Gibraltar 141
Giray Khans 123
Gobrecht, Christian 30, 34, 36, 38
Gobrecht Dollars 30

Gold 2½ Dollars 34
Gold Certificates 81
Gold Coinage, Canada 90, 99-103, 106
Gold Dollars, U.S. 34
Gold Five Dollars, U.S. 36
Gold Rush, California 34, 40
Gold Ten Dollars, U.S. 38
Gold Three Dollars, U.S. 36
Gold Twenty Dollars, U.S. 5, 40
Golden Horde 123
Grading 5-7, 74, 90
Grant, Ulysses S. 44, 47
Great Britain *(see also England)* 136, 195
Great Mongol 123
Great Seljuq 123
Greece 108, 110, 125, 162, 163, 195
Greek Imperial 113
Guadelupe 149, 195
Guatemala 149, 195
Guernsey 141
Guinea 169

H
Haiti 180, 196
Half Cents 4, 6, 7, 10, 11
Half Disme 10
Hamilton, Alexander 78, 80, 81, 84
Hamudid 123
Hard Times Tokens 64, 65
Hawaii 44, 69, 71, 79, 82, 84, 85, 196
Hibernia Coinage 58
Hobo Nickels 16
Holy Roman Empire 128, 131, 154
Honduras 185
Hong Kong 141, 196
Hungary 132, 133, 134, 159, 160, 196

I
Iceland 152, 153, 196
Iconographic Coins 123
Ilkhan 123
Impairments and "Do Nots" 7
India 122, 124, 139, 141, 145, 147, 170, 197
Indian Head Cents 12
Indian Subcontinent 170, 171
Indonesia 172, 197
Interest Bearing Notes 74, 86
Ionian Islands 142
Iran 112, 121, 164, 167, 197
Iraq 112, 121, 167, 197
Ireland 127, 139, 198
Islamic Coins 119, 122-124, 145, 164-167
Isle of Man 142
Israel 111, 168, 198
Issas 145
Italian Colonies 157, 158
Italian Somalia 157, 158
Italy 109, 114, 121, 129, 130, 157, 198

J
Jalayrid 123
Jamaica 142, 180, 199

Japan 177, 178, 199, 200
Jefferson, Thomas 5, 16, 48, 51, 80, 83
Jefferson Nickels 5, 16
Jersey 142
Jerusalem 111, 112, 122, 124
Jordan 166, 200
Julius Caesar 113, 115, 129

K
Kakwayhid 123
Kazakhstan 167
Kennedy, John F. 29, 70
Kennedy Half Dollars 29, 33
Kenya 169, 200
Khwarizmshah 123
Korea 177-179
Kyrgyzstan 167

L
Lafayette, Marquise de 47
Laos 172
Large Cents 4, 6, 7, 10, 11, 56, 64, 71
Large Denomination Silver, Gold and Platinum: Canada 99ff.
Latvia 160, 161
Lebanon 166
Leon 130, 131
Lewis and Clark 48
Liberia 168, 169
Liberty Nickels 15
Libya 165
Lincoln, Abraham 12, 45, 56, 66, 69, 70, 77, 80, 81, 82, 83, 84, 88
Lincoln Cents 12-14
Lithuania 133, 160, 161. 200
Livonian Order 134
Lombards 121
Low Countries 129, 150-152
Lower Canada 103
Luxembourg 129, 150, 152

M
Macao 147, 148
Macedonia 107, 108, 110, 111, 162, 163
Madagascar 146
Majorca 131
Malaysia 172
Mali 169
Mamluk 123
Maple Leaf Bullion Coins 90, 102, 103
Marshall Islands 173
Martinique 146
Maryland 60
Massachusetts 59, 60
Mauritius 8, 142
McKinley, Wm. 48, 79, 81
Medieval Islamic 119, 122-124
Merchants' Tokens and "Good Fors" 67
Mercury Dimes 5, 20, 21
Merovingian 121
Mexico 149, 180-182, 200, 201
Military Payment Certificates 88, 89
Mint Sets 53, 54

Mintmarks 5
Moldavia 135
Moldova 163
Mongolia 167
Mongols 122, 123, 134
Montenegro 163
Morgan Dollars 4, 6, 7, 32, 33
Morocco 164, 165, 201
Mozambique 148, 201
Muwahhidun 123
Muzaffarid 123

N
Namibia 169
National Bank Notes 78, 79
National Gold Bank Notes 80
Nepal 170, 171
Netherlands 126, 129, 150, 151, 201
Netherlands Antilles & Curacao 151
Netherlands East Indies 151
New Brunswick 104
New Caledonia 146
New England 60, 61
New Guinea 142
New Hampshire 61
New Jersey 61
New Testament Coins 112
New York 61, 62
New Zealand 142, 201
Newfoundland 104
Nicaragua 185, 201
Nickel Three Cent Pieces 15
Nigeria 169, 201
Niue 173
Norman 125, 126
Normandy 127
North Korea 179
North Vietnam 172
Norway 135, 152, 153, 201, 202
Nova Scotia 106

O
Obsoletes 75, 76
Olympic Coinage, Canada 99ff.
Ostrogoths 121
Ottoman Empire 122, 134, 164

P
Pacific 173
Pakistan 112, 121, 167, 202
Palestine 202
Panama 186, 202
Papal States 129, 130, 158
Paraguay 202
Parthia 112
Patterns 9, 10, 30, 56
Peace Dollars 4, 33, 56
Persia 108, 122
Persis 112
Personal Checks 89
Peru 149, 183, 185, 186, 202
Philippines 173, 202, 203
Philippines, U.S. 5, 77-73

Phoenicia 109, 111
Pitt Tokens 58
Plantation Tokens, American 57
Platinum Coins, Canada 90, 101, 102, 103
Poland 133, 160, 203
Portugal 131, 146, 147, 203
Portuguese Guinea 147
Portuguese India 147
Postage Stamps, Encased 66
Postal Currency 76
Powell, Colin 71
Pre Federal Coinage 9, 10
Prince Edward Island 106
Proof Sets 53
Provincial Coinage, Canada 103ff.
Prussia 154, 155, 160
Ptolemaic Egypt 112
Puerto Rico 79, 149, 150, 203

R
Ragusa 135
Ras-al-Khaima 166
Rasulid 122, 124
Reunion 146
Rhodesia & Nyasaland 143
Richard the Lionheart 126, 127
Roman Egypt 112
Roman Imperatorial 115
Roman Imperial 115-118
Roman Republic 113-115
Romania 135, 162, 163, 203
Roosevelt, Franklin 21, 70, 72, 173
Roosevelt, Theodore 4, 34, 36, 38, 40
Roosevelt Dimes 21, 22
Rosa Americana 57
Russia 134, 152, 159-163, 167, 203, 204
Rwanda 170, 204

S
Safavid 123
Saint-Gaudens, Augustus 5, 38, 40, 41, 42, 54
Saint-Gaudens Double Eagles 5, 40-42, 54
Saint Thomas & Prince 148
Saladin 123
Samanid 123
San Marino 157
Sasanian 121, 122
Sasanian Kushanshahs 122
Saudi Arabia 166, 204
Scandinavia 135, 152-154
Scotland 127, 136, 138, 139
Seated Liberty Dimes 19
Seated Liberty Half Dimes 18
Seated Liberty Half Dollars 26
Seated Liberty Quarters 22
Seated Liberty Silver Dollars 31
Seljuq 123
Serbia 134, 162, 163
1792 Mint Issues 4, 10
Seychelles 143
Sharjah 166

Shaybanid 123
Shield Nickels 15
Siam 171, 172
Siberia 162
Sicily 108, 109, 110, 129, 130, 157
Sierra Leone 170
Silver Certificates 82, 83
Silver Three Cent Pieces 14
Singapore 171, 172
Sinnock, John 21, 29
Slabs 7
Slavonia 134, 135
Slovakia 159, 160
Slovenia 163
Solomon Islands 143
South Africa 143, 170, 204
South East Asia 171-173
South Korea 179, 204
South Vietnam 172, 173
Southern Rhodesia 143
Spain 109, 113, 120, 121, 122, 123, 129, 130, 131, 148, 149, 183, 205
Spanish Empire 149, 150
Special Mint Sets 54
St. Pierre & Miquelon 146
Standing Liberty Quarters 24, 25
Straits Settlements 143
Sudan 165
Swaziland 170
Sweden 133, 135, 152, 153, 160, 205
Switzerland 132, 156, 157, 205
Syria 111, 113, 122, 124, 166

T
Tannu Tuva 167
Tanzania 170
Ten Cents, Canada 111, 113, 122, 124
Teutonic Knights 133, 134
Thailand 171, 172
Thrace 108, 110
Three Cent Pieces 14
Three-Legged Buffalo 16
Tibet 171
Timor 147, 148
Timurid 123
Togo 146
Tonga 173
Tonkin Protectorate 146
Trade Dollars 4, 31, 32
Transportation Tokens 68, 69
Transylvania 133
Treasury Notes 78
Trebizond 125
Trinidad & Tobago 180
Tripoli 124
Tulunid 123
Tunisia 146, 165
Turkey 164, 165, 204
Turkmenistan 167
Turkoman 122
Tuva 167
Twenty Cent Pieces 22
Twenty Cents, Canada 94

Twenty Five Cents, Canada 94
Two Cent Pieces 14

U
Uganda 170
Umayyad 122, 123
U.S. Philippines 5, 71, 72, 73
United Arab Emirates 166
United Kingdom and Ireland 136-139
United States Coins, history 4
United States Notes 80-82
Upper Canada 106
Uruguay 185
Uzbekistan 168

V
Valencia 131
Vandals 120

Vatican City and Papal States 158, 206
Venezuela 186
Vermont 62
Vietnam 171-173, 206
Vikings 126, 134
Virginia 62
Visigoths 121
Voce Populi Coins 58

W
Walking Liberty Half Dollars 5, 28
Wallachia 135
Washington, Booker T. 43, 47
Washington, George 4, 17, 24, 47, 48, 56,
    60, 62, 63, 70, 76, 77, 79, 80, 81, 83, 83,
    87
Washington, Martha 82
Washington Half Dollars 48

Washington Pieces 63
Washington Quarters 24, 25
Weinman, Adolph 5, 20
West African States 170
Western Samoa 173
White Huns 122

Y
Yemen 122, 123, 124, 167
Yugoslavia 162, 163, 206

Z
Zaire 170
Zambia 170
Zengid 124
Zimbabwe 170

PHOTO ACKNOWLEDGMENTS

Many of the illustrations in this book were used by the gracious permission of and are copyright © 1996:

Amos Press: 140: 1974, 1928; 141: 1971; 142: 1966, 1968; 146: 1972; 147: 1969, 1973; 148: 1973, 1971; 152: 1971; 156: 1971, 1777; 159: 1938; 163: Column I a; 166: 1971, 1970; 167: 1971, 1351; 169: 1970, 1971; 170: 1970, 1972, 1967; 171: 1973, 1971; 172: 1967; 173: 1974, 1983; 178: 1906; 179: 1 Won; 181: 1968, 1977; 183: 1972.

Allen G. Berman, Professional Numismatist: 7: 1963; 12: 1909 VDB Detail; 15: 1883 Reverse; 63: 1783; 68: All; 69: All; 70: All; 71: Column I, F.U.N.; 72: 1905, 1944, 1945; 73: 1944, 1903; 75: All; 76: All; 77: 3¢, 10¢; 81: All; 82: All; 84: All; 87: All; 88: All; 89: $30, $112; 99: $2; 106: 1857; 140: 1 a; 141: 1935; 145: 1964, 1971; 148: Detail; 149: 1980; 162: I & II; 163: I b, II a, b, III b, c; 167: 1993; 168: 1963; 169: 1994; 171: 1937; 172: 1941; 173: 1947, 1988; 174: Cowrie; 179: 1973; 182: 1994; 184: 1858, 1886, 1983; 185: 1934, 1985, 1943, 1870, 1880, 1980; 186: 1904, 1863, 1877; 187-206: All.

Paul Bosco: 178: 1882-83 2 Chon; 180: 1981; 184: 1824.

Bowers and Merena Galleries, Inc.: 6: Column II 1917 & 1892; 7: 1882 & 1908; 10: 1792 1 Cent; 14: Detail; 16 Detail; 17: 1796; 21: All; 25: All; 26: 1796; 29: 1965, 1976; 33: 1971, 1976, 1979; 36: 1796; 42: 1937; 43: Arkansas, California, Carver-Washington, Cincinnati, Cleveland; 44: Columbian, Connecticut, Elgin, Gettysburg; 45: Lynchburg, Maine, New Rochelle; 46: Robinson, Sesquicentennial; 47: Stone Mountain, B.T. Washington, York, Grant; 48: Louisiana Purchase, Pan-Pacific $18 & $2½, Washington; 49: $10 1984, 1986-90 All; 50: 1991; 54: 1966; 56: 1855; 57: ½ Penny; 59: All; 60: NE, Willow; 61: 1694, 1776, St. Patrick; 62: Excelsior, Eagle, 1788, 1714; 63: $1, $50, $10; 64: $5 1849, $10 1860, $5 Georgia, $5 Oregon, $5 Utah; 65: I All; 67: All.

Civil War Token Society: 65: Column III All; 66: All.

Charlton International, Inc.: 91: 1858, 1906, 1912, 1920, 1947, 1953; 92: 1¢, 1903-1922; 93: All; 94: 10¢; 95: 1902, 1947, 1967, 1973, 1992; 96: All; 97: 50¢, 1935, 1949, 1958, 1964; 98: All; 99: Column I, III; 100: $15, $20; 101: All; 102: I & II; 104: All; 105: I, II 1865, 1904 obv., III 1870, 1911; 106: 1823, 1856, 1864, 1861, Ship Token; 138: 1834.

Fairfield Coin and Collectibles: 182: 1991.

Dennis Gill: 141: 1941; 147: 1697; 158: 1918; 159: 1780.

Alex G. Malloy, Inc.: All ancient and medieval coins not otherwise listed are from the auctions and fixed price lists of Alex G. Malloy, Inc.

Numismatic Fine Arts: 108: Column I b; 110: II b; 111: III b; 112: II, III a; 115: III a, c, d; 116: I a, II a, III b; 117: I a, c, d, II b; 118: II b, III a, c; 121: I b, II; 126: I b, II b, III b; 128: I b, II b; 129: III b; 132: I a, II a; 133: I a; 135: II b; 137: 1688; 138: 1902; 146: 1642; 154: 1616; 156: 1955; 158: 1689, 1929; 162: 1927; 163 1917.

RaBenco, Inc.: 77: 5¢; 79: $5; 83: All; 86: $10.

Wayte Raymond, Inc.: 10: 1783, 1792 Quarter; 63: $50 Kohler; 103: Sou.

Stack's: 4: Column II; 6: I, II 1874 & 1893, III; 7: I 1794 & 1918; 9: 1776; 10: 1785, 1787, 1806; 11: I, II 1793, 1794, 1827; 12: 1852, 1909SVDB; 14: 2 Cent, 3 Cent; 15: 3 Cent, Shield 5 Cent, 1893 5 Cent; 16: All except detail; 18: 1837, 1867, 1805; 19: All; 20: All; 22: 1875, 1807, 1852; 23: 1892; 24: 1916, 1925; 26: 1795, 1807, 1837, 1844; 27: 1853; 28: All; 30: All; 31: 1869, 1883; 32: All; 33: 1934; 34: All; 35: 1836, 1892; 36: 1911, 1885, 1805; 37: All; 38: All; 39: All; 40: 1856; 41: 1893, 1907; 42: 1925, 1893, 1921; 43: Boone; 44: Grant, Hawaii, Hudson; 45: Missouri; 46: Pan Pacific, Roanoke, Spanish Trail; 47: Lafayette; 48: Lewis & Clark, McKinley, Sesquicentennial; 56: III; 57: 1972; 58: All; 60: II & III; 61: 1786; 62: Nova Eborac, 1795, Plow, 1773; 64: 1849 $10, $1, 1834; 71: 1¢, 25¢; 78: All; 79: $2; 80: All; 99: $5; 105: 1912 20¢; 137: 1672, II & III All; 138 I b, c, II c, III; 139: 1805, 1892; 140: I d; 141: 1842, 1797, 1808; 143: 1961, 1931; 144: 1933; 148: 1864; 150: 1895; 152: 1659; 154: 1730; 155: 1902, 1879; 156: 1892, 1894; 157: 1712; 161: 1832; 166: 1356; 169: 1896; 172: 1851; 179: 1970 Gold, 4 Peso; 181: 1822.

Superior Stamp and Coin: 95: 1928; 108: Column I a; 109: III a & b; 110: III; 111: I a, II; 115: III b; 116: II d, III c; 117: II b, III d; 119: II, III a; 120 II a; 141: 1889, 1877; 142: 1906, 1877, 1935; 143: 1939; 144: 1832; 146: 1835; 147: 1858; 151: I a-c, 1898; 153: 1648, 1727; 155: 1925; 163 1831, 1922; 165: 1927, 1943; 167: 1377; 168: 1949; 171: 1909; 178: 1837-58, 1898, 1885, 1925; 181: 1916, 1921; 183: 1853, 1869; 184: 1900.

AMERICAN NUMISMATIC ASSOCIATION

<u>10</u> <u>Outstanding</u> <u>Reasons</u> <u>why</u> <u>you</u> <u>should</u> <u>belong!</u>

<u>The</u> <u>Numismatist:</u> The official publication of the ANA is a monthly journal containing more than 140 pages of feature articles and columns. Advertising is accepted only from members, all of whom must abide by a strict code of ethics. All members, except Associates, receive this publication.

<u>Resource</u> <u>Center:</u> The ANA Resource Center houses the world's largest numismatic lending library. More than 30,000 titles as well as audio-visual programs, videotapes and 35mm- slide presentations cover every aspect of the hobby. Members can borrow these items for only the cost of postage and insurance.

<u>Research</u> <u>Services:</u> Our professional staff can provide free opinions, or for a nominal fee in-depth answers to your numismatic questions.

<u>Educational</u> <u>Conferences</u> <u>and</u> <u>Seminars:</u> Seminars at the Early Spring and Anniversary Conventions, as well as the week-long Summer Conference, offer a hands-on approach to learning.

<u>Programs</u> <u>for</u> <u>Young</u> <u>Collectors:</u> The ANA has developed a number of programs exclusively for young numismatists (YNs). In addition to *First Strike*, the quarterly supplement to *The Numismatist*, our anniversary conventions feature exciting activities for the budding numismatist. Summer Conference scholarships and an extensive awards program are designed to encourage and recognize the accomplishments of young collectors.

<u>Authentication:</u> The American Numismatic Association Authentication Bureau (ANAAB) provides an unbiased opinion as to the authenticity of your numismatic item.

<u>Mediation</u> <u>Services:</u> ANA members and dealers must adhere to a strict code of ethics. Any member committing unethical acts in dealings with others is subject to expulsion from the ANA. The Mediation Services Department will work with both parties in a disagreement to correct reported problems.

<u>MoneyMarket</u> <u>Catalog</u>: Everyday numismatic products, as well as novelty items and professional-quality equipment, can be ordered from this catalog issued by the ANA Museum Store.

<u>Conventions:</u> The ANA sponsors two numismatic conventions a year. These events spotlight the very best of the hobby. The bourse features foreign mints and eminent national and international dealers. Educational programs, exhibits, activities and tours are entertaining and educational.

<u>Club</u> <u>Network:</u> The ANA can put you in touch with coin clubs in your area.

For more information and an application write to:
American Numismatic Association
Department WP
818 N. Cascade Ave.
Colorado Springs, CO 80903
or call toll free: 1-800-367-9723

Warman's
THE SOURCE.

The more you know about antiques and collectibles, the better equipped you are to make the best purchasing decisions. That's the premise behind the titles in the Warman's Encyclopedia of Antiques and Collectibles.

Each volume in this unique series includes tens of thousands of listings with complete descriptions, hundreds of photos, accurate pricing by experts in their field, state-of-the-market reports (what's hot and what's not), references, reproduction alerts, and histories.

Warman's Americana & Collectibles

Whether you grew up in the 1930s or the 1980s, there is a strong chance that your childhood treasures are worth far more than you think. Before you throw anything away, look for it in this book. You may be surprised at what you find.

With *Warman's Americana & Collectibles* at your fingertips, you're in command. You have the competitive edge on what's hot and what's cooling off. Never rivaled, *Warman's* has become the "bible" for collectors and dealers, who describe it as informative, educational, easy to use, "on the money," and indispensable. More than just a price guide, it is an educational tool you'll use time and again. (Updated biannually.)

$16.95/$21.50 Canada

Warman's Paper

Paper ephemera is one of the hottest segments of the antiques and collectibles market. *Warman's Paper* covers more than 75 general topics (organized by type of item) and 150 collectible categories (organized by specific areas of collecting). Detailed price listings and more than 350 photos aid in identifying and valuing paper collectibles.

Also included is a mini-collector's guide that includes information on where to find paper ephemera, how to determine value, caring for paper, and keys to spotting restrikes, reproductions, copycats, fantasies, and fakes.

$18.95/$23.95 Canada

Warman's Antiques and Collectibles Price Guide

For nearly fifty years, *Warman's* has been serving the antiques and collectibles community with reliable, up-to-the-minute pricing and information. Now larger in both size and content, Warman's contains easy-to-read type and hundreds of new photos 200% bigger than in previous editions.

And that's not all! We've added two additional features—specialized auction houses and valuable information on reproductions—both in handy, easy-to-spot boxes. Collectors and dealers alike won't want to miss out on the newest edition. (Updated every March.)

$16.95/$21.50 Canada

OTHER BOOKS AVAILABLE FROM WALLACE-HOMESTEAD

All of the following books can be purchased from your local bookstore, antiques dealer, or can be borrowed from your public library. Books can also be purchased directly from **Chilton Book Company, One Chilton Way, Radnor, PA 19089-0203.** Include code number, title, and price when ordering. Add applicable sales tax and **$2.50** postage and handling for the first book plus **$.50** for each additional book shipped to the same address. VISA/Mastercard orders call **1-800-695-1214** and ask for Customer Service Department (AK, HI, & PA residents call **215-964-4730** and ask for Customer Service Department). Prices and availability are subject to change without notice. Please call for a current Wallace-Homestead catalog.

ANTIQUES

Code	Title/Author	Price
W5258	*American Clocks & Clockmakers*, Robert W. and Harriett Swedberg	$16.95
W6904	*American Family Farm Antiques, A Wallace-Homestead Price Guide*, Terri Clemens	$17.95
W6386	*Antique Radio Restoration Guide, 2nd Ed.*, David Johnson	$14.95
W6491	*Basic Book of Antiques and Collectibles, The, 3rd Ed.*, George Michael	$17.95
K0669	*Beatrix Potter & Bunnykins Price Guide, The*, Nick Tzimas and Doug Pinchin	$15.95
8395-9	*Brown Book of Brass Locomotives, The, 3rd Ed.*, John Glaab	$24.95
W6335	*Collecting Antique Linens, Lace, and Needlework*, Frances Johnson	$18.95
K0715	*Collecting Carnival Glass*, Marion Quentin-Baxendale	$24.95
K0464	*Collecting Lalique Glass*, Robert Prescott-Walker	$26.95
W5681	*Drugstore Tins and Their Prices*, Al Bergevin	$17.95
W5835	*Games: American Boxed Games and Their Makers, 1822-1992, with Values*, Bruce Whitehill	$19.95
W7404	*Guide to Old Radios: Pointers, Pictures, and Prices, 2nd Ed.*, David and Betty Johnson	$19.95
W4855	*Oriental Antiques & Art, An Identification and Value Guide*, Sandra Andacht	$21.95
A0966	*Royal Bayreuth: A Collector's Guide*, Mary McCaslin	$34.95
W5789	*Stereoviews: An Illustrated History and Price Guide*, John Waldsmith	$22.95
A0869	*Student Lamps of the Victorian Era*, Richard Miller and John Solverson	$34.95
W7463	*Warman's Antiques and Collectibles Price Guide 30th Edition*, Harry L. Rinker, ed.	$16.95
W7439	*Warman's Country Antiques & Collectibles, 3rd Ed.*, Dana Gehman Morykan and Harry L. Rinker	$19.95
W5770	*Warman's English & Continental Pottery & Porcelain, 2nd Ed.*, Susan and Al Bagdade	$19.95
W6963	*Warman's Jewelry*, Christie Romero	$18.95
W6734	*Warman's Pattern Glass*, Ellen Tischbein Schroy	$15.95
W0140	*Zalkin's Handbook of Thimbles & Sewing Implements*, Estelle Zalkin	$24.95*

COLLECTIBLES

Code	Title/Author	Price
W6491	*Basic Book of Antiques and Collectibles, The, 3rd Ed.*, George Michael	$17.95
W4464	*Check the Oil: Gas Station Collectibles with Prices*, Scott Anderson	$18.95
W7536	*Collectors' Information Bureau's Collectibles Market Guide & Price Index, 14th Ed.*	$24.95
W7498	*Collectors' Information Bureau's Collectibles Price Guide 1996, 6th Ed.*	$14.95
W7242	*Comics Collectibles and Their Values*, Stuart W. Wells III and Alex G. Malloy	$17.95
W7366	*Coykendall's Complete Guide to Sporting Collectibles*, Ralf Coykendall, Jr.	$22.95
W6912	*Drugstore Collectibles, A Wallace-Homestead Price Guide*, Patricia McDaniel	$17.95
W703X	*Encyclopedia of Black Collectibles, The, A Value and Identification Guide*, Dawn Reno	$19.95
W7056	*Gas Station Collectibles, A Wallace-Homestead Price Guide*, Mark Anderton and Sherry Mullen	$19.95
W6459	*Hake's Guide to Advertising Collectibles*, Ted Hake	$17.95
W6467	*Hake's Guide to Comic Character Collectibles*, Ted Hake	$17.95
W6475	*Hake's Guide to Cowboy Character Collectibles*, Ted Hake	$17.95
W6440	*Hake's Guide to Presidential Campaign Collectibles*, Ted Hake	$17.95
W5819	*Kitchen Collectibles: An Illustrated Price Guide*, Ellen M. Plante	$14.95
W6688	*Kitchen Collectibles: The Essential Buyer's Guide*, Diane Stoneback	$17.95
W6890	*Malloy's Sports Collectibles Value Guide*, Roderick A. Malloy	$17.95
W7293	*Petretti's Coca-Cola Collectibles Price Guide, 9th Ed.*, Allan Petretti	$39.95*
W6521	*Plastic Collectibles, Wallace-Homestead Price Guide to, Updated Prices*, Lyndi Stewart McNulty	$17.95
W6327	*Postwar Tin Toys: A Collector's Guide*, Jack Tempest	$24.95*
W5916	*Price Guide to Coca-Cola Collectibles*, Deborah Goldstein-Hill	$15.95
W6041	*Price Guide to Collectible Pin-Back Buttons, 1896-1986*, Ted Hake and Russ King	$19.95
W7196	*Price Guide to Flea Market Treasures, 3rd Ed.*, Harry L. Rinker Jr.	$19.95
A0966	*Ruby Glass of the 20th Century*, Naomi Over	$21.95
W6556	*Tomart's Price Guide to Garage Sale Gold*, Bob Welbaum, ed.	$17.95
W7129	*Transistor Radios: A Collector's Encyclopedia and Price Guide*, David and Robert Lane	$19.95
W7420	*Warman's Americana & Collectibles, 7th Ed.*, Harry L. Rinker, ed.	$16.95
W7439	*Warman's Country Antiques & Collectibles, 3rd Ed.*, Dana Gehman Morykan and Harry L. Rinker	$19.95
W6726	*Warman's Paper*, Norman E. Martinus and Harry L. Rinker	$18.95

COLLECTOR'S GUIDE SERIES

Code	Title/Author	Price
W6122	*Collector's Guide to American Pressed Glass, 1825-1915*, Kyle Husfloen	$18.95
W5320	*Collector's Guide to American Toy Trains*, Susan and Al Bagdade	$19.95
W5487	*Collector's Guide to Comic Books*, John Hegenberger	$12.95
W5800	*Collector's Guide to Decoys*, Gene and Linda Kangas	$17.95
W5479	*Collector's Guide to Early Photographs*, O. Henry Mace	$16.95
W5762	*Collector's Guide to Victoriana*, O. Henry Mace	$18.95

COUNTRY

Code	Title/Author	Price
W720X	*American Country Antiques, Book 14, Wallace-Homestead Price Guide To*, Don and Carol Raycraft	$16.95
W7234	*American Country Store, A Wallace-Homestead Price Guide*, Don and Carol Raycraft	$14.95
W7145	*American Stoneware, A Wallace-Homestead Price Guide*, Don and Carol Raycraft	$16.95
W6904	*American Family Farm Antiques, A Wallace-Homestead Price Guide*, Terri Clemens	$17.95
W6408	*Country Furniture, A Wallace-Homestead Price Guide*, Ellen M. Plante	$14.95
W7439	*Warman's Country Antiques & Collectibles, 3rd Ed.*, Dana Gehman Morykan and Harry L. Rinker	$19.95

FURNITURE

Code	Title/Author	Price
W6203	*American Oak Furniture Styles & Prices, Book I, 3rd. Ed.,* Robert W. and Harriett Swedberg	$16.95
W6602	*Colonial Revival Furniture with Prices,* David P. Lindquist and Caroline C. Warren	$14.95
W6408	*Country Furniture, A Wallace-Homestead Price Guide,* Ellen M. Plante	$14.95
W6629	*English and Continental Furniture with Prices,* David P. Lindquist and Caroline C. Warren	$18.95
W7412	*Four Centuries of American Furniture,* Oscar P. Fitzgerald	$24.95
W6645	*Victorian Furniture with Prices,* David P. Lindquist and Caroline C. Warren	$19.95

GLASS

Code	Title/Author	Price
W7137	*American Cut and Engraved Glass: The Brillant Period in Historical Perspective, Updated Prices,* Martha Louise Swan	$45.00*
W7161	*American Cut and Engraved Glass: The Brillant Period in Historical Perspective, Updated Prices,* price guide only, Martha Louise Swan	$ 6.00
K0715	*Collecting Carnival Glass,* Marion Quentin-Baxendale	$24.95
K0464	*Collecting Lalique Glass,* Robert Prescott-Walker	$26.95
A0478	*Collector's Guide to Black Glass, A,* Marlena Toohey	$15.95
A0907	*Definitive Guide to Shot Glasses, The,* Mark Pickvet	$19.95
W5452	*Early American Pattern Glass—1850 to 1910: Major Collectible Table Settings with Prices,* Bill Jenks and Jerry Luna	$29.95*
A0397	*Harry Northwood: The Early Years, 1881-1900,* William Heacock, James Measell, and Berry Wiggins	$21.95
A0745	*Harry Northwood: The Wheeling Years, 1901-1925,* William Heacock, James Measell, and Berry Wiggins	$34.95
A0073	*Imperial Glass Encyclopedia, Vol. I, A-Cane,* James Measell, ed.	$34.95
A009X	*Kemple Glass: 1945-1970,* John Burkholder and Thomas O'Conner	$34.95
A0826	*Made in Czechoslovakia,* Ruth A. Forsythe	$14.95
A0057	*Millersburg Glass,* Marie McGee and James Measell, ed.	$29.95
A0850	*New Martinsville Glass, 1900-1944,* James Measell	$34.95
A0001	*New Martinsville Glass, 1900-1944,* James Measell	$42.95*
W653X	*Oil Lamps: The Kerosene Era in North America, Updated Prices,* Catherine M.V. Thuro	$39.95*
A0103	*Pattern Glass Mugs,* John B. Mordock and Walter L. Adams	$34.95
A063X	*Phoenix & Consolidated Art Glass, 1926-1980,* Jack Wilson	$34.95*
W717X	*Phoenix & Consolidated Art Glass, 1926-1980, Comprehensive Price Guide*	$ 5.00
W7382	*Warman's Glass, 2nd. Ed.,* Ellen Tischbein Schroy	$19.95
W6734	*Warman's Pattern Glass,* Ellen Tischbein Schroy	$15.95
A0788	*Westmoreland Glass, 1950-1984, Vol. I,* Lorraine Kovar	$21.95
A0022	*Wheeling Glass, 1829-1939: Collection of the Oglesbay Institute of Glass Museum,* Gary E. Baker, Holly Hoover McCluskey, James S. Measell, Jane Shadel Spillman, and Kenneth M. Wilson	$34.95

JEWELRY

Code	Title/Author	Price
W6289	*Antique Jewelry with Prices, Updated Edition,* Doris J. Snell	$15.95
W5746	*Collectible Costume Jewelry, Rev. Ed.,* S. Sylvia Henzel	$16.95
W6963	*Warman's Jewelry,* Christie Romero	$18.95

PAPER

Code	Title/Author	Price
W7374	*Collecting Football Cards, A Complete Guide with Prices,* Mike Bonner	$15.95
W6866	*Cookbooks Worth Collecting,* Mary Barile	$17.95
W7307	*Encyclopedia of Antique Postcards, The,* Susan Brown Nicholson	$19.95
W7188	*Paper Collectibles: The Essential Buyer's Guide,* Robert Reed	$17.95
W5789	*Stereoviews: An Illustrated History and Price Guide,* John Waldsmith	$22.95
W6726	*Warman's Paper,* Norman E. Martinus and Harry L. Rinker	$18.95

POTTERY AND PORCELAIN

Code	Title/Author	Price
W7145	*American Stoneware, A Wallace-Homestead Price Guide,* Don and Carol Raycraft	$16.95
W698X	*Belleek, The Complete Collector's Guide and Illustrated Reference, 2nd Ed.,* Richard K. Degenhardt	$60.00*
K026X	*Character Jug Collectors Handbook, The, 6th Ed.,* Francis Salmon and Peter Miller	$24.95
K0561	*Clarice Cliff Price Guide, The, 1st Ed.,* Pat and Howard Watson	$24.95
K0022	*Collecting Carlton Ware,* Francis Salmon	$24.95
K0162	*Collecting Moorcroft,* Frances Salmon	$24.95
K312X	*Collecting Royal Winton Chintz,* Muriel Miller	$22.95
K0960	*Collecting Susie Cooper, 1st Ed.,* Francis Salmon	$24.95
K3227	*Crown Devon Collectors Handbook, 1st Ed., The,* Ray Barker	$19.95
K3413	*Doulton Figure Collectors Handbook, Fourth Edition, The,* Doug Pinchin, ed.	$19.95
K0251	*English Decorative Ceramics,* John Bartlett	$19.95
W7385	*Hummel: An Illustrated Handbook and Price Guide,* Ken Armke	$34.95*
A0826	*Made in Czechoslovakia,* Ruth A. Forsythe	$14.95
A0966	*Royal Bayreuth: A Collector's Guide,* Mary McCaslin	$34.95
W6742	*Stangl Pottery,* Harvey Duke	$19.95
K3618	*Wade Price Guide, The, 1st Ed.,* Robert Prescott-Walker	$24.95
W6939	*Warman's American Pottery & Porcelain,* Susan and Al Bagdade	$19.95
W5770	*Warman's English & Continental Pottery & Porcelain, 2nd Ed.,* Susan and Al Bagdade	$19.95
A0006	*World of Wade, The, Book 2,* Ian Warner and Mike Posgay	$35.95
A0014	*World of Wade, The, Book 2,* Ian Warner and Mike Posgay	$42.95*

Denotes hard cover edition

737.4   54,50⌡   PBK
Berman

Berman, Allen G.

Warman 's Coins & Currency

	DATE DUE		FEB 1 1 2008
Fe 28 '97	Se 25 '00	May 21 0	Ju 2 3 2008
Mar 14 '97	Fe 18 '99	Jul 3 01	OCT 2 3 2008
Ap 11 '97	No 26 '99	Sep 10 01	JAN 3 1 2012
Se 2 '97	Mar 2 0 0	Jul 26 0 2	
Oc 1 '97	4-15 00	Sep 9 0 2	
Nov 28 '97	Jun 29 00	MAR 3 1 2003	
Dec 15 '97	8-26-00	May 15 03	
Jan 20 '98	Oc 17 0 0	Jul 9 03	
Mar 10 '98	Jan 12 0	DEC 2 9 2004	
Apr 27 '98	Mar 8 01	MAY 3 0 2007	
Jun 12 '98	Ap 0 01	SEP 0 6 2007	